M000287171

Praise for *Trend Following*

"The way I see it, you have two choices—you can do what I did and work fo years, cobbling together scraps of information, seeking to create a money-m strategy, or you can spend a few days reading Covel's *Trend Following* and s three-decade learning curve."

—Larry Hite, profiled in *Marke*

"Michael Covel's *Trend Following*: Essential."

—Ed Seykota, profiled in *Marke*

"*Trend Following* by Michael Covel? I'm *long* this book."

—Bob Spear,

"[*Trend Following*] did a superb job of covering the philosophy and thinkir trend following (basically, why it works). You might call it the *Market Wiza* Trend Following."

—Van K. Tharp, PhD, profiled in *Mark*

"[*Trend Following*] documents a great deal of what has made trend followi managers a successful part of the money management landscape (how they risk and investment psychology). It serves as a strong educational justificat why investors should consider using trend following managers as a part of a portfolio strategy."

—Tom Basso, profiled in *The New Mark*

"I am very pleased to see Michael Covel's updated version of *Trend Follow* my favorite trading books out of the hundreds that I have read. He has dou size of this edition and expounded on the process used by legendary trend traders. The traders in this book made millions by getting on the right side and managing risk in diversified markets. This book should be studied by a trader or investor."

—Steve Burns, NewT

"*Trend Following*: Definitely required reading for the aspiring trader."

—David S. Druz, Tactical Investment Management

"A mandatory reference for anyone serious about alternative investments."

—Jon Sundt, Altergris

"Michael Covel does an excellent job of educating his readers about the little-known opportunities available to them through one of the proven best hedge fund strategies. This book is like gold to any smart investor."

—Christian Baha, Superfund

"Covel has created a very rare thing—a well-documented and thoroughly researched book on trend following that is also well written and easy to read. This is one book that traders at all levels will find of real value."

—John Mauldin, Mauldin Economics

"I think that Michael's *Trend Following* is an outstanding read from which all investors can learn to trade markets better by limiting their risks and maximizing their profits through a more disciplined approach to investments."

—Marc Faber
Managing Director, Marc Faber Limited
Editor, "Gloom, Boom & Doom Report"

Trend Following

Wiley Trading Series

Founded in 1807, John Wiley & Sons is the oldest independent publishing company in the United States. With offices in North America, Europe, Australia, and Asia, Wiley is globally committed to developing and marketing print and electronic products and services for our customers' professional and personal knowledge and understanding.

The Wiley Trading series features books by traders who have survived the market's ever changing temperament and have prospered—some by reinventing systems, others by getting back to basics. Whether a novice trader, professional or somewhere in-between, these books will provide the advice and strategies needed to prosper today and well into the future.

For more on this series, visit our website at www.WileyTrading.com.

Trend Following

Fifth Edition

How to Make a Fortune in Bull, Bear, and Black Swan Markets

Michael W. Covel

WILEY

Cover design: Wiley

Published by John Wiley & Sons, Inc., Hoboken, New Jersey.

The fourth edition of *Trend Following* was published by FT Press in 2009.

Published simultaneously in Canada.

Library of Congress Cataloging-in-Publication Data:

Names: Covel, Michael W., author.
Title: Trend following : how to make a fortune in bull, bear and black swan markets / Michael W. Covel.
Description: Fifth edition. | Hoboken : Wiley, 2017. | Series: Wiley trading | Revised edition of the author's Trend following. | Includes bibliographical references and index.
Identifiers: LCCN 2016056666 (print) | LCCN 2016057575 (ebook) | ISBN 9781119371878 (hardback) | ISBN 9781119371915 (ePDF) | ISBN 9781119371908 (ePub) |
Subjects: LCSH: Investments. | Stocks. | BISAC: BUSINESS & ECONOMICS / Commodities.
Classification: LCC HG4521 .C82 2017 (print) | LCC HG4521 (ebook) | DDC 332.6—dc23
LC record available at https://lccn.loc.gov/2016056666

10 9 8 7 6 5 4

“Get on the motorbike. *Relax*.” Cảm ơn Ánh.

He was impregnably armored by his good intentions and his ignorance.
—Graham Greene, *The Quiet American*

Yesterday don't matter if it's gone.
—The Rolling Stones, "Ruby Tuesday"

Contents

Foreword

True story: Not long after the financial crisis of 2008–09, I was dragged to a posh Long Island country club for some terribly boring social event (those tony golf places are not my idea of fun). On my way out the door, I was introduced to someone—let's just call him *Trader Guy*—who is described to me *sotto voce* as the wealthiest person in the club. The thinking apparently was "Hey, two finance guys! They should meet."

We exchange small talk. Trader Guy's diffidence makes it clear he has no interest in chatting. We are both heading out to the valet—these places won't let you park your own car—and a rather memorable few moments ensued.

Trader Guy knows who I am. My book on the financial crisis had come out the prior year; I had already been a regular in the financial media for a while. He knows my name and, truth be told, he could not possibly have cared less. If only to be polite to the host who introduced us, I ask what sort of trading he does. Trader Guy actually *sighs deeply*—then says to me, "I trade everything, I am a trend follower, you wouldn't understand."

Oh, really?

"What a coincidence" I say. "A friend of mine wrote a book on trend following."

By now, I have exhausted what little patience Trader Guy had with me to begin with. I actually *heard* his eyes roll.

"Listen, dude, it's really *cute* you have a friend who wrote a book on this, but there is only one book on the topic, every other one is crap. Your pal wasted trees writing *his*. The definitive book on the subject, the only one that matters, is called *Trend Following*. Everything else is a waste of your time."

I tried, I really tried so hard not to smirk.

As best as I could with a straight face, I casually say: "Yeah, *that's* the one. That's the book Mike—my friend Michael Covel—wrote. *Trend Following*.

Talk about an attitude adjustment: Trader Guy has a genuine *come-to-Jesus* moment, turning into a smitten schoolgirl: "*OhmygodOhmygodOhmygod*—you know Mike Covel? I love that book, I love *Trend Following*! I was a failing trader, about to get blown out of the business. I read *that* book, and it turned my whole life around. I owe that guy my entire career!"

Ahhh! The tables have turned. Now it is my turn to have a little fun:

"I keep telling Mike he needs to punch it up, make it more colorful, add a section on forecasting economic data, evaluating corporate management, and analyzing geopolitics. Make it *fresh and interesting.*"

Long pause as Trader Guy's jaw drops.

It takes him a few seconds before he realizes that: a) I am totally kidding; b) I understand how irrelevant those things are to trend followers, and; c) I am busting his chops for being such a hard ass before.

Trader Guy laughs as I am *now* deemed worthy. We are suddenly best buds: We chat about what we were short during the crisis (AIG, Lehman, Bear), the equity rally off of the lows (strong), and the gold run (at risk of breaking), dollar trending. His car pulls up, we keep talking. My car comes around, and we are still talking. Mr. Diffident has morphed into Mr. Conversationalist.

All of which goes a long way towards explaining why the book in your hands, now in its fifth edition, has become one of the most popular trading books ever written.

What are the characteristics that make *Trend Following* so unique? I have my own biases. I see the inherent and natural flaws of human psychology as an investor's biggest flaws. Like our inability to understand risk and data and statistics, our obsession to be right, and the ways our wetware constantly fool us into believing things that objectively are not true.

Hence, my top ten reasons I like *Trend Following* reflect all of that:

1. It is an objective, price-based approach.
2. News headlines, pundits, analysts, and opinions are not meaningful.
3. It has risk management built into it.

4. Specific views on "The Fundamentals" are not relevant.
5. It is methodical and systematic.
6. The same exact strategies apply across all asset classes.
7. It does not require any predictions.
8. Time frames are long-term in nature.
9. Economic data—Employment, GDP, Fed, etc.—are irrelevant.
10. It demands a very exacting personal discipline.

Readers may find that other aspects of trend following that resonate more for them. It depends on your own personality. But what does not vary for any trend follower is understanding the specific underlying philosophy, and having the discipline to follow that approach with unwavering, religious dedication.

I have a few complaints as well. It gives you nothing to talk about at cocktail parties or barbecues. It is less intellectually stimulating than say debating whether and when the FOMC should or should not (or will or will not) raise or lower rates next meeting. It can be boring. And, there are long stretches of time where the trend is neutral, and you are doing nothing.

Anyone can *learn* the methods Covel discusses here. Putting them into action requires commitment to the craft, and a military discipline. The Achilles heel of so many traders is a lack of precisely those qualities. As you will learn, *Trend Followers* must be willing to tough out some difficult sledding. It is an old joke but it's true: *If it was easy, everyone would be rich!*

But it is not easy. Anyone who has lived with a major drawdown understands how your own body responds. Physical and emotional tolls are not insignificant. You lose sleep, you have a low-grade headache for days or weeks at a time, and some people respond with physical nausea. The biggest issue comes in the hit to self-confidence. Riding out the loss of capital leads traders to question themselves and to doubt their methodology. They wonder if maybe it really is different this time. Market structures have changed, the Fed is doing something unprecedented, high-frequency trading is new, or perhaps it is ETFs, they think *something* is different this time around. "Perhaps if I just tweak the approach a little here this once . . ." are famous last words.

To those who master the techniques described herein, there are profits to be had. But it is not for everyone, and if you are unable or unwilling to ride out the losses, accept drawdowns in capital, be bored through periods of tedium and inactivity, to have the discipline to follow your strategy, to you I say, "Move along. Trend following is not for everyone."

For those who want to learn the craft of trading, have the personality and discipline, and are willing to do the heavy lifting, read on . . . you won't regret it.

—Barry L. Ritholtz
Chairman, Chief Investment Officer, Ritholtz Wealth Management
Columnist for Bloomberg View and The Washington Post
Host of Masters in Business radio podcast for Bloomberg

Preface

Men wanted for hazardous journey. Small wages. Bitter cold. Long months of complete darkness. Constant danger. Safe return doubtful. Honor and recognition in case of success.[1]

Want to take the financial journey to a new investing philosophy that might very well affect the rest of your moneymaking life? I can't guarantee the yellow brick road, but I can promise the red pill will leave you wide awake.

Nearly every time I strayed from the herd, I've made a lot of money. Wandering away from the action is the way to find the new action.

Jim Rogers

In late 2016 *The Wall Street Journal* reported that Steve Edmundson, the investment chief for the Nevada Public Employees' Retirement System, has no coworkers, rarely takes meetings, and eats leftovers at his desk. His daily trading strategy: Do as little as possible, usually nothing. The Nevada system's $35 billion in stocks and bonds are all in low-cost funds that mimic indexes. He may make one change to the portfolio a year.[2]

Not exactly a life changing revelation, I know, but that do-nothing, sit-on-your-hands investing premise doesn't stop with one-man shows. Dimensional Fund Advisors LP (DFA), the sixth-largest mutual fund manager, is drawing in nearly $2 billion in net assets per month at a time when investors are fleeing other firms. DFA is built on the bedrock belief that active management practiced by traditional stock pickers is futile, if not an absurdity. DFA's founders are pioneers of index funds.[3]

To receive my free interactive trend following presentation send a picture of your receipt to receipt@trendfollowing.com.

Now we are getting somewhere, because just about everyone has money tied up in an index fund—which in 2017 is not exactly pioneering. But the much larger issue at hand, unknown to most, is that there is an academic *theory* that allows anyone to confidently *index*.

Q: Do you pencil it in first?
A: No, you just start drawing.
Q: But don't you make mistakes?
A: There is no such thing as a mistake. A mistake is an opportunity to do something else. You have to leave it and let nature take it course.
Ralph Steadman, British artist best known for his work with American author Hunter S. Thompson, talking to Anthony Bourdain

The efficient market theory (EMT) states asset prices fully reflect all available information. This means it is *impossible* for average investors—or superstars, for that matter—to beat the market consistently on a risk-adjusted basis, since market prices should only react to new information or changes in discount rates. EMT, set in motion with Louis Bachelier's PhD thesis published in 1900, and developed by University of Chicago professor Eugene Fama, argues stocks always trade at fair value, making it impossible for investors to either purchase undervalued stocks or sell stocks for inflated prices.[4]

Let me drop the nuclear warhead on that perspective.

There is a mind-numbingly large hole in this cool-sounding theory. EMT by definition leaves the epic October 2008 stock market meltdown out of the academic equation. And for those who know about the sausage making of writing peer review papers or engineering a PhD, much of modern finance's foundation was bricked together with EMT mortar. Fama was ultimately awarded the 2013 Nobel Prize in Economic Sciences because his findings "changed market practice"—that is, the worldwide acceptance of index funds.

Those findings are the generally accepted status quo.

Not everyone, however, is a true believer guzzling the Kool-Aid.

One of the first and loudest critics of EMT was famed mathematician Benoit Mandelbrot. He saw EMT proponents sweep big events like 2008 under the carpet, like kids house cleaning for the first time, calling them "acts of God." French physicist Jean-Philippe Bouchaud sees EMT *marketing* in play: "The efficient market hypothesis is not only intellectually enticing, but also very reassuring for individual investors, who can buy stock shares without risking being outsmarted by more savvy investors."[5]

Bouchaud continues: "Classical economics is built on very strong assumptions that quickly become axioms: the rationality of economic agents, the invisible hand and market efficiency, etc. An economist once told me, to my bewilderment: 'These concepts are so strong that they supersede any empirical observation.' As Robert Nelson argued in his book, *Economics as Religion*, 'the marketplace has been *deified*.' In reality, markets are not efficient, humans tend to be overfocused in the short-term and blind in the long-term, and errors get amplified through social pressure and herding, ultimately leading to collective irrationality, panic and crashes. Free markets are wild markets."[6]

David Harding, a man you might not know yet, ratchets up the polemic by describing EMT in apocalyptic terms: "Imagine if the economy as we know it was built on a myth. Imagine if that myth was the foundation stone on which the mainstream financial systems that control the global economy have been erected—the great bazaars of stock markets, bond markets, fiendishly complex financial instruments, credit default swaps, futures and options on which the fortunes of billions rest. Imagine if the myth was the key cause of the global crash in 2008—and if its perpetuation today threatened another catastrophic crash in the future. We don't have to imagine. The myth is Efficient Market Theory (EMT)."[7]

Harding does not have a Nobel Prize, but he does have a net worth of $1.4 billion.[8] He is a flat-out financial heretic and would not be offended if you called him a punk rocker for his antiestablishment attitude. In prior centuries he absolutely would have been burned at the stake for his wholesale dressing down of the financial high priests. He knows to question EMT is seen as *madness* by academics, banks, pension funds, and endowments.[9]

The efficient market theory is about two questions: Can the market be beat and is the market price the right price? First, evidence says the market can be beat. Second, debating the right or wrong price is futile. There is only the market price and it's the most real, objective piece of data in finance. Don't make the market a morality tale.

Michael Covel

Interestingly, and with a bipolar flair, the Nobel committee split the 2013 Nobel Prize among economists with radically different theories. Robert Shiller, a man focused more on *behavior* and who shares the Nobel Prize with Fama, sees the contradictions: "I think that maybe he has a cognitive dissonance. [His] research shows that markets are not efficient. So what do you do if you are living in the University of Chicago? It's like being a Catholic priest and then discovering that God doesn't exist or something you can't deal with so you've got to somehow rationalize it."[10]

Harding goes further, explaining EMT *madness* in an everyman way: "This theory of rational markets treats economics like a physical science—like Newtonian physics—when in fact it is a human or social science. Human beings are prone to unpredictable behavior, to overreaction or slumbering inaction, to mania and panic. The markets that reflect this behavior do not assume some supra-human wisdom, they can and sometimes do reflect that volatility."[11]

Further translation: Human nature isn't *rational*. It blows bubbles and then pops bubbles—and you can see this going back hundreds of years:

When it is a question of money, everyone is of the same religion.

Voltaire

- Dutch Tulip Mania (1634–1637)
- The South Sea Bubble (1716–1720)

- The Mississippi Bubble (1716–1720)
- The British Railway Mania Bubble (1840s)
- The Panic of 1857
- The Florida Real Estate Bubble of the 1920s
- The stock market crash of 1929
- The 1973–1974 stock market crash
- Black Monday—the stock market crash of 1987
- Japan's bubble economy and crash, 1989–current
- Dot-com bubble (1999–2002)
- United States bear market (2007–2009)
- Flash Crash (2010)
- Chinese stock market crash (2015–2016)
- Brexit (2016)

Proponents of the theory [EMT] have never seemed interested in discordant evidence. Apparently, a reluctance to recant, and thereby to demystify the priesthood, is not limited to theologians.
Warren Buffett
The Warren Buffett Portfolio
1999

And on and on. . . .

But it's beyond being not rational. Those events, the human actions driving those booms and busts, are best described by academia's *prospect theory*, *cognitive dissonance*, *the bandwagon effect*, *loss aversion*, and assorted *heuristics* in judgment and decision-making—to name a few of the hundreds of biases inherent in people's lizard brains.

No doubt, the efficient versus not-efficient debate will not be resolved in these pages. Perhaps it will never be satisfactorily resolved in an academic *mine is bigger than yours* sense, which would not be surprising given that human beings and their egos, greed, fear, and money are knotted up so tight as to restrict brain blood flow. And please don't expect this work to be filled with the latest and greatest macroeconomic bubblegum predictions. You already know that is bullshit completely unrelated to making money—even if you have not yet admitted that fact to yourself.

Education rears disciples, imitators, and routinists, not pioneers of new ideas and creative geniuses. The schools are not nurseries of progress and improvement, but conservatories of tradition and unvarying modes of thought.
Ludwig von Mises

In the face of such chaos, complexity, and human frailty, my curiosity is quite simple. Answer a question: "Why does David Harding think he is *right* and, more importantly, how in the hell did he get all that money trading the likes of Apple, Tesla, gold, U.S. dollars, crude oil, NASDAQ, natural gas, lean hogs, palm oil, wheat, and coffee without investing in an index or having a fundamental expertise in any of those markets or the ability to predict directions?"

That is a worthy question, and the answer is a follow the big money adventure.

Trend Following

The 233,092 words in this book are the result of my near 20-year *hazardous journey* for the truth about this trading called *trend following*. To this day it still fills a void in a marketplace inundated with books about value investing, index investing, and fundamental analysis, but lacking few resources to explain *how* David Harding made his billion-dollar fortune with trend following.

Out of the gate let me break down the term *trend following* into its components. The first part is *trend*. Every trader needs a trend to make money. If you think about it, no matter what the technique, if there is not a trend after you buy, then you will not be able to sell at higher prices. *Following* is the next part of the term. We use this word because trend followers always wait for the trend to shift first, then *follow* it.[12]

You've got to guess at worst cases: No model will tell you that. My rule of thumb is double the worst that you have ever seen.

Cliff Asness

Every good trend following method should automatically limit the loss on any position, long or short, without limiting the gain. Whenever a trend, once established, reverses quickly, there is always a point, not far above or below the extreme reached prior to the reversal, at which evidence of a trend in the opposite direction is given. At that point any position held in the direction of the original trend should be reversed—or at least closed out—at a limited loss. Profits are not limited because whenever a trend, once established, continues in a sustained fashion without giving any evidence of trend reversal, the trend following principle requires a market position be maintained as long as the trend continues.[13]

A big reason this conceptually works is seen in the wonky-sounding Bayesian statistics. Named for Thomas Bayes (1701–1761), the belief is the true state of the world is best expressed in probabilities that continually update as new unbiased information appears, like a price trend that keeps updating and extending. New data stays connected to prior data—think of it chain-ganged together. Random dice rolls this is not.

Fish see the bait, but not the hook; men see the profit, but not the peril.

Chinese proverb

Trend following thus aims to capture the majority of a connected market trend up or down for outsized profit. It is designed for potential gains in all major asset classes—stocks, bonds, metals, currencies, and hundreds of other commodities. However straightforward the basics of trend following, it is a style of trading widely misunderstood by both average and pro investors, if it is known at all. Academic literature and real-world investors, for example, have put forth a host of strategies that, on the surface, appear unique, but at a high level they are all related to trend following.[14]

If you can't explain it simply, you don't understand it well enough.
Anonymous

That classic trend wisdom has long failed to be understood in academic circles—that is, until very recently. Notable voices in the academic community have come around to agree *momentum* exists—the source of trend following profit—but to confuse matters they describe two forms of momentum: time series momentum (i.e., trend following) and cross-sectional momentum (i.e., relative strength). I don't see a connection between the two, and I can guess carving out business and academic niches for assorted reasons is in play, but I do know which strategy has produced decades of real performance proof, and it's trend following.

The desire to enlighten this state of confusion is what launched my original research and ignited my passion, going all the way back to 1994. My plan was to be as objective as possible, pulling research data from wide sources:

- Month-by-month trend following performance histories.
- Hundreds of interviews conducted with subjects from top traders to Nobel Prize winners.
- Published interviews from dozens of trend followers over the last 50 years—details not found on Google.
- Charts of winning markets traded by trend followers.
- Charts of historical markets seen across financial disasters.

To be aware how fruitful the playful mood can be is to be immune to the propaganda of the alienated, which extols resentment as a fuel of achievement.
Eric Hoffer

If I could have utilized only data, numbers, charts, and graphs showing extreme trend following performance data, that would have been perfect—it is, after all, the raw, unassailable data.

Yet without a narrative explanation few readers would appreciate the ramifications of data mining. Robert Shiller has said "that there is a narrative basis for much of the human thought process, that the human mind can store facts around narratives, stories with a beginning and an end that have an emotional resonance. You can still memorize numbers, but you need stories. For example, the financial markets generate tons of numbers—dividends, prices, etc.—but they don't mean anything to us. We need either a story or a theory, but stories come first."[15]

Foundationally, my approach to researching and writing *Trend Following* became similar to the one described in the book *Good to Great*, in which researchers generated questions, accumulated data in an open-ended search for answers, and then debated it all—looking for stories, then for explanations that could lead to theories.

However, unlike *Good to Great,* which was about well-known public companies, to this day the strategy of trend following is still built around an underground network of relatively unknown traders who, except for the occasional misguided article, the mainstream press virtually ignores—and that has not changed in my 20 years. What I attempted with my first edition of *Trend Following* and with this newest edition is to lift the veil on this enormously successful strategy—how trend followers trade and what can be learned that anyone can apply to their portfolio for profit.

The credit bubble pushed the price of most financial assets far from fundamental value. The central bankers were rigging the market with their asymmetric approach to market volatility, where Alan Greenspan put a floor under the stock market but did not cap it with a ceiling. That ensured that the cost of waiting until after the event to clean up was unacceptably high.[16]

Throughout this effort I avoided institutionalized knowledge as defined by Wall Street banks, brokers and typical *long only* hedge funds. I did not start with JPMorgan Chase or Goldman Sachs. Instead I asked questions across all types of sources and then, objectively, doggedly, and very slowly—and even through some Deep Throat help—answers that made intuitive sense were revealed.

If there was one factor that motivated me to work in this manner, it was childlike curiosity—where you rip the toy open to the find the motor and locate the *essence*. For example, one of my earliest curiosities was about who profited when a famed British bank collapsed, making the front cover of *Time* magazine. My research alone unearthed a connection between this bank and a wildly successful trend follower now worth billions. This trader's trend-trading track record had me wondering, "How did he discover trend following in the first place?"

I also wanted to know who *won* when a two-billion-dollar hedge fund collapsed and almost sank the entire global economy. Why did the biggest banks on Wall Street, the so-called smart guys in charge of your retirement, invest $100 billion in this fund when there was so much obvious risk? Further, when I contrasted typical Wall Street losses during October 2008 to what trend following made during the same time in the great zero-sum game, it was hard to grasp why few market players were aware of the strategy. Other questions appeared:

***Question:** Some researchers argue that a market timing strategy based on buy/sell signals generated by a 50- or 200-day moving average offers a more appealing combination of risk and return than a buy and hold approach. What is your view?*
***Eugene Fama:** An ancient tale with no empirical support.*[17]

- How does trend following win in the zero-sum game of trading?
- Why has it been the most profitable style of trading?
- What is the philosophical framework of trend following success?
- What are the timeless principles?

- What is the trend following view of human behavior?
- Why is it enduring?

Many trend followers are still reclusive and extremely low key. One who has beaten the markets for over 40 years works out of a quiet office in a Florida coastal town. For Wall Street this approach is tantamount to sacrilege. It goes against all the customs, rituals, trappings, and myths embedded in so-called success. It is my hope my narratives, backed by data, will correct misconceptions of *winning* as a harried, intense workaholic posted 24/7 in front of 12 monitors while downing Red Bull.

I have noticed that everyone who ever told me that the markets are efficient is poor.
Larry Hite

One of my sources who helped break apart this puzzle was Charles Faulkner. He observed elite traders are almost "floating above the world, seeing it from a different perspective than the rest of other market participants." His insights go straight to the core:

- It doesn't matter what you think; it's what the market does that matters.
- What matters can be measured, so keep refining your measurements.
- You don't need to know when something will happen to know that it will happen.
- Successful trading is a probabilistic business, so plan accordingly.
- There is an edge to be gained in every aspect of your trading system.
- Everyone is fallible, even you, so your system must take this into account.
- Trading means losing as well as winning, something you must live with for success.

To adequately explain the genesis of this new edition, I need time travel. You see, my public trend following persona started in October 1996 with the launch of a simple four-page website. Armed with a political science degree from George Mason University, no connection to Wall Street or any fund and with zero academic respect or PhD credentials, it seemed perfectly appropriate to create the first trend following website.

The essence of trend following has been effective beyond my wildest dreams, and for me it has been more risky to diversify away from it than to embrace it wholeheartedly.
David Harding

And I did.

Loaded with original content, that rudimentary-looking site, turtletrader.com, generated millions of views, millions of dollars, and—unbeknownst to me at the time—respect among legions of beginner and professional traders alike.

Six years into that website, I decided it was time for a book—or maybe the book decided it was time for me. Larry Harris, the finance chair at the University of Southern California, randomly e-mailed me. He wanted me to review his new book because I was driving more interest in his whitepaper, *The Winners and Losers of the Zero-Sum Game*, than anyone else.

Without skipping a beat I said sure to a review of his book, but asked for an introduction to his publisher, since I was writing a book, too. He obliged and connected me even though my book at that moment was conceptual.

After two years of starts and stops, *Trend Following* was finally ready. And when the first edition hit the streets in April 2004, I had no idea whether *it* would sell 10 or 10,000 copies. But immediately the book made an under-the-radar splash, landing in Amazon's top 100—of all books. In fact, that first edition was so expected to fail by my first publisher you could only get it online—initially no bookstore.

It went on to sell over 100,000 copies with translations into German, Korean, Japanese, Chinese, Arabic, French, Portuguese, Russian, Thai, and Turkish. Its success led to four more books and the opportunity to direct a documentary film over the course of 2007 to 2009.

Most big startup breakouts are where people aren't paying attention.

Bill Gurley[18]

I never expected an obscure *trading* book first written 13 years ago would lead me to conversations with five Nobel Prize winners or face-to-face learning from trading legends Boone Pickens, David Harding, Ed Seykota, and literally hundreds more. This journey also led me to the world's top behavioral economists and psychologists from Daniel Kahneman and Robert Cialdini to Steven Pinker. And it opened the door to my podcast, which has run since 2012 and now has over five millions listens. My podcast has further featured guests ranging from Tim Ferriss to paleontologist Jack Horner of *Jurassic Park* fame—all connected philosophically to trend following thinking (at least in my mind).

Yet this wild ride has been far more than one-on-one conversations. The serendipity of *Trend Following* has led me around the world before live audiences in Chicago, New York City, Beijing, Hong Kong, Kuala Lumpur, Macau, Shanghai, Singapore, Tokyo, Paris, Vienna, and São Paulo. A speaking gig in front of 1,500 native German speakers at the Hofburg Palace, the former imperial palace in Vienna, Austria—that happened.

And it kept going. Audiences with China Asset Management to Singapore's Sovereign Wealth Fund GIC to regular investor audiences with well over a thousand people—everyone from new investor to pro who wanted to learn more about trend following, all allowed me to come into their world.

But I recall my first public presentation in support of *Trend Following*—fall 2004 at Legg Mason's headquarters in Baltimore, where their chief market strategist had invited me to lunch. Afterward, I was escorted up a flight of stairs to a nondescript door. Upon entering the room, I found it filled with young bankers listening to a speaker. Michael Mauboussin, then Legg Mason's chief investment strategist, motioned for me to sit. I instantly recognized the speaker as Bill Miller, then the fund manager of Legg Mason Value Trust. At the time Miller had beaten the S&P 500 index for 14 straight years—and was easily one of Wall Street's most successful and famed players.

If you're chasing the masses, you're almost certainly heading the wrong direction. The masses are ignoring you. It's the weird who are choosing to pay attention, to seek out what they care about.
Seth Godin

Miller then introduced me to the audience. Until that moment I had no idea I was up next. For the next hour, Miller from one side of the room, and Mauboussin from the other side, alternately peppered me with questions about trend following, risk management, and the TurtleTraders.

After the presentation I thanked Miller for the opportunity to make my case, but wanted to know how he learned about *Trend Following*. He said, "I surf Amazon for all types of books. I came across yours, bought it, liked it, and told all my people at Legg Mason they should read it."

At that moment I knew *Trend Following* might be catching on a little—at least in some very rarified circles. Forget sales—which were very good—I knew that if *Trend Following*'s message had struck a chord with Miller, who was not trading as a trend follower, I might be on to something life changing.

However, now it is time to bring this living work forward to 2017 and a whole new audience and generation for I have barely dented the broad consciousness of global investors. Roughly $80 trillion of investable assets sit squarely at the mercy of EMT inside buy and hold and/or passive index funds with only a quarter of 1 percent of assets in trend following strategies. Almost everyone's savings and retirement monies are literally a slave to wobbly economic theory that leaves the masses unprepared for the next smack down.

It is necessary for you to learn from others' mistakes. You will not live long enough to make them all yourself.
Hyman G. Rickover

That *slavery* is why I have yet again opened up the chest cavity on *Trend Following*. Not outpatient surgery to correct typos, but open-heart surgery to add thousands of details—big picture to minutia that bulk up the original to a new and improved *Schwarzenegger-on-steroids* edition. For starters, *Trend Following* is now divided into three sections:

1. *Trend Following*'s original chapters and principles, updated and extended.
2. Trend following interviews (new): Seven interviews from pros illuminate trend following's big picture with the requisite finer details.
3. Trend following research (new): Research contributions that add to the trend following conversation for average investors, professionals and scholars.

The river meanders because it can't think.
Richard Kenney

This is my most radical and extended volume. Content changes and additions are everywhere. It's now three books in one. I have added material in a way where you can take small steps or go for the deep dive—starting on almost any page. The tone is different, too. Toned down in some areas, toned up in others. Some of my younger *blank* and vinegar was expunged and reformulated to a new mature version, while staying true to the heart and soul of my origins. Last, some might complain there is too much information, too much content, and I am throwing the kitchen sink at the subject. If so, I will be happy with that criticism. Guilty as charged.

Now, if you're looking for guru secrets or easy money riches—please head on back to that OxyContin bender. There is no such thing. If you're in the mood for outlandish predictions, stories about the ultimate *gut* trader, or what it's like to work inside a Wall Street bank, or if you want to complain life is unfair and beg for the government to save you with a bailout—no one can help you on your path to irrelevance. Or, worse yet, if you maintain faith in EMT, steadfastly refusing to consider overwhelming contradictory evidence, maybe you can burn me in effigy along with Bouchaud and Harding. If you fit any of these problematic profiles, there is a good chance my words, and my politically incorrect perspective, will give you an aneurysm. Turn me off now.

"Trend" synonyms: tendency, movement, drift, swing, shift, course, current, direction, progression, inclination, leaning, bias, bent.

In the alternative, if you want outside-of-the-box *different*, the truth of how out-sized returns are made without any fundamental predictions or forecasts, this is it. And if you want the honest data-driven proof, I expect my *digging* will give everyone the necessary confidence to break their *comfort* addiction to the box they already know and go take a swing at making a fortune in bull, bear, and black swan markets.

—Michael W. Covel

Section I

Trend Following Principles

Trend Following

1

An object at rest stays at rest and an object in motion stays in motion with the same speed and in the same direction unless acted upon by an unbalanced force.
—Newton's First Law of Motion

Speculation is dealing with the uncertain conditions of the unknown future. Every human action is a speculation in that it is embedded in the flux of time.
—Ludwig von Mises[1]

Speculation

It might sound pedantic or perhaps that I am focusing on the extraneous, I am not: A speculator's ability to receive a *price* they can count on as *fact*—is the foundation of markets. Said another way, with no *price*, humanity is back to cavemen beating each other with clubs. Austrian economist Ludwig von Mises puts price discovery's value in perspective:

The aim is to make money, not to be right.
Ned Davis

> It is the very essence of prices that they are the offshoot of the actions of individuals and groups of individuals acting on their own behalf. The catallactic concept of exchange ratios and prices precludes anything that is the effect of actions of a central authority, of people resorting to

> violence and threats in the name of society or the state or of an armed pressure group. In declaring that it is not the business of the government to determine prices, we do not step beyond the borders of logical thinking. A government can no more determine prices than a goose can lay hen's eggs.[3]

The people that I know who are the most successful at trading are passionate about it. They fulfill what is the first requirement: developing intuitions about something they care about deeply, in this case, trading.
Charles Faulkner[2]

Although government can't determine prices in the long run, in the short-term, government will attempt to directly *rig* the market system via QE, ZIRP, NIRP, or whatever acronym sure to follow.

However, speculation is all there is for making choices about those market prices. Learning how best to speculate using prices is not only a worthy endeavor—it is a survival-of-the-fittest concept that traces back to the earliest literature of Wall Street.

From *Young America on Wall Street* (1857), quoting a French poem about a latter-day millionaire:

> Monday, I started my land operations;
> Tuesday, owed millions, by all calculations;
> Wednesday, my brown-stone palace began;
> Thursday, I drove out a spanking new span;
> Friday, I gave a magnificent ball;
> Saturday, smashed—with just nothing at all.[4]

There is nothing wrong with that turn of events. It's normal. It's the expected up and down. Luck is always in play, but so is skill. From *The Theory of Stock Exchange Theory* (1874):

Who will check the 'fact checkers?' Who will watch the watchmen?
Anonymous

> A man who wins by haphazard speculation, who chances to operate successfully until he has filled his pockets, and retires with his gains from so fascinating an arena, is one in a hundred. Any one who knows anything of Stock Exchange speculation will confirm the statement that, to the ordinary run of men, the game is not worth the candle. There are, however, conditions under which speculation, in a market where ten or fifty thousand pounds can be lost in half an hour, may, under given conditions, be systematically practiced profitably. First, and most important perhaps of all those conditions, is the temperament of the speculator. When it is known in a market that a great speculator is selling, weak bulls are speedily frightened out, and when he has such an object in view it is his *game* to intimidate with all the force

of his prestige and the power of his capital. Such a man must have a concrete hardness of indifference through which nothing can penetrate to his heart. It is as necessary to the success of his operations that he posses no more regard for the feelings or pockets of other people than a hungry tiger would for him if he were airing himself unconcernedly in a Bengal jungle. He has a purpose in view, just as a surgeon has when the amputation of a leg has been decided upon. The speculator's sole aim in the operation is the profit, towards which he cuts his way, regardless of the nature of the obstacles to be overcome, just as the knife is plunged into the flesh, severing the arteries, muscles, and sinews that surround the bone, which it is the object to reach and saw through. For a man to tread a path in which he must systematically not only disregard the interest of other people, but deliberately calculate upon the weaknesses of human nature which characterize the crowd, in order to work upon them for his own ends, it is obvious that he must be constituted in a quite exceptional manner, and not in a way that it is at all desirable others should attempt to imitate. If uninitiated people who enter the arena in which some of the professional speculators flourish, were to spend some months in gathering information and in close observance of the modus operandi, so far as they can get to see and hear, many of them would soon be persuaded that they were utterly useless at such work, and would retire, thanking their stars. The haphazard man, who is the antithesis of the professional speculator, will generally be found as differently constituted as are the results of his operations. The man who makes a study and business of speculating, investigating every detail that it seems necessary to probe until he has adapted it to the rest of his machinery, will be found to be a hard-grained man, sailing very close to the wind, while your persistently haphazard man is mostly a person of flabby character, and no less flabby mind, as easily frightened off a line that he has set himself to follow, in the innocence of a heart that expands with a delusive consciousness of possessing power, as a stray rabbit. Such a class of man is to be found by hundreds in the haunts of the stock markets, and they are always fidgeting in and out, first as little bulls, and then as little bears, disappearing after a sharp panic like flies from a joint of meat that is rudely disturbed by the shop-boy, with the important difference that whereas the flies always get something, the speculators invariably drop their money.[5]

Too many people simply give up too easily. You have to keep the desire to forge ahead, and you have to be able to take the bruises of unsuccess. Success is just one long street fight.

Milton Berle

From *How to Win and How to Lose* (1883) arguably the first trend-based market *player* arrives: "The shrewdest operator ever known on the London Stock Board was David Ricardo (1772–1823) who amassed an enormous fortune. In advice to a friend he sums up as the true secret of his success, the rule, every word of which is golden. 'Keep down your losses—never let them get away from you. Let your profits take care of themselves.'"[6]

That precept is huge. *Timeless.* If you were to put Ricardo into language of modern day computer science 134 years later you would say, *optimal stopping* or *win-stay, lose-shift* or *A/B testing*. More clarification from 1883 keeps the focus on taking a loss: "Speculation is looked upon as being so much more risky than other avocations cause its results are more sudden and startling, though not one whit more disastrous. Statistics show that ninety-five out of one hundred men fail in mercantile life. The proportion is not greater among speculators: quicker action is obtained whether it be favorable or unfavorable, and it does not take five or ten years' time to find that you are playing a losing game."[7]

A study on human behavior shows 90% of the population can be classified into four basic personality types: Optimistic, Pessimistic, Trusting and Envious. Envious, at 30%, is the most common.
Universidad Carlos III de Madrid

No one is saying that attitude comes naturally. From *The Art of Investing* (1888): "Then, in theory, it is so easy to win by speculation! To buy at a low figure and sell at a higher, or to sell at a high figure and afterward buy at a lower, seems such a simple operation! It almost looks as if you could go into Wall Street and pick up money from the sidewalks."[8]

Intense study, practice, is the rock solid foundation. From *Gold Bricks of Speculation* (1904):

> Speculation is inherent in the human constitution, and men have a legal and moral right to speculate, provided they do so reasonably, intelligently and at their own risks. Reasonable speculation is such speculation as cannot seriously or permanently affect the resources or position of the persons indulging in it. Intelligent speculation is such speculation as is indulged in only after a thorough investigation and study of the subject of the speculation. The professional speculator is in the market not for the purpose of either depressing or raising prices. He is as ready to make money on a rise as on a fall in prices. In either case he will try to ascertain what the probable tendency of the market is before he embarks in any undertaking. No speculator or clique of speculators in their senses would undertake to try to depress prices in the face of a rising market.[9]

From *Investments and Speculation* (1911) it's easy to see free-market capitalism and less government as optimal:

> Call it what you will, speculation will always be with us. Prudes may frown upon it, superficial thinkers may confuse it with the commonest forms of gambling, and sociologists may dream of the day when envy, ambition and covetousness will be a thing of the past and the human race can exist in peace without these human traits, but their agitations and outcries can no more check speculation than human ingenuity can devise a scheme to control the tides. What the blood is to the human body, speculation is to business. It is absolutely a necessary part of it. The only difference, if there is at all a difference, is in the form it assumes. What would business be without incentive? In fact incentive is all there is at the bottom of speculation. Men are willing to take risks to acquire wealth. They are willing to stake their capital upon opportunities, which appeal to their judgment. From the pioneer who heedlessly plunges into a trackless waste to find a new home with greater opportunities for the acquisition of wealth, to the modern capitalist, who, to control the trade in a given commodity, plans gigantic trusts, is a long line of speculators, as speculation is behind all their ambitions. The inventor who is, apparently, of all men the least of speculators, takes greatest speculative chances, for he uses up time and energy to shape his ideas into some form where they can be of practical use and should he fail has wasted them utterly and lost all. Illustration after illustration could be given to demonstrate how speculation in a greater of less degree enters into the material welfare of each individual. Without speculation no business could progress. It is the dynamic power behind every incentive to activity and progress. It is the desire for gain, which prompts the inception of every venture. If it is all that, then it can be readily seen how necessary speculation is. In fact, speculation in its highest form has shaped the course of history and often changed the map of the world. Intelligent speculation is no crime. It is not gambling. It is merely pitting human shrewdness against the uncertainties of the future. For that matter, life itself is a speculation in which ministers, prudes and agitators hope to avoid sickness and accident and live their allotted span of life. Between speculation and gambling there is as much difference as there is between night and day. Speculation commands

The free market punishes irresponsibility. Government rewards it.

Harry Browne

The absolute number doesn't matter, it's the trend over time.

Seth Godin

> the exercise of the greatest measure of acumen, where gambling trusts everything to luck and the turn of a card. Experience has demonstrated far too convincingly that wherever speculation has been leashed by the iron bonds of the law, the effect has been almost an immediate stoppage in the material progress of the country.[10]

And finally from *Psychology of the Stock Market* (1912), one year before the Federal Reserve System was established, the behavioral school comes into focus:

> The psychological aspects of speculation may be considered from two points of view, equally important. One question is: "What effect do varying mental attitudes of the public have upon the course of prices?" "How is the character of the market influenced by psychological conditions?" A second consideration is: "How does the mental attitude of the individual trader affect his chances of success?" To what extent, and how, can he overcome the obstacles placed in his pathway by his own hopes and fears, his timidities and his obstinacies? [11]

Gaslighting is a form of manipulation that seeks to sow seeds of doubt in a targeted individual or members of a group, hoping to make targets question their own memory, perception, and sanity.
Wikipedia

This wisdom is clean, clear, and instantly *true* for those awake. These days, however, speculation is often positioned as a pejorative among the intelligentsia. While I enjoy Oliver Stone's outsider status, his film *Wall Street: Money Never Sleeps* (2010) paints speculation quite differently, as his film's main character Gordon Gecko profanes, "The mother of all evil is speculation."[12]

Stone is not alone in making an enemy out of speculation. New age guru Deepak Chopra makes the sweeping generalization that "Wall Street is broken for sure because it succumbed to greed and corruption and pure speculation with no values."

Wall Street, the phrase, can mean *anything*. If Chopra is talking big bank bailouts it is easy to agree with him, but pure speculation practiced *honestly* is far from valueless. Politicians, too, love the sport of ripping speculators, an enduring ritual. United States socialist Bernie Sanders was predictable: "I'm not much into speculation." The character Bobby Axelrod of *Billions* counters Sanders: "What have I done wrong? Really? Except make money. Succeed. All these rules and regulations? Arbitrary. Chalked up by politicians for their own ends."

Axelrod is of course a fictional, fast and loose day trader built on inside information, but his *words*, words uttered by many an honest man over the millennia, expose in raw form the hatred inferior minds have toward speculation and reinforce it as a worthy endeavor—at least for those disconnected from *The Matrix*.

Winning versus Losing

It is typical the general public equates *winning* in the markets with abusing the financial market system—you know the horror stories so I won't overwhelm you. However, there are players with the utmost integrity who achieve spectacular returns year after year. Examine their beliefs and self-perceptions and you will understand what keeps them *honest*. But before you examine their perspectives, take a moment to consider your own.

The joy of winning and the pain of losing are right up there with the pain of winning and the joy of losing. Also to consider are the joy and pain of not participating. The relative strengths of these feelings tend to increase with the distance of the trader from his commitment to being a trader.

Ed Seykota[13]

For example, at the end of the 1990s or let's say summer 2007 or even fall 2016 for that matter, when investors were feeling more secure financially on *paper*, the you-know-what hit the fan or was about to, and by the time it was over, they had lost significant money. They became angry with analysts, experts, brokers, and money managers whose advice they had guzzled down. Now they know they will not meet their investment goals or come close to the mythological retirement. They've religiously held on to their remaining investments hoping they will eventually turn around, but 401(k) decisions are paralyzing. They still believe indexing or buying and holding is the way to go—after all, they've been sold that meme for decades. But now as a final act of desperation, they give up—they rationalize winning as only dumb luck.

Still others lost even more in October 2008, but, win or lose, they enjoy the thrill in the hopes of the one trade that makes them rich. Investing gurus, stock tips, and all of that is their entertainment. Plus they love to boast about their investments—ego needs attention, after all. Yes, they are depressed and angry when they lose, but when they win it feels terrific—it's the heroin-junkie high. Since their main goal is to invest for quick profits, they will keep doing what they've always done. After all, there was one time a few years ago when a *tip* made a nice profit they still dream about.

If you think education is expensive, try ignorance.

Derek Bok

Stop.

There is a much better way to think: Your approach becomes objective, moving as close as you can to rational. You have enough confidence in your own decision making that you never seek out investment recommendations. You're content to wait patiently for the right opportunity. And you're never too proud to buy a stock making new highs, even all-time highs. For you, investing opportunities are market *breakouts*. Conversely, when wrong, you exit immediately, no questions asked. You view loss as an opportunity to learn, move on, and save money to play another day. Obsessing on the past is pointless. You approach trading as a business, making note of what you buy or sell and why in the same matter-of-fact way you balance your checkbook. By not personalizing your trading decisions, your emotional indecision has the chance to decrease.

The first perspective is that of a market loser; the latter a winner. Don't be in a hurry to choose your approach until you know what the choice entails. And look, don't be shy about it. You have to want the money. You have to want to get ahead and be rich—the critics' condemnation, the player hating, the rank jealousy be damned. Speculation is not only honorable—it is life. Profit-seeking speculation is the absolute driving force of markets and without it there is only disintegration.[14]

Nothing has changed during the 21 years [over 40 years now] we've been managing money. Government regulation and intervention have been, are, and will continue to be present for as long as society needs rules by which to live. Today's governmental intervention or decree is tomorrow's opportunity. For example, governments often act in the same way that cartels act. Easily the most dominant and effective cartel has been OPEC, and even OPEC has been unable to create an ideal world from the standpoint of pricing its product. Free markets will always find their own means of price discovery.
Keith Campbell[15]

Investor versus Trader

Wide swaths of the population think as investors in search of a bargain. However, if you were to learn the most consistent market winners call themselves traders, you would want to know why. Simply put, they don't invest—they trade.

Investors put their money, or capital, into a market, such as stocks or real estate, with the assumption that value will always increase over time: "I am *long* and never wrong!" As value increases, their investment and psychological reinforcement also increase. But investors have no plan when their value drops. They hold on to their investment, hoping the value will go back up. Investors succeed in bull markets and lose in bear markets—like clockwork.

This is because investors have zero plan to respond when losses mount. They always choose to *hang tight* and continue to lose. And if mainstream press continually positions investing as *good* or *safe* and trading as *bad* or *risky*, average investors will be reluctant to align themselves with trading. Better to trust the mutual fund, and government systems, and fall asleep.

A trader, on the other hand, has a defined plan or strategy to put capital to work to achieve profit. Traders don't care what they buy or what they sell as long as they end up with more money than their starting capital. They are not investing in anything. They are trading. It is a critical distinction.

Trader Tom Basso believes a person is a trader whether or not he or she is trading. Some mistakenly think they must be in and out of the markets every day to call themselves traders. What makes someone a trader has more to do with their perspective on life more than making a given trade. For example, a great trader's perspective must include extreme patience. Like the African lion waiting days for the right moment to strike its unsuspecting prey, great trading strategy can wait weeks or months for the right trade with the right odds, and only then pull the trigger.

He who lives by the crystal ball will eat shattered glass.

Ray Dalio

Additionally, and ideally, traders will go *short* as often as they go *long*, enabling them to make money in both up and down markets. However, many traders won't or can't go short. They struggle with the counterintuitive concept of making money on market declines. I would hope the confusion associated with making money in down markets will dissipate, but it won't. Human nature believes in only *up*.

Fundamental versus Technical

There are two basic trading theories. The first is fundamental analysis. It is the study of external factors that affect the supply and demand. Fundamental analysis uses factors such as Federal Reserve meetings, 24/7 news, weather reports, regulatory knowledge, price-earnings ratios, and balance sheet projections to make buy and sell decisions. By monitoring all *fundamentals*, one can supposedly *predict* a change in direction before that change has been reflected in the price of the market, with the belief you can then make money from that knowledge. That means you can sit around, ponder the viability of Uber's autonomous car fleet, make your bets on whatever markets, and the easy bling money rolls in.

Whenever we get a period of poor performance, most investors conclude something must be fixed. They ask if the markets have changed. But trend following presupposes change.

John W. Henry[16]

The vast majority of Wall Street is fundamental analysis alone. They are the bankers, academics, brokers, and analysts who always have an opinion or prediction, rain or shine. Many of these Wall Street players have serenaded millions with fundamental stories for decades. Gullible and naïve investors buy into rosy fundamental projections riding bubbles straight up with no clue how to exit. Consider an exchange with President George W. Bush before the Great Recession:

> **Question:** "I'm a financial advisor here in Virginia, and I wanted to ask you what your thoughts are on the market going forward for 2008 and if any of your policies would make any difference?"
>
> **President Bush:** "No (laughter), I'm not going to answer your question. If I were an investor, I would be looking at the basic fundamentals of the economy. Early on in my Presidency, somebody asked me about the stock market, and I thought I was a financial genius, and it was a mistake (laughter). The fundamentals of this nation are strong. One of the interesting developments has been the role of exports in overall GDP growth. When you open up markets for goods and services, and we're treated fairly, we can compete just about with anybody, anywhere. And exports have been an integral part, at least of the 3rd quarter growth. But far be it for me—I apologize—for not being in the position to answer your question. But I don't think you want your President opining on whether the Dow Jones is going to—(laughter)—be going up or down."

With the possible exception of things like box scores, race results, and stock market tabulations, there is no such thing as objective journalism. The phrase itself is a pompous contradiction in terms.
Hunter S. Thompson

The President's view is a cardboard cutout of the type of fundamental view shared by the vast majority of market participants. An excerpt from Yahoo! Finance outlining a typical market day is instantly familiar: "It started off decent, but ended up the fourth straight down day for stocks. Early on, the indices were in the green, mostly as a continuation from the bounce Monday afternoon, but as the day wore on and the markets failed to show any upward momentum, the breakdown finally occurred. The impetus this time was attributed to the weakness in the dollar, even though the dollar was down early in the day while stocks were up. Also, oil prices popped higher on wishful thinking statements from a Venezuelan official about OPEC cutting production. Whether or not these factors were simply excuses for selling, or truly perceived as fundamental factors hardly matters."

One of our basic philosophical tendencies is that change is constant, change is random, and trends will reappear if we go through a period of non-trending markets. It's only a precursor to future trends and we feel if there is an extended period of non-trending markets, this really does set up a base for very dynamic trends in the future.
Research at John W. Henry[17]

Millions consume news or fake news drivel such as this every minute, hour, day, year, and decade. Thousands have watched the likes of CNBC's Jim Cramer's *Mad Money* show promote similar projections for what seems like decades (actually back to 2005). But predictions based off fundamental analysis are a crapshoot guessing game, as you will never know all fundamentals in what has become an ever-expanding fact and fact-less society.

But instead of helping people to understand *news* is not at all critical to their moneymaking decision making, politicians across the globe are gearing up to stamp out the supposed scourge of *fake news*. For example, State of California Assembly member Jimmy Gomez introduced Assembly Bill (AB) 155 in 2017 "to ensure that upcoming generations of online readers possess the analytical skills needed to spot fake news. The bill would direct the *Instructional Quality Commission* to develop and adopt curriculum standards and frameworks that incorporate civic online reasoning, for English Language Arts, Mathematics, History, Social Science, and Science."

[Insert your own Orwellian reference.]

Trader Ed Seykota notes across the board cognitive dissonance in play with a simple story: "One evening, while having dinner with a fundamentalist, I accidentally knocked a sharp knife off the edge of the table. He watched the knife twirl through the air, as it came to rest with the pointed end sticking into his shoe. 'Why didn't you move your foot?' I exclaimed. 'I was waiting for it to come back up,' he replied."[18]

Our ace in the hole is that the governments usually screw things up and don't maintain their sound money and policy coordination. And about the time we're ready to give up on what usually has worked, and proclaim that the world has now changed, the governments help us out by creating unwise policy that helps produce dislocations and trends.

Jerry Parker[20]

Everyone knows an investor waiting for their market to come back, and it often never does. The financial website Motley Fool has a backstory, a narrative behind its start that reinforces the folly of fundamental analysis: "It all started with chocolate pudding. When they were young, brothers David and Tom Gardner learned about stocks and the business world from their father at the supermarket. Dad, a lawyer and economist, would tell them, 'See that pudding? We own the company that makes it! Every time someone buys that pudding, it's good for our company. So go get some more!' The lesson stuck."[19]

The Motley Fools' David and Tom Gardner's pudding story is *cute*, but it's misleading in design. Their plan gets you in, but it doesn't get you out or tell you how much of that pudding stock you should buy. Many low information types believe that easy to digest narrative. I can only scream inside my head: "Houston, we've got a freaking problem!"

Ultimately, it is the dollar-weighted collective opinion of all market participants that determines whether a stock goes up or down. This consensus is revealed by analyzing price.

Mark Abraham

A second market theory, technical analysis, operates in stark contrast to the funnymentals. This approach is based on the belief at any given point in time, market prices reflect all known factors affecting supply and demand. Instead of evaluating fundamental factors, technical analysis looks at the market prices themselves. But an understanding of technical analysis can quickly become confusing and controversial. There are essentially two forms of technical analysis. One is based on an ability to read charts or use indicators to *predict* market direction.

And predictive technical analysis rightly deserves poignant criticism:

> "I often hear people swear they make money with technical analysis. Do they really? The answer, of course, is that they do. People make money using all sorts of strategies, including some involving tealeaves and sunspots. The real question is: Do they make more money than they would investing in a blind index fund that mimics the performance of the market as a whole? Most academic financial experts believe in some form of the random-walk theory and consider technical analysis almost indistinguishable from a pseudoscience whose predictions are either worthless or, at best, so barely discernibly better than chance as to be unexploitable because of transaction costs." [21]

Now walking into client meetings we hardly ever have a discussion around why trend following works—the battle has been won.
Anthony Todd

This is the view of technical analysis held by most who think they know of it—that it is a form of chart reading, astrology, moon cycle analysis, chart pattern wiggle feelings, Elliott waves to the first, second, third, fourth, and fifth degree, and—Barry Ritholtz's favorite one to skewer—the *Death Cross*. Big bank equity research departments add to confusion by asking the wrong question: "The question of whether technical analysis works has been a topic of contention for over three decades. Can past prices forecast future performance?"[22]

It gets worse. Consider a recent *Red Alert* example from HSBC: "The Head & Shoulders Top with the neckline acting as resistance comes on top of a potentially bearish Elliot Wave irregular flat pattern and the fact that the index is now backing off from the old 2015 highs. A close below 17,992 would be very bearish. Pressure would ease above 18,449."[23]

Good luck with that.

There is a second type of technical analysis that neither predicts or forecasts. This type is based on *reacting* to price action, as trend trader Martin Estlander notes: "We identify market trends, we do not predict them. Our models are kept reactive at all times."[24]

Mebane Faber expands on *reaction* by noting three criteria are necessary for a model to be simple enough to follow, yet mechanical enough to remove emotion and subjective decision making:

1. Simple, purely mechanical logic
2. The same model and parameters for every asset class
3. Price-based only[25]

Instead of trying to predict market direction (an impossible chore), trend following reacts to movements whenever they occur. This enables a focus on the actual price risk, while avoiding becoming emotionally connected with direction, duration, and fundamental expectations.

This price analysis never allows entry at the exact bottom of a trend or an exit at the exact top. And you won't necessarily trade every day or week. Instead, trend following waits patiently for the right conditions. There is no forcing an opportunity not there. And with this view there are not exact performance goals. Some want a strategy that dictates, "I must make $400 a day." The trend following counter is, "Sure, but what if markets don't move on a given day?" Trend following works because you don't try to outthink it. You are a trend *follower*, not a trend *predictor*.[26]

It is not the strongest of the species that survive, nor the most intelligent, but the ones most responsive to change.

Charles Darwin

Discretionary versus Systematic

There are investors and traders, and trading can be fundamentally or technically based. Further, technical trading can either be *predictive* or *reactive*. However, there is more distinction. Traders can be discretionary or mechanical.

Trader John W. Henry makes a clear distinction between the two strategies: "I believe that an investment strategy can only be as successful as the discipline of the manager to adhere to the requirements in the face of market adversity. Unlike discretionary traders, whose decisions may be subject to behavioral biases, I practice a disciplined investment process."[27]

When Henry speaks of decisions that may be subject to behavioral biases, he is referring to those who make their buy and sell decisions on fundamentals, the current environment, or any number of other whatever factors. It's a never-ending parade of data they can supposedly sift through and utilize. In other words, they use their discretion—hence, the use of *discretionary* to describe their approach.

Investing should be more like watching paint dry or watching grass grow. If you want excitement, take $800 and go to Las Vegas.

Paul Samuelson

Decisions made at the *discretion* of the trader can be changed or second-guessed nonstop. These discretionary gut-trading decisions will be colored by personal bias. I have yet to see a multi-decade track record produced by gut trading. It's 100 percent fantasy. Many imagine the process is like a fighter pilot strapped into the cockpit armed with an instinctive feel, or even an innate gift. It's not that.

Now, a trader's initial choice to launch a trading system is discretionary. You must make discretionary decisions such as choosing a system, selecting your portfolio, and determining a risk percentage (some would argue even these aspects can be made systematically too). However, after you've decided on the system-orientation basics, you can systematize these discretionary decisions and make them mechanical.

Mechanical or systematic trading systems are based on objective rules. Traders put rules into computer programs to get in (buy) and out (sell) of a market. A mechanical trading system eliminates emotional vacillation. It forces discipline to stick with the process. If you rely on mechanical trading system rules, and break them with discretion, you are guaranteed to go broke.

Henry puts into perspective the downsides of discretionary thinking: "Unlike discretionary traders, whose decisions may be subject to behavioral biases, we practice a disciplined investment process. By quantifying the circumstances under which key investment decisions are made, our methodology offers investors a consistent approach to markets, unswayed by judgmental bias."[28]

Maybe it is rigid to say it's against the rules to use a little discretion. You might think, "How boring to live like a CPA." Where's the *fun* if all you ever do is follow a mechanical model? Successfully making fortunes isn't about excitement. It's about winning. A researcher at Campbell & Company, one of the oldest and most successful trend following firms, is adamant: "One of our strengths is to follow our models and not use discretion. This rule is written in stone at Campbell."[29]

The trend is your friend except at the end when it bends.
Ed Seykota[30]

Trend trader Ewan Kirk adds:

> Systematic trading involves coming up with a statistical model of the markets. Assuming that model has worked in the past, and that you have developed and researched and tested your model correctly, then your hypothesis is that it's likely to keep working in the future. So the actual execution of trades is just continuing to follow what the model says. Now that sounds quite mechanical. In fact, it's no different than the way any good investor works. Why would you invest with Warren Buffett? Because, over the past 30 years, Warren Buffett has made money, and you're assuming that's going to continue in the future. Conceptually, that's no different than what we do.[31]

Traders Todd Hurlbut and Ted Parkhill further note the perils in discretion: "We are systematic. We have seen examples where managers either start to doubt and then start tinkering so there is what today is called style shift or worse where a manager dramatically changes the approach to what could be called style 'flip.'"[32]

Hiding in Plain Sight

Trend following, and assorted derivatives of price-based trading, is not a new concept. It goes back across names like David Ricardo, Jesse Livermore, Richard Wyckoff, Arthur Cutten, Charles Dow, Henry Clews, William Dunnigan, Richard Donchian, Nicolas Darvas, Amos Hostetter, and Richard Russell. Believe it or not, it literally goes back centuries, with data to prove it (see Chapter 19 and 20 in Section III, "Trend Following Research").

AQR's Cliff Asness clarifies: "Historically, it's been a strategy pursued primarily by futures traders and in the last 10–20 years by hedge funds. The trading strategy employed by most managed futures funds boils down to some type of trend following strategy, which is also known as momentum investing."[33]

Even traders not typically associated with trend following eventually find their way. In *Hedge Fund Market Wizards*, Jack Schwager asked Ed Thorpe, an American mathematics professor, author, hedge fund manager, and blackjack player best known as the "father of the wearable computer," if he believed "there are trends inherent in the markets?" Thorpe replied: "Yes. Ten years ago, I wouldn't have believed it. But a few years ago, I spent a fair amount of time looking at the strategy. My conclusion was that it works, but that it was risky enough so that it was hard to stay with it."[34]

Defining a trend is like defining love. We know it when we see it, but we are rarely sure exactly what it is. Fung and Hsieh's paper goes a long way to doing for trends what poets have been trying to do for love since time immemorial. They give us a working model that quantitatively defines their value for us. Traders will not be surprised to learn that trend following advisors performed best during extreme market moves, especially during bad months for equities.[36]

Thorpe noted he used trend following, too. And so it goes; price-based trend strategies discovered by new and old generations at different times. Salem Abraham, now an established trend following veteran, began researching the markets in his early twenties by asking a simple question: "Who is making money?" His answer was "trend followers" and his journey began.[35]

Still, not many have made the journey. During the Dot-com era of the late 1990s, throughout the Fed-induced S&P run-up after March 2009, and even today into 2017, many with zero strategy have made money in other ways, so trend following becomes a blip on the radar screen—seemingly not so important.

And since trend following has nothing to do with high-frequency trading, short-term trading, cutting-edge technologies or Wall Street hocus pocus nonsense, its appeal is universally lost during extraordinary delusions unleashed inside the madness of crowds—that is, until bubbles pop. Trend following is not *sexy* until after the masses get poached and bleed out.

Change is not merely necessary to life—it is life.
Alvin Toffler

Nonetheless, if you look at how much money trend following has made before, during, and after assorted market bubbles, it becomes far more relevant to the bottom line of astute market players.

Yet, even when over the top trend following success is thrown onto the table, skeptical investors can be tough sells. They might say markets have changed and trend following no longer works. But philosophically trend following hasn't changed and won't change, even though markets might not always cooperate.

Let's put change in perspective. Markets behave the same as they did hundreds of years ago. In other words, markets are the same today because they always change—humans are involved, after all. This behavioral view is the philosophical underpinning of trend following. A few years ago, for example, the German mark had significant trading volume. Then the euro replaced the mark. This was a huge change, yet a typical one. If you are flexible and have a plan of attack—a solid strategy—market changes, like changes in life, won't kill you. Trend followers traded the mark; now they trade the euro. That's how to *think*.

Accepting that inevitability of change is an initial step to understanding. One trend follower elaborates:

> But what won't change? Change. When a period of difficult performance continues, however, most investors' natural conclusion is that something must be done to fix the problem. Having been through these draw downs before, we know that they are unpleasant, but they do not signal that something is necessarily wrong with the future. During these periods, almost everyone asks the same question in these exact words: "Have the markets changed?" I always tell them the truth: "Yes." Not only have they changed, but they will continue to change as they have throughout history. Trend following presupposes change. It is based on change.[37]

Markets of course are built by design to go up, down, and sideways. They *trend* or *chop*. They *flow* or don't. They are consistent, then they *surprise*. No one accurately can forecast a trend's beginning or end until it becomes a matter of record. However, if your trading strategy is designed to adapt, you can take advantage of changes:

> If you have a valid basic philosophy, the fact that things change turns out to be a benefit. At least you can survive. At the very least, you will survive over the long-term. But if you don't have a valid basic philosophy, you

> won't be successful because change will eventually kill you. I knew I could not predict anything, and that is why we decided to follow trends, and that is why we've been so successful. We simply follow trends. No matter how ridiculous those trends appear to be at the beginning, and no matter how extended or how irrational they seem at the end, we follow trends.[38]

A valid basic philosophy means a trading strategy that can be defined, quantified, written down, and measured in terms of numbers. Trend following does not guess at buys and sells. It knows what to do because valid basic philosophy is codified into a specific plan for all contingencies.

The people who excel in any field are people who realize that the moment is there to be seized—that there are opportunities at every turn. They are more alive to the moment.

Charles Faulkner[39]

The Man Group, one of the largest trend following traders, describes the source behind their profits:

> ...trends as a persistent price phenomenon that stems from changes in risk premiums—the amount of return investors demand to compensate the risks they are taking. Risk premiums vary massively over time in response to new market information, changes in economic environment, or even intangible factors such as shifts in investor sentiment. When risk premiums decrease or increase, underlying assets have to be priced again. Because investors typically have different expectations, large shifts in markets result over several months or even years as expectations are gradually adjusted. As long as there is uncertainty about the future, there will be trends for trend followers to capture.

Change Is Life

Patrick Welton saw no evidence trend following has devolved. He constructed 120 trend following models. Some were reversal based, and some not. Some were breakout-style trading systems based on price action, and others relied on volatility and band-style breakouts. The average holding periods ranged from two weeks to one year. The results gave almost identical performance characteristics.

The four most expensive words in the English language are: this time it's different.

Sir John Templeton

Welton addressed head on the misconception that the sources of return for trend following had changed. He pointed out starting from first principles, it was a fact the source of return for trend following resulted from sustained market price movements. Human reaction to such events (read: Daniel Kahneman), and the stream of information describing them, takes time and runs its course unpredictably. The resulting magnitude and rate of price change could not be reliably forecast. This is the precise reason why trend following works.[40]

They are like surfboard riders, who study the movements of the waves, not in order to understand why they behave as they do, but simply in order to be on hand whenever they surge, to catch them at their crest, or as soon thereafter as possible to ride them as far as they possibly can, and to dissemble before they change direction.
Morton S. Baratz[41]

One fund consultant confronted trend trading skeptics decades before trend following's huge October 2008 positive returns:

> [In the 1980s] on a tour of Germany sponsored by the Deutsche Terminborse, several advisors and pool operators were making a presentation to a group of German institutional investors. Among them were two trend-based traders, Campbell and John W. Henry. During the question-and-answer period, one man stood and proclaimed: "But isn't it true that Trend Following is dead?" At this point, the moderator asked that slides displaying the performance histories for Campbell and Henry be displayed again. The moderator marched through the declines, saying, "Here's the first obituary for trend-based trading. Here's the next one . . . and the next but these traders today are at new highs, and they consistently decline to honor the tombstones that skeptics keep erecting every time there's a losing period." Campbell and Henry have made their investors hundreds of millions of dollars since that time. It might, therefore, be a mistake to write yet another series of obituaries.[42]

Markets don't move from one state to another in a straight line: There are periods of countertrend shock and volatility. We spend most of our time trying to find ways to deal with those unsettling but inevitable events. That being said, it is really not difficult to put together a simple trend following system that can generate positive returns over a realistic holding period and there are many, many commercial systems that have been generating strong, albeit volatile, returns for a long time. So there are definitely firm grounds for believing in Santa Claus.
Paul Mulvaney

Like sunrise, sunset you can always expect a new trend following obituary, oblivious to the data, and rooted in purposeful ignorance, will be written every few years by an agenda-driven press, EMT defenders, and player haters despite the incredible amounts of money made by trend following practitioners.

Perplexed at Wall Street's lack of acceptance, one trend follower sees the danger in trying to be *right*: "How can someone buy high and short low and be successful for two decades unless the underlying nature of markets is to trend? On the other hand, I've seen year-after-year, brilliant men buying low and selling high for a while successfully and then going broke because they thought they understood why a certain investment instrument had to perform in accordance with their personal logic."[43]

Trend following trader Paul Mulvaney made the point: "One thing to bear in mind is that we have made no changes to our trend following strategy since 2005. So in a way we take the ancient Spartan view that everything that needed to be said about long-term trend following has already been said." He continued: "In recent years our research has focused on execution algorithms—but those are of minor importance versus the strategic trend following *philosophy*."

Here is Mulvaney's philosophy in performance data format:

Monthly Net Returns (%)

	JAN	FEB	MAR	APR	MAY	JUN	JUL	AUG	SEP	OCT	NOV	DEC	YEAR
2016	5.94	10.75	−13.52	−2.84	−8.35	27.33	−1.01	−13.30	18.22				**16.72**
2015	6.93	−0.50	3.84	−7.98	4.13	−6.07	4.77	−9.23	6.15	−11.05	13.52	−2.10	**−0.77**
2014	−1.46	1.36	4.65	2.67	−4.47	2.37	2.25	9.33	17.69	−1.67	13.05	9.05	**67.36**
2013	10.46	7.39	9.29	9.73	0.13	−3.15	−4.03	−10.90	2.61	7.29	11.58	−1.24	**43.12**
2012	−3.75	0.78	5.21	−1.08	−0.90	−18.12	11.38	−6.26	−8.58	−15.07	−0.97	0.76	**−33.72**
2011	2.07	9.78	−4.62	6.07	−11.82	−7.41	11.15	1.59	−4.20	−14.14	12.05	−1.64	**−5.26**
2010	−3.84	−7.15	−5.15	2.02	−8.77	0.53	−12.03	14.59	16.46	22.29	−5.36	25.30	**34.90**
2009	1.60	−0.03	−3.36	−5.51	−1.30	−6.81	−0.53	10.85	1.32	−7.86	10.70	−3.19	**−5.90**
2008	21.65	28.86	−7.96	−8.58	5.35	8.51	−18.78	−6.73	11.58	45.49	6.97	5.30	**108.87**
2007	0.56	−5.18	−8.82	2.59	4.70	4.85	−16.89	−19.40	3.92	13.72	−8.59	8.47	**−23.14**
2006	11.09	−2.70	13.05	11.46	−4.27	−6.10	−5.20	1.95	1.00	−0.13	0.56	1.60	**21.94**
2005	−4.28	0.54	2.30	−9.28	−4.08	5.32	6.62	2.78	13.57	−5.64	15.27	8.35	**32.34**
2004	4.19	8.45	2.37	−11.50	−6.99	−0.73	−0.41	−6.21	7.76	0.76	9.63	−4.94	**−0.10**
2003	13.20	7.22	−12.83	1.45	7.64	−7.61	−6.33	0.07	6.66	15.32	−0.27	5.35	**29.28**
2002	—	—	−7.52	1.55	6.75	7.38	5.95	5.44	5.13	−7.73	−5.08	7.80	**19.37**
2001	−9.62	18.76	13.46	−15.25	−0.66	5.39	−1.26	—	—	—	—	—	**6.69**
2000	−5.02	2.52	−8.40	−0.27	6.97	1.55	−1.25	12.68	−4.36	1.96	9.05	8.90	**24.51**
1999					−0.29	−0.14	−2.22	2.13	−4.81	−4.80	7.01	4.84	**1.09**

Mark Spitznagel, a trader focused on *tails* and a close associate of Nassim Taleb, would characterize Mulvaney's returns as "lumpy" with "extreme asymmetric payoffs"—exactly how he would refer to his trading world. And whether using Spitznagel's strategy, or Mulvaney's go-for-the-gusto high-octane strategy, an opportunistic plan of attack knows you aim to lose battles, but win the war.

By honest I don't mean that you only tell what's true. But you make clear the entire situation. You make clear all the information that is required for somebody else who is intelligent to make up their mind.

Richard Feynman

Let me be clear, though: Mulvaney's track record is but one example for industrious types to go reverse-engineer, to learn step by step how those volatile but overall *up* numbers came to be. His performance table is an initial shot across the bow to bring you into the trend following, month-to-month mindset of no benchmarks. But trend following is much more than one trend following track record alone—this strategy has performed consistently for more than a century across an untold number of traders. And the reasons to explain why markets have tended to trend more often than not include investors' behavioral biases, market frictions, hedging demands, and never-ending market interventions launched by central banks and governments.[44]

Follow the Trend to the End When It Bends

In an increasingly uncertain and downright unfriendly world, it is extremely efficient and effective to base decision making on the single, simple, reliable truth of price. The 24/7 never-ending fundamental data barrage, such as price-earnings ratios, crop reports, and economic studies, plays right into the tendency to make trading more complicated than it need be. Yet by factoring in every possible fundamental piece of data, which is impossible, you still would not know how much and when to buy, or how much and when to sell. The truth of *price* always wins if the debate is grounded in reason. Price is the only fact.

That said, even if you digest price as the key trading variable, it is not unusual for traders to focus on only one market—usually individual stocks in their home country to the exclusion of all other global opportunities. Seeking a maximum degree of comfort, many follow their one familiar market's movements faithfully every day. They never dream of branching out into currencies or futures or coffee or gold. The idea you could know enough about Tesla and soybeans to trade them the same might be unfathomable, but think about what cotton, crude oil, Cisco, GE, the U.S. dollar, the Australian dollar, wheat, Apple, Google, and Berkshire Hathaway all have in common: price action.

Warren Buffett says in the long run the stock market is a weighing machine and in the short term it is a voting mechanism. He exploits the weighing machine and we exploit the voting mechanism.
David Harding

Market prices, traded prices, are the unequivocal objective data reflecting the sum total of all views. Accepting that truth allows you to compare and study prices, measuring their movements, even if you don't know a damn thing about fundamentals. You could absolutely look at individual price histories or charts, without knowing which market is which, and trade them successfully. That is not what they teach at Harvard or Wharton, but it is the foundation of making millions as a trend following trader.

Further, don't try to guess how far a trend will extend. You can't. You will never know how high or how low any market might go. Peter Borish, former second-in-command with Paul Tudor Jones, lays bare the trader's only concern: "Price makes news, not the other way around. A market is going to go where a market is going to go."[45]

The concept of price as the paramount trading signal is too simple for Wall Street to accept. This confusion or misinformation is seen across the mainstream press where they always emphasize the *wrong* numbers. Bill Griffeth, of CNBC, "At some point, investing is an act of faith. If you can't believe the numbers, annual reports, etc., what numbers can you believe?"

He misses the point. It doesn't matter whether you can or cannot believe an earnings statement. All of those numbers can be doctored, fixed, cooked, or faked. The traded market price can't be fixed. It's the only number you can believe. You can see it every day. However, this does not diminish confusion. Alan Sloan, a finance reporter, doesn't get it: "If some of the smartest people on Wall Street can't trust the numbers, you wonder who can trust the numbers."

I know Sloan is droning on about balance sheets and price-earnings ratios. You can't trust those numbers—*ever*. Bad actors can always alter them. Even if you knew accurate balance sheet numbers, that info doesn't necessarily correlate with buying and selling at the right time.

A critical lesson from an old-pro trend trader:

> Political uncertainty is one reason why investment decisions are not driven by discretionary judgments. How, for example, do you measure the impact of statements from [central bankers and treasury chiefs]? Even if we knew all the linkages between fundamentals and prices, unclear policy comments would limit our ability to generate returns . . . trying to interpret the tea leaves in Humphrey-Hawkins testimony or the minds of Japanese policy authorities does not lend itself to disciplined systematic investing. Instead of trying to play a loser's game of handicapping policy statements, our models let market prices do the talking. Prices may be volatile, but they do not cloud the truth in market reactions. Our job is to systematically sift price data to find trends and act on them and not let the latest news flashes sway our market opinions.[46]

Ed Seykota is a genius and a great trader who has been phenomenally successful. When I first met Ed he had recently graduated from MIT and had developed some of the first computer programs for testing and trading technical systems. . . . Ed provided an excellent role model. For example, one time, he was short silver and the market just kept eking down, a half penny a day. Everyone else seemed to be bullish, talking about why silver had to go up because it was so cheap, but Ed just stayed short. Ed said, "The trend is down, and I'm going to stay short until the trend changes." I learned patience from him in the way he followed the trend.

Michael Marcus[48]

William Eckhardt, a trend follower and former partner of Richard Dennis (see my book *TurtleTrader*), describes how price is to live and die by: "An important feature of our approach is that we work almost exclusively with price, past and current. . . . Price is definitely the variable traders live and die by, so it is the obvious candidate for investigation. . . . Pure price systems are close enough to the North Pole that any departure tends to bring you farther south."[47]

Understanding how a trend follower implements that philosophy is illustrated in Ed Seykota's sugar story. He had been buying sugar—thousands of sugar futures contracts. And every day, the market was closing limit up. Every day, the market was going nonstop higher and higher. Seykota kept buying more and more sugar each day limit up. An outside broker was watching all of Seykota's action. And one day the broker called him after the market close, and since he had extra contracts of sugar that were not balanced out, he said to Seykota, "I bet you want to buy these other 5,000 contracts of sugar." Seykota replied, "Sold."

After the market closes limit up for days in a row, Seykota says, "Sure, I'll buy more sugar contracts at the absolute top of the market." Everybody instinctively wants to buy sugar on the dip or on the retracement. Let it come down lower they pine. "I want a bargain" is their thinking—even if the bargain never appears. Trend following works by doing the opposite: It buys higher highs and sells short lower lows.

Be less curious about people and more curious about ideas.
Marie Curie

Good Traders Confuse Price

The trading histories of Julian Robertson and Louis Bacon, two famed hedge fund titans, underscore the importance of price for decision making.

After the Dot-com crisis Julian Robertson shut his long-running hedge fund down. He was a global macro trader who relied on fundamentals for decision making. Robertson had a close relationship with another global macro trader, Louis Bacon. Bacon was extremely secretive to the extent that it was nearly impossible to find out his performance numbers unless you were a client. Although Bacon did not advertise himself as a trend follower, he was focused on price action:

"If a stock goes from 100 to 90, an investor who looks at fundamentals will think maybe it's a better buy. But with Louis [Bacon], he will figure he must have been wrong about something and get out." Contrast that, say, with [Julian] Robertson, who, even after shutting down his firm, was doggedly holding on to massive positions in such stocks as U.S. Airways Group and United Asset Management Corp. . . . [Bacon made the comment] in an investor letter that 'those traders with a futures background are more sensitive to market action, whereas value-based equity traders are trained to react less to the market and focus much more on their assessment of a company's or situation's viability.'"[49]

Every successful trader is a trend follower even if they don't use the technique, admit it, or know it.

The wisest trend follower I know has said that every five years some famous trader blows up and everyone declares trend following to be dead. Then, five years later, some famous trader blows up and everyone declares trend following to be dead. Then, five years later . . . was the problem trend following or the trader?
Anonymous

Trend followers know to pick the trend start is a masochistic exercise. When trends start they often come from flat markets that don't appear to be trending anywhere—it's choppy, up-and-down, trendless, go-nowhere market action. The solution is to take small bets early to see if the trend will mature and get big enough to ride.

An executive at trend following pioneer Graham Capital Management clarifies, "The ability of trend following strategies to succeed depends on two obvious but important assumptions about markets. First, it assumes that price trends occur regularly in markets. Secondly, it assumes that trading systems can be created to profit from these trends. The basic trading strategy that all trend followers try to systematize is to 'cut losses' and 'let profits run.'"[50]

I asked Charles Faulkner to expand:

> The first rule of trading is to, "Cut your losses, and let your profits run." And then, that it's the hardest thing to do. Seldom do any of them wonder why, and yet this is exactly where the efficient market theory breaks down, and the psychological nature of the markets shows through. When we lose or misplace something, we expect to find it later. The cat comes back. We find our car keys. But we know a dollar on the street will not be there with the next person who passes by. So experience teaches us that losses are unlikely and gains are hard. "A bird in the hand is worth two in the bush." This is when I tell them that they earn their trading profits by doing the hard thing—by going against human nature. This is where the discipline comes in, the psychological preparation, the months of system testing that give the trader the confidence to actually trade against his natural tendencies.

If cutting losses and letting profits run is the trend following mantra, it is because harsh reality dictates you can't play the game if you run out of money. No money, no honey! Trend trader Christopher Cruden sarcastically builds the thought: "I would prefer to finish with a certain currency forecast, based upon my own fundamental reading of the market and one that underpins my personal investment philosophy. . . . The only problem is I can't tell you when this will happen or which event will be first. On that basis alone, it seems best to stay with our systematic approach."[52]

A good example of not letting profits run can be seen in trading strategies that take profits off the table before the trend is over. For example, one broker told me one of his strategies was to ride a stock up for a 30 percent gain and then exit. That was his strategy. Let it go up 30 percent

Trend following is similar to being long options because the stop loss creates a limited downside, and the continuation of the trend creates the large upside. This is why the phrase for this approach to trading is to cut losses and to let profits run. Of course, if trends continually fail to materialize, these limited losses can accumulate to large losses. This is also true for any option purchase strategy. For trend followers, the option premium is paid for after an unsuccessful trade is closed when a stop loss has been reached. The premium can also be paid after markets have moved a great deal, profits have been made, and a reversal causes a trailing stop to be hit, and some of the profits reversed.

President, Graham Capital Management[51]

In Patton, *my favorite scene is when U.S. General George S. Patton has just spent weeks studying the writing of his German adversary Field Marshall Erwin Rommel and is crushing him in an epic tank battle in Tunisia. Patton, sensing victory as he peers onto the battlefield from his command post, growls, "Rommel, you magnificent bastard. I read your book!"*

Paul Tudor Jones in George Soros' *The Alchemy of Finance*

and get out. Sounds reasonable. However, a strategy that uses profit targets is problematic at a root level. It goes square against the math of getting rich, which is always without question to let your profits run. If you can't predict the end or top of a trend, don't get out early and risk leaving profits on the table—you will need the biggest winners after all to pay for the smaller losers.

Bull market babies don't survive, they revert to the mean.
Michael Covel

For example, let's say you start with $50,000. The market takes off and your account swells to $80,000. You could, at this point, quickly pull your $30,000 profit off the table. Your wrong thinking is if you don't take those profits immediately, they will be gone.

Trend followers know that a $50,000 account may go to $80,000, back to $55,000, back up to $90,000, and from there, perhaps, all the way up to $200,000. The person who took profits at $80,000 is not around to take the ride up to $200,000. Letting your profits run is tough psychologically. But understand in trying to protect every penny of your profit you never make big profits. Those are the stark choices for the big boy game.

You are going to have ups and downs in your trading account. Get over it. Losses are a part of the trading game no matter the strategy. If you want no losses, if you want positive returns every month, well, you could have had your money with the Ponzi scheme of Bernard Madoff and his fake monthly 1 percent performance, but you know how that turned out. You can't make money if you are not willing to lose. It's like breathing in, but not willing to breathe out.[53]

Think of it this way: If you don't have losses, you are not taking risks. If you don't risk, you won't ever win big. Losses aren't the problem. You must always *cut* them. Ignore losses with no plan, let them build up, and they will come back to wipe out your account.

I began to realize that the big money must necessarily be in the big swing.
Jesse Livermore

Theoretically, really big losses rarely befall trend following strategy because it eliminates or reverses positions as soon as the market goes against it. The rationale for hanging in is that any price move could be the beginning of a trend, and the occasional big breakout justifies a string of small losses.[54]

Surf the Waves

I am fortunate to have learned from trader Ed Seykota starting in 2001 with our first Virgin Islands meeting, through a 2012 panel with Larry Hite, and up to his 2016 podcast appearance. But early on he told me a story about being in Bermuda with a new trader who wanted *secrets.* "Give me the quick-and-dirty version of your magical trading secrets," the neophyte beamed.

Seykota took the new trader out to the beach. They stood there watching the waves break against the shoreline. The newbie asked, "What's your point?"

Seykota said, "Go down to the shoreline where the waves break. Now begin to time them. Run out with the waves as they recede and run in as the waves come in. Can you see how you could get into rhythm with the waves? You follow the waves out and you follow them in. You follow their lead."

The truth of trend following is its philosophical underpinnings are relevant not only to trading, but to life in general, from business to personal relationships. The old-pro trend followers were clear with me, in their words and actions: Trend following works best when pursued with the right *mindset* and unbridled *passion.*

Many people would sooner die than think; in fact, they do so.

Bertrand Russell

First, consider the role of proper mindset. As Stanford psychologist Carol Dweck teaches, "In a fixed mindset, people believe their basic qualities, like their intelligence or talent, are simply fixed traits. They spend their time documenting their intelligence or talent instead of developing them. They also believe that talent alone creates success—without effort. They're wrong. In a growth mindset, people believe that their most basic abilities can be developed through dedication and hard work—brains and talent are just the starting point. This view creates a love of learning and a resilience that is essential for great accomplishment. Virtually all great people have had these qualities."[55]

Second, trading coach and psychologist Brett Steenbarger argues the passion point: "Find your passion: the work that stimulates, fascinates, and endlessly challenges you. Identify what you find meaningful and rewarding, and pour yourself into it. If your passion happens to be the markets, you will find the fortitude to outlast your learning curve and to develop the mastery needed to become a professional. If your passion is not the markets, then invest your funds with someone who possesses an objective track record and whose investment aims match your own. Then go forth and pour yourself into those facets of life that will keep you springing out of bed each morning, eager to face each day."[56]

In my experience it became crystal clear when used within the context of mindset and passion, the term *trend following* can be substituted in this edition for other aspects of life. That insight crystallized in a passage from Brenda Ueland's 1938 book on creative writing: "Whenever I say *writing* in this book, I also mean anything you love and want to do or to make. It may be a six-act tragedy in blank verse, it may be dressmaking or acrobatics, or inventing a new system of double entry accounting . . . but you must be sure that your imagination and love are behind it, that you are not working just from grim resolution, i.e., to impress people."[57]

Among people who take the trouble to understand what the business is about instead of assuming it involves speculating on live cattle, it is readily understood.
Campbell & Company[58]

Successful trend followers don't trade with grim resolve or with the intention to impress. They are playing a game to win and enjoying every moment of it. Like other high-level performers, think professional athletes and world-class musicians, they understand how critical it is to maintain a winning attitude for success. And as Larry Hite told me, good trend following traders ask questions:

> The first question you have to ask yourself: "who are you?" I'm not kidding. And don't look at your driver's license! But what you got to say to yourself: "What am I comfortable doing?" Am I an arbitrager? Am I a short-term trader? It is really important that you understand who you are and what you want to do. The next thing you have to ask yourself, one of the real details, "What are you going to do?" What are you going to do exactly? What has to be done? Is it hard to you? Is it easy? Do you have the materials to do it? One of the great things about the market is the markets don't care about you. The market doesn't care what color you are. The markets don't care if you are short or tall. They don't care about anything. They don't care whether you leave or stay. The last question you have to ask yourself: "What follows?" You have to ask yourself, "If I do this and it works, where am I? What have I got?" Now what I've said may really sound like it's pretty simple and common sense, [but think about the failed hedge fund Long-Term Capital Management] those were some very, very smart people [Nobel Prize winners] who did some pretty *stupid* things. And they did it because they didn't ask themselves the basic questions.

If you take emotion—would be, could be, should be—out of it, and look at what is, and quantify it, I think you have a big advantage over most human beings.
John W. Henry[59]

Armed with Hite's marching orders let's dive deeper into what it takes for trend following excellence.

Summary Food for Thought

- Galileo Galilei: "All truths are easy to understand once they are discovered; the point is to discover them."
- Hendrik Houthakker (1961): "Price changes are not purely random, but follow certain longer run trends." Inspired by Benoit Mandelbrot, Houthakker was an early EMT critic.
- Ed Seykota: "All profitable systems trade trends; the difference in price necessary to create the profit implies a trend."
- Prices, not traders, predict the future.
- If you don't have losses, you are not taking risks. If you don't risk, you can't win anything.
- Price goes either up, down, or sideways. No advance in technology, leap of modern science, or radical shift in perception will alter this fact.
- What if they told you the best way to get to point B, without bumping into walls, would be to bump into walls and not worry about it? Don't worry about getting to point B, but enjoy bumping into walls.[61]
- Trend following strategy is not for trading alone. The MIT blackjack team led by Mike Aponte (podcast episode #22) pursued very similar strategies, as do venture capitalists like Marc Andreessen. Film producer Jason Blum also uses an edge-seeking strategy to produce films.
- To receive my free interactive trend following presentation send a picture of your receipt to receipt@trendfollowing.com.

A trend is a trend is a trend. Gertrude Stein would have said if she were a trader, "Once you have a game plan, the differences are pretty idiosyncratic."

Richard Dennis[60]

2 Great Trend Followers

Most of us don't have the discipline to stay focused on a single goal for five, ten, or twenty years, giving up everything to bring it off, but that's what's necessary to become an Olympic champion, a world class surgeon, or a Kirov ballerina. Even then, of course, it may be all in vain. You may make a single mistake that wipes out all the work. It may ruin the sweet, lovable self you were at seventeen. That old adage is true: You can do anything in life; you just can't do everything. That's what Bacon meant when he said a wife and children were hostages to fortune. If you put them first, you probably won't run the three-and-a-half-minute-mile, make your first $10 million, write the great American novel, or go around the world on a motorcycle. Such goals take complete dedication.

—Jim Rogers[1]

The wise and most efficient way to understand trend following is not by only learning rules that make up the strategy, or by studying behavioral work, but by reviewing every last detail of the traders who practice it—Anthony Robbins modeling 101. However, many are reluctant to concede they might do better with mentoring or guidance—even if only from a *book*. Although they will sign up for a cooking or language class, and bet their money on social media avatars, they won't take advantage of insights from those who have made fortunes. They prefer reinventing the wheel instead of modeling behavior from proven top performers. However, the evidence shows modeling is critical for trend following success.

Ultimately, I've also come to realize through nearly 20 years of research if you take trend following performance data seriously, you make a choice. You can accept the data as fact, make an honest assessment of yourself and your approach to making money, and make a commitment to change. Or you can pretend the performance of trend following traders doesn't exist and stay on passive indexing autopilot while waiting for the inevitable *correction*.

People are mathaphobic.
David Harding

Author Tom Friedman sees the immense benefits in thinking wide. He knows the first step to the contrarian philosophy is that of a *generalist*:

> The great strategists of the past kept forests as well as the trees in view. They were generalists, and they operated from an ecological perspective. They understood the world is a web, in which adjustments made here are bound to have effects over there—that everything is interconnected. Where, though, might one find generalists today? . . . The dominant trend within universities and the think tanks is toward ever-narrower specialization: a higher premium is placed on functioning deeply within a single field than broadly across several. And yet without some awareness of the whole—without some sense of how means converge to accomplish or to frustrate ends—there can be no strategy. And without strategy, there is only drift.[2]

Technical trading is not glamorous. It will rarely tell that you bought at the lows and sold at the highs. But trading should be a business, and a systematic program is a plan to profit over time, rather than from a single trade. High expectations are essential to success, but unrealistic ones just waste time. Computers do not tell the user how to make profits in the market; they can only verify our own ideas.
Cognitrend

The traders I have profiled in *Trend Following* see the playing field as generalists. They see what is important and cut the extraneous. Charles Faulkner notes you must also know *you*:

> Being able to trade your system instead of your psychology means separating yourself from your trading. This can begin with your language. "I'm in the trading business" and "I work as a trader" are very different from "I'm a trader" or "I own a few stocks and bonds" (from a major East Coast speculator). The market wizards I've met seem to live by William Blake's phrase, "I must make my own system or be enslaved by another's." They have made their own systems—in their trading and in their lives and in their language. They don't allow others to define them or their terms. And they are sometimes considered abrupt, difficult, iconoclastic, or full of themselves as a result. And they know the greater truth—they are themselves and they know what works for them.

David Harding is a trend following trader not originally profiled in my first edition. He has established himself as a leader of a new generation of trend followers which includes Leda Braga, Cliff Asness, Martin Lueck, Anthony Todd, Svante Bergström, Gerard van Vliet, Ewan Kirk, Martin Estlander, Zbigniew Hermaszewski, Natasha Reeve-Gray, and Jean-Philippe Bouchaud.

After Harding, I reintroduce all the legendary trend following pros. They provide timeless insights, motivation and lessons for all aspiring trend following traders—from the brand new with zero experience to professionals with perhaps all the wrong experience. There are fantastic lessons from the superstar names, no doubt, but 100 years from now those names will be different. The names *always* change, but trend following strategy endures.

When I first got into commodities, no one was interested in a diversified approach. There were cocoa men, cotton men, grain men—they were worlds apart. I was almost the first one who decided to look at all commodities together. Nobody before had looked at the whole picture and had taken a diversified position with the idea of cutting losses short and going with a trend.

Richard Donchian

David Harding

David Harding has had rock and roll success as a trend following trader. Today, his trend following fund for clients exceeds $30 billion in assets, give or take a billion or two to the upside. He had a long stretch where his firm made 20 percent a year, but has dropped some with his explosion of assets under management.

Born in London and reared in Oxfordshire, Harding was always interested in investing—a result of his father's influence, a horticulturalist who enjoyed betting on the markets. His mother by comparison was a French teacher. As a young man he had a natural inclination for science and quickly found a way to put the talent to use. Early in his career he took a job at Sabre Fund Management where he designed trading systems. Soon thereafter he met Michael Adam and Martin Lueck. The trio went on to launch Adam, Harding, and Lueck (AHL) a trend following firm managing money for clients. In a few years the Man Group bought AHL out and built its trend following firm and systems into a monster with billions under management.[3] Harding, while wealthy from the sale, knew much of Man Group's success was built around his trading systems. But he wanted more than to rest on his buyout winnings, and over time built his new firm Winton Capital into a juggernaut. All that success comes with a certain philosophical underpinning. But before jumping into his philosophy, consider his performance (see Table 2.1):

TABLE 2.1: Monthly Performance Data for Winton Futures Fund (%)

	Jan	Feb	Mar	Apr	May	Jun	Jul	Aug	Sep	Oct	Nov	Dec	Year
2016	3.51%	1.76%	–2.92%	–1.49%	–1.64%	5.21%	0.73%	–1.72%	–0.30%	–2.64%	–1.23%		**–1.06%**
2015	2.89%	–0.01%	2.04%	–3.24%	0.11%	–3.15%	3.90%	–4.27%	3.47%	–1.42%	3.44%	–1.58%	**1.72%**
2014	–2.04%	2.29%	–0.57%	1.81%	1.92%	0.18%	–2.09%	3.98%	–0.39%	3.55%	5.28%	0.64%	**15.23%**
2013	2.27%	–0.35%	2.06%	3.05%	–1.85%	–2.18%	–1.18%	–2.92%	3.09%	2.77%	2.70%	0.52%	**7.98%**
2012	0.66%	–0.80%	–0.66%	0.02%	0.06%	–3.39%	4.32%	–1.15%	–2.25%	–2.55%	1.18%	1.51%	**–3.24%**
2011	0.11%	1.62%	0.20%	3.06%	–2.22%	–2.55%	4.64%	1.55%	0.20%	–2.35%	0.94%	1.54%	**6.68%**
2010	–2.51%	2.29%	4.64%	1.58%	–0.85%	1.46%	–2.83%	4.92%	0.84%	2.62%	–2.23%	3.89%	**14.27%**
2009	0.92%	–0.32%	–1.78%	–3.08%	–2.08%	–1.31%	–1.55%	0.31%	2.73%	–1.54%	5.01%	–2.53%	**–5.38%**
2008	3.92%	8.21%	–0.92%	–0.97%	1.95%	5.22%	–4.66%	–3.09%	–0.38%	3.65%	4.48%	1.93%	**20.25%**
2007	4.03%	–6.39%	–4.13%	6.13%	5.04%	1.83%	–1.38%	–0.96%	6.83%	2.38%	2.45%	0.12%	**16.13%**
2006	3.93%	–2.74%	3.88%	5.68%	–3.21%	–1.34%	–0.62%	4.58%	–1.43%	1.43%	3.10%	2.03%	**15.83%**
2005	–5.16%	5.72%	4.70%	–4.03%	6.49%	2.85%	–2.15%	7.66%	–6.50%	–3.02%	7.05%	–4.59%	**7.65%**
2004	2.65%	11.93%	–0.50%	–8.27%	–0.16%	–3.12%	0.88%	2.64%	4.78%	3.37%	6.38%	–0.58%	**20.31%**
2003	5.30%	11.95%	–11.14%	2.07%	10.18%	–5.85%	–1.15%	0.69%	0.71%	5.46%	–2.68%	10.00%	**25.52%**
2002	–10.81%	–6.14%	11.44%	–4.66%	–3.80%	7.32%	4.79%	5.48%	7.42%	–7.76%	–1.09%	13.46%	**12.86%**
2001	4.58%	0.57%	7.48%	–5.23%	–3.32%	–2.95%	0.72%	0.02%	4.48%	12.45%	–7.56%	–4.02%	**5.56%**
2000	–3.66%	1.75%	–3.13%	1.53%	–0.50%	–1.28%	–4.33%	2.82%	–7.54%	2.50%	7.10%	16.04%	**9.72%**
1999	–1.51%	3.55%	–4.24%	10.09%	–8.58%	5.31%	–1.93%	–3.64%	–0.16%	–6.13%	13.12%	9.20%	**13.24%**
1998	1.50%	3.27%	8.02%	–1.48%	8.53%	3.23%	1.35%	11.06%	4.52%	–5.65%	1.18%	9.19%	**53.26%**
1997										–12.97%	9.96%	8.34%	**3.68%**

I have had the opportunity to talk with Harding on multiple occasions. He always comes across as down-to-earth, a hard worker, but also highly competitive. He wants to win. Harding did not start out with the silver spoon. He worked. To hear him describe it, he engaged in the sort of deliberate practice that Anders Ericsson researched:

> I worked for a company [early on], and the people who ran that took a very old-fashioned approach to trading. About 10 people and I spent the first half of every day drawing about 400 charts by hand. It was very tedious. I did this for about two years. The act of laboriously updating these charts forces you to focus in much more minute detail on data than you normally would, and over a period of time, I became completely convinced the market was not efficient, contrary to the theory at the time.[4] I became convinced that markets weren't efficient and absolutely trended. . . . We trade everything using trend following systems, and it works. By simulation, you come up with ideas and hypotheses, and you test those. Over the years, what we've done, essentially, is conduct experiments. But instead of using a microscope or a telescope, the computer is our laboratory instrument. And instead of looking at the stars, we're looking at data and simulation languages . . . it's counterintuitive to think in terms of statistics and probability. It takes discipline and training; it tortures the machinery. People are much better, for instance, at judging whether another person is cheating in a human relationship. We're hugely social creatures. We're keen on our intuition. But when our intuition is wrong, we'll still be very resistant to being corrected. What are traders' biggest failures about understanding risk? There's a human desire to seek spurious certainty. We try to come to a yes-no answer, one that's absolute, when the right answer might be neither yes nor no. People see things in black and white when often they need to be comfortable with shades of gray.[5]

One of the only things I could say with certainty was that markets trend because I can observe trends in any financial market, in any time era.

Michael Platt

Hedge Fund Market Wizards

Shades of gray are tough medicine to swallow, a tough philosophy to believe down in your core. No one wants to think that hardcore when it comes to money. You might want to imagine uniform precision as possible, but if the guys who make the most money think like Harding, it's smart to try and think that way, too. At the end of the day, perhaps the best lessons I took from Harding came from his original internally published book, *The Winton Papers*. His decision-making philosophy should be absorbed before anyone ever puts a dollar to work in the markets:

> The aggregate effect of shared mental biases and imitation results in patterns of behavior, which while they are nonconsistent with Mr. Spock-like, rational decision-making or with informational efficiency, are demonstrably systematic. The market equivalent of these behavioral patterns is trending, whereby prices tend to move persistently in one direction or another in response to information. The widespread adoption of investing fashions, like indexation, introduces market mechanisms, which magnify herding behavior on a large scale.[6]

Although Harding's words were written before the events of 2008, his insights explain the crash that followed. To those who want to learn how to trade, to those who don't want to affix blame for down performance, Harding offers a way out. But he knows his agnostic approach has critics: "Most people believe it doesn't work or if it did it soon won't work. We almost never do anything based on our opinions. If we do it's based on opinions about mathematical phenomenon and statistical distribution, not opinions about Fed policy."

Summary Food for Thought

- David Harding on EMT: "Economists, academics, modelers, gurus and geeks need to recognize that though a grand and beautifully simple theory applying across financial markets may be desirable, it is most likely impossible."
- Harding: "… the essence of trend following has been effective beyond my wildest dreams and, for me it has been more risky to diversify away from it …"
- Harding: "As the years have unfolded and I have had experience of the seemingly magical phenomenon of trends, my prejudice in favor of this unloved and unheralded investment approach has hardened. To a statistician this is called a Bayesian Philosophy."
- Harding: "Humans are prone to unpredictable behavior, to overreaction or slumbering inaction, to mania and panic."

Bill Dunn

Bill Dunn's firm made 50 percent in 2002 when the majority of investors were losing big from the Dot-com blowout. The firm made 21 percent in the one month of October 2008 when most of Wall Street was melting down. And into 2017 the firm's track record exceeds 40+ years. Dunn Capital performance data is a clear, consistent, and dramatic demonstration of trend following.

Dunn was the original founder and chairman of Dunn Capital Management, Inc. By his original design the firm has always traded for above average returns. Dunn has no defined target for return (other than positive). There is nothing in their risk management that precludes annual returns approaching 100 percent. There is no policy, for example, if a Dunn portfolio was up 50 percent by mid-year, they would rest, and dial back for the rest of the year. Further, since 1984 their track record shows 10 drawdowns in excess of 25 percent (Did you know Warren Buffet has drawdowns too?). But whatever the level of volatility, this independent, self-disciplined, and long-term trend follower never deviates from the core strategy:

Whenever you can, count.
Sir Francis Galton[8]

> We have a risk budgeting scheme that certainly was ahead of its time in 1974 and is still—in our opinion—state of the art in [2017].[7]

It is easy to believe that Dunn Capital adheres to core rules set forth 40 years ago if you understand sound business principles: "Essentially, whatever you find will be as true 10 years from now, 20 years from now, 30 or 50 years from now as it is today and as it was 50 years ago. And if you can put your finger on those truths, then you've made a contribution."[9]

Dunn Capital has always believed in order to make money you must live with volatility. Clients who invest must have absolute no-questions-asked trust in the firm's decision making. This trend follower has no patience for questions about their ability to take and accept losses. This "full throttle" approach has proven itself for 40 years, making everyone involved, owners and clients, rich.

The novice trader is at a disadvantage because the intuitions that he is going to have about the market are going to be the ones that are typical of beginners. The expert is someone who sees beyond those typical responses.
Charles Faulkner[10]

The Dunn *risk-budgeting scheme* or money management is based on objective decision making. "Caution is costly" could be the motto. At a certain point if they enter a market and if the market goes down to a point, they exit. To Dunn, trading without a predefined exit strategy is a recipe for disaster.

Dunn Capital's risk management system enables the firm to balance overall portfolio volatility—something the average or even professional investor ignores. The more volatile a market, the less they trade. The less volatile a market, the more they trade. For Dunn, if risk-taking is a necessary means to potential profit, then position sizing should always be titrated to maintain the targeted risk constraint, which in turn should be set at the maximum level acceptable.

Like so many others who share his libertarian views, Bill Dunn's journey to Free Minds *and* Free Markets *began in 1963 when he read Ayn Rand's short collection of essays on ethics.*
Reason Magazine[11]

The Dunn system of risk management ensures discipline:

> One of our areas of expertise in the risk-budgeting process is how risk is going to be allocated to say a yen trade and how much risk is going to be allocated to an S&P trade and what is the optimal balance of that for a full 22 market portfolio. The risk parameters are really defined by their buy and sell signals so it is just a matter of how much you are going to commit to that trade so that if it goes against you, you are going to lose only x percent.[12]

Extreme Performance Numbers

Like Dunn Capital's philosophy this chart (Figure 2.1) assumes an *in-your-face* attitude and that is not negative. That performance data compares returns if you had hypothetically invested $1,000 with Dunn and $1,000 with the S&P. It demands a choice—either put your money with Dunn, learn to trend follow yourself, or pretend trend following does not exist.

March 2006: Changed from market-specific parameter set selection to portfolio-wide parameter set selection. Increased the number of parameter sets from 3 to 100+. Increased markets traded from 26 (financial) to 52 (fully diversified). January 2013–Present: WMA utilizes a dynamic risk management methodology referred to as the Adaptive Risk Profile ("ARP"), which gears exposure to current market conditions. ARP serves to establish the size of WMA's portfolio positions based on a proprietary metric that incorporates expected returns, volatility and inter-market correlations. The program's risk target varies daily and is high only when a preponderance of the signals are in agreement and the correlation matrix of WMA's positions is favorable. Monthly VaR at the 99% confidence level is expected to be in the range of –22% to –8%, with an average monthly VaR of 15%. This translates into an annualized volatility of ~23% over time. Previously (November 1984–December 2012) WMA targeted a static monthly VaR of –20% at the 99% confidence level. During that time (339 months), the 20% monthly loss level was penetrated 4 times, or 1.18%.

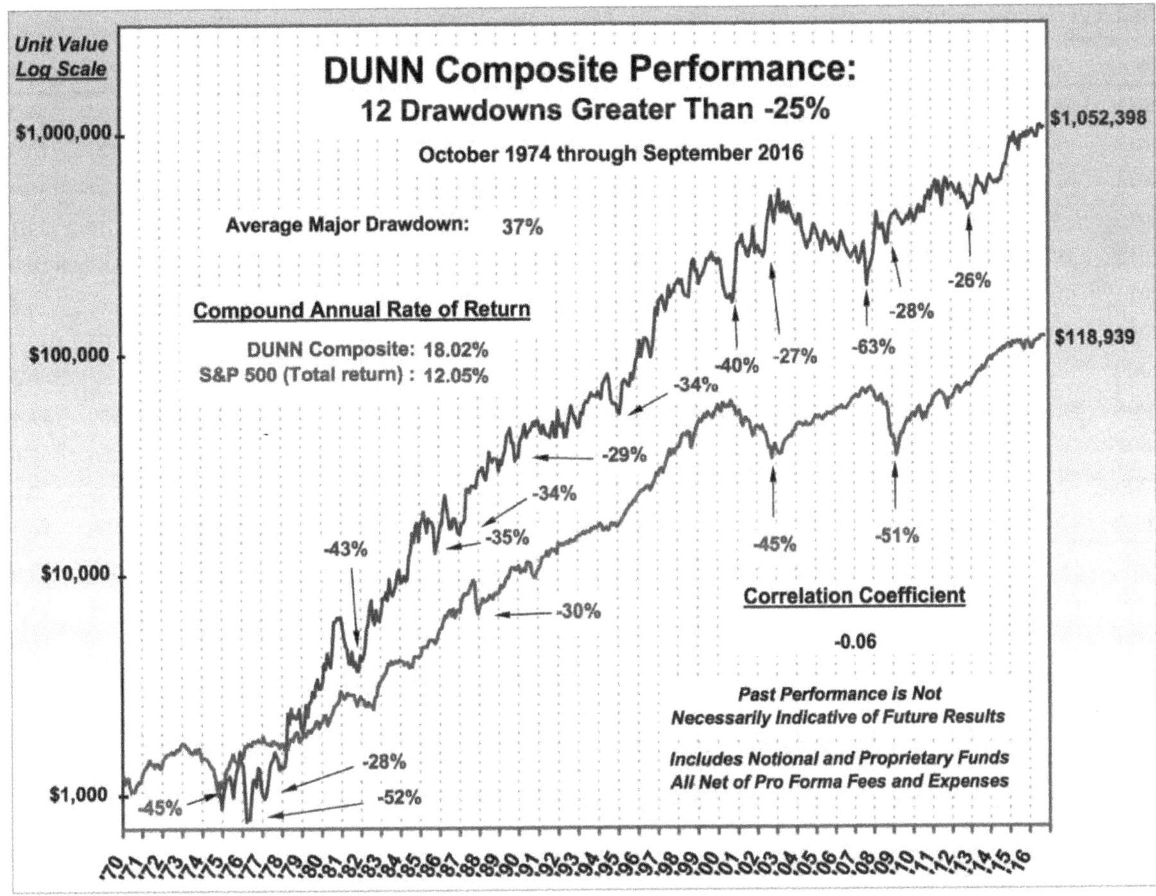

FIGURE 2.1: Dunn Capital Management: Composite Performance 1974–2016

Next, consider two charts that reflect different periods of Dunn Capital's trading history but tell the same story about their approach. The first one (Figure 2.2) is a Japanese yen trade from December 1994 to June 1996, where Dunn made a monumental killing.

Nineteen ninety-five was obviously a great year for Dunn Capital. And in 2003 Bill Dunn walked through his trend following homerun with an audience that came away with an invaluable lesson:

> This is 18 months of the Japanese yen and as you can see, it went up and down and there was some significant trends so we should have had an opportunity to make some money and it turns out we did. Because the WMA is a reversal system, it's always in the market, it's either long

TABLE 2.2: Monthly Performance Data for Dunn Capital Management WMA Program 1984–2016 (%)

Year	Jan	Feb	Mar	Apr	May	Jun	Jul	Aug	Sep	Oct	Nov	Dec	YTD
2016	4.16	2.52	-4.04	-3.38	0.16	12.42	0.38	-3.54	1.46	-12.18	-3.72	2.17	**-5.39**
2015	8.52	-3.87	9.30	-10.78	4.65	-10.72	16.60	-2.41	4.97	-3.85	6.10	-4.24	**10.92**
2014	-4.35	-1.76	-1.91	2.23	-2.33	4.04	-1.12	9.83	7.04	0.22	13.43	7.22	**35.65**
2013	-0.23	16.79	3.22	10.59	-6.67	-1.66	-0.45	-4.81	-4.56	5.81	10.00	4.40	**34.16**
2012	-3.10	-4.96	-2.96	2.77	7.69	-13.23	4.53	-4.17	-4.37	-6.59	3.23	2.64	**-18.62**
2011	3.69	6.17	-12.06	11.78	-10.05	-12.59	19.93	10.40	-2.64	-9.00	5.26	1.25	**6.36**
2010	-6.61	3.97	9.83	4.22	-7.26	5.02	-4.39	16.96	-1.44	8.22	-8.73	10.95	**30.75**
2009	0.89	3.07	-3.05	-4.65	-1.08	-4.98	1.84	3.16	4.54	-4.14	11.00	-5.84	**-0.58**
2008	19.94	29.55	-10.13	-6.55	1.67	3.56	-10.18	-9.26	1.02	21.09	7.77	2.59	**51.45**
2007	6.21	-8.30	-3.36	8.22	11.77	7.39	-17.75	-22.63	16.90	3.00	7.78	6.55	**7.60**
2006	-3.63	-1.37	12.42	9.38	-7.78	-1.63	-5.69	-8.76	-5.22	5.93	4.33	7.86	**3.08**
2005	-4.09	-6.72	-4.04	-15.01	13.03	12.23	-1.89	-5.46	-3.51	-0.94	6.00	-3.88	**-16.41**
2004	-2.86	8.38	-2.90	-18.35	-6.84	-9.86	-5.16	9.29	1.58	7.93	5.32	-0.69	**-16.68**
2003	6.94	13.83	-22.44	1.57	9.45	-8.07	-4.75	16.70	-7.63	-4.23	-4.45	-4.47	**-13.41**
2002	3.03	-8.07	2.39	-5.71	5.41	24.24	14.82	10.50	9.10	-12.27	-12.70	21.34	**54.06**
2001	7.72	0.55	6.26	-8.96	-0.91	-8.31	0.09	6.47	1.13	20.74	-23.52	6.73	**1.10**
2000	6.85	-2.94	-17.34	-12.36	-7.59	-3.95	0.56	3.29	-9.70	9.12	28.04	29.39	**13.08**
1999	-13.18	3.91	4.22	4.09	7.63	9.61	0.52	5.77	3.60	-7.01	1.35	-5.44	**13.34**
1998	4.25	-5.30	3.99	-11.05	-4.76	-0.38	-1.37	27.51	16.18	3.79	-13.72	0.32	**13.72**
1997	17.83	-0.15	2.21	-6.47	-5.88	10.38	16.84	-10.21	6.45	-0.64	9.82	1.55	**44.60**
1996	15.78	-13.33	9.55	9.17	-1.18	0.60	-12.40	-5.20	12.55	20.28	26.94	-7.09	**58.21**
1995	0.49	13.71	24.41	3.80	-2.60	-3.59	0.63	18.46	-6.52	10.82	11.16	4.44	**98.69**
1994	-1.71	-5.34	14.90	6.97	5.21	3.29	-13.38	-17.67	-4.68	-1.02	0.74	-4.22	**-19.33**
1993	2.90	13.99	-3.28	12.37	3.76	0.58	7.41	8.42	-5.02	1.59	1.03	6.10	**60.28**
1992	-14.53	-0.90	4.04	-15.10	-0.36	13.04	11.43	9.18	-8.23	-5.42	-4.30	-8.15	**-21.78**
1991	-7.05	-4.51	10.30	-4.49	-4.99	-0.46	-2.54	9.93	9.23	-14.93	1.20	31.22	**16.91**
1990	23.45	5.35	6.11	6.80	-11.23	3.99	1.37	2.07	3.76	-0.40	5.44	-1.19	**51.55**
1989	21.10	-4.23	9.30	6.09	20.02	3.21	8.15	-13.02	-1.56	-16.65	7.34	-5.42	**30.51**
1988	0.73	4.34	-6.55	-2.47	3.88	-0.56	-1.83	-2.65	1.98	1.92	-0.72	-16.70	**-18.72**
1987	8.81	-1.75	7.18	31.63	-2.69	-4.61	5.97	-2.98	5.50	-5.59	17.76	1.96	**72.15**
1986	-1.50	24.55	11.93	-5.59	-5.98	-13.98	-4.20	12.45	0.64	-2.79	-6.18	-0.11	**3.56**
1985	6.23	10.03	-7.25	-13.09	21.66	-6.79	-8.36	-13.48	-30.68	6.69	13.61	10.02	**-21.68**
1984											-10.95	18.01	**5.09**

or short, trying to follow and identify the major trends. So while this is the first signal that's shown on the chart and is long, we obviously must have been short coming in to this big rise. The rise was enough to tell us we should quit being short and start being long and it seemed like a pretty smart thing do and after we saw that big rise up.[13]

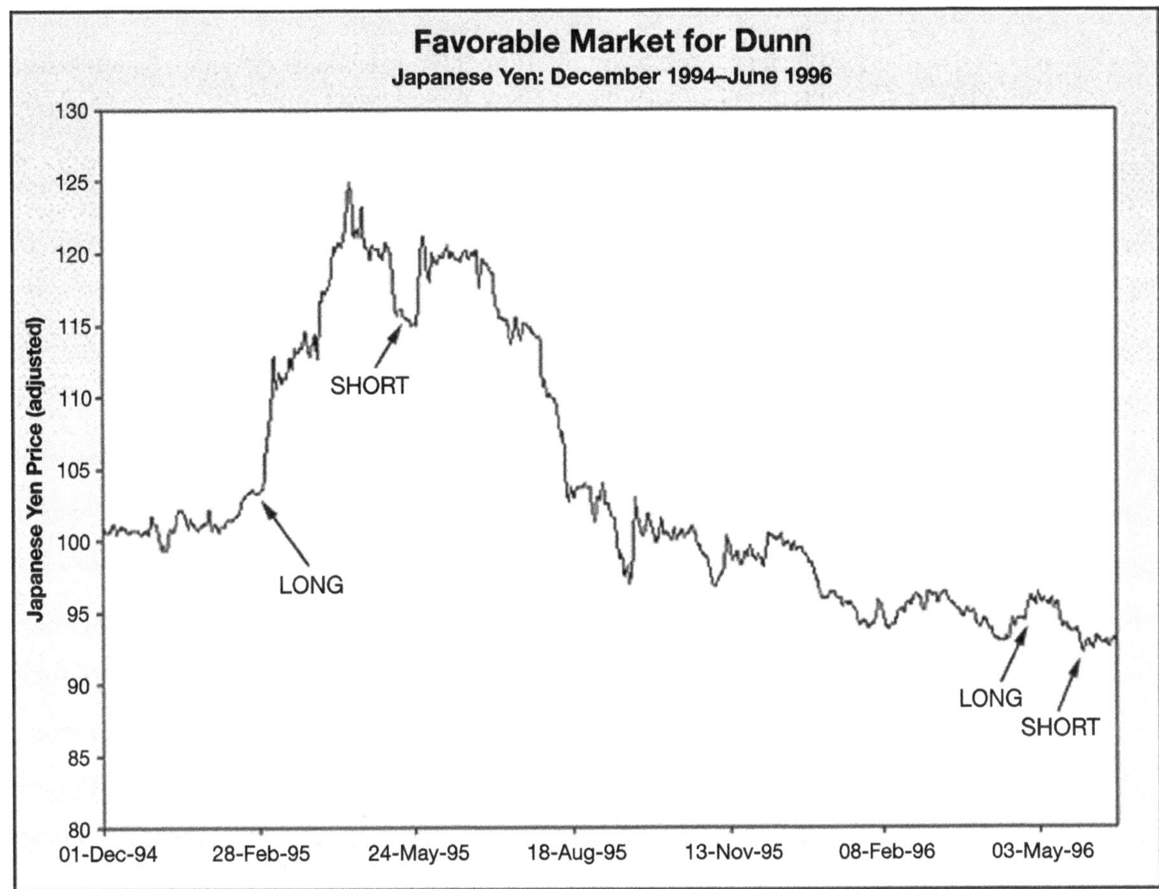

FIGURE 2.2: Dunn Capital's Japanese Yen Trade Source: Dunn Capital Management

Dunn Capital is riding the trend up that first big hill of the yen in March 1995. They are making decisions within the context of their mechanical system. Bill Dunn continues: "Then we have significant retracement, which caused a short signal for the WMA program; our model has always incorporated near-term volatility and this volatility as we went long was far less than the volatility that was going on when we went short."[14]

Bill Dunn summarizes the trade: "Now also because the volatility was very high here, this rise was not enough to give us a long signal and as a result, we rode this short position for nearly a year all the way down—where we got a long signal that was wrong and we reversed and went down to short. Now that was a very, very good market for our program, but some markets are not so good."[15]

The confidence in Bill Dunn's tone and delivery cannot be replicated in print. I feel fortunate to have the original tape.

The beginning is the most important part of the work.
Plato

Be Nimble

Bill Dunn, with a straight face after riding a trend to great profit, once noted: "The recent volatility in the energy complex has been quite exciting and potentially rewarding for the nimble."[16]

What does Dunn mean by *nimble*? They mean they are ready to make decisions based on market movement. When an opportunity to get on a potential trend appears, they are prepared. They take the leap. They are nimble when relying on their system; they react to the Japanese yen move with precise rules because they trust their trading plan and risk management.

The second chart is the British pound (Figure 2.3) where, unlike the Japanese yen, the market proved unfavorable for Dunn Capital. It was a whipsaw market, which is always difficult for trend followers. You can see how they entered and were stopped out; then entered and were stopped out again. Remember, trend following doesn't predict market direction or duration, it reacts—so small losses are always part of the game. Dunn managed the small losses because the British pound was only a portion of their portfolio. Their yen trade more than made up for losses on the British pound trade, because no matter how uncomfortable others are with that approach, for Dunn, big winners offset small losers in the long run.

If you told Bill Dunn his approach made you uncomfortable, he would be blunt:

> "We don't make market predictions. We just ride the bucking bronco."[17]

Dunn's failed British pound trades demonstrate exactly what he means when he says, "We just ride the bucking bronco." In hindsight you might ask yourself why was Dunn Capital trading the British pound if they were losing. The simple answer is they nor anyone else could

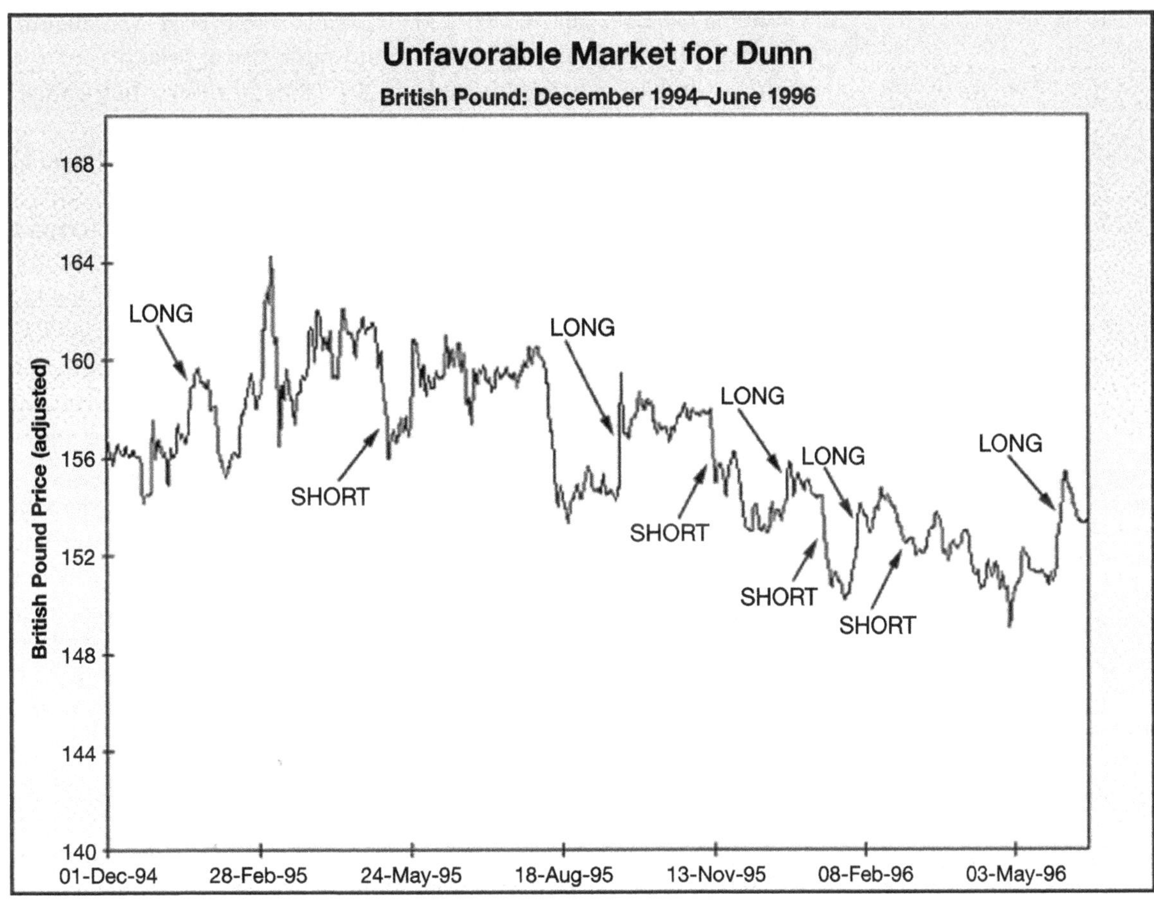

FIGURE 2.3: Dunn Capital's British Pound Trade Source: Dunn Capital Management

have predicted whether or not the British pound would be the next great home run. The real question is, "Do you stay out of the game because you can't predict how the game is going to unfold?"

Early Years

Bill Dunn grew up in Kansas City and Southern California. After graduating from high school, he served three years with the U.S. Marine Corps. In the ensuing years he received a bachelor degree in engineering physics from the University of Kansas in 1960 and a doctorate in theoretical physics from Northwestern University. For the next two years he held research and faculty positions at the University of California and Pomona College. He then worked for organizations near Washington, D.C., developing and testing logistical and operational systems for the Department of Defense. He enjoyed the R&D side of things, but wanted to go beyond theoretical. The markets became his real world.

Around the age of 35 Dunn *got it.* He was working out of his home in suburban Fairfax, Virginia when he came across a newsletter touting a commodity trading system "which almost sounded too good to be true." Upon testing, it turned out to be the case and he set about developing his new system. Using daily data, Dunn's original system looked for big trends as defined by a percentage of a price move from a recent low or high. It traded each market three to five times a year, automatically reversing if the trend moved in the other direction. Dunn determined position size by risking 2 percent to 6 percent of equity under management on each trade.[18]

Gas Station Proprietor: *"Look, I need to know what I stand to win."*

Anton Chigurh: *"Everything."*

Gas Station Proprietor: *"How's that?"*

Anton Chigurh: *"You stand to win everything. Call it."*

Gas Station Proprietor: *"Alright. Heads then."*

[Chigurh removes his hand, revealing the coin is indeed heads]

Anton Chigurh: *"Well done."*[21]

It's not uncommon for long-term trend followers to have trades in place for well over a year, hence the term *long.* If you want day-trading insanity or the feeling of exhilaration in Las Vegas, Dunn Capital is not the firm you should choose as the trading role model. Following their computerized trading system, Dunn holds long-term positions in major trends, typically trading only two to five times per year in each market. Their original system was a reversal system, whereby it is always in the market either long or short. Dunn notes proudly they have held winning positions for as long as a year and a half.[19]

Early on Bill Dunn needed more capital to execute his particular plan of attack on trading. He found it in the person of Ralph Klopenstein. Ralph helped launch Dunn by giving him a $200,000 house account to manage. Dunn, still a Defense Department systems analyst, realized his trading hobby would require a whole lot of other people's money to properly use his promising system.[20]

That's a great lesson: When you stop trying to please others and concentrate on pleasing yourself you become aware of what you are passionate about in life. And when that happens, all sorts of supporters come out of the woodwork to help you achieve your goals. Bill Dunn is serendipity proof positive.

Life inside Dunn Capital

Years back Marty Bergin (podcast episode #525) arranged for me to visit Stuart, Florida and spend a day at Dunn Capital. In one of those classic small-world stories Bergin had been my baseball coach when I was 16 in Northern Virginia outside Washington D.C. Today, he is the president and owner of Dunn Capital while Bill Dunn remains chairman emeritus.

Amazingly, their long time office is on a quiet street located off a waterway in the heart of Stuart, a quiet retirement community 30 miles from West Palm Beach. There is no grand entrance at Dunn Capital, so after you enter, your only recourse is to see if anyone is in. It feels more like an accountant's office than a high-powered trading firm. In fact, the atmosphere is no atmosphere. Dunn is a shining example of why location, pretentious offices, and intense activity have little to do with long-term trading success.

There are not hundreds of employees at Dunn Capital because it doesn't take armies to run the fund. Plus, not all employees are traders. One issue to deal with when running a fund is not necessarily trading, but accounting and regulatory concerns. No one at Dunn is tied to screens discretionarily trading. Trades are systematically entered only after an alarm goes off indicating a buy or sell signal.

Confidence comes from success, to be sure, but it can also come from recognizing that a lot of carefully examined failures are themselves one path to success.

Denise Shekerjian[22]

Another reason Dunn Capital has less infrastructure is because they have a few relatively well-chosen clients. In fact, Bill Dunn was fond of saying, "If people want to invest with me, they know where to find me." Dunn's investors benefit from the fact there is no disconnect between their bottom line as a fund manager and the investor's bottom line—to wit, trading profits.

Dunn Capital is different than many because they compound absolute returns. They leave their own money on the table by reinvesting in the fund. As a result, Dunn's assets are not only made up of clients, but owners and employees too, all systematically reinvesting profits over a very long time.

By focusing on profits and incentive fees Dunn Capital makes money only when the fund (read: clients) makes money. They don't charge a management fee. With no management fee, there is no incentive to constantly raise capital. The only incentive is to make money. If Dunn makes money, the firm gets a portion of the profits. Compounding, or reinvesting your profits, makes sense if you're serious about making money, and Dunn is serious.

In the time I spent with Bill Dunn, Marty Bergin and other staff I was impressed with their matter-of-fact, no-BS attitude. In fact, the very first time I met Bill Dunn he was wearing khakis and a Hawaiian shirt, and made it clear while he looked out over the waterways of Florida, it was his reasoned way or the highway.

No Profit Targets

Dunn Capital doesn't say, "We want 15 percent a year." The market can't be ordered to give a trader a steady 15 percent rate of return, but even if it could, is a steady 15 percent the right way in the first place? If you started with $1,000, what rate of return would you rather have over a period of three years: +15 percent, +15 percent, and +15 percent or the unpredictable –5 percent, +50 percent, and +20 percent? At the end of three years the first hypothetical investment opportunity would be worth $1,520 but the second investment would be worth $1,710. The second one would be a stream of returns representative of a Dunn type trading style.

You can't dial in a return for a given year. There are no profit targets that work. Bill Dunn explained:

> We only have two systems. The first system is the one I started with in 1974. The other system, we developed and launched in 1989. The major strategic elements of these two models—how and when to trade, how much to buy and sell—have never changed in almost 30 years. We expect change. None of the things that have happened in the development of new markets over the past 30 years strike us as making the marketplace different in any essential way. The markets are just the markets. I know that is unusual. I know in the past five years a lot of competitors have purposefully lowered the risk on their models i.e., they are deleveraging them or trying to mix them with other things to reduce the volatility. Of course, they have also reduced their returns.[23]

He is addressing a critical issue: reducing risk to reduce volatility for nervous clients. The result is always lower absolute returns. If you remain fixated on volatility as an enemy, instead of seeing volatility as the source of profit, you will never *get* this.

Money management is the true survival key.
Bill Dunn[24]

Dunn Capital by definition is very good at using risk management—more commonly called money management, or as Van Tharp calls it, position sizing—to their advantage. In June 2002 Dunn returned 24.26 percent, then followed that with 14.84 percent for July. By that time he was up 37 percent for the same year in which buy-and-holders of the NASDAQ for this period were crushed. Dunn Capital finished 2002 up more than 50 percent. Their 2008 performance was huge again—a big up year when most of the world was collapsing.

How does Dunn do it:

- *Cuts losses.*
- *Never changes core strategy*: Dunn Capital's performance is not a result of human judgment. Their trend following is quantitative and systematic with no discretionary overrides of system-generated trade signals. This is foreign to those who watch CNBC for stock tips. Dunn's trading style doesn't drift.
- *Long-term holding*: For holding periods of approximately 3.75 years and beyond, all returns are positive for Dunn Capital. Lesson? Stay with a system for the long haul and do well.
- *Compounding*: Dunn Capital compounds relentlessly. The firm plows profits back into their trading system and builds upon fresh gains.
- *Recovery*: Dunn Capital had losing years of 27.1 percent in 1976 and 32.0 percent in 1981, followed by multi-year gains of 500 percent and 300 percent, respectively. You must be able to accept drawdowns and understand that recovery is around the corner.
- *Going short*: Dunn Capital goes short as often as he goes long. Buy-and-holders generally never consider the short side. If you are not biased to trend direction, you can win either way.

Dunn Capital has had its share of drawdowns, but their approach remains clear and calm: "Some experience losses and then wait for gains, which they hope will come soon . . . But sometimes they don't come soon and sometimes they don't come at all. And the traders perish."[25]

Nevertheless, don't think for a second you are not going to suffer drawdowns, either by trading like Dunn Capital or letting them manage your money. And drawdowns—a.k.a. your account going down—will make you feel like you need an extra dose of Prilosec.

There are great lessons to be learned from Dunn Capital's performance data, but I found insight in their writings as well[26]:

1. As global monetary, fiscal, and political conditions grow increasingly unsustainable, the trend following strategy that Dunn Capital steadfastly employs may possibly be one of the few beneficiaries.
2. The only thing that can be said with certainty about the current state of the world economy is that there are many large, unsustainable imbalances and structural problems that must be corrected. Perhaps the equity markets are correctly predicting a rapid return to more

stable and prosperous times. Perhaps not. Regardless, there seems to be more than ample fodder for the creation of substantial trends in the coming months.

3. On the truly bright side, it is comforting to know that the opinions expressed in this letter will have absolutely no bearing on the time-tested methods that Dunn Capital uses to generate trading profits and manage risk.

Change is not merely necessary to life—it is life.
Alvin Toffler

I love that even though Bill Dunn, Marty Bergin and the firm have strong political opinions, they know opinions mean zilch when it comes to proper trading. Their political and economic opinions do not form the basis of when to buy and sell. These problems prevent clients from seeing Dunn Capital's perspective:

- Clients usually do not understand trend following's nature. They often panic and pull out just before the big move makes a lot of money.
- Clients may start asking for the trader to change their approach. Although they may not have articulated this directly to the fund manager, they really wanted the trend following strategy customized for them before investing their money in the first place. The manager is then faced with a difficult decision: Take the client's money and make money through management fees (which can be lucrative) or trade the capital as originally designed. Trading a trend following system as originally designed is the optimal path in the long run.

There must be a match between trader and client as Bill Dunn noted: "A person must be an optimist to be in this business, but I also believe it's a cyclical phenomenon for several other reasons. In our 18 years [40+ now] of experience, we've had to endure a number of long and nasty periods during which we've asked ourselves this same question. In late 1981, our accounts had lost about 42 percent over the previous 12 months, and we and our clients were starting to wonder if we would ever see good markets again. We continued to trade our thoroughly researched system, but our largest client got cold feet and withdrew about 70 percent of our total equity under management. You guessed it. Our next month was up 18 percent, and in the 36 months following, their withdrawal of our accounts made 430 percent!"[27]

Check Your Ego

Dunn Capital once posted a want ad that caught my eye. Part of it read: "Candidates . . . must NOT be constrained by any active non-compete agreement and will be required to enter into a confidentiality and non-compete agreement. Only long-term, team players need apply (no prima donnas). Salary: competitive base salary, commensurate with experience, with bonus potential and attractive benefits, beginning at $65,000."[28]

Notice that Dunn Capital says, "No prima donnas." Readers of this ad can choose either to work for Dunn or attempt to be Dunn on their own, but they cannot have both. Trend following demands taking personal responsibility for one's actions, and Dunn Capital makes it clear they are responsible.

An interesting trait seen in many trend followers is their honesty. If you listen closely to their words and review their performance, they tell you exactly what they are doing and why. Dunn Capital is a great example in action.

Men's expectations manifest in trends.

John W. Henry[29]

Summary Food for Thought

- Dunn Capital's performance data is one of the clearest, most consistent, and dramatic demonstrations of trend following success available.
- Originally, Dunn Capital's designed risk was a 1 percent chance of a 20 percent or greater loss in a given month. In January 2013 Dunn Implemented an Adaptive Risk Profile. Dunn's VaR target is no longer static. Now the firm targets a dynamic monthly VaR between 8–22 percent based on market conditions. Dunn recalibrates its portfolio daily to gear the risk to what it measures as the favorability of markets to trend following. The average monthly VaR going forward should be about 15 percent, which translates into an annualized volatility of ~23 percent over time.

John W. Henry

Since my first edition, John W. Henry has retired to his hobbies as owner of the Boston Red Sox and the Liverpool Football Club. His current net worth of $2.2 billion started with trading—because let's face it owning those teams required capital. Guess where he got the money to buy? Trend following. And given the timelessness of his wisdom, investors will improve their financial condition by considering John W. Henry's trading career.

Interestingly, the early performance data of Dunn Capital and John W. Henry shows them to be trend followers cut from similar cloth—high octane. They are both astonishingly successful self-made men who started without formal association to Wall Street. They developed trading systems in the 1970s that made them millions of dollars. Their correlated performance data showed they both traded for absolute returns and often traded in the same trends at the same time.

Henry captured some of the great trends of his generation. By all available evidence Henry was on the other side of the Barings Bank blowout in 1995. In the zero-sum game, he won what Barings Bank lost. In 2002, Henry was up 40 percent while the NASDAQ was spiraling downwards. He, like Dunn, didn't have a strategy that could be remotely considered "active" or "day trading," but when his trading system told him, "It's time," he literally blew the doors off the barn with spectacular returns in short order. Did he have down years? Yes, from time to time, but he was right there again making huge money in 2008 when everyone else was losing.

Also, as the owner of the Boston Red Sox, Henry applies the basic tenets of trend following—simple heuristics for decision making, mathematics, statistics, and application of a system—to the world of sports.

There is no Holy Grail. There is no perfect way to capture that move from $100/ounce to $800/ounce in gold.
John W. Henry[30]

Prediction Is Futile

Henry was always blunt about prediction fantasies:

> I don't believe that I am the only person who cannot predict future prices. No one consistently can predict anything, especially investors. Prices, not investors, predict the future. Despite this, investors hope or believe that they can predict the future, or someone else can. A lot of them look to you to predict what the next macroeconomic cycle will be. We rely on the fact that other investors are convinced that they can predict the future, and I believe that's where our profits come from. I believe it's that simple.

Because trend following is primarily based on a single piece of data—the price—it is difficult to paint the true story of what that means. Henry was always able to articulate clearly and consistently how he traded, year after year, to those willing to listen *carefully*. To generate his profits, he relied on the fact other traders thought they could predict where the market will go and often ended up as losers. Henry would tell you that he routinely won the losses of the market losers in the zero-sum trading game.

On the Farm

John W. Henry was born in Quincy, Illinois, to a successful farming family. For a Midwestern farm boy in the 1950s, there was nothing in the world like baseball, and from the time nine-year-old Henry went to his first major league game, he was hooked. In the summer he would listen to the great St. Louis Cardinals broadcaster Harry Caray night after night. Henry described himself as having average intelligence, but a knack for numbers. And like many young baseball fans, he crunched batting averages in his head.

Henry attended community colleges and took numerous night courses, but never received his college degree. It wasn't for lack of interest, however. When he was attending a class taught by Harvey Brody at UCLA, they collaborated on and published a strategy for beating blackjack odds. When his father died, Henry took over the family farms, teaching himself hedging techniques on the side. He began speculating in corn, wheat, and soybeans. And it wasn't long before he was trading for clients. In 1981, he founded John W. Henry and Company, Inc. in Newport Beach, California.[31]

Henry's first managed account was staked with $16,000 and he now owns the Boston Red Sox. Don't you think the best question to ask is, "How?" A former president at his trading firm speaks to their success:

> There has been surprisingly little change. Models we developed 20 years ago are still in place today. Obviously, we trade a different mix of markets. We've also added new programs over the last 20 years, but relative to many of our peers, we have not made significant adjustments in our trading models. We believe that markets are always changing and adjusting, and the information that's important to investors will also change. In the 1980s, everyone was interested in the money supply figures . . . everyone would wait by their phones until that number came out. In the 1990s, the information du jour was unemployment numbers. But people's reactions to the markets are fairly stable. Uncertainty creates

How are we able to make money by following trends year in and year out? Trends develop because there's an accumulating consensus on future prices, consequently there's an evolution to the believed true price value over time. Because investors are human and they make mistakes, they're never 100 percent sure of their vision and whether or not their view is correct. So price adjustments take time as they fluctuate and a new consensus is formed in the face of changing market conditions and new facts. For some changes, this consensus is easy to reach, but there are other events that take time to formulate a market view. It's those events that take time that form the basis of our profits.

John W. Henry

> trends and that's what we're trying to exploit. Even if you have better and faster dissemination of information, the one thing we haven't really improved is people's ability to process information. We're trying to exploit people's reaction, which is embedded in prices and leads to trends. These reactions are fairly stable and may not require major adjustments of models.[32]

He reiterates an important philosophical tenet of trend following: In looking at the long-term, change is constant. And because change is constant, uncertainty is constant. And from uncertainty, trends emerge. It is the exploitation of these trends that forms the basis of trend following profit. All of your cutting-edge technology or news reading is not going to help you trade trends.

We have made our business managing risk. We are comfortable with risk and we get our reward from risk.
John W. Henry[34]

When I spoke with Henry's president, he sounded like classic traders from 100 years earlier:

- "We stick to our knitting."
- "Most people don't have the discipline to do what they need to do."
- "We like to keep it sophisticatedly simple."
- "Our best trading days are when we don't trade."
- "We make more money the less we trade."
- "Some of our best trades are when we are sitting on our hands doing nothing."
- "We don't want to be the smartest person in the market. Trying to be the smart person in the market is a losing game."

He was not being flippant. His tone was matter of fact. He wanted people to understand why his firm succeeded. A few years ago he gave a great analogy about the emotional ups and downs: "Looking at the year as a mountain ride . . . Anyone who has ridden the trains in mountainous Switzerland will remember the feeling of anxiety and expectations as you ascend and descend the rugged terrain. During the decline, there is anxiety because you often do not know how far you will fall. Expectations are heightened as you rise out of the valley because you cannot always see the top of the mountain."[33]

Life is a school of probability.
Walter Bagehot[35]

Worldview Philosophy

Trend followers like Henry could not have developed his trading systems without first deciding how he was going to view the world. Through experience, education, and research, he came to an understanding of how markets work before he determined how to trade them. What he found was market trends are more pervasive than people think, and trends could have been traded in the same way 200 years ago as they are today.

Henry spent years studying historical price data from the eighteenth and nineteenth centuries in order to prove his research. When he explained his philosophy he was crystal clear about what it was and what it was not:

- *Long-term trend identification*: Trading systems ignore short-term volatility in the attempt to capture superior returns during major trending markets. Trends can last as long as a few months or years.
- *Highly disciplined investment process*: Methodology is designed to keep discretionary decision making to a minimum.
- *Risk management*: Traders adhere to a strict formulaic risk management system that includes market exposure weightings, stop-loss provisions, and capital commitment guidelines that attempt to preserve capital during trendless or volatile periods.
- *Global diversification*: By participating in more than 70 markets and not focusing on one country or region, they have access to opportunities that less diversified firms may miss.

The game of speculation is the most uniformly fascinating game in the world. But it is not a game for the stupid, the mentally lazy, the person of inferior emotional balance, or the get-rich-quick adventurer. They will die poor.

Jesse Livermore

The uninformed dismiss trend following as predictive technical analysis. Henry was not a predictive indicator guru: "Some people call what we do technical analysis, but we just identify and follow trends. It's like, if you are in the fashion world, you have to follow trends, or you're yesterday's news. But as with technical analysis, trend followers believe that markets are smarter than any of their individual participants. In fact, they make it their business not to try to figure out why markets are going up or down or where they're going to stop."[36]

Henry's use of fashion as a metaphor goes beyond obvious comparison between trends in clothing and in markets. To be fashionable you have no choice but to follow trends. Likewise, trend followers have no choice but to react and follow trends, and like those who follow fashion early, successful trend followers exploit trends long before the public is clued in.

Trend followers would agree with H. L. Mencken when he said, "We are here and it is now. Further than that, all human knowledge is moonshine." They understand attending to what is taking place in the market from moment to moment isn't a technique; it is what is and that is all. The moment, the here and now, is the only place that is truly measurable.

Henry illustrated the point in a coffee trade: "All fundamentals were bearish: The International Coffee Organization was unable to agree on a package to support prices, there was an oversupply of coffee, and the freeze season was over in Brazil . . . his system signaled an unusually large long position in coffee. He bought, placing 2 percent of the portfolio on the trade. The system was right. Coffee rallied to $2.75 per lb. from $1.32 in the last quarter of the year, and he made a 70 percent return. 'The best trades are the ones I dislike the most. The market knows more than I do.'"[37]

What You Think You Know Gets You in Trouble

Henry knew the complicated, difficult elements of trend following were not about what you must master, but what you must eliminate from your market view.

On why long-term approaches work best:

"There is an overwhelming desire to act in the face of adverse market moves. Usually it is termed 'avoiding volatility' with the assumption that volatility is bad. However, I found avoiding volatility really inhibits the ability to stay with the long-term trend. The desire to have close stops to preserve open trade equity has tremendous costs over decades. Long-term systems do not avoid volatility; they patiently sit through it. This reduces the occurrence of being forced out of a position that is in the middle of a long-term major move."[38]

We don't predict the future, but we do know that the next five years will not look like the last five years. That just doesn't happen. Markets change. And our results over the next three years will not replicate the last three. They never do.
John W. Henry[39]

On stocks: "The current thinking is that stocks have outperformed everything else for 200 years. They may have a little relevance for the next 25 years. But there is no one in the year 2000 that you can convince to jettison the belief that 200 years of performance will not cause stocks to grow to the sky. Right now people believe in data that supports the inevitable growth in prices of stocks within a new landscape or new economy. What will be new to them is an inevitable bear market."[40]

For all his talk about avoiding predictions, Henry is making one here. He is predicting stocks can't go up forever because eventually trends reverse themselves. He is also pointing out that as a trend follower he was prepared to take action and profit (which he did during the market crash of October 2008).

Starting with Research

Henry has influenced many traders. One of his former associates presented these observations in his new firm's marketing materials:

- The time frame of the trading system is long-term in nature, with the majority of profitable trades lasting longer than six weeks and some lasting for several months.
- The system is neutral in markets until a signal to take a position is generated.
- It is not uncommon for markets to stay neutral for months at a time, waiting for prices to reach a level that warrants a long or short position.
- The system incorporates predefined levels of initial trade risk. If a new trade turns quickly unprofitable, the risk control parameters in place for every trade will force a liquidation when the preset stop-loss level is reached. In such situations, a trade can last for as little as one day.

This same employee participated in a conference seminar while at Henry's firm. The conference was sparsely attended and, as happens when someone speaks to a small audience, the conversation became more informal and more revealing:

> We are very well aware of the trends that have taken place in the last 20 years and we are just curious to see are we in a period in this century that trend following seems to work? Have we lucked out that we happen to be in this industry during trends for the last decade or two? We went back to the 1800s and looked at interest rates, currency fluctuations, and grain prices to see if there was as much volatility in an era that most people don't know much about as there has been this decade. Much to our relief and maybe also surprise, we found out that there were just as many trends, currencies, interest rates, and grain prices back in the 1800s as there has been exhibited this last decade. Once again, we saw the trends were relatively random, unpredictable, and just further supported our philosophy of being fully diversified, and don't alter your system to work in any specific time period.

There are only a limited number of Fed meetings a year; however, this is supposed to help us infer the direction of interest rates and help us manage risk on a daily basis. How do you manage risk in markets that move 24 hours a day, when the fundamental inputs do not come frequently? In the grain markets, crop reports are fairly limited, and demand information comes with significant lags, if at all. Under these types of conditions, simple approaches, such as following prices, may be better.

Mark S. Rzepczynski[41]

He added:

> Hours and hours were spent in the depths of the university library archives. They gave us Xerox burns on our hands, I think, photo-copying

> grain prices, and interest rate data—not only in the U.S., but also around the world. We looked at overseas interest rates back to that time period. A lot of it is a little bit sketchy, but it was enough to give us the fact that things really jumped around back then as they do now.[42]

We can't always take advantage of a particular period. But in an uncertain world, perhaps the investment philosophy that makes the most sense, if you study the implications carefully, is trend following. Trend following consists of buying high and selling low. But trends are an integral, underlying reality in life. How can someone buy high and sell low and be successful for two decades unless the underlying nature of markets is to trend? On the other hand, I've seen year-after-year, brilliant men buying low and selling high for a while successfully and then going broke because they thought they understood why a certain investment instrument had to perform in accordance with their personal logic.
John W. Henry[43]

It reminded me of the scene in the *Wizard of Oz* when Toto pulls back the curtain to reveal how the wizard works his magic. It was clear there were no secret formulas or hidden strategies. There were no short cuts. This was slow, painstaking trench warfare in the bowels of a research library, armed only with a photocopier to memorialize price histories.

Years later I was inspired to do my own price research. My objective in the moment was not to use price data in a trading system, but to see also how little markets had changed. One of the best places to research historical market data in newspapers and magazines from over 100 years ago is the U.S. National Agricultural Library. Don't be misled by the word *Agricultural*. You can review the stacks at this library and spend hours poring over magazines from the 1800s. Like Henry's firm, I discovered through weeks of research that markets were indeed the same then as now.

On the Record

I had the chance to hear Henry speak in person at a FIA Research Division Dinner in New York City years back. This was only months after the Barings Bank debacle. During the Q&A Henry revealed the qualities shared by all successful trend followers. He refused to waste time discussing fundamentals and offered a genuine appreciation of the nature of change:

> **Moderator:** The question that always comes up for technicians is, "Do you believe the markets have changed?"
>
> **Henry:** It always comes up whenever there are losses, especially prolonged losses. I heard it, in fact, when I started my career 14 years ago. They were worrying, "Is there too much money going into trend following?" You laugh, but I can show you evidence in writing of this. My feeling is that markets are always changing. But if you have a basic philosophy that's sound, you're going to be able to take advantage of those changes to greater or lesser degrees. It is the same with using good, sound business

> principles—the changing world is not going to materially hurt you if your principles are designed to adapt. So the markets have changed. But that's to be expected and it's good.
>
> **Female Voice:** John, you're noted for your discipline. How did you create that, and how do you maintain that?
>
> **Henry:** Well, you create discipline by having a strategy you really believe in. If you really believe in your strategy, that brings about discipline. If you don't believe in it, in other words, if you haven't done your homework properly, and haven't made assumptions that you can really live with when you're faced with difficult periods, then it won't work. It really doesn't take much discipline, if you have a tremendous confidence in what you're doing.
>
> **Male Voice:** I'd like to know if your systems are completely black box.
>
> **Henry:** We don't use any black boxes. I know people refer to technical trend following as black box, but what you have is really a certain philosophy of trading. Our philosophy is that there is an inherent return in trend following. I know CTAs that have been around a lot longer than I have, who have been trading trends: Bill Dunn, Millburn, and others who have done rather well over the last 20 to 30 years. I don't think it's luck year after year after year.

Everything flows.

Heraclitus

Leda Braga, the most successful female trend follower today, builds on Henry's earlier message with comparable timelessness: "We're actually a white box, the white of the mind. We are fully auditable. If you are a pension fund with long-term liabilities, you want some reassurance that the business is sustainable. The hedge fund business is filled with very talented people, but talented people retire. What we do, this effort to articulate the investment process through algorithms, through equations, through code, means that the intellectual property exists in its own right. If I disappear tomorrow, it's fine."[44]

As a side note, what that John W. Henry transcript cannot recreate on the page is the audience reaction. I remember looking around at the Henry fans jammed into that Wall Street hotel suite and thinking, "Everyone in this room is far more interested in viewing Henry as a personality—a rock star—instead of knowing what he does to make money."

Change Is Overrated

Henry was publicly forthright for years. For instance, his presentation in Geneva, Switzerland, could have been a semester course in trend following for those open to the message: "We began trading our first program, in 1981 and this was after quite a bit of research into the practical aspects of a basic philosophy of what drives markets. The world was frighteningly different in those days than it is today when I was designing what turned out to be a trend following system. That approach—a mechanical and mathematical system—has not really changed at all. Yet the system continues to be successful today, even though there has been virtually no change to it over the last 18 years."[45]

I always know what's happening on the court. I see a situation occur, and I respond.
Larry Bird

I can't help but notice the "we haven't changed our system" chorus is not only sung by Dunn, but by Henry and many other trend followers. Consider an example of a winning trend for Henry (see Figure 2.4): "We took a position around March or April 1998 in the South African rand, short (which would be this particular chart; this is the dollar going up against the rand). You can see it takes time for these things and if you're patient, you can have huge profits, especially if you don't set a profit objective."[46]

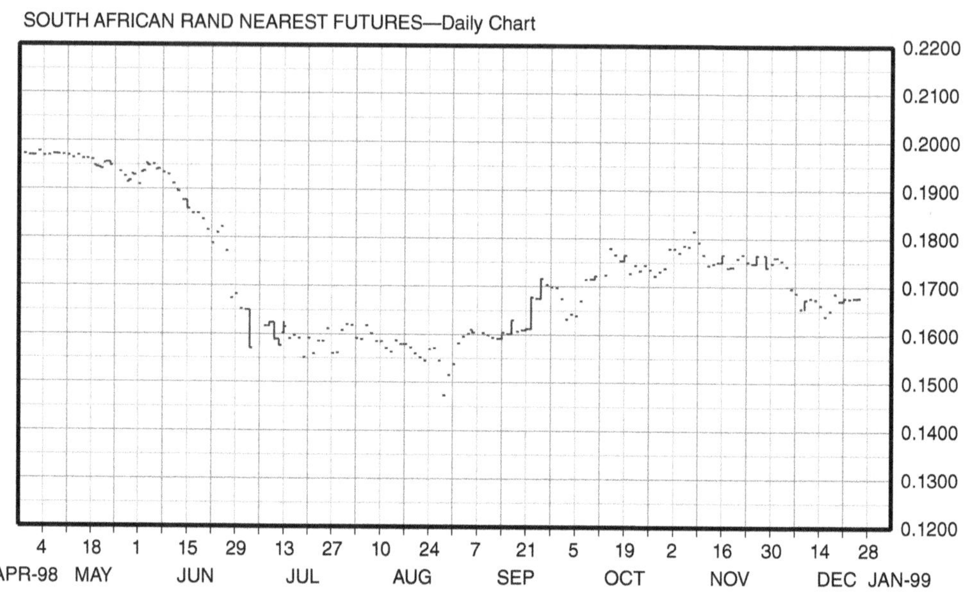

FIGURE 2.4: Henry South African Rand Trade Source: Barchart.com

Moreover, Henry did well in the historical Japanese yen trade shown in Figure 2.5. Henry concluded: "You can see that in this enormous move, when the dollar/yen went from 100 to 80 in that particular month we were up 11% just in the Japanese yen that quarter."[47]

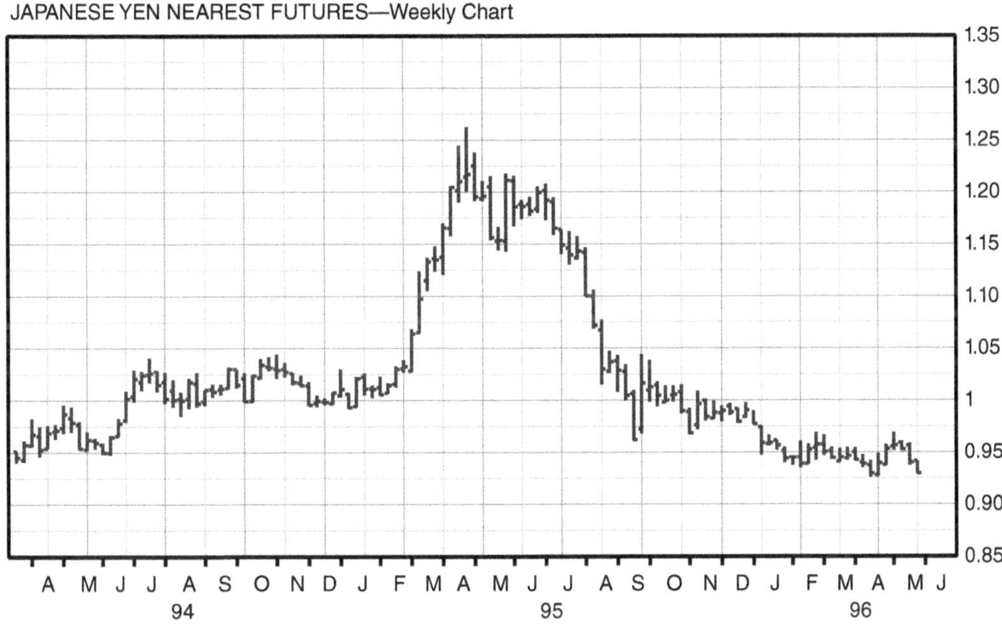

FIGURE 2.5: Henry Japanese Yen Trade Source: Barchart.com

Fade the Fed

Overreaction to Federal Reserve announcements is part of Wall Street life. Some so-called pros take the Federal Reserve's words and act on them even if there is no way to know what any of it means. And does it make logical sense to worry about what the Fed is going to do if there is no way to decipher it? The Fed to the best of my knowledge has never offered any statement you could rely on that says, "Buy 10,000 shares of GOOG now and sell here."

Henry's trend following system was never predicated on the Fed's statements: "I know that when the Fed first raises interest rates after months of lowering them, you do not see them the next day lowering interest rates. And they don't raise rates and then a few days later or a few weeks later lower them. They raise, raise, raise, raise . . . [pause] . . . raise, raise, raise. And then once they lower, they don't raise, lower, raise, lower, raise, lower. Rather they lower, lower, lower, lower. There are trends that tend to exist, whether they are capital flows or interest rates . . . if you have enough discipline, or if you only trade a few markets, you don't need a computer to trade this way."[48]

Henry knows the human mind creates anxiety by conjuring up terrifying future market scenarios. He kept focused in the present on what he could control—his system. That attitude for dealing with the Fed never changes, no matter who is playing the game.

Trading Retirement

The chief obstacle is that we are quick to be satisfied with ourselves. If we find someone to call us good men, cautious and principled, we acknowledge him. We are not content with a moderate eulogy, but accept as our due whatever flattery has shamelessly heaped upon us. We agree with those who call us best and wisest, although we know they often utter many falsehoods: we indulge ourselves so greatly that we want to be praised for a virtue which is the opposite of our behavior. A man hears himself called 'most merciful' while he is inflicting torture... So it follows that we don't want to change because we believe we are already excellent.
Seneca

John W. Henry shut his trend following firm down in 2012, but most of his assets under management were pulled in 2007 before the financial crisis in October 2008. That meant billions in Merrill Lynch assets left Henry's firm and went to other trend following firms (e.g., firms in London). And by the time 2008 unfolded, his money under management had decreased so much that even his great 2008 performance was not enough.

Many will tell you John W. Henry was simply too volatile for *modern* tastes (whatever modern means exactly), and when taking a look at his programs' track records, there were big numbers on both sides. Take his Financials & Metals 36 percent annualized volatility for example, or the multiple years with above 40 percent gains or more than 17 percent losses, and you can see that Henry's model was one of high risk for high return.[49]

Not surprisingly, his exit from trend following has left some confused. This 2016 note in my inbox illustrates: "I recently purchased your *Trend Following* book (2009 edition) and have been eagerly reading it for the past several days. After reading about the success of John W. Henry, I decided to look him up and discovered he had to close his firm a few years ago after experiencing *unsustainable losses.* In your book, you frequently discuss how time and time again critics argue that trend following is dead, yet they are consistently proven wrong. My question is, if trend following is such a reliable strategy, how could one of the most successful trend followers *collapse*? In general, I agree with all of the points you make in your book, but I worry that if someone who is exceedingly versed in the methods of trend following can lose huge sums of money, then someone like me, with absolutely no experience using trend following techniques, is also bound to fail."

Great question. An insider with Henry at the time provided insights instructive for the confused or skeptical:

- "It is a fallacy to say John W. Henry collapsed." His clients moved on to other trend following firms. Firm assets went from over $2 billion to $150 million in around 1.5 years.
- The firm did not close because of "unsustainable" losses but more from a re-deployment of his talents and investment capital.
- Big funds are all about "distribution." That means keeping brokers happy, as they live and die with commissions. Henry's peers weathered the storm.
- Competition replaced older firms who did not respond to vagaries of the brokerage industry. Trend following assets under management exploded inside several London-based firms (e.g., Winton, Aspect, Cantab, etc.).
- Henry essentially moved into venture capital. Red Sox Baseball was not a *hobby*—it was a business transaction. He also bought Fenway Park, the broadcasting, the *Boston Globe*, and Liverpool Football Club (U.K.). People don't think of Henry as a venture capitalist, but he became one.
- Henry still trades his own money as a trend follower with "two" of his original "guys" there.

As an investor you have to dig deep past headline reading. You have to understand all issues associated with any investment—trend following included. And if you think trend following *died* because John W. Henry or any other one person stopped running a trend fund, you may want to ponder a more complete view, not the incomplete one. Go do the autopsy. Find out *why*. And hypothetically, even if John W. Henry was the only trend follower to have ever walked the planet, his public 30-year track record requires an objective post mortem.

Win or lose, everybody gets what they want out of the market. Some people seem to like to lose, so they win by losing money.

Ed Seykota[50]

Summary Food for Thought

- John W. Henry's first managed fund was staked with $16,000 in 1981. He now owns the Boston Red Sox.
- Henry had a four-point investment philosophy: long-term trend identification, highly disciplined investment process, risk management, and global diversification.

Ed Seykota

After you enter the world of markets you will eventually run across *Market Wizards* by Jack Schwager. Of all the trader interviews in *Market Wizards* the most memorable is with Ed Seykota. While some may perceive him as extremely direct, most will agree his thinking is unique. One profound and now famous statement of his: "Everybody gets what they want out of the market." This was a response to a question about trading, but I feel certain Seykota would say it also applies to life.

Even though he is almost unknown to both traders and laymen alike, Seykota's achievements rank him as one of the great trend followers (and traders) of all time. I first met him at a small beachside café. I had received an invitation from him to get together to discuss the outreach possibilities of the Internet. During that first meeting, he asked me what I thought Richard Dennis was looking for when he hired his student traders, the Turtles (Seykota knew my website www.turtletrader.com). My reply was to say Dennis was looking for students who could think in terms of *odds*. His response was to ask me if my reply was my own thinking or something I was told by someone else. This was my indoctrination to his *direct* nature.

Fortune tellers live in the future. So do people who want to put things off. So do fundamentalists.
Ed Seykota[51]

This story passed along from an associate is pure Seykota:

> I attended a day-long seminar in February 1995 in Toronto, Canada where Seykota was one of the guest speakers. The whole audience peppered him with questions like: Do you like gold, where do you think the Canadian $ is headed, how do you know when there is a top, how do you know when the trend is up etc.? To each of these, he replied: "I like gold—it's shiny, pretty—makes nice jewelry" or "I have no idea where the Canadian dollar is headed or the trend is up when price is moving up, etc." His replies were simple, straight-forward answers to the questions asked of him. Later, I learned through the event organizer that a large majority of the audience (who paid good money, presumably to learn the "secrets" of trading from a Market Wizard) were not impressed. Many felt they had wasted their time and money listening to him. Seykota's message couldn't be clearer to anyone who cared to listen. The answers were found in the very questions each person asked. Don't ask, "How do you know the trend is moving up?" Instead, ask, "What is going to tell me the trend is

> up?" Not, "What do you think of gold?" Instead, ask, "Am I correctly trading gold?" Seykota's answers effectively placed everyone in front of a huge mirror, reflecting their trading self back at them. If you don't even know the question to ask about trading, much less the answers, get out of the business and spend your life doing something you enjoy.[52]

Think about how you would have reacted to his speech.

Performance

Seykota earned, after fees, nearly 60 percent on average each year from 1990 to 2000 managing proprietary money in his managed futures program.[53]

But he is different than Harding, Henry, and Dunn. He literally has been a one-man shop his entire career. There is no fancy office or other employees. He does not hold himself out as a fund manager and he is extremely selective of clients. He doesn't care whether people have money or that they want him to trade or not. Seykota takes big risks and he gets big rewards—that takes a strong stomach.

> *Pyramiding instructions appear on dollar bills. Add smaller and smaller amounts on the way up. Keep your eye open at the top.*
>
> Ed Seykota[54]

Seykota was born in 1946. He earned his Bachelor of Science from MIT in 1969 and by 1972 had embarked on the trading career he pursues to this day—investing for his own account and the accounts of a few select others. He was self-taught, but influenced in his career by Amos Hostetter and Richard Donchian.

Originally, he took a job with a major broker. He then conceived and developed the first commercial computerized trading system for client money in the futures markets. And according to *Market Wizards*, he increased one client's account from $5,000 to $15,000,000 in 12 years.

His trading is largely confined to the few minutes it takes to run his internally written computer program, which generates trading signals for the next day. He also mentors traders through his website and his Trading Tribe, a widespread community of like-minded traders. He has served as a teacher and mentor to some great traders, including Michael Marcus and David Druz.

The Secret

Seykota debunks market ignorance with terse, Zen-like statements that force the listener to look inward: "The biggest secret about success is that there isn't any big secret about it, or if there is, then it's a secret from me, too. The idea of searching for some secret for trading success misses the point."[55]

That self-deprecating response emphasizes process over outcome, but don't be misled by his modesty, for he gets impatient with hypocrisy and mindlessness. He is a fearless trader and does not suffer fools gladly. Yet when he remembers his first trade, I saw the passion: "The first trade I remember, I was about five years old in Portland, Oregon. My father gave me a gold-colored medallion, a sales promotion trinket. I traded it to a neighbor kid for five magnifying lenses. I felt as though I had participated in a rite of passage. Later, when I was 13, my father showed me how to buy stocks. He explained that I should buy when the price broke out of the top of a box and to sell when it broke out of the bottom. And that's how I got started."[56]

Later on he was more directly inspired: "I saw a letter published by Richard Donchian, which implied that a purely mechanical trend following system could beat the markets. This too seemed impossible to me. So I wrote computer programs (on punch cards in those days) to test the theories. Amazingly, his [Donchian] theories tested true. To this day, I'm not sure I understand why or whether I really need to. Anyhow, studying the markets, and backing up my opinions with money, was so fascinating compared to my other career opportunities at the time, that I began trading full time for a living."[57]

The guy with discretion has what, a crystal ball?
Leda Braga

Trading was now in his blood, and at age 23 he went out on his own with about a half-dozen accounts in the $10,000–25,000 range.[58] He found an alternative to the Wall Street career built only on commissions. From the beginning he worked for incentive fees alone. If he made money for his clients, he got paid. If he did not make money, he did not get paid. Most brokers, index fund managers, and hedge funds don't work like that.

Never Mind the Cheese

As a new trader, Seykota passed through Commodities Corporation, a trader training ground in Princeton, New Jersey. One of his mentors was Amos Hostetter. Hostetter made phenomenal amounts of money trading. When a market's supply-and-demand prospects looked promising, Hostetter would put up one-third of his ultimate position. If he lost 25 percent he'd get out. "Never mind the cheese," he'd crack, "let me out of the trap." But when the market swung his way he'd add another third, taking a final position when prices climbed half as high as he thought they'd go. Hostetter's strategies were so successful they were computerized so other traders could learn to duplicate his success.[59]

His get-out-of-the-trap strategies influenced many top traders of the last 30 years. Who else passed through Commodities Corp.? Traders with names like Paul Tudor Jones, Bruce Kovner, Louis Bacon, and Michael Marcus paid their dues there. Interestingly, in the mid-1990s, long after the majority of well-known trend followers had left, I visited Commodities Corporation's offices.

Midway through the tour, I bumped into a stressed-out energy trader. After a few minutes of conversation, we began to chat about his trading style, which was based on fundamentals. Throughout the entire conversation, he was glued to the monitor. When I brought up trend following, he assured me it did not work. I was surprised that a trader working for a famous firm, known for training brilliant trend followers, was completely blinded to even the possibility that trend following worked. I realized then even those closest to trend following's roots had no appreciation for it.

I believe babies are born as innovative personalities, but our social processes work to stamp out exploration and questioning.

Jay Forrester

System Dynamics

Along with Hostetter, MIT's Jay Forrester was a strong influence on the then young Seykota: "One of my mentors, Jay Forrester, was a stickler for clear writing, a sign of clear thinking."[60]

Forrester taught Seykota about system dynamics, which is a method for studying the world around us. Unlike other scientists, who study the world by breaking it up into smaller and smaller pieces, system dynamicists look at things as a whole. The central concept to system dynamics is understanding how all the objects in a system interact with one another. A system can be anything from a steam engine, to a bank account, to a basketball team. The objects and people in a system interact through *feedback* loops, where a change in one variable affects other variables over time, which in turn affects the original variable, and so on. An example of this is money in a bank account. Money in the bank earns interest, which increases the size of the account. Now the account is larger, it earns even more interest, which adds more money to the account. This goes on and on. What system dynamics attempts to do is understand the basic structure of a system, and thus understand the behavior it can produce. Many of these systems and problems that are analyzed can be built as models on a computer. System dynamics takes advantage of the fact a computer model can be of much greater complexity and carry out more simultaneous calculations than can the mental model of the human mind.[61]

This type of thought process and computer modeling is not only a foundation of his success, but also can be seen across the entire trend following success landscape.

If a gambler places bets on the input symbol to a communication channel and bets his money in the same proportion each time a particular symbol is received, his capital will grow (or shrink) exponentially. If the odds are consistent with the probabilities of occurrence of the transmitted symbols (i.e., equal to their reciprocals), the maximum value of this exponential rate of growth will be equal to the rate of transmission of information. If the odds are not fair, i.e., not consistent with the transmitted symbol probabilities but consistent with some other set of probabilities, the maximum exponential rate of growth will be larger than it would have been with no channel by an amount equal to the rate of transmission of information.
J. L. Kelly, Jr[62]

FAQs

Examples of Seykota's *clear* wisdom[63]:

To avoid whipsaw losses, stop trading.

Lesson: You will have losses. Accept them.

Here's the essence of risk management: Risk no more than you can afford to lose, and also risk enough so that a win is meaningful. If there is no such amount, don't play.

Lesson: Position sizing or money management is crucial.

Trend following is an exercise in observing and responding to the ever-present moment of now. Traders who predict the future dwell upon a nonexistent place, and to the extent they also park their ability to act out there, they can miss opportunities to act in the now.

Lesson: All you have is now. It is much better to react to the fact of market movements in present time than a future time that doesn't exist.

Markets are fundamentally volatile. No way around it. Your problem is not in the math. There is no math to get you out of having to experience uncertainty.

For a system trader, it's way more important to have your trading size down than it is to fine tune your entry and exit points.
David Druz[64]

Lesson: You can crunch all the numbers you like, but your "gut" still has to handle the ups and downs. You have to live with and feel the uncertainty.

I recall, in the old days, people showing a lot of concern that markets are different and trend following methods no longer work.

Lesson: Today or yesterday, skeptics abound. They sound like broken records in their desires to see trend following debunked.

It can be very expensive to try to convince the markets you are right.

Lesson: Go with the flow. Leave your personal or fundamental opinions at the door. Do you want to be right or make money? Losers try to convince everyone they are right.

When magazine covers get pretty emotional, get out of the position. There's nothing else in the magazine that works very well, but the covers are pretty good. This is not an indictment of the magazine people, it's just that at the end of a big move there is a communal psychological abreaction that shows up on the covers of magazines.[65]

Lesson: Crowd psychology is real and the price reflects all.

Students

Seykota's track record is impressive, but one of his students, Easan Katir, offered a warning:

> Journalists, interviewers, and such like to hedge their praise and use phrases such as "one of the best traders," etc. If one looks at Ed Seykota's model account record and compares it with anyone else, historical or contemporary, he is the best trader in history, period. Isn't he? Who else comes close? I don't know of anyone. Livermore made fortunes, but had drawdowns to zero. There are numerous examples of managers with a few years of meteoric returns who subsequently blow up. The household names, Buffet and Soros, are less than half of Ed's return each year. One might apply filters such as Sharpe ratios, AUM, etc., and perhaps massage the results. But as far as the one central metric—raw percentage profit—Ed is above anyone else I know, and I've been around managing money for 20 years.

The difference between a successful person and others is not a lack of strength, not a lack of knowledge, but rather a lack of will.

Vince Lombardi

Jason Russell provided a glimpse into the Seykota process:

> Through working with Ed, I have learned many things in the past couple of years, one of the most important being: Apply trend following to your life as well as to your trading. Freeing yourself from the need to understand "why" is as useful when dealing with family, friends, and

foes as it is when entering or exiting a trade. It also has the added benefit of making you a much better trader.

Russell further sees the *simplicity*:

> There is simplicity beyond sophistication. Ed spends a lot of time there. He listens, he feels, he speaks with clarity. He is a master of his craft. Before working with Ed, I spent years learning, reading, and earning various designations. All of this has been useful as it provides me with a high level of technical proficiency. However, somehow through this whole process, I have gained a strong appreciation for simplifying. Miles Davis was once asked what went through his mind when he listened to his own music. He said: "I always listen to what I can leave out." That sounds like Ed.

David Druz, featured in my book *The Little Book of Trading* (Wiley, 2011), described working with Seykota:

Apprenticing with Ed Seykota is like getting a drink of water at a fire hydrant.
Thomas Vician Jr.

> It was one of the most incredible experiences of my life. He is the smartest trader I have ever seen. I don't think anybody comes close. He has the greatest insights into how markets work and how people operate. It's almost scary being in his presence. It was tough surviving working with him because of the mental gymnastics involved. If you have a personality weakness, he finds it—fast. But it's a positive thing because successful traders must understand themselves and their psychological weaknesses. My time with Ed was one of the greatest times of my life and gave me tremendous confidence—but I don't trade any differently because of it. A guy like Ed Seykota is magic.[66]

Seykota would be the first to say he is no magician. Although it may be human nature to attribute phenomenal trading success to magical powers, trend following is a form of trial and error. The errors are all the small losses incurred while trying to find those big trends.

Jim Hamer felt it was important to talk life beyond the markets:

> I lived with Ed and his family for a little over two months in early 1997. One of the more amazing things I observed about Ed is that he has gifts

in so many areas, trading being just one of them. He showed me a music video that he produced many years ago. It was an excellent production. He also recorded an album several years before the video. He is a very talented musician. My favorite song was Bull Market, which he used to play for me on his acoustic guitar. During the time I was with him, he was very involved in experiments that attempted to redefine airflows as they relate to the Bernoulli Principle. He spent an enormous amount of time putting together academic papers and sending them to several experts in the field concerning this work. He is the consummate scientist. One day, we took a "field trip" to visit Ed's state legislator to discuss Charter School legislation and the impact on Ed's children and the students of Nevada. Not long after I left, Ed ran for the local school board. He has a keen interest in and knowledge of education. Ed Seykota will never be defined solely by trading. He has a love of learning and is a modern-day Renaissance man.

You've got to have a longer perspective and confidence in the veracity of the approach that you're using.
Campbell and Company[67]

Summary Food for Thought

- Ed Seykota: "Win or lose, everybody gets what they want out of the market. Some people seem to like to lose, so they win by losing money."
- Seykota: "To avoid whipsaw losses, stop trading."
- Seykota: "Until you master the basic literature and spend some time with successful traders, you might consider confining your trading to the supermarket."
- Seykota: "I don't predict a non-existing future."

Keith Campbell

Measure what is measurable, and make measurable what is not so.
Galileo Galilei[68]

Considering he founded one of the largest (in terms of client assets) and oldest trend following firms, Keith Campbell and his firm, Campbell & Company, were nearly non-existent for their first three decades. Back in the day a search revealed little to no information. Like many of the earliest trend following traders their returns and legacy are a matter of public record (if you know where to look), but as 2017 shows the firm has evolved.

As the world of funds and quant strategy has changed and investor needs have expanded, Campbell's approach has shifted some. While still possessing a trend following core expertise, the firm also offers a number of strategies oriented around other alpha generators. Several members of their firm have appeared on my podcast and their transparency in discussing their evolution is refreshing.

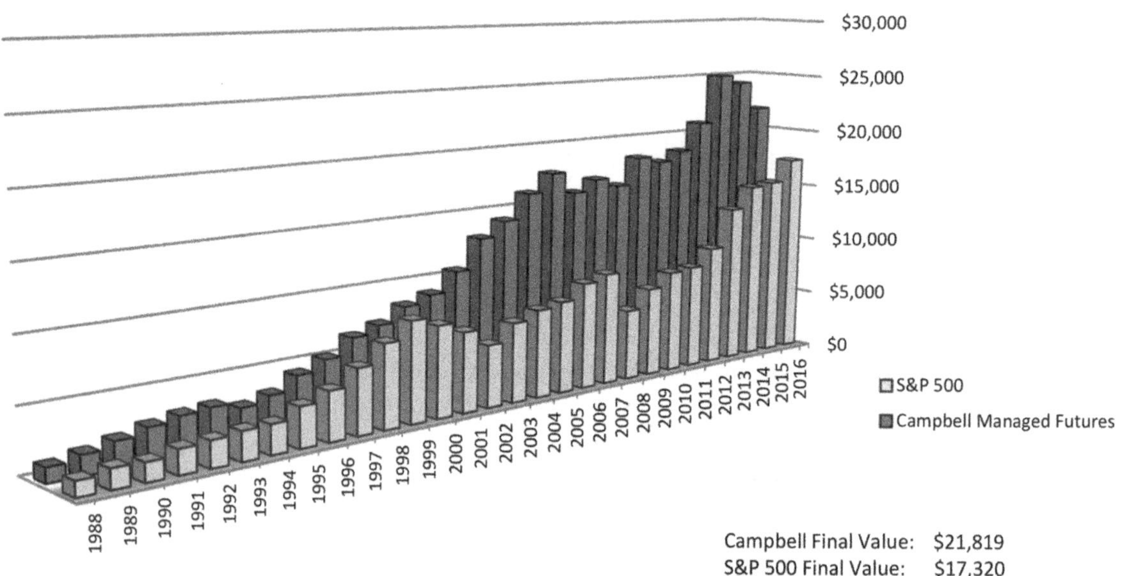

FIGURE 2.6: Hypothetical $1,000 Growth Chart for Campbell & Company

But for a moment let's go back in time to the roots. In the 1960s Keith Campbell took a job in California where he could both ski and surf—a healthy motivation! When his roommate moved out of their apartment he advertised for a replacement and ended up with Chet Conrad, a commodity broker. Campbell recalled that, "(Conrad) got me into trading as a customer. But he was always moaning he didn't have enough money to trade." Campbell then put together $60,000 from 12 investors to form his first futures fund with three advisors—a fundamentalist, a bar chartist, and a point-and-figure advocate. When that fund struggled he started the Campbell Fund and took it over on January 1, 1972. A few years later, Campbell and Conrad went their separate ways. Conrad relocated to Lake Tahoe, Nevada, on a gutsy sugar trade that turned a borrowed $10,000 into $3 million. Campbell remained with his fund and now has seen his firm through formal succession plans to ensure continuity of leadership (he stepped away from overseeing day to day operations).[69]

The mathematics are very important, but it's only one piece of the puzzle. The most important thing overall is the total investment process, of which the signal generator is an important part. Portfolio structuring, risk management, execution strategies, capital management, and leverage management may not be directly connected to the algorithm that generates the buy and sell signals, but they are all hugely important.

Campbell & Company[71]

Yet it is unfair to refer to Campbell & Company with the word "commodity" alone because Campbell trades far more than commodities. They currently deploy several dozen models across commodities, fixed income, foreign exchange and cash equities. They've also evolved risk management enhancements that allow strategies with constant or dynamic risk targets. Will Andrews, CEO at Campbell & Company: "We have great pride in our diversified flagships and our experience in trend following. That continues to be the core of our offering, but we recognize the need for a broader set of strategies and access points for our evolving client base."

But I still love that early Campbell wisdom—those legendary pearls. For example, one Campbell executive noted back in the day: "I'm very uncomfortable with black box trading where I'm dealing with algorithms I don't understand. Everything we do we could do on the back of an envelope with a pencil."[70]

That back-of-an-envelope remark is a revelation to those that imagine trend following trading as overly complex. And by no means do I imply running a multi-billion dollar fund with multiple strategies is *simple* (it's not), but trend following as a strategy can always be explained on the back of an envelope—even if it's a big envelope. The real lesson with Campbell, like with other great trend followers, is the discipline to stick to rules in tough times.

Mike Harris, President at Campbell & Company, however, wanted me to see Campbell today too, "We've also seen investor interest come full circle. After years of being pushed to offer solutions beyond trend following, more recently we've seen renewed interest in pure trend strategies and the potential 'Crisis Alpha' they can provide. Our dynamic trend strategy is a good example of responding to this interest. We've been able to combine our years of expertise in trend following with a sophisticated dynamic risk-targeting framework that's designed with the specific goal of delivering returns during equity crisis periods. Many investors have told us that they look to trend following allocations specifically for that equity crisis protection so we've developed programs with that focus."

Campbell versus Benchmarks

While I am no proponent of benchmarking, the following chart (Table 2.3) shows drawdown comparisons across asset classes:

TABLE 2.3: Worst-Case Cumulative Percentage Decline, January 1988–December 2016

S&P—51%	10/07–02/09
Fidelity Magellan—73%	03/00–02/09
Campbell Managed Futures—29%	07/93–01/95
Bloomberg Barclay U.S. Aggregate Index—5%	1/94–06/94

Many skeptics like to think trend followers are the only ones with drawdowns. The chart, however, shows the truth of drawdowns across several indexes and fund types. The key is to accept drawdowns and be able to manage them when they occur. Otherwise, you are left watching the NASDAQ drop 77 percent peak to trough over 2000–2002 with no plan on what to do next.

Still, Campbell's strategies were often doubted by Wall Street, especially the *old-guard efficient market types* that griped about the *riskiness* of trend following. Campbell counters: "A common perception is that futures markets are extremely volatile, and that investing in futures is therefore very risky, much riskier than equity investments. The reality is that, while not for everyone, generally futures prices are less volatile than common stock prices. It is the amount of leverage available in futures, which creates the perception of high risk, not market volatility. The actual risk involved in futures trading depends, among other things, upon how much leverage is used."[72]

Campbell & Company analyzes only technical market data, not any economic factors external to market prices.[73]

Managing leverage is crucial component for risk management regardless of strategy. It is a key part that allows traders to keep coming back day after day and year after year to trade and win.

Correlation and Consistency

Most trend followers earn their returns at different times than common benchmark measures, such as the S&P stock index. Campbell (see Table 2.4) is lowly correlated with major stock market indexes.

TABLE 2.4: Correlation Analysis between Campbell Composite and S&P 500 Index, January 1988–December 2016

Both Positive	132 of 348 Months
Opposite	160 of 348 Months
Both Negative	56 of 348 Months

SOURCE: Campbell & Company

Even more remarkable than the low correlation to the S&P, Campbell's performance (see Table 2.5) is consistent over total months, total years, and five rolling time windows:

TABLE 2.5: Past Consistency Campbell Managed Futures, January 1988–December 2016 (estimates)

January 1988–December 2016 (estimates)	Number of Time Periods	Number of Profitable Periods	Number of Unprofitable Periods	Percentage Profitable
Total Months	348	199	149	57.18
Total Years	29	23	6	79.31
12-Month Rolling Windows	337	271	66	80.42
24-Month Rolling Windows	325	283	42	87.08
36-Month Rolling Windows	313	292	21	93.29
48-Month Rolling Windows	301	289	12	96.01
60-Month Rolling Windows	289	286	3	98.96

SOURCE: Campbell & Company

Qualitatively you are not terribly more knowledgeable about Campbell & Company now. But quantitatively their performance numbers demonstrate something way more than an anomaly or *luck*.

Summary Food for Thought

Our trend following methods do not pretend to determine the value of what we are trading, nor do they determine what that value ought to be, but they do produce absolute returns fairly consistently.

Campbell & Company[74]

- Will Andrews: "With 45 years of experience the one thing we know is that the markets never stop evolving and you must evolve with them."
- Mike Harris: "This brave new world and its unknowns are scary for most people but we see it as a potential opportunity as a lot of re-pricing could need to happen. A dramatic drop in correlation between asset classes and markets improves opportunities. Markets are slow to price in changes, which often leads to trends. We can capture large moves, whether up or down."

Jerry Parker

I first visited Jerry Parker's original office in Manakin-Sabot, Virginia, in 1994. Manakin-Sabot is a rural Richmond suburb. It's in the *sticks.* I make that point because a few months before I was in Salomon Brothers' office in lower Manhattan, gazing for the first time across their huge trading floor, which seemed like the epicenter of Wall Street. The light bulb of geographic irrelevance went off when Parker's unpretentious offices in Manakin-Sabot hit my eyes. You never would have guessed this was where the thoughtful, laid-back CEO of Chesapeake Capital Management managed over $1 billion.

Technical traders do not need to have a particular expertise in each market that they trade. They don't need to be an authority on meteorological phenomena, geopolitical occurrences or the economic impact of specific worldwide events on a particular market.
Jerry Parker[75]

Parker grew up in Lynchburg, Virginia, and graduated from the University of Virginia. He was working as an accountant in Richmond when he applied to Richard Dennis' training program and was the first student Dennis accepted. Pragmatic and consistent, he went on to start his own money management firm, Chesapeake Capital, in 1988. He made the decision to risk less and make less for clients, so he took his Turtle approach, a trend following strategy and ratcheted it down a few degrees. In other words, he took an aggressive system for making money and customized it to investors who were comfortable with lower leverage.

Even though he was shooting for lower risk he returned 61.82 percent on his money in one incredible year of 1993. That put his firm on the map. However, he is generally in the 12–14 percent return range today. His more conservative approach to trend following is different than Dunn who has always pushed systems for absolute returns. Parker does it a little differently, but no less successfully. I have always walked away from him impressed each time at how straightforward and unassuming he was.

Skeptics

Parker gave a rare speech at the height of the Dot-com bubble. His address covered a full range of trend following philosophies. However skeptical Parker's audience, it did not prevent him from offering simple, direct, and solid advice about trading to those willing to accept it.

- *Dangers of a buy and hold mentality*: "The strategy of buy and hold is bad. Hold for what? A key to successful traders is their ability to leverage investments . . . many [traders] are too conservative in their willingness to leverage."[76]

- *Folly of predicting where markets may be headed*: "I don't know nor do I care. The system that we use at Chesapeake is about the market knowing where it's going."[77]
- *His trend following trading system*: "This flies in the face of what clients want: fancy schools, huge research, an intuitive approach that knows what's going to happen before it happens, e.g., be overweight in the stock market before the rate cut. But obviously you can't know what's going to happen before it happens, and maybe the rate cut is the start of a major trend, and maybe it's okay to get in after. That's our approach. No bias short or long."[78]
- *Counter-trend or day trading*: "The reason for it is a lot of traders as well as clients don't like trend following. It's not intuitive, not natural, too long-term, not exciting enough."[79]
- *The wishful thinking of market disaster victims*: "They said 'the market's wrong, it'll come back.' The market is never wrong."[80]

Ask yourself if you want to be right or do you want to win. They are different questions.

I participated in the Richard Dennis "Turtle Program." The methods we were taught and the trading experience received were all a technical approach to trading the commodity markets. The most important experience that led me to utilize a technical approach was the amount of success that I experienced trading Rich's system.

Jerry Parker[82]

Intelligence

Trend following success is much more predicated on discipline than pure academic achievement. Parker is candid about *intelligence*: "We have a system in which we do not have to rely on our intellectual capabilities. One of the main reasons why what we do works in the markets is that no one can figure out what is happening."[81]

The great trend followers admit pure IQ is no savior. They also know the latest news of the day does not figure into decisions about when to buy, when to sell, or how much to buy or sell. Parker adds, "Our pride and opinions should not interfere with sound trading approaches."[83]

Salem Abraham

Salem Abraham does it differently than most. He truly proves physical location is meaningless. It would be hard to find a financial firm in the United States as removed from Wall Street, geographically and culturally, as Abraham Trading Company. Housed in the same building where his grandfather Malouf Abraham once chewed the fat with local politicians and ranchers, the company has evolved into one of the nation's most unusual trading operations.[84]

It was while he was a student at Notre Dame University that Abraham found he had a natural ability for and interest in trading. Like Greg Smith, one of Seykota's students, he researched which traders were the most successful and discovered trend following. Abraham returned home to the family ranch in Canadian, Texas, after graduating and discussed the idea of trading for a living with his "granddad," who cautiously agreed to help him get started as a trader. According to Abraham he was to "try it out for six months," and then discard the idea ("throw the quote machine out the window") if he failed.[85]

There was no failure for Abraham. He quickly developed a Wall Street business in the most anti–Wall Street way. Abraham's firm's culture is astonishingly different: "No one at the company has an Ivy League degree. Most of the employees at Abraham Trading have backgrounds working at the area's feedlots or natural-gas drilling and pipeline companies. Their training in the complexities of trading and arbitrage is provided on the job. 'This beats shoveling manure at 6 am in the morning,' said Geoff Dockray, who was hired as a clerk for Mr. Abraham after working at a feedlot near Canadian. The financial markets are complicated but they're not as relentless as dealing with livestock all the time."[86]

Abraham's meat-and-potatoes approach to trading: "The underlying premise of Abraham Trading's approach is that commodity interests will, from time to time, enter into periods of major price change to either a higher or lower level. These price changes are known as trends, which have been observed and recorded since the beginning of market history. There is every reason to believe that in free markets prices will continue to trend. The trading approach used by Abraham is designed to exploit these price moves."[87]

The only cardinal evil on earth is that of placing your prime concern within other men. I've always demanded a certain quality in the people I liked. I've always recognized it at once—and it's the only quality I respect in men. I chose my friends by that. Now I know what it is. A self-sufficient ego. Nothing else matters.
Ayn Rand[88]

When asked about his relationship with Jerry Parker, Abraham gave an example of six degrees of separation: "We do in fact know Jerry Parker with Chesapeake Capital. The shortest version I can give you is he is my dad's sister's husband's brother's daughter's husband. I'm not sure you can call that related but something like that. I first learned about the futures industry by talking to him while he visited in-laws in Texas."

The lesson learned: Keep your eyes open to possibilities, as you never know when opportunity will appear. At the time, however, Parker knew Abraham's age (and success) could cause problems: "Sometimes people have a tendency to resent a young guy who's making so much money. I just think he has a lot of guts."[89]

The core lesson to be learned from Abraham is that if you want to become a trend follower, get out there and meet the players. Parker and Abraham are realists. They play the zero-sum game hard in similar ways and excel at it, but they have also found a way to balance their lives. Without compromising integrity they have found a way to apply their trend trading philosophy.

Summary Food for Thought

- Jerry Parker: "A key to successful traders is their ability to leverage investments. Many traders are too conservative in their willingness to leverage."
- Parker: "A lot of traders as well as clients don't like trend following. It's not intuitive, not natural, too long-term, not exciting enough."
- Parker: "The market is never wrong."
- More on Jerry Parker and Salem Abraham can be found in my second book, *TurtleTrader*.

Richard Dennis

Richard Dennis is retired. His exit was often misinterpreted by the press as a death knell for trend following. It is true Dennis' career had big ups and downs, but trend following never stopped.

Dennis was born and raised in Chicago in close proximity to the exchanges. He began trading as a teenager with $400 saved from his pizza delivery job. Because he was too young to qualify for membership on the exchange, he would send signals to his father who would do the actual trading. At 17 he finally landed a job in the pit as a runner on the exchange floor and started trading.[90]

Trading was even more teachable than I imagined. In a strange sort of way, it was almost humbling.
Richard Dennis[91]

TurtleTraders

Eventually, Dennis would achieve fantastic wealth with profits in the hundreds of millions of dollars. However, his real fame would come from his experiment in teaching trading to new traders.

In 1983 he made a bet with his partner William Eckhardt. Dennis believed trading could be taught. Eckhardt belonged to the "you're born with it or you're not" camp. They decided to experiment by seeing whether they could teach novices successful trading. Twenty-plus students were accepted into two separate training programs. Legend has it Dennis named his students "Turtles" after visiting a turtle-breeding farm in Singapore.

I agree with the metaphysics of technical analysis that the fundamentals are discounted. You don't get any profits from fundamental analysis; you get profit from buying and selling. So why stick with the appearance when you can go right to the reality of price and analyze it better?
Richard Dennis[93]

How did it start? Dennis ran classified ads saying *Trader Wanted* and was immediately overwhelmed by some 1,000 queries from would-be traders. He picked 20+ novices, trained them for two weeks, and then gave them money to trade for his firm. His Turtles included two professional gamblers, a fantasy-game designer, an accountant, and a juggler. Jerry Parker, the former accountant who now manages more than $1 billion, was one of several who went on to become top money managers.[92]

Although Dennis appears to own the mantle of trend following teaching professor, there are many other trend followers, including Seykota, Dunn, and Henry, who have served as teachers to successful traders. Also keep in mind not all the Turtles turned out winners. After they left Dennis's tutelage several Turtles failed (i.e., Curtis Faith, who later served jail time). Perhaps, too, after some Turtles went out on their own they could not cope without the safety net. Jerry Parker is a monster exception to that theory—he is absolutely the most successful of the Turtles.

This is not a criticism of the system Dennis taught his students. It is rather an acknowledgment that some could not stick with his trading system. In stark contrast, Bill Dunn was completely unknown to the general public when the Turtles burst onto the scene in the 1980s. Since that time Dunn has slowly overtaken all Turtles in terms of absolute performance. I wonder if something about the initial one-man shop of Dunn set in motion habits enabling his firm to roar past the Turtles, who had the head start. For years, many Turtles also refused to acknowledge they were trend followers, while Dunn was candid. Maybe the hype and mystery set forward in the *Market Wizards* books did not help in the long run.

There's nothing quite as good or bad as trading. They give you a number every day. That's what's good about it, and that's what's bad about it. That's what makes it hard. That's what makes it worth doing.
Richard Dennis[94]

Nevertheless, the story of the Turtles is so amazing still in 2017 that the criteria Dennis used to select his students is insightful.

Selection Process

Dale Dellutri, a former executive at Dennis's firm, managed the Turtle group. He said they were looking for "smarts and for people who had odd ideas." Ultimately, they selected several blackjack players, an actor, a security guard, and a designer of the fantasy game Dungeons & Dragons. One of the ways they screened candidates was by having them answer true-or-false questions.

The following true-or-false questions were sent to the Turtles and were used to decide who was picked and who went home:

1. One should favor being long or being short, whichever one is comfortable with.
2. On initiation, one should know precisely at what price to liquidate if a profit occurs.
3. One should trade the same number of contracts in all markets.
4. If one has $100,000 to risk, one ought to risk $25,000 on every trade.
5. On initiation, one should know precisely where to liquidate if a loss occurs.
6. You can never go broke taking profits.
7. It helps to have the fundamentals in your favor before you initiate.
8. A gap up is a good place to initiate if an uptrend has started.
9. If you anticipate buy stops in the market, wait until they are finished and buy a little higher than that.
10. Of three types of orders (market, stop, and resting), market orders cost the least skid.
11. The more bullish news you hear and the more people are going long, the less likely the uptrend is to continue after a substantial uptrend.
12. The majority of traders are always wrong.
13. Trading bigger is an overall handicap to one's trading performance.
14. Larger traders can "muscle" markets to their advantage.
15. Vacations are important for traders to keep the proper perspective.
16. Under trading is almost never a problem.
17. Ideally, average profits should be about three or four times average losses.
18. A trader should be willing to let profits turn into losses.
19. A very high percentage of trades should be profits.
20. A trader should like to take losses.
21. It is especially relevant when the market is higher than it's been in 4 and 13 weeks.
22. Needing and wanting money are good motivators to good trading.
23. One's natural inclinations are good guides to decision making in trading.
24. Luck is an ingredient in successful trading over the long run.

All a company report and balance sheet can tell you is the past and the present. They cannot tell future.
Nicolas Darvas

25. When you're long, "limit up" is a good place to take a profit.
26. It takes money to make money.
27. It's good to follow hunches in trading.
28. There are players in each market one should not trade against.
29. All speculators die broke.
30. The market can be understood better through social psychology than through economics.
31. Taking a loss should be a difficult decision for traders.
32. After a big profit, the next trend following trade is more likely to be a loss.
33. Trends are not likely to persist.
34. Almost all information about a commodity is at least a little useful in helping make decisions.
35. It's better to be an expert in one to two markets rather than try to trade 10 or more markets.
36. In a winning streak, total risk should rise dramatically.
37. Trading stocks is similar to trading commodities.
38. It's a good idea to know how much you are ahead or behind during a trading session.
39. A losing month is an indication of doing something wrong.
40. A losing week is an indication of doing something wrong.
41. The big money in trading is made when one can get long at lows after a big downtrend.
42. It's good to average down when buying.
43. After a long trend, the market requires more consolidation before another trend starts.
44. It's important to know what to do if trading in commodities doesn't succeed.
45. It is not helpful to watch every quote in the markets one trades.
46. It is a good idea to put on or take off a position all at once.
47. Diversification in commodities is better than always being in one or two markets.
48. If a day's profit or loss makes a significant difference to your net worth, you're overtrading.
49. A trader learns more from his losses than his profits.
50. Except for commission and brokerage fees, execution "costs" for entering orders are minimal over the course of a year.

Always say 'yes' to the present moment. Surrender to what is. Say 'yes' to life and see how life starts suddenly to start working for you rather than against you.
Eckhart Tolle

51. It's easier to trade well than to trade poorly.
52. It's important to know what success in trading will do for you later in life.
53. Uptrends end when everyone gets bearish.
54. The more bullish news you hear, the less likely a market is to break out on the upside.
55. For an off-floor trader, a long-term trade ought to last three or four weeks or less.
56. Others' opinions of the market are good to follow.
57. Volume and open interest are as important as price action.
58. Daily strength and weakness is a good guide for liquidating long-term positions with big profits.
59. Off-floor traders should spread different markets of different market groups.
60. The more people are going long, the less likely an uptrend is to continue in the beginning of a trend.
61. Off-floor traders should not spread different delivery months of the same commodity.
62. Buying dips and selling rallies is a good strategy.
63. It's important to take a profit most of the time.

Chance is commonly viewed as a self-correcting process in which a deviation in one direction induces a deviation in the opposite direction to restore the equilibrium. In fact, deviations are not corrected as a chance process unfolds, they are merely diluted.

Amos Tversky

Not all were true or false. Dennis also asked essay questions:

1. What were your standard test results on college entrance exams?
2. Name a book or movie you like and why.
3. Name a historical figure you like and why.
4. Why would you like to succeed at this job?
5. Name a risky thing you have done and why.
6. Explain a decision you have made under pressure and why that was your decision.
7. Hope, fear, and greed are said to be enemies of good traders. Explain a decision you may have made under one of these influences and how you view that decision now.
8. What are some good qualities you have that might help in trading?
9. What are some bad qualities you have that might hurt in trading?
10. In trading would you rather be good or lucky? Why?
11. Is there anything else you'd like to add?

No trader can control volatility completely, but you can improve your odds.
Student of Richard Dennis

Those questions might seem simplistic, but Dennis did not care: "I suppose I didn't like the idea that everyone thought I was crazy or going to fail, but it didn't make any substantial difference because I had an idea what I wanted to do and how I wanted to do it."[95]

Dennis placed passion to achieve at the top. You have to wake up with inner drive and desire to make it happen. You have to go for it. He also outlined the trend following problem with profit targets—a key lesson taught to the Turtles: "When you have a position, you put it on for a reason, and you've got to keep it until the reason no longer exists. Don't take profits just for the sake of taking profits."[96] Dennis made it clear if you didn't know when a trend would end, but you did know it could go significantly higher, then don't get off.

Whatever you use should be applied in some quantitative, rigorous fashion. You should use science to determine what works and quantify it. I'm still surprised today at how I can expect so strongly that a trading methodology will be profitable but, after running it though a simulation, I discover it's a loser.
Paul Rabar[97]

Yet even though some of his Turtle students had successful money management careers, Dennis did not do well when trading for clients. His most recent stab at managing money for others resulted in a compounded annual return of 26.9 percent (after fees). That included two years when performance was over 100 percent.

But he stopped trading for clients after a drawdown in 2000. His clients pulled their money right before his trading would have rebounded. Doubt me? Use Dunn Capital or any other trend follower as a proxy and you will see what happened in the fall of 2000. If those impatient clients had stayed with Dennis they would have been richly rewarded.

One of the most crucial lessons a trader can learn is trading for your own account and for clients are different. John W. Henry was blunt with me saying it was never easy losing money for clients. On the other hand, traders who concentrate on expanding their own capital have a great advantage. Fund managers must always deal with the pressure and expectations of clients.

I don't think trading strategies are as vulnerable to not working if people know about them, as most traders believe. If what you are doing is right, it will work even if people have a general idea about it. I always say that you could publish trading rules in the newspaper and no one would follow them. A key is consistency and discipline.
Richard Dennis[98]

Summary Food for Thought

- Richard Dennis: "Trading was even more teachable than I imagined. In a strange sort of way, it was almost humbling."
- Dennis: "When you have a position, you put it on for a reason, and you've got to keep it until the reason no longer exists. Don't take profits just for the sake of taking profits. You have to have a strategy to trade, know how it works, and follow through on it."
- Dennis: "You don't get any profits from fundamental analysis; you get profit from buying and selling."

- The narrative of Richard Dennis and his students can be found in my book *TurtleTrader.*

Richard Donchian

Richard Donchian is known as the father of trend following. His original technical trading system became the foundation on which later trend followers built their systems. From the time he started the industry's first managed fund in 1949 until his death, he shared his research and served as a teacher and mentor to numerous present-day trend followers.

Donchian was born in 1905 in Hartford, Connecticut. He graduated from Yale in 1928 with a BA in economics. He was so fascinated by trading that even after losing his investments in the 1929 stock market crash, he returned to work on Wall Street.

In 1930 he managed to borrow some capital to trade shares in Auburn Auto, what William Baldwin in his article on Donchian called, "the Apple Computer of its day." The moment after he made several thousand dollars on the trade he became a market *technician*, charting prices and formulating buy and sell strategies without concern for an investment's basic value.[100]

From 1933 to 1935 Donchian wrote a technical market letter for Hemphill, Noyes & Co. He stopped his financial career to serve as an Air Force statistical control officer in World War II, but returned to Wall Street after the war and became a market letter writer for Shearson Hamill & Company. He began to keep detailed technical records on futures prices, recording daily price data in a ledger book. Barbara Dixon, one of his students, observed how he computed his moving averages and posted his own charts by hand, developing his trend following signals—without the benefit of an accurate database, software, or any computing capability. His jacket pockets were always loaded down with pencils and a pencil sharpener.[102]

Dixon makes it clear her mentor's work preceded and prefigured that of academic theorists who developed the modern theory of finance. Long before Harvard's John Litner published his quantitative analysis of the benefits of including managed futures in a portfolio with stocks and bonds, Donchian used concepts like diversification and risk control that won William Sharpe and Harry Markowitz Nobel prizes in economics in 1990.[103]

I became a computer applicant of Dick's [Donchian] ideas. He was one of the only people at the time who was doing simulation of any kind. He was generous with his ideas, making a point to share what he knew; it delighted him to get others to try systems. He inspired a great many people and spawned a whole generation of traders, providing courage and a road map.

Ed Seykota[99]

We started our database using punch cards in 1968, and we collected commodity price data back to July 1959. We back-tested the 5 and 20 and the weekly rules for Dick. I think the weekly method was the best thing that anyone had ever done. Of all Dick's contributions, the weekly rules helped identify the trend and helped you act on it. Dick is one of those people who today likes to beat the computer—only he did it by hand.

Dennis D. Dunn[101]

Personification of Persistence

Richard Donchian was not an overnight sensation. After 42 years, Donchian was still managing only $200,000. Then, in his mid-60s, everything came together, and a decade later, he was managing $27 million at Shearson American Express, making $1 million a year in fees and commissions and another million in trading profits on his own money.[104]

Donchian of course didn't predict price movements; he followed them. His explanation for his success was simple and as old as the Dow Theory itself: "Trends persist." He added: "A lot of people say things like: Gold has got to come down. It went up too fast. That's why 85 percent of commodities investors lose money. The fundamentals are supposed to be bullish in copper. But I'm on the short side now because the trend is down."[106]

These classic Donchian trading rules were first published over 75 years ago:

I remember in 1979 or 1980, at one of the early MAR conferences, being impressed by the fact that I counted 19 CTAs who were managing public funds, and I could directly identify 16 of the 19 with Dick Donchian. They had either worked for him or had had monies invested with him. To me, that's the best evidence of his impact in the early days. Dick has always been very proud of the fact that his people have prospered. He also was proud that after too many years in which his was the lone voice in the wilderness, his thinking eventually came to be the dominant thinking of the industry.
Brett Elam[105]

General Guides

1. Beware of acting immediately on a widespread public opinion. Even if correct, it will usually delay the move.
2. From a period of dullness and inactivity, watch for and prepare to follow a move in the direction in which volume increases.
3. Limit losses and ride profits, irrespective of all other rules.
4. Light commitments are advisable when market position is not certain. Clearly defined moves are signaled frequently enough to make life interesting and concentration on these moves will prevent unprofitable whip-sawing.
5. Seldom take a position in the direction of an immediately preceding three-day move. Wait for a one-day reversal.
6. Judicious use of stop orders is a valuable aid to profitable trading. Stops may be used to protect profits, to limit losses, and from certain formations such as triangular foci to take positions. Stop orders are apt to be more valuable and less treacherous if used in proper relation to the chart formation.
7. In a market in which upswings are likely to equal or exceed downswings, heavier position should be taken for the upswings for percentage reasons—a decline from 50 to 25 will net only 50 percent profit, whereas an advance from 25 to 50 will net 100 percent profit.

8. In taking a position, price orders are allowable. In closing a position, use market orders.
9. Buy strong-acting, strong-background commodities and sell weak ones, subject to all other rules.
10. Moves in which rails lead or participate strongly are usually more worth following than moves in which rails lag.
11. A study of the capitalization of a company, the degree of activity of an issue, and whether an issue is a lethargic truck horse or a spirited race horse is fully as important as a study of statistical reports.

Donchian Technical Guidelines

1. A move followed by a sideways range often precedes another move of almost equal extent in the same direction as the original move. Generally, when the second move from the sideways range has run its course, a counter move approaching the sideways range may be expected.

Losing an illusion makes you wiser than finding a truth.

Ludwig Borne

2. Reversal or resistance to a move is likely to be encountered:
   a. On reaching levels at which in the past, the commodity has fluctuated for a considerable length of time within a narrow range
   b. On approaching highs or lows
3. Watch for good buying or selling opportunities when trend lines are approached, especially on medium or dull volume. Be sure such a line has not been hugged or hit too frequently.
4. Watch for "crawling along" or repeated bumping of minor or major trend lines and prepare to see such trend lines broken.
5. Breaking of minor trend lines counter to the major trend gives most other important position taking signals. Positions can be taken or reversed on stop at such places.
6. Triangles of ether slope may mean either accumulation or distribution depending on other considerations, although triangles are usually broken on the flat side.
7. Watch for volume climax, especially after a long move.
8. Don't count on gaps being closed unless you can distinguish between breakaway gaps, normal gaps, and exhaustion gaps.

9. During a move, take or increase positions in the direction of the move at the market the morning following any one-day reversal, however slight the reversal may be, especially if volume declines on the reversal.

Students

Barbara Dixon was one of the more successful female trend traders in the business. She graduated from Vassar College in 1969, but because she was a woman and a history major, no one would hire her as a stockbroker. Undaunted, she finally took a job at Shearson as a secretary for Donchian. Dixon received three years of invaluable tutelage in trend following under Donchian. When Donchian moved to Connecticut she stayed behind to strike out on her own in 1973. Before long she had some 40 accounts ranging from $20,000 to well over $1 million.

Can one know absolutely when price will trend? No. Does one have to know absolutely in order to have a profitable business? No. In fact, a great number of businesses are based on the probability that a time-based series will trend. In fact, if you look at insurance, gambling, and other related businesses, you will come to the conclusion that even a small positive edge can mean great profits.
Forum Post

Dixon saw uncomplicated genius in Donchian's trading: "I'm not a mathematician. I believe that the simple solution is the most elegant and the best. Nobody has ever been able to demonstrate to me that a complex mathematical equation can answer the question, 'Is the market moving in an uptrend, downtrend, or sideways?' Any better than looking at a price chart and having simple rules to define those three sets of circumstances. These are the same rules I used back in the late 70s."[107]

Donchian was once again ahead of his time when he taught the importance of fast and simple decision making. Dixon was fond of pointing out a good system is one that keeps you alive and your equity intact when trends evaporate. She explained that the reason for any system is to get you into the market when a trend establishes. Her message: "Don't give up the system even after a string of losses . . . that is important because that's just when the profits are due."[108]

She also doesn't attempt to predict price moves, nor expect to be right every time. She knows she can't forecast the top or bottom of a price move. The hope is it continues indefinitely because you expect to make money over the long run, but on individual trades you admit when you're wrong and move on.[109]

Today most market players still fixate on the new and fresh fast-money idea of the day, yet I still find almost every word Donchian (or Dixon) wrote newer, fresher and more honest than anything currently broadcast on CNBC. My favorite Donchian wisdom tackles an issue that people are still struggling with in 2017: "It doesn't matter if you're trading stocks or soybeans. Trading is trading, and the name of the game is increasing your wealth. A trader's job description is stunningly simple: Don't lose money. This is of utmost importance to new traders, who are often told 'do your research.' This is good advice, but should be considered carefully. Research alone won't ensure a profit, and at the end of the day, your main goal should be to make money, not to get an A in How to Read a Balance Sheet."

Richard Donchian's blunt and a-touch-too-honest talk may explain why the Ivy League's finance curriculums do not include his exploits.

Summary Food for Thought

Nobody will deny that there is at least some roughness everywhere.

Benoit Mandelbrot

- Richard Donchian's account dropped below zero following the 1929 stock market crash.
- Donchian was one of the Pentagon whiz kids in World War II working closely with Robert McNamara.
- Donchian did not start his trend following fund until age 65. He traded into his nineties and personally trained legions in the art of trend following and trained women at a time when women had little respect on Wall Street.
- Donchian: "Nobody has ever been able to demonstrate to me that a complex mathematical equation can answer the question, 'Is the market moving in an up trend, downtrend, or sideways.'"

Jesse Livermore and Dickson Watts

Richard Donchian had *influences*. And Jesse Livermore, born in South Acton, Massachusetts in 1877, was a big one. At the age of 15 he went to Boston and began working in Paine Webber's Boston brokerage office. He studied price movements and began to trade their price fluctuations. When Livermore was in his 20s he moved to New York City to speculate. After 40 years of trading he developed a knack for speculating on price movements. One of his foremost rules: "Never act on tips."

The unofficial biography of Livermore was *Reminiscences of a Stock Operator*, first published in 1923 and written by journalist Edwin Lefevre. Readers likely guessed Lefevre as a pseudonym for Livermore himself. *Reminiscences of a Stock Operator* went on to become a Wall Street classic. Numerous quotations and euphemisms from the book are so embedded in trading lore traders today don't have the slightest idea where they originated[110]:

1. It takes a man a long time to learn all the lessons of his mistakes. They say there are two sides to everything. But there is only one side to the stock market; and it is not the bull side or the bear side, but the right side.
2. I think it was a long step forward in my trading education when I realized at last that when old Mr. Partridge kept on telling the other customers, "Well, you know this is a bull market!" he really meant to tell them that the big money was not in the individual fluctuations but in the main movements—that is, not in reading the tape, but in sizing up the entire market and its trend.
3. The reason is that a man may see straight and clearly and yet become impatient or doubtful when the market takes its time about doing as he figured it must do. That is why so many men in Wall Street, who are not at all in the sucker class, not even in the third grade, nevertheless lose money. The market does not beat them. They beat themselves, because though they have brains they cannot sit tight. Old Turkey was dead right in doing and saying what he did. He had not only the courage of his convictions but the intelligent patience to sit tight.
4. The average man doesn't wish to be told that it is a bull or bear market. What he desires is to be told specifically which particular stock to buy or sell. He wants to get something for nothing. He does not wish to work. He doesn't even wish to have to think. It is too much bother to have to count the money that he picks up from the ground.
5. A man will risk half his fortune in the stock market with less reflection than he devotes to the selection of a medium-priced automobile.

We love volatility and days like the one in which the stock market took a big plunge, for being on the right side of moving markets is what makes us money. A stagnant market in any commodity, such as grain has experienced recently, means there's no opportunity for us to make money.
Dinesh Desai[111]

Think about the wild speculation that took place during the Dotcom bubble of the late 1990s, the wild speculation that ended with the October 2008 market crash, the current-day Federal Reserve market propping, and then remember Livermore was referring to a market environment nearly 100 years ago.

Livermore did write one book: *How to Trade in Stocks: The Livermore Formula for Combining Time, Element and Price.* It was published in 1940. The book is difficult to find, but a little persistence paid off. Livermore was by no means a perfect trader (and he says so). He was no role model. His trading style was bold and extremely volatile. He went broke several times making and losing millions. Yet his personal trading does not detract from his wisdom.

One early trend trader who had an influence on Livermore was Dickson Watts. Watts was president of the New York Cotton Exchange between 1878 and 1880. His mindset still inspires in 2017:

> All business is more or less speculation. The term *speculation*, however, is commonly restricted to business of exceptional uncertainty. The uninitiated believe that chance is so large a part of speculation that it is subject to no rules, is governed by no laws. This is a serious error.
>
> Let's first consider the qualities essential to the equipment of a speculator:
>
> 1. **Self-reliance:** A man must think for himself, must follow his own convictions. Self-trust is the foundation of successful effort.
> 2. **Judgment:** That equipoise, that nice adjustment of the facilities one to the other, which is called good judgment, is an essential to the speculator.
> 3. **Courage:** That is, confidence to act on the decisions of the mind. In speculation, there is value in Mirabeau's dictum: Be bold, still be bold; always be bold.
> 4. **Prudence:** The power of measuring the danger, together with a certain alertness and watchfulness, is important. There should be a balance of these two, prudence and courage; prudence in contemplation, courage in execution. Connected with these qualities, properly an outgrowth of them, is a third, viz: promptness. The mind convinced, the act should follow. Think, act, promptly.
> 5. **Pliability:** The ability to change an opinion, the power of revision. "He who observes," says Emerson, "and observes again, is always formidable."
>
> These qualifications are mandatory to achieve successful speculation, but they must be conducted in a balanced manner. A deficiency or an over plus of one quality will destroy the effectiveness of all. The possession of such faculties, in a proper adjustment is, of course, uncommon. In speculation, as in life, few succeed, many fail.[112]

Bottomless wonders spring from simple rules, which are repeated without end.
Benoit Mandelbrot

Jesse Livermore's take is less academic and more emotional than Watts's, but spot on enduring: "Wall Street never changes, the pockets change, the suckers change, the stocks change, but Wall Street never changes, because human nature never changes."

Summary Food for Thought

Neither a state nor a bank ever have had unrestricted power of issuing paper money without abusing that power.
David Ricardo

- David Ricardo (1772–1823) inspired and influenced Watts, Livermore, and Donchian. He was arguably the very first trend following trader.
- Seeing the invisible, otherwise known as *risk*.
- Michael Melissinos: "The trend following philosophy is based on adapting to evolving conditions in the now. It's about learning from the past in order to make the right decisions today. The goal is not to eliminate losses from investing, but to manage them in a way that doesn't kill us."
- Bill Gurley on not pursuing Google: "I go back, and the learning is that if you have remarkably asymmetric returns you have to ask yourself, 'how high could up be and what could go right?' Because it's not a 50/50 thing. If you thought there was a 20% chance you should still do it because the upside is so high."[113]
- Miles Davis: "When you hit a wrong note, it's the next note that makes it good or bad."

Performance Proof 3

Even if you are a minority of one, the truth is the truth.
—Gandhi

What we've got here is failure to communicate. Some men you just can't reach, so you get what we had here last week, which is the way he wants it.
—Cool Hand Luke

Anyone can tell you they have a successful method or system, but the only objective measurement is raw data. If a claim is to be made, it must be supported. The numbers in this volume, across numerous third-party reporting services and inside disclosures on file with American and international regulatory authorities, don't lie. You could be the skeptic and say: "Hold on, the numbers could be faked!" That doesn't fly with decades of data across unrelated traders located in dozens of countries. This is not about one isolated Bernie Madoff track record open to hanky-panky. Thus, in reviewing legendary trend following performance histories and assorted research studies I alone might own (my insider investigation methods are a whole other book), I zeroed in on six key data concepts:

It is a capital mistake to theorize before one has data.
Sir Arthur Conan Doyle[1]

1. Absolute returns
2. Volatility

3. Drawdowns
4. Correlation
5. Zero sum
6. Berkshire Hathaway

Absolute Returns

An absolute return trading strategy means you are trying to make the most money possible. Author Alexander Ineichen defines it succinctly: An absolute return manager is essentially an asset manager without a benchmark—Bench marking can be viewed as a method of restricting investment managers so as to limit the potential for surprises, either positive or negative.[2]

Trend following in its purest form doesn't track or attempt to mimic any particular index—ever. If trend following had a coat of arms, *Absolute Returns* would be emblazoned upon it. It thrives and profits from the *surprises* benchmarking artificially stops.

This ain't clipping coupons. No risk, no return. No balls, no babies.
Anonymous

However, not all trend followers are shooting for absolute returns or the most amount of money possible. Not all play the game full tilt. Jerry Parker, for example, purposefully aims for lower returns to cater to a different client base (those who want less risk and less return).

But John W. Henry long made the case "[that] the overall objective is to provide absolute returns. Relative return managers, such as most traditional equity or fixed-income managers, are measured on how they perform relative to some pre-determined benchmark. We have no such investment benchmark, so its aim is to achieve returns in all market conditions, and is thus considered an absolute return manager."[3]

Shoot for a benchmark in returns and you run with the crowd. Benchmarks such as the S&P might make you feel safe, even when that feeling is clearly artificial. Trend following, on the other hand, understands that trading for absolute returns and not from blind adherence to benchmarks is the best way to handle uncertainty.

The concept of indexing and benchmarking is very useful in the EMT world of traditional long-only passive investing, but it has almost zero usefulness for an absolute return process. Again, it gets back to what it takes to achieve an absolute return—you need an enormous amount of latitude and freedom in executing a trading strategy to ensure capital preservation and achieve a positive return. At its core, the concept of absolute return investing is antithetical to benchmarking, which encourages traditional managers to have similarly structured portfolios and look at their performance on a relative basis.[4]

If you base your trading strategy on benchmark comparisons, it doesn't matter whether you are a talented trader or not because all decisions are about the *averages*. Why is any trading skill relevant? It's not. That's why 80 percent of mutual funds don't beat averages.

Volatility versus Risk

There are organizations that rank and track monthly performance numbers. One organization gives a *star ranking* (like Morningstar):

> The quantitative rating system employed ranks and rates the performance of all commodity trading advisors (CTA) . . . Ratings are given in four categories: a) equity, b) performance, c) risk exposure, and d) risk-adjusted returns. In each category, the highest possible rating is five stars and the lowest possible rating is one star. The actual statistics on which the percentiles are based as follows:
>
> 1. Performance: Rate of Return
> 2. Risk: Standard Deviation
> 3. Risk Adjusted: Sharpe Ratio
> 4. Equity: Assets[5]

The class of those who have the ability to think their own thoughts is separated by an unbridgeable gulf from the class of those who cannot.

Ludwig von Mises[6]

Dunn Capital once received one star for *risk*, the implication being that an investment with Dunn is more *risky*. However, these rankings don't give accurate information on Dunn's true risk. This rating group uses standard deviation as their measure of risk. But this is a measure of volatility and not necessarily risk. High volatility alone does not necessarily mean higher risk.

It's doubtful Dunn, with a track record exceeding 40 years, is overly concerned about being inaccurately penalized, but using standard deviation as a risk measurement does distort a true understanding.

Volatility is the tendency for prices to change unexpectedly.[7]

This same firm's ranking of then-active trader Victor Niederhoffer demonstrates the star system's weakness. At the time of Niederhoffer's public-trading demise in 1997, he was rated as four stars for *risk*. Based on Niederhoffer's past performance, the rankings were saying he was a much safer bet than Dunn. Obviously the star system failed for people who believed Niederhoffer was less *risky*. Standard deviation as a risk measure does trend following an injustice. One of my goals is to dispel the simplistic notion trend following is *risky* or that all trend following strategies have high standard deviations, which means they are *bad*.

A good illustration begins with this 10-year chart of various trend following performances (see Table 3.1).

TABLE 3.1(a): Absolute Return: Annualized ROR (January 1993–June 2003)

Trading Managers	Annualized ROR	Compounded ROR
1. Eckhardt Trading Co. (Higher Leverage)	31.14%	1,622.80%
2. Dunn Capital Management, Inc. (World Monetary Asset)	27.55%	1,186.82%
3. Dolphin Capital Management Inc. (Global Diversified I)	23.47%	815.33%
4. Eckhardt Trading Co. (Standard)	22.46%	739.10%
5. KMJ Capital Management, Inc. (Currency)	21.95%	703.59%
6. Beach Capital Management Ltd. (Discretionary)	21.54%	675.29%
7. Mark J. Walsh & Company (Standard)	20.67%	618.88%
8. Saxon Investment Corp. (Diversified)	19.25%	534.83%
9. Man Inv. Products, Ltd. (AHL Composite Pro Forma)	7.66%	451.77%
10. John W. Henry & Company, Inc. (Global Diversified)	17.14%	426.40%
11. John W. Henry & Company, Inc. (Financial & Metals)	17.07%	423.08%
12. Dreiss Research Corporation (Diversified)	16.47%	395.71%
13. Abraham Trading (Diversified)	15.91%	371.08%
14. Dunn Capital Management, Inc. (Targets of Opportunity System)	14.43%	311.66%
15. Rabar Market Research (Diversified)	14.09%	299.15%
16. John W. Henry & Company, Inc. (International Foreign Exchange)	13.89%	291.82%
17. Hyman Beck & Company, Inc. (Global Portfolio)	12.98%	260.18%
18. Campbell & Company (Fin. Met. & Energy—Large)	12.73%	251.92%
19. Chesapeake Capital Corporation (Diversified)	12.70%	250.92%
20. Millburn Ridgefield Corporation (Diversified)	11.84%	223.88%
21. Campbell & Company (Global Diversified—Large)	11.64%	217.75%
22. Tamiso & Co., LLC (Original Currency Account)	11.42%	211.29%
23. JPD Enterprises, Inc. (Global Diversified)	11.14%	203.03%

TABLE 3.1(b): Trailing Performance and Sharpe Comparison through December 2016

Commodity Trading Advisors	Vol	Performance					Sharpe					
	60 Mo.	12 Mo.	24 Mo.	36 Mo.	48 Mo.	60 Mo.	12 Mo.	24 Mo.	36 Mo.	48 Mo.	60 Mo.	ODR*
AQR Capital Mgt. (Managed Futures — Class I)	10%	-8%	-7%	2%	12%	15%	-0.80	-0.27	0.13	0.34	0.35	1.47
Aspect (Diversified)	13%	-9%	-2%	29%	24%	10%	-0.86	0.00	0.64	0.45	0.21	1.02
Campbell & Company (Managed Futures)	12%	-10%	-13%	5%	18%	23%	-0.87	-0.47	0.18	0.40	0.40	1.09
DUNN World Monetary and Agriculture (WMA) Program	23%	-5%	5%	42%	91%	55%	-0.18	0.21	0.62	0.81	0.50	1.34
DUNN WMA Institutional Program	11%	-1%	4%	23%	41%	31%	-0.08	0.24	0.65	0.82	0.56	1.32
Graham Diversified (Diversified k4D-10V)	10%	-8%	-7%	10%	22%	16%	-1.01	-0.39	0.36	0.53	0.36	1.13
ISAM (Systematic Program)	17%	-12%	1%	64%	47%	21%	-0.78	0.13	0.93	0.61	0.30	1.64
Lynx Asset Mgmt Bermuda	15%	-3%	-12%	12%	25%	16%	-0.15	-0.34	0.32	0.45	0.28	0.87
Man Investments (AHL Diversified)	12%	-8%	-10%	18%	15%	14%	-0.66	-0.32	0.49	0.33	0.27	0.99
Transtrend B.V. (Enhanced Risk — USD)	12%	8%	5%	23%	23%	22%	0.60	0.23	0.57	0.47	0.38	1.14
Winton Capital (Diversified)	9%	-3%	-2%	11%	22%	17%	-0.38	-0.09	0.42	0.55	0.39	1.15
Barclays CTA Index	5%	-1%	-2%	5%	4%	2%	-0.20	-0.24	0.37	0.22	0.10	1.15

Data Source: BarclayHedge

**The Offensive/Defensive Ratio ("ODR") calculation measures the Average Winning Months/Average Losing Months. Programs with a higher ODR indicates the program is successful at releasing the upside potential when the environment is good; conversely they are good at limiting losses when times are less favorable for the strategy.*

Just saying a trader is volatile and thus *bad* makes little sense if you examine absolute return performance (Table 3.1). Raw absolute returns should count for something far more than fear or career risk—they equal the only way to massive wealth.

Nonetheless, volatility (what standard deviation measures) is still a pejorative for most market participants. Volatility scares them, even when a young student can quickly analyze any historical data series to see volatility is normal and expected. But most investors try to run away from the hint of volatility—even when running is not possible. Some markets and traders are more volatile than others, but degrees of volatility are basic facts of life. To trend following, volatility is the precursor to profit. If you have no volatility, you have no opportunity for profit.

The press is always confused as seen in *BusinessWeek*: "Trend followers are trying to make sense out of their dismal recent returns. 'When you look past the superficial question of how we did, you look under the hood and see immense change in the global markets,' says John W. Henry's president. 'Volatility is just a harbinger of new trends to come.' Maybe. But futures traders are supposed to make money by exploiting volatility. Performance isn't a 'superficial question' if you were among the thousands of commodity-fund customers who lost money when the currency markets went bonkers."[8]

Focusing on one period in isolation while ignoring a complete performance history misrepresents the full picture. I wondered if this reporter had written a follow-up article correcting his observations about trend following, because the following year trend trader Dunn produced a 60.25 percent return, and trend trader Parker produced a 61.82 percent return. It didn't surprise me *BusinessWeek* archives revealed no correction.

Some suggested a few years ago that trend following had been marginalized. The answer is we haven't been marginalized—[trend following] has played a key role in helping protect a lot of people's wealth this year.
Mark Rzepczynski[9]

Volatility

Hedge fund researcher Nicola Meaden compared monthly standard deviations (volatility as measured from the mean) and semi-standard deviations (volatility measured on the downside only) and found that although trend following arguably experiences higher volatility, it is often concentrated on the upside (positive returns), not the downside (negative returns).

Trend following performance is thus unfairly penalized by performance measures such as the Sharpe ratio. The Sharpe ratio ignores whether volatility is on the plus or minus side because it does not account for the difference between the standard deviation and the semi-standard deviation. The actual formula is identical, with one exception—the semi-standard deviation looks only at observations below the mean. If the semi-standard deviation is lower than the standard deviation, the historical pull away from the mean has to be on the plus side. If it is higher, the pull away from the mean is on the minus side. Meaden points out the huge difference that puts trend following volatility on the upside if you compare monthly standard (12.51) and semi-standard (5.79) deviation.[10]

Here is another way of thinking about upside volatility: Ponder a market going up. You enter at $100 and the market goes to $150. Then the market drops to $125. Is that necessarily bad? No. Because after going from $100 to $150 and then dropping back to $125 the market might then zoom up to $175. This is upside volatility in action. Even Harry Markowitz (see podcast episode #235), who won the Nobel Prize for his mean-variance theory, has noted semi-variance is a better *risk* measure. He has even said he might not have won that Nobel Prize if he built CAPM around semi-variance.

Quite simply, Trend following has greater upside volatility and less downside volatility than traditional equity indices because it exits losing trades quickly. Trend trader Graham Capital mitigates the fear: "A trend follower achieves positive returns by correctly targeting market direction and minimizing the cost of this portfolio. Thus, while trend following is sometimes referred to as being 'long volatility,' trend followers technically do not trade volatility, although they often benefit from it."[11]

The question, then, is not how to reduce volatility (you can't control the market after all), but how to manage it through proper position sizing or money management. You have to get used to riding the bucking bronco. Great trend traders don't see straight-up equity curves in their accounts, so you are in good company when it comes to the up and down nature of making big money.

Trading is a zero-sum game in an important accounting sense. In a zero-sum game, the total gains of the winners are exactly equal to the total losses of the losers.[12]

Larry Harris

John W. Henry sees the distinction: "Risk is very different from volatility. A lot of people believe there is no difference, but there's a huge difference and I can spend an hour on that topic. Suffice it to say that we embrace both volatility and risk and, for us, risk is that we're going to lose if we risk two tenths of one percent on a particular trade. That is, to us, real risk. Giving back a profit to you probably seems like risk, to us it seems like volatility."

Henry's world-view didn't avoid high volatility. The last thing he wanted to experience is volatility that forced him out of a major trend before he could make a profit. Dinesh Desai, a trend follower from the

1980s, was fond of saying he *loved* volatility. Being on the right side of a volatile market was the reason he retired rich.

Even with predictable and ongoing volatility debates, trend following has one of the longest-standing track records in the hedge fund industry and has consistently demonstrated its diversifying power. The ability to take short positions objectively is absolutely crucial. As a strategy with a relatively low Sharpe ratio, it needs to be well understood by investors, so the size of positions is in line with their particular risk tolerance.[13]

However, the skeptics and critics always view high volatility as only *bad*. For example, a fund manager with $1.5 billion in assets remains on the sidelines, refusing to believe in trend following: "My biggest source of hesitancy about the asset class [trend following] is its reliance on technical analysis. Trading advisors do seem to profit, but because they rarely incorporate economic data, they simply ride price trends until they reverse. The end result of this crude approach is a subpar return to risk ratio." Another money manager opines: "Why should I give money to a AA baseball player when I can hire someone in the major leagues?"[14]

Some people seem to like to lose, so they win by losing money.
Ed Seykota[15]

Looking at the absolute performance of great trend traders and calling it AA baseball makes little objective sense. I doubt this guy made it past October 2008, unless he was bailed out. Of course, the funds and banks that all blew out then were all considered *Major League*. But if you can get beyond the "volatility is the devil" propaganda it's easy to see how you can benefit from volatility.

Trend follower Jason Russell says it well:

> Volatility matters when you feel it. All the charts, ratios, and advanced math in the world mean nothing when you break down, vomit, or cry due to the volatility in your portfolio. I call this the *vomitility* threshold. Understanding your threshold is important for it is at this point that you lose all confidence and throw in the towel. Traders, portfolio managers, and mathematicians seem well equipped to describe risk with a battery of formulas and ratios they use to measure volatility. However, even if you can easily handle the math, it can be a challenge to truly conceptualize it. I can sum it up as follows: Surrender to the reality that volatility exists or volatility will introduce you to the reality that surrender exists.

Building on Russell's point David Harding was asked: "You've attracted quite a lot of new money into the fund since you've launched, but particularly in the last couple of years. *Why*?"

Harding replied, "The market has bought what actually is quite a complicated story. [Our story] is not simple. In our early years, we were impeded by the terrific performance of Dot-com stocks. Later people became very attracted to certain types of hedge funds, which produced very smooth and steady returns; something which we've never purported to do. But now that the story has been got across better, people are, I think, realizing that [we are] a good horse to back in the race."

Drawdowns

With trend following, however, comes the inevitable drawdown. A drawdown is any losing period during an investment record. It is defined as the percent retrenchment from an equity peak to an equity valley. A drawdown is in effect from the time an equity retrenchment begins until a new equity high is reached—that is, in terms of time, a drawdown encompasses both the period from equity peak to equity valley (length) and the time from the equity valley to a new equity high (recovery).[16]

For example, if you start from $100,000 and drop to $50,000, you are in a 50 percent drawdown. You could also say you have lost 50 percent. The drawdown is thus a reduction in your account equity. Yes, that happens for buy and holders, too, but the big difference is that trend following has an exit strategy built in. Not surprisingly, many investors and regulators have made drawdown for trend following a dirty word, while leaving mutual funds free to disguise their true drawdowns.

Dunn Capital's retort:

> Investors should be aware of the volatility inherent to [our] trading programs. Because the same portfolio risk profile is intrinsic to all . . . programs, investors in any . . . program can be expected to experience volatility similar to our composite record. During 40+ years of trading, the composite record, on a month-to-month basis, has experienced eight serious losses exceeding 25 percent. The eighth such loss equaled 40 percent, beginning in September 1999 and extending through September 2000. This loss was recovered in the three-month period ending in December 2000. The most serious loss in our entire history occurred over a four-month period, which ended in February 1976 and equaled 52 percent [Dunn did have a 57 percent drawdown in 2007, which it recovered from and made new highs as recently as July 2016].

If you were to put all the trend following models side by side, you would probably find that most made profits and incurred losses in the same markets. They were all looking at the same charts and obtaining the same perception of opportunity.

Marc Goodman
Kenmar Asset Allocation[17]

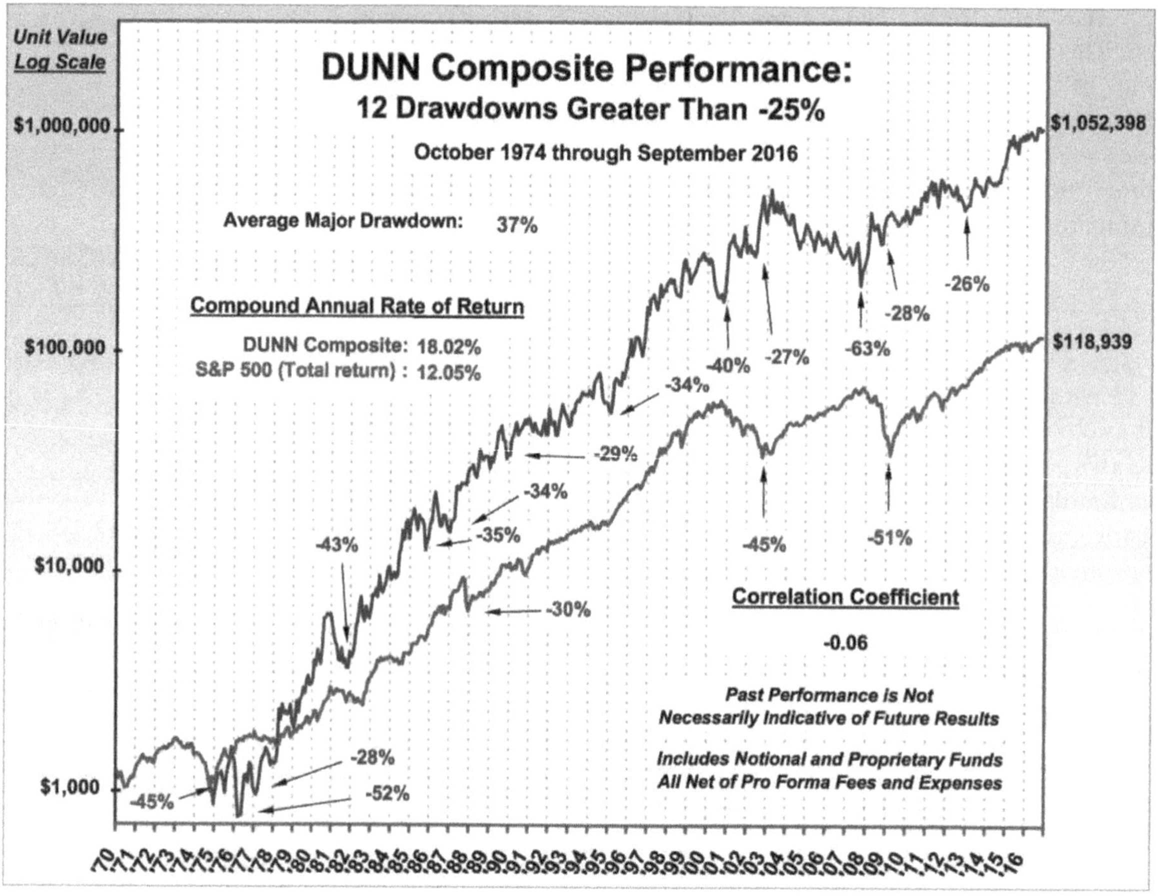

FIGURE 3.1: Drawdown Chart Source: Dunn Capital Management

Dunn Capital Management's documents include a summary of serious past losses. The summary explains that the firm has suffered through seven difficult periods of losses of 25 percent or more. Every potential investor receives a copy: "If the investor is not willing to live through this, they are not the right investor for the portfolio."[19]

Clients should be prepared to endure similar or worse periods in the future. The inability (or unwillingness) to do so will probably result in serious loss, without the opportunity for subsequent recovery.[18]

Unless you understand Dunn's philosophy, you might refuse to invest, even though that 40-year plus track record is the envy of Monday morning quarterbacks. Examine their drawdown history in Figure 3.1. I used this same chart in Chapter 2 to illustrate performance, but it serves another purpose.

Imagine the valleys between the peaks are filled with water. First, place a piece of paper over the chart and then slowly move the paper to the right and uncover the chart. Imagine you have made a large investment in the fund. How do you feel as you move the page? How long can you remain underwater? How deep can you dive? Do you pull out the calculator and figure out what you could have earned at the bank? Do you figure out you lost enough to buy a vacation, car, house, or perhaps solve the hunger crisis of a small nation?

Obviously you don't want to overhaul a program in response to one year just because something didn't work. That's when you're almost guaranteed that it would have worked the next year had you kept it in there.

Eclipse Capital

To the eyes-wide-open player this drawdown chart (Figure 3.1) is tolerable because of the absolute returns over the long-term, but that doesn't make it easy to accept. An accurate discussion of drawdown inevitably leads to the recovery conversation, which means bringing capital back to the point where a drawdown began. Historically, trend following has quickly made money back during recovery from drawdowns.

However, you can't neglect the math associated with losing money and making it back. What if you start with $100 and it drops to $50? You are now in a 50 percent drawdown. How much do you have to make to get back to breakeven (Table 3.2)? You need 100 percent to get back. That's right—when you go down 50 percent you need to make back 100 percent to get back to breakeven. Notice as drawdown increases (see Table 3.2), the percent gain necessary to recover to the breakeven point increases at a much faster rate. Trend following strategy lives with this chart daily. It handles this math:

The 25 or 50 biggest trend followers are essentially going to make money in the same places. What differentiates them from one another are portfolio and risk management.[20]

TABLE 3.2: Drawdown Recovery Chart

Size of Drawdown	Percent Gain to Recover
5%	5.3%
10%	11.1%
15%	17.6%
20%	25.0%
25%	33.3%
30%	42.9%
40%	66.7%
50%	100%
60%	150%
70%	233%
80%	400%
90%	900%
100%	Ruin

Unless you can watch your stock holding decline by 50% without becoming panic-stricken, you should not be in the stock market.

Warren Buffett

***Note:** Since 1980 Berkshire Hathaway has had drawdowns of –51%, –49%, –37%, and –37%. In addition, Charles Munger Partnership dropped –31.9% in 1973 and –31.5% in 1974.*

David Harding goes after drawdown *haters*:

> A key measure of track record quality and strategy "riskiness" in the managed futures industry is drawdown, which measures the decline in net asset value from the historic high point. Under the Commodity Futures Trading Commission's mandatory disclosure regime, managed futures advisors are obliged to disclose as part of their capsule performance record their "worst peak-to-valley drawdown." As a description of an aspect of historical performance, drawdown has one key positive attribute: It refers to a physical reality, and as such, it is less abstract than concepts such as volatility. It represents the amount by which you are less well off than you were; or, put differently, it measures the magnitude of the loss an investor could have incurred by investing with the manager in the past. Managers are obliged to wear their worst historical drawdown like a scarlet letter for the rest of their lives.[21]

We have not made any changes because of a drawdown. While we have made minor changes since the program started trading in 1974, over the course of the years the basic concepts have never changed. The majority of the trading parameters and the buy and sell signals largely have remained the same.
Bill Dunn[22]

If the complete story of an absolute return trading strategy is understood, drawdown fear is mitigated.

However, you can't eliminate catastrophic risk, much less drawdowns, from trading. A great example of getting scared at the wrong time during a drawdown can be seen in this trader's story: "I [once] opened an account for a client. At the time we were down 10–12 percent, and I explained the drawdown and our expectation for losses. Suddenly, when his account went down 20 percent, he became very anxious. He eventually closed his account. He made the business decision to stop trading because of the pain he was feeling from the drawdown. I continued to track his account hypothetically so I could see what would happen if he would have continued trading."

You have to keep trading the way you were before the drawdown and also be patient. There's always part of a trader's psyche that wants to make losses back tomorrow. But traders need to remember you lose it really fast, but you make it up slowly. You may think you can make it up fast, but it doesn't work that way.
David Druz[23]

He added: "As it turns out, he closed his account within 2 days of the drawdown low. Had he stayed invested he would be up +121.1 percent from his closing value, and +71.6 percent from his starting value (through October 2008). I am reminded of a statement quoted many times from Peter Lynch, the manager of the Fidelity Magellan Fund. In light of Lynch's trading success, he revealed over 50 percent of the investors in his fund lost money. He explained the reason—most investors pulled out at the wrong time. They traded with their gut and treated drawdowns as a cancer, rather than the natural ebb and flow of trading."

Interestingly, there is another perspective on drawdowns that few consider. When you look at trend following performance data—for example,

Dunn's track record—you can't help but notice certain times look better than others to invest.

Some clients do look at that performance chart and *buy* when the fund is experiencing a drawdown. Because if Dunn is down 30 percent and you know from analysis of past performance data that recovery from drawdowns can be quick, then buying while on sale is an option. This is commonly referred to as equity curve trading. Trend trader Tom Basso:

> I haven't met a trader yet that wouldn't say privately that he would tend to buy his program on a drawdown, particularly systematic traders. But, investors seem to not add money when, to traders, it seems to be most logical to do so . . . Why don't investors invest on drawdowns? I believe the answer to that question lies in the investing psychology of buying a drawdown. The human mind can easily extrapolate three months of negative returns into "how long at this rate will it take to lose 50 percent or everything?" Rather than seeing the bargain and the positive return to risk, they see only the negative and forecast more of the same into the future.[24]

Not only do some trend followers tell clients to buy into their funds during a drawdown, they also buy into their own funds during the drawdowns. I know employees at top trend following funds who are too happy when they are in a drawdown because they can buy their fund *cheap*.

Other trading styles have drawdowns, too. For example, some of the best names on Wall Street (non-trend followers) had tough sledding in 2008—but they don't have the drawdown stigma associated with trend following:

- Warren Buffett (Berkshire Hathaway): –43 percent
- Ken Heebner (CMG Focus Fund): –56 percent
- Harry Lange (Fidelity Magellan): –59 percent
- Bill Miller (Legg Mason Value Trust): –50 percent
- Ken Griffin (Citadel): –44 percent
- Carl Icahn (Icahn Enterprises): –81 percent
- T. Boone Pickens: Down $2 billion since July 2008
- Kirk Kerkorian: Down $693 million on Ford shares alone

It is paramount to determine how quickly you can recover from a drawdown and get back to making new money again—regardless of trading strategy.

Correlation coefficient: A statistical measure of the interdependence of two or more random variables. Fundamentally, the value indicates how much of a change in one variable is explained by a change in another.[25]

Campbell & Company, a trend following managed futures firm with almost [billions] in assets under management, has returned 17.65 percent since its inception in 1972, proving that performance can be sustainable over the long-term.[26]

If an investor had invested 10 percent of his or her portfolio in the Millburn Diversified Portfolio from February 1977 through August 2003 he or she would have increased the return on his or her traditional portfolio by 73 basis points (a 6.2 percent increase) and decreased risk (as measured by standard deviation) by 0.26 of a percent (an 8.2 percent decrease).

Millburn Corporation

Correlation

Correlation comparisons help to show trend following as a legitimate style and demonstrate the similarity in strategy used among trend followers. Correlation is not only important in assembling the portfolio you trade, but it is also a critical tool for analyzing and comparing performance histories of trend followers.

In a research paper titled *Learning to Love Non-Correlation*, correlation is defined as a statistical term giving the strength of linear relationship between two random variables. It is the historical tendency of one thing to move in tandem with another. The correlation coefficient is a number from –1 to +1, with –1 being the perfectly opposite behavior of two investments (e.g., up 5 percent every time the other is down 5 percent). The +1 reflects identical investment results (up or down the same amount each period). The further away from +1 one gets (and thus closer to –1), the better a diversifier one investment is for the other. But to keep things simple, another description of correlation is instructive: the tendency for one investment to zig while another zags.[27]

When I was young I thought that money was the most important thing in life; now that I am old I know that it is.
Oscar Wilde

Let's look an an example. I took the monthly performance numbers of trend followers and computed their correlation coefficients. Comparing correlations gave the evidence that trend followers trade typically the same markets in the same way at the same time.

Look at the correlation chart (see Table 3.3(a)) and ask yourself: "Why do two trend followers who don't work in the same office, who are on opposite sides of the continent, have the same three losing months in a row with similar percentage losses?" Then ask: "Why do they have the same winning month, then the same two losing months, and then the same three winning months in a row?" The relationship is there because they can respond only to what the market offers. The market offers trends to everyone equally. They're all looking at the same market, aiming for the same target of opportunity. Table 3.3(b) also shows trend followers using similar techniques.

Interestingly, correlation can be a touchy subject. The Turtles were all grateful to Richard Dennis for his mentoring, but some were ambivalent over time, obviously indebted to Dennis, but struggling to achieve their own identity: "One Turtle says his system is 95 percent Dennis' system and the rest his 'own flair . . . I'm a long way from someone who follows the system mechanically . . . but by far, the structure of what I do is based on Richard's systems, and certainly, philosophically, everything I do in terms of trading is based on what I learned from Richard.'"[28]

TABLE 3.3(a): Correlation: Trend Followers

	AbrDiv	CamFin	CheDiv	DUNWor	EckSta	JohFin	ManAHL	MarSta	RabDiv
AbrDiv	1.00	0.56	0.81	0.33	0.57	0.55	0.56	0.75	0.75
CamFin	0.56	1.00	0.59	0.62	0.60	0.56	0.51	0.57	0.55
CheDiv	0.81	0.59	1.00	0.41	0.53	0.55	0.60	0.72	0.75
DUNWor	0.33	0.62	0.41	1.00	0.57	0.62	0.61	0.51	0.45
EckSta	0.57	0.60	0.53	0.57	1.00	0.57	0.58	0.74	0.71
JohFin	0.55	0.56	0.55	0.62	0.57	1.00	0.53	0.55	0.50
ManAHL	0.56	0.51	0.60	0.61	0.58	0.53	1.00	0.57	0.59
MarSta	0.75	0.57	0.72	0.51	0.74	0.55	0.57	1.00	0.68
RabDiv	0.75	0.55	0.75	0.45	0.71	0.50	0.59	0.68	1.00

AbrDiv: Abraham Trading; CamFin: Campbell & Company; CheDiv: Chesapeake Capital Corporation; DUNWor: DUNN Capital Management, Inc.; EckSta: Eckhardt Trading Co.; JohFin: John W. Henry & Company, Inc.; ManAHL: Man Inv. Products, Ltd.; MarSta: Mark J. Walsh & Company; RabDiv: Rabar Market Research.

TABLE 3.3(b): Further Correlation: Trend Followers

	AQR	Aspect	Campbell	DUNN WMA	Graham	ISAM	Lynx	Man	Transtrend	Winton
AQR		77%	80%	78%	70%	76%	79%	63%	73%	67%
Aspect	77%		76%	75%	70%	85%	75%	71%	77%	80%
Campbell	80%	76%		72%	72%	75%	77%	70%	74%	67%
DUNN WMA	78%	75%	72%		69%	73%	75%	59%	72%	72%
Graham	70%	70%	72%	69%		72%	79%	64%	66%	80%
ISAM	76%	85%	75%	73%	72%		73%	77%	75%	67%
Lynx	79%	75%	77%	75%	79%	73%		64%	83%	79%
Man	63%	71%	70%	59%	64%	77%	64%		66%	66%
Transtrend	73%	77%	74%	72%	66%	75%	83%	66%		75%
Winton	67%	80%	67%	72%	80%	67%	79%	66%	75%	
Average	67%	69%	67%	68%	65%	68%	69%	60%	67%	66%
Barclays CTA Index	83%	78%	82%	70%	76%	82%	88%	67%	86%	73%
S&P 500	–21%	–1%	2%	–8%	15%	–19%	14%	6%	–1%	16%

Data Source: BarclayHedge

* Average excludes Barclay CTA Index and S&P 500

Even when correlation data shows similar patterns among Dennis's Turtle students, the desire to differentiate is stronger than their need to honestly address obvious similarities in their return streams: "There no longer is a turtle trading style in my mind. We've all evolved and developed systems that are very different from those we were taught, and that independent evolution suggests that the dissimilarities to trading between turtles are always increasing."[29]

A Turtle correlation chart paints another picture. The relationship is there to judge. The data (Table 3.4) is the ultimate arbiter:

TABLE 3.4: Correlation among Turtles

	Chesapeake	Eckhardt	Hawksbill	JPD	Rabar
Chesapeake	1	0.53	0.62	0.75	0.75
Eckhardt	0.53	1	0.7	0.7	0.71
Hawksbill	0.62	0.7	1	0.73	0.76
JPD	0.75	0.7	0.73	1	0.87
Rabar	0.75	0.71	0.76	0.87	1

Correlation coefficients gauge how closely an advisor's performance resembles another advisor. Values exceeding 0.66 might be viewed as having significant positive performance correlation. Consequently, values exceeding –0.66 might be viewed as having significant negative performance correlation. Data is for Chesapeake Capital Corporation, Eckhardt Trading Co., Hawksbill Capital Management, JPD Enterprises Inc., and Rabar Market Research.

If they can get you asking the wrong questions, they don't have to worry about answers.
Thomas Pynchon

There is more to the story than correlation, however. Although correlations show Turtles trade in a similar way, their returns differ due to their individual leverage and portfolio choices. Some traders use more leverage, others less. TurtleTrader Jerry Parker explains, "The bigger the trade, the greater the returns and the greater the drawdowns. It's a double-edged sword."[30]

Zero Sum

The zero-sum nature of many markets is arguably the most important concept in markets. Larry Harris, chair in finance at the Marshall School of Business at University of Southern California: "Trading is a zero-sum game when gains and losses are measured relative to the market average. In a zero-sum game, someone can win only if somebody else loses."[31]

Harris told me he was amazed at how many people came from my websites to download his white paper on zero-sum trading—the topic left out of most strategy discussions. It's one winner and one loser.

The Winners and Losers of the Zero-Sum Game: The Origins of Trading Profits, Price Efficiency and Market Liquidity, *see http://turtletrader.com/zerosum.pdf.*

Harris examines the factors that determine who wins and who loses in market transactions. He does this by categorizing traders by type and then evaluating speculative trading styles to determine whether the styles lead to profits or losses: "Winning traders can only profit to the extent that other traders are willing to lose. Traders are willing to lose when they obtain external benefits from trading. The most important external benefits are expected returns from holding risky securities that represent deferred consumption. Hedging and gambling provide other external benefits. Markets would not exist without utilitarian traders. Their trading losses fund the winning traders who make prices efficient and provide liquidity."[32]

There are those who absolutely do not accept that there must be a loser for them to be a winner. They cannot live with the fact everyone can't be a winner. Although they want to win, many do not want to live with the guilt by their winning, someone else has to lose. This is a poorly thought out yet all too common view of the losing trader's mindset.

Harris is clear on what separates winners from losers:

> On any given transaction, the chances of winning or losing may be near even. In the long run, however, winners profit from trading because they have some persistent advantages that allow them to win slightly more often or occasionally much bigger than losers win. . . .
>
> To trade profitably in the long run, you must know your edge, you must know when it exists, and you must focus your trading to exploit it when you can. If you have no edge, you should not trade for profit. If you know you have no edge, but you must trade for other reasons, you should organize your trading to minimize your losses to those who do have an edge. Recognizing your edge is a prerequisite to predicting whether trading will be profitable.[33]

Nobel Prize winner and cofounder of famed trend following incubator Commodities Corporation Paul Samuelson adds, "For every trader betting on higher prices, another is betting on lower prices. These trades are matched. In the stock market, all investors (buyers and sellers) can profit in a rising market, and all can lose in a falling market. In futures markets, one trader's gain is another's loss."

I was talking to myself, saying like, 'Just relax, man. The comeback is so great already. Let it fly off your racquet and just see what happens.' I think that's the mindset I got to have, as well, in the finals. Sort of a nothing-to-lose mentality. It's been nice these last six matches to have that mentality. It worked very well so I'll keep that up.

Roger Federer on pep talk he gave himself in the fifth set of his 18th grand slam win

Dennis Gartman adds to the perspective: "In the world of futures speculation, for every long there is an equal and opposite short. That is, unlike the world of equity trading where there needn't be equal numbers of longs versus shorts, in the world of futures dealing there is. Money is neither made, nor lost, in futures; it is simply moved from one pocket to the next as margins are swapped at the close of trading each day. Thus, every time there is a buyer betting that prices shall rise in the future, there is an equal seller taking the very opposite bet, betting that prices will fall."

These observations will save your skin if you're willing to accept the truth, but as you can see throughout this volume, many are either ignorant to zero-sum thinking, choose to ignore it, or refuse to believe it condemned to exist inside biases.

George Soros

The trading success of famed speculator George Soros is well known. In 1992 he was labeled the man who broke the British pound for placing a $10 billion bet against the pound that netted him at least $1 billion in profit.[34]

Yet even successful pros sometimes miss a key point. Years back, Soros appeared on *Nightline*, an old-school ABC news program. This exchange between Soros and then-host Ted Koppel goes to the zero-sum understanding—or lack thereof:

> **Ted Koppel:** As you describe it, the market is, of course, a game in which there are real consequences. When you bet and you win, that's good for you, it's bad for those against whom you have bet. There are always losers in this kind of a game?
>
> **George Soros:** No. See, it's not a zero-sum game. It's very important to realize.
>
> **Ted Koppel:** Well, it's not zero-sum in terms of investors. But, for example, when you bet against the British pound that was not good for the British economy?
>
> **George Soros:** Well, it happened to be quite good for the British economy. It was not, let's say, good for the British treasury because they were on the

> other side of the trade . . . It's not—your gain is not necessarily somebody else's loss.
>
> **Ted Koppel:** Because—put it in easily understandable terms—I mean if you could have profited by destroying Malaysia's currency, would you have shrunk from that?
>
> **George Soros:** Not necessarily because that would have been an unintended consequence of my action. And it's not my job as a participant to calculate the consequences. This is what a market is. That's the nature of a market. So I'm a participant in the market.

Soros opens a can of worms with his description of zero-sum. From a blog post that incorrectly analyzes Soros' interview: "Cosmetically, Koppel wipes the floor with Soros. He's able to portray Soros as a person who destroys lives and economies without a second thought, as well as simplify, beyond belief, something that should not be simplified."[35]

What objectivity and the study of philosophy requires is not an "open mind," but an active mind—a mind able and eagerly willing to examine ideas, but to examine them critically.

Ayn Rand[36]

This is nonsense. The fact Soros is a player in the market does not establish him as a destroyer of lives. You might disagree with Soros's political ideology, but you can't question his morality for participation in markets. You have a 401(k) plan designed to generate profits from the market—like Soros. Others, such as Lawrence Parks, a union activist, correctly state that Soros is in a zero-sum game, but Parks then goes jealous by declaring zero-sum unfair and harsh for the *working-man*:

> Since currency and derivative trading are zero-sum games, every dollar "won" requires that a dollar was "lost." Haven't they realized what a losing proposition this has been? What's more, why do they keep playing at a losing game? The answer is that the losers are all of us. And, while neither rich nor stupid, we've been given no choice but to continue to lose. And every time one of these fiat currencies cannot be "defended," the workers, seniors, and business owners of that country—folks like us—suffer big time. Indeed, as their currencies are devalued, workers' savings and future payments, such as their pensions, denominated in those currencies lose purchasing power. Interest rates increase. Through no fault of their own, working people lose their jobs in addition to their savings. There have been press reports that, after a lifetime of working and saving, people in Indonesia are eating bark off the trees and boiling grass

> soup. While not a secret, it is astonishing to learn how sanguine the beneficiaries have become of their advantage over the rest of us. For example, famed financier George Soros in his recent *The Crisis of Global Capitalism* plainly divulges: "The Bank of England was on the other side of my transactions and I was taking money out of the pockets of British taxpayers." To me, the results of this wealth transfer are inescapable.[37]

Parks says his only choice is to lose. He loses, his union loses—it's a pity party. It seems *everyone* loses in the zero-sum game (even though Parks' fund will of course have their assets invested in the very funds he criticizes). Look, there are winners and losers and he knows that. Yes, the zero-sum speculation game is indeed a wealth transfer. The winners profit from the losers. Life is not fair. If you don't like being a loser in the zero-sum game, then it is time to consider how the winners play the game.

Trying to understand Soros's reasons for denying zero-sum would be speculation on my part. Soros is not always the zero-sum winner, either. He was on the losing side of the zero-sum game during the Long-Term Capital Management fiasco in 1998, in which he lost $2 billion. He also had severe trouble in the 2000 technology meltdown: "With bets that went sour on technology stocks and on Europe's new currency, the five funds run by Soros Fund Management have suffered a 20 percent decline this year and, at $14.4 billion, are down roughly a third from a peak of $22 billion in August 1998."[38]

These wins and losses took a toll on Soros: "Maybe I don't understand the market. Maybe the music has stopped but people are still dancing. I am anxious to reduce my market exposure and be more conservative. We will accept lower returns because we will cut the risk profile."[39]

Don't Blame Zero-Sum

Long-time Federal Judge Milton Pollack's ruling that dismissed class action suits illustrates zero-sum confusion. He minces no words in warning *whiners* about the game they are playing:

> Seeking to lay the blame for the enormous Internet bubble solely at the feet of a single actor, Merrill Lynch, plaintiffs would have this Court conclude that the federal securities laws were meant to underwrite, subsidize, and encourage their rash speculation in joining a

> freewheeling casino that lured thousands obsessed with the fantasy of Olympian riches, but which delivered such riches to only a scant handful of lucky winners. Those few lucky winners, who are not before the Court, now hold the monies that the unlucky plaintiffs have lost, fair and square, and they will never return those monies to plaintiffs. Had plaintiffs themselves won the game instead of losing, they would have owed not a single penny of their winnings to those they left to hold the bag (or to defendants).[40]

A 96-year-old judge bluntly telling plaintiffs to take responsibility for their own actions was no doubt painful for those seeking an incompetence bailout. Pollack flatly nails the losers for trying to circumvent the zero-sum market process via the judicial process.

It's all a matter of perspective. What some consider a catastrophic flood, others deem a cleansing bath.

Gregory J. Millman[41]

The harsh reality of speculation is you only have yourself to blame for decisions you make with your money. You can make ongoing losing or winning decisions. It's your choice. David Druz, a longtime trend follower, takes Judge Pollack's ruling a step further spelling out the practical effects:

> Everyone who enters the market thinks they will win, but obviously there are losers as well. Somebody has to be losing to you if you are winning, so we always like to stress that you should know from whom you're going to take profits, because if you're buying, the guy that's selling thinks he's going to be right, too.

The market is a brutal place. Forget trying to be liked. Need a friend? Get a dog. The market doesn't know you and never will. If you are going to win, someone else has to lose. If you don't like these survival-of-the-fittest rules, then stay out of the zero-sum game.

If all it took to beat the markets was a Ph.D. in mathematics, there'd be a hell of a lot of rich mathematicians out there.

Bill Dries[42]

Berkshire Hathaway

Amidst the recent celebration of Berkshire Hathaway's 50 years of investment returns, trend following trader Bernard Drury and his firm Drury Capital wondered if a portfolio holding Berkshire (BRKA), already hugely successful, could nonetheless be improved by combining holdings of BRKA with other assets. An ideal candidate for investment alongside BRKA would be an asset with both positive returns on a stand-alone basis as well as low correlation to BRKA.

In 1983, Dr. John Linter published the classic paper, "The Potential Role of Managed Commodity-Financial Futures Accounts (and/or Funds) in Portfolios of Stocks and Bonds." In this study he pointed to gains in risk-adjusted rates of return that potentially could be obtained by combining equity investment with managed futures.

If you have sound philosophy, and superior strategy, the day-to-day slows down. If you don't have such every distraction appears consequential.
Michael Covel

To examine a portfolio combination of stocks and managed futures (read: trend following), Drury focused on Berkshire because of its legendary performance. On the managed futures side, Drury's trend following fund satisfies the requirements of having both strong performance and almost-zero correlation to Berkshire.

While Drury cannot cite the same longevity as Berkshire, it has been in continuous operation for almost 19 years. At least for these years, it is useful to examine Drury in relation to Berkshire for a possible improvement of overall portfolio returns. The two performance records, taken individually during this period, are broadly similar. (See Table 3.5.)

TABLE 3.5: May 1997 to February 2015: Drury and BRKA

	Drury	BRKA	50% Drury/50% BRKA
Rate of Return (ROR)	11.3%	10.4%	10.9%
Standard Deviation (Vol)	20.0%	20.6%	14.4%
Drawdown (DD)	32.5%	44.5%	23.9%
ROR/DD	0.35	0.23	0.50
ROR/Vol	0.57	0.50	0.83

Source: Drury Capital

Valeant is like ITT and Harold Geneen come back to life, only the guy is worse this time...Valeant, of course, was a sewer.
Charlie Munger
2015, 2016

The correlation between the two return streams is 0.01. Despite the overall similarity of returns, the paths to producing these returns have nothing in common. Consequently, as modern portfolio theory would predict, the performance of a portfolio holding Berkshire is potentially improved by adding a noncorrelated Drury. (It is of course equally true a portfolio holding only Drury is potentially improved by being coupled with a noncorrelated asset such as Berkshire).

A look at the efficient frontier for this two-asset portfolio suggests a blend of approximately 50/50 would have produced the highest ratio of ROR versus standard deviation of returns:

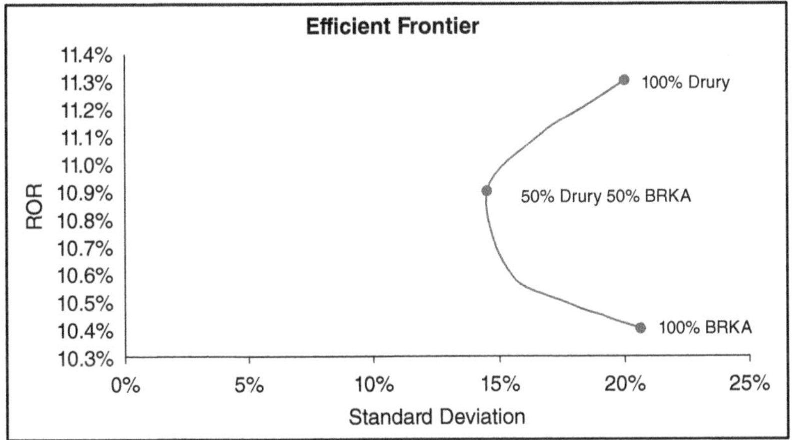

The portfolio with 50 percent each in Berkshire and Drury raised the risk-adjusted ROR to a level higher than either could achieve individually. For the holder of Berkshire, the diversification reduced the portfolio volatility by almost one-third and reduced the depth of the peak-to-trough drawdown by almost half. Finally, perhaps even remarkably, the combination of Berkshire holdings with this noncorrelated asset cut the length of the drawdown associated with holding Berkshire alone by a whopping 43 months. This means instead of experiencing a 61-month period (December 2007–January 2013) underwater, relative to the latest high price, while holding Berkshire shares alone, the combined portfolio reduced the underwater period to only 18 months. (By the same token, of course, the underwater period of holding Drury alone is reduced from 55 months to the same 18 months).

There are no facts about the future, just opinions. Anyone who asserts with conviction what he thinks will happen in the macro future is overstating his foresight, whether out of ignorance, hubris or dishonesty.

Howard Marks

TABLE 3.6: May 1997 to February 2015 Drawdown December 2007–January 2013

	Drury	BRKA	50% Drury 50% BRKA
Drawdown	32.5%	44.5%	23.9%
Peak to trough (months)	32	14	10
Trough to peak (months)	23	47	8
Total (months)	55	61	18

SOURCE: Yahoo! Finance and Drury Capital

Columbia University professor Benjamin Graham led academia and Wall Street with pioneering work across value investing. Famously, Warren Buffett was one of his students in the 1940s. And years later, the Nobel Prize–winning work of Harry Markowitz explored the effects of combining noncorrelated assets to improve risk-adjusted returns. Markowitz is credited with the often-repeated quip that "diversification is the only free lunch in finance." Thus it's not surprising that adding Drury's trend following as diversification to Buffett and Berkshire clearly enhances an overall portfolio return while reducing volatility.

Ultimately, performance data is the driver, the only truth we can take in for analysis. If there is no data, no believable narrative can be used to explain anything. And trend following data is a very clever way to illustrate human behavior with numbers—and it happens to also be proof of concept any skeptic would want before jumping into the deep end to deploy their risk capital. Yet where does trend following performance data come from *exactly*?

Summary Food for Thought

- "F-You money": If you trade for absolute returns you have the chance for F-You money—the money it would take to leave your job and never work again.
- Ewan Kirk: "When people ask: 'What do you think is going to happen in the future?' We always say: 'We don't know.' I can't really project whether next year will be a good year or a bad year."
- Absolute return means trying to make the most possible.
- In a zero-sum game the total gains of the winners are exactly equal to the total losses of the losers.
- George Crapple: "So while it may be a zero-sum game, a lot of people don't care. It's not that they're stupid; it's not speculative frenzy; they're just using these markets for a completely different purpose [hedging]."
- The U.S. Army War College introduced the acronym VUCA to describe general conditions post Cold War: volatile, uncertain, complex and ambiguous.
- Mark Rzepczynski: "If a manager cannot explain what he does and his edge in 45 minutes, you should not invest."[43]

Bernard Drury graciously contributed for this section. Percentage change in stock price month over month as of each month end across the period covered. BRKA stock prices from Yahoo! Finance.

Note: You can review trend following performance going back decades. Send an email for online sources: www.trendfollowing.com/contact.

Big Events, Crashes, and Panics 4

Of all the beliefs on Wall Street, price momentum makes efficient market theorists howl the loudest.
—James O'Shaughnessy

Rare events are always unexpected, otherwise they would not occur.
—Nassim Taleb[1]

Remember the Gomer Pyle character from The Andy Griffith show? I can see Gomer saying his classic TV line now:

"*Surprise, surprise, surprise.*"

To comprehend trend following's true impact you must look at its performance across the biggest events, bubbles and crashes of the last 50 years where it won huge profits in the zero-sum game of *surprises*.

An investment in Dunn Capital acts as a hedge against unpredictable market crises.
Dunn Capital Management

While world governments and Wall Street are notorious for country wipeouts, central bank errors, corporate collapses, bank implosions, and fund blow-ups that transfer capital from losers to winners, the winners are almost always missing from after-the-fact analysis. Like clockwork, the press is over-the-top fascinated with the losers when surprises roll in. Following their lead, the public also gets caught up in the losers' drama, oblivious to: Who were the winners and why did they win?

Sometimes they get close to the insight: "Each time there's a derivatives disaster I get the same question: If Barings was the loser, who was the winner? If Orange County was the loser: Who was the winner? If Procter & Gamble was the loser: Who was the winner?"[2]

I'd say that Procter & Gamble did what their name says, they proctored and gambled. And now they're complaining.
Leo Melamed

Prominent finance academics searching for winners often come up short, as Christopher Culp of the University of Chicago lamented: "It's a zero-sum game. For every loser there's a winner, but you can't always be specific about who the winner is."[3]

When big market events happen, smart people know the losers' losses are going somewhere, but time passes and they stop thinking about it or forget the original goal. Reflecting on an implosion is not pleasant: "Fear is still in the bones of some pension fund trustees—after Mr. Leeson brought down Barings Bank. The failure of Barings Bank is probably the most often cited derivatives disaster. While the futures market had been the instrument used by Nick Leeson to play the zero-sum game and someone made a lot of money being short the Nikkei futures Mr. Leeson was buying."[4]

Someone did make a lot of money trading short to Leeson's long. But most of Main Street and Wall Street look at it through the wrong lens. Michael Mauboussin sees standard finance theory coming up short when explaining winners during high-impact times: "One of the major challenges in investing is how to capture (or avoid) low-probability, high-impact events. Unfortunately, standard finance theory has little to say about the subject."[5]

The unexpected events so many bemoan are a source of outsized trend following profits. High impact and unexpected events, the black swans, have made many in this book very wealthy. One trader explains trend following's success during uncertain times:

It often seems that trends create events more than events create trends. The event itself is usually a reflection of everyone getting it *as Ed [Seykota] calls it,* an aha. *By this time, the trend followers usually have well-established positions.*
Jason Russell[6]

> For markets to move in tandem, there has to be a common perception or consensus about economic conditions that drives it. When a major "event" occurs in the middle of such a consensus, such as the Russian debt default of August 1998, the terrorist attacks of September 11, 2001, or the corporate accounting scandals of 2002 [and the 2008 equity market crash], it will often accelerate existing trends already in place . . . "events" do not happen in a vacuum . . . This is the reason trend following rarely gets caught on the wrong side of an "event." Additionally, the stop loss trading style will limit exposure when it does—When this consensus is further confronted by an "event," such as a major country default, the "event" will reinforce the crisis mentality already in place and drive those trends toward their

> final conclusion. Because trend following generally can be characterized as having a "long option" profile, it typically benefits greatly when these occurrences happen.[7]

Said more bluntly: "Even unlikely events must come to pass eventually. Therefore, anyone who accepts a small risk of losing everything will lose everything, sooner or later. The ultimate compound return rate is acutely sensitive to fat tails."[8] However, big events also generate plenty of inane analysis by focusing on the unanswerable like questions posed by Thomas Ho and Sang Lee, authors of *The Oxford Guide to Financial Modeling*[9]:

1. What do these events tell us about our society?
2. Are these financial losses the dark sides of all the benefits of financial derivatives?
3. Should we change the way we do things?
4. Should society accept these financial losses as part of the "survival of the fittest" in the world of business?
5. Should legislation be used to avoid these events?

On Saturday, February 25, 1995, Mike Killian, who almost single-handedly built Barings Far East customer brokerage business over the past seven years, was awakened at 4:30 a.m. in his Portland, Ore., home. It was Fred Hochenberger from the Barings Hong Kong office.

"Are you sitting down?" Hochenberger asked a sleepy Killian.

"No, I'm lying down."

"Have you heard any rumors?"

Killian, perplexed, said no.

"I think we're bust."

"Is this a crank call?" Killian asked.

"There's a really ugly story coming out that perhaps Nick Leeson has taken the company down."[10]

It is not unusual to see market wins and losses positioned as a morality tale to be solved by government. This drama absolves the losers' guilt for poor strategies (i.e., Amaranth, Bear Stearns, Bernard Madoff, LTCM, Lehman Brothers, Deutsche Bank, Valeant, etc.). Yet the market is no place for politics or social engineering. No law will ever change human nature. As Dwight D. Eisenhower noted: "The search for a scapegoat is the easiest of all hunting expeditions."

Bottom line, trend following performance histories during the 2016 Brexit event, the 2014–2016 oil implosion, the 2008 market crash, the 2000–2002 Dot-com bubble, the 1998 Long-Term Capital Management (LTCM) crisis, the 1997 Asian contagion, and the 1995 Barings Bank and 1993 Metallgesellschaft collapses answer the all-important question: "Who won and why?"

Event 1: Great Recession

The world changed as stock markets crashed during October 2008. Millions lost trillions of dollars when buy-and-hold-tight strategies imploded. The Dow, S&P, and NASDAQ fell like stones, with the carnage carrying over into 2009. Everyone felt it: jobs lost, firms going under, and fear all around. No one made money during this time. Everyone lost. That was the *meme*.

Hold on—is that true? It is not. There were winners during October 2008 and they made fortunes ranging from +5 percent to +40 percent in that single month. And trend following strategy was the winner. First, let me state how it did not win:

One reason for this paucity of early information is suggested by the following part of the term trend following. The implication is one of passivity, of reaction, rather than of bold, assertive action—and human nature shows a distinct preference for the latter. Also, trend following appears to be too simple an idea to be taken seriously. Indeed, simple ideas can take a very long time to be accepted; think of the concept of a negative number, or of zero: simple to us, but problematic to our ancestors.

Stig Ostgaard
Turtle

1. Trend following did not know stock markets would crash in October 2008.
2. Trend following did not make money from only shorting stocks in October 2008.

Trend following made money from many different markets; from oil to bonds to currencies to stocks to commodities, markets that trended up and down. It always does well in times of wild and extended price swings, in part because systems programmed into computers make calculated, emotionless buys and sells.

"We are not going to be the first to get in or the first to get out, but we are generally able to capture 80 percent of the trends," opined a Superfund associate. For example, consider performance from January 2008 through October 2008:

- January: –2.21 percent
- February: 14.17 percent
- March: 1.59 percent
- April: –1.23 percent
- May: 6.52 percent
- June: 9.88 percent
- July: –10.26 percent
- August: –8.36 percent
- September: 2.59 percent
- October: 17.52 percent

This was not the only trend following trader winning big. Consider others during the period:

- One fund run by John W. Henry was up 72.4 percent through October 2008.

- TransTrend, a Dutch-based trend following trader managing more than $1 billion in assets, saw one of its funds go up 71.75 percent from January through November 2008.
- Clarke Capital Management saw its $72.2 million fund gain 82.2 percent through October 2008. As but one example of his winning bets, Clarke shorted crude oil when it was around $140, and then stayed with the trade down to $80 before exiting, thereby collecting the bulk of the trend.
- Trend following trader Bernard Drury started selling S&P 500 index futures short in November 2007. The index went down about 36 percent and the largest Drury fund roared up 56.9 percent through October 2008.[11]
- Paul Mulvaney, another trend following trader who has used a much longer timeframe in his trading (weekly bars), saw his fund post a 45.49 percent return for the month of October 2008—yes, in one month.

If you average out the returns per dollar per year on [trend following] managed futures funds, they're between lousy and negative.

Charlie Munger
2007 Annual Shareholder Meeting

Note: *Berkshire Hathaway dropped –51% over 2007–2009.*

Another trend follower provided insights into his 2008 performance: "October 2008 provides a prime example of how [we] can produce gains in volatile and otherwise adverse market conditions. During this month and preceding months, [our] trading system not only profited from trends that were gaining momentum, but also responded to historic volatility by reducing or eliminating positions, and thus risk exposure, in markets in which trends were growing stale."

How did they do it? "In February 2008, a sustained downward trend in the U.S. dollar against various currencies accelerated. This coincided with a significant rally in gold and energy markets. Many trend following trading systems . . . profited from short positions in the U.S. dollar [see Figure 4.1] and long positions in gold and energies."

They described the unfolding market chaos: "At the same time, several world stocks indices exhibited signs of weakness. By June, however, gold stumbled nearly $200 from recent highs above $1,000 per ounce [see Figure 4.2]. [We were able] to continue capturing gains in the U.S. dollar, energies, and stocks while reducing its long exposure to gold as returns in this market faltered."

They clarified how events led to October 2008:

The other level of trend following is something else entirely. This is the meta-level, which sits above the tableau of material and psychological cause and effect, allowing participants to observe the behavior of the markets as a whole and to design intelligent, premeditated responses to market action. This is the level of trend following from which we as traders should—and usually do—operate.

Stig Ostgaard
Turtle

> During July and August, profitable trends in the U.S. dollar, energies, and grains exhausted themselves. It was at this juncture that the our system repositioned itself for results in October despite short-term drawdowns

FIGURE 4.1: U.S. Dollar Short Trade

FIGURE 4.2: Long Gold Trade

during these two months. While speculative traders may have viewed the precipitous drop in energies and other commodities as an opportunity to add to their long positions, we identified the end of sustained trends in these markets and significantly reduced its positions, and therefore its risk, particularly in the U.S. dollar. Meanwhile, our system began identifying emerging trends in world treasury markets [see Figure 4.3], as well as meats and industrial metals.

Figure 4.3 shows the patience trend following had to endure in the face of extreme volatility:

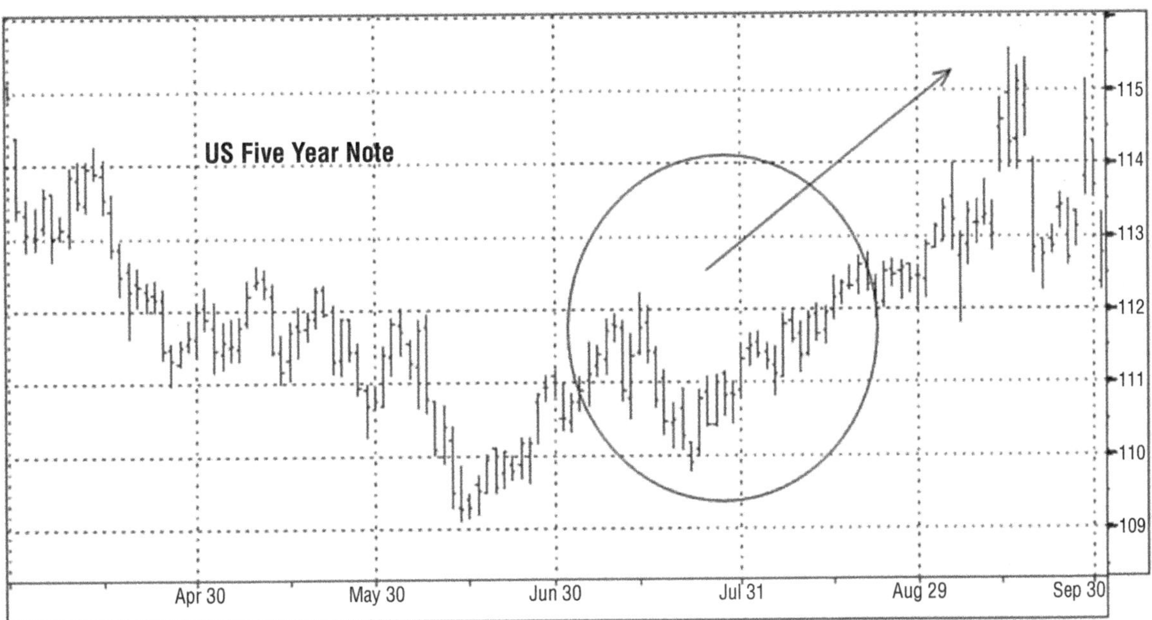

FIGURE 4.3: Long Five-Year Notes Trade

As October 2008 unfolded, my associate offered a behind-the-scenes take: "Approaching October, we were ready to take advantage of changing market conditions both because of positions we no longer held as well as positions we had entered during the subpar return periods of July and August. For example, we had avoided the potential for substantial losses from an 18.3 percent decline in gold futures and a 32 percent collapse in crude oil [see Figure 4.4] by reducing long exposure to these markets before their substantial October declines."

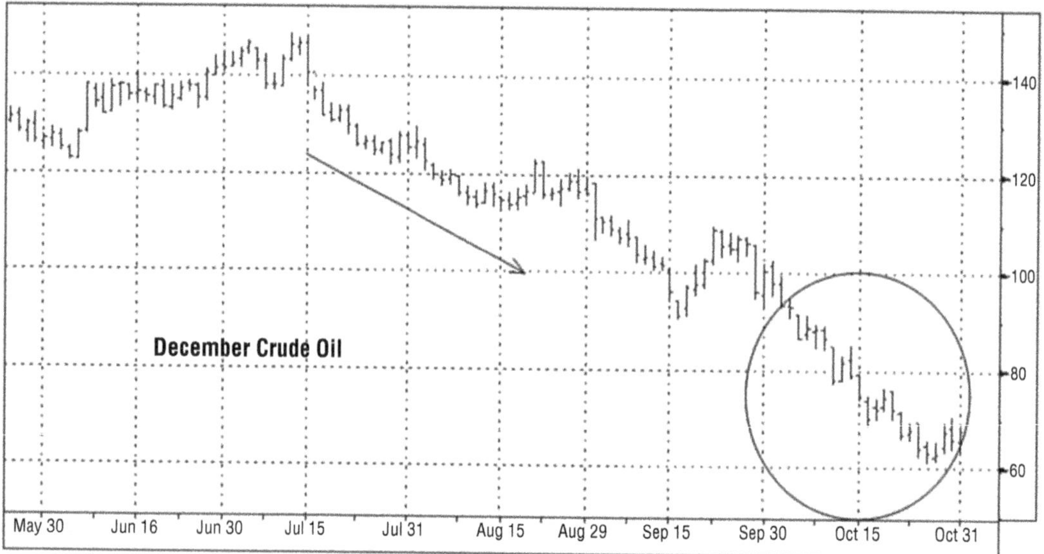

FIGURE 4.4: Crude Oil Short Trade

Trend following also captured a major trend in the Nikkei 225 (see Figure 4.5):

FIGURE 4.5: Nikkei 225 Short Trade

But this is not about predictions, so when trends changed, the gears switched: "After having been short the U.S. dollar for most of the first half of 2008, by October, we had established positions designed to profit from the reversal of the U.S. dollar trend in July and August. At that point, currencies such as the British pound began to decline against the dollar [see Figure 4.6]."

It may surprise many to know that in my method of trading, when I see by my records that an upward trend is in progress, I become a buyer as soon as a stock makes a new high on its movement, after having had a normal reaction. The same applies whenever I take the short side. Why? Because I am following the trend at the time.

Jesse Livermore (1940)

Trend following realized the bulk of October profits as a result of the ability to capitalize on different market conditions while limiting losses based on a combination of diversification, flexibility, risk management, and discipline. While a substantial portion of trend following's October profits were derived from short positions in the stock indices and world currencies, trend following also realized profits from long bond positions. It avoided major losses by reducing exposure to gold and energies as well.

Although not as large as some trend following traders in terms of assets under management, another trader offered insights into his 2008 performance. He took me through his trades where he saw monster returns while other market players gasped for air.

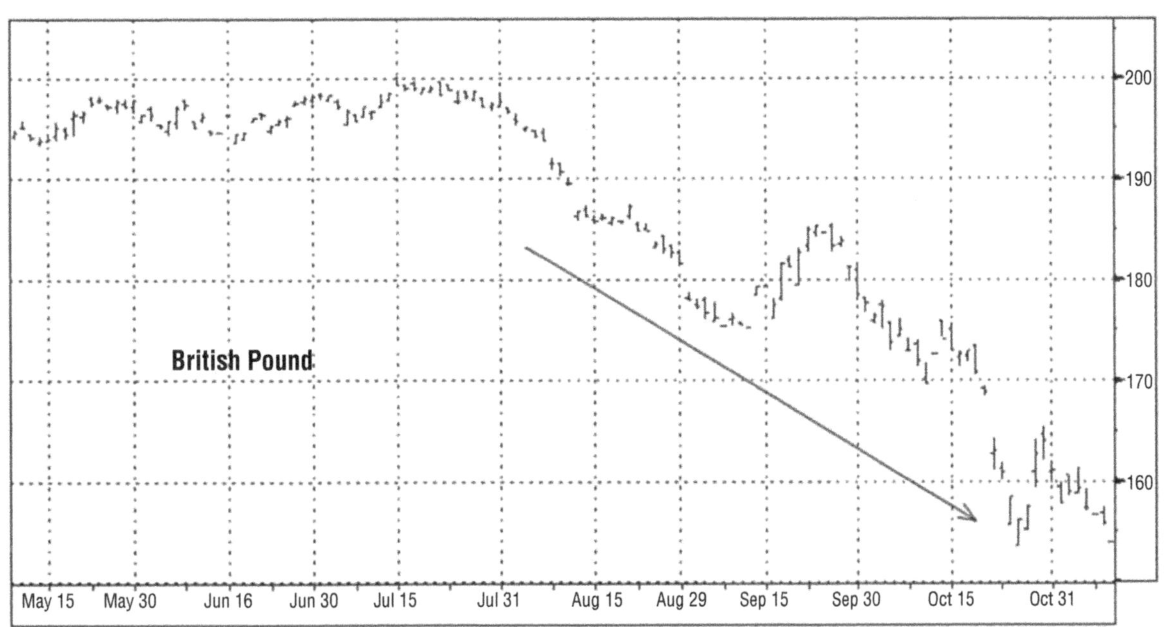

FIGURE 4.6: British Pound Short Trade

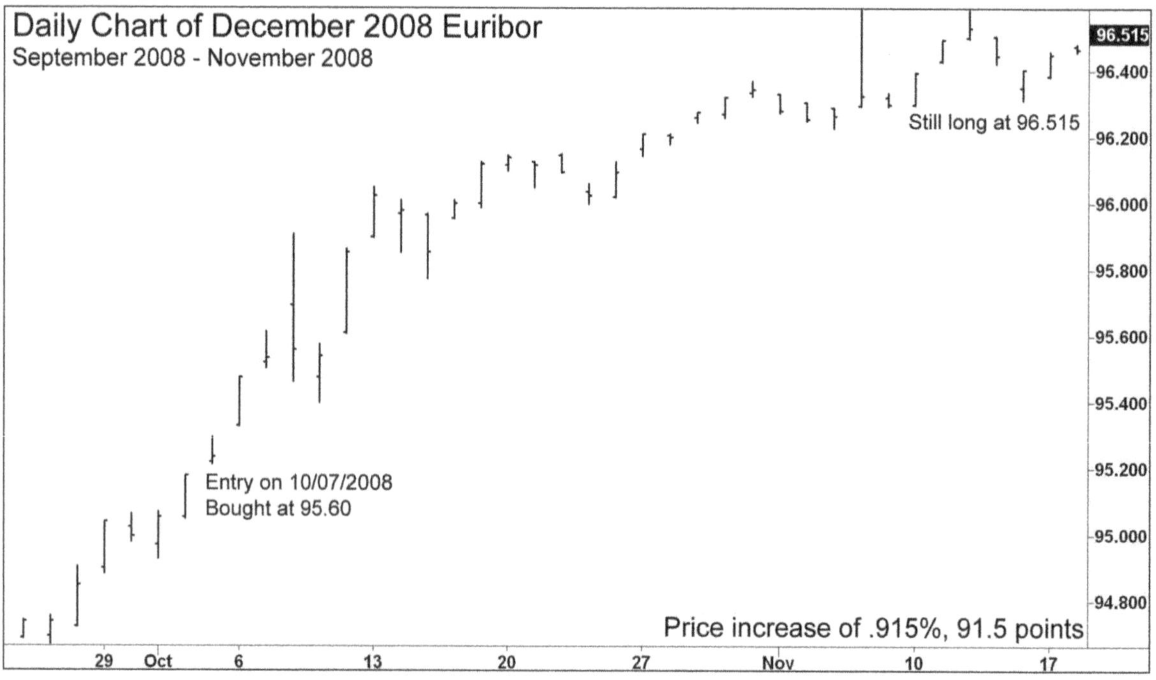

FIGURE 4.7: Long December 2008 Euribor Trade

First he outlined a European interest rate trade (see Figure 4.7): "In the midst of the global financial crisis, we received signals on many short-term interest rates. The Euribor is a short-term interest rate futures contract traded at the EUREX. We bought on October 7 and are still long (through December 2008). Central banks around the globe began dropping interest rates to ward off equity market declines. Lower interest rates mean higher Euribor futures prices. Fundamentals did not drive our decisions."

He further explained how he profited from a short-term interest rate, the EuroSwiss (see Figure 4.8): "The EuroSwiss is another short-term interest rate futures contract. We entered this position well before the global equity market crash."

Consider his explanation about trading *hogs* (see Figure 4.9): "The Hog position was one of the most beautiful trends that I've seen in years. As the U.S. dollar rallied, nearly every commodity tied to the dollar moved violently. Although our larger portfolio gains happened in October, this position profited throughout the fall of 2008."

FIGURE 4.8: Long December 2008 EuroSwiss Trade

FIGURE 4.9: Short December 2008 Lean Hogs Trade

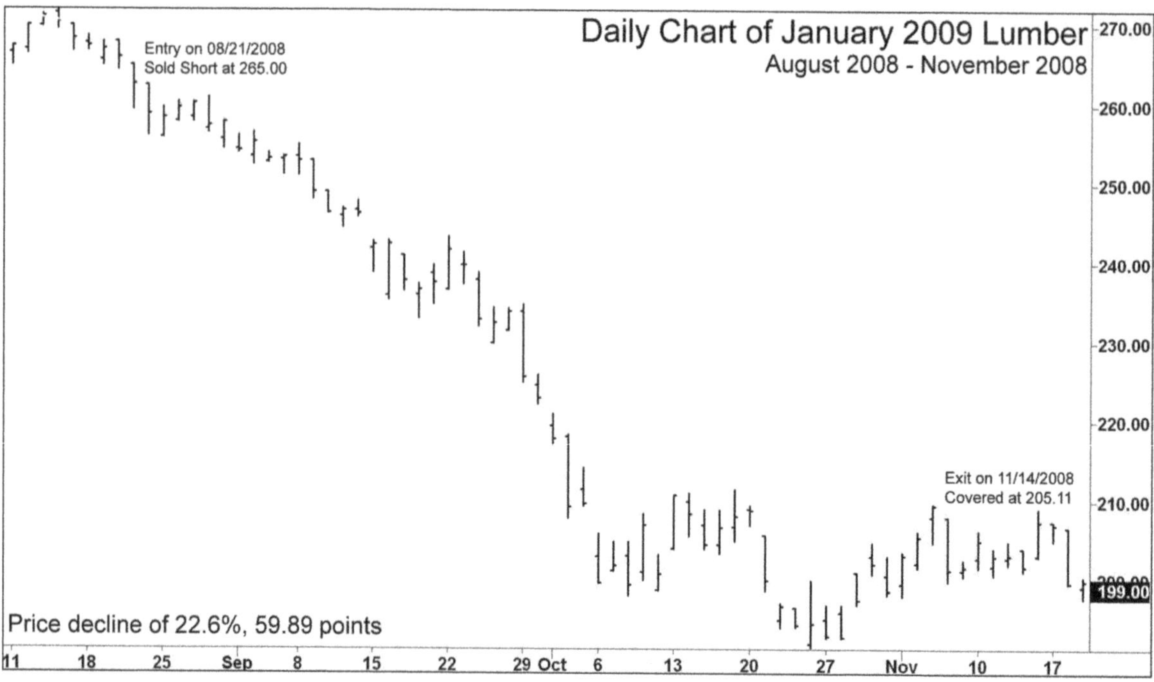

FIGURE 4.10: Short January 2009 Lumber Trade

Many professional speculators, including in particular exponents of the so-called Dow Theory widely publicized by popular financial journals, have adopted systems based in the main on the principle that it is advantageous to swim with the tide.
Alfred Cowles (1937)

Sure, people love to focus on *stocks*, but lumber of all things offered huge gains (see Figure 4.10): "Lumber was another great market over the fall of 2008. Lumber fell due to the housing crisis in the U.S. Lower demand means lower lumber prices. We sold the market short in the late summer and held the position until mid-November. However, it is important to keep in mind that we went short based off of price action, not fundamentals."

For you Starbucks connoisseurs, the coffee market fall 2008 was another major move (see Figure 4.11): "Although traded in London, Robusta Coffee is denominated in U.S. dollars. The move up in Robusta Coffee was helped in large part from a strengthening U.S. dollar. A higher dollar means less purchasing power in other currencies, pushing Robusta lower. My fundamental views once again mean little, we just followed the trend."

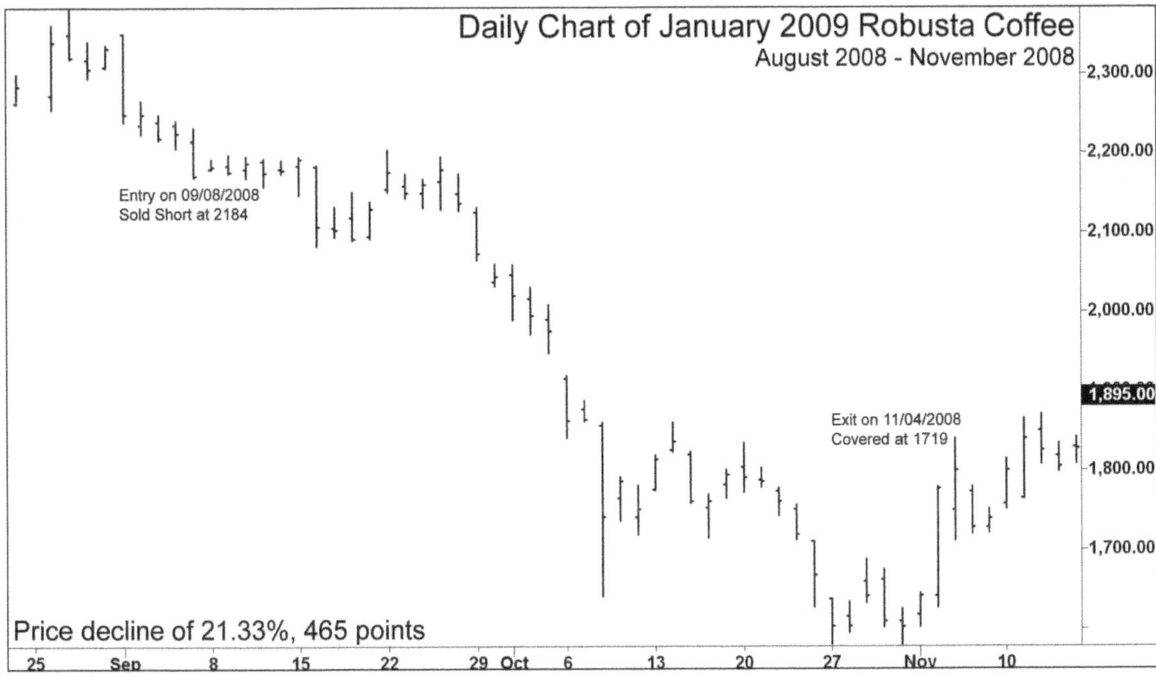

FIGURE 4.11: Short January 2009 Robusta Coffee Trade

Perhaps no other market than the U.S. dollar was more consequential for trend following. It did not matter whether the strategy made money in the dollar going long or going short—it was agnostic to direction (see Figure 4.12): "The trend up in the U.S. dollar was cut into two segments. We saw more volatility in this contract than others, simply due to the U.S. equity markets. Although our entries and exits are tied to highs and lows in the U.S. dollar futures, moves in the U.S. equity markets influenced the price as well. The rise of this contract created opportunities in many of the other markets we trade, because they are so closely tied to the price of the dollar."

All you can do with trend following is take what markets give you. The goal is to make money in whatever market is trending and not fall in love with one particular market to the exclusion of another, better market opportunity.

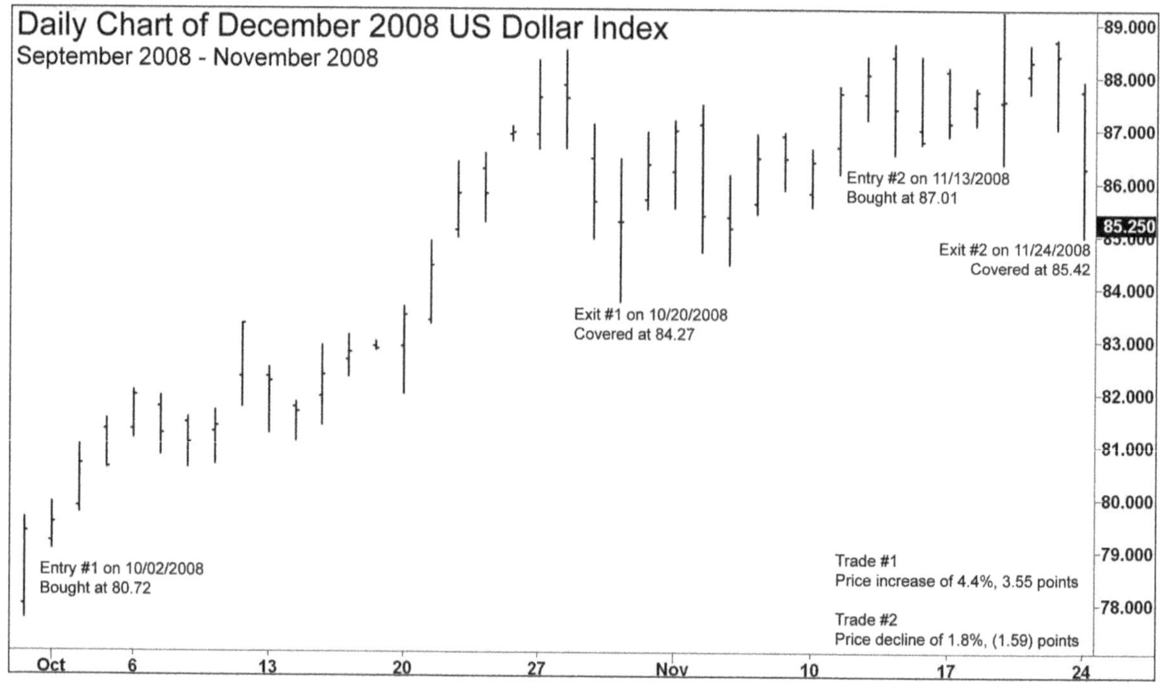

FIGURE 4.12: Long December 2008 U.S. Dollar Trade

Day-to-Day Analysis

We think that forecasting should be thought of in the light of measuring the direction of today's trend and then turning to the Law of Inertia (momentum) for assurance that probabilities favor the continuation of that trend for an unknown period of time into the future. This is trend following, and it does not require us to don the garment of the mystic and look into the crystal balls of the future.
William Dunnigan (1954)

The market crash of 2008 offered fantastic evidence showing trend following as vastly different than the passive index mindset. Figure 4.13 shows daily data from trend follower Salem Abraham and lets you see day-to-day performance differences between his trend following fund and the S&P. For those who hear about trend trading wins in October 2008 and immediately want to scream *lucky*, look closely at the Abraham data. It is a great proxy for the other trend following traders as well.

Even though gains by the likes of Abraham and Mulvaney might make logical sense, in hindsight their performance is not easy to accept for indoctrinated EMT minds. Consider feedback from a reader attempting to sell his firm on trend following benefits:

> I have been in discussions with trend following trader Mulvaney Capital Management since the summer for a company in which I was the COO. The board thought my ideas were too risky and that I tried to hit too many homeruns by potentially hiring Mulvaney. This particular [firm I

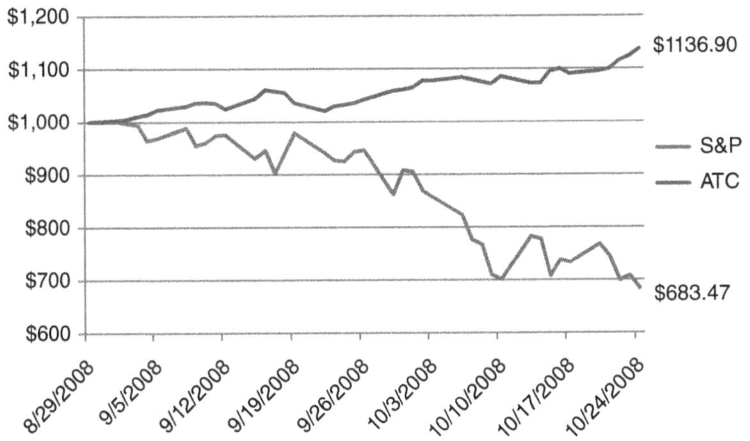

Abraham Trading

vs.

S&P 500

Sept. 1, 2008 to Oct. 24, 2008

Sept. 1, 2008 to Oct. 24, 2008		
	S&P 500	ATC
Average	−0.87%	0.33%
Std. Dev.	4.08%	0.87%
Correlation	−0.39	

Daily ROR Comparison

Date	S&P	ATC
9/1/2008	0.00%	0.32%
9/2/2008	−0.41%	0.26%
9/3/2008	−0.20%	0.50%
9/4/2008	−2.99%	0.33%
9/5/2008	0.44%	0.86%
9/8/2008	2.05%	0.67%
9/9/2008	−3.41%	0.62%
9/10/2008	0.61%	0.05%
9/11/2008	1.38%	−0.12%
9/12/2008	0.21%	−1.09%

Date	S&P	ATC
9/15/2008	−4.71%	1.95%
9/16/2008	1.75%	1.62%
9/17/2008	−4.71%	−0.33%
9/18/2008	4.33%	−0.25%
9/19/2008	4.03%	−1.78%
9/22/2008	−3.82%	−1.46%
9/23/2008	−1.56%	0.83%
9/24/2008	−0.20%	0.26%
9/25/2008	1.97%	0.35%
9/26/2008	0.34%	0.61%

Date	S&P	ATC
9/29/2008	−8.81%	1.56%
9/30/2008	5.27%	0.24%
10/1/2008	−0.32%	0.33%
10/2/2008	−4.03%	1.23%
10/3/2008	−1.35%	0.06%
10/6/2008	−3.85%	0.52%
10/7/2008	−5.74%	−0.41%
10/8/2008	−1.13%	−0.39%
10/9/2008	−7.62%	−0.33%
10/10/2008	−1.18%	1.34%

Date	S&P	ATC
10/13/2008	11.58%	−1.16%
10/14/2008	−0.53%	−0.03%
10/15/2008	−9.03%	2.06%
10/16/2008	4.25%	0.48%
10/17/2008	−0.62%	−0.88%
10/20/2008	4.77%	0.44%
10/21/2008	−3.08%	0.37%
10/22/2008	−6.10%	1.42%
10/23/2008	1.26%	0.78%
10/24/2008	−3.45%	1.17%

FIGURE 4.13: Abraham Trading Compared to the S&P

was with] lost $30 million in September and October [2008]. I showed them the Mulvaney performance: $15 million invested in 1999 equated to $71 million today and $30 million over the same period equated to $142 million. After my presentation at a board meeting, I returned to my office and was told [that] next week . . . I was being eliminated as I was too big of a risk taker. My only other investment in my short tenure was with Abraham Trading and the returns equated to nearly positive 12 percent for the same time period. This was the only positive investment for the organization over that period. So much for my risk taking.

Logically, it is difficult to keep saying trend following is *risky* especially in the face of those *risky* leveraged, long-only buy and hold approaches that cratered in 2008, but Wall Street is not logical.

Event 2: Dot-com Bubble

Conventional capital market theory is based on a linear view of the world, one in which investors have rational expectations; they adjust immediately to information about the markets and behave as if they know precisely how the structure of the economy works. Markets are highly efficient, but not perfectly so. Inefficiencies are inherent in the economy or in the structure of markets themselves . . . we believe inefficiencies in markets can be exploited through a combination of trend detection and risk management.
John W. Henry[12]

The period from 2000–2002 was littered with volatile up-and-down markets. Although the prime story for that three-year period was the Nasdaq meltdown, several subplots unfolded, ranging from the September 11 surprise to the Enron debacle to major trend following drawdowns and subsequent recoveries to new highs. It is interesting to note how trend following performed, for example, compared to the 2002 S&P and NASDAQ (see Table 4.1).

TABLE 4.1: 2002 Performance Histories for Trend Followers

Bill Dunn	+54.23%
Salem Abraham	+21.37%
John W. Henry	+45.06%
Jerry Parker	+11.10%
David Druz	+33.17%
William Eckhardt	+14.05%
Mulvaney Capital	+19.37%
S&P	–23.27
NASDAQ	–31.53%
Dow	–16.76

Figures 4.14 through 4.21 show what trends they were riding to produce this performance.

Drawdowns and Recoveries

It's no secret for the majority of 2000, trend following as a strategy was in a drawdown. It went down significantly heading into the last few months of the year (Figures 4.14 through 4.21). Some press and skeptics were eagerly calling the strategy finished, kaput.

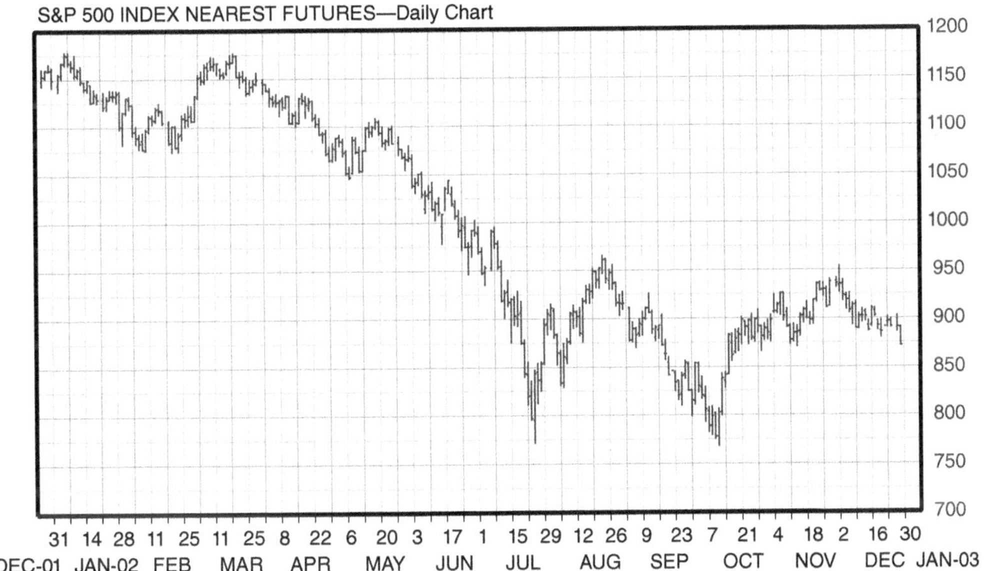

FIGURE 4.14: Trend Followers and the S&P Chart, January 2002–December 2002
Source: Barchart.com

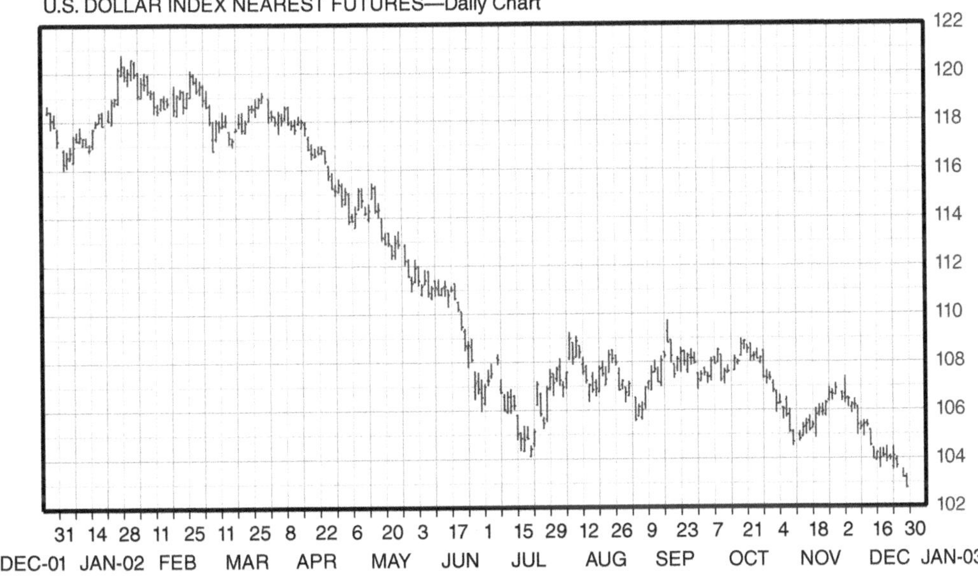

FIGURE 4.15: Trend Followers and the Dollar Chart, January 2002–December 2002
Source: Barchart.com

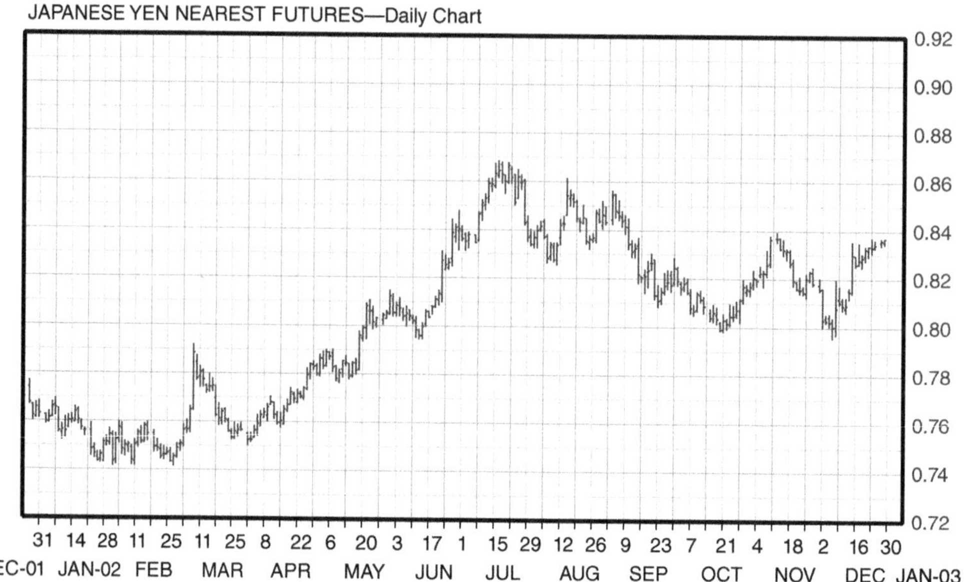

FIGURE 4.16: Trend Followers and the Yen Chart, January 2002–December 2002
Source: Barchart.com

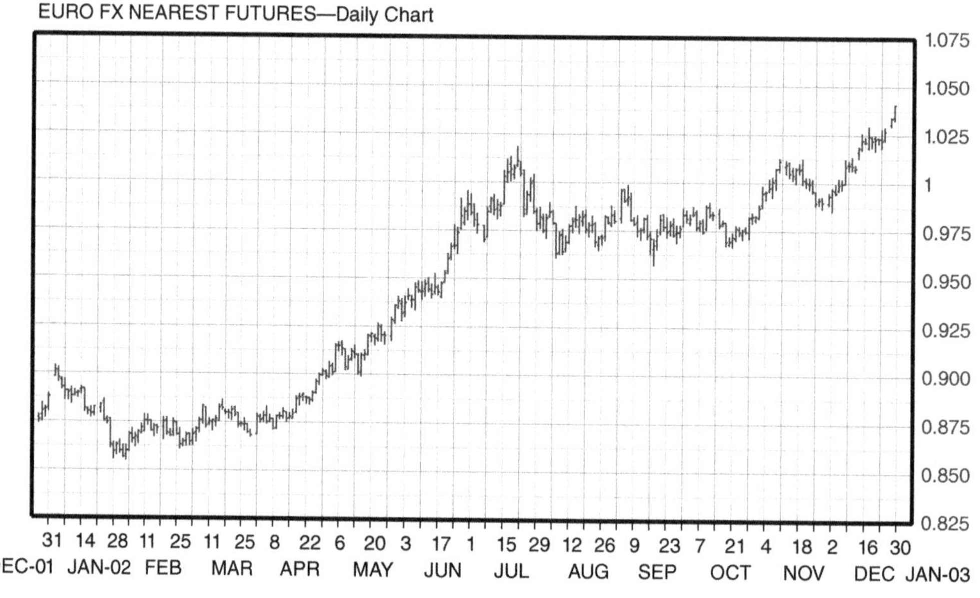

FIGURE 4.17: Trend Followers and the Euro Chart, January 2002–December 2002
Source: Barchart.com

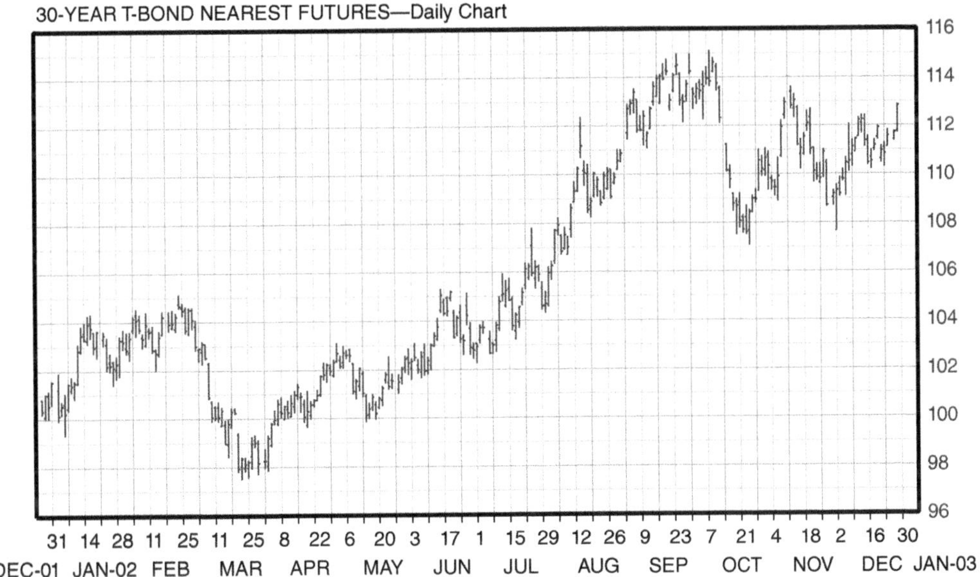

FIGURE 4.18: Trend Followers and the T-Bond Chart, January 2002–December 2002
Source: Barchart.com

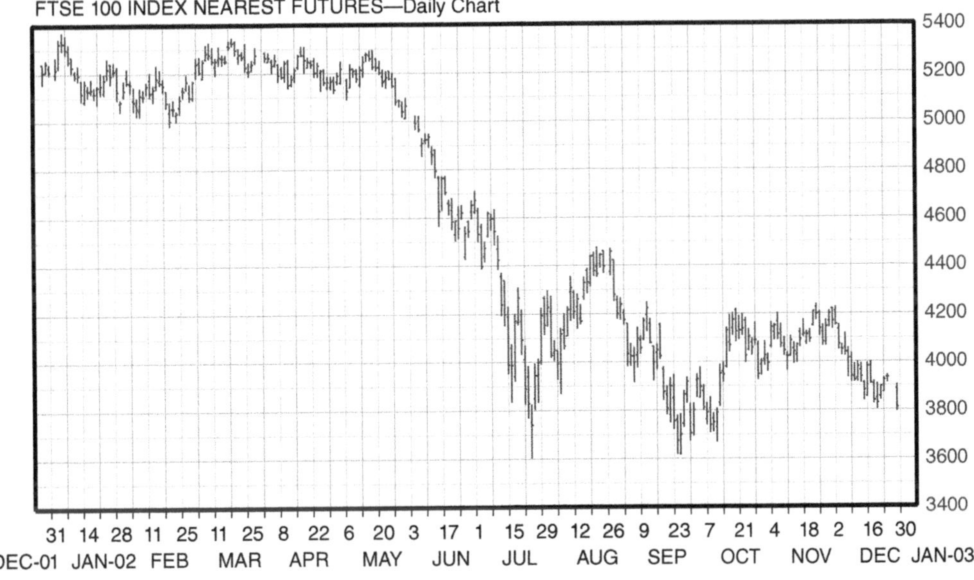

FIGURE 4.19: Trend Followers and the FTSE Chart, January 2002–December 2002
Source: Barchart.com

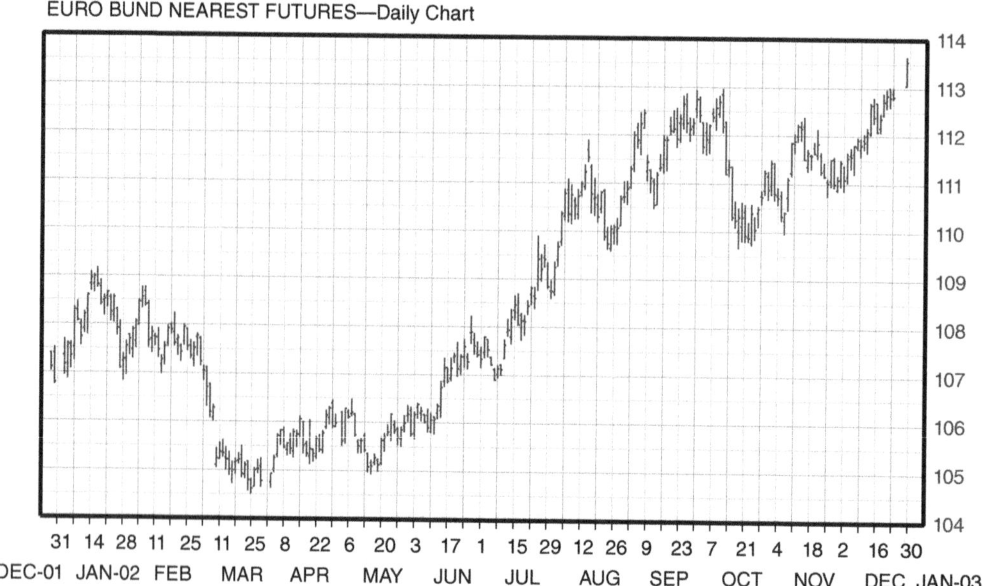

FIGURE 4.20: Trend Followers and the Euro-Bund, January 2002–December 2002
Source: Barchart.com

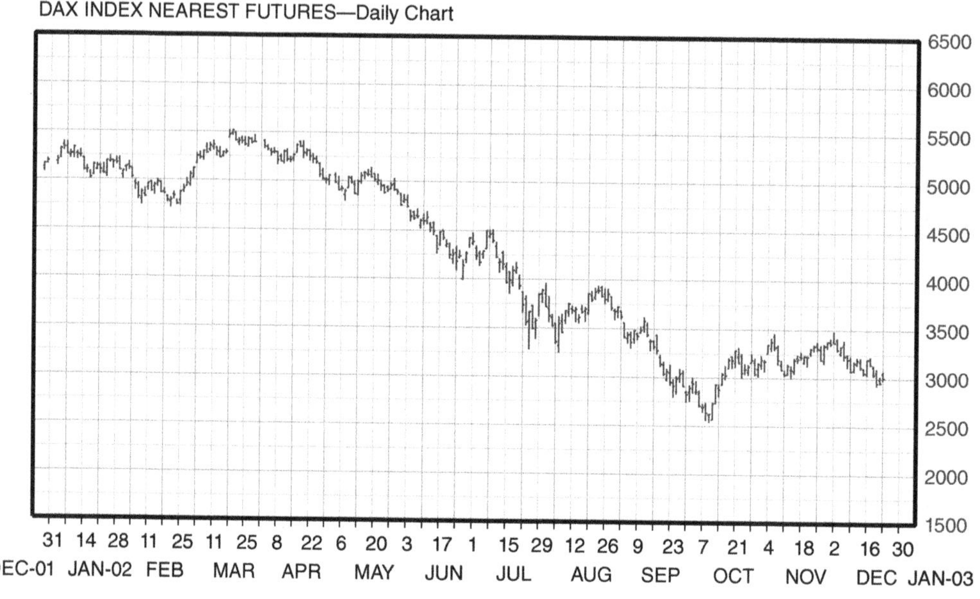

FIGURE 4.21: Trend Followers and the DAX, January 2002–December 2002
Source: Barchart.com

I was not surprised when a *Barron's* reporter contacted me for my opinion given the popularity of my trend following site at the time. She appeared to have it in for Henry and Dunn and was looking for confirmation that trend following was *dead.* I pointed out drawdowns had occurred in the past, but that over the long haul trend following has made tremendous amounts of money. She ignored those facts:

"John W. Henry isn't alone in experiencing hard times. But the firm's losses are among the most staggering . . . The company's hardest-hit trend following trading program, called Financial & Metals, was down 18.7 percent in 1999 . . . Henry, whom one rival calls 'our industry's Dave Kingman,' definitely swings for the fences. (Kingman hit 442 home runs during his 16 seasons in the majors, but he also struck out more than 1,800 times.) It's unclear whether John W. Henry will make changes to his trading program, one he cooked up decades ago while on a vacation to Norway."[14]

Convergent styles:
- *World knowable*
- *Stable world*
- *Mean-reverting*
- *Short volatility*
- *Arbitrage-based*

Divergent styles:
- *World uncertain*
- *Unstable world*
- *Mean-fleeing*
- *Long volatility*
- *Trend Following*

Mark S. Rzepczynski[13]

You have to wonder if this *Barron's* reporter had taken the time to read Henry's speech from November 2000 before writing her December article. Henry was hinting at new success around the corner: "Unfortunately, markets do not step to a drummer we control. The period we have just been through has been terrifically painful for investors, brokers, general partners, and trading advisors. Drawdowns affect everyone emotionally, psychologically, and physically when they persist. It becomes very easy to envision a scenario in which things never get better. However, experience tells us that things inevitably look bleakest before the tide turns."[15]

Don't be fooled by the calm. That's always the time to change course, not when you're just about to get hit by the typhoon. The way to avoid being caught in such a storm is to identify the confluence of factors and to change course even though right now the sky is blue, the winds are gentle, and the water seems calm . . . After all look how calm and sunny it is outside.

Thomas Friedman
The World Is Flat

The tide was indeed turning. On January 10, 2001, this same reporter sent me an e-mail to say she was doing a follow-up story and wanted a comment. I was impressed she was willing to set the record straight because Dunn made 28 percent in November 2000 and 29 percent in December 2000. Henry made 13 percent in November 2000 and 23 percent in December 2000. Here's her follow-up:

> Wall Street's biggest commodity-trading advisers posted a dramatic turnaround in the fourth quarter, turning last year's heart-stopping losses into gains for the year. "This rebound is not a surprise," says Michael Covel, of TurtleTrader.com, which tracks trend followers . . . Henry, a high-profile commodities-trading firm in Boca Raton, Florida, profiled by Barron's last month, posted a 20.3 percent return last year in its largest trading program which was down 13.7 percent for the first nine months of the year, powered back 39.2 percent in the fourth quarter.[16]

How was Henry able to power back 39.2 percent in the fourth quarter of 2000 after posting a loss of 13.7 percent for the first nine months of the year? What trends did he ride? Where was his target of opportunity? The answers can be found in Enron, California, and natural gas.

After having experienced a 40.0 percent decline through September 2000, Dunn Capital Management finished 2000 with a 17.3 percent asset weighted composite return. Dunn's 75.5 percent gain in the fourth quarter delivered $590 million to its investors; its annualized composite compound return since the firm's inception over 26 years ago is now 24.3 percent.[17]

Enron, California, and Natural Gas

If you examine the natural gas market during the last few months of 2000 and almost all of 2001, you can see obvious trend trading opportunity. For trend following, the natural gas market's massive trend up and down were the source of immense profit.

The losers of course were Enron and the State of California. Enron's collapse is a classic case of greed, fear, and ultimately incompetence on an epic scale. From Enron's upper management's manipulation of the facts, to the employees who purposefully ignored the manipulations, to the State of California's inept attempts to play energy markets, everyone should have been accountable for foolishness. That said, in the zero-sum game everyone is responsible, whether they admit it or not.

The Enron debacle is stunning when you consider the losers. The number of investors who deluded themselves into thinking they were on a path to quick riches is incalculable. Portfolio managers of pension funds, university endowments, individual investors . . . everyone was caught up in the exhilaration of a company that seemed to go in only one direction—up. Owners of Enron stock never stopped seeing the pot of gold. They looked the other way and suspended their disbelief to celebrate the zooming share price.

Q: Why didn't Wall Street realize that Enron was a fraud?
A: Because Wall Street relies on stock analysts. These are people who do research on companies and then, no matter what they find, even if the company has burned to the ground, enthusiastically recommend that investors buy the stock.
Dave Barry

However, there was a gargantuan misstep: They had no strategy to sell when the exit time arrived as the Enron trend turned hard the other way. That Enron crash chart (see Figure 4.22) is now famous. And there was only one piece of data needed to judge Enron: the share price. At its peak the company's stock traded at $90 a share, but it collapsed to 50¢ a share. Why would anyone with a pulse hold onto a stock that goes from $90 to 50¢? Even if Enron was the biggest scam ever propagated, hopeful investors who held on all the way down to 50¢ a share are as responsible as Jeff Skilling. Blind investors bear responsibility for not selling and losing their money. The chart was telling anyone who cared that the trend had not only changed, but Enron was going to zero and fast.

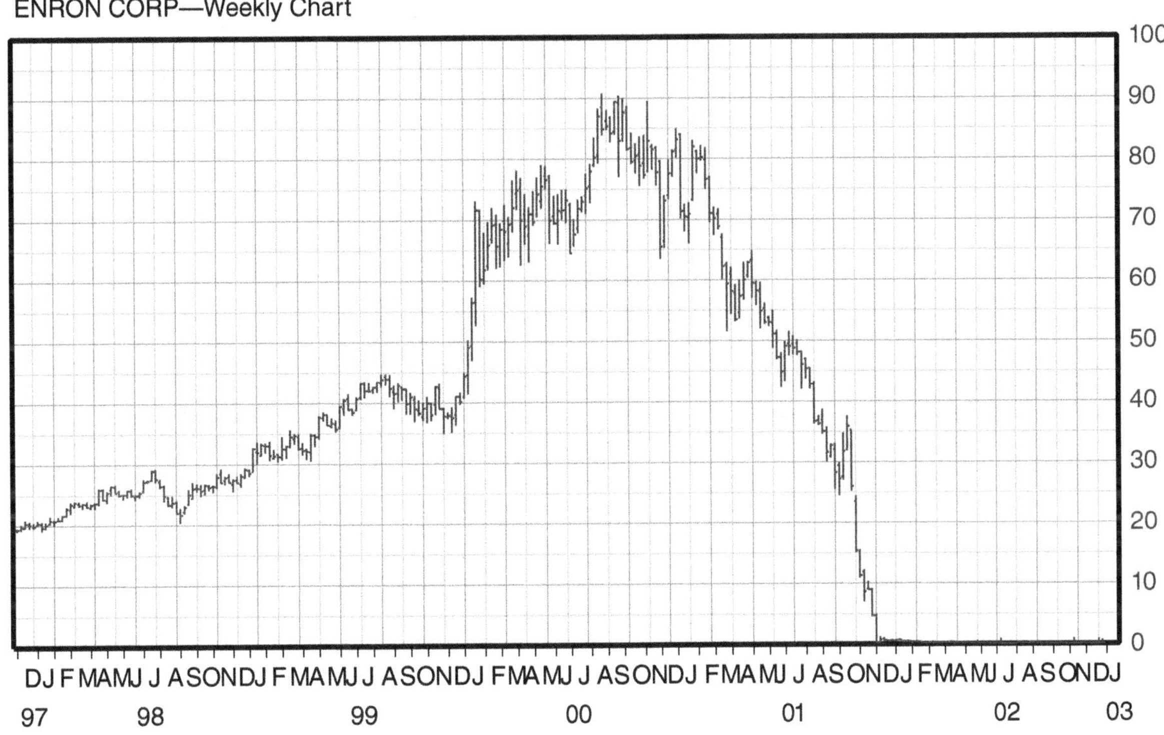

FIGURE 4.22: Enron Stock Chart Source: Barchart.com

Not only were there massive winners and losers in Enron stock, but huge losses were also seen in natural gas during the 2000–2001 California energy crisis. Enron was a primary supplier for California natural gas. And California, bound by its own flawed deregulation schemes, freely signed long-term contracts with energy trading firms buying Enron natural gas for their electricity .

They say patience is a virtue. For me patience is synonymous with discipline. You must have the discipline to know that markets change and poor periods are followed by good period. Longevity in this business—I have seen it again and again—is measured by discipline.

John W. Henry[18]

Not surprisingly, with inexperienced players and bad agreements in place, Enron and the State of California forgot natural gas was just another market. Like any market it was subject to go up or down for any number of reasons. Eventually natural gas spiked up and then down in ferocious trends. Unfortunately, neither Enron nor the State of California had a plan in place to deal with price changes.

Feeling abused, California complained loudly. California Senator Diane Feinstein maintained they had no culpability in the *game*: "I am writing to request an additional hearing to pursue what role Enron had in the California energy crisis with respect to market manipulation and price gouging. Enron's ability to deal in complex unregulated financial derivatives in the natural gas market while controlling a tremendous share of the gas trading market provided Enron the ability to manipulate market prices. This was very likely a key factor in driving up gas and electricity prices leading to the California energy crisis."

It has been said the Enron crisis cost California $45 billion over two years in higher electricity costs and slowed economic growth. When you look at the charts of natural gas (see Figure 4.23) and Enron (see Figure 4.22), you have to question Feinstein's basic understanding of markets:

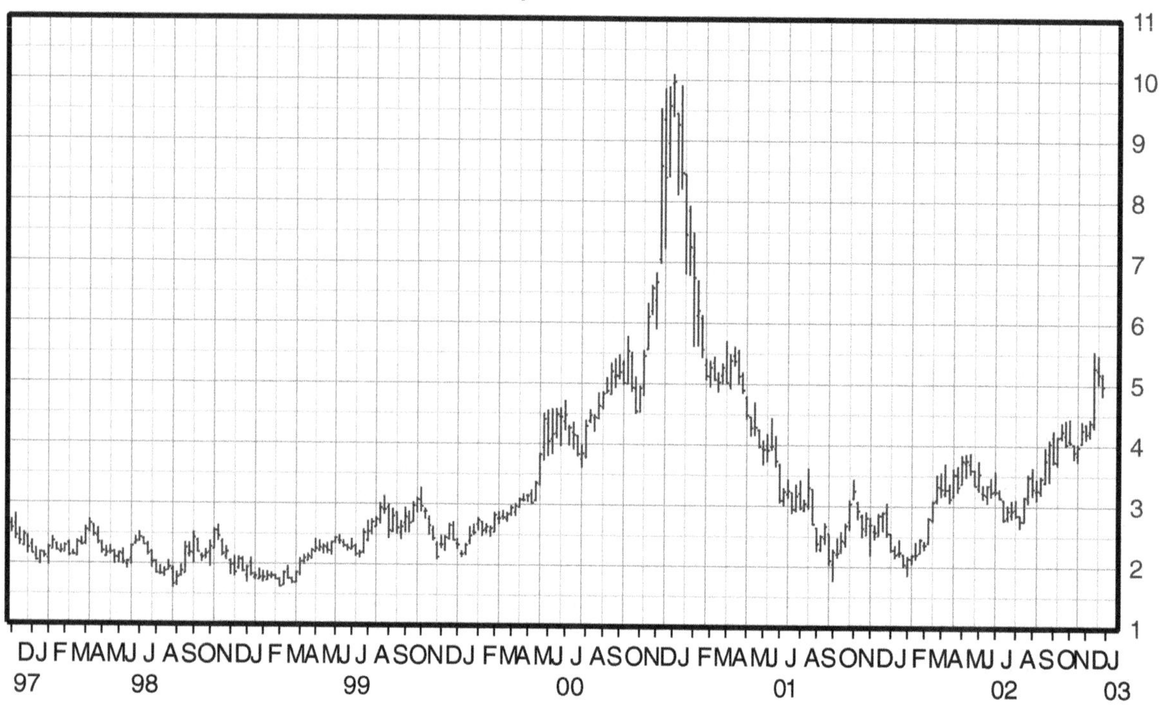

FIGURE 4.23: Natural Gas Stock Chart Source: Barchart.com

Why did California lock itself into stringent agreements with firms like Enron? Why did California, through its own deals, trade outside typical market structures? Why couldn't they deal with a changing natural gas price? The State of California alone is at fault for its inept decisions.

Anyone at any time can trade natural gas. Anyone can hedge a natural gas position. The opportunity to speculate and hedge is there for everyone. It is not a *novel* concept. Trend following traders were playing the natural gas game, too, riding it up and down for profit, as Table 4.2 demonstrates.

Among the hottest funds this year [2002] is Dunn Capital Management, which is up more than 50 percent. The firm from Stuart, Florida, profited on trades on Japan's Nikkei, Germany's DAX, and Britain's FTSE stock indexes, as well as on bond and Eurodollar interest-rate futures.[19]

TABLE 4.2: Trend Followers' Performance

Dunn Capital Management WMA	
October 2000:	+9.12%
November 2000:	+28.04%
December 2000:	+29.39%
January 2001:	+7.72%
John W. Henry Financials and Metals	
October 2000:	+9.39%
November 2000:	+13.33%
December 2000:	+23.02%
January 2001:	+3.34%
Graham Capital Management K4	
October 2000:	+1.44%
November 2000:	+7.41%
December 2000:	+9.37%
January 2001:	+2.37%
Man Investments	
October 2000:	+4.54%
November 2000:	+10.30%
December 2000:	+10.76%
January 2001:	+1.49%
Campbell & Company Financials and Metals	
October 2000:	+3.19%
November 2000:	+5.98%
December 2000:	+2.38%
January 2001:	–1.09%

The thing you have to worry about is the thing you haven't thought about.

Howard Marks

Chesapeake Capital	
October 2000:	–0.62%
November 2000:	+7.42%
December 2000:	+8.80%
January 2001:	–0.43%
Abraham Trading	
October 2000:	+9.51%
November 2000:	+8.58%
December 2000:	–0.18%
January 2001:	+2.28%

One Enron employee lashed out at the sordid affair: "My fellow (former) colleagues have no one to blame other than themselves for allowing such disastrous losses to occur in their retirement accounts. An abdication of personal responsibility should not be rewarded. It is a sad consequence, but it is reality."[20]

From private mutual fund companies like Janus to retirement funds managed by State governments, none of them had a plan for exiting Enron. They all bought the stock assuming it would only go up, but walking away was never part of their plan. "Hold on forever" was the mantra. Yet the Enron story is more profound than the tale of one company's disaster. It is the all too typical story of inept individuals managing billions of retirement wealth. Losses in Enron were staggering:

- Japanese banks lost $805.4 million.
- Abbey National Bank lost £95 million.
- John Hancock Financial Services lost $102 million.
- British Petroleum retirement lost $55 million on Enron debt.

David Brady, a Stein Roe Focus Fund manager: "Where did I go wrong? If I learned anything, I learned the same old lessons . . . The numbers just didn't add up. If you had looked at the numbers the balance sheet would have showed you the real problems."

Notice he blames balance sheets and not his choices. Public retirement accounts led by essentially DMV workers recklessly bet on Enron to go up forever as well:

- The Kansas Public Employees Retirement System had about $1.2 million invested in about 82,000 shares of Enron stock. "It was based on (Enron's) spectacular earnings growth and many analysts recommended it as a hot stock," said David Brant, Kansas Securities Commissioner.
- The retirement fund for the City of Fort Worth lost nearly $1 million in Enron.
- The Teacher Retirement System of Texas first invested in Enron in June 1994. It realized a net loss of approximately $23.3 million from its Enron stock holdings and $12.4 million in net unrealized losses from its current bond holdings in Enron. Jim Simms of Amarillo, a board member for six years and chairman of the board, said: "We're human beings—when you're investing money you'll have some winners and some losers . . . You can't protect yourself when you're being fed inaccurate information . . . We had all the precautions in place."

The best way I can explain it is that many investors believed that our returns were in some way inferior to the returns of many other hedge fund strategies, because of a perception of higher volatility, and lower absolute returns. The additional . . . benefits of low correlation, transparency, liquidity, and effective regulation somehow escaped their attention.

Campbell & Company[21]

There were no precautions in place. No fail-safes. No stops. Enron's fall from grace was no different than any other corporate implosion, although the losers (such as those in Table 4.3), as this quote reminds, always need to call it *new* to rationalize losses. However, the game never changes, even if the company names do.

An interesting aspect of the Enron fiasco was the close relationship between the Enron share price and natural gas. To lose money in Enron stock was to lose money in natural gas. They were connected at the hip. Enron acted as a derivative for natural gas. The company presented mutual funds and pension funds an opportunity to get into natural gas speculation even if their mission statement had them limited to stocks. Using Enron as a proxy, mutual and pension funds were able to ride natural gas to the top without ever taking a position in natural gas. Not only was everyone buying and holding Enron; they were, for all intents and purposes, buying and holding natural gas. The data makes the case:

TABLE 4.3: Largest Shareholders in Enron (Percent Fund in Enron Shares)

Alliance Premier Growth (4.1%)
Fidelity Magellan (0.2%)
AIM Value (1%)
Putnam Investors (1.7%)
Morgan Stanley Dividend Growth (0.9%)
Janus Fund (2.9%)
Janus Twenty (2.8%)
Janus Mercury (3.6%)
Janus Growth and Income (2.7%)
Rydex Utility (8%)
Fidelity Select Natural Gas (5.7%)
Dessauer Global Equity (5.6%)
Merrill Lynch Focus Twenty (5.8%)
AIM Global Technology (5.3%)
Janus 2 (4.7%)
Janus Special Situations (4.6%)
Stein Roe Focus (4.2%)
Alliance Premier Growth (4.1%)
Merrill Lynch Growth (4.1%)

All the intensive research these firms performed did not protect them, or their investors, from massive losses. It is particularly noteworthy [that] Janus, whose commercials tout their superior research efforts and skills, [held] over 16 million shares. On April 30, 2001, the last time it reported individual fund holdings, 11 Janus funds collectively owned more than 5 percent of Enron. As of Sept. 30, Janus still owned more than 5 percent of Enron. Another touter of their superior stock-picking skills is the Fidelity family of funds. As of September 30, 2001, together they owned 154 million shares. So much for the value or research [of Janus and Fidelity].

Larry Swedroe[22]

September 11, 2001

September 11, 2001 demonstrates unpredictable on a grand scale. How could anyone know in advance where the safe place to be was? Before considering September 11 specifically, consider Ed Seykota's words in general: "A surprise is an event that catches someone unaware. If you are already on the trend, the surprises seem to happen to the other guys."[23]

We don't see things as they are. We see things as we are.

Anaïs Nin

No one predicted a terrorist attack would close Wall Street for four days. Although it was difficult to stay focused on the rigors of everyday life, trend following maintained. It confronted markets as it always had—with a plan set in motion long before the unexpected event happened.

Trend following was short stocks and long bonds ahead of the attack because those markets were already headed in that direction. For example, Sunrise Capital Partners noted how lucky they were to be positioned ahead of the attack. Further, Campbell & Company made the case that currency markets had followed through with continued trends. "The U.S. dollar had already begun to weaken before the attacks, hence Campbell was short that market." Campbell had been *long* bonds and *short* a number of global stock index futures contracts ahead of the attack because of established trends.[24]

Although Enron, the California energy crisis, and September 11th are vivid illustrations of the zero-sum game with trend following as the winner, the story of Long-Term Capital Management in the summer of 1998 is an even better case study.

Event 3: Long-Term Capital Management

Long-Term Capital Management (LTCM) was a hedge fund that went bust in 1998. The story of who lost has been told repeatedly over the years; however, because trading is a zero-sum game, exploring the winners was the real story. LTCM is a classic saga of the zero-sum game played out in grand fashion with trend following again as the winner.

Trillion Dollar Bet, a PBS special, described how LTCM came to be. In 1973, three economists—Fischer Black, Myron Scholes, and Robert C. Merton—discovered an elegant formula that revolutionized modern finance. This mathematical Holy Grail, the Black–Scholes option pricing formula, was sparse and deceptively simple. It earned Scholes and Merton a Nobel Prize and attracted the attention of John Meriwether, the legendary bond trader of Salomon Brothers.

The most damaging consequence of the LTCM episode is, therefore, the harm done by the perception that Federal Reserve policy makers do not have the faith to take their own medicine. How can they persuade the Russians or the Japanese to let big institutions fail if they are afraid to do the same themselves?[27]

LTCM promised to use complex mathematical models to make investors wealthy beyond their wildest dreams. It attracted the elite of Wall Street's investors and initially reaped fantastic profits managing money. Ultimately, theories collided with reality and sent the company spiraling out of control.[25]

This was not supposed to happen: "They were immediately seen as a unique enterprise. They had the best minds. They had a former vice chairman of the Federal Reserve. They had John Meriwether . . . So they were seen by individual investors, but particularly by banks and institutions that went in with them, as a ticket to easy street."[26]

To understand the LTCM fiasco you again need to look at modern finance's foundations. Merton Miller and his colleague Eugene F. Fama launched what became the efficient market theory: "The premise of the theory is that stock prices are always right; therefore, no one can divine the market's future direction, which in turn, must be 'random.' For prices to be right, of course, the people who set them must be both rational and well informed."[28]

In other words, Miller and Fama believed perfectly rational people would never pay more or less than any financial instrument was worth. As a fervent supporter of the efficient market theory, Myron Scholes was certain markets could not make mistakes. His associate, Robert Merton, took it a step further with his continuous-time finance theory, which essentially wrapped the financial universe into a supposedly tidy ball.[29]

Merton's markets were as smooth as well-brewed java, in which prices would flow like cream. He assumed . . . the price of a share of IBM would never plunge directly from 80 to 60 but would always stop at 79¾, 79½, and 79¼ along the way.[30]

If LTCM's universe was supposed to be in a tidy ball, it might have been because academic life—where Merton and Scholes pioneered their theories—was tidy. LTCM's founders believed the market was a perfect normal distribution with no outliers, no fat tails, and no unexpected events. Problems began the moment these assumptions were accepted.

After Merton, Scholes, and Meriwether had Wall Street convinced the markets were a nice, neat, and continuous normal distribution and there was no risk and the party was on, LTCM began using mammoth leverage for the soon to come risk-free returns.

UBS said last week it would take a SFr950m ($686m) charge reflecting losses relating to its equity investment in LTCM, which was linked to an options deal that the former Union Bank of Switzerland had done with the hedge fund before merging with Swiss Bank Corporation to create the new UBS.[31]

Approximately 55 major banks gave LTCM financing including Bankers Trust, Bear Stearns, Chase Manhattan, Goldman Sachs, J.P. Morgan, Lehman Brothers, Merrill Lynch, Morgan Stanley, and Dean Witter. Eventually, LTCM would have $100 billion in borrowed assets and more than $1 trillion worth of exposure in markets everywhere. This type of leverage was not a problem initially—or so it seemed. Merton was even said to have remarked to Miller, "You could think of LTCM's strategy as a gigantic vacuum cleaner sucking up nickels across the world."

However, it was too complicated, too leveraged, and devoid of anything remotely resembling trend following risk management. The Organisation for Economic Co-operation and Development outlined a single trade example that uncovered LTCM's overall trading strategy. It was a bet on the convergence of yield spreads between French bonds (OATs) and German bonds (bunds). When the spread between the OATs and the bunds went to 60 basis points in the forward market, LTCM decided to double its position. That deal was one leg of an even more complex convergence bet, which included hedged positions in Spanish peseta and Italian lira bonds.[32]

The result of all these complex convergences was no one had a clue what LTCM was up to risk-wise, including LTCM itself. Its professors ran a secretive and closed operation so convoluted that regulators and investors had no idea what, when, or how much they were trading. Not being able to price an instrument or trade freely in and out of it on a daily basis ignores what Wall Street calls transparency. Jerry Parker sees the differences between LTCM and his trading:

> We've always had 100 percent transparency . . . The good thing about CTAs is their strategies are usually straightforward, not something that only a few people in the world can understand. We're trend following and systems-based, something you can easily describe to a client . . . People who aren't willing to show clients their positions are in trouble . . . One of the problems was that people put too much money in these funds such as Long-Term Capital Management. We ask for just 10 percent of risk capital, and clients know they may make 10 percent one month and lose 10 percent the next month. The ultimate error is to put a ton of money with geniuses who never lose money. When all hell breaks loose, those guys lose everything.[33]

Even more than LTCM's lack of transparency, the larger failure involved *lightning* as one critic noted: "I don't yet know the balance between whether this was a random event or whether this was negligence on theirs and their creditors' parts. If a random bolt of lightning hits you when you're standing in the middle of the field, it feels like a random event. But if your business is to stand in random fields during lightning storms, then you should anticipate, perhaps a little more robustly, the risks you're taking on."[35]

The Black–Scholes option pricing formula did not factor in the *randomness* of human behavior—only one example of the negligence that ultimately would cause lightning bolts to zap LTCM in August and September 1998. When lightning struck LTCM, trend following was assessing the same markets—playing the zero-sum game on the other side. In hindsight, the University of Chicago professors were clearly aware of the problem as Nobel Laureate Professor Merton Miller noted: "Models that they were using, not just Black–Scholes models, but other kinds of models, were based on normal behavior in the markets and when the behavior got wild, no models were able to put up with it."[36]

Last month [August 1998], during one of the most stressful points in market performance, our largest portfolio, Financial and Metals, was up [an estimated] 17.7 percent. Of the $2.4 billion that we manage, I think just slightly over half of it is in the Financial and Metals Portfolio. This was not a direct result of the decline in the U.S. market—as I said we don't trade in the S&P 500—but rather an example of the typical predictable investor behavior in the face of trouble. In reverting to rules of thumb, in this case, the flight to quality, global bonds rose, global stock markets plunged, and a shift in foreign exchange rates occurred. However, the magnitude of the moves was the only real surprise for us. The trends which were demonstrated during late August had been in place for weeks or months beforehand.

John W. Henry[34]

If only the principals at LTCM had remembered Albert Einstein's quote that elegance was for tailors, part of his observation about how beautiful formulas could pose problems in the real world. LTCM had the beautiful formulas, but they were not for the real world. Eugene Fama, Scholes's thesis advisor, had deep reservations about his student's options pricing model: "If the population of price changes is strictly normal [distribution], on the average for any stock . . . an observation more than five standard deviations from the mean should be observed about once every 7,000 years. In fact, such observations seem to occur about once every three to four years."[37]

For most investors, August 1998 was the month from hell. Not for William Dunn, though. His firm, Dunn Capital Management, with $900 million under management, had one of its best runs in years. He's up 25.4 percent so far this year, and 23.7 percent in August alone.[38]

LTCM lost 44 percent of its capital, or $1.9 billion, in August 1998 alone. In a letter to LTCM's 100 investors dated September 1998, John W. Meriwether wrote: "As you are all too aware, events surrounding the collapse of Russia caused large and dramatically increasing volatility in global markets throughout August. We are down 44 percent for the month of August and 52 percent for the year to date. Losses of this magnitude are a shock to us as they surely are to you, especially in light of the historical volatility of the fund."[39]

At the time of Meriwether's letter, LTCM's history consisted of only four short years, and although its "losses of this magnitude" might have shocked LTCM, its clients, and the lender banks to whom it owed over $100 billion, those trading losses became the source of profits for trend following. Amazingly, years later, Scholes still seemed to have a problem with accepting personal responsibility for his action in the zero-sum game: "In August of 1998, after the Russian default, you know, all the relations that tended to exist in a recent past seemed to disappear."[40]

Ultimately, the Fed, along with major world banks, most of which were heavily invested in LTCM, bailed the firm out. I believe if this bailout was not allowed to happen there would have been no precedent for the October 2008 bailouts, which made LTCM look like a walk in the park. The LTCM bailout stopped normal market forces. It set in motion the events of the next 10 years culminating in the fall of 2008. And the fixing of 2008, tracing back to LTCM's fixing, brings the world up to today—waiting for the next one.

The Losers

CNN outlined LTCM losers:

- Everest Capital, a Bermuda-based hedge fund, lost $1.3 billion. The endowments of Yale and Brown Universities were invested in Everest.
- George Soros' Quantum Fund lost $2 billion.

- High Risk Opportunity Fund, a $450 million fund run by III Offshore Advisors, went bust.
- The Tiger Fund run by Julian Robertson lost $3.3 billion in August and September of 1998.
- Liechtenstein Global Trust lost $30 million.
- Bank of Italy lost $100 million.
- Credit Suisse lost $55 million.
- UBS lost $690 million.
- Sandy Weill lost $10 million.
- Dresdner lost $145 million.

"There are two kinds of people who lose money: those who know nothing and those who know everything." With two Nobel Prize winners in the house, LTCM clearly fits the second case.[42]

The Winners

As dramatic as the LTCM blowout story is, the real lessons you can learn are from the winners. Campbell & Company was candid:

> If you look back to the early part of 1998, you will see it was a similar period in terms of industry returns. It was a very sad time all the way through July. And then out of nowhere it came, the collapse or the near-collapse of Russia in August and the LTCM crisis. All of a sudden, August was up 10 percent and September and October were up 4 percent or 5 percent, and many CTAs pulled down an 18 percent or 20 percent year out of nowhere. It's very hard to put your head back where you were three months before that and say it looked like a very gloomy business without much of a future and all of a sudden we're the place it's all at. The hedge fund world had fallen apart, equities had gone into the toilet, and managed futures were king and on the front page of *The Wall Street Journal*. So some of this is the psychology of what we do.[41]

The Fed's intervention was misguided and unnecessary because LTCM would not have failed anyway, and the Fed's concerns about the effects of LTCM's failure on financial markets were exaggerated. In the short run, the intervention helped the shareholders and managers of LTCM to get a better deal for themselves than they would otherwise have obtained.[43]

Trend following performance data for August and September 1998 looks like one continuous credit card swipe from LTCM to trend following—a zero-sum transfer swipe. During the exact period that LTCM lost $1.9 billion in assets, the aggregate profits (see Table 4.4) of Bill Dunn, John W. Henry, Jerry Parker, Keith Campbell, and Man exceeded $1 billion dollars.

Crunch the numbers on Dunn Capital Management's World Monetary Assets (WMA) fund. Their fund made nearly $300 million for the months of August and September 1998 alone. For example, here are markets from which trend following strategy profited (see Figures 4.24–4.31).

One of the former top executives of LTCM gave a lecture in which he defended the gamble that the fund had made. What he said was, "Look, when I drive home every night in the fall, I see all these leaves scattered around the base of the trees . . . There is a statistical distribution that governs the way they fall, and I can be pretty accurate in figuring out what that distribution is going to be. But one day, I came home and the leaves were in little piles. Does that falsify my theory that there are statistical rules governing how leaves fall? No. It was a man-made event." In other words, the Russians, by defaulting on their bonds, did something that they were not supposed to do, a once-in-a-lifetime, rule-breaking event . . . this is just the point: In the markets, unlike in the physical universe, the rules of the game can be changed. Central banks can decide to default on government-backed securities.

Malcolm Gladwell[44]

TABLE 4.4: Trend Following Profits August–September 1998

Dunn Capital Management WMA	
July 1998	–1.37%, 575,000,000
August 1998	+27.51%, 732,000,000
September 1998	+16.8%, 862,000,000
Dunn Capital Management TOPS	
July 1998	–1.08%, 133,000,000
August 1998	+9.48%, 150,000,000
September 1998	+12.90%, 172,000,000
John W. Henry Financials and Metals	
July 1998	–0.92%, 959,000,000
August 1998	+17.50, 1,095,000,000
September 1998	+15.26, 1,240,000,000
Campbell & Company Financials and Metals	
July 1998	–3.68, 917,000,000
August 1998	+9.23, 1,007,000,000
September 1998	+2.97, 1,043,000,000
Chesapeake Capital	
July 1998	+3.03, 1,111,000,000
August 1998	+7.27, 1,197,000,000
September 1998	–0.59, 1,179,000,000
Man Investments	
July 1998	+1.06, 1,636,000,000
August 1998	+14.51, 1,960,000,000
September 1998	+3.57, 2,081,000,000

Note: Percent returns for each month and total money under management in that fund.

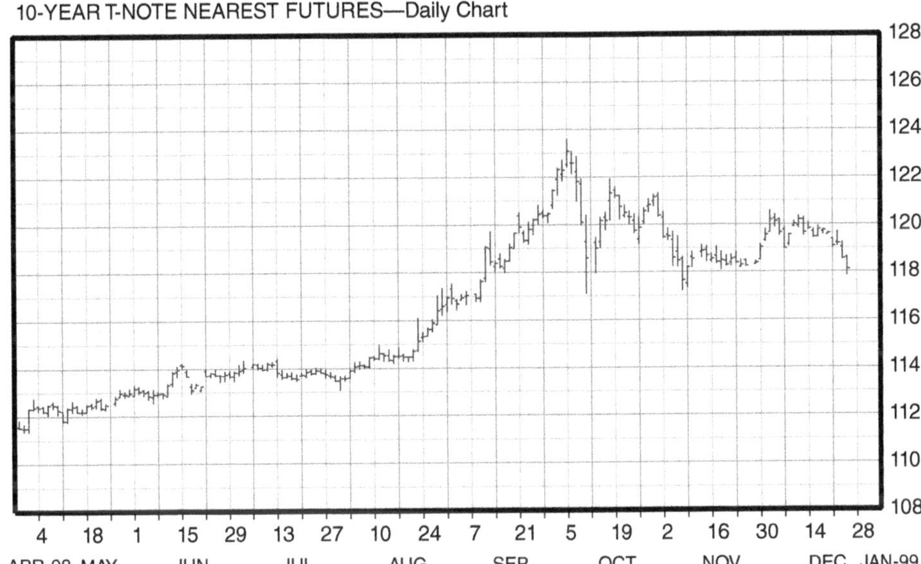

FIGURE 4.24: Trend Followers and 10-Year T-Note, May 1998–December 1998
Source: Barchart.com

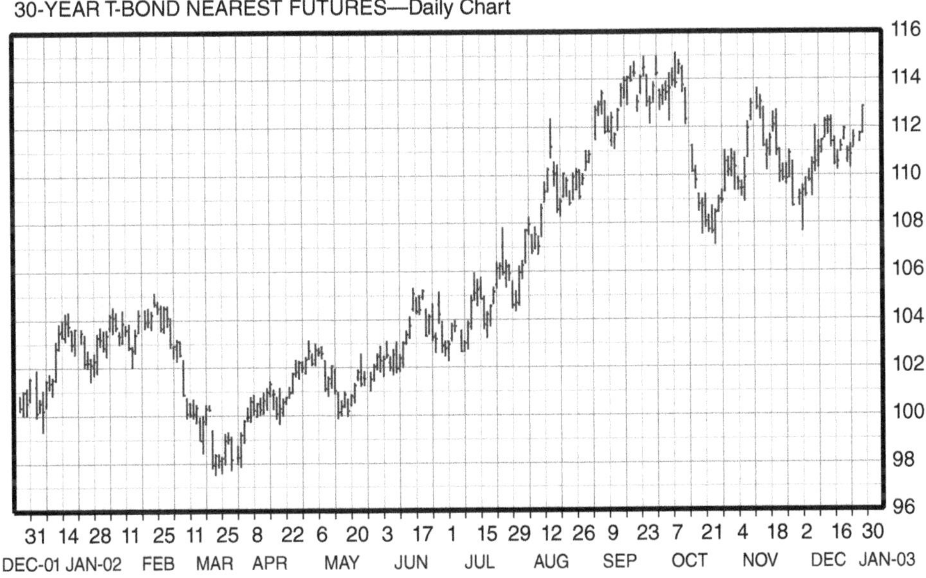

FIGURE 4.25: Trend Followers and U.S. T-Bond, May 1998–December 1998
Source: Barchart.com

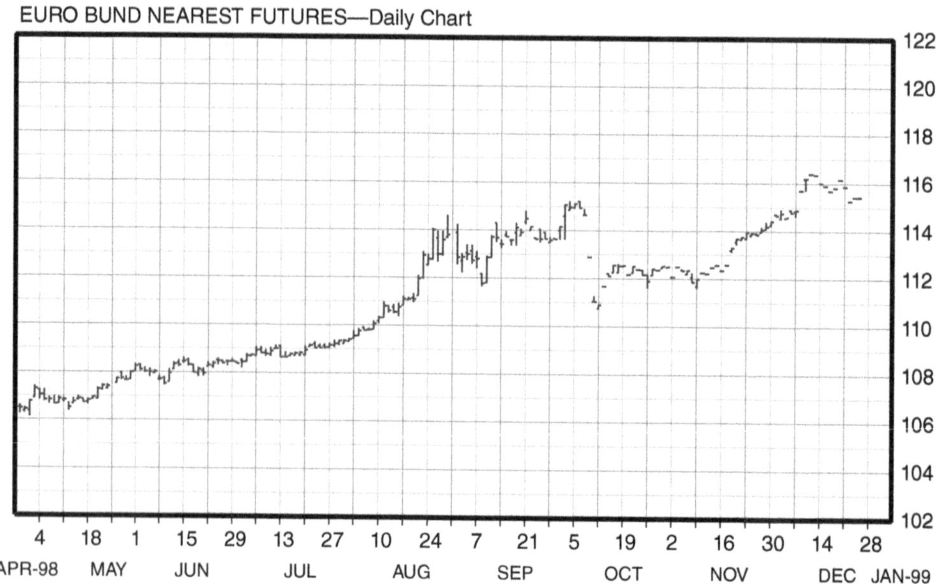

FIGURE 4.26: Trend Followers and German Bund, May 1998–December 1998
Source: Barchart.com

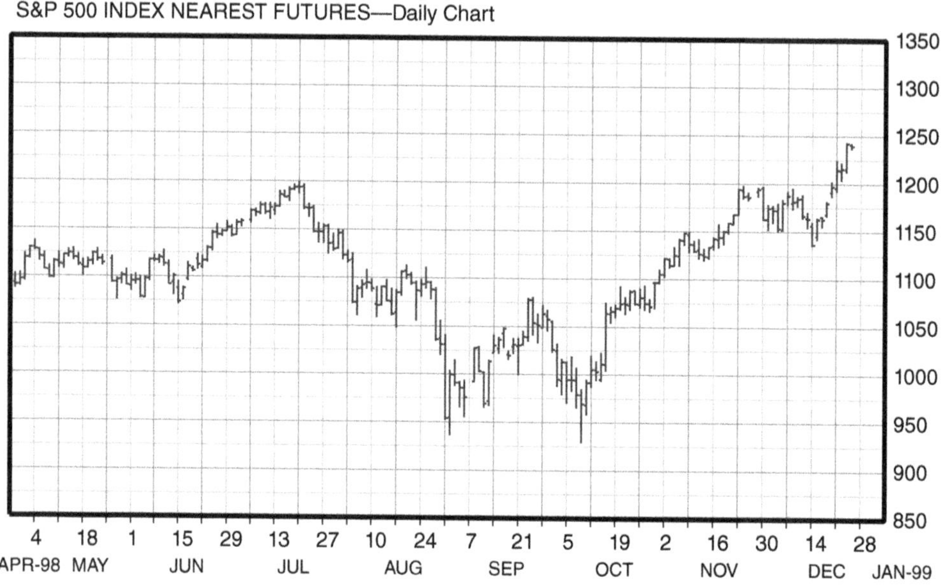

FIGURE 4.27: Trend Followers and S&P, May 1998–December 1998
Source: Barchart.com

FIGURE 4.28: Trend Followers and Swiss Franc, May 1998–December 1998
Source: Barchart.com

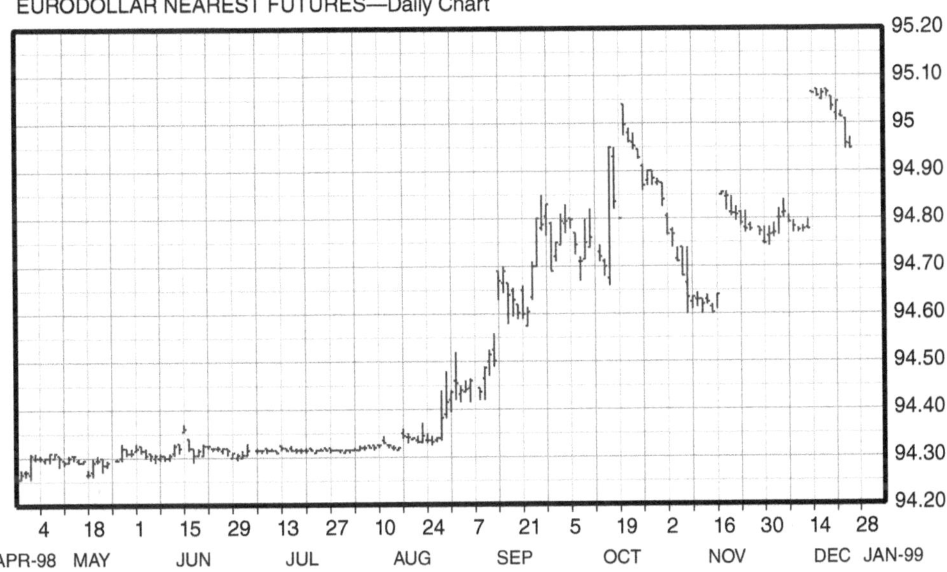

FIGURE 4.29: Trend Followers and Eurodollar, May 1998–December 1998
Source: Barchart.com

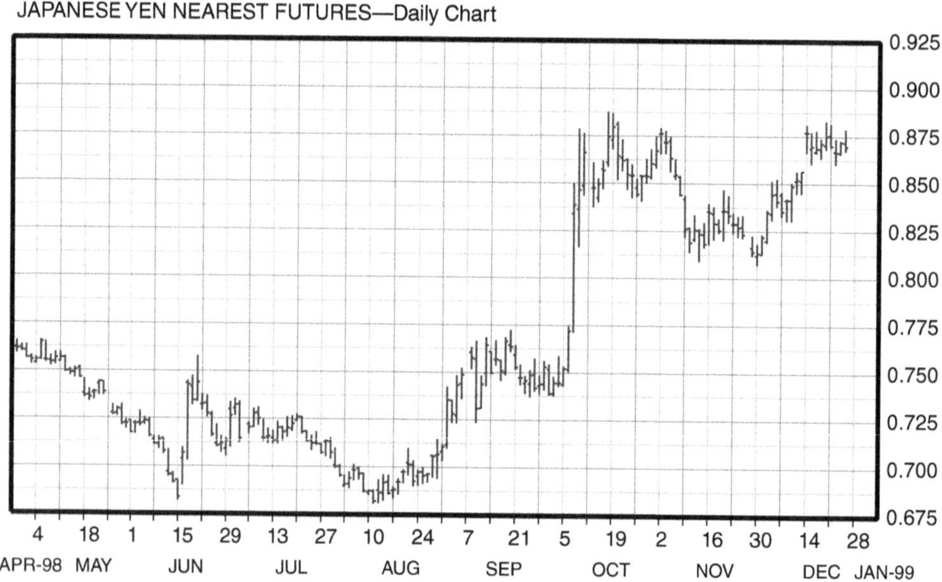

FIGURE 4.30: Trend Followers and Yen, May 1998–December 1998
Source: Barchart.com

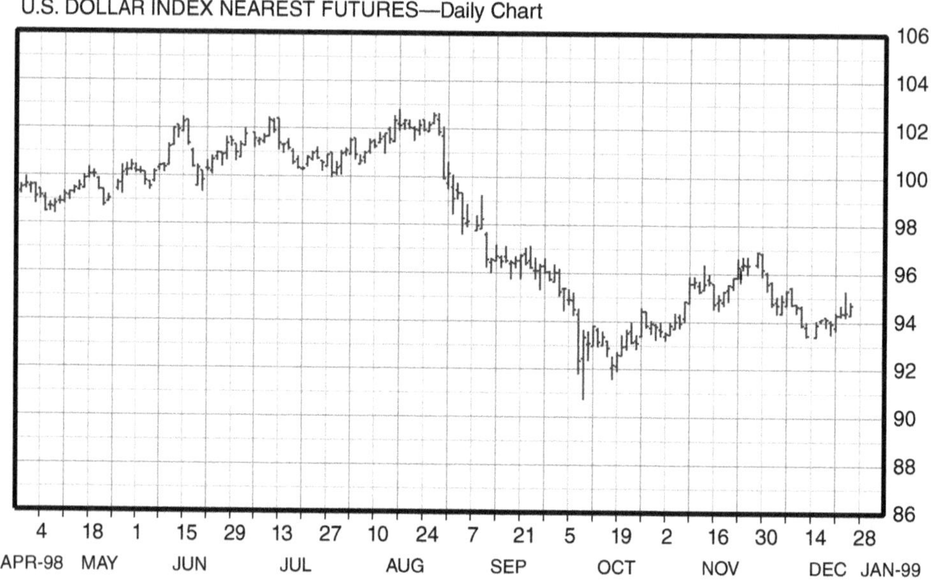

FIGURE 4.31: Trend Followers and Dollar Index, May 1998–December 1998
Source: Barchart.com

LTCM's failure lessons are now taught by all prominent business schools, but they leave out the winning lessons trend follower Jerry Parker teaches:

- *Transparent*—By and large, trend followers trade markets on regulated exchanges. They are not cooking up new derivatives in basements. Trend followers typically trade on freely traded markets where a price that everyone can see enables anyone to buy or sell. Trend followers have nothing in common with the derivatives fiascos that damaged Orange County or Procter and Gamble.
- *Understandable*—Trend following strategies can be understood by anybody. No high-level math only PhDs can comprehend.
- *No rock stars*—There are individuals who not only want to make money, but also want a rock star as their portfolio manager. They want to think that the strategy being used to make them money is exciting and state-of-the-art. Trend followers are not in the game for notoriety, only to win.

It isn't that they can't see the solution. It is that they can't see the problem.
G. K. Chesterton[45]

I always wonder what would have happened and how much more money trend following models would have made if LTCM had been allowed to implode without preferential government interference. And I asked Dunn Capital whether they thought LTCM's bailout was proper. They replied with a one-word answer: *No.* Bill Dunn responded with even more clarity:

> I believe the Long-Term Capital Management collapse was caused by:
>
> 1. Their trading approach was based on the theory prices and relationships between prices tend to vary, but they also tend to return to their mean value over long periods of time. So in practice, they probably looked at a market (or a spread between markets) and determined what its mean value was and where the current price was in relation to their estimate of its "true mean" value. If the current price was below the mean, a "buy" was indicated, and if it was above the mean, a "sell" was indicated. (I don't know what their exit strategy was.)
> 2. The main problem with the above is that as market prices move further against your position, you will be experiencing losses in your open positions and your above trading approach would suggest that adding to the current position will prove to be even more profitable

than originally expected. Unless this market very quickly turns and starts its anticipated return to its mean, additional losses will be suffered and the potential for profit will seem to become even greater, although elusive.

3. This problem can only be overcome by either adopting a strict entry and exit strategy that is believed to promote survivability or by having a nearly unlimited amount of capital/credit to withstand the occasional extreme excursions from the mean, or better yet, adopt both of these ideas.
4. But the situation became even more unstable when LTCM ventured into highly illiquid investment vehicles and also became a very major part of these very thin markets.
5. In the end, they became overextended and they ran out of capital before any anticipated reversion to the mean could bail them out.

Those who cannot or will not learn from the past always set themselves up for another August–September 1998 lightening bolt. Another LTCM fiasco is always in the offing since the Black–Scholes way of life, where the world is a normal distribution, is still considered a viable approach to investing in 2017. Philip Anderson, joint winner of a Nobel Prize in Physics, sees the dangers in normal distribution thinking: "Much of the real world is controlled as much by the 'tails' of distributions as by means or averages: by the exceptional, not the mean; by the catastrophe, not the steady drip; by the very rich, not the 'middle class.' We need to free ourselves from 'average' thinking."[46]

And breaking out from average thinking starts with hitting home runs (i.e., trend following) instead of hitting supposed sure-fire singles (i.e., LTCM).

Footnotes to LTCM

- Myron Scholes went on to form a new fund, Platinum Grove, after LTCM's demise. With Scholes as chairman, Platinum Grove lost $600 million dollars during 2007–2008.
- A great story about LTCM hiring Goldman Sachs to assist raising cash during the crisis: "LTCM gave their derivatives positions to Goldman Sachs as part of their due diligence: 'Goldman Sachs traders stayed up all night using the LTCM data to front-run their clients in markets

around the world. Goldman, led by Jon Corzine, was in similar spread trades as LTCM, and was losing billions itself. With the LTCM data, Goldman unwound trades like a precision guided missile instead of a machine gun firing indiscriminately. Ultimately Goldman failed to raise money for LTCM, but it was mission accomplished in terms of gaining inside information. If Goldman could not save the system, it would at least save itself.'"[47]

Event 4: Asian Contagion

The 1997 *Asian Contagion* was another event where trend following won out. To this day in 2017 if you drive around Bangkok, Thailand or Kuala Lumpur, Malaysia, you can still see unfinished skyscrapers left as artifacts of yet another financial implosion. One of the biggest losers during this meltdown was infamous trader Victor Niederhoffer. Always opinionated, bombastic, and for most of his trading career, exceptionally successful, Niederhoffer's trading demise was swift.

We make a lot more money trading at the level we do. The trade-off is volatility, but if it doesn't cause you to perish, then you're better off in the long run.

Dunn Capital[49]

Niederhoffer played a big game, whether at speculating, chess, or squash. He challenged grandmasters in chess and he won repeated titles as a national squash champion. He regularly bet hundreds of millions of dollars and consistently won until Monday, October 27, 1997. That day he lost an estimated $50 million to $100 million, and his three hedge funds, Limited Partners of Niederhoffer Intermarket Fund L.P., Limited Partners of Niederhoffer Friends Partnership L.P., and Niederhoffer Global Systems S.A., bellied up.[48]

Imagine receiving this letter faxed from Niederhoffer on Wednesday, October 29, 1997:

To:

Limited Partners of Niederhoffer Intermarket Fund, L.P.

Limited Partners of Niederhoffer Friends Partnership, L.P.

Shareholders of Niederhoffer Global Systems, S.A.

Dear Customers:

As you no doubt are aware, the New York stock market dropped precipitously on Monday, October 27, 1997. That drop followed large declines on

(Continued)

On Wednesday Niederhoffer told investors in three hedge funds he runs that their stakes had been "wiped out" Monday by losses that culminated from three days of falling stock prices and big hits earlier this year in Thailand.[50]

(Continued)

two previous days. This precipitous decline caused substantial losses in the fund's positions, particularly their positions in puts on the Standard & Poor's 500 Index. As you also know from my previous correspondence with you, the funds suffered substantial losses earlier in the year as a result of the collapse in the East Asian markets, especially in Thailand.

The cumulation [sic] of these adverse developments led to the situation where, at the close of business on Monday, the funds were unable to meet minimum capital requirements for the maintenance of their margin accounts. It is not yet clear what is the precise extent (if any) to which the funds' equity balances are negative. We have been working with our broker-dealers since Monday evening to try to meet the funds' obligations in an orderly fashion. However, right now, the indications are that the entire equity positions in the funds has been wiped out.

Sadly, it would appear that if it had been possible to delay liquidating most of the funds' accounts for one more day, a liquidation could have been avoided. Nevertheless, we cannot deal with "would have been." We took risks. We were successful for a long time. This time we did not succeed, and I regret to say that all of us have suffered some very large losses.[51]

There are so many ways to lose, but so few ways to win. Perhaps the best way to achieve victory is to master all the rules for disaster, and then concentrate on avoiding them.
Victor Niederhoffer

Niederhoffer seems unable to acknowledge that he, alone, was to blame for his losses in the zero-sum game. He did it. It was his strategy. No one else did it for him and using the unexpected as an excuse is no excuse. It is interesting to note his trading performance was long heralded as low risk. He made money almost every month. Compared to trend following drawdowns he was the golden boy making money as consistently as a casino. Who would want to place money with trend following and potentially tolerate a steep drawdown when they could put money with Niederhoffer, who seemed to combine similar performance with what appeared to be far less risk and almost no drawdown? That's how the narrative looked before Niederhoffer's flame out .

But the idea Niederhoffer was devoid of risk disappeared quickly with his trading firm's 1997 demise. Examine his performance numbers during that year (Table 4.5):

TABLE 4.5: Niederhoffer Performance[52]

Date	VAMI	ROR	Quarter ROR	Yearly ROR	Amount Managed
Jan-97	11755	4.42%			
Feb-97	11633	–1.04%			
Mar-97	10905	–6.26%	–3.13%		$130.0M
Apr-97	11639	6.73%			
May-97	11140	–4.28%			
Jun-97	10296	–7.58%	–5.58%		$115.0M
Jul-97	11163	8.42%			
Aug-97	5561	–50.18%			
Sep-97	7100	27.67%	–31.04%		$88.0M
Oct-97	1	–99.99%			
Nov-97	1	0.00%			
Dec-97	1	0.00%	–99.99%	–99.99%	0

When reviewing Niederhoffer's performance meltdown (see Table 4.5), keep in mind in the last issue of *The Stark Report* where his performance was still listed, his ranking was as follows:

Return: four stars

Risk: four stars

Risk Adjusted: four stars

Equity: five stars[54]

I felt there were very definite economic trends that were established from knowledge and the ability to know what events meant. I was looking for a way to participate in [those] major trends when they occurred, even though they were unexpected.

Bill Dunn[53]

The star rankings gave the impression Niederhoffer was risk-free. However, his trading, like LTCM's, was predicated on a world of normal distributions. Measuring him with standard deviation as the risk measure gave an imperfect view of Niederhoffer's true risk. Some observers were well aware of problems in Niederhoffer's contrarian style long before the flameout. Frank J. Franiak spoke out six months earlier: "It's a matter of time before something goes wrong."[55]

But Niederhoffer loyalists were concerned only with whether the profits were continually coming in even if his strategy was deeply flawed

Victor Niederhoffer looked at markets as a casino where people act as gamblers and where their behavior can be understood by studying gamblers. He regularly made small amounts of money trading on that theory. There was a flaw in his approach, however. If there is a . . . tide . . . he can be seriously hurt because he doesn't have a proper fail-safe mechanism.
George Soros[57]

and potentially dangerous. His clients were enamored: "Whatever voodoo he uses, it works," said Timothy P. Horne, chairman of Watts Industries Inc. (and a Niederhoffer customer since 1982).[56]

The vast majority of Niederhoffer clients did not realize until after their accounts were toast that *voodoo* doesn't work.

Niederhoffer on Trend Following

Five years after his blowout, Niederhoffer began ripping trend following: "Granted that some users of trend following have achieved success. Doubtless their intelligence and insights are quite superior to our own. But it's at times like this, when everything seems to be coming up roses for the trend followers' theories and reputations, that it's worthwhile to step back and consider some fundamental questions: Is their central rule; is the trend is your friend valid? Might reported results, good or bad, be best explained as due to chance?" He added: "But first, a warning: We do not believe in trend following. We are not members of the Market Technicians Association or the International Federation of Technical Analysts or the TurtleTrader Trend Followers Hall of Fame. In fact, we are on the enemies' lists of such organizations."[58]

In statistical terms, I figure I have traded about 2 million contracts—with an average profit of $70 per contract. This average profit is approximately 700 standard deviations away from randomness, a departure that would occur by chance alone about as frequently as the spare parts in an automotive salvage lot might spontaneously assemble themselves into a McDonald's restaurant.
Victor Niederhoffer[61]

Niederhoffer continued: "No test of 'the trend is your friend' is possible, because the rule is never put forward in the form of a testable hypothesis. Something is always slippery, subjective, or even mystical about the rule's interpretation and execution."[59] Even though the market is the ultimate arbiter (it's always *right*), Niederhoffer still didn't let go:

> In my dream, I am long IBM, or priceline.com, or worst of all, Krung Thai Bank, the state owned bank in Thailand that fell from $200 to pennies while I held in 1997. The rest of the dream is always the same. My stock plunges. Massive margin calls are being issued. Related stocks jump off cliffs in sympathy. Delta hedges are selling more stocks short to rebalance their positions. The naked options I am short are going through the roof. Millions of investors are blindly following the headlines. Listless as zombies, they are liquidating their stocks at any price and piling into money market funds with an after tax yield of –1 percent. "Stop you fools!" I scream. "There's no danger! Can't you see? The headlines are inducing you to lean the wrong way! Unless you get your balance, you'll lose everything—your wealth, your home!"[60]

Many smart players to this day view Niederhoffer as brilliant, and I see his wisdom in some work and hope to have him on my podcast one day. But markets are unforgiving. Get the risk wrong, and it's obituaries.

Event 5: Barings Bank

The first few months of 1995 go down as one of the most eventful periods in the history of speculative trading. The market events of that period, by themselves, could be the subject of a Harvard PhD finance course. But twenty years later, despite the enduring significance, the events have been forgotten and no Harvard class ever materialized.

Niederhoffer is an inveterate contrarian. He feeds off panic, making short-term bets when prices get frothy. He condemns the common strategy of trend following, which helped make his buddy George Soros super-rich: "A delusion."[62]

What happened? A rogue trader, Nick Leeson, overextended Barings Bank in the Nikkei 225, the Japanese equivalent to the Dow, by speculating that the index would go higher. It tanked instead, and Barings—the Queen's bank, one of the oldest, most well established banks in England—collapsed, losing $2.2 billion.

Who won the Barings Bank sweepstakes? That question was never asked by anyone—not *The Wall Street Journal* nor *Investor's Business Daily*. Was the world interested only in a story about failure and not the slightest bit curious about where $2.2 billion went? Trend following was sitting at the table devouring Leeson's mistakes.

The majority of traders do not have the discipline to plan 3, 6, and 12 months ahead for unforeseen changes in markets. However, planning for the unexpected is an essential ingredient of trend following strategy. Huge moves to profit from are always on the horizon if you are reacting to the market and not trying to predict it.

Despite his envy and admiration, [Nassim Taleb] did not want to be Victor Niederhoffer—not then, not now, and not even for a moment in between. For when he looked around him, at the books and the tennis court and the folk art on the walls—when he contemplated the countless millions that Niederhoffer had made over the years—he could not escape the thought that it might all have been the result of sheer, dumb luck.

Malcolm Gladwell[63]

Sadly, most market players only know to make decisions based on their perceptions of what the market direction will be. After they make their directional choice, they are blinded to any other option. They keep searching for validation to support their analysis even if they are losing colossal money—like Nick Leeson. Before the Kobe earthquake in early January 1995, with the Nikkei trading in a range of 19,000 to 19,500, Leeson had long futures positions of approximately 3,000 contracts on the Osaka Stock Exchange. After the Kobe earthquake of January 17, his buildup of Nikkei positions intensified and Leeson kept buying as the Nikkei sank.[64]

Who Won?

Observe the Nikkei 225 (see Figure 4.32) from September 1994 until June 1995. Barings' lost assets directly padded the pockets of disciplined trend following traders.

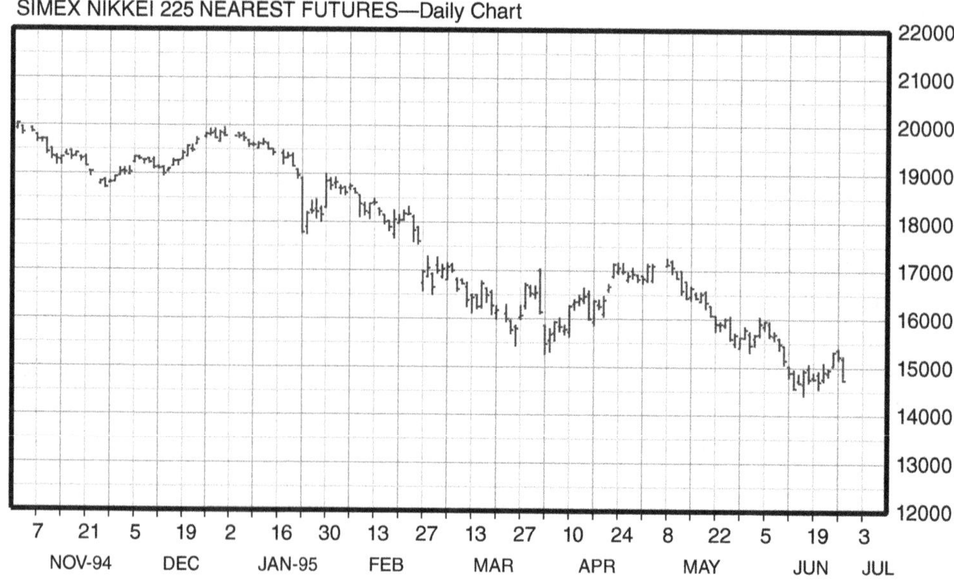

FIGURE 4.32: Nikkei 225 September 1994–June 1995
Source: Barchart.com

A few months after Barings, John W. Henry's performance (see Table 4.6) made the case clear:

TABLE 4.6: John W. Henry Trading Programs

Name of Program	01–95	02–95	03–95
Financials and Metals	$648	$733	$827
	–3.8	15.7	15.3
Global Diversified	$107	$120	$128
	–6.9	13.5	8.5
Original	$54	$64	$73
	2.1	17.9	16.6
Global Financial	$7	$9	$14
	–4.1	25.6	44.4

Note: Total money under management in millions with monthly percent returns.

Dean Witter (now Morgan Stanley) was Henry's broker at the time: "I have over $250 million with Henry . . . I have been pleased to see how well the Original [Henry] Program has done so far in 1995: up over 50 percent through April 18 [1995]."[65]

Other trend followers brought home huge gains in February and March of 1995 (see Table 4.7). However, their winnings arguably were more from the Japanese yen trend up and down:

TABLE 4.7: 1995 Trend Following Performance

Name	01–95	02–95	03–95
Chesapeake	$549	$515	$836
	-3.2	-4.4	8.6
Rabar	$148	$189	$223
	-9.4	14.0	15.2
Campbell (Fin/Metals)	$255	$253	$277
	-4.53	5.85	9.58
Mark J. Walsh	$20	$22	$29
	-16.4	17.0	32.3
Abraham	$78	$93	$97
	-7.9	1.2	6.6
Dunn (WMA)	$178	$202	$250
	0.5	13.7	24.4
Dunn (TOPS)	$63	$69	$81
	-7.6	9.9	22.7
Millburn Ridgefield	$183	$192	$233
	-6.5	8.7	19.4

Note: Total money under management in millions with monthly percent returns.

In my opinion, luck is far and away the most important determinant in our lives. Various events of infinitesimal probability—where you are born, to whom you are born, who you marry, where you take your first job, which school you choose—have an enormous impact on our lives. People tend to deny that luck is an important determinant. We like explanations. For instance, during a basketball game, there are innumerable random events. If a guy hits three in a row, he's really hot. Most of the time, it's random. Of course, the announcer doesn't want to say, "Oh my! Another random event!" That's not exciting, so he'll give a reason. But it is just luck. Not all of our luck is good, but there is more good luck behind our performance than even I like to acknowledge.

Jim Simons[66]

There might be slight differences in leverage and signal timing, but even a quick glance makes clear: Immense trends equaled monster profits for almost all trend followers. Henry confirmed in 1998, albeit cryptically, his massive zero-sum Barings win:

> The inflation story, of course, is not the most dramatic example. More recently Asia is another example of how one-time big events can lead to trends that offer us opportunity, and really shape our world. Whether

> you believe the causal story of banking excesses in Asia or not, there was a clear adjustment in the Asian economies that has been, and will continue to be, drawn out. Under these situations, it's natural that trends will develop, and recognizing these trends allows us to capitalize on the errors or mistakes of other market participants. Because, after all, we're involved in a zero-sum game.[67]

Henry and Leeson were indeed involved in the age-old zero-sum game—like in so many other historical examples. They both bellied up to the table, but there was one big difference—Henry had an actual strategy. What Leeson had nobody knows, but as long as he was making money, his bosses in England did not care. Yes, they cared after he destroyed the bank, but by then it was too late.

In the course of the next 12 months it became more and more obvious that other traders were formulating trading strategies that exploited MG's need to liquidate its expiring long position. At the end of each trading month, as MG tried to liquidate its long positions by buying the offsetting shorts, other traders would add their short positions to MG's, creating the paper market equivalent of a glut in supply that initially exceeded the number of longs, driving prices down until the market reached equilibrium. The combined force of MG's selling its long position in the prompt contract and other traders increasing their short positions was severe downward pressure on crude prices as the prompt month contract neared expiration.[69]

Event 6: Metallgesellschaft

Metallgesellschaft (MG) now has a new name and a new identity as a specialty chemicals plant and process-engineering concern. However, after 119 years of success as a German metals, trading, and construction conglomerate, it became best known for its high-profile trading loss of $1.5 billion (2.3 billion Deutsche Marks at the time).[68]

You know what's coming—another zero-sum lesson in action. And while I am sure some might feel that an event this long ago holds no value—pause that thought and consider greed and fear.

The story starts with MG long crude oil futures on the New York Mercantile Exchange (NYMEX) through most of 1993. During that time period MG lost between $1.3 and $2.1 billion; the winners were trend followers. Over the course of 1993, crude oil futures (see Figure 4.33) slowly declined from May through December.

You know the drill. There is always someone on the other side of a trade. The difficulty of course lies in determining who is on the opposite side of a position if only one side is publicly known. The fact MG lost was well known, but who won was my curiosity in the mid to late 1990s. And in the aftermath of the MG losses, a variety of explanations developed. The financial world was treated to academic mumbo jumbo from MBA students analyzing why MG lost as well as articles condemning energy futures. The actual explanation for implosion is simple: MG had zero trading strategy and lost.

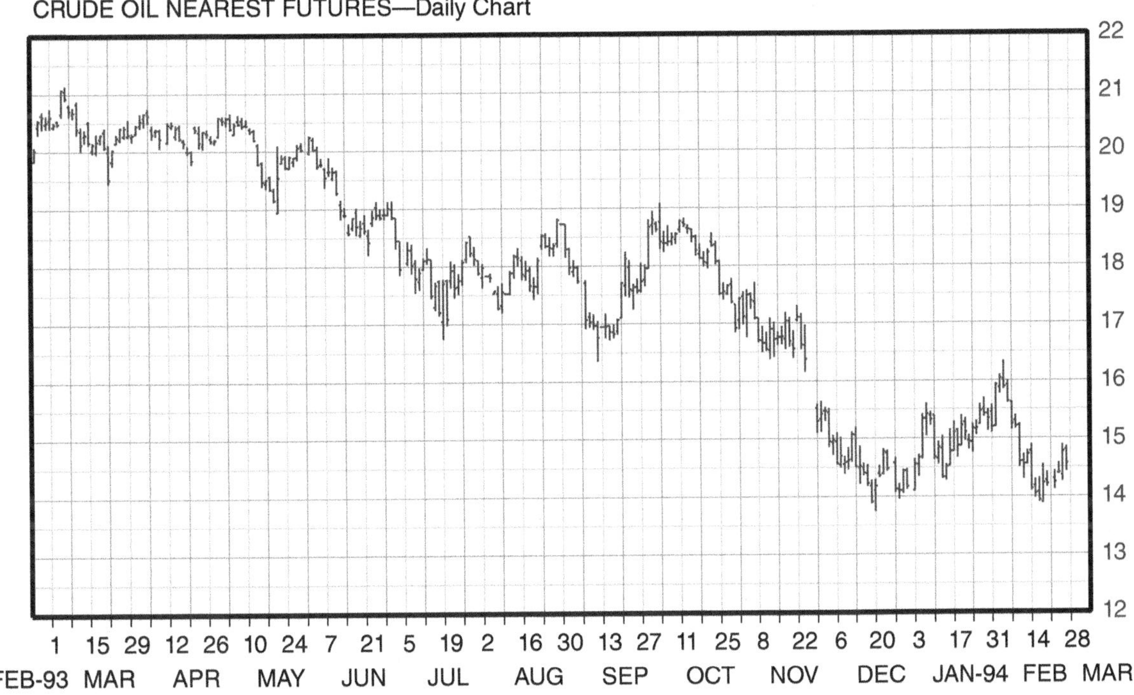

FIGURE 4.33: Crude Oil Futures, February 1993–February 1994 Source: Barchart.com

Trend following players had a major role in MG's demise, and the job of explaining this was made easy with publicly available trend following performance data (see Table 4.8).

The key to explaining Table 4.8 lies in the months of July 1993, December 1993 and January 1994. Those months do not require much more than a casual glance at correlations to confirm the similarity in

TABLE 4.8: Trend Follower Performance, June 1993–January 1994

	6–93	7–93	8–93	9–93	10–93	11–93	12–93	1–94
Abraham	–1.2	6.6	–5.3	1.2	–6.6	3.5	12.5	-1.45
Chesapeake	1.0	9.5	5.8	–2.7	–0.1	1.1	5.8	-3.33
JPD	–6.9	10.2	–2.1	–4.1	–2.0	2.7	8.6	-3.9
Rabar	–1.3	14.8	–3.9	–4.1	–6.0	5.6	10.1	-10.5
Saxon	–2.7	20.5	–14.3	–2.1	–1.1	6.6	17.1	-10.8

trend following strategies. Trend following made money in July and December and lost in January.

One of the few things the post-mortems seem to have glossed over is the trap that MG had gotten itself into by becoming the dominant participant in the futures markets. By the fall of 1993, some traders had come to anticipate the rollovers of MG's positions. As long as its huge position was in the market, MG hung there like a big piñata inviting others to hit it each month. The self-entrapping nature of its positions is what is missing from Edwards and Canter's, and even Culp and Miller's, defenses of MG.[70]

The academics, media, and everyone else, it seems, figured out professional traders were shorting energy markets and putting extensive pressure on MG. What the academics never found out or never seemed to be too interested to find out was who those professional traders were. The performance data was out there for everybody to look at. It wasn't a secret. I found it on file with the United States Commodity Futures Trading Commission.

Every day trend following models dictate how many contracts or shares to trade based on total capital on hand at that time. For example, after trend following traders initiated positions and were rewarded with strong profits in July they were willing to risk those profits again. In August, with nice profits in hand, they were willing to risk those profits and still lose a fixed percentage based on original stops. They were willing to let profits on the table turn into losses. They let the market tell them when the trend was over (January 1994).

In the fall of 1993, trend followers continued to hold established short positions in crude oil futures. MG was long crude oil futures and desperately trying to stay afloat while trend followers waited like predators. However, trend followers were not short; they were aggressively short, reinvesting profits back into additional short crude oil positions as the market decreased more and more.

On the losing side of this zero-sum game, MG refused to take a loss early on. In fact, the whole MG affair would have been a footnote in trading history if they had exited after the July price decline. Instead, MG stayed in the game in hopes of an upward trend to make up for losses. They wanted to *get back* at the market and *break even*—a common psychological issue that bedevils new to pro traders to this day. But MG obviously had no inkling of the steely discipline of their trend following opponents. Not one trend follower was going to exit anytime soon. The price told them the trend was down. An exit would have violated one of trend following's most fundamental rules, one of the most fundamental rules across all of successful trading: Let your winners run.

According to the NYMEX, MG held the futures position equivalent of 55 million barrels of gasoline and heating oil.[71]

As the story winds down, crude oil begins its final descent in late November and into December. At this time, MG management liquidated their positions and further fueled the November and December crude oil price drop. Ultimately, all good trends must end. And trend followers would eventually begin their crude oil futures exit in January 1994. If you look at the performance of trend followers in January

1994 (see Table 4.8), you can see what they lost for the month as they extricated themselves from their history-making profits of 1993 (see Table 4.9):

TABLE 4.9: 1993 Trend Following Returns

Name	% Return
Abraham Trading	+34.29%
Chesapeake Capital	+61.82%
Man Investments	+24.49%
Rabar Market Research	+49.55%
Dunn WMA	+60.25%
John W. Henry	+46.85%
Mark J. Walsh	+74.93%
Eckhardt Trading	+57.95%

"What's one and one and one and one and one and one and one and one and one and one?"

"I don't know," said Alice. "I lost count."

Lewis Carroll[72]

There is no shortage of big events in the past 50 years to show the prowess of trend following. However, there are rabid skeptics who suspect they know the Achilles' heel of trend following strategy—the 1987 stock market crash.

Event 7: Black Monday

One of my favorite questions that I still hear to this day: "How did trend following do during the 1987 Black Monday stock crash?" "How did it do during a 20-standard-deviation event?" Their tone always says what they think the answer will be or what they hope it will be—that trend following was killed that day. I now must be the bearer of bad news for those skeptics. The fall of 1987 (see Tables 4.10 and 4.11) produced *historic* gains for trend following:

The S&P lost 29.6 percent of its value during the 1987 crash and took until May 1989 to recover. EAFE Index, Jaguar, and Quantum performances were highly correlated to that of the broad market. Over the full period, Financial and Metals Portfolio earned nearly 260 percent on a composite basis.

John W. Henry[73]

TABLE 4.10: October–November 1987 Stock Market Crash

Name	% Return
S&P 500	–28%
John W. Henry Original Investment Program	+58.2%
John W. Henry Financials and Metals Portfolio	+69.7%

Success demands singleness of purpose.
Vince Lombardi

TABLE 4.11: Trend Following Performance 1987

Name	% Return
Chesapeake Capital	+38.78%
JPD	+96.80%
Rabar	+78.20%
John W. Henry (Financials and Metals)	+251.00%
Campbell & Company (Financials and Metals)	+64.38%
Millburn Ridgefield	+32.68%
Dunn Capital Management (WMA)	+72.15%
Mark J. Walsh	+143%
Man Investments	+42.54%

A speculative mania is a wonderful thing for our program. We do as much of that as possible. Unfortunately, in saying that, I sound a little bit anti–common man, man on the street. What's bad for the general public is very good for our program.
Toby Crabel

I also pulled *The Economist* from March 1987, which to my fortunate surprise included quotes and references to a then 26-year-old David Harding and a then 31-year old Larry Hite. Highlights:

- Technical analysis of financial markets starts with the assumption markets follow trends determined by previous patterns of price behavior, and that rarely, if ever, move randomly.
- A chartist will attempt to discern a trend by spotting recognizable movements in the price of a security or commodity which confirm a *break out*, either up or down, from the range within which the price has previously been trading.
- Larry Hite compared a computer to an anvil. Ideas can be hammered out on it and discarded if they do not come up to scratch.
- David Harding's computer system not only generates buy and sell signals; it also shows how long an investment should be held. Only 50 percent of his trades are profitable, but winners are on average 3× bigger than losers.
- 1987 critics call Harding and Hite's trend following efforts a *fad.*[75]

"When you have eliminated the impossible, whatever remains, however improbable, must be the truth."
Sir Arthur Conan Doyle[74]

I was having dinner with Larry Hite in late 2016 and I brought up that he was called a 1987 fad. But his mantra doesn't change. What he said in 1987, he says in 2017. The evidence is in. All we can do is trust evidence, until it changes.

A main reason trend following trading has done so well for so long is because it has no quarterly performance constraints. Both Wall Street and Main Street measure success on the artificial constraints of the calendar. Trend following does not. For example, looking back at the end of 2008 you can see that without October 2008's home run, trend following would have had a different performance profile. History now would be remembered differently.

The notion of quarterly performance measures implies you can predict the market or achieve profit targets. Quarters as a measurement might not be real, but they provide a comfortable structure for investors who mistakenly believe they can demand consistent profits. This demand for consistency has led to a constant search for the Holy Grail or *hot hand*, to the detriment of ever winning consistently.

Imagine playing football where there are four quarters, and you have to score in each quarter to win. Imagine placing more importance on scoring in each quarter than winning the game. Now a great trend trader says, "I might score 28 points in any of the four quarters. I might score at any point in the game, but the object, at the end of the game, is to win." If a trend following trader scores 28 points in the first quarter and no points in the next three quarters, and wins, who cares when he scored?

Blaming derivatives for financial losses is akin to blaming cars for drunk driving fatalities.

Christopher L. Culp[76]

Trend followers are home run hitters taking what the market gives them no matter when it arrives. Absolute return traders have no profit targets. They view the world as a rolling return. I asked Bill Dunn how they address quarterly performance measures popular on Wall Street. I wanted to know exactly how they educate clients to appreciate big event hunting. His response: "Clients must already have an appreciation for the pitfalls of relying on short-term performance data before they can appreciate us."

That's blunt talk for a serious game.

On the other hand, after he retired, Julian Robertson publicly slammed his constraints, comparing them to a necessary but incompetent baseball umpire: "One of the great investors likened it to a batter not having an umpire. If you don't have an umpire, you can wait for the fat pitch. The trouble with investing for other people, particularly in a hedge fund, is that you do have an umpire—called quarterly performance."

Jason Gerlach, of trend following firm Sunrise Capital, provided even more event data buttressing the issues with calendar-mandated benchmarks. The S&P contrasted against a trend following index shows the historical performance differential when historical events hit:

TIME PERIOD	EVENT	S&P 500 INDEX PERFORMANCE	BARCLAY CTA INDEX PERFORMANCE
1987 Q4	Black Monday	–22.53%	+13.77%
2002 Q3	WorldCom scandal	–17.28%	+6.77%
2001 Q3	9/11	–14.68%	+2.62%
2011 Q3	European debt crisis	–13.87%	+1.65%
1990 Q3	Iraq invades Kuwait	–13.75%	+5.82%
2002 Q2	Dot-com bubble	–13.40%	+8.20%
2001 Q1	Tech bear market	–11.86%	+3.75%
1998 Q3	Russian default/LTCM	–9.95%	+8.95%
2008 Q1	Credit crisis	–9.45%	+6.91%
2008 Q3	Credit crisis/bailout	–8.37%	–3.02%
2000 Q4	Dot-com bubble burst	–7.83%	+9.86%
2015 Q3	Fed policy uncertainty	–6.40%	–0.27%
1999 Q3	Y2K anxiety	–6.25%	–0.79%
1994 Q1	Fed rate hikes	–3.79%	–2.76%
2007 Q4	Credit crisis	–3.33%	+4.07%
2003 Q1	Second Gulf War	–3.15%	+0.72%
1990 Q1	Recession/oil spike	–2.99%	+5.43%

Source: *Sunrise Capital*

Big money is made in the stock market by being on the right side of the major moves. The idea is to get in harmony with the market. It's suicidal to fight trends. They have a higher probability of continuing than not.
Martin Zweig

Kieron Nutbrown, while not researching trend following, provided a chronology of financial crises and market panics dating from the Middle Ages to present day:

- 1255: Overexpansion of credit led to banking failures in 1255–62 in Italy
- 1294: Edward I default to the Ricciardi of Lucca during war with France
- 1298: Seizure of the Gran Tavola of Sienna by Philip IV of France
- 1307: Liquidation of the Knights Templar by Philip IV
- 1311: Edward II default to the Frescobaldi of Florence
- 1326: Bankruptcy of the Scali of Florence and Asti of Sienna
- 1342: Edward III default to the Florentine banks during the Hundred Years' War

- 1345: Bankruptcy of the Bardi and Peruzzi; depression, Great crash of the 1340s
- 1380: Ciompi Revolt in Florence. Crash of the early 1380s
- 1401: Italian bankers expelled from Aragon in 1401, England in 1403, France in 1410
- 1433: Fiscal crisis in Florence after wars with Milan and Lucca
- 1464: Death of Cosimo de Medici: loans called in; wave of bankruptcies in Florence
- 1470: Edward IV default to the Medici during the Wars of the Roses
- 1478: Bruges branch of the Medici bank liquidated on bad debts
- 1494: Overthrow of the Medici after the capture of Florence by Charles VIII of France
- 1525: Siege of Genoa by forces of Spain and the Holy Roman Empire; coup in 1527
- 1557: Philip II of Spain restructuring of debts inherited from Charles V
- 1566: Start of the Dutch Revolt against Spain: disruption of Spanish trade
- 1575: Philip II default: Financial crisis of 1575–79 affected Genoese creditors
- 1596: Philip II default: Financial crisis of 1596 severely affected Genoese businessmen
- 1607: Spanish state bankruptcy: failure of Genoese banks
- 1619: Kipper-und-Wipperzeit: Monetary crisis at the outbreak of the Thirty Years' War
- 1627: Spanish bankruptcy: collapse of Genoese banks and the Fuggers
- 1637: End of the Dutch Tulipmania; also, Dutch East India Company shares, canals
- 1648: French state bankruptcy, eliminated the Italian bankers
- 1652: Outbreak of the First Anglo-Dutch War: attacks by Britain on Dutch shipping
- 1666: Second Anglo-Dutch War: disruption of the Dutch spice fleet
- 1672: Rampjaar (Disaster Year) in Holland: French/English invasion
- 1696: English government debt crisis during the Nine Years' War against France

It's frightening to think that you might not know something, but more frightening to think that, by and large, the world is run by people who have faith that they know exactly what is going on.

Amos Tversky

- 1705: English crisis during the War of the Spanish Succession against France
- 1720: Collapse of the South Sea Bubble in England and Mississippi Bubble in France
- 1761: English government debt crisis over the Seven Years' War against France
- 1769: Collapse of the Bengal Bubble in East India Company stock
- 1772: Credit Crisis in London and the American colonies
- 1783: Economic depression in Britain and America after the Revolutionary War
- 1792: Boom and bust in the First Bank of the United States after Hamilton's refunding
- 1797: Land speculation bubble burst. Bank run in England on fear of French invasion
- 1802: Boom and bust after the Peace of Amiens between Britain and France
- 1807: Jefferson's Embargo Act: restriction of trade with Britain
- 1812: Outbreak of the War of 1812 between America and Britain
- 1819: Land bubble burst; bank failures. Tightening by the Second Bank of the U.S.
- 1825: Emerging market (Latin America) bubble burst in London
- 1837: Collapse of bubbles in canals, cotton, and land; run on banks
- 1847: Collapse of railway boom in London (following Bank Charter Act)
- 1857: Global market panic; railway bubble; failure of Ohio Life Co.
- 1866: Failure of Overend Gurney and Co. in London; banking crisis
- 1869: Black Friday in New York: collapse of Gould and Fisk gold speculation
- 1873: Railroad bubble; Jay Cooke failure; end of silver coinage
- 1877: Great Railroad Strike: deflation and wage cuts following the Panic of 1873
- 1884: Tightening by New York City national banks; bank failures in New York
- 1893: Railroad bubble burst, bank failures, run on gold reserves; Sherman Silver Act

There are three kinds of intelligence: one kind understands things for itself, the other appreciates what others can understand, the third understands neither for itself nor through others. This first kind is excellent, the second good, and the third kind useless.
Niccolo Machiavelli

- 1896: Run on silver reserves; commodity price declines; National Bank of Illinois failure
- 1901: Cornering of Northern Pacific Railway stock
- 1907: Bankers' Panic: cornering of United Copper Co.; failure of Knickerbocker Trust Co.
- 1910: Enforcement of Sherman Antitrust Act: breakup of Standard Oil Co.
- 1913: Drain of gold reserves to Europe in lead-up to WWI
- 1921: Depression of 1920–21: demobilization, monetary tightening; severe deflation
- 1929: Wall Street Crash/Black Tuesday: collapse of 1920s boom
- 1932: Great Depression trough: widespread bank failures
- 1938: Monetary and fiscal tightening following New Deal: Roosevelt Recession
- 1942: Response to Japanese/German successes in WWII
- 1948: Monetary tightening by the Federal Reserve; recession of 1949
- 1953: Monetary tightening to combat post–Korean War inflation in 1952
- 1957: Eisenhower Recession: monetary tightening to combat inflation
- 1962: Kennedy Slide/Flash Crash; Cuban Missile Crisis
- 1969: Nixon Recession: monetary and fiscal tightening to combat inflation and deficit
- 1974: Oil crisis (OPEC embargo): rising inflation and unemployment; stagflation
- 1979: Energy crisis (Iranian Revolution): monetary tightening under Paul Volcker
- 1982: Continued Fed tightening on energy crisis; defaults by Mexico, Brazil, Argentina
- 1984: Continental Illinois bank failure and seizure by the FDIC
- 1987: Black Monday: global market crash, collapse of speculative boom
- 1990: Gulf War: spike in oil price; recession of 1990–92
- 1994: Tequila Crisis: Mexico peso devaluation; Federal Reserve rate hikes
- 1998: Asia crisis (began 1997), Russia default, LTCM failure

There is no profit taking per se. We only exit on stop-losses, because profit taking would interfere with the unlimited upside potential we have, in theory, on every position. Our stop-loss policy is an actuarial model that analyzes the probability and consequences of hitting stops placed at various prices relative to the current market level. This allows us to estimate the expected loss associated with each possible exit point and hence to construct an optimal liquidation schedule.

Paul Mulvaney

- 2001: Collapse of Dot-com bubble; 9/11 attacks; corporate accounting scandals
- 2008: Collapse of housing bubble; Global Financial Crisis; Lehman, AIG etc. failures
- 2011: U.S. debt ceiling crisis and credit rating downgrade; eurozone sovereign debt crisis
- 2015: End of the Federal Reserve's zero interest rate policy (quantitative easing ended 2014)
- 2016: Brexit

In omnia paratus. Prepared for all things.

The surprise event list will never stop expanding. They say history is never the same, but it sure rhymes more often than not. That rhyming was why the following passage was added to my second edition in Fall 2005. It was commentary from *The Economist* circa February 2004:

The success of options valuation is the story of a simple, asymptotically correct idea, taken more seriously than it deserved, and then used extravagantly, with hubris, as a crutch to human thinking.
Emanuel Derman[78]

> The size of banks' bets is rising rapidly the world over. This is because potential returns have fallen as fast as markets have risen, so banks have had to bet more in order to continue generating huge profits. The present situation "is not dissimilar" to the one that preceded the collapse of LTCM . . . banks are "walking themselves to the edge of the cliff." This is because—as all past financial crises have shown—the risk-management models they use woefully underestimate the savage effects of big shocks, when everybody is trying to wriggle out of their positions at the same time . . . By regulatory fiat, when banks' positions sour, they must either stump up more capital or reduce their exposures. Invariably, when markets are panicking, they do the latter. Because everyone else is heading for the exits at the same time, these become more than a little crowded, moving prices against those trying to get out, and requiring still more unwinding of positions. It has happened many times before with more or less calamitous consequences . . . There are any number of potential flashpoints: a rout in the dollar, say, or a huge spike in the oil price, or a big emerging market getting into trouble again. If it does happen, the chain reaction could be particularly devastating this time.[77]

That *prediction* unfolded like a movie script in 2008. And it's guaranteed to unfold again—though no one can accurately predict the next tsunami's landfall.

Former LTCM counsel sees we are on borrowed time: "The reason to revisit the story [LTCM] now is to show how the 2008 panic was foretold by 1998's events. Circumstances were different in 1998 and 2008, yet the dynamics were the same. Disturbingly, the next panic is now foretold by both 1998 and 2008. No lessons were learned. Elites simply expanded the bailout each time. Except next time the panic will be too large, and the bailout too small to stop it."[80] Nassim Taleb clarified further in easily understood lay terms in November 2016: "The market has been on *Novocain* since 2009."

It seems LTCM could have survived one Nobel prize winner, but with two, they were doomed.

Frederic Townsend[79]

Still, numbed, and awash in zombie-film fascination, the average Joe will sit there, as Hunter S. Thompson crooned: "In a nation ruled by swine, all pigs are upward-mobile—and the rest of us are fucked until we can put our acts together: Not necessarily to Win, but mainly to keep from Losing Completely. We owe that to ourselves and our crippled self-image as something better than a nation of *panicked sheep.*"

Enjoy the ride. You can't stop it.

I'd rather be the second person going in the right door, then the first person going in the wrong door. React > predict.

Larry Tentarelli

Summary Food for Thought

- Trend following is generally on the right side of *surprise.*
- "It was a stunning development!"
- Value-at-risk (VAR) models measure volatility, not risk.
- Hunt Taylor: "The single worst descriptor of negative events is the hundred-year flood. Am I wrong? How many hundred-year floods have we lived through in this room? Statistically maybe we should have lived through one and we lived through seven now at this point."
- *Young America in Wall Street* (1857): "The sooner the people of the United States make up their minds that the financial simoom of 1857 eclipses every other crisis since the time that Columbus was under obligations to a North American savage for a raccoon steak, the better."
- Thomas F. Woodlock (1866–1945): "The principles of successful stock speculation are based on the supposition that people will continue in the future to make the mistakes that they have made in the past."
- Peter Tchir: "My concern is that when something comes to bite us in the butt, it's not going to be something we've traditionally looked at. And it's going to take a while for the markets to adjust."[81]
- Morgan Housel: "A normal person isn't capable of leveraging their portfolio 100-to-1, losing everything when the market sneezes, and

Corporations make good and bad decisions every day offers one dealer. P&G made a bad trading decision. But if they came in with a Pampers diapers line that flopped, you wouldn't have hearings in Congress, would you?[82]

When the mind is in a state of uncertainty, the smallest impulse directs it to either side. [Lat., Dum in dubio est animus, paulo momento huc illuc impellitur.]

Terence (Publius Terentius Afer)

blaming it on a 25-sigma event. You need a PhD in physics to convince yourself of that."

- Wolfgang Münchau: "The curse of our time is fake maths. Think of it as fake news for numerically literate intellectuals: it is the abuse of statistics and economic models to peddle one's own political prejudice. The fakeness of the maths lies in an exaggerated inference. Economic models have their uses, as do opinion polls. They provide information to policymakers and markets. But nobody can see through the fog of the future."

Thinking Outside the Box

5

How to hit home runs: I swing as hard as I can, and I try to swing right through the ball . . . The harder you grip the bat, the more you can swing it through the ball, and the farther the ball will go. I swing big, with everything I've got. I hit big or I miss big. I like to live as big as I can.

—Babe Ruth

What is striking is that the leading thinkers across varied fields—including horse betting, casino gambling, and investing—all emphasize the same point. We call it the Babe Ruth effect: even though Ruth struck out a lot, he was one of baseball's greatest hitters.

—Michael J. Mauboussin[1]

Since the first edition of *Trend Following*, sports analytics has exploded. In the last decade professional sports have undergone a remodeling, with teams scrambling to change strategies to accommodate untold new trends in statistical analysis. There haven't necessarily been major rule changes, nor have there been any substantial changes to the venues or the equipment. Instead, the renaissance is rooted in an unconventional process known as *sabermetrics*.[3]

Today, every major professional sports team either has an analytics department or an analytics expert on staff. The popularity of data driven decision making in sports has trickled down to the fans too,

Lenny [Dykstra] didn't let his mind mess him up. . . . Only a psychological freak could approach a 100-mph fastball aimed not all that far from his head with total confidence. "Lenny was so perfectly designed, emotionally, to play the game of baseball. . . . He was able to instantly forget any failure and draw strength from every success. He had no concept of failure."

Moneyball[2]

as they are consuming more analytical content than ever. There are now entire websites dedicated to the research and analysis of sports statistics, i.e., FiveThirtyEight.com.* The use of analytics has enabled organizations and players to build a more efficient mousetrap, and it will impact every aspect of high school, collegiate, and professional sports.[4]

From my perspective, the sports analytics revolution also happens to offer an instructive way for traders to digest trend following from an alternate vantage. Sabermetrics might be the best *new* illustration for bringing people into the study of *numbers* to the exclusion of fundamentals.

Baseball

Failure is not fatal, but failure to change might be.
John Wooden

Baseball has always been a passion of mine. My playing career went from Little League into college for one year, and I've watched more baseball than I care to admit. My childhood friend Kevin Gallaher even made the Houston Astros 40-man roster for a few years in the 1990s. We played and talked baseball on almost every team for 10 years as kids, then into high school and during summers while in college. To this day I admire from afar, for example, David Ortiz's 2016 hitting in his last season and at his age (40): 38 homeruns, 48 doubles, 127 runs batted in, and a .315 batting average. Awesome.

I love this game and the numbers that go with it. And I've known instinctively for some time that baseball and trend following have much in common. But it wasn't until the revolution, when everyone was acknowledging the *numbers*, that the similarities truly hit me. Not surprisingly, this was about the time trend follower John W. Henry bought the Boston Red Sox.

Henry connects baseball and trend following in Michael Lewis's *Moneyball*: "People in both fields [stock market and baseball] operate with beliefs and biases. To the extent that you can eliminate both and replace them with data, you gain a clear advantage. Many people think they are smarter than others in the stock market and that the market itself has no intrinsic intelligence as if it's inert. Many people think they are smarter than others in baseball and that the game on the field is simply what they think through their set of images/beliefs. Actual data

---

* Note: More on Nate Silver in Chapter 9.

from the market means more than individual perception/belief. The same is true in baseball."[5]

And as is evident in trend following performance data, trend followers like David Harding, Bill Dunn, and John W. Henry swing for the fence. They hit home runs in performance. If they coached a baseball team they would be Earl Weaver, the former manager of the Baltimore Orioles. He designed his offenses to maximize the chance of a three-run homer. He didn't bunt, and he had a special taste for guys who got on base and guys who hit home runs.[6]

The general complacency of baseball people—even those of undoubted intelligence—toward mathematical examination of what they regard properly and strictly as their own dish of tea is not too astonishing. I would be willing to go as far as pretending to understand why none of four competent and successful executives of second-division ball clubs were most reluctant to employ probabilistic methods of any description . . . but they did not even want to hear about them!

Earnshaw Cook[7]

Ed Seykota uses a clever baseball analogy to explain his view of absolute returns (and home runs): "When you're up to bat, it doesn't pay to *hedge* your swing. True for stocks and true for [Barry] Bonds."[9] Lesson: If you are going to play, play hard. Swing with determination and if you miss, so be it. You will get another swing.

Babe Ruth, hero of the Yankees, hero of baseball, and arguably one of the greatest sports legends of all time was known for his prolific home runs. However, he had another habit not talked about as much: striking out. In fact, even with a lifetime batting average of .342, he spent a lot of time going back to the dugout *out*. From a pure numbers perspective, he saw more failure than success. Ruth understood the big home runs helped more than the strikeouts hurt. He summarized his philosophy: "Every strike brings me closer to the next home run."

Richard Driehaus, a successful trader who has made millions trading trends, backed Ruth: "A third paradigm [pushed in the financial press] is don't try to hit home runs—you make the most money by hitting a lot of singles. I couldn't disagree more. I believe you can make the most money hitting home runs. But, you also need a discipline to avoid striking out. That is my sell, discipline. I try to cut my losses and let my winners run."[10]

Life is too dynamic to remain static.

John W. Henry[8]

But swinging for the fence is often characterized as reckless by the indoctrinated and or uninitiated. One trading competitor once said John W. Henry was Dave Kingman, referring to the ex-ballplayer famous for either hitting home runs or striking out. Henry saw talk as unfair: "I've been doing this for 20 years, and every time there's a change in the market, they say I should change my ways. But every time there's a period when we don't do well, it's followed by one in which we do extraordinarily well."[11] Henry's multi-decade performance was much closer to Babe Ruth's than Kingman's. Consider the actual hitting statistics of Ruth and Kingman (see Table 5.1).

Even before he trained with legend Richard Dennis, Jim DiMaria had learned an important trading principle in the less lucrative arena of baseball statistics: The players who score the most runs are home run hitters, not those with consistent batting records. "It's the same with trading. Consistency is something to strive for, but it's not always optimal. Trading is a waiting game. You sit and wait and make a lot of money all at once. The profits tend to come in bunches. The secret is to go sideways between the home runs, not lose too much between them."[12]

"What kind of people are getting rich these days? People like John W. Henry." That is, people on the nerdly end of the spectrum who have a comfort with both statistical analysis and decision-making in an uncertain environment.

Michael Lewis[13]

When John W. Henry purchased the Boston Red Sox, he understood that a combination of good management and hard science was the most efficient way to run a major league baseball team. As a trend follower, Henry had been exploiting market inefficiencies for decades.

Michael Lewis[14]

TABLE 5.1: Babe Ruth versus Dave Kingman

	Babe Ruth	Dave Kingman
At Bats	8,399	6,677
Hits	2,873	1,575
Runs	2,174	901
Home Runs	714	442
Batting Average	.342	.236
Slugging	.690	.478

Compare the slugging percentages. Kingman could not be considered a great run producer by any measure. On the other hand, John W. Henry's performance numbers were consistently outsized. He had a great slugging percentage. Of course, most want the fantasy: big homeruns, but zero strikeouts.

To further illustrate, consider a modern-day example: blue-collar Joe versus the entrepreneur. Blue-collar Joe is paid the same sum every two weeks like clockwork. In terms of *winning percentage*, blue collar Joe is king: His ratio of hours worked to hours paid is one to one, a perfect 100 percent. He has a steady job and a steady life. But the security he feels is an illusion—his paycheck comes at the whim of his local economy, his industry, and even the foreman of his plant. The pay isn't exactly impressive; it gives him a solid, livable life, but not much more.

In contrast, consider the entrepreneur, the trader or the trend follower. Paydays are wildly irregular. He frequently goes for months, sometimes years, without seeing tangible reward for his sweat and toil. The winning percentage is, in a word, pathetic. For every 10 big ideas or trades he has, 7 of them wind up in the circular file. Of the remaining three, two of those fizzle out within a year—another big chunk of time, money, and effort down the drain. However, don't feel too sorry for the poor entrepreneur or trend trader who spends time losing. He has a passion for life, he controls his own destiny, and his last idea/trade paid off with a seven-figure check.

Billy Beane

Famed sports agent Leigh Steinberg sets the modern sports-and-numbers stage: "Winning in team sports has always been a function of superior ownership, front offices and coaching. Decision making as which players to draft, trade, develop, coach and which system to play have traditionally been made by a *gut* feeling or adherence to past traditions. But then came Oakland Athletics' General Manager, former ballplayer Billy Beane."[15]

Moneyball made Beane's no fancy stadium, poor owner story famous. In fact, his small-market team's payroll is miniscule compared to the Yankees. However, his teams have been some of the best and they have reached the playoffs a lot.

The philosophy Billy Beane helped unleash has proved almost all of the old baseball truisms to be false, i.e., talent, character, chemistry. The genius behind sabermetrics was a mechanical engineer named Earnshaw Cook, who, in the early 1960s, compiled reams of data that overturned baseball's conventional wisdom. However, when he presented the data to executives at struggling teams, they pushed him away. Cook then wrote a book called *Percentage Baseball*, based on his statistical research that was irrefutable.[16]

Look closer at Beane's approach to baseball and you learn he uses actuarial analysis to determine the odds of a high school pitcher becoming a major leaguer. And, in drafting and acquiring talent, he relies on those sabermetric truths. For instance, if a team draws a lot of walks and hits a lot of home runs while giving up few of each, that team will win a lot of ballgames. Not surprisingly, Beane has stocked his team with sluggers who take walks and control pitchers who rarely give up home runs.[19]

> *When I started writing I thought if I proved X was a stupid thing to do that people would stop doing X. I was wrong.*
>
> Bill James

> *There is a core of institutional investment managers, primarily in Europe, who manage billions of dollars for clients, who have waited for me to fail for more than 20 years. They have an inherent bias against the notion that data or mechanical formulas can lead to success over time in markets. They have personally watched my success now for more than 20 years. Yet, if anything, they are now no more convinced than they were 20 years ago that I am going to be successful in the future using data over analysis. I am not legendary on Wall Street or off. Bill James is, and I assume the inherent bias against him within baseball will increase now that he has taken sides.*
>
> John W. Henry[17]

Bill James

What Earnshaw Cook started, Bill James took to a deity level. James defined sabermetrics as "the search for objective knowledge about baseball." Thus, sabermetrics attempts to answer objective questions about baseball, such as "which player on the Red Sox contributed the most to the team's offense?" or "How many home runs will Ken Griffey hit next year?" It cannot deal with the subjective judgments, which are also important to the game, such as "Who is your favorite player?" or "That was a great game."[20] Sabermetrics challenges our perceptions, which are often misguided from emotional bias.[21]

James' enduring work from his 1981 Baseball Abstract illustrates his unique take by contrasting sports writing with sabermetrics:

1. Sports writing draws on the available evidence, and forces conclusions by selecting and arranging that evidence so that it points in the direction

desired. Sabermetrics introduces new evidence, previously unknown data derived from original source material.[22]

John W. Henry knew a dispassionate statistical investigation could be used to help shape a baseball team. "It is remarkably similar, I just happened to apply 'quant' to an area that's extremely lucrative."[18]

2. Sports writing designs its analysis to fit the situation being discussed; sabermetrics designs methods which would be applicable not only in the present case but in any other comparable situation. The sportswriter says this player is better than that one because this player had 20 more home runs, 10 more doubles, and 40 more walks and those things are more important than a players 60 extra base hits and 31 extra stolen bases, and besides, there is always defense and if all else fails, team leadership. If player C is introduced into this discussion, he is a whole new article. Sabermetrics puts into place formulas, schematic designs, or theories of relationships, which could compare not only this player to that one, but to any player who might be introduced into the discussion.[23]

The nature of markets is to trend. The nature of life is to trend.
John W. Henry[26]

3. Sportswriters characteristically begin their analysis with a position on an issue; sabermetrics begins with the issue itself. The most over-used form in journalism is the diatribe, the endless impassioned and quasi-logical pitches for the cause of the day—Mike Norris for the Cy Young Award, Rickey Henderson for MVP, Gil Hodges for the Hall of Fame, everybody for lower salaries and let's all line up against the DH. Sports writing "analysis" is largely an adversary process, with the most successful sportswriter being the one who is the most effective advocate of his position.... sabermetrics by its nature is unemotional, and non-committal. The sportswriter attempts to be a good lawyer; the sabermetrician, a fair judge.[24]

I feel I've had an advantage over the years because I am clear about a couple of things: It is part of the nature of life itself to trend, and I will never have a complete or full understanding of anything. Therefore, all investment decisions should be based on what can be measured rather than what might be predicted or felt.
John W. Henry[27]

Trend following's connection with baseball picked up major steam when John W. Henry hired Bill James. James, the consummate outsider, was brought in to statistically enrich Henry's Red Sox with his numbers-centric perspective. But James' controversial views are harsh medicine for old-time baseball professionals. For example, he was blunt in his negative assessment of Don Zimmer, the former Yankees coach, and others: "An assortment of half-wits, nincompoops, and Neanderthals like Don Zimmer who are not only allowed to pontificate on whatever strikes them, but are actually solicited and employed to do this."[25]

Bad feelings from the baseball establishment toward James are mutual: "A little fat guy with a beard who knows nothing about nothing," is how Hall of Fame manager Sparky Anderson once described James, who's neither short nor fat.[28]

Personalities aside, John W. Henry knew baseball strategy had to change. Henry was convinced baseball was putting too much emphasis on tools—baseball jargon for athletic ability—and not enough on performance. The on-the-field success of the Oakland A's, then the only team using sabermetrics, confirmed Henry's view. Henry's first team, the Florida Marlins, would draft athletes, while the A's would draft baseball players.[29]

Part of the problem, from both Henry and James's perspective, was the old guard's love of an Adonis athlete over pure production—hitting, power, and plate discipline. Would you rather have Tim Tebow, who looks the physical part, or David Ortiz, with the Hall of Fame statistics and a healthy midsection? To Henry, in both baseball and trend trading, *producing* must be the goal: "People in both baseball and the financial markets operate with beliefs and biases. To the extent you can eliminate both and replace them with data, you gain a clear advantage. Many people think they are smarter than others in the stock market, and that the market itself has no intrinsic intelligence—as if it's inert. Similarly, many people think they are smarter than others in baseball, and that the game on the field is simply what they think it is, filtered through their set of images and beliefs. But actual data from the market means more than individual perception/belief. And the same is true in baseball."[31]

For nearly 25 years, there's been a huge food fight in baseball. The argument was basic: How do you evaluate a player? On one side were general managers, scouts and managers. For the most part, they evaluated players the old-fashioned way—with their eyes, stopwatches, and radar guns and by looking at statistics which were popularized in the nineteenth century. Their mind-set was always, "How fast does he run? How hard does he throw? What's his batting average? Does he look like a major leaguer should look?" On the other side—led by statistical gurus such as Bill James and Pete Palmer, and assisted by countless lesser seamheads *(including, at times, me)—were the geeks, the outsiders, mere fans, who thought they knew better.*

Thomas Boswell
The Washington Post[30]

Stats Take Over

Boston Red Sox Nation still debates whether Pedro Martinez should have been lifted in the eighth inning of game 7 of the 2003 American League Championship Series against the Yankees. He was left in, and the Yankees rallied from three runs down to win the series. Red Sox manager Grady Little was blamed for Boston's loss and fired soon thereafter. Many wondered if he was unfairly scapegoated for a decision others might have made, too. After all, Martinez was his ace, and the manager's *gut* told him to stay with his ace.

It's like any field. There's a vested interest in maintaining the status quo so you don't have to learn anything new.

Rob Neyer
ESPN[32]

Perhaps in this situation, Martinez gets through the eighth 9 times out of 10. After all, the percentage of innings in which a pitcher gives up three or more runs is small, and Martinez was a Hall of Fame pitcher. However, the numbers say leaving him in was the absolutely wrong decision. After 105 pitches in a given start, his batting average against rises to .370. He ended up throwing 123 pitches in Game 7.

The firing of Grady Little ultimately was all about *numbers*:

> Grady isn't a stats guy, plain and simple. He's an old school manager who goes with his gut and defers to his partially informed conscience when making decisions. Contrast this with the front office, which has transformed itself into a sabermetric, number-crunching machine, and the divide is clear as day—Fast forward to the eighth inning of Game 7 of the ALCS. Grady sends Pedro back onto the mound to the surprise of many who assumed he would be yanked after throwing exactly 100 pitches. Opponents hit .364 off Pedro this year after his 105th pitch—even Tony Clark could hit Pedro in the late innings.[33]

I had learned something from publishing Moneyball. *I learned that if you look long enough for an argument against reason, you will find it.*
Michael Lewis[34]

The late, great Stephen Jay Gould, a numbers man himself (read his fantastic *The Median Isn't the Message* about cancer treatments online) and lifelong baseball fan, offered indirect insight into the decision-making process that left Pedro Martinez in:

> Everybody knows about hot hands. The only problem is that no such phenomenon exists. The Stanford psychologist Amos Tversky studied every basket made by the Philadelphia 76ers for more than a season. He found, first of all, that probabilities of making a second basket did not rise following a successful shot. Moreover, the number of "runs," or baskets in succession, was no greater than what a standard random, or coin-tossing, model would predict. Of course Larry Bird, the great forward of the Boston Celtics, will have more sequences of five than Joe Airball—but not because he has greater will or gets in that magic rhythm more often. Bird has longer runs because his average success rate is so much higher, and random models predict more frequent and longer sequences. If Bird shoots field goals at 0.6 probability of success, he will get five in a row about once every 13 sequences (0.65). If Joe, by contrast, shoots only 0.3, he will get his five straight only about once in 412 times. In other words, we need no special explanation for the apparent pattern of long runs. There is no ineffable "causality of circumstance" (if I may call it that), no definite reason born of the particulars that make for heroic myths—courage in the clinch, strength in

adversity, etc. You only have to know a person's ordinary play in order to predict his sequences.[35]

Gould's friend, Ed Purcell, a Nobel laureate in Physics, conducted intense research on baseball streaks. He concluded that nothing ever happened in baseball above and beyond the frequency predicted by coin-tossing models. The longest runs of wins and losses are as long as they should be.[36]

Had Grady Little played the *numbers* the Red Sox would not have waited until 2004 to finally win the World Series (which they won again in 2007 and 2013). In fact, the 2016 World Series pitted the Chicago Cubs against the Cleveland Indians—two very sabermetrics baseball clubs run by Theo Epstein and Terry Francona, the very two men who most helped John W. Henry win the 2004 and 2007 World Series. One argument against analytics 10 years ago was it would make baseball boring, but the 2016 playoffs were viewed as very exciting. These teams were doing things differently, a big reason for the excitement. Plus, the Chicago Cubs won their first world championship in 108 years—now that's a number![38]

When Grady Little let Pedro continue pitching into the eighth in Game 7 of the ALCS against the Yankees, he provided the perfect demonstrator of why the Red Sox fired him after his second winning season in Boston. Little explained his move (which allowed the Yankees to tie and eventually win) after the game: "We trained him to work just like that deep into a game. When he tells me he has enough in the tank to keep going, that's the man I want out there. That's no different than what we've done the last two years." In fact, the stats said just the opposite. Pedro pitched into the eighth only five times in his 29 regular-season starts, and simply didn't pitch well after he'd thrown 100 pitches, the number he'd tossed before taking the mound in the eighth. In fact, during 2003, opponents' batting averages went up .139 after Pedro tossed his 105th pitch—strong evidence that he'd continue to weaken. That it would turn out badly was likely, as most everyone knew—and as the Red Sox computers knew.[37]

However, let's be clear: This is not only a baseball evolution. Since Billy Beane first started utilizing statistical predictors, every Major League Baseball team has adopted a copycat system to an extent, the NFL now hires analytics executives, and the NBA has introduced the most sophisticated technologies in terms of performance information.[39]

Look no further than the NBA's Golden State Warriors and Stephen Curry: "What's really interesting is sometimes in venture capital and doing startups the whole world can be wrong," said the team's primary owner, Joe Lacob, a longtime partner at Silicon Valley venture capital firm Kleiner Perkins Caufield & Byers. "No one really executed a game plan—a team-building architecture—around the 3-pointer."[40]

From the beginning of his ownership, Lacob placed unusually strong emphasis on *numbers*. Their initial data research yielded many insights, but the Warriors eventually zeroed in on the 3-point line. NBA players made roughly the same percentage of shots from 23 feet as they did from 24. But because the three-point line ran between them, the values of those two shots were radically different. Shot attempts from 23 feet had an average value of 0.76 points, while 24-footers were worth 1.09. This, the Warriors concluded, was an opportunity. By moving back a few inches before shooting, a basketball player could improve his rate of return by 43 percent.[41]

That type of thinking and what many of these new data sources have in common is an emphasis on *process*. Outcomes such as strikes, walks, home runs, three-point shooting, and so forth—are already well tracked. But this new generation of data allows analysts to understand how those outcomes are generated, perhaps even down to the level of a player's brain activity.[42]

Nonetheless it will be a fight every step of the way, as curmudgeonly New York Mets manager Terry Collins growled in early 2016:

> I'm not sure how much an old-school guy can add to the game today. It's become a young man's game, especially with all of the technology stuff you've got to be involved in. I'm not very good at it. I don't enjoy it like other people do. I'm not going to sit there today and look at all of these [expletive] numbers and try to predict this guy is going to be a great player. OPS this. OPS that. GPS. LCSs. DSDs. You know who has good numbers? Good [expletive] players. That's just me. I don't have to apologize to anybody.[43]

Ego is a *killer.*

Jack Lambert couldn't get on the field as a backup linebacker. . . . The kid in front of him was really their leader, kind of the heart and soul of the Kent State defense. . . . Through a series of circumstances the kid dropped out of school and went to work for Mick Jagger; he was his security guy on tour with the Stones, and Lambert became the starting middle linebacker. He probably would have never played had that not happened. And you have a Hall of Fame player. Sometimes things take a turn, and then once some players get that opportunity and they get in there—the Tom Bradys of the world, or whoever—you can't get them out of there—[like] Lou Gehrig.[44]

Bill Belichick
October 2016
New England Patriots press conference

Summary Food for Thought

- Thinking in terms of odds, finding that edge, is a common denominator for baseball and trend following.
- Bill James: "I always admire people who have the courage to confront the conventional wisdom—people within the system. Those of us on the outside, it's easy for us to say whatever we think, because there are no consequences to it. It's much harder to say, 'I think the conventional wisdom is full of beans, and I'm not going to go along with it,' when you're inside the system and exposed to the possibility of actual failure. I think the people who do this drive the world to get better, whereas the people who snipe at anybody who dares suggest that the conventional wisdom is malarkey are, in my view, gutless conspirators in the mediocrity of the universe."
- Leonard Koppett in *A Thinking Man's Guide to Baseball* (1967): "Statistics are the lifeblood of baseball. In no other sport are so many available and studied so assiduously by participants and fans. Much of the game's appeal, as a conversation piece, lies in the opportunity the

Sabermetrics is an unlikely marriage between mathematicians and jock culture.[45]

fan gets to back up opinions and arguments with convincing figures, and it is entirely possible that more American boys have mastered long division by dealing with batting averages than in any other way."

- Paul Fisher: "A passion for statistics is the earmark of a literate people."
- Steven Pinker: "Cognitive psychology tells us that the unaided human mind is vulnerable to many fallacies and illusions because of its reliance on its memory for vivid anecdotes rather than systematic statistics."
- Jameis Winston on staying NFL focused: "We're just trying to be 1-0 every week. It's so easy to think about the future, but it doesn't help you."

The truth of a theory is in your mind, not in your eyes.
Albert Einstein[46]

Human Behavior 6

Human nature never changes. Therefore, the stock market never changes. Only the faces, the pockets, the suckers, and the manipulators, the wars, the disasters and the technologies change. The market itself never changes. How can it? Human nature never changes, and human nature runs the market—not reason, not economics, and certainly not logic. It is our human emotions that drive the market, as they do most other things on this planet.

—Jesse Livermore (1940)

We are not really interested in people who are experts at the French stock market or German bond markets due to the technical nature of the trading . . . it does not take a huge monster infrastructure: neither Harvard MBAs nor people from Goldman Sachs . . . I would hate it if the success of Chesapeake was based on my being some great genius. It's the system that wins. Fundamental economics are nice but useless in trading. True fundamentals are always unknown. Our system allows for no intellectual capability.

—Jerry Parker[1]

Simple, robust solutions are easier to find than robust people or firms willing to apply them.

Jason Russell[2]

Trend following is as much about observing and understanding human behavior as it is about moving averages, breakouts, and position sizing. Understanding human behavior and how it relates with markets is commonly referred to as *behavioral economics* or *behavioral finance*. It evolved from the contradiction between classical economic theory (EMT) and reality. The assumption people act rationally, have identical values and access to information, and use rational decision making is one preposterous assumption.

There is an old Hindhu saying: 'The World is as we are'. Are you tired of seeing the condition of the world around you? Start by changing yourself. Be the change you want to see in world. Be what you want to attract more in your life. Being loving to yourself is the fastest way to enjoy a more fun and productive life.
Charles Poliquin

However, trend following strategies only work if price trends continue. But why should trends continue? If prices initially underreact to either good or bad news, trends tend to continue as prices slowly move to fully reflect changes in fundamental value. These trends have the potential to continue even further as investors herd (or chase trends). Herding can cause prices to overreact and move beyond fundamental value after the initial under-reaction. Naturally, all trends must eventually end, as deviation from fair value cannot continue infinitely.[3]

Said another way, people are irrational as hell and seldom make rational decisions even if they think they do. That's not my one-man opinion either. I have had the good fortune to learn from and interview the top minds in the field of behavioral economics and finance, including Nobel Prize winners Daniel Kahneman and Vernon Smith, Dan Ariely, Colin Camerer, Christopher Chabris, Robert Cialdini, K. Anders Ericsson, Gerd Gigerenzer, Donald MacKenzie, Spyros Makridakis, Terrance Odean, Steven Pinker, Laurie Santos, Hersh Shefrin, Daniel Simons, Paul Slovic, Didier Sornette, Meir Statman, Brett Steenbarger, and Philip Tetlock to name a few of the best minds in the field. (You can find these interviews on my podcast at www.trendfollowing.com/behavior.)

You can see their contributions to the academic nomenclature: *confirmation bias, sunk cost fallacy, availability heuristic, attentional bias, frequency illusion, anchoring, contrast effect, clustering illusion, insensitivity to sample size, neglect of probability, anecdotal fallacy, halo effect, in-group bias, curse of knowledge, illusion of transparency,* and *hindsight bias,* to name a few of hundreds.

History does not repeat itself; people keep forgetting it. No matter how many stock market bubbles there have been, or will be, investors and their advisors always treat the current one as permanent, sometimes even calling it a new era. *In the meantime, others, myself included, have abandoned all hope of people permanently remembering the lessons of history.*[4]

I believe you can also see their work and all of these assorted biases conceptualized inside systematic trend following strategy. I have yet to see another rules-based approach that tackles EMT's deficiencies head on while giving credence to the behavioral school, and then tying it all together with irrefutable proof in the form of month-by-month track records—going back literally decades.

Prospect Theory

Investment bubbles have always been a part of human market history. For example, seventeenth-century speculators in the Netherlands drove prices of tulip bulbs to such absurd levels some bulbs were priced more than *houses*. The inevitable crash followed. Since then, from the Great Depression to the Dot-com implosion to October 2008, investors can't and will never steer clear of manias. They repeatedly make the same mistakes over and over.

Daniel Kahneman, who was the first psychologist to win the Nobel Prize in Economics (see my podcast episode #212), attributed market manias to investors' illusion of control, calling the illusion *prospect theory*. He studied the intellectual underpinnings of investing—how traders estimate odds and calculate risks—to prove how often people act from the mistaken belief they know more than they do.

To be a good trader, you need to trade with your eyes open, recognize real trends and turns, and not waste time or energy on regrets and wishful thinking.

Alexander Elder

Kahneman and his associate Amos Tversky found a typical person acts on what they christen the *law of small numbers*—basing broad predictions on narrow samples of data. For instance, if you buy a fund that's beaten the market three years in a row, you become convinced it's on a hot streak. People are unable to stop themselves from overgeneralizing the importance of a few supporting facts. Limited statistical evidence satisfies, no matter how inadequate the depiction of reality.[5]

They also determined people dislike losses so much they make irrational decisions to avoid them. This helps explain why some investors sell winning stocks too early, but hold on to losers too long. It is human nature to take the profit from a winner quickly on the assumption it won't last for long, while sticking with a loser in the futile hope it will bounce back.[6]

Trend following by design knows if you don't cut your losses, if you don't exit with a small loss, loss will grow like a cancer. And the more you struggle with your small loss, unable to accept it, the larger it will become and the harder it will be to deal with it in the future—if you are still solvent by then. The problem with accepting a loss is it forces people to admit they are wrong. Human beings don't like being wrong—ego rules decision making.

Knowing others is wisdom;
Knowing the self is enlightenment.
Mastering others requires force;
Mastering self needs strength.

Lao Tsu[7]

Accordingly, a discussion of why investors are their own worst enemies starts with sunk costs. A *sunk cost* is a cost that has already incurred that you can't recoup. One you don't get back. Thinking in sunk costs lets you see a loss for what it is—a loss. Although sunk costs should not influence present decisions, humans have a hard time letting go. An investor might buy more of a stock even though it is tanking because of their initial decision to buy it ("I am right!"). That investor archetype can then say proudly, "I bought on a discount!" Now, if the price of the stock never goes up again, as is so often the case, his theory implodes with the concrete lesson of a big loss.

"Take your small loss and go home" is the trend following pièce de résistance. However, too many market players are ambivalent when dealing with sunk costs. Although intellectually people know there is nothing they can do about money already spent and they should move on, emotionally people dwell and worry literally their whole lives.

An experiment with a $10 theater ticket demonstrates the irrationality of sunk costs. Kahneman told one group of students to imagine they have arrived at the theater only to discover they have lost their ticket. "Would you pay another $10 to buy another ticket?" A second group was told to imagine they are going to the play but haven't bought a ticket in advance. When they arrive at the theater, they realize they have lost a $10 bill. Would they still buy a ticket? In both cases, the students were presented with essentially the same simple question: Would you want to spend $10 to see the play? Eighty-eight percent of the second group, which had lost the $10 bill, opted to buy the ticket. However, the first group, the ticket losers, focusing on sunk costs, tended to ask the question in a different way: Am I willing to spend $20 to see a $10 play? Only 46 percent said yes.[8]

Plenty of people are motivated by external factors such as a big salary or the status that comes from having an impressive title or being part of a prestigious company. By contrast, those with leadership potential are motivated by a deeply embedded desire to achieve for the sake of achievement.
Daniel Goleman[9]

This wide spectrum of market behaviors and biases that guarantee losses is endless. These behaviors, the antithesis of trend following, include:

- *Lack of discipline*: It takes an accumulation of knowledge and sharp focus to trade successfully. Many would rather listen to the advice of others than learn for themselves. They are lazy when it comes to the education needed for trading. To quote Fox Mulder's office poster in *The X-Files*: "I Want to Believe!"
- *Impatience*: The human mind has an insatiable need for action. It might be the adrenaline rush or the "gambler's high." Proper trading, however, is about patience and objective decision making, not action addiction.
- *No objectivity*: The inability to disengage emotionally from the market kills investors—literally. Losers in the market "marry" positions. They have no prenuptial agreement with the market.
- *Greed*: The quick money types aim to pick tops or bottoms in the hope they'll be able to "time" trades to guarantee profits. Their desire for quick profits blinds them to the real hard work for winning.

- *Refusal to accept truth*: Media types can't believe truth is price action. As a result, they follow every other fundamental variable (an impossibility), setting the stage for inevitable losses.
- *Impulsive behavior*: Gamblers often jump into a market based on the morning paper's lead. But by the time news has been published, markets have discounted it. Thinking if you act quickly, somehow you will beat everybody else in the great day-trading high frequency race, is the grand recipe for your failure.
- *Inability to stay in the present*: You can't spend your time thinking about how you're going to spend your profits. Trading because you have to have money is the state of mind that keeps you from ever finding the goal.
- *False parallels*: Just because the market behaved one way in 1995 or 2015 does not mean a similar pattern today will give the same result tomorrow.

There is little doubt if you try to bridge the gap between the present and the future with your market predictions, you will be in a continual state of uncertainty whether you admit it or not. Scientists have investigated the impact of extended uncertainty. The conclusion: People react the same way to uncertainty that other animals do when faced with a threat—shifting into *fight-or-flight* mode. Some don't like that fatalistic conclusion, as it leaves them feeling like *cognitive cripples*.

Yet unlike the animal's environment, where the threat passes quickly one way or another, human lives are spent in constant stressful situations, many of which never go away or ever arrive. According to neuroscientist Robert Sapolsky, human beings, unlike other animals, can—and often do—experience stress by imagining stressful situations: "For 99 percent of the beasts on this planet, stressful situations include about three minutes of screaming terror, after which the threat is over or you are over. Humans turn on the exact same stress response thinking about 30-year mortgages. Yet, while thinking about a mortgage is not life threatening, the stress is probably going to last much longer than three minutes. The biggest public health problem in the developed world 50 years from now will be depression."[10]

Traders not prepared for the inevitability of loss will become depressed when they lose money. They will look everywhere except inside, blaming others or events to avoid taking responsibility for their actions. Instead of understanding their own emotional state, they chase

NLP is short for Neuro-Linguistic Programming. The name sounds high tech, yet it is purely descriptive. Neuro refers to neurology, our nervous system—the mental pathways our five senses take which allow us to see, hear, feel, taste, and smell. Linguistic refers to our language ability; how we put together words and phrases to express ourselves, as well as how our silent language of movement and gestures reveals our states, thinking styles and more. Programming, taken from computer science, refers to the idea that our thoughts, feelings and actions are like computer software programs. When we change those programs, just as when we change or upgrade software, we immediately get positive changes in our performance. We get immediate improvements in how we think, feel, act and live.

Charles Faulkner[11]

easy bucks and holy grails to avoid real thinking. It's a cat chasing its tail while running in circles.

Fat, drunk, and stupid is no way to go through life, son.
Dean Wormer
Animal House[13]

You see, some want more money, but feel guilty about admitting those true feelings. A few have lots of money, but want even more and feel guilty. Take a moment to think through your motivations for trading. If you have any reason for trading other than to make money, find something else to do, get a dog, whatever, and avoid the stress. There is nothing good or bad about money. Money is a tool—nothing more, nothing less.

Ayn Rand articulates nonjudgmental and rational attitudes about money:

> You think that money is the root of all evil? Have you ever asked what is the root of money? Money is a tool of exchange, which can't exist unless there are goods produced and men able to produce them. Money is the material shape of the principle that men who wish to deal with one another must deal by trade and give value for value. Money is not the tool of the moochers, who claim your product by tears, or of the looters, who take it from you by force. Money is made possible only by the men who produce. Is this what you consider *evil*?[12]

Self-Knowledge Keys

1. Know what you want. Know who you are, not who you think you should be. Self-awareness gives you the power to pursue what really feeds your soul and the belief that you deserve it.

2. Know the cost of getting what you want. Realize the trade-offs of every choice. People often think if they are clever they can make choices without experiencing any downside. Any road you choose means there is a road you won't experience.

3. Be willing to pay the cost. People often try to negotiate to win a choice without cost. Every choice involves a price; we get to decide what cost we want to pay.[14]

Human behavior *should* reflect a rational approach to money. People are *supposed* to refuse to pay too much for a watch because of the social cachet of a label, but they *still* pay. They are *supposed* to make intelligent objective choices that maximize wealth and financial security, but they don't.

Then what is the motivation behind someone who runs up credit card debt at 25 percent interest, but would never think of dipping into savings to pay off that debt? What is the explanation for people who spend time researching a new car or designer kitchen, but when it comes time to invest, they refuse to learn and then trust some kid banker fresh out of college with their life savings? *Cognitive dissonance* is in play: Some problems run deeper, springing from limiting, unconscious beliefs. For instance, a trader who has labeled himself a one-for-trader, or who learned as a child the biblical story "it's easier for a camel to pass through the eye of a needle than for a rich man to enter the kingdom of God," may subconsciously sabotage his trading to respect his beliefs. They're deeply ingrained in us . . . but if all ethical people think money is bad, "Who's going to get the money?"[15]

David Harding knows deep in his bones the need for proper risk thinking in all of life. At the University of Cambridge he created a professorship to help improve people's understanding of the mathematics of risk. Questions requiring a scientific ability to assess the chances of something happening—or not happening—arise all the time. Here are some examples:

- Following the poisoning of the Russian ex-spy Alexander Litvinenko, traces of polonium-210 were found at various locations in London he had visited. Statistically, how probable is it that someone who visited the same locations at a later stage would contract radiation poisoning?
- An apparently healthy woman is judged to be at risk of breast cancer and is advised to undergo a mastectomy. Should she do so?
- A person has to cross a main road to reach a few shops. Should he walk straight across the road, or use an available footbridge instead?
- How sensible would it be for me to invest in the stock market today? Might delaying improve my prospects greatly?
- A 29-year-old man decides to marry his girlfriend of three years. What is the chance he will meet a more suitable partner at a later stage?

It may readily be conceived that if men passionately bent upon physical gratifications desire greatly, they are also easily discouraged; as their ultimate object is to enjoy, the means to reach that object must be prompt and easy or the trouble of acquiring the gratification would be greater than the gratification itself. Their prevailing frame of mind, then, is at once ardent and relaxed, violent and enervated. Death is often less dreaded by them than perseverance in continuous efforts to one end.

Alexis de Tocqueville[16]

As these examples show, risks must considered in the most ordinary of situations and high-pressure environments alike. But always be careful to not torture the statistics as a form of confirmation bias.

Note: My Gerd Gigerenzer podcasts, episodes 193 and 295, offer more on this topic.

Emotional Intelligence

People want to believe if they are able to discern patterns, count cycles, etc. they will *win*. As a result they are continually making connections and drawing parallels not there. They miss seeing the evidence staring back. Ironically, the real pattern they miss is the pattern of acting with complete confidence to make decisions, right or wrong, in the face of the unknown. The less personal confidence, the more frustrating and demoralizing experiences will be. The more you learn about the markets and yourself, the more confidence unfolds. The greater your confidence, the more effective you become as a trader.

Psychologist Daniel Goleman's bestseller, *Emotional Intelligence*, is a powerful case for broadening the meaning of intelligence to include emotions. Drawing on brain and behavioral research, Goleman demonstrated why people with high IQs often flounder, while people with modest IQs often do extremely well. The factors that influence how well people do in life include self-awareness, self-discipline, intuition, empathy, and an ability to enter the flow of life—character traits most traders would not consider particularly useful for garnering profits from the markets.[17]

You see, Dr. Stadler, people don't want to think. And the deeper they get into trouble, the less they want to think. But by some sort of instinct, they feel that they ought to and it makes them feel guilty. So they'll bless and follow anyone who gives them a justification for not thinking.
Ayn Rand[20]

Being self-aware also means understanding what you want out of life. You know what your goals and values are and you are able to stick to them. For example, if you're offered a high-paying job that doesn't square with your values or your long-term goals, you can turn it down promptly and without regret. If an employee breaches corporate ethics, you deal with it instead of making a half-hearted response because you're pretending it won't happen again.[18]

However, Goleman is not saying you should repress your feelings of anxiety, fear, anger, or sadness. You must acknowledge and understand your emotions for what they are. Like animals, biological impulses drive emotions. There is no way to escape them, but you can learn to self-regulate your feelings and, in so doing, manage them. Self-regulation is the ongoing inner conversation emotionally intelligent engage in to be free from being prisoners of their feelings. If you are able to engage in such a conversation, you still feel bad moods and emotional impulses as everyone else does, but you can learn to control them and even to channel them in useful ways.[19]

A trend follower's ability to delay gratification, stifle his impulsiveness, and shake off the market's inevitable setbacks and upsets, makes him not only a successful trader, but a leader. Goleman found effective leaders all have a high degree of emotional intelligence along with the relevant IQ and technical skills. While other threshold capabilities were entry-level requirements for executive positions, emotional intelligence was the sine qua non of leadership. Without emotional intelligence, someone can have superior training, an incisive and analytical mind, and infinite creativity, but still won't be a great leader.[22]

Over-familiarization with something—an idea, say or a method, or an object—is a trap. Creativity requires something new, a different interpretation, a break from the twin opiates of habit and cliché.
Denise Shekerjian[21]

However, few people live or trade in a vacuum. That sense of being cut off from the world is a common consequence for modern man. This doesn't necessarily mean you need a group of colleagues to hang out with around the water cooler, but objectivity comes from having a balanced life and that means making sure you don't sit at your screen alone 24/7. Who needs or wants to sit there like that anyway?

When popular opinion is nearly unanimous, contrary thinking tends to be most profitable. The reason is that once the crowd takes a position, it creates a short-term, self-fulfilling prophecy. But when a change occurs, everyone seems to change his mind at once.

Gustave Le Bon[24]

Neuro-Linguistic Programming

One of the reasons Richard Dennis and Richard Donchian have been able to teach trend following is found in the field of Neuro-Linguistic Programming (NLP). Top NLP teacher Charles Faulkner sees how to gain the *mental edge*: "NLP's techniques involve moving out negative mental beliefs and replacing them with positive ones. Think of an unpleasant trade as you do that, what happens if you take a breath and go 'ah,' push it out and then trade with it? Much better. People go through fifths of scotch trying to get that feeling. When you get agitated, go 'whoosh' and just step out of it that way and you'll find it's less. Do it again and you'll be at zero real fast."[23]

I first met Faulkner at a trading seminar in 2001. He has the natural gift for explanation. He urges traders to take matters into their own hands and to believe, "I am competent to be confident. I know what's going on in these markets. If I don't know, I get out."[27]

Walk into the college classroom, and you will hear your professors teaching your children that man can be certain of nothing; that his consciousness has no validity whatsoever; that he can learn no facts and no laws of existence; that he's incapable of knowing an objective reality.

Ayn Rand[25]

I found Faulkner's *Swiss skiing* example to be especially insightful. He noted until the 1950s, most thought skiing was a matter of natural talent you had or you didn't have. Then films were made of some of Europe's greatest skiers to identify the movements that characterized them. It was found that all had certain techniques in common. All kinds of people could learn to be good skiers if the movements that made a great skier and the essence of their skills, could be identified to be taught to others. This essence of skills was called a model, and the model, or set of basic principles, could be applied to any endeavor.[28]

Trading Tribe

Ed Seykota has served as a teacher and mentor to hundreds of traders in his Trading Tribe, a global network of groups of traders who meet to work through challenges: "The trading tribe is an association of traders who commit to excellence, personal growth, and supporting and receiving support from other traders."[29]

I model human excellence.

Charles Faulkner[26]

Reason is the main resource of man in his struggle for survival.
Ludwig von Mises[30]

What feels good is often the wrong thing to do.
William Eckhardt[31]

"My life has stopped, but I continue to age," deadpans Karen Levine, a Wharton School MBA who has worked at General Mills (GIS), Unilever, Deloitte Consulting, Condé Nast, and Hearst. But in real terms, Levine made more in 1988 fresh out of Harvard College than she earns today. During her two years of battling unemployment, Levine has worked for $8 an hour at Pottery Barn and for $18 an hour as a temp for a Wall Street trading firm. "I can't even afford a dog."[34]

Seykota's tribe works on the psychological and emotional issues crucial to successful trading—and life for that matter. Faulkner relays a story about his finely honed intuition: "I am reminded of an experience that Seykota shared with a group. He said when he looks at a market, that everyone else thinks has exhausted its up trend, that is often when he likes to get in. When I asked him how he made this determination, he said he put the chart on the other side of the room and if it looked like it was going up, then he would buy it . . . Of course this trade was seen through the eyes of someone with deep insight into the market behavior."[32]

Seykota doesn't pretend to have all the answers, but he is extremely good at turning the mirror back on students so they focus on the self. His precision with language forces one to pay attention. One of his students broke down his teachings into breathing exercises—for me, an immediate connection to yoga and meditation: "The mind is a filter, letting only some information in . . . When you're designing systems or setting stops, it's an ever-present part of what you do. My goal is to get in touch with those subconscious processes. A lot of what Seykota does is a breathing technique to achieve an altered state of consciousness where you somehow relax your conscious filters. We did it both unstructured and in a structured way, with ideas to concentrate on, such as, 'Why do I always do this when I'm trading?'"[33]

I am nearly five years into my yoga practice. If you have never tried it, please do. In my experience it is my single best tool to de-clutter the mind. You may also enjoy my podcast episode with Andy Puddicombe (#261)—a mediation expert.

More bullet point insights from my conversations with Seykota (podcast episodes #208 and #355):

- One use of the Trading Tribe Process (TTP) is to locate and dissolve the feelings that stand between you and following your system.
- When you notice all things happen now, and when you take responsibility for your experience, you notice that even *noise* results from your intention. At that point, you can clarify your intention and remove the noise. The entire length of the chain of events exists in the ever-evolving moment of now—and at all points of now, you might choose to see your result equals your intention. Alternatively, you might choose to avoid responsibility, especially for the noise, and then try to find exogenous *causes*.
- Analysis leads to solving and fixing. TTP leads to dissolving and noticing things already work right. Incontrovertible solvers tend to use

TTP as an analytical tool—until they happen to experience a desire to solve things.
- Take responsibility for your experience and see intentions equal result. Deny responsibility and a delta between intentions and results may appear.
- Your real trading system is the set of feelings you are unwilling to experience.
- In tracking your feelings and in tracking the markets, take whatever comes up and go with it. Trying to force a feeling is like trying to force a market. You might find some joy in the process of allowing feelings and markets to come and go as you experience them.

The illiterate of the twenty-first century will not be those who cannot read and write, but those who cannot learn, unlearn, and relearn.
Alvin Toffler

It might seem counterintuitive that a successful trader would spend significant time delving into *feelings*, but Seykota is blunt: "It is a dominant idea in Western society that we should separate emotion and rationality. Advances in science show that such a separation is not only impossible but also undesirable."[35]

Many legendary trend followers have known about these *advances in science* for 50 years. I wonder if they should have also been awarded Nobel Prizes for prospect theory because their track records are the single best market examples of the theory in action.

Human beings never think for themselves, they find it too uncomfortable. For the most part, members of our species simply repeat what they are told—and become upset if they are exposed to any different view. The characteristic human trait is not awareness but conformity . . . Other animals fight for territory or food; but, uniquely in the animal kingdom, human beings fight for their beliefs . . . The reason is that beliefs guide behavior, which has evolutionary importance among human beings. But at a time when our behavior may well lead us to extinction, I see no reason to assume we have any awareness at all. We are stubborn, self-destructive conformists. Any other view of our species is just a self-congratulatory delusion.
Michael Crichton[37]

Curiosity, Not PhDs

Try and recall what it was like to experience simple childlike curiosity with no agenda other than to know. The curiosity I am talking about is open-ended and enthusiastic. Kids have wide-eyed wonderment when they take apart their first toy to figure out how it works.

Emotional issues aside, many traders remain fixated on academic intelligence as their only path to get to the top. William Eckhardt, co-father of the Turtles, knows their energies are misplaced: "I haven't seen much correlation between good trading and intelligence. Some outstanding traders are quite intelligent, but a few are not. Many outstandingly intelligent people are horrible traders. Average intelligence is enough. Beyond that, emotional makeup is more important."[36]

When it comes to being an outstanding trader, emotional intelligence (EQ) is as important as IQ—shoot, let's face it, it's way more important. When people are conditioned to appear book smart, they are afraid to be curious, afraid to fail. They think by asking questions

Having an education is one thing, being educated is another.

Lee Kuan Yew
Former Prime Minister of Singapore[38]

they'll be perceived as ignorant, although in truth, by not questioning the world, people get into even more trouble (i.e., lose money). Still, the issues for others might be more nuanced. They don't fear the question, but fear the answer. Yet the *answer* might be the information that requires a legitimate integration into your life or it might prove you dead wrong. Open-ended curiosity lets you take a step back and see everything for what it is right now, in the moment of now.

However, like clockwork, many spend time listening to someone feed information or instruct them. They are judged on how well they can regurgitate information back to whomever offered it. When it comes time to take responsibility for decision making, too many are waiting for someone to lead them. Curiosity has been lobotomized from the masses. Government father figures provide comfort and safety—even if they are artificial and unreliable.

When teaching children, a good chess teacher devises ways to get students through the pain of losing, since they lose a lot when first learning the game. By learning how to handle defeat, the young students can learn how to win.[40]

For example, in the book *Memos from the Chairman*, Ace Greenberg told his then-employees, "Our first desire is to promote from within. If somebody with an MBA degree applies for the job, we will certainly not hold it against them, but we are really looking for people with PSD [poor, smart, and a deep desire to be rich] degrees. They built this firm and there are plenty around because our competition seems to be restricting themselves to MBAs."[39]

Recall the 2008 Wall Street escapade. All of the so-called best and brightest traders, those armed with Ivy League educations and Goldman Sachs pedigrees, they imploded, only to be bailed out by the government. They played by the *rules* their whole life. They went to the *right* schools. They were at the *right* investment banks. They had fabulous CV's back to first grade. They were rewarded for playing the *role*, but then 2008 hit. I am sure many went back to school for an MBA or PhD in the hope if they could learn more *rules*, and then it would be okay.

Anyone with average intelligence can learn to trade. This is not rocket science.

William Eckhardt

But ignoring opinions and contributions of others to be *right* is not particularly *pleasing* behavior as Charles Faulkner notes: "One doesn't have to be a student to want to please people or want to be right. I would claim serious students (and professors) know there is much they don't know, and are less interested in what is right. On the other hand, those that know little often feel the need to be in the right about it. People pleasing is an entirely different dimension, though people that need to be right are usually experienced at ignoring others, and therefore, failing to please them."

Sigmund Freud goes to the heart of curiosity imbalances: "What a distressing contrast there is between the radiant intelligence of the child and the feeble mentality of the average adult." As simplistic as it sounds, maintaining childlike wonder and enthusiasm keeps mental doors open for fresh insights. It is very possible to disengage your ego and think of yourself as still evolving, but there will be some heavy lifting on your end.

Never call on intuition. It calls on you.[41]

Commitment

You must be committed to winning. If you don't want to win, and don't have it deep in your gut, there's a good chance you don't have a snowball's chance in hell to win. Commitment to trend following trading is the same commitment you would make to any new endeavor in life. If you're committed to excellence, you will figure it all out one way or another. No commitment? Then you lose, pony up to the bar for a pint, and kvetch.

A top CEO recently spoke before a Harvard MBA class. After his presentation, the students asked questions. One of the questions was, "What should we do?" The CEO replied, "Take the rest of the money you have not spent on tuition and do something else."

For example, if you're trying to be a pro baseball player, you keep pushing. You never give up. By the time you get to the major leagues, it was years of work. However, the only reason you have that outcome is because you made the commitment at the outset to win. Everyone wants the big leagues and big money, but most are not committed to making it happen with relentless drive.

Charles Faulkner, always seeking to tone me down, sees it differently: "I see it more as a matter of choosing between what is in accord with your nature or changing your nature to accord with your dreams. Most people don't recognize this as a choice point. Few realize it is possible to hold dreams constant and vary behavior until they are good at what they need to be good at. And usually, there is a bit of both."

We delude ourselves that we proceed in a rational manner and weight all of the pros and cons of various alternatives. But this is seldom the case. Quite often, "I decided in favor of X" is no more than "I liked X" . . . We buy the cars we like, choose the jobs and houses we find attractive, and then justify these choices by various reasons.[42]

If you're going to chase success, the basic principles, the basic psychological requirements are the same, no matter what you do in life. You still have to wake up every day with a deep desire to be successful. You have to be consistently focused every day, day after day. You can't wake up and say, "I'm going to give a little bit of effort today and see what happens. If it doesn't work out for me, I can say I tried and complain to my wife or girlfriend." You can't jump helter skelter because the newspaper or some journalism student posing as a market analyst blurts out, "Here's the get-rich-quick scheme for today!"

That's not the way real achievement works. Behave like that and you will fail. Consider simple trading *do not's* from Amos Hostetter, the wise sage of famed trend following incubator Commodities Corporation:

Focus on the moment, not the monsters that may or may not be up ahead.
Ryan Holiday

- Don't sacrifice your position for fluctuations.
- Don't expect the market to end in a blaze of glory. Look out for warnings.
- Don't expect the tape to be a lecturer. It's enough to see that something is wrong.
- Never try to sell at the top. It isn't wise. Sell after a reaction if there is no rally.
- Don't imagine that a market that has once sold at 150 must be cheap at 130.
- Don't buck the market trend.
- Don't look for the breaks. Look out for warnings.
- Don't try to make an average from a losing game.
- Never keep goods that show a loss, and sell those that show a profit. Get out with the least loss, and sit tight for greater profits.

The strategies of human reason probably did not develop, in either evolution or any single individual, without the guiding force of the mechanisms of biological regulation, of which emotion and feeling are notable expressions. Moreover, even after reasoning strategies become established in the formative years, their effective deployment probably depends, to a considerable extent, on the continued ability to experience feelings.[43]

Hostetter also saw the dangers inherent in human nature:

- Fearful of profit and one acts too soon.
- Hope for a change in the forces against one.
- Lack of confidence in one's own judgment.
- Never cease to do your own thinking.
- A man must not swear eternal allegiance to either the bear or bull side.
- An individual fails to stick to facts!
- People believe what it pleases them to believe.

Imagine those simple rules were handed out in January 2008 to every investor with their life savings in index funds, mutual funds, etc. Hostetter was telling you how to avoid October 2008 long before it ever happened. Interestingly, one of Commodities Corporation's founders was Paul Samuelson, the Nobel Prize winner. In 1965, Samuelson published a version of the efficient markets hypothesis that described "a world in which all reliably predictable events are priced right, and only surprises would remain."[44]

"Only surprises would remain"?

That is the textbook definition of an elephant in the room. I wonder if Wikileaks has the secret documents with passive indexer proponents on record giving their creative rationalizations to bury Samuelson's 1965 *surprise* insight. But Samuelson was no dummy. He had *his* 1970s, '80s, and '90s fortune in Commodities Corporation's trend following system, the utilitarian-named TCS ("technical computer system"), and he made a bloody fortune from it. Samuelson gave credit where credit was due, to trend following: "[Amos] Hostetter was the most remarkable investor I ever knew."[45]

If you try to impose a rigid discipline while teaching a child or a chimp, you are working against the boundless curiosity and need for relaxed play that make learning possible in the first place . . . learning cannot be controlled; it is out of control by design. Learning emerges spontaneously, it proceeds in an individualistic and unpredictable way, and it achieves its goal in its own good time. Once triggered, learning will not stop—unless it is hijacked by conditioning.

Roger Fouts

Summary Food for Thought

- 改善 (Kaizen)
- Anfangen ist leicht, beharren eine Kunst.
- Grit: Love the grind.
- Sam Carpenter: "For too many of us, slowing down to examine things is not entertaining, and that's too bad because it is mandatory that we understand the machinery of our lives if we are to modify that machinery to produce the results we want."[46]
- Peter Thiel: "One of the things that's striking about talking to people who are politically working in D.C. is, it's so hard to tell what any of them actually do. It's a sort of place where people measure input, not output. You have a 15-minute monologue describing a 15-page résumé, starting in seventh grade."
- Winners take responsibility, losers place blame.
- "You tell everybody. Listen to me, Hatcher. You've got to tell them! Soylent Green is people! We've got to stop them somehow!"
- "Who is John Galt?"

Decision Making 7

"Would you tell me please which way I have to go from here?"
"That depends a good deal on where you want to go," said the cat.
—Lewis Carroll[1]

We see heuristics as the way the human mind can take advantage of the structure of information in the environment to arrive at reasonable decisions.
—Gerd Gigerenzer[2]

Trend following strategy approaches day-to-day trading decisions in a way most would not recognize: K.I.S.S. For example, each day millions of fundamental traders around the world attempt to evaluate a relentless onslaught of confusing, contradictory, and overwhelming market information, all to hopefully make profitable trading guesses for that day (e.g., the type of information on daily finance news).

Although they know decisions should be educated and, based on factual data, they see impulsive action as sound decision making, leaving them with absolutely no clue. They either end up paralyzed and make no decision, let someone else decide or guess. It's a vicious and repeating cycle of decision-making frustration.

Any individual decisions can be badly thought through, and yet be successful, or exceedingly well thought through, but be unsuccessful, because the recognized possibility of failure in fact occurs. But over time, more thoughtful decision making will lead to better overall results.
Robert Rubin[3]

Terrence Odean, a professor at the University of California, Berkeley, uses a roulette wheel to illustrate. He postulates that even if you knew the results for the last 10,000 roulette spins, knew what materials the roulette wheel is made of, and whatever hundred other pieces of information you could dream up as possibly being useful, you still will not know what matters: where the ball will land next.[4]

Ed Seykota takes Odean's thought a step further in critiquing decision making: "While fundamental analysis may help you understand how things work, it does not tell you when, or how much. Also, by the time a fundamental case presents, the move may already be over. Just around the recent high in the Live Cattle market, the fundamental reasons included Chinese Buying, Mad Cow Disease, and The Atkins' Diet."[5]

People who make decisions for a living are coming to realize that in complex or chaotic situations—a battlefield, a trading floor, or today's brutally competitive business environment—intuition usually beats rational analysis. And as science looks closer, it is coming to see that intuition is not a gift but a skill.[6]

Trend followers excel because they control what they know they can control. They know they can choose a level of risk. They know they can estimate volatility. They know the transaction costs. However, there is still plenty they know they do not know, but in the face of that uncertainty they still step up to the plate and swing. That ability to make a decision is core to trend trading philosophy—that is, swinging the bat without fear. Those decision-making skills might not appear worthy of endless discussion, but the philosophical framework of that decision making is critical to execution.

If we were to keep the trend following style in baseball terms, the question would be: "Do you want to play ball or not?" When the pitch comes—if it's your pitch, swing the bat. There is no time to wait for more information before you swing. In an uncertain world, if you wait until the data is clear, the ball has crossed the plate, you miss the pitch. You are *out*.

Occam's Razor

Nature operates in the shortest way possible.
Aristotle

Tackling the challenge of making smart decisions in a complicated market world is hardly new. As far back as the fourteenth century, when medieval life was as rigidly complex as its cathedrals, philosophers grappled with how to make simple decisions when pressed for time. In any scientific realm, especially when a new set of data requires the creation of a new theory, many hypotheses are proposed, studied, and rejected. And even when all unfit hypotheses are thrown out, several might remain. In some cases they reach the same end, but have different underlying assumptions. To choose among similar theories, scientists (and trend traders) use Occam's razor.

Occam's razor is a principle attributed to logician and Franciscan friar William of Occam. The principle states entities must not be multiplied unnecessarily. In its original Latin form, Occam's razor is *Pluralitas non est ponenda sine neccesitate.* This bit of Latin still underlies all scientific modeling and decision making. A common interpretation of the principle is the simplest of two or more competing theories is preferable.[7] Occam's razor does not guarantee the simplest solution will be correct, but it focuses priorities.

Heuristic: Serving to discover; using trial and error; teaching by enabling pupil to find things out.
Oxford Dictionary

Fast and Frugal Decision Making

In the field of cognitive science, economics, and trading, it has always been assumed the best decision makers have the time and ability to process vast amounts of information. Not true. The field of heuristics explores how to make constructive, positive choices by simplifying processes. Gerd Gigerenzer's *Simple Heuristics That Make Us Smart* shows how to cope with complexities using the simplest of decision-making tools. His premise: "Fast and frugal heuristics employ a minimum of time, knowledge, and computation to make adaptive choices in real environments."[8]

We could still imagine that there is a set of laws that determines events completely for some supernatural being who could observe the present state of the universe without disturbing it. However, such models of the universe are not of much interest to us mortals. It seems better to employ the principle known as Occam's razor and cut out all the features of the theory which cannot be observed.
Stephen Hawking[9]

For example, a component of fast and frugal heuristics is one-reason decision making. This is what trend followers do when faced with a trading decision: "One reason decision makers use only a single piece of information for making a decision—this is their common building block. Therefore, they can also stop their search as soon as the first reason is found that allows a decision to be made."[10]

Whether your decisions are about life in general or trading in particular, your decision-making process should not be complex for the sake of complexity. You make the trading decision, buy or sell, on a single piece of information of *price*. The great trend traders share character traits with other achievers across other fields such as quick reactions or being able to turn a position on a dime.[11]

I'm increasingly impressed with the kind of innovation and knowledge that doesn't come from preplanned effort, or from working towards a fixed goal, but from a kind of concentration on what one is doing. That seems very, very important to me. It's the actual process, the functioning, the going ahead with it.
J. Kirk T. Varanedoe
Museum of Modern Art
New York City

When you are faced with a decision, going with the first instinct is almost always the right choice. If you reflect and consider options and alternatives or try to second-guess, you will end up making the wrong decision or the same right decision, but only after taking valuable time to get there.

Gigerenzer elaborates: "Fast and frugal heuristics can guide behavior in challenging domains when the environment is changing rapidly (for example, in stock market investment), when the environment requires many decisions to be made in a successively dependent fashion. These particular features of social environments can be exploited by heuristics that make rapid decisions rather than gathering and processing information over a long period during which a fleeter-minded competitor could leap forward and gain an edge."[12]

Heart, guts, attitude and the ability to tolerate uncertainty are core to long-term winning.
Michael Covel

Consider how players catch—like in baseball. It may seem they would have to solve complex differential equations in their heads to predict the trajectory of the ball. In fact, baseball players use a simple heuristic. When a ball comes in high, the player fixates on the ball and starts running. The heuristic is to adjust the running speed so the angle of gaze remains constant—that is, the angle between the eye and the ball. The player can ignore all the information necessary to compute the trajectory, such as the ball's initial velocity, distance, and angle, and focus on one piece of information, the angle of gaze.[13]

Former baseball catcher Tim McCarver drew the same conclusion, and he is in no way a trained decision-making scientist:

To be uncertain is to be uncomfortable, but to be certain is to be ridiculous.
Proverb

> Before each delivery, the catcher flashes a hand signal to the pitcher indicating the best pitch to throw. Imagine that a strong batter faces a count of three balls and two strikes, with runners on first and third. What should the hurler serve up, a fastball high and inside, a slider low and away, or a change-up over the heart of the plate? By the way, Mark McGwire's up next. You have to put down a sign quickly. The first one is going to be the right one. For most baseball decisions you can train yourself to be right quicker than in five seconds.[14]

Leaving the trees could have been our first mistake. Our minds are suited for solving problems related to our survival, rather than being optimized for investment decisions. We all make mistakes when we make decisions.
James Montier

McCarver is talking about bare-bones decision making with incomplete information. "Be quick" is his central tenet. The transition from fast and frugal decision making by a baseball player, McCarver, to fast and frugal decision making by a baseball team owner and trader, John W. Henry, is remarkably smooth. Henry was one of the first to focus on the use of heuristics in trading.

At the New York Mercantile Exchange, the president of John W. Henry's firm talked fast and frugal:

> "We're a trend follower; we use just price information and volatility in order to make decisions. The reason why we do that is because we don't

> think that we can predict the future . . . [Further] I can't be an expert in every one of them [markets]. In fact I can't be an expert in any of them, so what I have to do is be able to be expert at being able to move faster when I see information that's important . . . So my way in which I can move faster is to just use the price information that's the aggregation of everyone's expectation . . . What we try to do is extract the appropriate signals as quickly as possible so we can act fast to limit our risk and also create opportunities . . . we're frugal in the senses that we use . . . very simple recognition heuristics . . . the price information itself . . . what could be an example of this? We like to think of those as non-linear models. But it's no different than what some people describe as breakout systems.[15]

His simple heuristic for making trading decisions is price action. But there is more:

Most people believe that great chess players strategize by thinking far into the future, by thinking 10 or 15 moves ahead. That's not true. Chess players look only as far into the future as they need to, and that usually means thinking just a few moves ahead. Thinking too far ahead is a waste of time: The information is uncertain. The situation is ambiguous. Chess is about controlling the situation at hand.[16]

> "Finding a price trend among noisy random price moves presents a challenge similar to that of filtering information from the noise in many other applications, such as astronomy, audio, ballistics, image processing, and macroeconomics. For example, engineers who track ballistic missiles based on noisy radar information attempt to filter out noise to determine the missile's direction. Similarly, macroeconomists and central bankers who receive imperfect economic data—such as estimates of GDP for countries and unemployment rates collected from many sources (with errors)—try to assess whether an economy is heading into a recession or is overheating. Investors trading on trends in financial markets face the similar challenge of assessing the direction prices are headed by filtering noisy price data. In the world of audio, Ray Dolby developed the Dolby system to reduce noise in music recordings and enhance the signal that the listener hears. Along the same lines, trend followers use quantitative tools to enhance the signal of the price trend and reduce the noise around it.[17]

The use of quantitative tools does not mean complicated analysis. The fewer trading decisions traders make—the better. This may seem counter-intuitive, but in a complex world where decisions have to be made with limited information and real-world time constraints, time to consider all possible alternatives is not an option.[18]

The 2016 study "The Enduring Effect of Time-Series Momentum on Stock Returns over Nearly 100 Years" provide[s] evidence that supports the view that time-series momentum (also referred to as trend following) is one of the few investment factors that meet five important criteria for inclusion in a portfolio; specifically, it is persistent, pervasive, robust, investable and intuitive. Their study covered the 88-year period from 1927 to 2014.[21]

Trend following is inherently *simple*, but very few want to believe—especially many respected market players—that something simple can make money consistently. The reason trend followers do well is because they stay focused and very disciplined. They execute their game plan—that is their real strength.[19]

Not everyone agrees with the science of fast and frugal heuristics. One group said, "This can't be true, it's all wrong, or it could never be replicated." Among them were financial advisors, who certainly didn't like the results. Another group said, "This is no surprise. I knew it all along. The stock market's all rumor, recognition, and psychology."[20]

However, staying exclusively with the simple heuristic of price is tricky. Traders can't help trying to *improve*. They become impatient or even bored with systems. Far too many like to make decisions even if those decisions are short-term emotional fixes that have zero to do with making a profit.

For example, let's say you have a buy signal for Google. You must buy the stock if it follows rules. You must trust the rules and your decision making to follow the rules. Don't make it more complicated than it is—buy when you get the signal. That's not to say that trend following in its entirety is elementary. However, the decisions that go along with it should be processes you can jot out on the back of a napkin.

Innovator's Dilemma

Qui court deux lievres a la fois, n'en prend aucun.

Clayton M. Christensen, author of *The Innovator's Dilemma*, understands trend following, even if not by the name I use. What Christensen understands are odds and reactions. He saw this as readers attempted to decipher his work:

"They were looking at *Innovator's Dilemma* for answers rather than for understanding. They were saying, 'tell me what to do' as opposed to 'help me understand so I can decide what to do.' . . . Wall Street analysts are theory-free investors. All they can do is react to the numbers. But the numbers they react to are measures of past performance, not future performance. That's why they go in big herds. Wall Street professionals and business consultants have enshrined as a virtue the notion you should be [fundamental] data-driven. That is the root of companies' inability to take action in a timely way."[22]

"Many are looking for highly complex ways of interacting with the markets, when most of the time it's only the simple ones that are going to work."[23]
Charles Faulkner

Christensen drives home again that you must make decisions without all the facts. You cannot foresee how a changing market will look until change has taken place, and then it's too late. Take, for example, an up and down stock such as Yahoo!. You probably said, "I should have bought here and sold there." But there was no way you could have predicted the future of Yahoo!. You could only act early before the direction of the trend was obvious. You must be in *ready, set, go* mode, long before pundits say the coast is clear. They are the herders Christensen slams—those in the *sheep* business.

Everything should be made as simple as possible, but not simpler.

Albert Einstein

Consider another decision-making story similar to Tim McCarver's baseball example. Years ago, the catcher and the pitcher called pitches. Today you still have a catcher and a pitcher, but the coaches are usually calling the pitches. Why? So the pitcher can execute exactly what he's told to do. When the typical Major League pitcher gets a signal to throw a curveball, he doesn't stand out there on the mound debating it. He says to himself, "This is the system we're using. I have a coach on the sidelines with a computer. He's studied and charted everything. He knows I should throw a curve ball. The only thing I'm going to worry about right now is throwing the curveball to the precise location that I'm supposed to throw it." The pitcher then can concentrate solely on execution—the best pitch possible he can throw right now.

Likewise, as a trend follower, you wake up and see the market move enough to cause you to take action, like a buy signal. For example, let's say the rule dictates buy at price level 20. You do it. You don't debate or second-guess it. Sure, that might feel boring and it might feel like you're not in control. It might feel like there should be something more exciting, more adrenaline-fueled, more *fun* for you to do, in which case consider a trip to the Spearmint Rhino in Vegas. If you want to win, however, you execute the signal as prescribed. That means you trade at price level 20 and throw the curve ball when called for by the coach. Fun, excitement, and glamour are not what you want. Executing correctly to win is what you want.

The Greek philosopher Archilochus tells us, the fox knows many things, but the hedgehog knows one great thing. The fox—artful, sly and astute—represents the financial institution that knows many things about complex markets and sophisticated marketing. The hedgehog—whose sharp spines give it almost impregnable armor when it curls into a ball—is the financial institution that knows only one great thing: long-term investment success is based on simplicity.

John C. Bogle

Process versus Outcome versus Gut

The decision-making process is that—a process. You can't make decisions based on what you want the outcome to be. Michael Mauboussin has long presented a compelling argument for *process*:

> In too many cases, investors dwell solely on outcomes without appropriate consideration of process. The focus on results is to some degree

> understandable. Results—the bottom line—are what ultimately matter. And results are typically easier to assess and more objective than evaluating processes. But investors often make the critical mistake of assuming that good outcomes are the result of a good process and that bad outcomes imply a bad process. In contrast, the best long-term performers in any probabilistic field—such as investing, sports team management, and pari-mutuel betting—all emphasize process over outcome.[24]

When the mind is exhausted of images, it invents its own.
Gary Snyder

Building on that wisdom, Edward Russo and Paul Schoemaker, professors in the field of decision making at Wharton, present a simple tool (see Figure 7.1) to map out the process versus outcome matrix:

		Outcome	
		Good	*Bad*
Process Used to Make the Decision	*Good*	Deserved Success	Bad Break
	Bad	Dumb Luck	Poetic Justice

FIGURE 7.1: Process versus Outcome[25]

The process versus outcome schematic shown in Figure 7.1 is built into trend trading systems. For example, imagine the process you use to make a decision is sound. If your outcome happens to be good, you can view your result as deserved. On the other hand, if you use a good process and your outcome turns out bad, you take solace with failure as a bad break, but you achieved it with a good process.

Always do whatever's next.
George Carlin

Trend trader Larry Hite put it another way: "There are four kinds of bets. There are good bets, bad bets, bets that you win, and bets that you lose. Winning a bad bet can be the most dangerous outcome of all, because a success of that kind can encourage you to take more bad bets in the future, when the odds will be running against you. You can also lose a good bet, no matter how sound the underlying proposition, but if you keep placing good bets, over time, the law of averages will be working for you."

That's sage advice from one of my favorite thinkers, but the romance of in-the-moment-no-process-gut decision making remains a strong pull in for modern world. From admiration of entrepreneurs and firefighters, to the popularity of books by Malcolm Gladwell and Gary Klein, to the outcomes of the last two U.S. presidential elections, instinct over process is positioned as ascendant. Many push intuition as the X factor separating men from the boys. Gut decisions, *they say*, are needed in moments of crisis when *they say* there is no time to weigh arguments or calculate the probability of every outcome. Gut decisions are made in situations, *they say*, where there is no precedent and consequently little evidence.[26]

There is a place for gut decision making in life choices, but it's not applicable to the markets. If you have no market process, and focus on profit outcomes alone, it will end badly. Guaranteed.

Confine yourself to the present.

Marcus Aurelius

Summary Food for Thought

- Ed Seykota: "One pretty good [heuristic] is: 'Trade with the Trend.'"
- Occam's razor dictates if two equal solutions, pick the simplest.
- Fearless decision makers have a plan and execute. They don't look back. If something changes, they adjust.
- Murray N. Rothbard: "If a formerly good entrepreneur should suddenly make a bad mistake, he will suffer losses proportionately; if a formerly poor entrepreneur makes a good forecast, he will make proportionate gains. The market is no respecter of past laurels, however large. Capital does not 'beget' profit. Only wise entrepreneurial decisions do that."
- Tom Asacker: "The process, not the proceeds."

The Scientific Method

8

An interviewer asked Ann Druyan (Carl Sagan's wife), "Didn't [Sagan] want to believe?" She responded, "He didn't want to believe. He wanted to know."

First principles, Clarice. Read Marcus Aurelius. Of each particular thing ask, "What is it in itself? What is its nature?"
—Hannibal Lecter[1]

Great trend followers approach trading as science and their foundation is the scientific method. At best, they view the world like physicists. And the following physics definition is dead-on applicable to trading success: "The science of nature, or of natural objects; that branch of science which treats of the laws and properties of matter, and the forces acting upon it; especially, that department of natural science which treats of the causes that modify the general properties of bodies; natural philosophy."[2]

If you can't measure it, you probably can't manage it . . . Things you measure tend to improve.
Ed Seykota[3]

Excellence in physics, or trend following, requires a solid grounding in *numbers*. Both disciplines work off models that describe relationships, and their common language, math, is finite. Physics and trend following thus work best when they constantly test models with real-world applications.

From error to error, one discovers the entire truth.
Sigmund Freud

Trading your money necessarily means dealing with numbers and varying quantities—like a physics experiment. But the connection goes deeper. Physics is at its core about developing mathematical models of our world. Those models may describe different types of complexity such as the movement of molecules in a gas or the dynamics of stars in a galaxy. And it turns out similar models can be applied to analogous complex behavior in financial markets.[4]

Although few would admit it, the truth is that the typical trader wants to be right on every single trade. He is desperately trying to create certainty where it just doesn't exist.
Mark Douglas

When I use the term *science of trading*, it is not a reference to the engineers or scientists who develop elegant and complex academic models prone to fragility (trend following is in the *antifragile* headspace). Keeping it simple is hard because it is hardest to do what is obvious. Famed physicist, Nobel Prize winner, and Manhattan Project scientist Richard Feynman beautifully sums up the needed mindset in his classic 1960s lecture:

> In general, we look for a new law by the following process. First, we guess it (audience laughter), no, don't laugh, that's really true. Then we compute the consequences of the guess, to see what, if this is right, if this law we guess is right, to see what it would imply and then we compare the computation results to nature, or we say compare to experiment or experience, compare it directly with observations to see if it works. If it disagrees with experiment, it's wrong. In that simple statement is the key to science. It doesn't make any difference how beautiful your guess is, it doesn't matter how smart you are, who made the guess, or what his name is. If it disagrees with experiment, it's wrong. That's all there is to it.

He added:

It is remarkable that a science which began with the consideration of games of chance should have become the most important object of human knowledge . . . The most important questions of life are, for the most part, really only problems of probability.
Pierre-Simon Marquis de Laplace[6]

> It is much more likely that the reports on flying saucers are the result of the known irrational characteristics of terrestrial intelligence, rather than the unknown rational efforts of extraterrestrial intelligence. It's just more likely, that's all. And it's a good guess. We always try to guess the most likely explanation, keeping in the back of our mind that if it doesn't work, then we must discuss the other possibilities.[5]

Critical Thinking

Trend followers, like physicists, approach the investing landscape with an open mind. They examine, experiment and A/B test to find solid ground. Like physicists they think critically and develop the ability to ask the *right* questions, including:

- Digging deep to face the real problem, instead of mindlessly going for the easy superficial query.

- Being completely honest regarding the real reason you might want an answer.
- Discovering how to interpret information before asking the question—in other words, questions that offer the opportunity to make a midcourse correction.
- Facing cold, hard facts about human nature.
- Facing the reality of where the new answer might lead.
- Facing subjective takes on the world and factoring in objective data.
- Seek questions that engender important details that might be missed because people did not ask.[7]

Do not believe in anything simply because you have heard it. Do not believe in anything simply because it is spoken and rumored by many. Do not believe in anything simply because it is found written in your religious books. Do not believe in anything merely on the authority of your teachers and elders. Do not believe in traditions because they have been handed down for many generations. But after observation and analysis, when you find that anything agrees with reason and is conducive to the good and benefit of one and all, then accept it and live up to it.

Buddha

Charles Faulkner prioritized his favorites: "The questions that are most critical—in both senses of that word—are the ones that question our assumptions, our assumptions of what is or is not a fact or a truth or possible. After this comes questions that assist statistical thinking."

You must be determined to know what is real. You do not avoid asking a question if you're suspicious you might not like the answer. You do not ask self-serving questions that reinforce an opinion you already have. You do not ask mindless questions or accept mindless answers. You are content to ask questions knowing there might not be an answer. This is not an easy process for the masses.

Most go the wrong way every time. The questions become superficial and ill-informed because they have not taken ownership. Instead they ask dead-end questions, "Is this going to be on the test?" Their questions demonstrate a complete lack of desire to think. They might as well be sitting in silence with minds on pause. To think critically, you must want to stimulate your intellect with questions that lead to more questions. You must undo the damage previous traditional *rote memorization* schooling has done to your curiosity. You need to want to resuscitate your mind.[8]

Probability theory is the underpinning of the modern world. Current research in both physical and social sciences cannot be understood without it. Today's politics, tomorrow's weather report, and next week's satellites depend on it.[9]

Linear versus Nonlinear

Chaos theory dictates a nonlinear universe. Our world does not move in a straight line. Spending your time looking for *perfect* is an exercise in futility. The future is unknown no matter how educated the fundamental forecast. Manus J. Donahue III, author of *An Introduction to*

Chaos Theory and Fractal Geometry, paints a picture of our chaotic, nonlinear world:

I'd say the non-normal distribution is what we arbitrage. That is what you make profits from.
Richard Dennis

> The world of mathematics has been confined to the linear world for centuries. That is to say, mathematicians and physicists have overlooked dynamical systems as random and unpredictable. The only systems that could be understood in the past were those that were believed to be linear, that is to say, systems that follow predictable patterns and arrangements. Linear equations, linear functions, linear algebra, linear programming, and linear accelerators are all areas that have been understood and mastered by the human race. However, the problem arises that we humans do not live in an even remotely linear world; in fact, our world must indeed be categorized as nonlinear; hence, proportion and linearity is scarce. How may one go about pursuing and understanding a nonlinear system in a world that is confined to the easy, logical linearity of everything? This is the question that scientists and mathematicians became burdened with in the nineteenth century; hence, a new science and mathematics was derived: chaos theory.[10]

Although a nonlinear acceptance is new for many, it is not a new principle inside trend following trading. The big events such as the 2008 market crash, or Brexit 2016, are examples of nonlinear events. Trend following won during these events because it's built to expect the unexpected. Lack of linearity, or cause and effect, was not unanticipated. How did trend following manage this preparation for events no one could predict? What set it apart is that trend following, deep down, is statistical thinking.

Gerd Gigerenzer notes the power of statistical thinking:

Everyone's entitled to their own opinion, but they're not entitled to their own facts.
Daniel Patrick Moynihan[11]

> At the beginning of the twentieth century, the father of modern science fiction, Herbert George Wells, said in his writings on politics, "If we want to have an educated citizenship in a modern technological society, we need to teach them three things: reading, writing, and statistical thinking." At the beginning of the twenty-first century, how far have we gotten with this program? In our society, we teach most citizens reading and writing from the time they are children, but not statistical thinking.[12]

One of my favorite examples of statistical thinking is a case study involving the birth ratio of boys and girls. There are two hospitals. In the first one, 120 babies are born every day; in the other, only 12. On average the ratio of boys to girls born every day in each hospital is 50/50. However, one day in one of those hospitals twice as many girls are born as boys. In which hospital was it more likely to happen? The answer is obvious to numbers thinking, but as research shows it's not so obvious for the untrained: It is much more likely to happen in the small hospital. The probability of a random deviation of a particular size from the population mean decreases with the increase in the sample size.[13]

I have no special talents. I am only passionately curious.

Albert Einstein

Statistical puzzles about birth and gender tie directly to trend following. Take two traders who on average win 40 percent of the time with winners being three times as large as losers. One has a history of 1,000 trades and the other has a history of 10 trades. Who has a better chance in the next 10 trades to have only 10 percent of total trades turn out as winners (instead of the typical 40 percent)? The one with the 10-trade history has the better chance. More trades in a history mean a greater probability of adhering to the average. Fewer trades mean a greater probability of deviation from the average.

Consider a friend who receives a tip and makes quick money. He tells everyone about his newfound trading prowess. You are impressed. But you would be less impressed if you were a statistical thinker because you would realize immediately his *population* of tips was extremely small. He could as easily follow the next great stock tip and blow up. One tip means nothing. The sample is too small.

The difference between these two views is why great trend followers have grown from one-person shops to firms that routinely beat the so-called Wall Street powerhouses. Why did Wall Street sit by and allow trend traders to enter and dominate arenas they could, and perhaps should, have dominated? The answer lies in Wall Street and Mains Street's fascination with benchmarks. Wall Street is after index-like performance (*benchmarks*) because their clients think they can avoid risk and control return (fantasies die hard), whereas trend following is focused on absolute performance—monthly calendars be damned.

Standard deviation measures the uncertainty in a random variable (in this case, investment returns). It measures the degree of variation of returns around the mean (average) return. The higher the volatility of the investment returns, the higher the standard deviation will be.

National Institute of Standards and Technology[14]

On the other hand, large, established Wall Street firms grounded in EMT judge success with measures of central tendency. The large banks and brokerages view an average measure (mean) and the variation from average to determine whether they are winning or losing. They are beholden to investors' irrational desires. The trend following mindset is counter to their entire business model.

They go in wrong directions with their volatility understanding. Volatility around the mean (standard deviation) is the de facto Wall Street risk definition. Typical Wall Street types, *long-only* types, aim for consistency instead of absolute returns. As a result returns are average by design. They worship the normal distribution:

> Normal distributions are the bedrock of finance, including the random walk, capital asset pricing, value-at-risk, and Black-Scholes models. Value-at-risk (VaR) models, for example, attempt to quantify how much loss a portfolio may suffer with a given probability. While there are various forms of VaR models, a basic version relies on standard deviation as a measure of risk. Given a normal distribution, it is relatively straightforward to measure standard deviation, and hence risk. However, if price changes are not normally distributed, standard deviation can be a very misleading proxy for risk.[15]

Mathematics and science are two different notions, two different disciplines. By its nature, good mathematics is quite intuitive. Experimental science doesn't really work that way. Intuition is important. Making guesses is important. Thinking about the right experiments is important. But it's a little more broad and a little less deep, so the mathematics we use here can be sophisticated. But that's not really the point. We don't use very, very deep stuff. Certain of our statistical approaches can be very sophisticated. I'm not suggesting it's simple. I want a guy who knows enough math so that he can use those tools effectively but has a curiosity about how things work and enough imagination and tenacity to dope it out.
Jim Simons[16]

The problem with standard deviation as a risk measurement is seen when two traders have similar standard deviations, but show an entirely different distribution of returns. One might look like the familiar normal distribution, or bell curve. The other might show statistical characteristics known as kurtosis and skewness. In other words, the historical pattern of returns does not resemble a normal distribution.

Trend following never has and never will produce returns that exhibit a normal distribution. It will never produce consistent average returns that hit benchmarks quarter after quarter. When trend followers hit home runs in the zero-sum game and win huge profits from the likes of Barings Bank, Long-Term Capital Management, and the 2008 market crash, they are targeting the edges or those fat tails of a non-normally distributed world.

Jerry Parker, the most successful of the trained Turtles: "The way I describe it is that overlaying trend following on top of markets produce a non-normal distribution of trades. And that's sort of our edge—in these outlier trades. I don't know if we have an inherent rate of return, but when you place this trend following on top of markets, it can produce this distribution—the world is non-normal."[18]

Luck is largely responsible for my reputation for genius. I don't walk into the office in the morning and say, "Am I smart today?" I walk in and wonder, "Am I lucky today?"
Jim Simons[17]

Jean-Jacques Chenier, like Parker, knows markets are far less linear and efficient than the typical view. Remember, not everyone across markets plays to win. Some might be hedgers, playing to lose, using the markets as insurance: "The Bank of Japan will intervene to push the yen lower . . . a commercial bank in Japan will repatriate yen assets overseas just to window dress its balance sheets for the end of the fiscal year. These activities create liquidity but it is inefficient liquidity that can be exploited."[19]

To better understand Parker's words, it helps to break down the concepts of skew and kurtosis. *Skew* measures the statistical likelihood of a return in the tail of a distribution being higher or lower than commonly associated with a normal distribution. For example, a return series of –30 percent, 5 percent, 10 percent, and 15 percent has a mean of 0 percent. Only one return is less than 0 percent, whereas three are higher but the one that is negative is much farther from the mean (0 percent) than the positive ones. This is called negative skewness. Negative skewness occurs when the values to the left of (less than) the mean are fewer, but farther from the mean than the values to the right of the mean. Positive skewness occurs when the values to the right of (more than) the mean are fewer, but farther from the mean than the values to the left of the mean.[22]

Trend following exhibits a positive skew return profile. *Kurtosis*, on the other hand, measures the degree to which exceptional values, much larger or smaller than the average, occur more frequently (high kurtosis) or less frequently (low kurtosis) than in a normal (bell-shaped) distribution. High kurtosis results in exceptional values called *fat tails*, which indicate a higher percentage of very low and very high returns than would be expected with a normal distribution.[23]

Skew may be either positive or negative and affects distribution symmetry. Positive skew means there is a higher probability for a significant positive return than for a negative return the same distance from the mean. Skew will measure the direction of surprises. Outliers, or extremes in performance not normally associated with a distribution, will clearly affect skewness. The crash of 1987 is usually considered an extreme outlier. For example, a positive outlier will stretch the right-hand tail of the distribution. Because this method eliminates losing positions and holds profitable positions, historically there has been a tendency for positive outliers and a higher chance of positive returns. A negative skew results in a higher probability of a significantly negative event for the same distance from the mean.[24]

These concepts are not as entertaining as listening to the latest money honey paraded out by finance shows to serenade sweet nothings—literally nothings. Few see the use for statistical thinking when they can trust a hot model to think for them. If you forget these moneymaking basics, you will never see the reality great trend following

One would not expect to see a home-improvement volume with the title The New Reality of Plumbing. But the science of investing, at least as it is propagated by financial writers, undergoes a seeming revolution every couple of thousand points on the Dow.[20]

The risk-reducing formulas behind portfolio theory rely on a number of demanding and ultimately unfounded premises. First, they suggest that price changes are statistically independent from one another . . . The second assumption is that price changes are distributed in a pattern that conforms to a standard bell curve. Do financial data neatly conform to such assumptions? Of course, they never do.

Benoit B. Mandelbrot[21]

Skewness is a measure of symmetry, or more precisely, the lack of symmetry. A distribution, or data set, is symmetric if it looks the same to the left and right of the center point.

National Institute of Standards and Technology[25]

traders see—the reality of a making a fortune when the next black swan arrives.

Kurtosis is a measure of whether the data are peaked or flat relative to a normal distribution. That is, data sets with high kurtosis tend to have a distinct peak near the mean, decline rather rapidly, and have heavy tails. Data sets with low kurtosis tend to have a flat top near the mean rather than a sharp peak. A uniform distribution would be the extreme case.
National Institute of Standards and Technology[26]

Compounding

Jim Rogers's *Investment Biker* was one of my first Wall Street books. He brought so much passion and common sense to the table. Nearly 14 years later in early 2008, I interviewed him for my first documentary film (*Broke*) at his home in Singapore. (My Rogers visits never stopped; I saw him in 2014 and 2016, too). Even though I had been up for nearly 48 hours straight (going around the world does take 20 hours in the air) when I did the interview, the classic moneymaking lessons were on the table.

Rogers, who is not a technical trend following trader, but who has made a fortune trading trends, put the importance of compounding at the top of his list: "One of the biggest mistakes most investors make is believing they've always got to be doing something . . . the trick in investing is not to lose money . . . the losses will kill you. They ruin your compounding rate; and compounding is the magic of investing."[27]

For such a long time we thought that most data must have a normal distribution and therefore that the mean is meaningful. Much of the world around us is not normal . . . [and] it is so difficult to see the simplest things as they really are. We become so used to our assumptions that we can no longer see them or evidence against them. Instead of challenging our assumptions, we spend our time studying the details, the colors of the threads that we tear from the tapestry of the world. That is why science is hard.[28]

You can't get rich overnight, but with a proper compounding perspective you at least have the chance to make big money over a lifetime. For example, if you manage to make 50 percent a year in your trading you can compound an initial $20,000 account to over $616,000 in seven years. Is 50 percent unrealistic? Perhaps. However, do the math again using 25 percent. You can be a trend follower, make 25 percent a year, and spend all of your profits each year. Or you can apply trend following and possibly compound your 25 percent a year for 20 or more years and become *filthy* rich. Look at a hypothetical investment of $20,000 (see Table 8.1):

TABLE 8.1: Compounding Example

	30%	40%	50%
Year 1	$26,897	$29,642	$32,641
Year 2	$36,174	$43,933	$53,274
Year 3	$48,650	$65,115	$86,949
Year 4	$65,429	$96,509	$141,909
Year 5	$87,995	$143,039	$231,609
Year 6	$118,344	$212,002	$378,008
Year 7	$159,160	$314,214	$616,944

A trend example further illustrates the point. In October 1997 David Harding launched his Winton Futures Fund, which provided investors with annualized returns of 21 percent per year for his first 10 years. To put that in context, if you had been the buyer of Vincent van Gogh's "Irises" in 1947, you would have paid $80,000. The next time it changed hands, in 1987, it was bought for $53.9 million. This seems like a huge increase in value, but mathematically it's a compounded average annual growth rate of 17.7 percent, which is less than the annualized returns in Harding's fund.

Say goodbye to a nice, steady, equilibrium perspective. Equilibrium equals death. Things do not rock along smoothly, change in small increments. Change is catastrophic. We must learn to adapt because we cannot predict.[29]

The acceptance of compounding math is not intuitive in a world focused on prediction hocus pocus, instant gratification, and tweets by the bushel. However, if there is evidence trend following thrives and flourishes in a compounded nonlinear world, and there is, it's worth considering the specific people, operations and philosophies *religiously* at work against wider acceptance.

Summary Food for Thought

- Donald Rumsfeld: "Reports that say that something hasn't happened are always interesting to me, because as we know, there are known knowns; there are things we know we know. We also know there are known unknowns; that is to say we know there are some things we do not know. But there are also unknown unknowns—the ones we don't know we don't know. And if one looks throughout the history of our country and other free countries, it is the latter category that tends to be the difficult ones.[30]
- If you can't think in *numbers*, don't play the game.
- The *edges* of the bell curve are *opportunity*.
- Probable events are not always certain and extremely improbable events are not always impossible (i.e., Black Swans).
- Bill Bonner: "If you had asked a group of investors, in August 1929, what was likely to happen on Wall Street, you'd have heard a range of views. You might even have found a crank or two who predicted a market crash. But the majority view was nothing like what happened."[31]

Holy Grails

9

Jesse Livermore described Wall Street as a giant whorehouse, where brokers were pimps and stocks whores, and where customers queued to throw their money away.
—*The Economist*[1]

Tell the truth and then run.
—Proverb

Al Capone famously said: "It's a racket. Those stock market guys are crooked."

That's dead on.

The crooked abound. Or, to be kind, I will call them ignorant. Or, to be nice, I will call them wrong. I often wonder if my great-great-uncle Frank Mast (Balys Mastauskas; my grandfather's uncle) passed a little of that good-fight-attitude genetic material along. (Assistant State Attorney Mast is captured on the next page, face to face with famed crime boss Al Capone at a Chicago courthouse.)

The rackets found on Wall Street always overflow with Holy Grails—those predictions, secret formulas, and divine interpretations that promise otherworldly knowledge and riches. They are most often delivered in the investment world through a *black box*—a closed system where the inputs and outputs are known, but the internal analytical workings are left top secret, only for the high priests' consumption.

What is dangerous is for Americans not to be in the stock market. We're going to reach the point where stocks are correctly priced and we think that's 36,000 . . . It's not just a bubble. Far from it. The stock market is undervalued.
James Glassman
Dow 36,000[2]

Another psychological aspect that drives me to use timing techniques on my portfolio is understanding myself well enough to know that I could never sit in a buy and hold strategy for two years during 1973 and 1974, watch my portfolio go down 48 percent and do nothing, hoping it would come back someday.

Tom Basso

Al Capone (left) and Frank Mast

Whenever we see evidence that our rules *are even remotely correct, our sense of security is boosted. When we are faced with evidence contrary to our* rules, *we quickly rationalize it away.*[3]

With the title alone [Dow 36,000] *causing hysterics, placing this on your coffee table will elicit your guests to share their best Dot-com horror story. How they invested their $100,000 second mortgage in Cisco Systems at $80 after reading about it, waiting for it to become $500 (as predicted in this very book) only to see it dive to $17. Just the thought of this book gives me the chuckles.*

Amazon Review of Dow 36,000[4]

Black box positioning goes far beyond markets. It is not surprising in a modern, interconnected age when you take a smart guy, rows of computers, proprietary formulas, and code only the one smart guy can see, and then add a string of successful *forecasts*, boom—you end up with a nerdy, made-for-social-media superstar who suddenly makes *prediction* cool for the proletariat.

Nate Silver is that *it* guy. Consider:

- He successfully called the outcomes in 49 of the 50 states in the 2008 U.S. presidential election.
- He successfully called the outcomes in 50 of the 50 states in the 2012 U.S. presidential election.

Thus, Silver became the go-to smart numbers guy overnight. He went from baseball stats expert to political stats expert. His mathematical model for elections beat political journalists and commentators at their own game—so goes his Moneyball-for-politics narrative. In short order his followers on Twitter surpassed 1 million, his book became a bestseller, and FiveThirtyEight.com became ubiquitous—even offering investing insights such as, "Worried about The Stock Market? Whatever You Do, Don't Sell."

Yet for anyone who followed the 2016 presidential race, Silver's political predictions went bust. Over the course of 2016 Silver posted daily election odds that jumped around like a cat on fire—not exactly surprising if your new guru status forces you to offer forecasts every day of an election cycle for over a year.

He admitted in his laborious mea culpa, "How I Acted Like a Pundit and Screwed Up on Donald Trump" to not using his statistical models on Donald Trump's candidacy. He instead used educated guesses, which blew his statistical-model-made-me-famous-you-can-now-trust-I-am-not-a-typical-pundit-with-built-in-biases storyline out of the water. Worse yet, the way Silver outlined his predictions, he could say he was right no matter what happened. For Silver's followers, his 2016 hedged forecasts, his arguable *mathturbation*, doesn't matter:

History is not a good guide to the future.

Jerry Parker

> "Look at Nate's record. Trump was an *outlier.*"
>
> "There was not enough *historical* data."
>
> "He gets *most* of them right."
>
> "Nate's winning percentage is so *high.*"

Those weak retorts illustrate the faulty foundation in Silver's approach: He leaves out the surprises, the unusual, and unexpected. He has no way of predicting or accounting for those. On Trump's win, Silver said as much, "It's the most shocking political development of my lifetime." But no one can predict outliers, so if someone like Silver pretends he can—watch out. Spyros Makridakis, in his famed 1979 paper "Accuracy of Forecasting: An Empirical Investigation," showed simple beats complicated and moving averages beat tortuous econometric routines. Would moving averages also have predicted the two elections that made Silver a household name?

Only when the tide goes out do you discover who's been swimming naked.

Warren Buffett

Nonetheless, Silver defenders come back to the 49 out of 50 and 50 out of 50 in 2008 and 2012—proof, they say as they ignore 2016. But in 2008 and 2012, what percentage of those were *hard* calls? For example, California is blue no matter what. So there is always a huge risk in relying on strategy that gets the easy calls right and punts on the hard ones.

These are not terribly new inconsistencies to ponder. The efficient market theory—the strategy that runs the world's money—also has no solution for surprise (i.e., black swans). Silver illustrates the conundrum across a different discipline, but with the same pressing problem. In summer 2016, Nassim Taleb, father of the black swan, launched a detailed criticism of Silver into the public sphere: "@FiveThirtyEight is showing us a textbook case on how to be totally *clueless* about probability yet make a business in it."

From error [loss] to error [loss], one discovers the entire truth [trend].
Sigmund Freud

The intellectual cage match: Nassim Taleb versus Nate Silver.

Pick your side carefully, it just got real.

Buy and Hope

After the Spring 2000 stock market bubble implosion and after the October 2008 crash, passive indexing or buy and hold as a sound investing strategy both should have been permanently labeled junk science. Yet that did not happen. Investors still fall into the lemmings line and obey mantras such as "buy and hold for the long-term," "stay the course," and "buy the dips." These happy talk market prayers share the same problematic issue inherent in Nate Silver's weakness: no accounting for *surprise*.

I bought SNAP even when I was pretty positive I would not make a profit in the short run, but just because I am a fan of the product.
Chris Roh
25-year-old trading for 1 month
New York Post
March 13, 2017

Jerry Parker proffers the alternate case:

> Trend following is similar to a democracy. Sometimes it doesn't look so good, but it's better than anything else out there. It's a worse investment now, let's say, than it was in the '70s or '80s. But so what? What other choice do we have? Are we going to buy market breaks? Are we going to rely on buy and hold? Buy and hope, that's what I call it. Are we going to double up when we lose money? Are we going to do all these things that everyone else does? Eventually people will come to understand that trend following works in other markets, markets that produce trends.[5]

SNAP is tapping into the pride of ownership (for millennials) which we don't see often in the stock market.
Dan Schatt, Stockpile
New York Post
March 13, 2017

Consider the NASDAQ market crash of 1973–1974. The NASDAQ reached its high peak in December 1972. It then dropped by nearly 60 percent, hitting rock bottom in September 1974. The NASDAQ did not break permanently free of the 1973–1974 bear market until April 1980. Buy and hold did nothing for investors from December 1972 through March 1980. Investors would have made more money during this period in a 3 percent savings account. History repeated itself with the 77 percent drop in the NASDAQ from 2000–2002.

Making matters worse, pure buy and hold strategy during an extended market drop makes recovery back to breakeven difficult if not impossible. Buy and hold investors have been led to slaughter by an industry with powerful conflicts of interest. They believe armed only with tremendous patience, they will make a good long-term return. These investors expect to make back most, if not all, of any loss. They believe the best place for long-term capital is the stock market—long only—and if they give it 5 or 10 or 20 years they will rock and roll. Investors need to understand they can go 5, 10, and 20 years and make no return at all and even lose money.[6]

To compound problems, buy and hold panders to market revenge. Investors want their money back. They think, "I lost my money in XYZ stock, and I'm going to make my money back in the same stock come hell or high water no matter what." It's now personal. They can't fathom sunk costs or admit passive holding forever might have seriously unexamined fissures under the surface. They buy and hold no matter what happens, regardless of how many times they get kicked in the teeth. It's a version of Stockholm syndrome with bad investing strategy as the captor.

You will run out of money before a guru runs out of indicators.

Neal T. Weintraub

Jonathan Hoenig sees where many fall down: "I am a trader because my interest isn't in owning stocks per se, but in making money. And while I do trade in stocks (among other investments), I don't have blind faith that stocks will necessarily be higher by the time I'm ready to retire. If history has demonstrated anything, it's that we can't simply put our portfolios on autopilot and expect things to turn out for the best. You can't be a trader when you're right and an investor when you're wrong. That's how you lose."

If you use a system, you automatically have a seat belt on for protection. That keeps you from making portfolio buy sell decisions the next time CNN's Don Lemon postulates that a missing Malaysian Boeing 777 may have entered a black hole.

There is little point in exploring the Elliott Wave Theory because it is not a theory at all, but rather the banal observation that a price chart comprises a series of peaks and troughs. Depending on the time scale you use, there can be as many peaks and troughs as you care to imagine.[7]

Warren Buffett

Warren Buffett is positioned as the single biggest proponent of value investing and buy and holding—accurate or not. Like Sir Galahad, he has achieved his real Holy Grail, and I am the first to salute his immense success. However, can you achieve what he has via insurance companies and arcane tax advantages? No. He is the classic exception to the rule. There is only one Buffett. Unfortunately, many mistakenly assume Buffett is the simple buy and hold investor: "Honey, Warren made all of his money holding Coke for 40 years!" Uh, his $60+ billion net worth is far more complex than *that*.

Warren Buffett is not warning investors about potential risk when he recommends stock investing. I am concerned that people will just blindly follow that advice not realizing the risk until it is too late & then they sell at the bottom.
Julian Rubinstein
ValueWalk
March 5, 2017

For example, Buffett was once against financial derivatives: "'Things are less lucrative in the stock market. We have more money than ideas,' he said, adding that 6 percent to 7 percent was a fair rate of return in the current environment. The company has more than $37 billion in cash to invest. One place the money certainly won't go is derivatives. 'There's no place with as much potential for phony numbers as derivatives.' Buffett's billionaire vice chairman, Charlie Munger, couldn't resist chiming in. 'To say that derivative accounting is a sewer is an insult to sewage.'"[8]

Sixteen days later, Buffett changed tune: "Berkshire Hathaway Inc. announced today that it has sold $400 million of a new type of security, named 'SQUARZ,' in a private placement to qualified institutional investors . . . 'Despite the lack of precedent, a negative coupon security seemed possible in the present interest rate environment. I asked Goldman Sachs to create such an instrument and they responded promptly with the innovative security being announced today,' said Warren Buffett."[10]

If Buffett was forthright at first, what made him change two weeks later and create an instrument so complicated and secretive not even his press release could explain it? Even more confusing is that Buffett contradicted himself a year later, lambasting with vigor his financial Frankenstein creation: "Derivatives are financial weapons of mass destruction, carrying dangers, while now latent, are potentially lethal . . . We view them as time bombs, both for the parties that deal in them and the economic system."[11]

In 2008 Buffett was again trading derivatives, and helping to promote government bailouts. Still today, in 2017, his firm maintains massive derivative positions. The Buffett legend of value investing or buy and hold as his strategy to make billions has permeated the public consciousness with books by the literal dozens. And when he launches a new derivatives strategy against his legend, no one talks. Long-time fund manager Michael Steinhardt was the exception: "[Buffett] is the greatest PR person of recent times. And he has managed to achieve a snow job that has conned virtually everyone in the press to my knowledge . . . and it is remarkable that he continues to do it."[12]

Sun Microsystems probably has the best near-term outlook of any company I know.
James Cramer
September 7, 2000[9]

Warren Buffett is an investing icon and deserves high praise, but unlike trend following, where there are examples of multiple trend following winners, there is only one Warren Buffett. It makes you pause. Is he the sole *survivor*?

A few years back, I sat down with a trend trader. He has a 30-year-plus track record making on average 20 percent a year. The topic of Warren Buffett came up. While he was very respectful of Buffett, he was bewildered how some could call his trend following trading *luck*, but those same people could see Buffett as *skilled*. This trader pointed out the thousands of trades he has made. He noted his trend-trading peers also produced thousands of trades over decades. He saw it more logical to make an argument for Buffett's success much more connected to luck given the relatively few leveraged trades that helped make him so astronomically wealthy: Coke, Gillette, American Express, Goldman Sachs, and Wells Fargo.

Imagine you are at a car auction hoping to buy a beautiful red '66 Corvette. Imagine the car that is being auctioned before the Corvette is a 1955 Mercedes Gull Wing Coupe that sells for $750,000. The Corvette is up next and the Blue Book price is $35,000. What would you bid? Now imagine the car before yours was a "kit" car replica of the Gull Wing Mercedes that sold for $75,000. What would you pay now? Research has shown that incidental price data can affect what you are willing to pay. We have a tendency to pay more if the preceding price is considerably higher.

Jon C. Sundt

Losers Average Losers

There's a famous late 1980s picture of Paul Tudor Jones, the great macro trader profiled in *Market Wizards*, relaxing in his office. Tacked up on the wall behind him on a loose-leaf sheet of paper is the simple phrase in black magic marker, "Losers Average Losers."

Jones's wisdom was lost on James K. Glassman back during the Dot-com bubble "If you had Enron in your portfolio and didn't sell it at $90 or even at $10, don't feel embarrassed. As Alfred Harrison, a money manager at Alliance Capital Management Holding LP, which owned a ton of Enron, put it, 'On the surface it had always seemed to be a fairly good growth stock. We bought it all the way down.'"[13]

Glassman and Harrison were dead wrong. What they call dollar-cost averaging is averaging a loser (Enron) all the way down. Traders should feel sick if they average losers, not embarrassed. When you have a losing position, it is telling you something is wrong. As unbelievable as it seems to the novice, the longer a market declines, the more likely it is to continue declining (Google every white paper you can find post-2010 on "time series momentum"). Falling markets are never places to buy cheap—unless you expect to live forever, and that might not be enough if whatever market flops to zero.

When people say the market is over-valued and there's a bubble, whatever that means, they're talking about just a handful of stocks. Most of these stocks are reasonably priced. There's no reason for them to correct violently anytime in the year 2000.

Larry Wachtel
Prudential Securities
December 23, 1999[14]

In our zero-sum world if the trend is down it is not a buying opportunity, it is a selling opportunity—a time-to-go-*short* opportunity. Even worse, as an active money manager for clients, Glassman admitted to averaging losers as his strategy. To top it off he opined: "Could the typical small investor have discovered a year ago that Enron was on the brink of disaster? It's highly unlikely. Still, if you looked for the right thing, you would have never bought Enron in the first place."[15]

Hold on, there was a way to spot Enron's problems. The price going from $90 to 50 cents was a clear indication the brink of disaster was right around the corner hiding in plain sight. Jesse Livermore knew 80 years earlier how to avoid averaging losers:

Jan, the bottom line is, before the end of the year [2000], the NASDAQ and Dow will be at new record highs.
Myron Kandel
Anchor CNNfn
April 4, 2000[16]

> I have warned against averaging losses. That is a most common practice. Great numbers of people buy a stock, let us say at 50, and two or three days later if they can buy it at 47 they are seized with the urge to average down by buying another hundred shares, making a price of 48.5 on all. Having bought at 50 and being concerned over a three-point loss on a hundred shares, what rhyme or reason is there in adding another hundred shares and having the double worry when the price hits 44? At that point there would be a $600 loss on the first hundred shares and a $300 loss on the second shares. If one is to apply such an unsound principle, he should keep on averaging by buying 200 at 44, then 400 at 41, 800 at 38, 1,600 at 35, 3,200 at 32, 6,400 at 29, and so on. How many speculators could stand such pressure? So, at the risk of repetition and preaching, let me urge you to avoid averaging down.

Others have tried to average losers as well. Julian Robertson ran one of the biggest and most profitable hedge funds ever. However, his run ended. On March 30, 2000, CNN excerpted a letter Julian Robertson sent to Tiger's investors blaming his fund's problems on the rush to cash:

If you want a guarantee, buy a toaster.
Clint Eastwood

> As you have heard me say on a number of occasions, the key to Tiger's success over the years has been a steady commitment to buying the best stocks and shorting the worst. In a rational environment, this strategy functions well. But in an irrational market, where earnings and price considerations take a back seat to mouse clicks and momentum, such logic, as we have learned, does not count for much. The result of the demise of value investing and investor withdrawals has been financial erosion, stressful to us all. And there is no real indication that a quick end is in sight.[17]

Tiger's spiral downward started fall of 1998 when a catastrophic trade on dollar-yen cost the fund billions. An ex-Tiger employee was blunt: "There's a certain amount of hubris when you take a position so big you have to be right and so big you can't get out when you're wrong. That was something Julian never would have done when he was younger. That isn't good risk-return analysis."[18]

I am of the belief that the individual out there is actually not throwing money at things that they do not understand, and is actually using the news and using the information out there to make smart investment decisions.

Maria Bartiromo
CNBC
March 2001[19]

The problem: Tiger's shaky strategy foundation. Robertson was open to criticism: "Our mandate is to find the 200 best companies in the world and invest in them, and find the 200 worst companies in the world and go short on them. If the 200 best don't do better than the 200 worst, you probably should go into another business."

Sifting through information was Robertson's forte. According to one associate, "He can look at a long list of numbers in a financial statement he'd never seen before and say, 'That one is wrong,' and he's right." Although that talent is impressive, being able to read and critique a balance sheet doesn't necessarily translate into profits. What do Julian Robertson, "losers average losers," the Dot-com stock crash, and October 2008 have in common?

Bubbles.

The 2008 crash was no different than the tulip bulb bubble made famous in Holland. In 1720 when the South Sea Bubble was at its height, even Sir Isaac Newton, the greatest genius of his time, got sucked into the hysteria and he eventually lost £20,000. Wash, rinse, repeat.

Although bubbles appear as blips in history, the aftermath is long-term disaster, resulting in severe recessions and government interventions (QE, ZIRP, NIRP, and the Fed buying common stocks) that make it worse. Bubble collapses over the past 500 years have always thrown nations into recessions lasting a decade or longer. What lesson can be learned from mass delusion? Human nature continues to be the way it has always been and probably always will be.[20]

You have to say, "What if?" What if the stocks rally? What if they don't? Like a catcher, you have to wear a helmet.

Jonathan Hoenig

Today, sane investors should do more than trust a suit for financial well-being. Glancing at a pension statement once a quarter—the meat of EMT propaganda sold for 40 years—won't cut it in the modern world. You can no longer pretend it is *retirement* money and the nest egg will go right back up. Take a quick view of the Japanese Nikkei 225 stock index (see Figure 9.1). The index reached nearly 40,000 in 1989. Now, over 25 years later, it is still in the range of 20,000. The Japanese do not believe in buy and hold, and should you? With USA stocks at all time highs, interest rates at 0 to negative, can you pretend stocks will go up forever with no 50 percent decrease ever again?

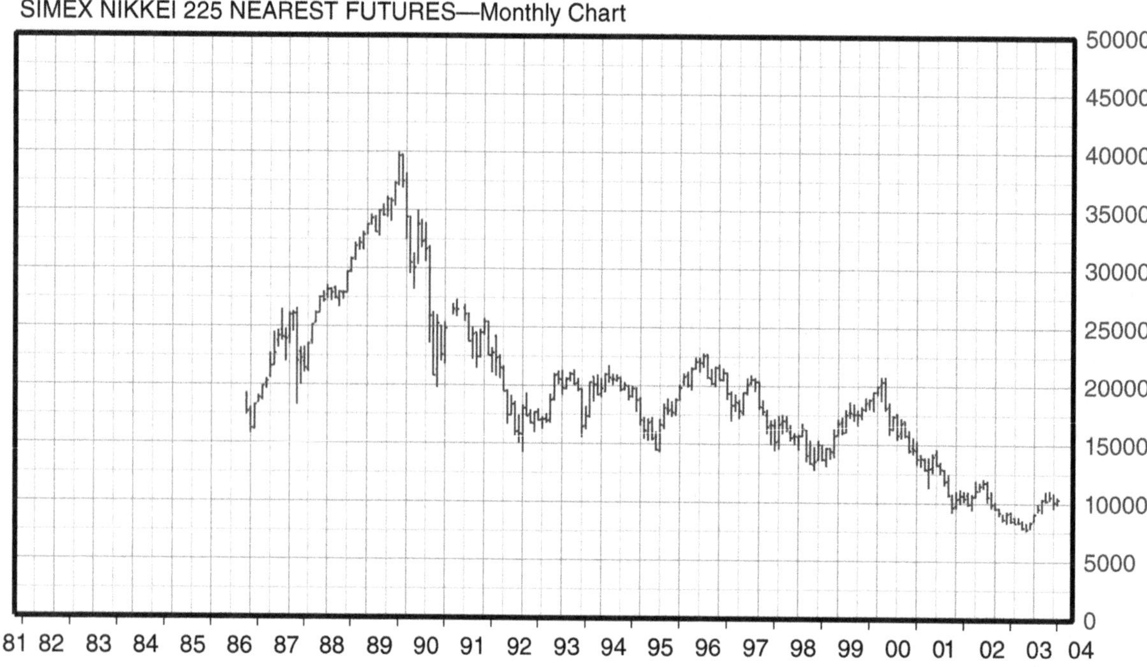

FIGURE 9.1: Weekly Chart Nikkei 225, 1985–2003 Source:Barchart.com

Going back in time, Table 9.1 shows a chart of the hot tech stocks of 1968:

TABLE 9.1: 1968 Tech Stocks

Company	1968 High	1970 Low	% Drop	P/E at High
Fairchild Camera	102.00	18.00	–82	443
Teledyne	72.00	13.00	–82	42
Control Data	163.00	28.00	–83	54
Mohawk Data	111.00	18.00	–84	285
Electronic Data	162.00	24.00	–85	352
Optical Scanning	146.00	16.00	–89	200
Itek	172.00	17.00	–90	71
University Computing	186.00	13.00	–93	118

Booms and busts all look the same: Boiling down to the terrible twins of greed and fear. Unfortunately for investors, journalists are too quick to use fear based copy to push investors into blindly accepting the new normal as their fait accompli:

> Now, with your portfolio trashed and Social Security looking insecure, you may be having nightmares about spending your retirement haunting the mac-and-cheese, early-bird specials, or about not being able to retire until six years after you've died. With the bull market gone, will the impending retirement of the post-World War II generation be the Boomer Bust?—If you work hard, save and adopt more realistic expectations, you can still retire rather than die in the harness. Earning maybe 9 percent on stocks isn't as good as the 20 percent that you might have grown used to. But it's not bad.[21]

Billionaire hedge fund manager Bill Ackman sold his 27.2 million shares in Valeant Pharmaceuticals at around $11 each. Ackman's Pershing Square Capital Management purchased Valeant at an average cost of $196 a share in 2015.

CNBC
March 13, 2017

Saying 9 percent compounded is not bad compared to 20 percent compounded mindlessly ignores the pure math. Imagine the last 25 years and two investments of $1,000 each. The first investment generated 9 percent for 25 years, and the second investment generated 20 percent for 25 years:

- $1,000 compounded at 9% for 25 years = $8,600.
- $1,000 compounded at 20% for 25 years = $95,000.

Here are two examples of not having a real compounding plan, but rather trusting buy and hope as the only strategy:

- "What do you do if you find yourself at retirement age without enough to retire on? You keep working," John Rother, AARP's policy director.
- "I've worked hard all my life and been a responsible citizen and it's not supposed to be threatened at this point," Gail Hovey who works for nonprofit groups in Hawaii.

What makes the Dow at 10,000 particularly noteworthy for us is that it means that the index has to rise a mere 26,000 more points to vindicate the prophecy of those two jokers who achieved 15 seconds of fame when we were in full bubble by predicting it would hit 36,000. We kind of miss them; they were always good for comic relief. Another 500 points and we've a hunch they'll be back peddling the same old moonshine.

Alan Abelson
Barron's
December 15, 2003[22]

No one wants to see Gail homeless. Yet, no one wants society to reward one group's harebrained mistakes with government bailouts paid for by a second group that did not make the same errors. Recall the 2008 bailouts and ponder the next round of bailouts sure to follow the next crash. Life should not be contorted into *fair* when it isn't. No political body should legislate outcomes. It is fine to compound trading gains, but it's not fine for government to compound idiocy.

Even well-paid top professionals running pension assets are always no-exit-plan buy and holders when the chaos reveals who is swimming naked: "Every major investor in the nation was heavily invested in WorldCom [Dot-com-era scam]. They were one of the largest corporations in America," stated the New York State comptroller.[23]

There is no greater source of conflict among researchers and practitioners in capital market theory than the validity of [trend following]. The vast majority of academic research condemns it as theoretically bankrupt and of no practical value . . . It is certainly understandable why many researchers would oppose [trend following]: the validity of [trend following] calls into question decades of careful theoretical modeling claiming the markets are efficient and investors are collectively, if not individually, rational.[24]

Their *plan* was the same idiocy employed by the State retirement plans of Michigan, Florida, and California that also lost in Dot-com bubble favorite WorldCom because they all had no exit strategy:

- The State of Michigan reported an unrealized loss of about $116 million on WorldCom
- The State of Florida reported an unrealized loss of about $90 million on WorldCom
- The California Public Employees Retirement System (CalPERS) reported an unrealized WorldCom loss of about $565 million

Referring to $8.4 million in WorldCom stock that dropped in value to only about $492,000, Robert Leggett of Kentucky Retirement Systems said, "Until you actually sell it, you haven't lost it."

Ouch. That is not logical.

Make sure as an observer of these players you too don't get caught up in the particular market or year—as if only the current day can teach a lesson. It's the wrong-headed psyche of these decision makers that's worth noting. Learning from losers after all is quite a smart strategy. Ed Seykota summed up the competitive playing field: "The best measure of your intention is the result you get."[25]

Avoiding Stupidity

CNBC anchor Joe Kernen's first interview with trend following trader David Harding instantly became a case study for the media zeitgeist. At the time of this interview, Harding's firm, Winton Capital, was managing $21 billion dollars in assets for clients via trend following strategies (today over $30 billion).

Kernen started the interview reading from a piece of paper describing Harding as a systematic trend follower who believes scientific research will succeed in the long run. He wondered out loud if *computers* were used and asked Harding to describe his trading strategy.[26]

Harding, on remote from London, responded his firm "goes with the flow." He said he follows trends and makes money going *long* on rising markets and *short* on declining markets. He said there had been enough trends for his firm to make money nearly every year for the last 15 years. [27]

Fundamental analysis creates what I call a reality gap between what should be and what is. The reality gap makes it extremely difficult to make anything but very long-term predictions that can be difficult to exploit, even if they are correct.

Mark Douglas

Kernen pounced, wondering whether he could blame Harding and other trend followers for oil and gold going higher and "for the pendulum swinging much further than it should on a fundamental basis."[28]

Harding thought there might be a kernel of truth to Kernen's point, but there was only so much time to elaborate. Kernen, under his breath, with a huge wide smile emerging, interjected: "Uh, yeah."[29]

Harding reminded Kernen his firm was limited by speculative position limits set by government and his trading size was tiny by comparison to major investment banks. Harding went on to further clarify he doesn't trade by a "gut feel." He added: "We don't just make it up." He also didn't apologize for his scientific approach to markets, an approach he defined as "rigorous."[30]

Kernen replied with a shot across the bow, bringing up failed hedge fund Long-Term Capital Management (LTCM). He saw it as ironic that LTCM folded in the same year (1998) Harding's firm launched: "I heard science and I heard you've never had a down year, and it just reminded me of LTCM." Kernen talked sarcastically about the Nobel Prize winners at LTCM, their "algorithms," and the fact they never had a down year until their blowup.[31]

Harding quickly clarified his firm did have a down year in 2009 and his performance success went back over two decades—23 years to be exact. He noted his first firm AHL (which he sold) was now the world's largest managed futures fund. He also addressed LTCM head-on, stating the book *When Genius Failed* (the story of LTCM blowing up) was "required reading" at his firm. [32]

Once an opponent throws down hypocrisy, inconsistency, cognitive dissonance, confirmation bias or a belief in the State as savior or daddy--the hammer comes down. We should all have that hammer.

Michael Covel

Kernen, with condescension, quipped: "I bet it is." He then went on to ask Harding if he could provide some of his best "picks." That question makes perfect sense for every fundamental trader who thinks he can predict the future, but it is a ridiculous question to ask a trend following trader. Harding replied he could not forecast markets: "I can't give you best picks." He pointed out his success comes from having a slight edge and proper betting.[33]

Kernen, still not about to acknowledge anything positive about trend following, smugly asked if Harding would know when the party was over.

Harding was nonplussed, noting that there has been a long history of successful trend following going back 40 years. He also compared recent trending markets to another era—the 1970s.[34]

Kernen, with little journalistic objectivity, shot back that he had heard those kinds of expressions before: "Please let there be another real estate boom because I spent all the money I made.' I heard commodities guys saying that for a while [too]." He then wrapped up with standard pleasantries and one last zinger saying that he hoped Harding could come back again "with the same moniker, same title."[35]

Consider a definition of critical thinking:

> Critical thinking is the intellectually disciplined process of actively and skillfully conceptualizing, applying, analyzing, synthesizing, and/or evaluating information gathered from, or generated by, observation, experience, reflection, reasoning, or communication, as a guide to belief and action. In its exemplary form, it is based on universal intellectual values that transcend subject matter divisions: clarity, accuracy, precision, consistency, relevance, sound evidence, good reasons, depth, breadth, and fairness.[36]

With that in mind:

Whoever wishes to foresee the future must consult the past; for human events ever resemble those of preceding times. This arises from the fact that they are produced by men who have been, and ever will be, animated by the same passions. The result is that the same problems always exist in every era.
Niccolo Machiavelli

1. Is it believable Joe Kernen, the anchor of CNBC's longest-running program, had no knowledge or comprehension of trend following, or other descriptions of it such as managed futures or CTAs? If he was forced to raise his right hand under the threat of perjury, do you think he would still have such limited understanding of trend following and managed futures?
2. When Kernen asked about trend followers purportedly pushing markets further than they should be fundamentally, did that mean he had a way to determine the correct price level of all markets at all times?
3. When Kernen brought up LTCM in attempt to compare Harding to its demise, did he not understand Harding did not believe in efficient markets? Had he ever looked at a monthly up-and-down track record of Harding or any trend follower?
4. Why ask a trend following trader for "picks"?
5. When Kernen asked Harding if he would come back with the same moniker and title, was he implying he believed Harding would

blow up soon and be back on CNBC under some reformulated firm name—like what the proprietors of LTCM did after their blowup? Has he ever asked Warren Buffett that question?

6. When you find yourself feeling manipulated by the press, remember: "People are sheep. TV is the shepherd."

Now I could easily see some painting this interview differently:

- "Harding set himself up for the LTCM tie-in by framing himself as a computer science shop looking at data and being black box."
- "You have to expect Kernen to kick you. That's what he does. Just like you know what you're going to get from Glenn Beck or Stephen Colbert."
- "Harding says, 'We are the smartest guys on the planet, trends work, and we look at a lot of data.'"

A reader who runs a fundamental advisory service wrote me:

> Whether Kernen's questions were clueless or not is really irrelevant. He did not argue with Harding on any point, and he gave Harding a good opportunity (within the time available) to explain how his firm implements trend following. [Kernen] was an "adult in the room." I'm thinking that's the way serious trend followers ought to consider presenting themselves instead of sarcasm and "we don't predict" as if that is an obvious answer to any question.

One of the things that's striking about talking to people who are politically working in D.C. is, it's so hard to tell what any of them actually do. It's a sort of place where people measure input, not output. You have a 15-minute monologue describing a 15-page résumé, starting in seventh grade.

Peter Thiel

The evidence does not bear those criticisms out. There is a deeper game at play beyond my questions. Joe Kernen is not devoid of academic intelligence. He holds a bachelor's degree from the University of Colorado in molecular, cellular, and developmental biology and a master's degree from MIT. He worked at several investment banks including Merrill Lynch. I am no Harding apologist, but I have spent time with him. That research time, coupled with his public career and track record, make him one of the most learned trend trading voices of the past 20 years.

Kernen had a pre-formulated agenda. His questioning was a transparent attempt to marginalize Harding and by extension trend following. Imagine if the interview started like this:

> We at CNBC believe in efficient markets and the use of fundamental analysis. Our business model also requires viewers to watch 24/7. Today, we have a guest on who has made billions with trend following trading, which does not require fundamental analysis or CNBC and makes a mockery of EMT. Would you like to know how to make money without ever watching our channel again? Welcome David Harding!

Anyone who doesn't take truth seriously in small matters cannot be trusted in large ones either.
Albert Einstein

You can bet no one at CNBC ever pulled any David Harding SEC filings. I did. Here is one:

> Winton's investment technique consists of trading a portfolio of over 100 contracts on major commodity exchanges and forward markets worldwide, employing a totally computerized, technical, trend-following trading system developed by its principals. This system tracks the daily price movements from these markets around the world, and carries out certain computations to determine each day how long or short the portfolio should be to maximize profit within a certain range of risk. If rising prices are anticipated, a long position will be established; a short position will be established if prices are expected to fall.
>
> The trading methods applied by Winton are proprietary, complex and confidential. Winton plans to continue the testing and reworking of its trading methodology and, therefore, retains the right to revise any methods or strategy, including the technical trading factors used, the commodity interests traded and/or the money management principles applied.
>
> Technical analysis refers to analysis based on data intrinsic to a market, such as price and volume. This is to be contrasted with fundamental analysis, which relies on factors external to a market, such as supply and demand. The Diversified Program uses no fundamental factors.
>
> A trend following system is one that attempts to take advantage of the observable tendency of the markets to trend, and to tend to make exaggerated movements in both upward and downward directions as a result of such trends. These exaggerated movements are largely explained as a result of the influence of behavioral biases, amongst market participants.
>
> A trend following system does not anticipate a trend. In fact, trend following systems are frequently unprofitable for long periods of time in

Happiness is not something you postpone for the future; it is something you design for the present.
Jim Rohn

particular markets or market groups, and occasionally they are unprofitable for spells of more than a year, even in large portfolios. However, in the experience of the principals, over a span of several of years, such an approach has proven to be consistently profitable.

The Winton trading system has been developed by relating the probability of the size and direction of future price movements with certain oscillators derived from past price movements, which characterize the degree of trending of each market at any time. While this is, to some degree, true of all trend-following systems, the unique edge possessed by the Winton system lies in the quality of the analysis underlying this relationship. This enables the system to suffer smaller losses during the inevitable whipsaw periods of market behavior and thus take better advantage of the significant trends when they occur, by focusing more resources on them.

The system was developed by research on price data of a variety of futures contracts between 1981 and 1991 (known as the "in sample data"), and subsequently tested on the data from 1991 to 1997 in order to assess its potential. It has subsequently been updated several times to incorporate more recent market data. This procedure seeks to avoid the risk of over-optimizing, which occurs when a system is allowed to fit itself to the historic data.

Harding and Winton are crystal clear that their world revolves around a non-discretionary system:

Trade selection is not subject to intervention by Winton's principals and therefore is not subject to the influences of individual judgment. As a mechanical trading system, the Winton model embodies all the expert knowledge required to analyze market data and direct trades, thus eliminating the risk of basing a trading program on one indispensable person. Equally as important is the fact that mechanical systems can be tested in simulation for long periods of time and the model's empirical characteristics can be measured.

The system's output is rigorously adhered to in trading the portfolio and intentionally no importance is given to any external or fundamental factors. Whilst it may be seen as unwise to ignore information of obvious value, such as that pertaining to political or economic

What we have been seeing worldwide, from India to the UK to the US, is the rebellion against the inner circle of no-skin-in-the-game policymaking "clerks" and journalists-insiders, that class of paternalistic semi-intellectual experts with some Ivy league, Oxford-Cambridge, or similar label-driven education who are telling the rest of us 1) what to do, 2) what to eat, 3) how to speak, 4) how to think... and 5) who to vote for.

Nassim Taleb

> developments, the disadvantage of this approach is far outweighed by the advantage of the discipline that rigorous adherence to such a system instills. Significant profits are often made by the Winton system, by holding on to positions for much longer than conventional wisdom would dictate. An individual taking trading decisions, and paying attention to day-to-day events, could easily be deflected from the chance of fully capitalizing on such trends, when not adhering to such a system.[37]

CNBC once invited *me* to their offices. They paid my Acela train travel from Washington, DC to New Jersey, so it seemed like a no-brainer opportunity to go behind the scenes of the evil empire. I had no specific knowledge of what they wanted, but the meeting was with producer Susan Krakower, who had invented Jim Cramer's show. Once there, it was clear they were looking for new content. The meeting was in a small, windowless office with Krakower and her two female lieutenants. A Jim Cramer poster hung behind her. It was exactly like when Jerry and George went to meet with NBC on *Seinfeld*.

The biggest cause of trouble in the world today is that the stupid people are so sure about things and the intelligent folks are so full of doubts.
Bertrand Russell

Krakower sat in front behind a large desk, and her two lieutenants flanked on either side. It was triangulation. They peppered me with small-talk questions, yet seemed to have no clue about my writings, research, or thinking. They had not read my books. They only had a headshot I had not seen before (something you might imagine an actor brings to a Hollywood casting call).

She asked me to hypothetically program 10 hours of CNBC air-time. The idea for new programming was blunt: trend following, not more stories. My inability to play the game did not help, and it was easy to see candor was taken as an insult. The conversation bounced around for 30 minutes and—surprise, surprise—there was no further dialogue.

Walking through CNBC's studios that day reminded me of *The Truman Show*: A constructed reality, a staged, scripted TV show. Except instead of it being one person (Jim Carrey's character) who does not know reality, CNBC's *fake* plays to a worldwide audience daily, week after week and year after year.

Analysts go on CNBC daily with unverifiable opinions, and to this day I know many viewers will think, "He sounds bright; he works for JPMorgan, and he's using a lot of financial jargon I don't understand, so he must know something I don't."

He doesn't know what will happen tomorrow.

The fact so many commentators said you could buy so many stocks in the middle of whatever bubble—and were entirely wrong—is proof positive the Wall Street opinion machine is not the answer, nor will they ever have the answer.

Even though there is never sound rationale for listening, of course many do, and they become angry when advice proves disastrous. At one point, one discredited analyst became a whipping boy for investors refusing to accept responsibility:

We are what we repeatedly do. Excellence, then, is not an act, but a habit.
Aristotle

- "Every time my broker mentions him, I get nauseous."
- "For the past few years, every time I'd call them, they'd say, 'He likes [name]' or 'He really likes [name].' As a result, I now own hundreds of shares of these duds."
- "So now when it comes to investment research, we need to think twice about the veracity of top-rate advice and stock picks from someone earning $20 million a year."
- "He should have warned that this epochal bubble was doomed to burst. After all he was the industry's greatest seer."
- "However unfair it is to blame just him, here's a situation when one person's contribution to wholesale disaster is impossible to overlook."
- "Telecommunications stocks were explosive. New companies went public, old companies saw spectacular growth, and he never once warned us that this was all a mirage."

I am not defending any analyst, but if investors have their life savings tied up in market predictions, they are in trouble no matter what. If one stock tanks, leaving a price trend evidence trail, or an entire sector implodes, investors can't whine. No one forced anyone to listen to anyone. It is a choice. Anyone who held Fannie, Freddie, AIG, Bear Stearns, or Lehman Brothers all the way down over the course of 2008, or most recently anyone who held Deutsche Bank or Valeant Pharmaceuticals all the way down, they have no one to blame except the person staring back in the mirror. Valeant, for example, dropped 95 percent since its August 2015 highs. Many of the world's most famous investors (i.e., Bill Ackman/Pershing Square) ignored that drop for an assortment of reasons to "hang on."

No human investigation can be called real science if it cannot be demonstrated mathematically.
Leonardo da Vinci

Yet, in a blame-everyone-else society, certain populations will always refuse responsibility for their decisions. Although they might have lost

Forecasts are financial candy. Forecasts give people who hate the feeling of uncertainty something emotionally soothing.
Student of Ed Seykota's

more than half their portfolio in the last 30 years, they still eagerly accept invitations like this beauty from a brokerage firm that technically imploded in 2008[38]:

> [Pick a name] cordially invites you to an educational workshop . . . Topics discussed:
>
> - Stock Market Forecast for [fill in the blank whatever year].
> - When will the recession end?
> - What do I do now?
> - What are the factors of a good stock market?
> - How did this bear market compare to others?

Never let the fear of striking out get in your way.
Babe Ruth

This firm has produced useless forecasts for decades and still does. But it went under in 2008, only to be rescued by a government-led buyout. Now, almost a decade later, clients have little memory of the then-artificial resuscitation needed to leave their life savings in the hands of all the wrong people.

And of course there is always more fun, games, and chaos on the way. No one knows the exact timing of the next pinprick, but you can bet another black swan is already gearing up for a Pearl Harbor sneak attack. On the other hand, if you are glued to every word from the talking heads for their supposed extra-special ability to forecast the trend change, you are in big trouble.[39]

The way we human beings operate helps to explain why speculative bubbles don't even need the Internet or social media in order to thrive. Looking at the chart of any asset price is enough for investors to reach similar (and hasty) conclusions without phones, e-mails, and such. In short, the fear of missing out is an indirect social contagion.[42]

Assets, once in motion, tend to stay in motion without changing direction, and that turns the old saw—buy low, sell high—on its ear.[40]

You think: "Can't everyone improve and get better?"

Some can, sure, but not all—no way.

Trend follower Jean-Philippe Bouchaud throws cold water on lizard brain decision-making improvements for the masses: "Human brains have most probably changed very little for the last two thousand years. This means that the neurological mechanisms responsible for the propensity to invest in bubbles are likely to influence the behavior of human investors for as long as they will be allowed to trade."[43]

Summary Food for Thought

- Things *happen.*
- Jerry Parker: "'I didn't see it coming.' No one did."
- Some feel forced to do *something* rather than sit there.
- Stop searching for *value.* Even if you locate value, that alone does not ensure your ability to buy, sell or bet right.
- Stock tips only indicate the *buy* side of the equation. They always leave out the *sell* side.
- Charlie Wright: "I have sat through hundreds of hours of seminars in which the presenter made it seem as if he or she had some secret method of divining where the markets were going. Either they were deluded or they were putting us on."
- Mark Twain: "If you tell the truth, you don't have to remember anything."
- Brian Fantana in *Anchorman*: "They've done studies, you know. Sixty percent of the time, it works every time."

Enron stock was rated as Can't Miss *until it became clear that the company was in desperate trouble, at which point analysts lowered the rating to* Sure Thing. *Only when Enron went completely under did a few bold analysts demote its stock to the lowest possible Wall Street analyst rating,* Hot Buy.

Dave Barry[41]

Trading Systems 10

If you don't risk anything, you risk even more.
—Erica Jong

No matter what kind of math you use, you wind up measuring volatility with your gut.
—Ed Seykota[1]

To manage human fallibilities, trend following has a process to counteract behavioral risk. Psychologist Daniel Crosby lays bare in his *Laws of Wealth* where that success foundation starts:

- Consistency
- Clarity
- Courageousness
- Conviction

Sometimes a cigar is just a cigar.
Attributed to Sigmund Freud

Building on those four C's, trend following reduces to *rules* that guide daily decision making.

These rules comprise what are commonly called trading systems. There is no limit to the number of different types of trading systems. But most trend following systems are similar as they seek to capture trends in big liquid markets.

Unlike so many Holy Grails, the never-ending fundamental predictions of this or that, trading systems are quantified. Dunn Capital, for example, has said their trading system has a "programmed risk of a 1 percent probability of suffering a monthly loss of 20 percent or more."[2] That's what I mean by quantifying. That's what serious people do.

At the end of the day, your job is to buy what goes up and to sell what goes down.
Paul Tudor Jones

Risk, Reward, and Uncertainty

Trend following is a precarious balance between risk and reward. If you want the big rewards, take big risks. If you want average rewards and an average life, take average risks. Charles Sanford's commencement address nails it:

It's much too early to tell. I think all we've learned is what we already knew, is that stocks have become like commodities, regrettably, and they go up to limit and they go down to limit. And we've also known over the years that when they go down, they go down faster than they go up.
Leon Cooperman[3]

> From an early age, we are all conditioned by our families, our schools, and virtually every other shaping force in our society to avoid risk. To take risks is inadvisable; to play it safe is the counsel we are accustomed both to receiving and to passing on. In the conventional wisdom, risk is asymmetrical: it has only one side, the bad side. In my experience—and all I presume to offer you today is observations drawn on my own experience, which is hardly the wisdom of the ages—in my experience, this conventional view of risk is shortsighted and often simply mistaken. My first observation is that successful people understand that risk, properly conceived, is often highly productive rather than something to avoid. They appreciate that risk is an advantage to be used rather than a pitfall to be skirted. Such people understand that taking calculated risks is quite different from being rash. This view of risk is not only unorthodox, it is paradoxical—the first of several paradoxes which I'm going to present to you today. This one might be encapsulated as follows: Playing it safe is dangerous. Far more often than you would realize, the real risk in life turns out to be the refusal to take a risk.[4]

The best place to live on this curve is the spot where you can deal with the emotional aspect of equity drawdown required to get the maximum return. How much heat can you stand? Money management is a thermostat—a control system for risk that keeps your trading within the comfort zone.
Gibbons Burke[5]

One of Major League Baseball's best pitchers, all of 24 years of age, died in a 2016 boating accident. Jose Fernández was almost guaranteed to make hundreds of millions of dollars—gone in an instant, perhaps due to a very bad risk choice.

There is no getting away from that reality. There will be failure. Therefore, get over yourself and accept that life is a big league game of chance. And if life is a game of chance, assessing odds in the face of risk is goal number one.

Money under a mattress is no good. The house you purchase could burn down or the real estate market might tank. Investing only in your startup is zero diversification. If your corporate job fails, you lose your employment and nest egg. Buy index mutual funds, pray that buy and hold will always work for you—that's dicey. There is no way to know what will happen next.

We see about 3,000 inbound referred opportunities per year. We narrow that down to a couple hundred that are taken particularly seriously. There are about 200 of these startups a year that are fundable by top VCs. About 15 of those will generate 95% of all the economic returns.

Marc Andreessen

To proceed in the face of risk, begin by accepting markets do not reward stupidity or ignorance in the long run. They reward brains, guts, and determination to find opportunity where others have overlooked and to press on where others fall short.

Every business opportunity is ultimately involved in assessing risk. Putting capital to work in the hopes of making it grow is the goal. The right decisions lead to success and the wrong ones lead to bankruptcy (Bear Stearns, Lehman Brothers, AIG, IndyMac, and so on). The key issues in a solid business plan:

- What is the market opportunity in the market niche?
- What is the solution to the market need?
- How big is the opportunity?
- How do you make money?
- How do you reach the market and sell?
- What is the competition?
- How are you better?
- How will you execute and manage the business?
- What are the risks?
- Why will you succeed?

It turns out that you don't need hundreds and hundreds of securities to be diversified. Much of the effective diversification comes with 20 or 30 well-selected securities. A number of studies have shown that the number of stocks needed to provide adequate diversification are anywhere from 10 to 30.

Mark S. Rzepczynski[6]

Those questions must be answered by everyone regardless of venture or discipline. It is paramount to answer to assess the risk of a business venture, a relationship, and it is just as important to answer honestly if you are going to trade.

Wise minds know the amount of risk taken in life is in direct proportion to how much you want to achieve. If you want to live boldly, you take bold moves. If your goals are meager, they can be reached easily with less risk of failure, but with greater risk of dissatisfaction. One of the saddest figures burns with desire to live big, but to avoid risk, embraces fear and lives lost. He is worse off than the man who tries and fails, or the man who never had desire.

Yet there is hope. If you study risk, you will find there are two kinds: blind risk and calculated risk. The first one, blind risk, is suspect. Blind risk is the calling card of laziness, the irrational hope, something for nothing, the cold twist of fate. Blind risk is the pointless gamble, the emotional decision, and the sucker play. The man who embraces blind risk demonstrates all the wisdom and intelligence of a drunk.

However, calculated risk builds fortunes, nations, and empires. Calculated risk and bold vision go hand in hand. To use your mind, to see the possibilities, to work things out logically and then to move forward in strength and confidence is what places humans above animal. Calculated risk lies at the heart of every great achievement and achiever since the dawn of time.

People tend to use discretion or gut feeling to determine the trade size.
David Druz[7]

Yet when it comes to trading most focus only on how to enter a market. They say, "I've got a way to beat the markets because this trading system I have is right 80 percent of the time. It's only wrong 20 percent of the time." They need to take a step back, "Okay. What does 80 percent right mean?" If 80 percent you don't win much, but 20 percent of the time you lose a lot, losses can far outweigh gains even though you're right 80 percent of the time. The magnitude of wins and losses is the *game*.

Lotteries, for example, reach jackpots of hundreds of millions of dollars or more all the time. And as the jackpot gets bigger, more buy tickets in the buying feeding frenzy. But as they buy more, the odds of winning do not increase. The ticket buyers still have a better chance of being struck by lightning.

For example, the odds of winning the California Super Lotto Jackpot are 1 in 18 million. If one purchases 50 Lotto tickets each week, he will win the jackpot about once every 5,000 years. If a car gets 25 miles per gallon, and a gallon of gas is bought for every Lotto ticket bought, there will be enough gas for about 750 round trips to the moon before the jackpot is won. If you know the odds are against you, don't play.

A man provided with paper, pencil, and rubber [eraser], and subject to strict discipline, is in effect a universal machine.
Alan Turing

Likewise, if your trading system says you have a 1 in 30,000 chance of winning, or roughly the same chance as being struck by lightning, you don't bet everything. You must have a mathematical expectation, an *edge*, or you won't win in the long run. For example, consider a coin-flipping game.

Imagine an unbiased coin toss game. Suppose also you bet that the next flip will be heads and the payoff will be even money when you win (you receive a $1 profit in addition to the return of the wager). The mathematical expectation is:

$$(.5)(1) + (.5)(-1) = 0$$

The mathematical expectation of any bet in any game is computed by multiplying each possible gain or loss by the probability of gain or loss. Then you add the two numbers. In this example, you can expect to gain nothing from playing this game. This is known as fair game, one in which a player has no advantage or disadvantage. Now, suppose the payoff was changed to 3/2, a gain of $1.50 in addition to a $1 bet—the expectation would change to:

$$(.5)(1.5) + (.5)(-1) = +.25$$

Playing this game 100 times would give a positive expectation of .25.[8]

This is the exact type of edge cultivated and honed inside trend following strategy. You might ask, "If everyone knows about expectation, how can I ever find my edge for success in the face of competition?"

Volatility, risk, and profit are closely related. Traders pay close attention to volatility because price changes affect their profits and losses. Periods of high volatility are highly risky to traders. Such periods, however, can also present them with opportunities for great profits.[9]

Good question. Consider a scene from the movie *A Beautiful Mind*, the film biography of mathematician John Nash. Nash and some of his mathematician buddies are in a bar when a sexy blonde and four brunettes walk in. After they admire the new arrivals, Nash and his friends decide to compete for the blonde. However, Nash has reservations, correctly observing if everyone goes for the same woman, they will just end up blocking each other out. Worse, they will offend the rest of the women not chosen. The only way for everyone to succeed is to ignore the blonde and hit on the brunettes. This scene dramatizes the Nash Equilibrium, his most important contribution to game theory. Nash proved in any competitive situation—war, chess, even picking up a date at a bar—if the participants are rational and they know that opponents are rational, there is only one optimal strategy. That theory won Nash a Nobel Prize in economics and transformed the way we think about competition in both games and the real world.[10]

Building off Nash's work Ed Seykota lays out a basic risk definition: "Risk is the possibility of loss." That is, if you own a stock, and there is a possibility of a price decline, you are at risk. The stock is not the risk, nor is loss the risk. The possibility of loss is risk. As long as you own the stock you are at risk. The only way to control risk is to exit. In the matter of trading stocks for profit, risk is unavoidable, and the best you can do is to manage the risk. Risk management is to direct and control the possibility of your loss. The activities of a risk manager are to measure risk and to increase and decrease risk by buying and selling. In general, good risk management combines several elements:

1. Clarifying trading and risk management systems until they can translate to computer code.
2. Include diversification and instrument selection in the back-testing process.
3. Back-testing and stress-testing to determine trading parameter sensitivity and optimal values.
4. Clear agreement among all parties regarding volatility and return expectations.
5. Maintenance of supportive relationships between investors and managers.
6. Above all, stick to the system.
7. See #6, above.

Five Questions

There is no such thing as a risk free investment. The real issue is not whether you want to take risk, but which risks and how many of them you are willing to accept.
Jim Little and Sol Waksman[11]

Answer the following five questions and you will have the core components of a trend following trading system—and be on your way to having your *edge*:

1. How does the system know what to buy or sell?
2. How does the system know how much to buy or sell?
3. How does the system buy or sell short?
4. How does the system get out of a losing position?
5. How does the system get out of a winning position?

These five questions are seminal to trend following, but no less important is attitude. Don't forget: "What do you want? Why are you trading? What are your strengths and weaknesses? Do you have any emotional issues? How disciplined are you? Are you easily convinced? How confident are you in yourself? How confident are you in your system? How much risk can you handle?"

When I discussed trading with Ed Seykota and Charles Faulkner, they both said the first step any person should take before trading is to complete a personal inventory:

- What is my nature and how well am I suited to trading?
- How much money do I want to make?
- What level of effort am I willing to make to reach my goals?
- What, if any, is my investing/trading experience?
- What resources can I bring to bear?
- What are my strengths and weaknesses?

If you have a $100,000 account and you're going to risk 5 percent, you'd have $5,000 to lose. If your examination of the charts shows that the price movement you're willing to risk equals $1,000 per contract, then you can trade five contracts. If you want to risk 10 percent, then do 10 contracts.

Craig Pauley[12]

Answering these questions is mandatory for when you are in the middle of the zero-sum game and adrenaline and sweat are flowing heavy—you can't afford to blink when chaos hits.

What Do You Buy or Sell?

Will you trade stocks? Currencies? Futures? Commodities? What markets will you choose? While some people might focus on limited, market-specific portfolios, such as currencies or bonds, others pursue a more widely diversified portfolio of markets. For example, the AHL Diversified Program (the largest trend following fund in the world, now run by Man Financial) trades a diversified portfolio of over 100 core markets on 36 exchanges. They trade stock indices, bonds, currencies, short-term interest rates, and commodities (e.g., energies, metals, and agriculturals; see Table 10.1):

TABLE 10.1: AHL Portfolio

Currencies	24.3%
Bonds	19.8%
Energies	19.2%
Stocks	15.1%
Interest rates	8.5%
Metals	8.2%
Agriculturals	4.9%

Large events happen more often than you would expect in systems that exhibit power law distributions.

Department of Physics
UC Santa Barbara

AHL does not have fundamental expertise. No trend following trader keeps fundamental experts on staff. They do not have an in-depth understanding of the companies that comprise whatever stock index. Their expertise is to take these different markets and "make them the same" through price analysis.

I learned not to worry so much about the outcome, but to concentrate on the step I was on and to try to do it as perfectly as I could when I was doing it.
Steve Wozniak

When you look at trend following performance losses are offset by winners. No one ever knows which market will be the big trend that pays for the losses—hence the need for diversification.

AHL is even more precise about diversification:

> The cornerstone of the AHL investment philosophy is that financial markets experience persistent anomalies or inefficiencies in the form of price trends. Trends are a manifestation of serial correlation in financial markets—the phenomenon whereby past price movements inform about future price behavior. Serial correlation can be explained by factors as obvious as crowd behavior, as well as more subtle factors, such as varying levels of information among different market participants. Although they vary in their intensity, duration, and frequency, price trends are universally recurrent across all sectors and markets. Trends are an attractive focus for active trading styles applied across a diverse range of global markets.

You can see AHL's words perform in practice by how another trend following trader described diversification:

> Portfolio diversification is often said to lose its importance after you have 7–10 different instruments in your portfolio. We found this simply not to be the case. Pre June 2007, we traded with 18 major markets in the program and we were in 7–8 of them most of the time. In short, our exposure was 7–8 markets at any one time, while signals in 18 were possible. After evaluating the program we discovered that most of our losses [at the time] were coming from one or two sectors that hit their maximum loss at roughly the same time. A breakout in the Ten Year Notes was most likely followed by a breakout in the Five Year Notes. Trading several highly correlated markets had led to exaggerated losses because these markets triggered a larger drawdown as they were stopped out together.

Talk is cheap. Show me the code.
Linus Torvalds

He increased his portfolio to over 40 markets with the goal of being in 15+ markets most of the time. And he still left his core trading system (entry and exits) the same. The turnaround in results was dramatic—all from changing the portfolio diversification.

Paul Mulvaney, for example, made over 40 percent in October 2008 alone. His performance was generated from these markets:

Currency: 8.91 percent

Interest Rates: 2.78 percent

Stocks: 14.59 percent

Metals: 9.83 percent

Energy: 3.43 percent

Crops: 7.84 percent

Livestock: 4.51 percent

Yes, that is one great outlier month. All months and sectors will not always be positive—clearly. But Mulvaney's performance during one of the worst months *ever* is a wakeup call to trend following possibilities. After all, author and film star Ben Stein famously said if you made money in October 2008, you were doing something *wrong*.

Now, fast-forward eight years. On June 23, 2016 51.9 percent of the United Kingdom voted to exit the European Union. Most prognosticators were surprised, if not shocked. Mulvaney's performance was +17 percent on June 24. His one-day Brexit performance, his greatest one-day return in the history of his firm, is a fantastic illustration of being on the right side of *surprise*. Long-time trend following trader Robert Rotella adds, "Qualitative examination of price movements suggests that markets were trending in the direction of the Brexit exit in the prior months. This is supported by systematic analysis over the same period."

There is never one perfect portfolio composition that will capture the next trend. Many trade different portfolios for untold different reasons. Generally speaking, trend followers trade the same markets. However, although larger trend following funds might avoid smaller markets, such as pork bellies or orange juice, other trend following traders might trade currency or bond-only portfolios. Salem Abraham, for example, once made a killing off cattle. Whatever markets chosen to trade, remain open to opportunity when it arrives.

There is a random distribution between wins and losses for any given set of variables that defines an edge. In other words, based on the past performance of your edge, you may know that out of the next 20 trades, 12 will be winners and 8 will be losers. What you don't know is the sequence of wins and losses or how much money the market is going to make available on the winning trades. This truth makes trading a probability or numbers game. When you really believe that trading is simply a probability game, concepts like "right" and "wrong" or "win" and "lose" no longer have the same significance. As a result, your expectations will be in harmony with the possibilities.

Mark Douglas

Author Tom Friedman makes the strong argument for sound strategy in a complex world: "If you can't see the world, and you can't see the interactions that are shaping the world, you cannot strategize about the world. And if you are going to deal with a system as complex and brutal as globalization, and prosper within it, you need a strategy for how to choose prosperity for your country or company."[13] Friedman knows all too well the real power brokers in today's frighteningly interconnected world are traders—not politicians.

How Much Do You Buy or Sell?

If you look at the past 30 years, there is only one fundamental investor who has consistently produced huge absolute returns—Warren Buffett. Compare that, however, with countless trend following traders who have outperformed throughout bull and bear market cycles. One of the keys to our success is to have a huge diversification of over 100 financial and commodity markets. A systematic, mechanical approach is the only way to successfully trade so many markets . . . every decision . . . from market entry, position sizing, stop placement . . . must be fully automated.
Christian Baha

The question many avoid at all costs is the question of money management. Also called risk management, position sizing, or bet sizing, it is a critical component to trend following success, as Gibbons Burke observes:

> Money management is like sex: Everyone does it, one way or another, but not many like to talk about it and some do it better than others. When any trader makes a decision to buy or sell short, they must also decide at that time how many shares or contracts to buy or sell—the order form on every brokerage page has a blank spot where the size of the order is specified. The essence of risk management is making a logical decision about how much to buy or sell when you fill in this blank. This decision determines the risk of the trade. Accept too much risk and you increase the odds that you will go bust; take too little risk and you will not be rewarded in sufficient quantity to beat the transaction costs and the overhead of your efforts. Good money management practice is about finding the sweet spot between these undesirable extremes.[14]

"I've only got a certain amount of money. How much do I trade?" If you have $100,000 and you want to trade Microsoft, well, how much of your $100,000 will you trade on Microsoft on your first trade? Will you trade all $100,000? What if you're wrong? What if you're wrong in a big way and you lose your entire $100,000 on one bet?

Trend following by design makes small bet sizes initially. So, if you start at $100,000 and you're going to risk 2 percent that equals $2,000. You might say to yourself, "I've got $100,000—why am I only risking

$2,000? What's the deal? I've got $100,000. $2,000 is nothing." That's not the point. You can't predict where the trend will go—you don't know up or down.

One trader's view on the initial risk decision: "There are traders who are unwilling to risk more than 1 percent, but I would find it surprising to hear of any trader who risks more than 5 percent of assets per trade. Bear in mind risking too little doesn't give the market the opportunity to allow your profitable trade to occur."[15]

It's not how right or how wrong you are that matters but how much you make when right and how much you do not lose when wrong.

George Soros

Think about money management as getting physically fit. Let's say you're a male athlete and you want peak performance. You weigh 185 pounds (84 kg) and you're six foot one (185 cm). Well, guess what? You can't lift weights six times a day for 12 hours a day for 30 straight days without hurting yourself during those 30 days. There's an optimum amount of lifting you can do in a day that gets you ahead without setting you back. You want to be at that optimal point, just as you want to get to an optimal point with money management.

Ed Seykota describes that optimal point with the concept of *heat*:

> Placing a trade with a predetermined stop-loss point can be compared to placing a bet: The more money risked, the larger the bet. Conservative betting produces conservative performance, while bold betting leads to spectacular ruin. A bold trader placing large bets feels pressure—or heat—from the volatility of the portfolio. A hot portfolio keeps more at risk than does a cold one. Portfolio heat seems to be associated with personality preference; bold traders prefer and are able to take more heat, while more conservative traders generally avoid the circumstances that give rise to heat. In portfolio management, we call the distributed bet size the heat of the portfolio. A diversified portfolio risking 2 percent on each of five instruments has a total heat of 10 percent, as does a portfolio risking 5 percent on each of two instruments.[16]

The Pareto principle, the 80/20 rule, the law of the vital few, states that, for many events, roughly 80% of the effects come from 20% of the causes.

Wikipedia

A student of Ed Seykota's adds: "There has to be some governor so I don't end up with a whole lot of risk. The size of the bet is small around 2 percent." Seykota calls his risk-adjusted equity "core equity" and the risk tolerance percentage "heat." Heat can be turned up or down to suit the trader's pain tolerance—as the heat gets higher, so do the gains, but only up to a point. Past that point more heat starts to reduce the gain. Traders must be able to select a heat level where they are comfortable.[17]

In limiting risk, people also limit the opportunity for gain. It is common, today, for investors to own six or eight mutual funds, each of which is likely to be invested in hundreds of stocks. This will, they hope, assure that no little bump, no little meltdown, overly upsets their portfolios. But since when was investing about avoiding the bumps?
Roger Lowenstein

Do you trade the same with $100,000 as you would $200,000? What if your $100,000 goes to $75,000? Tom Basso knows many traders usually begin trading small, say with one contract, and as they get more confident they might increase to 10 contracts. Eventually they attain a comfort level of 100 or 1,000 contracts where they may stay. Basso counsels against this. He stresses the goal is to keep things on constant leverage. His method of calculating the number of contracts to trade keeps him trading the same way even as equity increases or decreases.[18]

One of the reasons traders don't trade proportionally as capital increases is fear. Although it might feel comfortable when the math dictates you trade a certain number of shares or contracts at $50,000, when the math dictates trade a certain amount at $500,000, you might become risk-averse. So instead of trading the optimal amount at whatever capital you have, some trade less. This can be avoided by creating an abstract money world. Don't think about what money can buy; look at numbers like when playing Monopoly® or Risk®.

Dunn Capital speaks to "the money as a way to keep score" perspective: "Part of Dunn's approach is adjusting trading positions to the amount of equity under management. He says if his portfolio suffers a major drawdown, he adjusts positions to the new equity level. Unfortunately, he says, not enough traders follow this rather simple strategy."[19]

What are the three best market indicators? In order they are:

1. Price

2. Price

3. Price

If you start with $100,000 and you lose $25,000 you obviously now have $75,000. You must make your trading decisions off $75,000 not $100,000. You don't have $100,000 any more. However, Paul Mulvaney felt I was missing a critical aspect in money management: "Trend following is implicitly about dynamic rebalancing, which is why successful traders appear fearless. Many hedge fund methodologies make risk management a separate endeavor. In trend following it is part of the internal logic of the investment process."

When Do You Buy or Sell?

When do I buy? When do I sell? These are the questions that keep investors and traders up at night. Yet there is no reason why the buy and sell process should be a melodrama. Obsessing about when to buy or sell keeps your limited time focused on things you can't control.

For example, Apple has been trading between 100 and 120 for six months. All of a sudden Apple jumps, or breaks out, to a price level of 130. That type of upward movement from a range is an entry trigger for trend following strategy. They think, "I might not know that Apple is going to continue upward, but it's been going sideways for a while, and all of a sudden, the price has jumped to 130. I'm not in this game to try and find bargains or cheap places to buy. I'm in this game to follow trends, and the trend is up."

The good thing about science is that it's true whether or not you believe in it.

Neil deGrasse Tyson

One trend trader outlined the simplicity: "As our systems are designed to send a buy or sell signal only when a clear trend develops. By definition, we never get in at the beginning of a trend or get out at the top."[20] If your goal is to ride a trend that starts at 50 and goes to 100, it does not make a difference whether you got in at 52 or 60 or 70. Even if you got in at 70 and the trend went to 100, you still made a lot. Now, if you got in at 52 (and how you think you might predict the bottom, I will never know) you made more money than if you got in at 70. There are plenty of traders out there who think, "Oh, I couldn't get in at 52 so I won't get in at all even if I have the chance to get in at 70."

Richard Dennis smacks that thinking: "Anytime the market goes up a reasonable amount—say a strong day's work—after you've put on a position, it's probably worth adding to that position. I wouldn't want to wait for a retracement. That is everyone's favorite technique—to buy something strong that retraces. I don't see any justification in the statistics for that. When beans are at $8.00 and go to $9.00, if the choice is to buy them at $9.00 or buy them if they retrace to $8.80, I'd rather buy them at $9.00. They may never retrace to $8.80. Statistics would show that you make more money buying them and not waiting for a retracement."[21]

Even if people are somewhat familiar with Dennis's approach to trend trading, they still love the entry obsession—a misdirection of energy and focus. Seykota dead-panned, "The entry is a big concern before it happens, a small concern thereafter."[22]

You've got to think about big things while you're doing small things, so that all the small things go in the right direction.

Alvin Toffler

He is saying after you are in the trade, entry price isn't important. You have no idea how high the market is going to go or not. You should be concerned about protecting your downside in case the market goes against you, as opposed to creating drama associated with the *perfect* entry. After all, trend following trades can last extended time frames:

"Positions held for two to four months are not unusual, and some have been held for more than one year, says a spokesman. Historically, only 30–40 percent of trades have been profitable."[23]

The words of the great baseball player Ted Williams immediately come to mind: "Hitting a baseball, I've said it a thousand times, is the single most difficult thing to do in sport. If Joe Montana or Dan Marino completed 3 of every 10 passes they attempted, they would be ex-professional quarterbacks. If Larry Bird or Magic Johnson made 3 of every 10 shots they took, coaches would take the basketball away from them."[24]

Có chí làm quan, có gan làm giàu.

How is it possible to make money with only 40 percent winners? Trend following firm Campbell & Company is clear: "Say, for example, on the 60 percent, you lose 1 percent of your capital, but on the 40 percent winning trades you make 2 percent. Over longer periods of time, say a year or more, this would net 20 percent on a broadly diversified program."[25]

Trend following rules to enter and exit are driven by what is commonly called technical indicators. The technical indicator for trend following strategy is price action (i.e., breakout, moving average, etc.). However, many remain preoccupied with the hundreds upon hundreds of other indicators that promise *prediction*. They debate nonstop which is better, always assuming there must be something better. And they always yell at me that I didn't provide them the *secret*.

Technical indicators, however, are small components of the overall trading system. They are some of the tools needed in the trading toolkit, but not the kit itself. A technical indicator accounts for maybe 10 percent of the overall trading success. When some trader opines, "I tried indicator X and found it was worthless" or "I tried indicator Y and found it useful," that makes no sense. These statements imply an indicator is the actual trading system. By itself a technical indicator is meaningless. That means the suits that come on CNBC every week to talk *technicals* are *meaningless*? Yes.

People, they love blood. They love action. Not this talky, depressing, philosophical bullshit.

Michael Keaton
Birdman

When Do You Get Out of a Loser?

The time to think most clearly about why and when to exit is before getting in. In any trading system, the most important thing is to preserve your capital. A preset sell strategy gives you opportunity to not only preserve capital, but to also redeploy into more opportune markets. When do trend traders get out of a losing position? Fast! This is fundamental to trend following.

The logic of cutting losses and then cutting them even more has been around far longer than trend following, as Bernard Baruch notes: "If a speculator is correct half of the time, he is hitting a good average. Even being right 3 or 4 times out of 10 should yield a person a fortune if he has the sense to cut his losses quickly on the ventures where he is wrong."

You are buying and selling risk. As a technical trader, that's the only way to look at it.

Mark van Stolk[26]

For example, you enter GOOG with a 2 percent stop loss. This means if you lose 2 percent, you exit. Period. Get out. Don't debate it. Look back at the British pound trade in my Chapter 2 Dunn profile. That chart (see Figure 2.3) shows the constant starts and stops. Dunn keeps receiving entry signals and then exit signals. The trend is up and then it is down. He enters and then exits. Dunn knows he can't predict the direction of the British pound. He only knows he has received an entry signal, so he gets on board. Then he receives an exit right after that, so he gets out. Then another entry signal, then another exit comes. Dunn did say he "rides the bucking bronco."

Traders call these back-and-forth swings *whipsaws*. Whipsaws are quick ups and downs that go nowhere. Your trade is jerked, or whipsawed, back and forth, causing small losses due to lack of sustained trends. Seykota says the only way to avoid whipsaws is to stop trading (see his "Whipsaw" song on YouTube). Whipsaws are part of the game. Don't want to live with them—don't trade.

An old pro trader sent in a great story about his days at trend following incubator Commodities Corporation that makes the point:

> Back in the early '90s, Commodities Corporation (CC) brought a few Japanese traders in for some in-house "training." Of course the ultimate and true goal was to capture some big Japanese money. I was still in their good graces and CC asked me to have lunch with a couple of these gentlemen. They were new to the program, and I hoped to give them some insight into how I handled the process of trading. I told them they had to come up with a method or system that fitted who they were. Then I told them I thought it was great to find a mentor and I was available anytime they had questions or issues and that is still me today. I then began to discuss how important risk management was and

It became evident that the most direct way to make money and the one most compatible with my strengths was to be a position trader using computer models to develop the entry and exit points.

Michael J. Clarke

> that I was willing at that time to risk only 1 percent per bet in dealing with public money. I am more aggressive today, but that was then. I told them that losses were part of the process in finding winners. I will never forget as long as I shall live the youngest trader looked me square in the eye and with a very puzzled look asked "You have losses?" I knew right then these birds had a very long way to go and I often wonder what happened to them.

Reason's biological function is to preserve and promote life and to postpone its extinction as long as possible. Thinking and acting are not contrary to nature; they are, rather, the foremost features of man's nature. The most appropriate description of man as differentiated from nonhuman beings is: a being purposively struggling against the forces adverse to his life.
Ludwig von Mises[27]

Guaranteed that young trader moved onto another profession.

When Do You Get Out of a Winner?

You have seen the headline hype: "Use Japanese candlesticks to spot reversals" or "Determine support and resistance" or "Learn proper profit-taking." Stop. You can't spot reversals until they happen. There is no way to define the concept of support and resistance as 100 people could have 100 different definitions. These directions all try to do the impossible—predict. Tom Basso slams profit objectives: "A new trader approaches an old trend follower and asks, 'What's your objective on this trade?' The old trend follower replies that his objective is for the position to go to the moon."

Exiting a winning position can be a challenge because you have to be comfortable with letting a trend run as far as it can, crest, and then begin to decline before considering an exit with profits. Say you are up 100 percent in paper profits. If you cash in, those paper profits become real. But you have made a big mistake because you limited yourself in how much you could make. If you are long several positions, and there are huge open profits on the table, and the trend is still up—that is not the time to get out of a winner.

I have no ego in the stock market. If I make a mistake I admit it immediately and get out fast. If you could play roulette with the assurance that whenever you bet $100 you could get out for $98 if you lost your bet, wouldn't you call that good odds? I never bought a stock at the low or sold one at the high in my life. I am satisfied to be along for most of the ride.
Nicolas Darvas
***Time* Magazine**
May 25, 1959

Profit targets cap profits. For example, you enter at 100 and before you ever enter, you establish you will exit if the price reaches a 25 percent gain or 125. The idea of a profit target sounds wise at first blush. However, if you are riding a trend you have to let it go as far as it can go. You need to fully exploit the move. You don't want to exit at 125 and watch the trend go to 225.

Although profit targets keep you from getting to 225, they also play a damaging role in the overall trend following portfolio. Trend following needs those home runs to pay for its whipsaw losses. If you are artificially creating a profit target for no other reason than comfort, you are limiting potential for big trends. This, in turn, limits the ability to cover the small losses you've incurred. If you had used profit targets, there is no way you would have been around to win the huge profits from the events described in Chapter 4.

Trend following profits come from the meat, or middle, of a trend (see Figure 10.1):

Novice traders trade 5 to 10 times too big. They are taking 5 to 10% risks on a trade they should be taking 1 to 2 percent risks.

Bruce Kovner

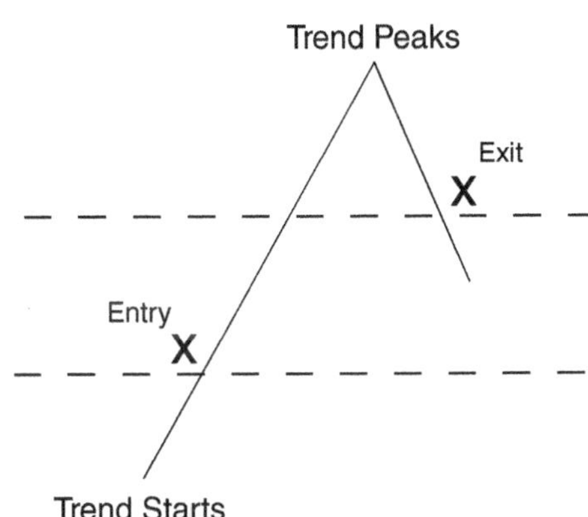

FIGURE 10.1: Trend Following Entry/Exit Example: The Middle Meat

Your Trading System

When you mechanize a trend following trading system, you take all discretionary judgments and build them into rules. For example, if you are uncomfortable with a high level of risk, you make a rule that sets a tolerable risk level. If you trade a currency-only portfolio, you make rules for that contingency from the outset. The logic is to *hardwire* all scenarios you could possibly see in advance across your portfolio. If a market rises 100 percent in short order you have rules that dictate the action to take. If a market loses 10 percent, follow the rules.

You must have an unambiguous plan established in advance. It also helps to constantly be aware of the downside. Larry Hite gives that legendary stoic perspective: "We approach markets backwards. The first thing we ask is not what can we make, but how much can we lose. We play a defensive game."[28]

Frequently Asked Questions

FAQ 1: Starting Capital

Ed Seykota was once asked how much money someone should have before starting to trade. He responded, "Good money management is equity invariant. I'd ask a trader who thinks he needs a certain amount before he can trade exactly what amount he would need to stop trading." There is no dollar amount too little or too big that allows you to sit back and assume your starting capital alone is the secret.

Numerous factors related to starting capital exist, not least of which is the personal discipline and ability to stick with it. Anyone who promises a certain amount of starting capital needed to *win* is full of it. However, what if you have unlimited resources? *Rich* can be a benefit or strike against you. Jaromir Jagr, the famous hockey player, and trend trader William Eckhardt have polar views on starting capital.

Information: the negative reciprocal value of probability.
Claude Shannon

Jagr is the riverboat gambler. He doesn't play the stock market but romps through it; last year, published reports estimated he took a hit [loss] of anywhere from $8 million to $20 million in the Dot-com market. He doesn't just have a girlfriend who is pretty and bright; he has a girlfriend who is a former Miss Slovakia and a second-year law student.[29] Jagr might be a great hockey player, but his approach is straight to the poorhouse. Backed by the millions he made playing hockey Jagr is the trader Eckhardt avoided:

> I know of a few multimillionaires who started trading with inherited wealth. In each case, they lost it all because they didn't feel the pain when they were losing. In those formative first years of trading, they felt they could afford to lose. You're much better off going into the market on a shoestring, feeling that you can't afford to lose. I'd rather bet on somebody starting out with a few thousand dollars than on somebody who came in with millions.[30]

I am hard-pressed to recall when any sort of bubble was accurately identified in real time on the cover of a major media publication. If anything, the opposite is true.
Barry Ritholtz

Consider net worth examples of trend following traders that started as one-man shops:

- Bruce Kovner is worth over $5.3 billion.[31]
- John W. Henry is worth $2.1 billion.[32] He used his trend following gains to buy the Boston Red Sox for $700 million.

- Bill Dunn made $80 million in 2008 when the rest of the world was blowing up.[33]
- Michael Marcus turned an initial $30,000 into $80 million. He also taught Bruce Kovner. Marcus was a student of Ed Seykota's.[34]
- David Harding is worth over $1.387 billion.[35]
- Kenneth Tropin made $120 million in 2008 as buy and hold collapsed. Earlier in his career he led John W. Henry's firm.[36]

People that work hard and legitimately do everything that they can, they tend to be luckier.

Julian Edelman
Patriots Football Team

That is inspirational. A small fraction of those huge fortunes is motivating—if you still have a pulse.

FAQ 2: Trend Following for Stocks

One of the great myths about trend following is it does not work on stocks. That is 100 percent false. Trends in stocks are no different than trends in currencies, commodities, or futures. Jerry Parker's trend following firm, for example, has adapted its system to stock trading and he is not alone (e.g., David Harding). He notes his system works well with stocks, particularly stocks in outlier moves that are in single industries.[37]

Bruce Terry, a disciple of Richard Donchian, dismisses out of hand the not-for-stocks meme: "Originally in the 1950s, technical models came out of studying stocks. Commodity Trading Advisors (CTA) applied these to futures. In the late 1970s and early 1980s, stocks were quiet and futures markets took off. That is how the CTA market started. It has come full circle. People are beginning to apply these models to stocks once again."[38]

From my leave-no-stone-unturned research, I am reminded of the opening line I found in a *Managed Account Reports* article from 1979: "Trading stocks and commodity futures by means of trend following techniques is an art with a long history."[39]

Whales only get harpooned when they come to the surface, and turtles can only move forward when they stick their neck out, but investors face risk no matter what they do.

Charles A. Jaffe

FAQ 3: Computers and Curve Fitting

Larry Hite knows a computer can't get up on the wrong side of the bed in the morning, which is why computers handle his decision making and implementation of his trading rules: "If your boyfriend or girlfriend breaks up with you, you'll feel one way; if you get engaged, you'll feel another way."[40]

It is useful to think of yourself as an intellectual nomad. In the world of the nomad, there is no carefully defined turf.
Thomas Friedman[42]

Hite would much rather have one smart guy working on a lone Macintosh than a team of well-paid timekeepers with an army of supercomputers. At the same time, however, Hite is adamant the real key to using computers successfully is the thinking that goes into the computer code. When someone asked him why go the computer route when people power is so important, he replied, "Because it works—it's countable and replicable. I'm a great fan of the scientific method. And the other things are not scientific. If I give you the algorithms, you should be able to get the same results I did. That to me means a great deal."[41]

However, technology can over-optimize or curve-fit a trading system to produce something that looks great on paper alone. Barbara Dixon, a Donchian student, notes: "When designing a system, I believe it's important to construct a set of rules that fit more like a mitten than like a glove. On the one hand, markets move in trends, but on the other hand, past results are not necessarily indicative of future performance. If you design a set of rules that fit the curve of your test data too perfectly, you run an enormous risk that it will fizzle under different future conditions."[43]

A robust trading system, one that is not curve-fit, must ideally trade all markets at all times in all conditions. Trend following parameters or rules must work across a range of values. System parameters that work over a range of values are considered robust. If the parameters of a system are slightly changed and the performance adjusts drastically, beware. For example, if a system works great at 20, but does not work at 19 or 21, that system is not robust. On the other hand, if a system parameter is 50 and it also works at 40 or 60, the system is much more robust and reliable.

If you think about it, it doesn't matter what you do because landings are most likely to be average. If a pilot had an exceptional landing, his next landing was likely to be average. If he had a poor landing, his next landing was likely to be average, also. By slicing the data and only looking at what follows good landings and praise, you only see part of the picture. You must consider how data was selected before you can draw conclusions.
James Simons

Trend trader David Druz has long championed robustness in trading systems. He dismisses trades of short-term traders who fight for quick hitting, arbitrage-style profits as pure noise. Traders who focus on short-term trading often miss the longer-term trends—those trends where long-term trend following often bags its biggest opportunities. To wait like that, you need complete faith in your trading system. However, you are in serious trouble if all you think you need to succeed at trading is the latest hardware and software. As Barbara Dixon warns: "Contemporary databases, software, and hardware allow system developers to test thousands of ideas almost instantaneously. I caution these people about the perils of curve fitting. I urge them to remember one of their primary goals is to achieve discipline, which will enable them to earn profits. With so many great tools, it's easy to change or modify a system and to develop indicators rather than rules, but is it always wise?"[44]

It is easy to get caught up in the computer program hype. Advertisements run nonstop everywhere promising instant riches. Fancy charting software will make you feel like Master of the Universe, but that is false security. When describing his early trading successes, John W. Henry made clear it was philosophy, not technology:

> In those days, there were no personal computers beyond the Apple. There were few, if any, flexible software packages available. These machines, far from being the ubiquitous tool seen everywhere in the world of finance and the world at large today, were the province of computer nerds . . . I set out to design a system for trading commodities. But things changed quickly and radically as soon as I started trading. My trading program, however, did not change at all. As I said, it hasn't changed even to this day.[45]

First, solve the problem. Then, write the code.
John Johnson

One of Henry's long-time associates elaborated: "Originally all of our testing was done mechanically with pencil and graph that turned into Lotus spreadsheets, which was still used extensively in a lot of our day to day work. With the advent of some of these new modeling systems like system writer, day trader and some of the other things, we've been able to model some of our systems on these products. Mostly just to back test what we already knew, that trend following works."[46]

Tom Basso clarifies: "You'll find that the more you're computerized, the more markets you'll be able to handle. Computers leverage your time if you know how to use them."[47] And Richard Donchian makes clear the *time* needed to execute successfully as a trend following trader:

> If you trade on a definite trend following, loss-limiting method, you can trade without taking a great deal of time from your regular business day. Because action is taken only when certain evidence is registered, you can spend a minute or two per market in the evening checking up on whether action-taking evidence is apparent, and then in one telephone call in the morning, place or change any orders in accord with what is indicated. Furthermore a definite method, which at all times includes precise criteria for closing out one's losing trades promptly, avoids . . . emotionally unnerving indecision.

The minute or two Donchian refers to takes preparation time. After you test your system and are satisfied with results enough to begin trading, the work is still not done. System results must be periodically compared to actual results to ensure that testing closely reflects real time. It is also helpful to keep a journal to record how well you stick to executing your system.

One trend trader trained at Commodities Corporation told me:

> Early in my trading career I found myself hung up on the "need" to be right rather than the "desire" to make money. I learned early that being "right," of having a high percentage of winners, had very little to do with my overall trading success. Those who have a need to be right with a high percentage of winners will find themselves passing on their best trading opportunities, assuming they use some degree of discretion in their trade selections. One of my trading buddies enjoys a trading success rate annually of around 15 percent winners with 50 percent losers and 35 percent breakeven trades. In 2005, he made over 300 percent on his initial beginning of year trading capital [of] a seven-figure account. This is a risk-reward numbers game and most who think it is something else usually face a "forced awareness" at some point in their trading careers. To further emphasize my point, everyone has seen ads on the Internet for systems being promoted at 90 percent accuracy. I bet 3/4 of these systems are based on a set of past criteria that have very little to do with their future performance. Let's say you do 100 trades in a calendar year. The average winning trade makes a net $100 so you make a net $9,000 in the "winners." Now the bad news is the 10 losing trades are for $1,000 so you lose a total of $1,000 for the year in a system that had 90 percent winners. Now, I realize this is a stretch from reality, but mathematically this is what happens once a trader commits capital to the so-called "sure thing" trading systems!

The obvious is always least understood.
Prince Klemens von Metternich

Trend following legend Ken Tropin was even more specific:

> In order for a system to be successful, it has to be what I call robust. Robust means I can test that system in a market I designed it around. Say I'm using it in the treasury bonds, and then if I switch that market and I try that system in the Euro, it still works. And if I change its

> parameters, it still works. And if I switch it over to corn—something totally different than treasury bonds—it still works. And if I look at some data that was out of sample from what I designed it around, it still works. Then I have something that might be interesting and have a chance of living in the future. Because the nature of data is it changes a little all the time. And so the key to success in systems trading is to have what I call a loose fitting suit. I can't have a suit that's so tight and perfectly proportioned to me that if I gain two pounds, it won't fit the data anymore.

Andrew Lo of MIT brings it back to simplicity:

> The first [rule of thumb] being that no matter how complex and subtle a strategy is and no matter how sophisticated it might be, it has to be possible to describe that strategy in relatively simple and intuitive terms to a sophisticated investor. In other words, regardless of how subtle and impressive and sophisticated the strategy is, I've never come across anything that couldn't be described in relatively straightforward terms as to what the value added of that strategy was.

FAQ 4: Day Trading Limits

When you trade with higher frequency, the profit you earn per trade decreases while transaction costs stay the same. This is not a winning strategy. However, many traders believe that short-term trading is less *risky*. Short-term trading by definition is not less risky, as evidenced by the catastrophic blowouts of Victor Niederhoffer and Long-Term Capital Management (LTCM). Do some short-term traders excel? Yes. However, think about the likes of whom you might be competing with when you are trading short-term, such as Jim Simons and Toby Crabel. Professional short-term traders, the HFT guys, have hundreds of staffers working as a team 24/7. They are playing for keeps, and looking to eat your lunch in the zero-sum world. You don't stand a chance Mr. Day Trading Dreamer.

Nearly every time I strayed from the herd, I've made a lot of money. Wandering away from the action is the way to find the new action.
Jim Rogers

But day trading flaws are invisible to many. Sumner Redstone, billionaire CEO of Viacom, talked of constantly watching Viacom's stock price, hour after hour, day after day. Although Redstone is a brilliant entrepreneur and has built one of the great media companies, his obsession with share price is pointless. Redstone might see his company as undervalued, but staring at the screen will not boost it.

FAQ 5: Wrong Way to View a Trade

Leo Melamed is chairman emeritus to the CME (episode #265 on my podcast). He is recognized as the founding father of financial futures. He was named to the top 10 most important Chicagoans in business of the twentieth century. Yet, with this tremendous resume and success, he is clearly not a trend following trader:

The idea behind digital computers may be explained by saying that these machines are intended to carry out any operations which could be done by a human computer.
Alan Turing

> The Hunt silver debacle also provided the setting for my worst trade. My company partner George Fawcett and I had become bullish on silver beginning in June 1978, when it was trading around $5.00 an ounce level. We were right in the market, and silver prices moved higher. In September 1979, silver reached the high price of $15.00 an ounce, and the profit we were each carrying was substantial. George and I had never before made that kind of money, it was truly a killing. How much higher would silver go? Wasn't it time to take the profit? Large profits, as I learned, were even more difficult to handle than large losses. I had a very good friend . . . with special expertise in the precious metals markets. . . . Since he knew I was long silver, I ventured to ask him his opinion. "Well, Leo," he responded, "you have done very well with your silver position and I really can't predict how much higher silver will go. But I'll tell you this, at $15.00, it is very expensive. On the basis of historical values, silver just doesn't warrant much higher prices." I never doubted that he gave me his honest and best opinion. I transmitted this information to George and we decided that if nothing happened by the end of the week, we would liquidate our positions and take our profits. That's exactly what we did. This was in late October 1979. So why was this my worst trade when in fact it was the biggest profit I had ever made up to that time? Because, within 30 days after we got out of our position, the Hunt silver corner took hold. It did not stop going higher until it hit $50.00 an ounce in January 1980. George and I had been long silver for nearly two years, and had we stayed with our position for just another 30 days, we would have been forced to take a huge profit. We both vowed never to calculate how many millions we left on the table.[48]

I can see why his 1979 silver trade was his *worst trade*. He described no predefined entry criteria. He never gives a reason why he and his partner were bullish on silver in 1978, nor does he explain why he entered the silver market other than it was at such a low price ($5.00). When the price of silver started to increase, he attempted to find out how high it would go, which is impossible. However, because he had no clearly defined exit rationale, he was uncertain when to get out. Without an exit strategy Melamed fell back on conventional trading wisdom that buying higher highs is wrong. He attempted to use fundamentals to justify that silver would not continue to increase and then set a profit target to get out. By having a profit target instead of an exit plan, Melamed lost out on millions of dollars of profit. Now, he has had a fantastic career, but his trade example contrasts sharply with trend following.

Lynx Asset Management, which uses mathematical models to decide when and which securities to buy and sell, posted a 5.1 percent gain on [Brexit] Friday in one of its funds. Capital Fund Management, a $7 billion firm in Paris, gained 4.2 percent that day in its Discus fund, while Systematica Investments, the $10.2 billion fund run by Leda Braga, gained 1.35 percent in its main BlueTrend fund.

Bloomberg

Rob Romaine brings it back to preparation: "The value of a disciplined trading systems approach is that it allows you to design your strategy during non-stressful times. Then, when the markets are tough, you need only to execute your plan rather than being forced to face difficult decisions under pressure when you are most likely to make mistakes."

Let me state emphatically the big picture point: If you are sitting in front of 20 monitors pretending to be Master of the Universe, like Bobby Axelrod in *Billions*, and imagining you can watch all those screens simultaneously and react cat-quick to thousands of pieces of real time data, give me a break. You can't, even though this guy would argue vociferously for his supernatural monitor scanning skills.

The computer model tells us when to get in and when to get out. The computer understands what the price is telling us about the trend of the market. All of the systems are designed to risk modest amounts of capital and to stay with winners as long as possible.

Ken Tropin

Summary Food for Thought

- Money is how you keep *score*.
- Ewan Kirk: "Have we changed things on the basis of what happened? The answer is no. We did not lose the faith. We are always grounded in research, and coming up with new ideas. If a model is losing money, but is within the statistical expectation, you can't just chop and change everything because you have a period of poorer performance."[49]
- Paul Tudor Jones: "I teach an undergrad class at the University of Virginia, and I tell my students, 'I'm going to save you from going to business school. Here, you're getting a hundred-grand class, and I'm going to give it to you in two thoughts, okay? You don't need to go to business school; you've only got to remember two things. The first is, you always want to be with whatever the predominant trend is. You don't ever want to be a contrarian investor.'"[50]
- Larry Tentarelli: "My biggest winners over time have come from two signals. Crossing > 200 SMA, and new 52-week highs. That's it."
- Josh Hawes and Paul King: "The four ways to make money trading: Making money when price moves, making money when price does not move, arbitrage, market making/scalping/high frequency trading."
- Seth Godin: "If someone needs directions, don't give them a globe. It'll merely waste their time. But if someone needs to understand the way things are, don't give them a map. They don't need directions, they need to see the big picture."
- Leo Tolstoy: "The two most powerful warriors are patience and time."

Life shrinks or expands in proportion to one's courage.
Anaïs Nin

The Game

Treat your life like a game.
—Ray Dalio

Trends come and go. Trend followers do too. Some stay longer than others.
—Ed Seykota[1]

In *Absolute Returns*, author Alexander Ineichen stresses that trading is nothing more than a *game*. There are three types of players in this game:

- Those who know they are in the game.
- Those who don't know they are in the game.
- Those who don't know they are in the game and have become the game.[2]

If, within a half of an hour of playing whatever game, and you don't know who the patsy is, you're the patsy or the *game*.

Throughout, I have introduced traders who didn't know they were in the game and became the game in the big events of Long-Term Capital Management, the Barings Bank collapse, the October 2008 market crash, and Brexit. I have introduced traders and investors who did

Larry Hite described a conversation with a friend who couldn't understand his absolute adherence to a mechanical trading system. His friend asked, "Larry, how can you trade the way you do? Isn't it boring?" Larry replied, "I don't trade for excitement; I trade to win."

not know they were in the game and who pursued Holy Grails that never panned out. And I introduced trend following traders who knew they were in a game and brought an edge to the table every time they played. If you know it's a game and you must know that by now, the choices are stark.

Acceptance

Many Turtles claim the biggest reason they no longer tolerate immense drawdowns or strive for colossal returns is because customers want a more conservative approach.[4]

If you're concerned this work will create a new generation of trend following traders, and that impact in the markets will negatively affect the frequency, direction, and intensity of trends (as well as an ability for everyone to make money), take note of timeless wisdom from trend follower Keith Campbell: "We are trend followers, not trend generators. At the beginning or end of a major trend, we may provide a little bump or a minor goose, but it will be an extremely superficial, temporary effect."[3]

He is 100 percent spot on. Recall Larry Harris in Chapter 3: Traders play the zero-sum game for numerous reasons. Not all play to win. However, trend following is about playing the zero-sum game to win. And let's face it, that attitude will cause feelings of intimidation, defensiveness, and jealousy. At the end of the day, for trend following trading to lose its effectiveness, dramatic changes must unfold:

Periods of above-average performance are alternated with periods of below-average performance. As soon as the inevitable, less attractive market environment commences, investors with wrong expectations are likely to become disgruntled. They will start complaining and with good reason: They will not understand why they lose money.
Transtrend

- *No more passive buy and hold*: Those believing in fundamental analysis (vast majority of market participants) would have to switch how they invest. Will they cease buy and hope, long-only index approaches and start trend following? *Never*. Globally there are $80 trillion dollars of investable assets, and only $200 billion are in trend following strategies. A quarter of 1 percent in trend following means no way.
- *Start trading both long and short*: Most will not sell *short* due fear, ignorance, or confusion. They trade long only. That changes when?
- *Index and mutual funds cease*: That is hard to do with retirement programs mandating *legally* that average Joe be 100 percent invested in certain instruments, while *legally* being precluded from other opportunities.
- *Embrace money management*: Most don't know how much to buy or how much to sell. They only worry about when to buy rarely thinking about when to sell. Recklessly bet 50% on one opportunity

alone that could have the odds of a coin flip? People do it all the time. Need even more proof? Las Vegas and Macau (China). Go see both firsthand.

- *Disprove Daniel Kahneman and Amos Tversky's work*: As long as there are human beings trading on markets and regardless if robots are involved or not, chaos will reign supreme. You want to fixate on robots and code as a game changing excuse? Hold on. Let me ask: "Who do you think programs the robots?" *People* write the algorithms that make the robots execute. There will always be excessive reactions up and down with trends to exploit for the systematically inclined.

The only way to make sense out of change is to plunge into it, move with it, and join the dance.

Alan Watts

- *End career risk*: Author Jason Zweig, "You might think a fund manager's job is to beat the market. But, in fact, a fund manager's job is to keep his job." That conflict kills trend following acceptance on Wall Street: "What? This trend following stuff doesn't spin off massive commissions for me? 'No, Mr. Jones you don't want that! Let me tell you about some news circulating around this great bio-tech-virtual-reality-porn penny stock…'" People love the *fantasy*.
- *Trust, but verify*: Too many don't have an understanding about process. They trust guys wearing $5000 suits no questions asked. They judge trading outcomes with zero understanding of the skill-luck interplay. Wealth alone is not wisdom—never forget that.
- *Central bank interventions go away*: Seizing control of your financial future is a must, especially in a world filled with crazed bankers hell bent on taking what you have left. The pressing fear: At the next bubble pop the system won't be able to raise asset prices again because the bullets will have left the chamber. At that moment everyone will officially be Japan—no more stock market wealth effect to trick investors into believing they are rich. The jig will be up. But the real problem isn't that central bankers are out of ammunition. The problem is they have the patient tied to the operating table, with zero anesthesia, performing Civil War era surgery—knowing full well the odds for survival with a hacksaw are brutal. Never, ever, underestimate how crazy things can get. When does central bank fun stop? It doesn't.
- *Stop asking "why?"*: Too many demand narratives for market moves. They must know *why*. Trend following doesn't need to know *why*.

The broad application of these principles globally in markets all around the world, Chinese porcelain, gold, silver, markets that exist, that don't exist today, markets that others are making lots of money in that we're not trading. We will eventually start broadening out and realizing that trend following is a great way to trade. What other way can you trade and get a handle on risk?

Jerry Parker[5]

Let's be candid: Most are more comfortable with the status quo—even if that means losing their life savings when the next black swan swims in—and at least then if the neighbors lose it all too, they can be happy in misery together. Accepting that all of their market knowledge is faulty would predictably trigger in investors a mega release of the stress hormone cortisol. Millions would rather zone out on Netflix, bicker on Facebook, post on Instagram, send troll tweets, farm digital crops, or pretend the next president will solve it all, than learn how to trade correctly for the chance at the life changing gain.

Markets may initially trend for fundamental reasons, but prices overshoot by ludicrous amounts. At some point, prices go up today simply because they went up yesterday.
Michael Platt

Don't Blame Me

It's not surprising that trend following is sometimes accused of throwing markets into disarray. Whenever a stock tanks, a bubble bursts, or scandal hits, winning traders catch the blame 9 times out of 10. The blame is never affixed to the little old lady in Omaha who lost her life savings gambling on biotech penny stocks. The blame is never placed on the masses that were gambling the Dow would go up forever, only to see it crater 50 percent. Few take responsibility for losses, and who better to target when the mob is feeling panicky than rich winners? Here are my favorite misconceptions that make trend following devil incarnate *evil*:

Future shock is the shattering stress and disorientation that we induce in individuals by subjecting them to too much change in too short a time.
Alvin Toffler

- *It trades futures, currencies, commodities, ETFs, etc.*: The vast majority of trend following traders trade on regulated exchanges. We can all trade there. If we can all go there, why is trend following singled out? Politics.
- *It uses leverage*: Great traders use the tools at their disposal, one of which is leverage. The key is not to overdo leverage like so many on Wall Street do time and time again.
- *It causes worldwide panics*: Trend following does no such thing; it reacts to unexpected events. There is no crystal ball.
- *It doesn't invest; it trades*: The markets are for *trading*, not *investing*. The markets reward winners, not losers. We can all choose and if we choose wrong, it's time to look in the mirror.

Most battles are won before they are ever fought.
General George S. Patton

Giving trend followers flak for making money on the downside ignores the skill involved: "Traders have always been an easy target for the press whenever the public is looking for someone to blame for volatile markets, and the press have singled out 'the short sellers.' Making money in down markets is portrayed as obscene and to blame for additional turbulence.

The industry is not about 'bad boys' manipulating the market and gambling; it is about specific trading skills practiced by highly experienced traders who are rewarded on performance alone."[6]

The notion that producing money in down markets is obscene is in itself obscene. Markets have rules. You can go long or you can go short. Serious players trying to make f-you money deal with the rules and don't make excuses. And if you don't know the rules, that's on *you*.

Jerry Parker, however, believes trend following must do better at explaining the inherent *skill* set: "Another mistake we made was defining ourselves as managed futures [industry term for trend following], where we immediately limit our universe. Is our expertise in that, or is our expertise in systematic trend following or model development? So maybe we trend follow with Chinese porcelain. Maybe we trend follow with gold and silver, or stock futures, or whatever the client needs. But a day will come when people will see that systematic trend following is one of the best ways to limit risk and create a portfolio that has some reasonable expectation of making money."[7]

In an unpredictable world, trend following is the best tool to manage risk and uncertainty while possibly producing out-sized returns. The performance sets of David Harding, Martin Lueck, Ken Tropin, Leda Braga, Ewan Kirk, Bill Dunn, Jean-Philippe Bouchaud, Jerry Parker, Keith Campbell, George Crapple, and Larry Hite, to name a few over the past 40 years, are incontrovertible facts.

The Sharpe ratio appears at first blush to reward returns (read: good) and penalize risks (read: bad). Upon closer inspection, things are not so simple. The standard deviation takes into account the distance of each return from the mean, positive or negative. By this token, large positive returns increase the perception of risk as though they could as easily be negative, which for a dynamic investment strategy may not be the case. Large positive returns are penalized and therefore the removal of the highest returns from the distribution can increase the Sharpe ratio: a case of "reductio ad absurdum" for Sharpe ratio as a universal measure of quality.

David Harding

Decrease Leverage, Decrease Return

Richard Dennis's Turtle students (see my book *TurtleTrader*) were originally instructed to make as much money as possible. They had no restrictions except to shoot for home runs. They were absolute return traders while under Dennis' guidance. However, when they went out solo to trade for clients, there was style drift. Many accepted clients who demanded less leverage and ultimately less return.

Dunn Capital knows to aim for and win big profits, trader and client must be synchronized. Dunn is adamant about alignment: "Now there is, of course, the possibility of turning down the leverage and trading more capital, but with less leverage. That works fine if the client will go along with you and you're charging management fees because you're charging management fees on the capital and then incentive fees on the profit. [We do] not charge any management fees to any of its clients . . . we care about the numbers that are generated."[9]

Everyone wants to invest when you're at new highs and making 50 percent a year. Everyone says they want to get in at a 10 percent drawdown or a 20 percent, or whatever, and no one ever does it. I just want to point out that right now, here is another chance to do just that—buy us at historical lows—and very few people are thinking in those terms. They want to buy the lows, but never seem to.

Richard Dennis[8]

Today is in the middle of June and there is a lot of talk about the weather, the grain situation, and whether it rains or snows or is dry. I have no idea. It's not the kind of thing I deal with. I don't have any way to use information like that. I don't think anyone else really does either. If I think it is going to rain, perhaps it's an indication of how I should dress for the day, but little else.[10]

Some might feel safer with watered-down trend following at a lower-vol, lower-reward, but the true way to the change your life money is through higher-vol, higher-reward. The key, regardless of leverage choice, is to be in concert, as trend trader Jason Russell prescribes: "Managers often say they are managing to long-term objectives but act to meet short-term objectives of clients who have not spent the time understanding what trend following means to them. As much as the managers, industry, and regulators try to educate and illustrate, the ultimate responsibility lies in the hands of the client."

Bottom line, trend following strategies stylistically vary due to volatility targets (leverage choices), speed (short or long-term trend targeting) and sector exposure (narrow or widely diversified). Trader Josh Hawes summed up the choices from another vantage: "There is fund level risk, account level risk, trading system-level risk and position level risk." Let that sink in before you leap.

Fortune Favors the Bold

Optimism means expecting the best, but confidence means knowing how to handle the worst.
Max Gunther[11]

It's more than the model, though. An associate drove home the point: "Trend trading and even trading in general isn't for everyone. As too few people check out what the day-to-day life of a trader is like, and trend trading specifically, I strongly recommend they find out before making a life-changing commitment."

Life-changing commitment means not needing to be right. Most must be *right* no matter what. They live to have others know they're right. They don't even want success. They don't want to win. They don't want money. They want to be absolutely *right*. The winners, on the other hand, they just want to *win*.

That's not all. You commit to patience in a trading process not structured on quarterly performance measures. You work hard to gain experience and great experience leads to discipline. You commit to the long-term. A *real* strategy might have one year when you are down 10 percent. The following year you might be down 15 percent. The next year you might be up 115 percent. If you quit at the end of the year two you never get to year three. That's the reality of sound strategy—for life or trading

Although this may seem a paradox, all exact science is dominated by the idea of approximation.
Bertrand Russell[12]

Larry Hite paints the picture of that risk choice:

> Life is nothing more than a series of bets and bets are really nothing more than questions and their answers. There is no real difference between,

"Should I take another hit on this Blackjack hand?" and "Should I get out of the way of that speeding and wildly careening bus?" Each shares two universal truths: a set of probabilities of potential outcomes and the singular outcome that takes place. Every day, we place hundreds, if not thousands, of bets—large and small, some seemingly well considered, and others made without a second thought. The vast majority of the latter, life's little gambles made without any thought, might certainly be trivial. "Should I tie my shoes?" Seems to offer no big risk, nor any big reward. While others, such as the aforementioned speeding and wildly careening bus, would seem to have greater impact on our lives. However, if deciding not to tie your shoes that morning causes you to trip and fall down in the middle of the road when you finally decide to fold your hand and give that careening bus plenty of leeway, well then, in hindsight the trivial has suddenly become paramount.

To receive my free interactive trend following presentation send a picture of your receipt to receipt@trendfollowing.com.

With trend following, you commit to a bigtime decision that's not trivial: Trade by yourself seizing opportunity, or let a trend following pro do it for you. There are pros and cons to both choices, but you won't know the best direction until you get in the game and stop with the *passive-buy-and-hope-long-only-everything-will-be-all-right-I-trust-the-Fed-implicitly-black-swans-are-extinct* insanity.

For unlike the foundation of the efficient market theory, trend following's enduring principles are not grounded in intricate algorithms or kept inside theorems with obvious holes. Trend following principles are solid proof that typical strategy seen across Wall Street and Main Street is at best built on a clumsy error or at worst a slick lie.

Our system of elite education manufactures young people who are smart and talented and driven, yes, but also anxious, timid, and lost, with little intellectual curiosity and a stunted sense of purpose: trapped in a bubble of privilege, heading meekly in the same direction, great at what they're doing but with no idea why they're doing it.

William Deresiewicz[13]

Note: This was the original ending for my first four editions, but for this 5th edition I added extensive new *Interviews* and *Research* sections.

Section II

Trend Following Interviews

To act without needing a reason, to sit still without knowing how, to ride the current of what is—This is the primal virtue.[1]
—Chuang-Tzu, *The Second Book of the Tao*

Trend following is my fun, but along the way I stumbled into another passion: interviews. During the writing of my second book, *TurtleTrader*, and during the production of my film, by necessity I developed interview skills. And in 2012 after my fourth book, *The Little Book of Trading*, I launched a podcast. It has gone far beyond trading to Charlie Rose guest diversity.

There is no magic trend following formula. There is a magic trend following thinking. *Find* that.
Michael Covel

Now, with 5 million plus listens, topics run the gamut: investments, economics, decision-making, health, human behavior, and entrepreneurship. My guests have included Nobel Prize winners: Robert Aumann, Angus Deaton, Daniel Kahneman, Harry Markowitz, and Vernon Smith. James Altucher, Dan Ariely, Robert Cialdini,

Kathleen Eisenhardt, Marc Faber, Tim Ferriss, Jason Fried, Gerd Gigerenzer, Sally Hogshead, Ryan Holiday, Jack Horner, Steven Kotler, Michael Mauboussin, Tucker Max, Steven Pinker, Barry Ritholtz, Jim Rogers, Jack Schwager, Philip Tetlock and Walter Williams have also appeared.

And I would argue that my collection of interviews with trend following traders and behavioral pros—the core thrust of *Trend Following*—is second to none. That's why with this new edition I include curated interviews. Think *Market Wizards,* but for trend following. These seven market pros bring the trend following wisdom you must know:

- Chapter 12: Ed Seykota
- Chapter 13: Martin Lueck
- Chapter 14: Jean-Philippe Bouchaud
- Chapter 15: Ewan Kirk
- Chapter 16: Alex Greyserman
- Chapter 17: Campbell Harvey
- Chapter 18: Lasse Heje Pedersen

Ed Seykota

12

Edward Arthur Seykota (see Chapter 2) pioneered systems trading using early punch-card computers to test ideas. In his influential best seller, *Market Wizards: Interviews with Top Traders*, author Jack Schwager devotes a chapter to Seykota and writes that his "achievements must certainly rank him as one of the best traders of our time."[1]

Michael: I know you look at trend following from not only a trading perspective, but a life perspective.

The stock market is never obvious. It is designed to fool most of the people, most of the time.

Jesse Livermore

Ed: I think if you're going to really be a trend follower you're going to have a lot of trouble limiting it to one area. Because let's say you have a trend following system. You say, "I'm going to have a diversified portfolio, a trend following portfolio. I'm going to free myself up from emotions. Emotions have always been a big problem here, so I'm going to have a diversified trend following portfolio or I'm going to invest in somebody else's portfolio and that's going to fix this emotional problem."

Then what happens? Their investment or their portfolio goes up and down and they get emotional problems with that. You don't really fix your emotions by having a system. What you do is you just move them up stream. You have constituents within the portfolio that used to bother you, and they went up or down, and then now you have a portfolio that goes up and down so you just move the problem upstream. Ultimately you have to say, "What is it that I'm feeling and what do I do when I feel these things and can I come up with better and more useful or productive ways of responding when the thing goes up and down?" Eventually, you've got to come to terms with that.

The best trend followers are the ones that have made peace with themselves, "This is what I do in the case of things going up or down, with the value increasing and decreasing. This is how I behave and this is how I act," and of course as you know, there are all kinds of things you can do when things go up. Some people, when something goes up, they sell. Some people when things go up, they buy and when they keep going up some people sell more and some people buy more. And if you go to extremes in either of those cases you're counterproductive, self-destructive. You've got to know how to do that and you've got to do it consistently. You've got to do it in your personal life.

I'm an optimist in the sense that I believe humans are noble and honorable, and some of them are really smart. . . . I have a somewhat more pessimistic view of people in groups.
Steve Jobs

If you do these things in your personal life as well it supports trend following. Because if you're not in alignment between your overall philosophy, how you behave as a person, and you try to do trend following, there's going to be conflicts. And so we in Trading Tribe hardly ever talk about actual trading or what the markets are doing. What we're working with is the emotional reaction to volatility or emotional reaction to loss or to structure or authority or all these other issues.

If people straighten these things out, their relationships with their significant others or their children get better. They report more satisfaction in all areas of life. And oh, incidentally, their trading is getting better. They don't quite know how that happened, but they've turned into a person that now can cope with uncertainty and can cope with volatility, and they couldn't do it before. You can't take a system and use that to medicate your feelings. Some people say, "I'm just going to suppress my feelings." Stiff upper lip approach, grin and bear it or clench your teeth and hope for the best.

I tend to go the other way, "What's the positive intention to these feelings?" Celebrate them. Find out the positive intention and as soon as you do that the feeling disappears and you go onto the next feeling. I'm more of the go with the flow on the feelings as well. There's a lot of different approaches.

By now, after we've been doing this a couple decades, we're developing a body of knowledge on how to do this and to what extent can we actually reprogram response patterns, and we're getting pretty good at this. You can follow what we're doing. I've put it all on my blog at www.seykota.com. All of this is free if people want to go on there. And we're documenting the growth of all kinds of people that are using this technology and it seems to be, to the extent they use it, working pretty well for them.

Michael: It always seems to me the place that one is trying to find is just some peace and contentment. To be able to sit in a room and not have this anxiety, worrying constantly, and if one has that, to work on that. I see parallels to your work in meditation when I read Zen scholars like Alan Watts. It seems like there's commonalities with some of your work and the Eastern thought process. Do you see that?

Ed: I believe every feeling has a positive intention. For instance, if you're in the house and you smell smoke, you hear crackling sounds, and notice the temperature going up in the room and you conclude that maybe the house is on fire. That would be a really good time to feel anxiety, take some action and respond to it.

EMT says everything I stand for and everything I have done my entire life is a complete waste of time.
David Harding

I'm not so sure you want to medicate your mind, anesthetize yourself and put yourself into a meditative state where you don't respond. That's not really what I'm saying. You want to notice the feeling you're having in the moment and act appropriately and you want to learn the difference between medicating a feeling and responding to it proactively.

I'm not suggesting you always aim towards peacefulness; sometimes you want to get busy. You might want to get busy and put a trade on or you might want to get busy and take some corrective action, some risk control. Or you might want to take some action and get into some opportunity. Whatever it is, you can learn to come into harmony with your feelings and to some extent it's nice to just be able to be peaceful and watch your feelings and watch your mind, and rest. It's important to rest particularly when you feel tired.

I don't recommend using either Trading Tribe technology, which I call TTP, the Trading Tribe Process, or anything else for medicinal purposes like a drug or alcohol or a sedative. There's a difference between using any of these technologies as a sedative and I don't think any of the Zen masters really recommend blissing out and staying there permanently. I think they want to be a little bit responsive and proactive to whatever feeling arises in the moment.

Time series momentum represents one of the most direct tests of the random walk hypothesis and a number of prominent behavioral and rational asset pricing theories. Our findings present new evidence and challenges for those theories and for future research.[2]

Michael: I love constant learning. What's the better way to handle expressing oneself? There's always a better way to do it.

Ed: I think so. I try. We're here in the moment. I'm learning something from you and I'm trying to be responsive. I'll think about this later and say, "Oh man, I really could have said that better." But that's how life is. I do the best I can in the moment and then I go back and maybe do it differently next time. I try to learn and study my responses and say, "Can I change the response?" And that's what we do in the Trading Tribe. We try to look at what our responses are to our feelings and then we practice identifying, "What is it we are doing? How are we getting the result we're getting and can we change our response patterns and get different results next time around?"

Michael: The only way you can learn is to extend yourself in front of somebody who has more experience, and once you extend yourself there's the chance that you might be forced to learn something that makes you feel like, "Wow, why didn't I just say it that way? I could have said it the way he just told me." But you wouldn't get to the point of knowing the better way until you've extended yourself the wrong way.

Ed: You set up an environment in which the goal is for people to help each other improve. This is true in the Trading Tribe and some companies have this down pretty well. Some other organizations too, where personal growth becomes important, people [may] correct you or offer advice and you say, "Thank you for helping me learn something."

In a lot of situations somebody will correct you or give you advice and then you get upset about it. You may say something to protect yourself, put them down, swear at them, tell them to keep their distance or whatever.

Knowing when to explore and knowing when to quit both have value.
Michael Covel

When you have an expansive economy and a company that's growing, everybody's trying to do better than the culture in that company. When you have growth, when you have a free competition society and free competition, you have a competitive startup firm.

And somebody says to somebody else there's a better way to do this, and they say, "Thank you for telling me." And they start doing it that way. When you get a survival company, one that's overly restrictive and political and there's regulations, you better mind your own business and don't go talking to somebody else about what they should be doing.

The environment in one case is pro personal growth and pro learning, and the other one is not. It's very territorial and very defensive. You can walk into companies and you can sense this right away. Some are open to grow and then they get mature. And if they start getting to the Govopoly model and they start going the other way . . .

Michael: One of the things that you do in your *Govopoly* book is talk about the strategy of trend following. And you offer trend following as a means to cope as we move towards this Govopoly system that you see as inevitable. But I would love for you to go back in time a little bit, if you will, because you've had an interesting career.

You've had some interesting mentors, interesting students, but there's a couple of traders in your early years that had a really strong influence on you. I would love for you to share wisdom or memories about two gentlemen in particular and that'd be Amos Hostetter and Richard Donchian.

Amos Hostetter, he was at Commodities Corporation and Richard Donchian at Hayden Stone. Two very accomplished early pioneers in the field of trend following.

Fear is only as deep as the mind allows.

Japanese Proverb

Ed: I'd be glad to share what I know. I knew Donchian a lot better than Hostetter. Donchian had noticed this system, the two-week rule in copper. Two-week rule: you buy something when it makes highs for two weeks and you sell it when it makes lows for two weeks. I asked him once, "How did you come up with the two-week rule?" And he said, "I don't exactly know and you're the first person that's ever asked." He said that he just kind of came up with it and I think that was the start of automated trend following [coming up to the two-week rule].

Before that, you can look at some of Livermore's writings and he had another system of pivot points and so forth. Donchian basically started the two-week rule. Now that won't work today. Back then you had different characteristics in the markets. And the two-week rule used to work in copper and then we found that you had to lengthen those and maybe made the weeks longer, six weeks or sometimes 30 or 40, 50 weeks or much more than that.

Donchian had this system and a couple of followers in his office. He didn't always follow it himself, but he had this system and he had people that were religiously following the system and they seemed to do pretty well. I came along and I studied his rule set. I had Donchian's rules and guidelines. And at about that time computers were starting to become within reach for people to use them, although they didn't have personal computers. They did have mainframes at some companies. And if you can believe this, I got to go into the major brokerage house at the time on the weekend. And I had access to their mainframe computers that they used to run the company.

There was a security guard and there was me. And I had access to the complete computer base of the whole company. I was just using it to do computer testing.

There is the plain fool, who does the wrong thing at all times everywhere, but there is the Wall Street fool, who thinks he must trade all the time.
Jesse Livermore

Michael: Were you pinching yourself at that time?

Ed: No, I thought it was just normal. I said, "I want to do this research" and they said okay. In those days nobody ever thought about anybody trying to go in there and do anything nefarious. I was just in there doing research. In those days you wouldn't even think about something like that. But these days you couldn't get anywhere close to the inner workings of a brokerage house.

[I used] all their discs, their history and everything. They were just sitting around in this big room. It was a huge room with all these mainframe computers and the tape drives and so forth. You probably have more computation power in your cellphone now. In those days that was quite the thing so I would run back tests that you could do now in probably a second or two. It would take a half hour, 45 minutes to do one set of tests and I was using punch cards. It was a different era back then.

Michael: During the early days there weren't a huge number of peers that you could bounce ideas off. You knew Donchian but unlike today where there's a much wider network and people are connected on the Internet [you didn't have that then].

Ed: I took Donchian's work; he had a letter that he would publish. Every week he would publish a letter which would have his rules on it, and it would also have a kind of a model account and you could follow along. And the idea was you would follow along and place your orders with him. I guess that was the way that was supposed to work. I tested his rules and came back and said, "The rules internally are not consistent. You can't program all these rules at the same time because they conflict with each other."

Investing should be like watching paint dry or watching grass grow. If you want excitement . . . go to Las Vegas.

Paul Samuelson

I started taking rule sets that were non-conflicting. I tried to tune it up and say, "Here's what we can do," and I would try different experiments with the rules. Then I would check it with some brokers and traders in the office and I'd say, "I'm going to change this. I'm going to make the system less responsive so the market has to go up more before you start to buy it, make the time constants longer," and people would say, "That's going to make it more risky because your stops are going to be further away." Then we would test it and we would get the exact opposite results.

All these things were very counterintuitive. I did some of the first testing and you're right, there wasn't any standard. Now I've got this on my website and if you want to replicate some of these tests and learn how to do it, you can. There's a template and you can do it on your Excel spreadsheet or whatever. Enough people have done it that they all get the same result to the penny. So I'm pretty confident I've got the right answer up there.

In those days there wasn't anybody else. I was just curious, and I said, "How does this work?" and Donchian had set it up as a system. I said, "Okay I'm going to simulate it. I'll go back in the computer and see if I get the same results that Donchian's getting. I'll try to set up a diversified portfolio" and we did that. The company I was with marketed it for a while. We had a diversified portfolio and it was all run on computer by a service bureau. We would enter the data every day, then get the result and then we would put the orders in.

The company I was with couldn't stick to it and they also couldn't resist the temptation of trying to get the customers to trade more often than the system wanted them to trade. The problem with this system was it *worked* and it made money for the clients, but the problem was it made far less money for the brokerage house. Because they were used to day traders, they were used to people coming in and lasting a few months, losing their money, moving on and doing something else. That's the way the brokerage house was set up. People would come in, try to trade, lose their money, and leave.

The three-to-five million dollar figure is not a random picked number. That amount is about what we are able to recoup on the movies if we don't get a wide release. In a worst case scenario, we break even and maybe lose a little money but not very much, and everyone gets paid scale . . . That budget is reverse-engineered to thinking that if the movie isn't in wide release, at least we get our money back and can keep our doors open.

Jason Blum
Film Producer[3]

They said, "The commissions are like a tenth of what they used to be. They're just staying with positions and this is going to wreck our business model." And so there were all kinds of pressures to get people to trade more often . . . like you pointed out in some of your letters to me. Well, they've got fancy names for it now like disposition effect. But in those days, people just didn't want to hold on to something. It would go up a little a bit and they would want to take their profit. Went down a little bit, they wanted to add more and hope it'll go back up.

You had lots of pressures against following systems in those days and so I invented something that no one really wanted. Then I left and I went out on my own. Found clients and I found that some of the most important things was developing a relationship with the clients. So that they knew what to expect and they knew what was going on. If the client was not aligned to it and if you didn't have emotional rapport and understand the system is more than the mathematics [there was trouble]. The system is the mathematics plus the willingness to follow the system. And when you increase your world view to include the investor himself and his emotional responses to what's going on is when you finally get the system to include everything—you can design a system that works.

But just going into a computer and tuning up their software and saying "Here's the right set of parameters," Well, great, you've got something that theoretically will work for some theoretical robot that'll follow it, but there aren't a whole lot of robots that have got money these days. Maybe someday, but right now you've got human beings with human feelings and unless you include that into your system design, the wheels are going to come off the cart around the corner.

Michael: You sum up so much of your ethos in those last few sentences for those paying attention. Correct me if I'm wrong, but it seems like you've been highly motivated by the puzzle aspect of figuring things out.

Ed: Yes, I like puzzles. I've got a huge collection of what you might call bar room puzzles—these metal detanglement puzzles where you have metal pieces that fit together and you've got to figure out how to get them apart or together. I've got a huge collection of those and in the morning I do chess puzzles. I just like figuring things out. That's always been something that I've enjoyed doing. I don't know exactly where that comes from. I've been able to incorporate that in my life in such a way that it's useful.

I think the puzzle aspect of what I did in the markets, or what I did with my *Govopoly* book, is what's driven me. I want to understand how it works. Then if it works and makes money, that's great. It's nice to make money, but I wouldn't have done it in the first place. I'd maybe figure out some other way of making money. But the puzzle was what got me. I said, "I've got to figure this out."

"This guy Donchian, he's got this thing that's mechanical, it's making money, how can that be? How can you get something that's mechanical that can make money for nothing without doing any work? How can that be?" And so I kind of got attracted to looking at it.

I don't think I would have gone into it for just the money, it was the puzzle. It was, "How does this work? How does this actually work? Can I build a model? Can I understand this?" And then when you understand it, then it becomes interesting to explain it to people for a while—whether you put it on the website or you write a book. Then you go on, and look for a new puzzle.

In short, we suffer from an "illusion of control" that fools us into thinking the future is more predictable and less uncertain than it really is. Or worse, we believe we can influence chance events through our own actions.

Spyros Makridakis[4]

Michael: Go back in time: you're in those mainframe rooms, and you're by yourself and you're struggling. There's got to be a struggle to try and figure this all out. Was it just pure excitement at the time? This internal excitement that was driving you to keep going and going till you got the puzzle solved?

Ed: Well, that's a good question. That's one of the best questions I've ever heard. What motivates somebody who's a researcher? What motivates them to go? Is it that pleasure or the puzzle, or is it the discomfort of not knowing? It's deeper than that. It's just that's what I do. *That's what I do*. I do that and I play banjo and I get lost in it. That's my meditation, I have to do it. If I can't play music something dies.

And the same with solving puzzles. That's who I am and that's what I do. And I don't think of it as there's something that pushes me to do it. That's just who I am and that's what I *have* to do.

Michael: I sometimes feel like my career's the same way. I don't necessarily know *why*, I'm just driven to do what I do and I'm not necessarily sure what I even do, but I just do it.

Ed: I like that, and you're good at it. And that's one of the places we succeed at in the Trading Tribe when we get people to this place you're at—where you find out who you are and what you do and you just do it. You express yourself and create a value by expressing exactly who you are and not pretending to be somebody else. That's a very high state. Congratulations for being there. It'd be a different world if everybody could get there, and I would hope people would follow in your footsteps. I've watched your career over many years and I've seen you keep expanding and getting closer to who you are, and now you're really blooming and you're really making a big contribution. So good job.

We find that whole communities suddenly fix their minds upon one object, and go mad in its pursuit; that millions of people become simultaneously impressed with one delusion, and run after it, till their attention is caught by some new folly more captivating than the first.
Charles Mackay
***Extraordinary Popular Delusions and the Madness of Crowds*[5]**

Michael: I'm not going to tell the exact story, but you influenced me greatly when I met you for the first time in 2001, and I can still remember some of the things that you said to me. And for some people they might have felt threatened. I don't think I felt threatened. I was like, "Okay, what has he just said to me? Why is he saying it? What's the deeper meaning?"

In many ways, as you talk about your love of puzzles, I felt like you were giving me a puzzle. "Michael, you might want to consider this. . . ." And so then of course I just considered *that* and you didn't give specific instructions, you gave some big-picture insights. That's probably how you like to be. You want to see if there's more puzzle finders out there.

Ed: Yes, and you're open—you wanted to do something. You wanted to go somewhere. You were on a growth path. And then you viewed ideas from me and other people. And you've surrounded yourself with an amazing group of people who have amazing amounts of ability, knowledge, wisdom, and resources.

You've surrounded yourself with one of the most advanced group of mentors possible. You just like to do that. I think you had an attraction. You attracted people like that and then you enjoyed hearing what they had to say. The people on your podcasts, and people in your life, all are people with strong opinions, all people that make you think and make you grow. You just have some kind of an affinity for people like that, and that's part of what makes you good at what you do.

When reading, don't let a single word escape your attention; one word may be worth a thousand pieces of gold.

Chinese proverb

Michael: If they keep talking to me, I should keep talking to them. That seems like a good rule. If really smart people will agree to talk to me, I should probably talk to them because then I wouldn't be that smart. [Laughter]

Ed: [Laughter] It seems to be working.

Martin Lueck

13

Martin Lueck co-founded Aspect Capital in September 1997. Lueck oversees the research team, which is responsible for generating and analyzing fundamental research hypotheses for development of all Aspect's Investment programs. Prior to founding Aspect, Lueck was with Adam, Harding and Lueck Limited (AHL), which he co-founded in February 1987 with Michael Adam and David Harding. Man Group plc completed the purchase of AHL in 1994. Lueck holds an MA in Physics from Oxford University.[1]

Michael: I'm thinking of all the assorted conferences that I've been at and I was wondering if we have crossed paths [in person].

Martin: The one I remember seeing you at . . . there's a picture of it on your website. You had Larry Hite and Ed Seykota [on stage in Chicago].

Martin: You had him on stage with . . . it wasn't a ukulele . . . he got out his banjo.

Michael: Yes, "The Whipsaw Song." You were in the audience for that?

Martin: I was in the audience for that.

Michael: That was probably an interesting audience. When you're on stage for one of those things you're in your own little world and you don't realize that's a pretty interesting audience [all trend followers at an annual event] at that moment in time.

Martin: Exactly. It's voyeuristic because you guys are having so much fun and you could be in a bar, the three of you, and the rest of us are like voyeurs.

The burnt customer certainly prefers to believe that he has been robbed rather than that he has been a fool on the advice of fools.[2]

Fred Schwed
Where Are the Customers' Yachts?

Michael: I sometimes wonder if it is something that comes with age when you loosen up, or do you think guys like Larry and Ed were always that way?

Martin: A bit of both. Obviously I don't know Ed at all but Larry's always been older than me and that will never change. Probably he's always been wiser than me. And actually I haven't seen him for a while, so whether he still gets wiser or whether he has just sort of plateaued and that wisdom is enough to carry him through, I don't know.

Michael: Yes, I have interviews with just me and Larry in his office that I can't release . . . they're awesome wisdom but there's a lot of color there that I can't put out.

The genesis of any [trading] idea, has to be a hypothesis about market behavior.
Anthony Todd

Martin: Yes, I can believe that . . . Michael, listen, it's a pleasure finally to speak with you. I have your book on my desk and have owned this for many, many years, so thank you for everything you've done for the industry.

Michael: Well, thank you. Thanks for the nice words.

Martin: I'm surprised we haven't spoken.

Michael: Yes. I should share a quick story with you. The first time I met one of your old friends, the head of Winton Capital, I was in his office and it was in 2005. And we had just met. It was just me and him and his dog. He started pulling up a screen showing me equity curves of assorted well-known U.S. CTAs and then superimposing his equity curve and then just giving me that wry smile of like, "Did you somehow miss me?" That was my first inkling of the London CTA scene, so to speak.

Martin: Yes.

Michael: There's been an exponential explosion of all of you guys . . . that's just out of this world.

Martin: It's an interesting story.

Michael: When did you first know in your mind, this quantitative style, this systematic style of trend following trading, coding it and trading it over a diversified basket of markets, when did you know in your heart of hearts this had changed your life or at least you knew this could make some money?

Martin: Wow. Michael [Adam], David [Harding], and I never quite had the luxury, if you could call it that, of having a role model. It wasn't as though we looked out at the investment universe and said, "I want to be that person," or, "I want to do that thing." Certainly, for Michael and I, because we go back further than our relationship with David. We were at boarding school together from age 13 and then we were at Oxford together. After Oxford, Michael went to work for his father who ran a small physical commodity broking business in London. I went and took my first job at Nomura trying to sell Japanese equities to European investors. And I didn't know what an equity was when I started that job, clutching my physics degree.

I was just fascinated by the analysis that Michael had started doing, prompted by his father. Michael's father said, "Here boy, buy one of those newfangled computers." Personal computers were just beginning to reach the shores of the U.K. in the 1980s and Michael bought a Hewlett-Packard 9816 [personal computer]. His father handed him a book of technical trading methods and said, "See whether there's anything in this."

You know the saying, "Human see, human do."
Julius
***Planet of the Apes* (1968)**

It's really been so gradual. Just over time I left Nomura, and joined Mike. This whole time-series analysis just lent itself to the nerdy physicist's approach. We just discovered some *things*. We tested every model that we could encode from that great book. We distilled them down to some fundamental rule sets. We tried them on a range of markets and at that time, the range of markets that we had available to us sitting in the commodity world of London... what did we have? Cocoa, coffee, sugar, aluminum, copper, silver. Something like that.

The financial commodities were really in their infancy. Only a few years later, and largely once we'd met David, we started expanding the application of these models to a more diverse set of markets.

Michael: People love that depth. People want to know what's going on inside the mind [of early guys].

Martin: There is no one moment where we said, "Ah yes, we have created the great imitator of . . ." who was around in those days? Richard Dennis, John W. Henry, the Mint gentleman [Larry Hite]. But, we didn't know that. As we started things we didn't know there was that U.S. industry.

Michael: Mid-late '80s?

Martin: Even early '80s. I started working with Mike in 1984. He was working for his father from early 1983. The earliest AHL track records stretches from 1983. We met David, I want to say in '85 or '86, and there was a bit of a tussle. David was working for Saber Asset Management and was the understudy to a great chartist, a man named Robin Edwards who ran a fund—very systematic but no computers involved—and David was a Cambridge-trained scientist. And he immediately saw the potential for using computers to encode Robin's chart approach.

The Saber folks tried to hire Mike and me out of Mike's father's business and that wasn't going to happen, so in the end we got David to join us in Mike's father's business. And then at the beginning of 1987 there was a little family tiff which resulted in the three headstrong boys leaving with one client and setting up AHL.

Michael: But at the moment you set up AHL, had you made enough money at that moment in time that you felt like, "I've got a little breathing room," or was it still kind of, "We're not really sure what's going to happen yet."

Martin: We didn't have a bean, *not a bean*. In fact, blood is thicker than water. Michael's dad, had built his business over the years, and it had morphed from that commodity broking firm into a small asset management business based on models the three of us were developing. He had a very, in those days, parochial or patrician's approach to managing money and to the clients. And it was just a difference of opinion. We said. "Look, you can't behave that way with your client's money, you can't take a paternal view of it, you have to be completely transparent," and we set off on our own.

Everything is worth what its purchaser will pay for it.
Publilius Syrus

But we didn't have a bean and Michael's father actually lent Michael £20,000 that we spent on computer gear and rent until we had generated enough fees that we could go and rent our own office and pay his father back. Gosh, it was a very long time before we had confidence in what we were doing actually.

Michael: A two-part question: What were you calling the style of trading amongst yourselves that you were executing? And number two, talk about some of the early coding and how you went about the early coding. This was not the age where you could walk out and buy TradeStation or Mechanica software. This was hard coding in the bowels, so to speak.

Martin: Two parts to that. What did we call it? I don't know. Yes, it was trend following and it wasn't long before we woke up to the fact that there was an industry here because we had friends in the brokerage community—through Michael's father's connections—there was a metal broker in London back in the '80s called Rudolf Wolf.

The roots of [our] managed futures was a client would open a managed account and give authorization for the manager, in our case AHL, to manage that money. It was brokers like Rudolf Wolf and some of the early physical commodity brokers that helped us and educated us in what the rest of the industry was doing. We knew pretty quickly that this was trend following and we started to get exposure to a much broader set of markets.

In terms of the modeling and the development, you had in Michael and me in particular real techie wonks. Certainly I would not get a job now as a developer but back in the day that's what we loved to do. Those Hewlett-Packard 9816s . . . actually the operating system was written in Pascal. And we learned Pascal and built our models in Pascal, and very quickly we built an environment that allowed you to encode trading ideas much more simply.

The first principle is that you must not fool yourself and you are the easiest person to fool.

Richard Feynman

You didn't need to write them all in Pascal and compile the darn thing and blah, blah, blah. It was effectively an inline simulation language which got developed in the days of AHL once we became part of the Man Group, and it was a well-funded exercise. We had code writers, developers just working on that interpreted language, so it was a precursor to many of those TradeStations. And for a while in the period between AHL and Aspect, certainly, Mike Adam had a version of that. Actually it wasn't his but it was a similar product that he was marketing commercially. The software development was very much intertwined with the model development.

Michael: I was thinking about the notion of achievement. Everyone, if they're pushing in some way, is achieving, we're all striving and it's sometimes hard to reflect on that because you're saying, "Hey, we just started doing this and it starts working and we just keep at it. We keep our nose to the grindstone and there's some ups and there's some downs and next thing you know, 30, 40 years later, boom, boom, boom, something interesting is there."

Then for outsiders they look back now and see the very successful firm Aspect today but they don't really think about the progression, the evolution.

Martin: That's so true of so much in life. It's very hard to join dots when the dots don't exist. You can join the dots with hindsight. If I was being really glib, there was a while where [it was just] the three of us [and] none of us got those fancy jobs in investment banking that all of our slick friends at university got . . . There was a period where [we were] three scientists, nerding around with the models and the simulations, the back data, some of Michael's father's money, and, "Heavens, this stuff works!"

The more we got into it, the more animated and the more excited we got . . . so it was revenge of the nerds for a little while. Then it was an investment bank in a box because . . . in the early days of AHL we did a number of different things—not only model development and asset management; Michael was already keen on commercializing that piece of software. I spent a fair bit of time using the software to provide consultancy services for financial businesses and what came to light . . . was that you could fairly easily model the behavior and the profitability of investment banks.

I grow old learning something new every day.
Solon
Athenian statesman

We did a piece of work for a London gilt trading house. We modeled how many people, their risk limits, what kind of investment horizon . . . they had the front book traders that were making a market, and they had the back book traders that were holding the house book if you will, and we modeled the behavior of those things and said, "Roughly this looks like the profitability of your business," and the folks, the executives, their jaws dropped. They went wide-eyed because we basically modeled their business.

We went around telling everyone, Goldman, Salomon, just get rid of all of your traders, they're very expensive and they have hangovers, you can build it all on computers. We believed ourselves of course but everyone thought we were completely nuts. By and large [now] that's what's happened.

Michael: Today Aspect is 100 percent systematic. I'm guessing that there was a moment when you're doing all this homework, in the early stages of this industry, and seeing the results, but when did you have that "aha!" moment, "Wow, we should really take the human discretion out and automate this." When was that moment?

Martin: I draw attention to two things. The first was just an awareness that your ability to rationalize the available information, if you could do that pretty quickly and get rid of the noise, we'd all be much better traders. I tell a story about those early AHL days. Mike and I came up with a game and it was just a piece of code that would randomly sample one of the markets in our database, and it might invert it and it might multiply it by a random factor. You couldn't tell what the market was but it would obviously keep the integrity of the price series and it would present a chunk of time series to you. It would then ask you to buy or sell and you'd buy or sell. Then it would move forward a day and then you'd buy or sell, and move forward a day and so on and so forth.

And with that kind of rapid-fire decision making, actually, we were pretty good discretionary traders. If you blow each of those ticks up into a 24-hour period, with news coming at you and fear and greed and the chaos of normal life, you become a lousy trader. That was the first inkling that taking the emotion out of it, just reducing it to the raw information, has to be a good thing.

The 50–50–90 rule: Anytime you have a 50–50 chance of getting something right, there's a 90% probability you'll get it wrong.

Andy Rooney

The second thing turns out to be the importance of risk management, because what a lot of people focus on in any model development is the models. Are you going long? Are you going short? How do you feel about this market or that? And that's all well and good, and you obviously need to develop those models and be able to articulate what the underlying drivers are, but what many people miss is the risk management component.

What a lot of people do is focus on systematizing models, and then portfolio construction or/and the risk management piece they leave to discretion. Somewhere in the genesis of Aspect Capital we realized that's absolutely a crucial thing to get right. You need to be able to systematize not only your models that interpret the price data and determine the confidence you have in that particular trend, but also you need to be able to systematize your portfolio construction process and your risk management process.

The manager that says "I am 95 percent systematic and 5 percent discretionary" is 100 percent discretionary. That's not necessarily a bad thing. I'm not saying there aren't geniuses out there who are discretionary, but it means you can't rely on the scientific process. You can't rely on the quality and the integrity of the simulation and research process if there's the hint that you're just going to step in and down-gear the portfolio when the going gets tough, or you're going to knock out a few markets when they seem to be a little off the charts. Because you can't build that into your simulations and you can't know what you're going to do in the future.

Although we knew at the outset that it was a good thing to systematize, I've become more resolute in how important it is across the entire investment process.

Michael: You talk about that notion of 95 percent systematic and some portion of discretion. That was a very common marketing line in disclosure documents of trend following's CTAs for a long, long time. It was this mysterious we're 95 percent systematic but there's also this magical 5 percent discretion which is the reason you're giving us money.

I always used to think that didn't make any sense. Now, because you and other peers, associates, et cetera have gone the opposite direction and said, "Hey hold on," I don't think you could probably get away today saying in the trend following space, "We're 95 percent systematic." People that want to invest would probably say, "Explain that."

Let me remind you of the particular characteristics of all of these behavior systems that I am trying to focus on. It is that people are impinging on other people and adapting to other people. What people do affects what other people do.
Thomas C. Schelling

Martin: It's really dependent who you were talking to, and we all lived in fear in the early days of the black box label. Two things: I think that 5 percent discretionary was also to give some investors a sense there was a thought process and it wasn't just this ignorant machine clunking away. But also I come back to the point that people built the models and then . . . the overall risk target of the portfolio was something they would set discretionarily on how it felt that week, day, month, or epoch.

Michael: It was a weird point in time where we had not yet got to the point where there was an acceptance of the 100 percent systematic. There was this gray area in the marketing and for good or bad reasons, perhaps, as you're saying.

Martin: That's exactly right. And now it needs to be used judiciously so the idea of being systematic, the idea of being research driven as an investor, as a consultant doing your due diligence, you've got to scratch at that. Because as I give a bright young graduate an infinite amount of data and an infinite amount of processing power, they're going to come up with the works of Shakespeare or they're going to come up with models that just look staggering. And you and I know that you wouldn't put your money in them.

There is a difference between 100 percent systematic models that are based on curve fitting, back fitting, cloud patterns, data mining versus 100 percent systematic models that are based on rigorous hypothesis extraction testing and a whole barrage of statistical tests to make sure that you aren't fooling yourself—big, big difference.

Michael: I have to give a presentation shortly in a country in Asia . . . a pretty successful city. And I assumed they knew what I was going to talk about, and they wrote me and they said, "Hey, can you bring these particular charts for your presentation and tell us whether or not these charts are in a trend or not in a trend?"

Maybe we should teach schoolchildren probability theory and investment risk management.

Andrew Lo

It's amazing that people still . . . want to fixate on *their* markets. They're excited about their markets and they're not even thinking about diversification. That's not even on their horizon. They've just got their markets they're happy about and they want me to tell them something exciting about them. That's not how you look at it. You are saying, "What are the targets of opportunity, when that opportunity arrives we're going to do something with it but we can't force it." And I still think today, it's still not a widely understood concept.

Martin: I think that's right, and I've been in exactly those situations where, whether it's the local conference organizer who's asking you to tell them how great their local market is, or it's the drinks party where somebody's saying, "What do you think about gold?" I don't even know what country I'm in and which way up your stock index is, but I know it's in my portfolio. And I know it's one of the 150-plus assets that we monitor 24 hours a day that we always have a position in, and depending on how those trends have unfolded we will have a large position. And depending on how those trends have unfolded we will have a long position or a short position, and that's the beauty of it.

Many managers will have a different approach from ours, but I start from the very high level premise that all assets have an equal opportunity to manifest trends. The whole model building process is an attempt to preserve that opportunity and make it as broad and robust as possible.

What do I mean by that? What I mean is that if you build your model such that it captures some of the characteristics of different markets, you trade hogs subtly differently from how you trade Treasury bonds, for example. You can persuade yourself that you're building in some features of those markets, because clearly the world of hog traders is different than the world of bond traders.

But the dynamics of those markets at that level of resolution, there is, in our opinion, no persistency. All you can say about hogs and bonds is they have the potential to demonstrate trends. If I had looked at, say, equity markets over . . . if my dataset was, this is somewhat spurious, but say U.S. equity 2002 to 2007, I could conclude that equities don't go down, or not for long.

What if I look at bonds over the last 10 years? Bonds don't go down, do they? Never. You could build into your model certain biases or certain scenario expectations and that's what we try and eschew. We try and avoid those built-in biases. I am indifferent as to whether your regional equity market is in a roaring bull trend, which I know is what you want, conference organizers. Or whether it's in a terrible bear trend. I'm agnostic as to whether it's going up or it's down and I don't look at how different markets have performed historically and say, "My models are better at trading commodities than they are at trading financials and therefore I overweight the financials."

I try and keep it as completely agnostic directionally and asset allocation wise so that it can grab hold of any opportunity that presents itself.

Michael: When you're talking to people after all these decades, what percentage of the educated financial audience do you think grasps what you do at Aspect?

Martin: Fortunately, many more now. This is a terrible generalization and therefore probably not true, but from my small vantage point, 2008 was the "aha!" moment and before that, marketing what we did could sometimes be a struggle, and you know that . . . we [also] didn't help ourselves with the absurd fees that we used to charge back in the '80s.

The evolution of that to making ourselves look respectable and "I want to be a hedge fund too," all the way through to 2008, was where as a result of performance in 2009 the phone started ringing and the pension funds and the pension fund consultants that wouldn't take our calls up until that point said, "Explain again how this stuff works." And then they were really receptive.

Of course, you can't make it up because then, ironically, in the aftermath of the global financial crisis, you get a period where this stuff didn't perform as well as it had done historically and as well as our expectations would have led us to believe it can and it will. I think the vast majority of people now get what we do, but it wasn't until relatively recently that that's been the state of the world.

Michael: I put this in one of my books that TV Ben Stein said, "If you made money in October 2008 you were doing something wrong."

Martin: Really? [Laughter]

I know that two and two make four, and should be glad to prove it too if I could, though I must say if by any sort of process I could convert 2 and 2 into five it would give me much greater pleasure.

George Gordon

Michael: I know where he's coming from. I understand from his understanding of assorted trading strategies or investment strategies, and if you only believe those, then that's a fair thing to say. You're leaving some things out to say that, but I just love that line.

Martin: That is a great one, and none of us in our industry should think—and the respectable ones of us don't think—that we've ever finished. It's not like you've ever unlocked the secrets of the markets and my model is my model and now I'm off to the beach. Because (a) the markets never leave you alone and (b) there's always some new thing that you hadn't thought about.

I think very topical at the moment is the evolution of portfolio construction. The theory and the practice of portfolio construction.

The Swensen model of diversification was not just have U.S. equities, have global equities too. There you go, now you're diversified. I'm oversimplifying it, but certainly he has had and as far as I know has had no interest in quant strategies and at the time that was perceived to be a very valid and very useful form of diversification. And in 2008 that's why you get lines like, "If you made in money in October 2008 you were doing something wrong," Because the world view was so rigid.

It's exciting. It keeps me young. And it keeps my research team young and energized, because there's always some new worldview that you should explore.

Michael: I've had some of the brightest and most accomplished behavioral economists on my podcast, and what I really find amazing in talking to them is their work seems to be the embodiment of traders like yourself, your peers, the other associates in the industry. Going down the systematic quant trend strategy path was in many ways capturing what Daniel Kahneman was winning the Nobel Prize for, or what Vernon Smith was winning the Nobel Prize for.

But when I talk to them, there seems to be this disconnect where all these behavioral economists should be waking up to these quant trend strategies and saying, "Wow, what a wealth of interesting data and evidence for us to sink our teeth into." But there still seems to be a wall where they've not yet pulled the hood of the car up and looked under there and said, "Interesting."

Some of the greatest, most revolutionary advances in science have been given their initial expression in attractively modest terms, with no fanfare.
Daniel Dennett

Martin: I agree, Michael, and, "vive la différence," I'm very happy that those folks and the folks at Google have not woken up to it. But you talk about behavioral economists—one area that has sort of fascinated me is the building of agent models. If you can define players in your complex system, who are the hedgers? Who are the speculators? Who are the counter trend traders? All of that. You'd think you could come up with a bottom-up model for the markets, which perhaps, but I don't know, is that [what] behavioral economists are trying to do?

In my limited experience, candidly, don't bother. It's a very elegant mathematical model but it's very unlikely to be able to make you any money. The thing about what we do is that it's a bit rough and ready. The models are very sophisticated of course, and the mathematics is complicated, but you almost start from the premise that all markets will at some point display trends, and it's our job in these models to be able to capture those trends efficiently and not lose money in the periods where we're participating in those markets and they're not trending.

There you go. I've just defined what it is we do, but you'll notice that I haven't dwelt on, "And it's my job to tell you why those trends exist, where they come from and where they're going." If you fixate too much on that, which is the role of the behavioral economist—very fascinating field—but it's not what we do.

Michael: They seem to do a great job of really putting aside the efficient market theory and offering that human beings are not always rational, and bubbles exist, so I look at that very basic premise. Their work gets more complicated than that, but their basic premise, it dovetails right into your world in the sense that it's a foundational explanation for why you might be successful.

Martin: Yes, and it is, and it makes for great reading, and often there are "aha!" moments as you say, "Yes, well that's why we sophisticated monkeys behave the way we do, and long may it continue."

Michael: The world is a very interconnected place. Everyone is coming online. If a country doesn't have a liquid futures market, they're thinking about it. They would like one. How do you go about the process of bringing new potential trading opportunities into Aspect? I imagine you always stay excited because you're like, "Hey, we don't even know the next group of markets from the next country that's going to come online that can possibly offer us opportunity."

The past can't hurt you anymore, not unless you let it.

Alan Moore
V for Vendetta

What's great about trend following in many ways, it is the Indiana Jones of trading. Once you have your models, your systems and you know these markets in these countries are liquid and viable, you can go in.

Martin: Yes. It's an ongoing process and it's something we devote a fair bit of time and a fair bit of money to, because you've got to keep your head up. It's relatively easy to get started with the 50 most liquid markets out there in the world, and if you just ignore all of the new stuff that you're referring to, you miss a huge opportunity set.

Whenever there is a simple error that most laymen fall for, there is always a slightly more sophisticated version of the same problem that experts fall for.
Amos Tversky

As a business we have a regular cycle of reviewing news alerts and our brokers keep us prompted of what's new, what's coming. We like to have some back data, so we're not going to be market participants on day one of an exchange opening, because we've got to get the sort of characteristic heartbeat of liquidity patterns within that market before we can parameterize our execution algorithms. We've got to establish a little bit of history and then we've got to establish a threshold of viability. A threshold of liquidity because it's got to be worthwhile at a certain point having a one-basis-point allocation to a market where it isn't viable in the program.

There's a liquidity threshold. There's something like 6,000, is that right? Six thousand futures markets globally. You can very quickly cut off 80 percent of those on liquidity basis as being viable for what we do and then it's an evolving cycle. As liquidity picks up we will adapt our allocation in the portfolio. And the other feature of course is there may be constraints. For example, we can't currently trade the Chinese futures markets for our investors because external investors are not allowed to participate in those markets.

Similarly, access to Brazilian futures markets, which are vastly liquid, but there's a taxation situation that makes them extremely difficult and expensive to trade. So all of those markets we're tracking, we're collecting data, we are simulating the models on them and we're ready to go at the drop of a hat should the legislation change. We welcome that. We love the additional diversification that it affords the portfolio, because back to the starting point, if you just traded the same liquid 50 markets that maybe we started with in the 1980s, if that was your portfolio now and all other things were equal, you'd have less diversification in the portfolio. There's a long-term secular trend towards markets becoming more homogeneous over time, I believe. We are hungry for new access and new opportunities of diversification.

Michael: Why do you think you're so passionate?

Martin: I'm a one-trick pony. [laughter] This is what I've done in my career. I can't claim to be a scientist or a physicist, but that's what I studied. I got into that because I'm inquisitive,

I like precision, I like answers, I like engineering solutions to things. I know myself and I would be . . . a lousy discretionary trader. I like the application of sophisticated mathematical techniques and theories to extract signal from noise and I love working with a bunch of really, really smart, talented people. All of that keeps you passionate to keep learning and to keep competitive and to keep doing what we're doing better and better.

Michael: Even if the economics of this was much less—let's say it was good enough to earn a living—I get the feeling talking to you that this still would have been your passion and your path.

Martin: Absolutely. This is just great fun. I didn't set out on day one to be a great trader at all. As I said, I got into this working for Michael's father because I was fascinated by the application of computers to time-series data. That's what I've done my whole career. It doesn't really matter that the rewards have been very good. That's a nice feedback loop . . . actually, markets are a very swift judge of how precise and how honest you have been. So . . .

Michael: It's how to keep score.

Martin: It's how to keep score, exactly. That means that I'm not in an amorphous world of where people could say, "Wow, what a great article you've written." There's a *scorekeeper*.

You build on failure. You use it as a stepping stone. Close the door on the past. You don't try to forget the mistakes, but you don't dwell on it. You don't let it have any of your energy, or any of your time, or any of your space."

Johnny Cash

Jean-Philippe Bouchaud

14

Jean-Philippe Bouchaud is a French physicist. He is the founder and chairman of Capital Fund Management (CFM) and is a professor of physics at École Polytechnique.[1]

Skeptical scrutiny is the means, in both science and religion, by which deep thoughts can be winnowed from deep nonsense.

Carl Sagan

Michael: I want you to elaborate on your physics background, but bring that into this framework of classical economics. Classical economics, the rationality of economic agents, the supposed rationality, the invisible hand, market efficiency . . . But for some reason the idea of empirical data often gets left out of the equation—and I've seen this with some other traders that have had success—a physics background is different. It allows you to maybe look at the world through a wider lens.

Jean-Philippe: Yes, exactly, I'm surprised that you say all of this because that's more or less what my usual message is and you've captured all of it in a few words. Yes, it is true that I'm a physicist by training, and physics is of course learning through doing experiments. And you learn that theories are no good if they're not able to reproduce observations. And even if your theory is beautiful, if it doesn't fit, it doesn't fit. You just have to throw it in the dustbin and start again.

As a physicist approaching economics and finance back in the early '90s, that's what struck me most—that it is a lack of a statistical aspect to the way economics and finance theories are built . . . very much axiomatic in imagining how the world could be or should be. Then developing the theories without much care about what's going on out there.

I guess that for a while it was justified because data was not so easy to access, so the whole academic world has developed without data in a sense. And so people had to maybe supplement the lack of data by actions and by ways of thinking . . . That can happen too in physics, actually, so perhaps I was fortunate enough to enter the field when data became very easy to access. And when looking at data and trying to make sense of data through a kind of vivid light on the failures and drawbacks of efficient market theory and Gaussian statistics, Black–Scholes, all this to me was quite apparent . . . that it was not enough to understand the world.

Michael: You mention the Black–Scholes model. It's still in use. So even though that systematic underestimation of risk is well known by people like yourself, it's still in use.

This is a fundamental truth about any sort of practice: If you never push yourself beyond your comfort zone, you will never improve.
Anders Ericsson

Jean-Philippe: Yes, I know, I've been ranting about that for ages and one problem is students. You have to teach students something, and Black–Scholes is so easy to teach and it's so beautiful mathematically, that a lot of people just resent the idea of having to put it all down and start again with something more messy. Of course the world is messy, and being messy it's much harder to teach . . . to focus on the right things. By definition you have to form your intuition on something else than mathematics.

That's why physics is good at that, because it gives you a lot of examples where you can put your hand in the dirt and try to push on some button and see what happens. But the same should be more and more true with economics and finance now, through two channels. One is the availability of data and the possibility to make experiments on data, simulations, that is, and even without data you can do simulations. You can invent worlds of people trading according to some rule, or funds producing according to some rules, and implement whatever rule of thumb or feature of the world that you think should be there, and then just run the simulation and see what happens.

Then what's very striking when you do that—plus it's fun because you kind of play God. And second, very quickly you realize that some of the rules just don't work. They don't represent at all what is seen out there, and others seem to capture something that's very close to reality. So my impression is that by training people more and more with this type of background, this type of experimental background . . . experimenting with simulation is a strange notion, which even in physics it took a little time for people to accept that simulation was a legitimate way to do science.

I don't know if you know Mark Buchanan, he's a science writer and he wrote a few years back something I like a lot . . . just after the crisis in October 2008. He said the following:

"Done properly, computer simulation represents a kind of 'telescope for the mind,' multiplying human powers of analysis and insight just as a telescope does our powers of vision. With simulations we can discover relationships that the unaided human mind, or even the human mind aided with the best mathematical analysis, would never grasp." For me, this is the essence of what the physics way of doing things has brought to the game.

Michael: So people don't think that you're giving an interesting marketing story about a physics background for your trading firm, your firm does not hire traders?

Jean-Philippe: Yes, it only hires physicists. And okay, people can think that, but we've been saying the exact same thing since the mid-90s. The everyday life of CFM is driven by data. It's banging our heads against data and trying to make sense of what we see and make models inspired by what we see.

We're rarely rational when we vote because we're rarely rational, period.
Robert M. Sapolsky

[Another reason] that it's not pure marketing is we're very strange as a trading firm to have published something like 100 science papers in the last 20 years, all published in academic journals, which shows that it's really in our DNA to consider science as the right way to do things.

Michael: Let's jump right into my primary reason for reaching out to you, which was seeing your paper ["Two Centuries of Trend Following"; see Chapter 20], which really didn't have any big fanfare. Just all of a sudden it appeared in the Internet ether. . . . I wonder if you might lay out a scenario for how that paper came to be and then we can discuss the specifics inside.

Jean-Philippe: This particular paper was in the back of our minds for a long time. There are two reasons for it to appear right now. One may fall in what you call marketing, which is that we're launching . . . a fund called "Institutional Systematic Diversified," and part of that fund is based on long-term trend following. So it is true that we needed to give some support to why we're doing that.

When it comes to money, the best investments were probably the ones I did not make.
Marc Faber

The second thing is that we recently in the course of the very last few years have had access to much longer time periods than we had in the past. We've been able to go back to the beginning of the nineteenth century on commodities and indices in terms of data. This allowed us to back test quite a number of ideas and in particular trend following. To our surprise we realized that the strategy has been extremely consistent as long as we could go back in the past.

This seemed to us to be a very interesting finding in the year where the Nobel Prize was given to Fama, Shiller, and Hansen. But this debate on the efficient market theory, on which I've been pretty vocal myself in the last 10 years, it is ironic that it's given to Fama who was still arguing there's no bubbles, there's no crashes. That the market went down in 2008 in anticipation of the crisis and not the other way around, and that everything is perfect.

Trend following, momentum in general, is something that efficient market theorists have a real difficulty to explain because that's completely out of the framework. It's very hard to evoke some kind of risk premium that would be associated with trend following. So it has to mean that markets are not that efficient.

There's a lot of other clear discrepancies between theories and reality, but this one is a very genuine and clear one which talks to everybody. Just looking at the trend on a long time scale is giving information on the future motion of the market. It really means that all public information is not included in the price right now. For me it's both from an intellectual and commercial point of view a very interesting finding.

I'd be a bum on the street with a tin cup if the markets were efficient.
Warren Buffett

Michael: The statement that jumped out at me was, and this is from your paper, "The existence of trends is one of the most statistically significant anomalies in financial markets." That's a powerful statement.

Jean-Philippe: We've been looking at financial markets in the last 20 years and it's very hard to find extremely significant statistical effects. You can find them on the high-frequency side, but then there's a lot of murky things around high frequency. First of all, costs are tremendous if you want to trade at high frequency. It's not clear that all the high-frequency anomalies that have a strong statistical signature are, as economists would say, very relevant from an economics point of view.

On the other hand, these very slow trends where a lot of money can pile in and has piled in, is of course much more mind-boggling in a way, and also has to be taken into account both for academics but also from the point of view of professionals.

Michael: Other interesting facts in the paper, perhaps this is obvious if data is going back to the early 1800s, but trend predates trend following, which I thought was interesting. It's actually a very small percentage of traders employing trend following models that make up the volume.

It's a wonderful thing to be optimistic. It keeps you healthy and it keeps you resilient.

Daniel Kahneman

Jean-Philippe: Yes, I agree. Well, you can see it both ways. I would say that traders on aggregate using trends is probably the reason why trends are there in the first place, and people using trends have been around for 200 years. That's my interpretation of what we see—there's a lot of people, even small people, who on aggregate play the role of trend followers and therefore create these trends.

Michael: You mentioned Fama and the split Nobel Prize. I had a chance to speak with Harry Markowitz recently, who's very lucid [89 years young now], and the point that I made, "Harry, did you find it interesting that when you wrote back in the 1950s this is what we should be doing, that within a few decades, other academics had taken what you said we should be doing and had said this is what we are doing?" His response was, "I think you're going to have to talk to the behavioral economists about that." He didn't want to touch it, but his point is that I never said this is what it is, this is what we should be doing. Other people interpreted him to come up with these, as you might say, hard axioms that became rules—the foundation of the efficient market theory.

Jean-Philippe: Yes, it is a strange field in the sense there's clearly interaction between what people do and what people observe, and the use of Black–Scholes in 1987 is rather a vivid example of how things can go wrong when wrong models are used. That's what makes the subject fascinating for a physicist, because you have to go kind of one step further and try to understand how the models themselves might change the game.

Actually we came up with a simple model on how trend could lead to trend or mean reversion could lead to mean reversion. It's not clear that we could imagine a world where people would follow mean reversion rather than trends, but it seems that humans have such a propensity to follow trends. There's a lot of very interesting psychological experiments where you can show that when a small child sees three points aligning on a line, it gives him pleasure. . . . We're wired in to extrapolate past trends, and that's probably a way to extrapolate the motion of a tiger jumping on us or something that makes us alive today.

My intuition is that it's much harder to go against the trend than it is to follow the trend. Again, there's a lot of very interesting psychological or even biological experiments showing there's a lot of things [for instance] . . . hormones going in and out of our body in the two situations. One when we're conforming to the crowd and the other when we're not conforming to the crowd. There's a pain associated with not conforming to what's going on.

Men, it has been well said, think in herds; it will be seen that they go mad in herds, while they only recover their senses slowly, one by one.
Charles Mackay
Extraordinary Popular Delusions and the Madness of Crowds[2]

Michael: Classical economics has no framework through which to understand wild markets—and *wild* is your phrasing. Could you talk to the idea of classical economics not having the ability to have a framework to see those wild markets, to see through them? And when you use the word *wild*, what does that mean to you?

Jean-Philippe: Yes, you're referring to a paper that I wrote "In Nature," which was just after the unraveling of the crisis, and this made me react very strongly because I felt that this was in the cards. And of course other people had seen it coming, but I was not too happy with the way economists had been dismissing all the attempts to introduce a little more wildness in the description of economic systems and financial markets.

Actually, wild is the reference to Benoit Mandelbrot. Mandelbrot introduced fractals, of course. He's introduced also the idea of distributions without the second moment, without variance or infinite variance and distribution with infinite means. That's his classification of randomness, if you want. He would call benign randomness, the ones that the economists love, Gaussian and things . . . where you can replace a heterogeneous system with its average. We know for example that this relates to Piketty's book [*Capital in the Twenty-First Century*] as well that the distribution of anything in economics is so broadly distributed, that very often it just doesn't make sense at all to replace a collection of people by an average people—or, a representative agent, would be the classical word.

But coming back to Mandelbrot, benign randomness is the one that I just described, whereas wild randomness is the one that is difficult to tame and it's difficult to tame because it's hard to speak about averages and variances. That's really what I was referring to when using the word *wild*.

Now why is economics in general not able to capture these big swings? It's very strange. It's because the models are constructed to be intrinsically stable. It's like people insist on the fact that a rational world is a stable world and so your model should be stable. So models in economics came up with equilibrium points which are intrinsically stable. That is if you perturb them by a small amount, they're going to naturally go back to the equilibrium. This is so much ingrained in the model that it's by definition impossible to have a crisis.

Nature is written in mathematical language.
Galileo Galilei
1564–1642
Italian Physicist

What's interesting is that when you remove a few of these rational assumptions and introduce market imperfections, then it's very easy to find situations where the rational equilibrium of economics, even if it still exists, is actually unstable, and if it's deterred by small external shocks in such a way the system goes out of whack for a while, this is what we would call a crisis.

Mathematical analysis is there to allow us to not only describe, but anticipate to some extent, or at least make space for, crisis in the economic world. And to me this is a fascinating topic of research on which we've been focusing in the last few years.

Michael: You sound like you're having fun with this subject. You get to wake up every day and have fun.

Jean-Philippe: Yes, exactly. That's totally true and I'm happy you say that.

Michael: What I have loved over the years, talking to you today, and many of your peers, is that when one accepts uncertainty, there's a certain honesty to it. I feel a lot of discomfort when people are so certain about what's going to happen.

Mathematics is the science of what is clear by itself.
Carl Gustav Jacob Jacobi
1804–1851
German mathematician

Jean-Philippe: I think that's the big difference between physicists and economists, and there's a lot to be written about this. In a sense I would say that we're privileged as physicists because we don't have to talk to politicians and we don't have to make statements about how the world is supposed to work, in the sense that nobody's relying on us to make political decisions. I think there's a huge amount of pressure on economists because they're under the spotlight. They have to come up with stories and decisions and this means that it's very hard for them to take a step back and say, "Okay, I'm really going to try to understand what's going on here and maybe it's going to take me 10 years or 20 years, but at the end of the day we'll have a better theory for the world."

Okay, well all this is great, but what am I going to say to my minister of finance when he asks me, "Should I raise tax or should I do this or that?" It's true that it puts people in a bad situation because they can't think long-term, and as you've just said, as physicists by training, what we love is to be able to think that we understand something.

If we fail, well, it's okay. There's nothing wrong in failing. We know that physics has had so many revolutions and so many things that people were absolutely convinced were true, turned out wrong in the end. It's an incredibly good backside against what you said earlier . . . against certainty and some form of arrogance as well.

Michael: To a degree you're expecting failure, and maybe the economists, they can't acknowledge there might be failure.

Mathematics knows no races or geographic boundaries; for mathematics, the cultural world is one country.
David Hilbert
1862–1943
German mathematician

Jean-Philippe: Yes, because their theory's construction is completely different for sociological reasons as well.

Michael: I appreciate you taking the time.

Jean-Philippe: Very happy to meet you someday. Of course we like your book [*TurtleTrader*]. As you saw, it's actually referenced in our paper, and I'm very happy to have been able to talk to you.

Ewan Kirk

15

Ewan Kirk is the CEO and co-founder of Cantab Capital Partners, a systematic hedge fund based in Cambridge, England. Kirk was previously partner-in-charge of Goldman Sachs's quantitative strategies group in Europe. His group was responsible for all of Goldman Sachs's quantitative technology across commodities, currencies, interest rates, credit, and equities.[1]

Michael: A guy with a PhD in mathematical physics going to Goldman Sachs . . . you weren't the guy that was living and breathing trading when you got there, were you?

Ewan: Not at all, no. When I turned up for my first interview with Goldman Sachs in 1992, I didn't actually know who Goldman Sachs were. I thought they were a bank but apart from that I wasn't entirely sure. So no, I didn't live or breathe trading, I didn't even live or breathe quantitative finance.

Michael: They were looking for a certain type of thinker, a certain type of thinking?

The Federal Reserve is not currently forecasting a recession.

Ben Bernanke
January 10, 2008

Ewan: Yes, they were looking for somebody who had some sort of mathematical background, and computer programming was also important. I say this to just about everybody that we interview, that it's sort of useless being a mathematician, being a statistician without being able to computer-program . . . it's like being a novelist who can't write. The way that you express your views or express your ideas is through programming computers. And so I was a reasonably good computer programmer. I had a background in quant and Goldman very kindly took a punt on me.

Michael: I saw that your cofounder called programming, *today's literacy*. You have to have it.

Ewan: It's today's literacy. And that strand runs through a lot of my career, but also runs through what we do at Cantab trading programs. I myself have just spent the last two or three weeks programming up a piece of our infrastructure. There's no rest for the wicked, as they say.

Michael: It's going to look to the reader that there's this perfect physics, mathematical background, but you're also a guy that allowed yourself to turn up at a black tie dinner wearing a kilt.

Ewan: Yes, that's true. [laughter]

Michael: You're not a cavalier guy. Obviously, you're very grounded, you think in terms of risk, but what was your thinking there? What is your thought process that you allow yourself to stand out like that?

Ewan: The truth is, of course, that for somebody who like myself originally came from Scotland, the traditional black tie dress is a kilt and all of the attendant bits and pieces with that. It's not like I turned up in a clown costume.

Michael: I hope you did not infer that's what I was saying!

Ewan: No, no I'm smiling as I'm saying this. I do think that one thing that Goldman Sachs was very good at doing, and presumably still is, is it's tolerant to some degree of idiosyncrasy. Certainly in the early days Goldman was a partnership with maybe 150 partners running their small businesses. That made it very much a meritocracy, very much a "what have you done for me today" kind of thing. Me turning up in a kilt is not the strangest thing that I've seen, but it's a place where, really much more so than other banks, certainly in the '90s, it is a place where all Goldman was interested in—were you good at your job. Within certain limits, obviously turning up in a clown costume at a client meeting would probably be a very quick way of getting fired.

A real decision is measured by the fact that you've taken a new action. If there's no action, you haven't truly decided.
Tony Robbins

Michael: I took it as you saying, "I'm going to march to some music that is standard but I'm going to think outside the box. I'm not going to just be the guy that's clocking in."

Ewan: I probably couldn't violently disagree with that view. I think yes, there's certainly some of that in me, to not just be *the guy*. Although, to put this in context . . . to take that as an example, Goldman Sachs is a very serious, very successful U.S. corporate and there's a limit to how outside the box you can think in a bank, and quite rightly too. Banks are responsible for a lot of risk for their customers, they have a fiduciary duty in lots of cases. Yes, you can be a little bit idiosyncratic sometimes, but at the end of the day it is a big U.S. corporate.

Michael: When I look at the success of the London CTAs [trend followers], the London Quants, many trend following backgrounds, why did the switch happen? Why did London become the spot? For example, so many of the long-standing, early, pioneer trend following CTAs were from the U.S. What was the switch flip?

In today's world if you worry about what anybody thinks about your decisions, you're going to drive yourself to a problem. A big problem. Alcohol, or something. You just gotta put your nose to the grindstone and believe in yourself, believe you're making the right call and just go.[2]

Jon Gruden

Ewan: That's a good question. It's not one I immediately have an answer for but I can speculate. If you think about the very early trend following, the history of the industry is, the very early trend following, the Turtles. We're talking mid-80s there, maybe early '90s. The kickoff for the London, or maybe better to call it the European scene, probably happened in the mid to late '90s with AHL, obviously the granddaddy of us all. And then Winton, Blue Trend, and Aspect and ourselves, and a whole plethora of really great firms in Europe.

Partly the reason why we maybe managed to become more successful or grow was more the scientific approach to investment and statistics. I look back at some of these things that I see in the old tattered books about average true range and breakouts and it seems like the dark ages. We are thinking in a much more statistical sense, much more scientific. And it's not just enough that it happens to work.

Maybe we can thank David Harding and the rest of the team at AHL for building that into the consciousness and then it just takes off. The question there, "Why didn't the CTAs in the U.S. follow that lead?" I clearly believe that [there should be] a more scientific approach to investing, a rigorous statistical approach to it, I clearly believe that that's better than just a rule that happens to have worked in the past. It's not clear to me why that would then not be transplanted back.

I remember, even though we started in 2006, 2007, I do remember people asking me . . . again particularly in the States . . . why do you weight your positions by risk? Why don't you just take a constant lot quantity? One lot of this or ten lots of this and ten lots of that and ten lots of the next thing? That's just madness in a world where you have a contract like the wheat contract which is maybe, I don't know, $20,000 and the nickel contract which is $250,000. It's just an insane way of doing it.

But it was the tradition and our industry is quite conservative. There's a small subset of investors who want the new thing . . . believe maybe that there's some fabulous technique out there that's just going to predict what the S&P's going to be tomorrow. But there are also people who want it to be the way it was and anything that steps outside that is maybe a little bit different.

You are not special. You are not a beautiful or unique snowflake. You're the same decaying organic matter as everything else.
Chuck Palahniuk
Fight Club

Michael: You're talking to clients and you have to tell the new client, or this could be a very experienced client perhaps not experienced with your strategy yet, and you ultimately have to bring up the conversation of, "Look, losses are statistically inevitable, you can't get around that fact." There's still a significant number of people in the population, whether they're very astute about investing or not so astute—they still don't want to imagine losses as part of the game.

Ewan: Yes, people are desperate to invest in something which never loses money and that is of course why Bernard Madoff existed. There's a great phrase by John Maynard Keynes where he said, "In the field filled with fraud and deception demand creates his own supply." Everyone is desperate to invest in something that doesn't lose money. I'd like to invest in things that don't lose money. I'd like to come up with a strategy that never loses money. Of course we all want that.

But the reality of almost all investing: If you're really good, really lucky, you've got a very long track record, maybe 20, 30 years, and you've never changed your strategy over that period, which of course none of these things are really true for anybody—then maybe the best you can look for is a Sharpe ratio of .8, .9, maybe 1. I know there are some more liquid, say, stat arb strategies, which can outperform that for a long period of time, and then of course August 2007 happens. But broadly, a good investment strategy, an outstanding investment strategy is something which over a long period of time has a Sharpe ratio of 1. Investors should really want that. So a 20 percent volatility with an average 20 percent return, that would be great. But a 20 percent volatility every two years is going to have a drawdown of 15 percent statistically. Every four years it's going to have a drawdown of 20 percent.

This is just what happens. Even if the system truly has that return profile, it's going to experience those kinds of drawdowns and it's going to experience losses. I have a little spreadsheet that I sometimes show to clients when I'm discussing this which . . . broadly, we don't really use spreadsheets but it's a nice little tool . . . which simulates five years of returns, daily returns, from something which is a 20 percent return, 20 percent volatility process. Effectively a Monte Carlo simulation if you want to call it that.

My approach works not by making valid predictions but by allowing me to correct false ones.

George Soros

And every time you press F9 on this spreadsheet it draws another graph of another realization of this random but positive process. You don't have to press F9 very often before you get a history which loses money in a straight line for five years, which has a 40 percent drawdown. Remember, this is something which is guaranteed to make 20 percent per annum over a long enough period.

The expectation of losses is something that everyone should build into their investment process at all times and it's something that investors do. The majority of our investors are institutions. They're pension funds, they're insurance companies, they're sovereign wealth funds, they're endowments. To be very fair to these investors, they are really quite sophisticated and they understand that. Sometimes when you're speaking to maybe high net worth individuals or smaller family offices, the desire there to protect capital is much stronger. You have to be extremely clear about the fact there are things that will happen in the future which will be unpleasant.

The other thing you have to do is explain to investors when you're making money that it probably won't last.

Michael: Do you see the demand for that discretionary macro trader or hedge fund that says, "Trust me, I have the experience. I can call the direction. I can position these multiple futures contracts across all these different markets. Just trust my discretion." Do you see the demand for that waning?

Speculative bubbles do not end like a short story, novel, or play. There is no final denouement that brings all the strands of a narrative into an impressive final conclusion. In the real world, we never know when the story is over.
Robert Shiller

Ewan: Obviously, by the time somebody's sitting on the other side of a table from me, they're probably not going to be asking me that question and I am of course very clear about the fact, and particularly when people say, "Do you take risk off, do you put it on? How about taking off your bond position or adding more this." I'm very clear about the fact I cannot see into the future. I'm not psychic, so therefore I don't have any skill in that. My skills lie elsewhere.

Maybe nobody has skills like that, maybe it is just impossible. I could certainly argue both sides of that. The demand for discretionary trading probably comes from the reactive demand. It's extremely hard to write a model, well it's impossible to write a model, that can react to every last move in the market or react to a piece of information that's coming in.

September 11 is probably a very good example of a piece of information that arrived, the world changed at two minutes past nine and systematic models knew nothing about it, whereas discretionary traders clearly did. In those kind of events it's quite possible that discretionary traders will outperform, and I can understand why people have that demand for it.

But it is an extremely difficult job to be a good macro trader. We all know of those people who have great reputations in doing that. It's maybe only a handful of people.

Of course, the interesting thing about macro trading is that everyone wants to be a macro trader. It's really interesting when you hear stock pickers talk discretionary equity long short, people-talk. Very often what they're talking about is macro things. We think the market's going up, we think it's going down, we're doing this and then therefore we're going to buy these stocks. And quite often macro decisions are wrapped up in security analysis which they probably shouldn't be.

I really think trading [on a] macro discretionary basis is one of the world's hardest jobs and it's possible the people who are successful at it may just be the lucky pennies, I don't know. I don't have hugely strong views on this but it is a very hard job.

Michael: When the macro discretionary guys hear that everything you do is systematic from strategy selection, asset allocation, portfolio construction, position sizing, execution, and risk control, that's got to cause some people to go, "What the blank?" There's got to be that aha! moment of, "This is an approach that's *different*."

Ewan: I don't think we are exceptional. Obviously whilst I know my peers well socially, I don't know what they do and how they sell themselves. But I would be surprised if any of the large European CTAs are talking about how they intervene in what they do [to make discretionary] decisions. There is that little bit from people who say, "We have a model but we occasionally intervene." My opinion, "That's not systematic trading."

In systematic trading, and I've used this phrasing before, it's almost like being pregnant—you either are or you aren't. You can't just be a little bit systematic. I often say to people who are maybe pitching me with systems that are a model that they then put a discretionary label on, "Why don't you just run two books. Run the model in one book and run your discretionary overlay as another book and then just see which one makes money."

This is a way for people to hide really quite complex decisions. Remember what we're all trying to do is we're trying to say, "What's more likely to go up tomorrow and what's more likely to go down tomorrow?" And that's the decision. Now what we have, and many other people like us, is we have lots of complex, or sometimes simple, models which have been tested statistically over many, many years, and then they're weighted using very sophisticated weighting algorithms and costs control measures and all of those other things. Literally millions of lines of code running. And all we're trying to do is forecast whether or not something's going to go up or down tomorrow.

Very often people intervene in their models by saying things like, "Vol is going to come off tomorrow," or "Correlations are going to go up," or "I don't think this model's going to work as well tomorrow." That's a very complex statement. The amount of analysis you would have to do to say, for example, a trend following model isn't working very well, is unlikely to work tomorrow . . . the idea that you can do that for something as complex as a model which is running on 120 different assets, with risk weighting and cost control measures on top of it, seems to me to be unlikely.

Michael: Why don't you talk about part of your process under the hood? In the sense that you like the idea of proving a strategy is broken rather than it's right.

Ewan: Yes, I don't think I'm the first person to come up with that, in that effectively that is the scientific method which has been working pretty well for humans since the Greeks came up with it. Science is about proving things wrong, it's not about proving things right. What you're trying to do is break your strategy. You can never really prove that a strategy works or doesn't work. Finance, despite pundits and newspapers and people in the television and maybe even people on podcasts, filling what they say with certainty, "This is going to happen. This is the best way of doing things. Our systems are better than somebody else's systems. Our stock portfolio is better than somebody else. I know this, I know that." Finance is full of all of that but in fact finance is dominated by randomness. Randomness is everything, and so because randomness is everything you need to be uncertain. You need to have a lack of conviction and dogma in certain things because you want to be able to prove that things are wrong.

Religion is a culture of faith; science is a culture of doubt.
Richard Feynman

When we come up with a new strategy or a new idea or a new trading system, what we're trying to do is, at least when we're simulating it and running it through all the systems, what we're trying to do is find out what's wrong with it. And then if you get what is literally months of testing and retesting and rethinking about it, and thinking about things, different environments and so on—if it gets through months of that, then maybe it's going to work in the future.

These are all very weak, uncertain statements, but to a great extent our philosophy of what we do is around that uncertainty and lack of conviction. There are certain things I've got conviction about. Obviously, I've got conviction about the importance of technology. I've got conviction about the importance of risk weighting or coherent portfolio design. All of those things I've got a lot of conviction about, but I don't have conviction about any particular technique. You just do what you think is best and what you think will be persistent.

Michael: It seems like until the last handful of years in the fund management arena, so many people desire certainty and thus it's refreshing to hear, "I don't know. I'm doing the best that I can, but I don't know. And I really don't think anyone else knows."

Ewan: What we are trying to do as scientists in finance is a little bit like sort of dimly being able to forecast what the weather is going to be like tomorrow. It's like meteorology in that sense. It's full of uncertainty and technology helps and the models aren't perfect and even the biggest computers in the world don't forecast the weather very well five days forward, but meteorologists are trying hard to improve that both in the technology side and better theories about atmospheric circulation. And, they're maybe not too bad at forecasting the weather tomorrow in certain places, probably not in the U.K. because it's so rainy.

Apparently people don't like the truth, but I do like it; I like it because it upsets a lot of people. If you show them enough times that their arguments are bullshit, then maybe just once, one of them will say, 'Oh! Wait a minute—I was wrong.' I live for that happening. Rare, I assure you.

Lemmy
Motörhead

In the past, a lot of investment has really been people looking at the sky and saying, "Look at that cloud, it looks like a dog." That probably captures the realism of the world. The other way of thinking about this is very often, and rightly, when something happens, either when you make money or lose money, or when a model does something or whatever it might be, there's always the question that everyone asks, whether or not it's internally people at Cantab or our investors or journalists, "Why did this happen?"

It's a great question, "Why did this happen?" What we try and do is approach the problem from the perspective of the reason why *this* happened was chance. Now prove that it wasn't chance. Very often that's quite hard. You have a bad month or you have a great month, people say, "What happened?" Can we prove that it's any different from chance? Quite often the answer to that question is no. It's just a different mindset.

Obviously, you have to approach problems in lots of different ways, but approaching a problem from the mindset of, "This might just be a result of random noise, let's see if we can prove that it isn't," is intellectually satisfying if nothing else. It's quite a powerful technique.

Michael: I saw this great article about you, featured in *The New York Times,* and I went through some comments, and I noticed some were highly negative. The thrust of the comments were that you don't bring value to the economy. And I thought to myself, because I know something about what you do and what your peers do, those comments misunderstand. Many of your investors, even if they're institutional investors, are representing the small guy. It's the small guy's retirement money that often makes it into the big institutional account.

Maybe people don't see that, yes, you might not be accepting Ma and Pa's retail account, that's not your position, but I think someone misses the point and misses the boat when they make that criticism. What's your feeling on that?

One of the things that I love to do is travel around the world and look at archaeological sites. Because archaeology gives us an opportunity to study past civilizations, and see where they succeeded and where they failed. Use science to work backwards and say, "Well, really, what were they thinking?"
Nathan Myhrvold

Ewan: This is a hard question to answer. The question is, "Are we doing something that is socially useful? Are we doing a good thing for the economy?" Once you start going down that route, What is useful to the economy or useful to society?" The world only needs one car manufacturer, it doesn't need hundreds of car manufacturers, it doesn't need hundreds of models. Every car manufacturer is kind of not doing something useful for the economy.

Nobody really needs an expensive meal at an expensive restaurant, so expensive meals and expensive restaurants aren't really doing anything useful to the economy. Nobody needs podcasts, we can live without them. Once you get into that, then you're getting into some dangerous water.

We are, I believe, over time are providing something which is valuable to our investors. We are doing that as well as we can. We're constantly trying to add little incremental improvements that make the returns better. We won't make money every month and we won't make money every year and sometimes we lose money and sometimes we make money. But we are doing the best we can to produce positive returns for investors.

And our investors are, as you say, a wide variety of people. They're pension funds, it's mum and dad, as we say here in the U.K., who are investing in this, and although this is not quite the same as finding a cure for cancer and it's certainly not the same as landing a probe on a comet, which are fantastic things to do. This is what we do. We probably at the margin make the returns of our investors' portfolios better in some way, either higher or lower risk or less correlated and so on.

Where I think there's much more of a problem is with people doing something not socially useful like when relatively simple strategies are dressed up as something very complex. People effectively just being an index tracker doing long-only things, like just tracking the S&P index but charging 2 and 20 for it. That's a very bad thing to do. At least I believe that what we do is something that is intellectually rigorous. It's probably a good thing.

The other thing to remember of course is that trend following, systematic trading, the money comes from somewhere. If we make money for investors, somebody loses it.

Michael: If you lose it, someone's gaining it.

Ewan: Someone's gaining it. We would believe and hope that over time we will make money more often than lose. We will over time get positive returns, but it does mean that somebody is losing. It's a very hard question to answer.

Michael: There's a game out there that everybody can play, everybody can pony up to the table, develop a strategy, and it is the ultimate game where everyone can try. I look at it like, "If you don't like it, go try."

Ultimately, the libertarian in me says we've got a lot of better things to do on this planet than draw those types of conclusions, and perhaps, if you look closely you can see those positive things. But of course we all know that some people will never see all positive things. You can't convince everybody.

Ewan: That's probably true. I'm obviously always weary about talking about politics in any public forum because it's not my job to do that. But I do believe that we do a relatively good thing. If nothing else, I provide employment for 50 people in Cambridge, which is the small-business side of what we do as well. It's important to remember that this little community we have is an employer and it pays people money and does all these things as well.

Financial crises are an unfortunate but necessary consequence of modern capitalism.

Andrew Lo

I do believe that we run good small businesses and that is a good thing. One of the things that I'm very pleased about is that in 2006, I reckon I sat in a small office with two computers and a server that gave us electric shocks every time we touched it, and from that we have built a business. It's a small business and it's a business like any small business that can go through bad times and could potentially go bust. And all the efforts associated with running small, medium-sized enterprises means we've managed to survive for eight or nine years now and I'm really pleased about that. If I'm proud of anything, I'm proud of that.

Many areas of modern life rely on scientific research and are guided by well-defined rules that are applied systematically. When flying aeroplanes or developing new medicines we rely on physics, maths, statistics and computer science. Taking these disciplines and applying them to investment research is a natural step.
Ewan Kirk

Michael: That's inspirational. I'd love for you to expand on the idea that you like to ask clients what they like. Not necessarily force things on clients. If you could expand on that—because clearly some clients are not going to have the technical market know-how that you do—so there's going to be some desire for guidance. Could you expand on seeking client feedback?

Ewan: That's maybe taking it a little bit out of context. It is important to understand what your client's utility function is, to use that scientific phrase. What are they looking for? What do they expect from an investment? That sort of informs the way that you explain things to them. As you say, generally, although all of our clients are very knowledgeable and sophisticated in lots of different areas, and of course they have to cover all types of investments and all types of asset allocation, they're almost certainly less knowledgeable than us in the very area that we do, systematic macro trading or systematic micro trading.

The point here is that you do have to understand your client's drivers. What is it they are looking for in their portfolio? What do they expect? It isn't a question of us sort of sitting on one side of the table saying, "What do you want? We've got it. You just ask, we'll give you that." But understanding what drives the decision-making process, who their stake holders are. [For example], we have two products. We have our original quantitative fund which is higher volatility, it's 20 percent, it's high octane, it's 2/20 fee, so it's very much in that mold of high-octane very diversified systematic macro and micro trading.

We also have another product which is lower volatility. It's 10 percent volatility. It's much more scalable. It's got more basic trend and more basic value strategies in there, and it's available to investors at a half and ten. Now, understanding your investor means that you can understand what their internal desires are: What do they need? Maybe they want low cost, very functional, but they want a low-cost system where it's lower volatility and the headline numbers are smaller.

We all know that investing in a 20 percent volatility product is too risky, then all you have to do is invest half your money in the 20 percent volatility product and keep half of it in your pocket, and you've got a 10 percent volatility investment. But somehow that doesn't feel the same as a 10 percent volatility product, for reasons that I really don't get. The pure mathematician in me says that's nuts. But nonetheless it is true and I'm human, too, obviously, and I feel that.

It is important to understand your investor, who their stake holders are, and by understanding that and communicating with investors at the right level. None of our investors need to know or cares about the deep statistical details which might be embedded in some non-linear Bayesian-regression portfolio algorithm. That sounds great but they kind of don't care and they shouldn't care about that.

But they should care about things like culture, technology, people, the search processes, and these are all things that we can explain and want to explain in great detail. And if you can understand what your investor needs and wants, then maybe you can explain those things better.

I always feel that I'm not really in that camp of—and our industry is quite bad at this—"If I told you about my models I'd have to shoot you." That's quite common, that sort of, "I have to be massively secret, can't tell you about it," thing. That's wrong. We as an industry are managing money for people, and it's their money, and they have the right to know, and we have the obligation to tell them what it is we're doing with it.

Michael: That probably has been one of the reasons that you guys have gone from zero to significant in fairly short order, in a very competitive space.

Ewan: Yes, well, we have. I'll refer you to my previous [explanation] about randomness. Yes, some of that is of course luck. We had a good run; we didn't have such a good year last year, we're having a good year this year. Some of this is randomness, but . . . apart from being open and transparent and supporting investors and all these things that you have to be, the other strand that runs through everything we do is that sort of aggregation of marginal improvements. Little, small, marginal improvements that really in and of themselves maybe just don't make much of a difference.

Let's say, we work out some way of saving ourselves half a basis point in costs a day. That doesn't seem like very much, half a basis point, that's a tiny amount of money, but it adds up to nearly a percent and a half over the course of a year. That's great. Fine, we'll have that. And lots of those little marginal improvements are probably what distinguishes good funds from less good funds.

One of the things you have to remember in life is that not everybody's going to think that you're great. I'm quite pragmatic about these things. There's valid criticisms about systematic trading, there's valid criticisms about the finance industry. You've got to take those criticisms on board, understand why they've happened. There's been a lot of, as we know, lots of stuff in the press, bad things have happened in finance.

People are right to criticize. I'm not going to get annoyed about it because maybe some of the criticisms aren't bad. We certainly don't have any monopoly on the truth.

Michael: As somebody who has watched this particular space for a long time and going back many, many decades, there is something noble about the systematic guys that have done this for a long time. There is something generally consistent that you can hang onto in this systematic space. Like you said, though, maybe things break and it all falls apart at some point in time, but, knock on wood for several decades or more, it's done pretty well.

We all fool ourselves from time to time in order to keep our thoughts and beliefs consistent with what we have already done or decided.
Robert B. Cialdini

Ewan: I think people in the systematic space, we try harder, to use that old Avis ad, we do try. I know just about everyone in the European space. I know that everyone is completely focused on just doing the best thing they can, and that's great. There's very few charlatans or people that are just knocking together any old rubbish just so they can raise some assets. People try really hard and sometimes we fail, but on average the industry succeeds.

Michael: That's how it goes though, right? It's not necessarily consistency, it can just come, boom, and you all of a sudden have a September 2014 and everyone goes, "Where did that come from?" Hold on, that's trend following.

Ewan: That's the way it works. That's an interesting thing for people. When people say, "Trend following hasn't worked for three years." I explain, if you take a simple trend following model and run it across 100 assets, when trend following's working really well it's maybe working on 60 assets and not working on 40, and when it's not working it's working on 45 assets and not working on 55 assets.

There's never really been a period in history where trend following hasn't worked on something, it just hasn't worked enough. And . . . I've got to be careful always to say, "We're not a trend follower alone, we do lots of other stuff: trends in bonds, trends in ags, trends in the yen, trends in energy." This is all working out really well and we're in one of those golden periods where trends are working on a lot of different things.

That too won't last. Over time there'll be ups and downs, but over a long enough period of time, trend following, and more generally systematic macro trading, has done incredibly well and presumably—and this is the little scientist in uncertainty in me coming out—and presumably with a reasonable degree of probability it will continue to work in the future.

Where all think alike, no one thinks very much.
Walter Lippmann

Michael: If anyone out there looks at a systematic quant track record and it's all black ink, then you've got trouble.

Ewan: I refer you to my previous answer about Bernard Madoff.

Alex Greyserman 16

Alex Greyserman is a member of the ISAM Systematic Trend Investment Committee. He has worked with Larry Hite since 1989, initially as research director at Mint Investment Management Co. ("Mint"), responsible for research and development of trading strategies and overall portfolio risk management. Greyserman co-authored, *Trend Following with Managed Futures: The Search for Crisis Alpha*."[1]

Alex: Are you are still [living] in God knows what country?

Michael: Oh, I love it! Yes, well let's just leave it like that. That keeps the audience guessing . . . "God knows what country." We'll circle back to that on the end maybe!

Let me jump right to the heart of the matter. When I last talked to you and Larry Hite we were right in the middle of the weekly parade of 26-year-old *Financial Times* reporters writing about trend following as dead. And then something funny happened along the way to the parade. Even in a zero interest rate environment, in a relatively low volatility environment, all of a sudden you and your peers started to make quite a bit of trend following money.

I don't care what town you're born in, what city, what country. If you're a child, you are curious about your environment. You're overturning rocks. You're plucking leaves off of trees and petals off of flowers, looking inside, and you're doing things that create disorder in the lives of the adults around you.
Neil deGrasse Tyson

I know we don't want this to sound like an infomercial, but it's educational in the sense that many people probably don't know [the real performance] when they see all these obituaries written about trend following. Well, it just hasn't worked out that way, has it?

Alex: I've been around long enough to probably have seen four or five of these obituaries written, maybe even more over the years, and we're still here. We've seen this in our 800-year study. This is not some voodoo arbitrage strategy that extracts something from somewhere that's not understood where it could just easily end. This is a strategy that harvests natural [occurrences] in markets. The only way you can, I guess, permanently kill a trend following strategy is to declare all markets to go sideways forever, or to declare that no market will ever move significantly away from some sort of equilibrium, and that just doesn't happen for long enough periods of time.

I'm looking at the yield of the 10-year note and all prognosticators have said that, "Oh, that can't go to where it is now," and here it is, but that's the nature of trend following.

Michael: Look at crude oil. There's been all kinds of fundamental opinions about why oil has to go up or why it's at the right price and this and that, and then wham-bam thank you ma'am, the price dropped pretty significantly.

The most erroneous stories are those we think we know best—and therefore never scrutinize or question.
Stephen Jay Gould

Alex: Yes, and nobody knows where it's going to go, but it's just the nature of people to figure, "Ok things are not going to move far away from where they are." Yet the same people will invest most of their money in stocks and hope that they'll go up a hundred percent. This is why this kind of strategy [trend following] adds value over time.

Michael: It's important for people to realize you're not saying that you know what's going to happen tomorrow. You're not saying that stocks are going to continue to go down (or up), but there's another way to think except being only *long* stocks. There's something else out there.

You've been in the middle of that something else for a long time. I would love for you to go back in time. You work with one of the most colorful people that I've ever met. I would like for you to talk about your first meeting. How old you were, your background in your first meeting with Larry Hite, and how you guys have come to have this great career together.

Alex: Yes, it was kind of a fork in a road as I look back. You know the joke: if you get a fork in a road, you take it. I came to interview with Larry in 1989. I was a kid out of school. I didn't know anything about trend following and certainly not managed futures or details, I just needed a job. I was making $28,000 a year and Larry offered me $32,000. I still have the offer sheet.

Michael: Hold on. You say out of school, were you 22, 26? Grad school, undergrad?

Alex: 21, 22.

Michael: Okay, young guy.

Alex: Yes. Didn't really know who Larry Hite was. This was in Millburn, New Jersey, and he was one of the guys that interviewed me. Now the interesting thing is the *Market Wizards* book had either just come out or was coming out, I don't recall whether there was the actual book on the shelf or a draft of the book on the shelf, but somebody gave me in the office the chapter about Larry to read while I was waiting. And I remember just flipping to . . . I'm paraphrasing Jack Schwager's question, something like, "What's your edge?" or something like that.

As somewhat of a scientist out of school, I would normally have expected some quite scientific answer, because I heard that Mint did something quantitative, so some sort of rocket science answer for what people did in 1989. But then I read this psychology stuff about how we know what we don't know and I was like, "You've got to be kidding me? What am I doing here?"

Michael: That was a line from Larry.

No one is dumb who is curious. The people who don't ask questions remain clueless throughout their lives.

Neil deGrasse Tyson

Alex: Yes, Larry said that his edge is that he knows what he doesn't know.

Michael: And you're reading this before you go into the interview?

Alex: Yes, I'm reading this before I'm going into the interview. The interview was, "Okay, whatever, go home," but then typically you have to follow up and write a letter or e-mail, "It was a great interview. Tell the headhunter that I really want this job." I couldn't figure out whether I really wanted to tell him that I wanted this job because actually I was confused.

Larry gave a talk in my class at Columbia recently. I teach a class at Columbia. He gave a talk to a bunch of grad students and he confused the hell out of them too. [Laughter] Because it takes times to sink in . . .

Michael: He makes those simple statements, but the depth of those simple statements is not to be underestimated.

Alex: Yes, later on I've obviously learned what all that means. It's the respect for risk and not getting very emotionally attached to any one strategy and those kinds of things, which allow you to survive for decades and decades in the markets. But initially, just like recently in my class, I have 80, 90 graduate PhD students, and here comes the Market Wizard. And they start asking him things they think a Market Wizard should know, like where gold is going next week or which way the market's going because he's some sort of a wizard. He of course says he has no idea. He just needs to know what he doesn't know and if he gets into a trade and if he's wrong then he has to get out of it. [Larry's view] is so powerful but yet so simple.

To go back to my story, really it's the fact that he offered me a couple of thousand dollars more that I ended up taking the job. I really had no idea, no way to appreciate that and no idea how to judge Mint or what Larry did, I just . . . I dove in.

Michael: How quickly did you know once you were hired and you got into the office and you're around Larry, how quickly did you know this was going to possibly be your passion for the rest of your career? How quickly did you start to have that feeling?

Absence of evidence is not evidence of absence.
Carl Sagan

Alex: Probably still took a couple of years. I saw the system was making money, but it took a couple of years to kind of sink in . . . what this is about. I was like most geeks in the beginning and just trying to find the Holy Grail, but it's your realization that no matter how smart you are . . . I see this with all my students. I joke that I try to bring their IQ down after they take my class rather than go up. Obviously, their IQs are high to begin with but if you have the kind of investment IQ where you think you know everything, you'll end up failing.

It took a while to establish the right mental equilibrium. This is by the way where it's hard to hire the right people in this area because you need a combination of two things that almost never go together, which is very, very smart people that are also very, very humble. To survive in this business, you need to have the right balance. If you get too smart and not humble enough, you get too emotionally attached.

There's lots of people out there in the world who are very humble but maybe not smart enough to do at least the basic arithmetic of the strategies. It took a while [for the strategy] to sink in, but I've been in this for 25 years and have learned not to get too emotionally attached to people declaring trend following dead. On the other hand you want not to feel like we're walking on water when we are up 30 percent on the year.

These things come and go but over time it works. But I wanted to make one point about trend following that is confusing to people. They focus too much on the S&P, obviously because it's in everybody's portfolios, but they think, "Ok, the value of trend following is just to time the short side of the S&P." I have a lot of allocators who are asking me, "Well, what's my position in the S&P?" If I say I'm long because trend following is long, then they say, "Oh, but that's not a diversifying investment. Why do I need trend following?"

If I say I'm short then they say, "Okay, maybe that's too late," and they try to overthink this. The value of trend following is not just getting the right side of the S&P trade. It may or may not happen. The truth is the systems are not that great in any one market. The value of trend following is that we can do this over . . . 150 markets or however many markets one can find, and really have a diversified, uncorrelated investment. That's what this is about. That's why it's worked [in our book] for 800 years.

Don't bet your deli to win a pickle.

Larry Hite

If you look back at my first experience with equity markets . . . gosh, shucks, it was in 1987. Mint made 60 percent in that year. This was before I started at Mint, so this is in the history books. But they didn't make that from necessarily timing Black Monday. . . . It makes money anyhow. Some corn trades and other things in other markets and the same thing in '01, '02. Same thing in 2008. The value of trend following is not a one-market thing, it's a harvesting of natural human behavior in 150 different markets.

Michael: I see many papers about trend following in the classical sense like you're talking about. But in the last bunch of years there's been a lot of papers about momentum and they specifically focus only on equities. There's some confusion that comes from some of the academic work where it's been attempting to attach momentum only to an equity perspective and ignoring what you're talking about as this great diversification.

Alex: Yes, so maybe this is slightly nerdy but there is a difference between so-called cross-sectional momentum, which is almost what all academic papers [talk about with] equities . . . this would be some kind of relative [strength], one stock to another, and time-series momentum is what trend following is.

We trend follow any given market whether it's going up and down, really unrelated to other markets. It's related in terms of the correlation and how much you risk, but not in terms of the signal. We could have no position in all markets except for one. All these equity papers are dealing with this cross-sectional momentum where you compare one stock to another and things like that, and they get into the efficient markets of whether it should exist, doesn't exist. It's overcomplicating things. When we have 800 years of data and simple—not simple strategies but simple concepts—you buy high and you sell higher and you sell short when it's going down and you cover lower, that works. In fact, some of the academic papers out call it time-series momentum. That's what this is.

By the way, anything in equities is invariably probably going to correlate to equities even if you try to make it uncorrelated to equities. What adds value is trend following—whether it's bonds or commodities or emissions or iron ore, or obviously currencies. Then people ask me, "What about the interventions and the government this and the government that?" Meanwhile look where the bond yields are and how far they've gone. Things can go quite far.

The solution often turns out more beautiful than the puzzle.
Richard Dawkins

Michael: The subtitle of your book has the phrase "Crisis Alpha." It's clear to anybody that looks at the data during these crisis periods, this time series [trend following], does perform exceptionally well. There's no guarantee that things will work out that way in the future, but it's performed that way.

But what's interesting about the last bunch of months, we really weren't at a crisis period, but there's still those trend following performances coming out from a fairly low-volatility, zero interest rates environment. If somebody was to couch trend following as only crisis alpha [also known as a black swan], that would be a mistake?

Alex: Yes, in fact some people in our space have tried to make some kind of an excuse for some lackluster performance by calling this a tail hedge and saying, "There was no tail." That's a total mistake. Trend following has two great features that you probably can't find in almost any other investment. First, it's totally uncorrelated. If you start with that and look at the history of trend following for 10 years, 20 years, or 800 years, it generates a return stream with zero to slightly negative correlation to all other asset classes.

If we take that as given, when you have 800 years of data, it's pretty close to a given, it's totally uncorrelated. It also happens to be quite negatively correlated in many periods when you want a negative correlation which is the crisis periods. Because it tends to make money from whether it's inflation shocks or downturns in equities or something else going on somewhere. Typically, volatility picks up during those periods and it makes money somewhere, but it's not only that. You could take out all the crisis alpha periods, all the crisis periods, and it's still a great investment.

I'd argue it's a liquid investment because we trade liquid markets and so people will go in their 401(k) plan and have 5,000 versions of the same thing. Small cap, mid cap, mid cap . . . I heard this term recently . . . "smid cap," small to mid-cap or large cap and international and this and that. And how many versions are there of being *long only*? Which are all 80 percent to 90 percent correlated, 70 percent correlated at least.

Of course, you get a little diversification from that, so, fair enough, but imagine in that same 401(k) plan or whatever list of instruments, now there was something called X, Y, Z. It wasn't labeled trend following and somebody remembers, "Oh, I read something bad about trend following." It's just another investment, another mutual fund or another fund that somebody can put their money into. You look at it and you say, "Wow, this thing is just different," and it tends to work when other things don't.

How much closer do you get to a Holy Grail? Maybe, that's too strong of a statement, but in terms of the possibilities of what one can invest in, how much better can it be? It's totally diversifying and there's a good chance, no guarantee, but there's a good chance that it'll perform in the periods when other things don't. So you go back to optimization 101, any kind of optimization of the portfolio should tell you to have some allocation to that thing. In fact, we're writing a paper right now on the topic of how costly is it to not have trend following in your portfolio. How much do you give up by actually not having it? Not in any particular year

If you can laugh at your mistakes, it's a good thing.
Ozzy Osbourne

but over time. It's quite costly because you're actually avoiding a tremendously diversifying asset class.

Michael: Let me jump into the idea of benchmarking and specifically those institutional managers out there that are fixating on stocks—the long-only prism. Your firm has to deal with that. It's a constant education process, and if you look at a situation like CalPERS, they had a very small percentage, relatively speaking, with perhaps managers like ISAM. I don't know if they had an investment with ISAM or not but I'm just saying in general in trend following.

What can be asserted without evidence can also be dismissed without evidence.
Christopher Hitchens

I wonder if you could maybe relay a story about watching people convert or watching people not convert to this way of thinking?

Alex: We do this all day long. We have major pension fund investors, so some people get it. It's interesting that in some parts of the world, maybe it's Australia, Canada, Middle East . . . and the part of the world that you're in, Japan, that kind of area, historically have been diversification friendly. It's almost a mental mindset, maybe, because the Japanese market certainly hasn't been going up in a straight line, right?

They have a lot of currency movements and [maybe] . . . those parts of the world are just friendly to the concept of diversification. Trend following will follow from there, but you first have to have the concept of moving somebody away from 100 percent equities.

The U.S. is somehow emotionally attached to this idea that everything will go up forever. Obviously some institutions have allocations to this. The CalPERS thing, by the way, probably was not a managed futures issue, it was just the size of the hedge funds. They actually had a decent allocation to manage futures. But, with some institutions, it depends on their appetite for embracing diversification and as you used the word "benchmark," whether some form of diversification is in the benchmark.

What's the benchmark of the institution? And if the benchmark doesn't allow for this kind of diversification, then we can talk to them until the cows come home, they probably won't risk their career by putting it in. Because at the end of the day, 1 percent allocation to trend following is not going to make any difference. It has to be 5,

10, and we have institutions who have investments with us or with some of our peers at that level, but their investment committee has embraced that in terms of their benchmark. And they just in general embrace the concept of diversification.

To some people it's so obvious: "I can't believe that we even considered not doing it." To some people it's, "Okay, stocks go up forever, so why do I need to bother?"

Michael: I think that it would take a Japanese-style stock market [crash] perhaps to get some people to say, "We have to change." There's going to be some out there that as long as equities go up seemingly in a straight line, even though there's been some 50 percent drawdowns in the last 15 years, they're going to be hard to convince.

Alex: Especially in the U.S. Like no matter what it's just all about, "Equities go straight up, equities go straight up." I don't know if it'll take a Japanese type of downturn, but some sort of a shock in the system. But again, I'm trying to tell people it's not that you just have to have that shock. Why not have a diversifying, uncorrelated investment in your portfolio that can do well when other things don't. You don't have to appeal to somebody's sense that, "Wow, this is only going to make money if [stocks] go down 100 percent."

If you personalize losses, you can't trade.

Bruce Kovner

People try to overthink the environmental factors for trend following and then they try to time them. Some people got it into their heads that this only works when volatility's high. Well, you said a minute ago that volatility hasn't been particularly high recently and we've done well. There's no law that says crude oil can't go from 100-something down to 85 or something like that, in a fairly smooth line.

You don't have to have massive volatility. There was a stomach virus [that] affected lean hogs recently that made prices go way up and not particularly with tremendous volatility, it was just a fundamental event. This whole down movement in interest rates over the years hasn't been particularly highly volatile. Somebody said to me, "Oh, this strategy only works in high-volatility environments so I'll wait till there's a high-volatility environment." Well, things are not that easy. [Laughter] By the time you get to a high-volatility environment or it doesn't work because you have too much intervention—well, wait a second, intervention has caused the biggest trend of all time in fixed income.

Michael: They want to trade your trend following strategy . . . No, they want to trade you.

Alex: Yes, they want to trade me. People years ago used to want to time equity markets, too. Remember that? People would try to time equity markets, get in and out, fun timing, all this. It's not that simple, it's not supposed to be that simple. What you're supposed to do is have a handful of diversifying investments and that's what's going to take your portfolio to the promised land. I tell people the worst thing you can do is to try and time a trend follower.

To try to time it when they're doing well, "I should give them more money" and when they're doing poorly, "I should take money away." That is actually the worst kind of investment you can make.

Michael: You are a professor. You have many, many PhD candidate students at Columbia. Let's say hypothetically because you're the top guy now or one of the top guys now, so they come to the office, the new employee comes to the office. Obviously, in this day and age they're going to know something about ISAM, they're going to know something about you, they're going to know something about Larry before they sit down with you. But you have to introduce the science of trend following to that new candidate, that new person that you want to join your team. How do you start?

If you hear a "prominent" economist using the word "equilibrium," or "normal distribution," do not argue with him; just ignore him, or try to put a rat down his shirt.[2]
Nassim Taleb

Alex: We have all these things like adaptive market hypothesis and behavioral theory and things like that, but at the end of the day what I would tell people is the markets are some sort of a risk transfer mechanism. You cannot assume that just because you're smart you will suck money out of the markets. If you think of it like a poker game, it could be a zero-sum game. You could be the best player, but then your profits will come down not because your skill goes down, but because the other people at the table will just leave the game.

Is it a game of zero-sum kind of outsmarting people? Or is it a natural phenomenon in the markets, almost kind of like providing insurance? Larry talked about this in our last talk about relating trend following to insurance. I say there are natural occurring things in the markets. Let's start with something other than trend following, so we've got an analogy.

Value investing, right? It's been scientifically, dare I say, proven or shown with data that value investing works because a lot of investors don't want to hold those stocks when they go down, and you actually are in an economic rent-type of risk premium if you hold them. There are other examples in the markets where you're actually providing value to the markets by doing a certain thing. That's what makes it lasting. Because there's no way for 800 years you could find some gimmick that makes money where you would only do that if nobody else knew about it. There's no way you can get away with that for 800 years. Somebody from my class will figure it out and then it'll be gone.

This happens a lot with some high-frequency traders and those things like that. The science is the natural element that what we're actually doing, what trend following is actually doing is providing liquidity to hedgers, and it's creating an equilibrium in the markets, and we have to get paid for that. That's why this has worked for 800 years. If the price of oil, for example, is going up, right now it's going down, but if it's going up, the airline companies will almost certainly need to sell oil to lock in the future price. They're not in the business of counter-trend trading; they just need to sell it to lock in the future price.

We at that point buy it—it gets just a little technical but it's conceptually establishing the fact that it's a natural occurring concept. The markets need players like us, otherwise you will have a whole bunch of hedgers and the markets won't exist.

Michael: You are speculators.

Alex: Yes, we're speculators and then actually we talk in [our] book, there's hedgers, speculators, risk transfer, and you need to have this. But it cannot be, when you think about evolutionary things, it cannot be a free lunch. If I made money in every single trend following trade, the hedgers will stop hedging. Sometimes their hedge turns out to be a good idea, sometimes they would have turned out better not to have hedged. Sometimes I will look better if I bought oil or I look better if I somehow ignored that trade. Of course, we take all trend following trades.

It's supposed to be slightly painful, but in the end if you look at the last 800 years, the data shows that equilibrium risk-adjusted returns are pretty good and they're slightly painful. That's why you can have a couple of bad years or you can have drawdowns. If it was too good you would have every hedger hiring a quant from my class and run moving-average systems to time their hedges.

It's the equilibrium of the markets that establishes this principle and that's what makes it work over 800 years. Trend following is almost unique in that area. A lot of convergent-type strategies are very limited in their capacity, very limited in what they can do, because if five other people discover it, it could be gone.

Success isn't permanent and failure isn't fatal.
Mike Ditka

It's a naturally occurring phenomenon in the markets and then it's just a matter of a handful of different ways of actually capturing it. But it's there. It almost cannot go away. It can temporarily not work but it just structurally cannot disappear, otherwise you might as well shut down the markets and go back to communism.

Michael: You were born in the former Soviet Union? What country were you born in, Alex?

Alex: Well, actually I don't know. I've had my passport changed several times. My U.S. passport originally used to say USSR because I came to the U.S. when the USSR still existed. So technically I was born in the former Soviet Union, but then they called me up and they said, "Okay, we need to change your passport because this new country got created called Ukraine and now we have to reprint your passport to say born in Ukraine."

But now, with what's going on there, they might call me tomorrow and say, "Okay, we have to reprint your passport, now you were born, I don't know, Russia or something else."

Michael: Here's where I want to go with bringing it up. It's not for a flippant reason. What age did you come to America?

Alex: Twelve.

Michael: Did you have an advantage coming from where you came? Was there a built-in drive, a motivation that you think gave you an advantage over other peers that you might have seen in America once you got to America?

Alex: I probably don't have hours to speak about the immigrant drive, but that's the immigrant drive that got me going on interviews in an area that I had no clue about. At that point it was sort of survival and making money, not this grand idea,

"I'm going to become a finance person." It's the bouncing around from washing dishes, which was my first job, to this to pay for schools. Certainly my parents didn't have money to really pay for anything back then. It's just the inherent immigrant drive to keep pushing.

I had a job before I went to the interview for Larry, but I just wanted to do better. I don't know if there was any other advantage other than just keep pushing, keep driving. Don't assume somebody's going to hand it to you. Larry, probably you've heard story's from him, he had a disadvantage with not being able to see and those kinds of things. I had a small disadvantage in the beginning, I couldn't even speak English, so that's why I had a dishwashing job. Nobody had to tell me what to do. If there's a pile of dishes, then I had to wash them.

Michael: Meeting Larry was an opportunistic-type thing because let's face it, I know from when I first met Larry, he gave me so much of his time and energy and we met so many times. I feel Larry's the type of guy that if he sees somebody trying and really pushing, he is the kind of guy that reaches down and says, "Okay, I'll give you my time. If you're really hungry I'll give you my time." I feel very fortunate to have met Larry. It's changed my life to meet people like Larry.

Study hard what interests you the most in the most undisciplined, irreverent and original manner possible.

Richard Feynman

Alex: I started at Mint not as some kind of a master. I started as a technical guy doing some programming. I was quite a low-level person. I could have stayed as a technologist for any number of years, but again it's that drive to see what else . . . I hung close to Larry, got to know about "know what you don't know" and what he means. I kept asking him about it and that's how I moved up.

I grabbed my opportunities. But again, that's not a Russian thing per se, it's just the immigrant drive. I've got to go get it, otherwise it's not going to come to me.

Michael: My great-grandfather came from Lithuania in the early 1900s, and they were in coal mines in Scranton and his kids became doctors and engineers, so it happens quick when they've got the drive.

Alex: Washing dishes obviously wasn't going to make me money, so I had to cut the loss there. I did work for one year out of school in an engineering role. I worked for RCA on high-definition television because I had a degree in electrical engineering. It was not losing me money per se, so it's not technically a losing trade, but it was not going to take me anywhere. I had to cut my losses there. I just trend followed my way into this. Trend following is a good general philosophy of life. It's not just on markets.

It's how people live anyway. This is why trend following in the markets works because that's how people are.

If you put in stops and run your profits and trade randomly you make money; and if you put in targets and no stops, and you trade randomly you lose money. So the old saw about cutting losses and running profits has some truth to it.
David Harding

Michael: When people look at trend following performance across the many managers out there, and we don't have to name names, people can go look at the performance—it's all freely available. I can see up and down months where trend following traders had a good month. You might see double the return for one particular trader versus another, but still it's pretty easy to see that there's dispersion amongst trend following CTAs, trend following managers. Why don't you talk about that dispersion?

Alex: Yes, by analogy to equities it's actually very simple. Initially this is complicated. This is why a lot of sophisticated investors like the institutions you asked me about have a hard time getting in, because they feel like they might make dumb decisions about the space and end up picking the so-called wrong manager, the wrong trend follower, because they have no understanding of what causes differences in performance, and they get a little emotional [over] what makes one manager better than the other. Well, is it who made more money last year, does that make them better? They don't know how to step in.

It's actually not that complicated if you make yourself aware that there's a couple of factors that drive performance. For example, by analogy to equities in the late '90s—this is where every Internet stock went up 100 percent every day and every brick-and-mortar stock stayed flat or went down.

You had this so-called dispersion between value and growth. Most investors understand that. That's why they'll have both in their portfolio. Sometimes you have dispersion between small cap and large cap. If you make just a few, let's call them sub-classifications, it's not just, okay, trend follower one, trend follower two, trend follower three. Okay, those are the trend followers but they have a particular focus. If this was equity manager one, two, three, the first one might have been growth focus, the second one might be value focus, the third might be small cap, fourth might be large cap.

There's going to be some correlation between them because those guys are in the stock market, but there's going to be some fair degree of dispersion, and in a year like 1999 it could have been a 100 percent degree in dispersion. Now investors in long-only say, "Ah, okay, I go to my Morningstar little matrix and then I need a little bit of value, a little bit of growth, so I kind of diversify." Same thing in the trend following space. You do a little bit of analysis and say, for example—the words are not the same—so it's not value growth, it's, for example, we introduce certain factors in the book like the *speed* of trading.

One of the best ways to make money is not to lose money.

Michael Milken

You could do trend following quite *slow* . . . either by choice or if you manage lots of money, maybe you have to be a little bit slower because of the size of your assets. Or you can be a little bit *faster*. And you can get different results and you can attribute that to the speed of trading. You can also have a market mix bias. You could trade only the large markets, again either by choice, or because you're big, or you can be quite a bit more diversified like, for example we are . . . trading a lot of smaller markets.

Sometimes those will cause performance differences. But if you would like to have a portfolio of two or three, a diversified portfolio of trend followers, it's not that hard. Just look at a couple of these factors and who's tilted too slow and who's tilted too fast and these kinds of things. Just by analogy to the whole value growth thing. Just a little bit of effort and then that can explain quite a bit of the dispersion between the managers.

It's not random because people are sometimes afraid of, "Wait, you have eight guys doing the same thing and you have like this massive difference in performance." I don't know, what is it? Some guy has a faster machine or bigger computers? And, they get scared because they've picked the wrong one. "What is it?"

It's not that. They're doing conceptually the same thing but they have certain portfolio tilts that can cause these differences, and with just a little bit of effort one can understand them.

I can live with doubt and uncertainty and not knowing. I think it is much more interesting to live not knowing than to have answers that might be wrong. If we will only allow that, as we progress, we remain unsure, we will leave opportunities for alternatives. We will not become enthusiastic for the fact, the knowledge, the absolute truth of the day, but remain always uncertain. In order to make progress, one must leave the door to the unknown ajar.
Richard Feynman

Michael: It's all the rage in conversations, the media, Fed watching—rate hikes. Interest rates going up. We don't necessarily know if there's going to be a higher rate environment? We don't necessarily know how that's going to affect trend following?

Alex: We've looked at it over the 800-year data set, "What happens in a rising interest rate environment?" But let's ask this question: You think equities might do well in that environment? I'm no prognosticator, but it's possible they won't. Will bonds do well in that environment? Well, almost certainly not, because rates go up, then bonds have to go down. I would put trend following as maybe one of the few things that might do well.

Trend followers are agnostic to direction. If yields go up, so the prices go down, we will be short bonds. Now it hasn't happened for many years that there have been substantial hikes in the markets, but if you look at the data, we have data on interest rates from 1395, Venice issued bonds in 1395 called Venetian Bonds. So we have centuries and centuries of data. Plenty of rising rates environments and I'll simply say we will make money being short bonds if that happens.

Now people ask technical questions, "If you're short bonds, you short carry, will that hurt you?" It's not really going to hurt us. There's going to be almost certainly inflationary pressure somewhere, so we'd probably make money off commodities. There'll be some interest we get on cash, as it's a technicality, but most trend followers put up T-bills as margins, so we'll make more money on margin. We'll make more money on something called the roll yield in commodities because we have to roll futures contracts.

When you put all this together it should be pretty good. At least we're going to have a pretty good chance of making money. A better chance of making money in a rising rate environment than a fixed-income portfolio, let's put it that way. And meanwhile, look, some macro funds out there—and not naming names—they have been betting on a rising rate environment for how long? And they've been losing money on *that*.

Of course, at some point rates will go up. It has to be a truism, maybe in our next life or something, but at some point they have to go up. But look at Japan, where's a law that says 10-year rates in the U.S. can't go down more? I don't know. Meanwhile we're making quite a bit of money on the trend that's in front of us now. When it turns there'll be a little bit of pain and then we'll make money the other way.

I'm a big fan of people that operate in the world of publish and iterate versus, you know, think, think, think, think.

Kevin Plank
Under Armour

This is the peril of timing, because you could sit there frozen like a deer in headlights, ignoring what's going on now, not making money out of it, betting on a rate hike. When is it going to happen? No one knows how to time those things, so just let a trend following system time it and meanwhile let's take the money, and put it in our pocket from rates going down. What's wrong with *that*?

Campbell Harvey

17

Campbell Harvey is a Canadian economist, known for his work on asset allocation with changing risk and risk premiums and emerging markets finance. He is currently the J. Paul Sticht Professor of International Business at Duke University's Fuqua School of Business in Durham, NC.[1]

> *We know that we know almost nothing. But the "almost nothing" we know isn't completely nothing, and we only bet on that.*
> **David Harding**

Michael: Outline your example that goes into American football and let people slowly come into your thinking.

Campbell: There are plenty of sports examples here. And football is one of them, where a team could have many wins in a row or a quarterback many passes in a row. And the issue: Is that due to skill, is it luck or is it a combination? It's also the case that a quarterback could appear to do quite poorly and not [make] that many passes. That doesn't necessarily mean that quarterback lacks skill, it could just be bad luck.

It's the same thing with investment managers where you can outperform the market many, many years in a row. It's not clear that's a result of skill or a result of just good luck. It is a vexing problem in finance: How do we separate the skill from the luck?

Michael: As you were talking about beating the market for many years in a row, I thought of someone. I'm quite fond of him. He's liked some of my work and I've had a chance to meet him several times. He had a fantastic run at Legg Mason, and that's Bill Miller. I think he beat the S&P for 14 years in a row. But then, at the end of the 14-year stretch there was a pretty significant drawdown in the '08 crisis. So as you make this point about skill versus luck, there's no doubt, it's not an easy subject.

The reason the trend following or the systematic investing industry has gotten big is because it has been successful. No one should miss that point.
David Harding

Campbell: No, it can be a combination, that's the thing. It's really interesting if you group the best-performing hedge funds or mutual funds and then hold those for the next period and just keep on doing that. You just buy the winners, like the extreme winners. You just have that as a strategy. Then what you find is that portfolio does poorly. Some at the very top probably were blessed with good luck.

That doesn't mean they're unskilled; it could still be skill, but they were skilled plus the luck that got them up there, and this is the way that I usually like to explain it. Suppose that you just like grab a whole bunch of dice, like a large number, let's say 36 dice. And you drop them on the table, and then you go pick out all of the ones that show six, and let's say there's about seven of them. You take all the other dice away off the table, then you drop the ones that all have six and you're going to get a combination of one, two, three.

It's going to average about three, and think of that as the people that did really well. The sixes are the people that were at the very top that did the best. Then when you threw those dice again, it's just natural that you're not going to get seven sixes from those dice. A lot of this has to do with regression to the mean and luck.

Michael: I was thinking of two traders. One very famous, one not so famous but just as successful, Jim Simons at Renaissance Technologies. He's had math formulas named after him. He will come out loudly and clearly, and always say, "Hey, I'm a very lucky guy." That's not taking away from his skill. I could think of the most famous U.S.A. investor, the wealthiest U.S.A. investor, he says, "Look, I won the Ovarian Lottery." That's Warren Buffett.

The notion of survivorship bias starts to become an interesting topic because if we look at a particular trading strategy or particular traders, and not to take anything away from Warren Buffett, but there's not a lot of other Warren Buffetts.

Campbell: That's true. Jim Simons, Warren Buffett are probably . . .

Michael: They're up there [as stars].

Campbell: They are up there and they are saying, "I was lucky." Really, that's a hard one to believe. I know Jim Simons and I don't know Warren Buffett. They do very different things. From what I know of Simons's operations, there's a lot of skill there, but as you say, again, it can be a combination of having skill and good luck.

Michael: You've got to have a strategy that puts you in a position to benefit when the unexpected happens. If one has a strategy that can operate like that . . . that starts to be skill-like.

Campbell: Definitely. Again, it might not always work . . .

Michael: Process versus outcome. You can have a great process and it doesn't necessarily mean that outcome's going to be beautiful every time.

Campbell: You mentioned survivorship bias. There is a kind of reverse type of bias and that is that some very skilled investment managers drop out because they've had bad luck. That's kind of a reverse survivorship bias.

Mean reversion works almost all the time, and then it stops and you are kind of out of business.
Jerry Parker

This is really important. This idea doesn't just apply to investment managers. Let me discuss, just for a minute, another research paper I have that does a psychometric survey of CEOs. What my paper finds is that CEOs are hugely more tolerant of risk than the lay population. Like by a factor of 10. It's extraordinary.

You can think of a scenario where these people that are very tolerant of risk enter a firm as a junior employee. They take a lot of risk and some of them, they get lucky, it turns out. Others don't get lucky and they drop out of the firm. Then these people that are taking a lot of risk with enough luck will rise to the top and be the CEO, whereas the person that's risk averse never takes that extra bit of risk and never experiences the good luck and is stuck in the middle.

This explains why CEOs happen to be very tolerant of risk. The interplay of that plus luck goes a long way to explain the psychometric qualities of CEOs.

Michael: I can think of two heads of investment banks who until the fall of 2008, for the vast population out there that understood what they did, they were Prince Charmings. Nothing could go wrong for them and that's Alan Greenberg at Bear Stearns and Richard Fuld at Lehman Brothers. These were guys that would fit right into the outline you were describing. But then on the back side of an entire career of taking more risk, waking up one day and the dice come up different.

Campbell: Exactly, and of course risk is two-sided, so there's an upside and a downside and this was an obvious negative realization. It's really hard because they were on a roll, so to speak. This could be bad luck or it could be lack of skill.

Michael: I often see people say, "Survivorship bias, they're the lucky ones left, what about all the other guys that failed?" The implication being that everyone that failed was as skilled and had the same technique or same strategy as those winners. I don't necessarily see that evidence. Sometimes we just assume they were equal but they're not necessarily equal or taking the same steps or strategies. Just another facet of this.

Campbell: Yes, totally agree. It could be a much different strategy, but in the end that's what they choose. You could think of every investor having a slightly different strategy. Some of them might be chasing real risk premia, some of them think they're chasing real risk premia but it turns out that it's not. Others are chasing mispricing in the market that might be fleeting. Indeed, it might turn the other way, that once you start buying, all of a sudden instead of something undervalued, it's overvalued.

The only sound reason for my buying a stock is that it is rising in price. If that is happening, no other reason is required. If that is not happening, no other reason is worth considering.
Nicolas Darvas

There's a myriad of different strategies out there and some of them will turn out because they should turn out. Like capturing a long-term risk premia and some of them will turn out just by luck.

Michael: Was it *random*?

Campbell: That's correct. We don't do a very good job at questioning the performance and saying, "Was this due to luck or was it due to skill?" We look at these investment manager stars and think they've got a huge amount of skill and we don't consider the other side. How much of that is luck?

As I said, goes both ways. And you know how often this happens, where you hire an investment manager? You look at the track record, it's a wonderful track record, you're comfortable with the track record. You invest with the manager and then they have like one or two years of subpar performance and then you fire them. As soon as you fire them, the next year they do great.

Well, what's the story there? It's a simple story like I mentioned with the dice. You have a couple of years of bad luck. Indeed, in the track record there's probably a couple of years like that, too, but you tend to ignore that. You fire the person at exactly the wrong time and you pay the price. Investors just don't do a very good job of attempting to weigh the balance of luck and skill.

Michael: One of the reasons many people get confused is we want to think in terms of a nice normal distribution, because it works great for weights and heights and all this kind of stuff. Everything's just normally distributed . . .

But in the real world of asset management in trading and investing, there's something called *skew*.

Talk sense to a fool and he calls you foolish.

Euripides
484 BC-406 BC

Campbell: This is an important component of my own research. There's a path-breaking paper published in 1952 by Harry Markowitz on how to optimize a portfolio. That paper led to a Nobel Prize for him in 1990. And what this paper does is it says what we want is a portfolio with the best possible target return but the lowest volatility for that level of target return.

Essentially this is the optimal tradeoff of an expected return and risk, and I'd like to put "risk" in quotations because in this path-breaking paper there's a footnote that's buried at the end of the paper that says, "This only is appropriate if the asset returns are normal and investors have no preference for skew."

Let me explain what that actually means. If the asset returns are so-called normally distributed, then there's no unusual tail behavior. That means there's no severe downside, there's no severe upside. The upside and the downside are exactly symmetric. With the usual measure of volatility, that's exactly what happens.

For example, you could have a stock that is going up dramatically. Maybe it goes up like 300, 400 percent and it's got a high level of volatility. You can have another stock that goes down dramatically, maybe goes down 95 percent, and it's got the exact same level of volatility. Volatility doesn't tell you anything about the direction. It's measuring the surprise in an absolute sense. Volatility is symmetric. It treats the upside and the downside the same.

October. This is one of the peculiarly dangerous months to speculate in stocks in. The others are July, January, September, April, November, May, March, June, December, August and February.
Mark Twain

Skew, on the other hand, tells us the balance between the upside and the downside. You could have two portfolios that have the same target return, the same volatility, but they've got a different skew. One has got an abnormally high probability of a severe downside, the other has got an abnormally high probability of severe upside. For any investor it's obvious which one to choose. You choose the one that has got more upside than downside.

I've been on a campaign for many years to try to change the way that we think of risk, to change the way that we actually do asset management or portfolio management. Take this asymmetry between the upside and the downside, and recognize that it is rare that any asset return is so-called normally distributed. Actually make that part of the portfolio management exercise and, equally as important, make it part of the risk management exercise.

I am tired of hearing about these 20-standard-deviation events, like what happened to Swiss franc. And there's many other examples during the financial crisis, the Russian crisis, etc. Twenty-standard-deviation events? It's not 20 standard deviations. It's only 20 if you believe naïvely these asset returns are normally distributed. They're not, so don't even tell me this. It doesn't make any sense.

Michael: I've had Harry Markowitz on my show. He was surprised at how the industry took his work, and he wasn't part of what happened, but they took his work and ran with it and that was essentially how modern finance got built off of his work. That's a fair synopsis, isn't it?

Campbell: Yes. That 1952 paper is an amazing paper. I've only mentioned one thing that he foresaw. I think that this was a simple framework he proposed. It works under special assumptions.

He was the one that recognized what those assumptions were, but then you're right, the industry goes with something and doesn't think about when is it appropriate to apply and when isn't it. When I teach finance at Duke University, as one of the main lessons for my students, we've got these models. But all these models are wrong, that's why they're called a model—you're simplifying reality.

And the issue of applying your skill is knowing when to apply a simplified framework and when not to. In certain situations, it's fine, other situations no. Harry is really the father of modern finance and that paper is just an incredible piece of work given that he saw not just the usefulness of his simplified framework, but he saw basically how to take it to the next level and to incorporate this idea of skew.

Michael: Your paper evaluating trading strategies caught my eye for one thing in particular . . . I assumed that I knew the advisor you were talking about, which was AHL—which is a managed futures trading [trend following] operation owned by Man out of London.

Campbell: It's a managed futures house that manages about $15 billion. At AHL they look at strategies all the time. They think very deeply about luck versus skill. There is a strategy that showed accumulative profit from 2004 through 2014. It's a graph and it's basically going straight up. It's an extraordinary strategy where it's got one year that has a very small negative return in 2004. It knocks the ball out of the park during the financial crisis. It's got about a 15 percent annualized return, 15 percent volatility, so the so-called Sharpe ratio of 1—extremely consistent. We're looking at this strategy and you can see people's head nodding, "Yes, this is the sort of thing we want to put some capital on." And then the very next slide is really surprising.

I actually went into the business thinking I could automate everything and that a machine would do it all.

Blair Hull

It adds to this graph the other 199 purely random strategies. All of a sudden this graph that was just one line going straight up is added to 199 things that basically are centered around zero. The exercise was to simulate 200 random strategies with a target return of zero, so every single one has no skill, and is purely generated numbers with 15 percent volatility.

You see the very top one, the very best one is the one that was shown first, and then you see at the bottom there's like a terrible one that earns 15 percent negative and everything in between. The idea is that by pure random chance, and that's what the random number generator is doing, by random chance you're going to see strategies that look great. You need to be careful if you're doing internal research. What you don't want is your researchers sifting through hundreds of strategies and picking off the top one, because when you put money on that top one in real time, it's going to do poorly.

Michael: This was AHL presenting, correct?

Campbell: They are leading edge in terms of thinking about luck versus skill. This was part of an exercise on how to avoid overfitting of back tests. That's why that exhibit is there, because it is a great example that you could easily be fooled by random strategies.

Michael: What is your perspective, your thoughts about the work of Nassim Taleb?

Campbell: That it fits in really well with my work on skewness. He talks about so-called black swan events and again, these events that are negative 20-standard-deviation events. It doesn't make any sense unless it's a normal distribution. Because within a normal distribution, the probability of something like that happening is like one event in the life of the universe, which doesn't make any sense.

It is easier to do many things than to do one thing continuously for a long time.
Marcus Fabius Quintilian
Roman Orator

He's talking about these things that you don't necessarily see in historical data, but then they happen. You could think of it as an extreme negative skew type of event. That works in pretty well because his view of the world, as my view of the world, is that it's not symmetrically distributed, it's not normally distributed, and I think that's important.

Michael: Many managed futures trading strategies obviously are trend following in nature and they're predicated on not knowing what's going to happen next. A lot of their risk premia come from the hedgers out there. People make arguments about where their source of profits come from . . .

There's a thinking, a long-standing thinking that goes behind this particular strategy, and you're making the point that, if you just sit down at your computer, and you really have not even philosophically thought through what the strategy is, and then you only want to trust some random systems that come up, you can wake up in trouble.

Even if initially all your investors are sold on the idea of 15 percent returns and 15 percent volatility and that sounds great, and you raise $1 billion, but if there's not a sound economic thinking behind the strategy, we all know what's going to happen.

Campbell: That's correct. This is the way that it should work. I do know from direct experience, this is the way that it does work at a firm like Man AHL, and maybe it's no surprise they've done so well with this. Basically a researcher would come up with an idea, but without looking at the data. They come up with an economic framework and then they actually pitch that framework in a seminar. I'll call it that—an academic seminar.

I fear not the man who has practiced 10,000 kicks once, but I fear the man who has practiced one kick 10,000 times.

Bruce Lee

They will get feedback and then the senior people will actually decide whether the economic idea makes enough sense that you actually go to the data. Let's say it does make sense, then the firm will give the researcher what's known as a random partition of the history of the data. They will give bits and pieces of the history to the researcher. The researcher will then test the economic idea, and this is the so-called in-sample testing, and then there'll be another seminar.

The results will be presented, and then a decision will be made whether to give the rest of the data to test it in a so-called out-of-sample test. It might be killed or it might go ahead to the out-of-sample. Let's say it actually goes to the other sample and let's say it does well, then there's a further stage where it will be invested in, but only invested with internal money.

It's multiple stages that you actually have to go through until it gets to the client, because you really don't want to put anything to client trading that might be a result of luck, because you don't want to disappoint your clients. All the incentives are running in the right direction to do the best possible thing for your client.

Michael: I was giving a presentation in Singapore, and I was speaking about the managed futures trading strategy of trend following. And at the end of the presentation this young lady raised her hand and she had this look that said she probably had been at Duke in one of your classes and was really was bright. She had that look that said, "Oh man, I'm in trouble. She's going to kill me. She's going to obliterate me. I'm dead."

She raises her hand and she immediately shot herself in the foot and I want you to explain why. She immediately said, "Okay, can you tell me about the Sharpe ratio of these strategies." I wanted to do a Vulcan mind meld and just say, "Hold on, don't just immediately assume the Sharpe ratio is the be-all end-all. Let's at least pick apart the pros and cons of the Sharpe ratio." But you could just see the indoctrination as she asked the question.

Campbell: Yes, incredibly naïve. But, this is the way it is in the industry on both sides, buy side, sell side, that people will look at an investment, look at the Sharpe ratio, which is the expected excess return usually over some benchmark divided by the volatility. They're only considering the volatility risk, and let me tell you the type of trouble that gets you into. If you do the Sharpe ratios of different investment styles or maybe even hedge fund returns, you'll see a wide variation in the average Sharpe ratios. You'll see gigantic Sharpe ratios for things like convertible arbitrage but more modest Sharpe ratios for things like managed futures [trend following]. The reason is very clear once you expand the way you think about risk.

Managed futures has got positive skew and it's almost by construction, because when things are going up you're buying. That's the same as replicating a long call option. When things are going down you're selling. That's like replicating a long put option. Effectively, you can think of managed futures as something with a long straddle-like performance which has got positive skew. They do really well in market meltdowns and they do well when the market's going up sharply.

The brain is like a muscle. When it is in use we feel very good. Understanding is joyous.
Carl Sagan

That is something that is rewarded by investors. They actually like that. It provides a hedge. Whereas these other Sharpe ratios, very high Sharpe ratio strategies, they get a severe negative skew. For them you need to have extra return on average because investors really don't like that severe downside.

You cannot compare two strategies based upon a Sharpe ratio if they have different skew properties. The Sharpe ratio does not take that into account. Indeed, it's very similar to what we were talking about earlier with the simple market, with its framework where you look at expected target return divided by volatility. Volatility is not a sufficient metric for risk; it is part of the story, it's not the entire story. If you make the mistake of just looking at volatility, then it's going to lead to a portfolio that will disappoint you.

Michael: Thinking back to that example with the young lady, I don't know if it was "I didn't want to listen" or "I don't understand" or "I've already got my mind made up." The indoctrination strikes me.

Campbell: Well, it's complicated because this sort of discussion is not even in the textbooks in finance. It's kind of surprising. So you can go through a top program [and not learn this].

Michael: That is the truest statement. Anyone reading right now that doubts you, I want them to go find where you're wrong.

Campbell: Yes, it's one of the reasons I don't use a textbook for what I teach. I teach out of my own notes and my own research articles. But this is something that you have to point a lot of fingers here, including pointing fingers at my own colleagues. I just don't think that we do a good job of explaining risk to our students. I think in my class, there's about three classes [where] we just sit down and think about what risk actually is.

A delusion is something that people believe in despite a total lack of evidence.

Richard Dawkins

Michael: You're making a fantastic point there. Put aside all the jargon and get people to conceptually wrap their arms around the idea of what skew is, and even getting rid of the word "skew," so to speak, and getting people to sit down and look at it all . . . a freshman in high school with no math training, if properly explained what's going on, could understand.

Campbell: Yes, I agree. Let me give the other insight from Markowitz's article that is relevant for this discussion. And that is that his framework assumes that you exactly know all of the inputs, you exactly know the volatilities, you exactly know correlations between assets, and you exactly know the target return. There's no uncertainty in any events, whereas in the practice of management there is uncertainty. So another dimension of risk is that you think the correlation is, let's say 0.5, but you're not sure, maybe it's 0.2, maybe it's 0.7, but it's certainly not exactly 0.5.

The same for the volatility. You think it's 15 but you're uncertain. Maybe it's 12, maybe it's 17. This is another dimension of risk. Most people think, "Risk is just the volatility." Another way of thinking about risk is, "What if you don't know what the volatility is?" Even deeper, what if you don't know the distribution? It's not normal, we kind of know that, but what is it?

I wish that I may never think the smiles of the great and powerful a sufficient inducement to turn aside from the straight path of honesty and the convictions of my own mind.
David Ricardo

Or the skew. We don't know what that downside tail actually is. We can maybe estimate it but we're not sure. All of this is *risk*, and it's rarely taken into account at this level that there's a difference between risk and uncertainty. People usually group those together and it shows they really haven't thought it through.

Michael: It would be a long story to get to the point as to why many of them have developed a faulty foundation, but the fact is that so many decision makers in charge of other people's money think that somehow or another there is a perfect prediction for tomorrow and that estimates are a bad thing, when estimates are basically all we've got.

It's really crazy that we've got to a position where so many people that think the world of investment management is supposed to be perfection. It's an insane notion.

Campbell: And unfortunately, the actual investors reinforce this, because they will judge the manager based upon the past quarter or the past year, and that leads to a different type of behavior on the part of the manager. I would much prefer, as I said earlier, take a look at the track record, you're comfortable with it, fine. And what I actually recommend is that the investment managers educate the client as to what could happen.

One way of doing that is really simple. Let's say I've got a 20-year track record, what I can do is to create with the real data from those 20 years an alternative history by kind of randomly sampling years and put them together. And then keep on doing that. Then it gives you a way to look at what things could look like given the track record.

The further a society drifts from truth, the more it will hate those who speak it.
Anonymous

Then when it actually happens, maybe you've got two years in a row of substandard performance, you can look at the history and say, "That's not unusual. That happens 25 percent of the time, given the track record." If you believe the actual track record and you actually analyze it in this way of creating alternative histories, then it really helps avoid the mistake of firing a skilled manager because they've had bad luck.

Michael: If I see 1 percent a month every month every year, I'm either thinking it's Bernie Madoff Junior or another Long-Term Capital Management. You can't make money every month. Maybe there's somebody with a high-frequency shop that's got some advantage that no one else has, but it just doesn't work that way.

Campbell: Yes, this is a great example. You've got somebody that is basically in a S&P 500 portfolio, but on top of the S&P 500 they're writing out-of-the-money put options and out-of-the-money call options. If there's not that much volatility you're collecting a premium. Month after month given that premium that you're collecting, they'd beat the market. One percent here, 2 percent, 1 percent, 2 percent. It keeps on going. It is foolish to think that is beating the market or alpha or whatever you want to call it. That's called taking risk, because if the market goes severely down, then you've got these put options you have to pay off. It magnifies the downside of holding the S&P 500 and on top of that it cuts off the upside because if the market goes up substantially you need to pay out for the call options.

Too many people simply give up too easily. You have to keep the desire to forge ahead, and you have to be able to take the bruises of unsuccess. Success is just one long street fight.

Milton Berle

All that does is to take a portfolio, the S&P 500, and tilt it towards negative skew, and that's the reason that you see a return pattern like this. People are getting a little extra return because at some point there's going to be a severe downside. That is important to take into account.

Michael: It's cliché, but that free lunch isn't always so free.

Lasse Heje Pedersen

18

The mental infection known as political correctness is one of the most dangerous intellectual afflictions ever to attack mankind. It appeals to pseudo-intellectuals everywhere, since it evokes the strong streak of cowardice notable among those wielding academic authority nowadays. Any empty-headed student with a powerful voice can claim someone (never specified) will be hurt by a hitherto harmless term, object or activity and be reasonably assured that the dons and professors in charge will show a white feather and do as the student demands. To a great extent PC is the revenge of the resentful underdog.

Paul Johnson[2]

Lasse Heje Pedersen is a Danish financial economist known for his research on liquidity risk and asset pricing. He is the John A. Paulson Professor of Finance and Alternative Investments at the New York University Stern School of Business. He is also a principal at AQR Capital Management.[1]

> **Michael:** *Efficiently Inefficient*, the title of your new work . . . you could say it's new ground, but we've all seen where the Nobel Prize was split between Fama and Shiller, and I'm guessing there was a certain inspiration for your title from that. If not, tell me the inspiration.
>
> **Lasse:** Yes, that's right. So there's been this long academic debate about whether the markets are efficient, and Eugene Fama, he stands for this view that markets are fully efficient and prices reflect the fundamental value of securities versus prices are inefficient. And Shiller, he sort of represents the opposite point of view, that market prices are irrational, they're driven by investors' irrationality and investors push prices far away from their fundamental values.
>
> I have a great respect for both Fama and Shiller. I know them both well, but I wanted to take a different point of view. One that is somewhere between, but also tries to be well-defined, saying that market prices are neither fully efficient nor completely inefficient.

But they are inefficient enough that smart asset managers and active investors have a chance to beat the market and be compensated for all the costs they have associated with actually becoming informed about asset prices and trading.

The term bubble should indicate a price that no reasonable future outcome can justify.
Cliff Asness

At the same time, market prices are efficient enough that the marginal investor is sort of indifferent about pursuing this active investing, with the benefits being better performance but the costs being transaction costs, asset management fees, and the costs associated with finding a good asset manager. There's that equilibrium in which markets are at the right place, and in between they're efficiently inefficient.

Michael: George Soros and David Harding are dogmatic about, "The efficient market hypothesis is . . . fill in the blank bad word," so how did the managers and traders in your book feel about your perspective?

Lasse: Yes, that's a great question. Definitely, you're right that many of these managers, they would certainly not feel that markets are fully efficient. They feel very strongly their job is to beat the market, and they succeed in that job not because they're just lucky but because markets are not efficient. You're right, David Harding's thought is strongly against the efficient market hypothesis.

A lot of these guys, at the same time, are sympathetic to this view that, yes, there is a [way] to have edge, but you must be very efficient to exploit these market inefficiencies. That's sort of another interpretation of the title, and I think they're actually quite sympathetic to this view. They don't think just anybody off the street can easily beat the market; you have to be really efficient to actually accomplish that.

Michael: Obviously, you know the managers and their styles, but what about your connection with them?

Lasse: I certainly knew of all of them, they're all extremely famous. I knew some of them well. I knew Cliff Asness, he's my colleague at AQR Capital Management, so he was the one by far I knew the best. I knew Myron Scholes quite well through my meeting him at academic conferences. I also knew John Paulson. He endowed a chair at NYU and I was lucky enough to actually hold the John Paulson chair.

Several of the others I had never met. It was really exciting and fun to meet these guys and get their perspective on how they invest, and try to get an opportunity to ask them exactly how they do it, what motivates them and what are the key drivers of their success.

Michael: Was there a common theme developing in how they thought regardless of style or technique?

Lasse: Obviously, they're all very smart. They are all extremely driven and ambitious. They are all disciplined and clear thinkers. In terms of their investment styles and methods, they're very different, but there are some common themes. Even though they use very different words, a lot of them are using trading strategies related to value investing and momentum trading.

The inability to predict outliers implies the inability to predict the course of history.

Nassim Taleb[3]

Cliff Asness has actually written academic papers and was one of the discoverers of momentum trading in stocks together with a few other academics. He talks a lot about value-momentum. But a guy like George Soros, he'll talk in very different terms. He will talk about trading on boom–bust cycles, for instance. But when he says he's riding the boom, in some sense he's a momentum trader, and when he positions himself for the bust, at that point he effectively becomes a value investor.

When you think about Lee Ainslie, who's a famous Tiger Cub, he's done very well in trading stocks globally. Obviously value investing and thinking about the quality of those companies is a key driver. And value is also a key driver for a short seller like James Chanos, who thinks about which company is overvalued, which company might be fraudulent or have some little bit of too creative accounting and so on—he wants to short those. And in shorting all value firms he's basically taking the short side of being a value investor.

Michael: You bring up a great point about terminology and jargon. I think to the classic phrase that Soros uses—reflexivity. It's a term with a certain philosophical bent to it. He's written several books. But a great place where you can take apart some of the jargon and perhaps with your best professorial hat is to describe the different types of momentum. AQR is obviously known for both types.

You mentioned Cliff and the type of momentum that he discovered. But time-series momentum, the type of momentum that might be more commonly called trend following, can you compare and contrast the two types of momentum?

Lasse: What's called momentum in stock trading—it's also called cross-sectional momentum—it means looking at the different stocks and seeing which stocks have outperformed other stocks. Then you will tend to go long the stocks that have been outperforming while at the same time shorting stocks that have been underperforming. Then you're basically hoping that those outperforming stocks over the last, let's say 6 to 12 months, will continue to outperform over the next month.

That is to be compared with what's called time-series momentum, which means looking typically at an index, whether it's a stock index or a currency or commodity, and basically seeing if it's going up and down. If it's been trending up over the last year, let's say. Time-series momentum is looking at markets in isolation, whereas cross-sectional momentum is looking at relative outperformance.

The more secretive or unjust an organization is, the more leaks induce fear and paranoia in its leadership and planning coterie. This must result in minimization of efficient internal communications mechanisms (an increase in cognitive "secrecy tax") and consequent system-wide cognitive decline resulting in decreased ability to hold onto power as the environment demands adaptation.
Julian Assange[4]

The difference is, for instance, let's say the whole stock market has been going down. In a cross-sectional momentum investment, you might go long stocks that have been dropping less in value. Suppose all the stocks in a given universe have been actually going down. Some of them have been going down less, so those are outperforming. A cross-sectional momentum investor would buy those and short those that drop by more.

Whereas the time-series momentum investor or managed futures type of investor, he would just short all of them. He would say, "They're all trending down, let me short all of them."

Michael: You mentioned the idea these very diverse traders and managers have commonalities. One of the commonalities is gamblers' ruin, risk of ruin.

Lasse: Yes, they're certainly all quite aware of risk management and several of them actually told me about some of their losing trades. A lot of them are very happy about their winning trades but they have learned a lot from their losing trades. It's really important that you learn from your losing trades, but also that you don't go bankrupt from them.

Michael: Are there any examples from a particular trader or manager and a losing trade that come to mind?

Lasse: Yes, certainly. Lee Ainslie talks about one particular losing trade when he had a great investment thesis. His analysis was correct but it turned out the management that were supposed to deliver on these great promises for that particular company, were not capable of doing it. He really learned the importance of management, and has since really paid very close attention to the management of the companies he invests in.

Also Chanos talks about a short position he had that kept moving against him for a variety of reasons. Fortunate for him, he has a position limit. So as the short position moves against him, it gets bigger and this is one of the risks of short selling. When you're short selling, you lose when the stock price goes up. When the stock price goes up, if you have a fixed number of shares, now you're actually short more dollars or bigger value and the risk potential increases. Therefore he has a position limit and he would actually reduce his position as the position moved against him and that helped him to limit losses in that particular trade.

Michael: Most people, if they're familiar with Julian Robertson and the Tiger Cub story, it's a fundamental style of thinking and trading. I thought what was interesting was your questioning to Lee Ainslie about his quantitative aspects of his trading methodology, particularly portfolio construction.

Lasse: Yes, that's right. He has a number of investment professionals who go out and meet with management and meet with different competitors to try to really understand the industry where each company operates. But at the same time, he told me they actually have a quantitative system to evaluate their positions, the risk exposures, and to help them make the portfolio construction as efficient as possible.

Michael: Looking at all these managers, looking at these traders, their track records, studying their performance, "Is there a *best* strategy?" There are different strategies for different reasons, but is there a strategy do you think across these managers, these traders, that's perhaps more repeatable? There's only one George Soros, there's only one Paulson. Do you see

You maniacs! You blew it up! Ah, damn you! God damn you all to hell!

George Taylor
Planet of the Apes (1968)

a particular style across this selection of traders that's more repeatable?

Lasse: I think what's common among these strategies is that there is not this magic effort by this genius, but we can actually understand at the core of many of these strategies there is an economic logic behind why they work. But at the same time they require tremendous skill and dedication and hard work to execute them well.

I talk about equity strategies, macro strategies, arbitrage strategies, and for each of these I try to understand what is the basic economics behind why they work, and how you could create a repeatable process that could deliver potential outperformance. It certainly has to be very difficult to do because otherwise these things would be arbitraged away.

Michael: In your work were you looking for the particular styles or were you looking for the particular manager and trader?

Lasse: I started with thinking about, "What are the various classic styles" and then for each of these eight styles that I identified I sought to get the most prominent current investor who's still active. I wrote down these eight names and I thought how am I going to get them to say yes. I started with the people I knew the best, and then when those guys said yes, I had a connection to someone who knew George Soros. Then Soros said yes, and when I started asking the next people it started getting easier when you have Paulson, Asness, Soros, and the like.

Active management is a zero-sum game before cost, and the winners have to win at the expense of the losers.
Eugene Fama

Michael: Something that Cliff Asness brings up, you have as a question in your work. You talk about the difference between the real world and the academic world. I like his answer because we can go back to a performance track record, for example, and you can say, "There was a three-year flat period, or there was a significant drawdown, but then you came out of it and everything was okay."

Cliff points out that in the real world it's not so easy to just look at track records like that.

Lasse: That's right, and he talks about when you're actually going through such a tough period, there's a time dilation, he calls it, where it seems like time is going much more slowly and it's really [painful] to have those losses, even if you have greater gains coming out of it. It's an extremely tough period.

That's part of the reason these strategies work in that it certainly is hard work to do it, but it's also really stressful and requires a lot of discipline to just continue to do the right thing. When you're starting to face losses there's a lot of temptation to panic or do various things that were not part of the original plan, because you think those will . . . be too difficult to handle otherwise.

Michael: Many traders and managers have to deal with clients and make sure clients are on board with the strategy and understand there can be down periods, etc. Which leads me to bring something up about Warren Buffett.

Many don't know that Warren Buffett has had multiple 50 percent drawdowns. I don't know the exact number but if you're going to produce the type of performance that he's produced over the years, you have to be willing to take and handle a significant down period. You talk about Buffett and his alpha. You put together significant insights where people can ponder, "Hold on, if Buffett's a value investor, why is he so much better than everyone else?" You broke it down and pulled apart why he is so much better.

Lasse: Yes, that's right. We got the data on Buffett's performance and we also looked at the performance of Berkshire Hathaway stock holdings too. As you know Buffett is running Berkshire Hathaway, and one way to look at his performance is to follow that stock price. But you could also see the publicly traded stocks that he holds. Berkshire Hathaway has to make a filing to the SEC about the publicly traded stocks they own, so we can put together a portfolio and simulate that portfolio at the same time.

Never underestimate the power of doing nothing.
Winnie the Pooh

The first thing we looked at is just how good is Warren Buffett? How good do you need to be to become one of the richest people in the world? And it turns out his Sharpe ratio is just over 0.7, between 0.7 and 0.8, which surprised a lot of people when we showed them this number, because a lot of people had assumed that he had a Sharpe ratio above 1 or even above 2, as a lot of hedge funds are bragging about numbers in that range. It turns out that he has had tremendously high returns, but he has also had quite significant risk, leaving him with a Sharpe ratio which is still incredibly impressive, because it's about double the Sharpe ratio of the market.

For the risk he's taking, which has been substantial, he's over the long haul been able to deliver double the return relative to that of the market. It's really an astonishing performance. Our research doesn't in any way try to diminish that incredible accomplishment, but when other researchers have looked at it, they have [simply] recognized he's a value investor. He talks about being a value investor, and you can also regress his return on the returns of being a value investor which is called a value factor.

A reliable way to make people believe in falsehoods is frequent repetition, because familiarity is not easily distinguished from truth. Authoritarian institutions and marketers have always known this fact.
Daniel Kahneman
Thinking, Fast and Slow

That factor explains some of his performance, but only a small part, and it leaves [out] a huge alpha that's a big unexplained part. What we then did is say, "Let's also regress on the return to what we call a quality investor." What he buys are not just cheap stocks but he also buys high-quality stocks. He talks about that in his speeches and his writings—that he really likes to buy high-quality companies at a reasonable price.

When we actually regress him on both the standard factor, including value factor, as well as what we call quality minus junk, and also a factor that captures more safe stocks, called betting against beta, then it turns out we can actually explain a large part of his performance, and get us a strategy that looks very much like his performance . . . to explain almost all his alpha.

What we interpret that to be is he is doing what he's saying he's doing. Yes, he's a value investor, he's a quality investor, he likes to buy stable, profitable, high-quality companies at a reasonable price, and those types of stocks have done well in general. The interesting finding is it's not just the quality firms that he has been buying that have done well and have been good investments, it's quality firms in general. Those types of stocks in general have performed well, and he has benefited from being a very early investor to recognize that and exploit it. And he's been able to leverage it through his insurance company in a very clever and very smart way and really perform extremely well as a result of those investment choices and that leverage strategy.

Michael: He definitely is using leverage to a degree that perhaps the novice investor might not understand, but obviously he's doing it in a very smart way—but he's not a trader devoid of leverage.

Lasse: Yes, that's right. He speaks quite negatively about leverage often and certainly there are risks to leverage. If you look at his portfolio and his performance you can see that he uses leverage in two ways. Number one is that you can simply look at his balance sheet and you can see that he has leverage. He has a number of liabilities, he's been issued bonds, for instance, as one source of leverage, and he has a lot of insurance-related liabilities. And we estimate his leverage is about 1.6 to 1.0. Meaning that for every dollar of equity capital he will then invest in $1.60 of companies.

Another way to see that he's using leverage? You remember I mentioned that we could simulate the performance of his portfolio of publicly traded stocks? We could look at the volatility, the risk of that strategy and then we can look at the risk or the volatility of Berkshire Hathaway's stock. Sometimes the volatility of Berkshire Hathaway stock is bigger than the volatility of his publicly traded stocks—that suddenly is consistent with the idea that . . . Berkshire applies leverage to the portfolio. If you add leverage to a portfolio, then you will tend to increase the risk and that sort of ranking of the risk is consistent with leverage.

A large fraction of traffic accidents are of the type "driver looked but failed to see." Here, drivers collide with pedestrians in plain view, with cars directly in front of them, and even run into trains. That's right—run into trains, not the other way around. In such cases, information from the world is entering the driver's eyes. But at some point along the way, this information is lost, causing the driver to lose connection with reality. They are looking, but they are not seeing.

Ronald A. Rensink

Michael: It's just a tool and he's using the tool wisely.

Lasse: That's right.

Michael: Let me move to a quote from Cliff Asness. "Good quant investment managers can really be thought of as financial economists who have codified their beliefs into a repeatable process. They're distinguished by their diversification, sticking to their process with discipline and the ability to engineer portfolio characteristics." For those traders out there today that call themselves more fundamentally driven or value, is there anybody that's not back testing their world now?

Lasse: Yes, there's a lot of discretionary traders that will look at a unique special situation that you might have a very hard time back testing. If you're an event-driven trader and there's a new type of event, perhaps you can't back test that, but perhaps you can still convince yourself that you're buying something at a discount to its fundamental value. You're relying on the general principle that buying things cheap has worked over the long-term. You might not be able to back test in a more scientific way this type of strategy, or if you're trading a new type of security and so on. The problem is still the majority of investing is done in a discretionary manner.

Michael: Do you think guys like Harding, guys like Asness, with this mindset of testing and this quantitative mindset, is it slowly making a dent in the consciousness where perhaps investors in the future are going to say, "We want more than discretionary ability." Are they winning over the head space? Or is it in the early stages?

How should we modify our beliefs in the light of additional information? Do we cling to old assumptions long after they've become untenable, or abandon them too readily at the first whisper of doubt? Bayesian reasoning promises to bring our views gradually into line with reality and sync up with the universe. The theorem itself can be stated simply. Beginning with a provisional hypothesis about the world (there are, of course, no other kinds), we assign to it an initial probability called the prior probability or simply the prior. After actively collecting or happening upon some potentially relevant evidence, we use Bayes's theorem to recalculate the probability of the hypothesis in light of the new evidence. This revised probability is called the posterior probability or simply the posterior.[5]

Lasse: I myself am a quant investor. I'm a sworn believer in using scientific methods to evaluate investment strategies. But at the same time I try to keep an open mind. I don't want to say that one method is better than the other method. You are right the more scientific way of investing has made large inroads over the last 20 years. But at the same time there is a role for discretionary strategies. I personally have great respect for some of the more discretionary traders.

When Chanos, for instance, is finding funny things in the accounting numbers in a way that you can't really get a computer to do right now, or when other discretionary traders are doing things that cannot easily be codified in a computer because it's more relying on more soft information or different case-by-case type of analysis. I personally have a great respect for that. So I'm not sure that we'll gravitate to everybody investing in one way. I think investing fundamentally will have many aspects and it's driven by people having different methods and different points of view. That's basically what creates a buyer and a seller. There are all these different ways of doing it.

Michael: Let's talk about the role of hedge funds in the economy. The typical understanding is there's often negative press, especially at chaotic moments. Words like "speculation" will be thrown around in a negative way. But there is a role for hedge funds in the economy and it's not just necessarily the investors themselves that invest in the particular fund. Some might say, "Why should I be concerned with assorted hedge funds? I'm not invested in these." Talk about the big picture role of hedge funds.

Lasse: Hedge funds can play a very positive role in the economy for a number of reasons. First of all, our free market economy basically allocates resources based on prices. If somebody invents a drug, they can cure a particular disease. He may not have enough capital to pursue that cure but he can . . . "this is a very promising idea that others can't understand" . . . he can then raise a lot of money through the capital markets and then build factories to pursue that idea.

Cross-Validation means assessing not only how well a model fits the data it's given, but how well it generalizes to data it hasn't seen.

Brian Christian[7]

Whereas another inventor who has perhaps a not very useful idea, he might have a difficult time raising money, and therefore the machines and the real capital, the factories, are allocated to the more promising idea. Now that whole notion relies on market prices being relatively efficient. The company with the more promising ideas, their stock price has to be higher. Their market cap has to be higher in order for them to be able to really raise more capital and build more machines.

This is incredibly important for the market economy and hedge funds, and other active investors are tending to buy low and sell high, so they tend to push prices in the right direction and make markets more efficient. Again, that's just incredibly important. They help to provide liquidity, make it easier to buy and sell for investors, make it easier for people to save for retirement. A lot of large pension funds are invested in these types of vehicles and hopefully hedge funds and other active investors contribute to their performance.

As the years have unfolded and I have had experience of the seemingly magical phenomenon of trends, my prejudice in favor of this unloved and unheralded investment approach has hardened. To a statistician this is called a Bayesian Philosophy. You start with your prejudices and modify them in the light of experience. I started with a weak belief in trend following because conventional opinion said it couldn't work. As I saw it work year after year my belief in it has hardened.

David Harding[6]

Of course they take large fees and they keep a lot of the benefits for their own sake, too. It's certainly fair to say that investors should be very concerned about the fees and to what extent they themselves enjoy the benefits of those investment strategies.

Michael: You asked a question to David Harding: "Does your research suggest that it's better to have the same type of model for every instrument or is it better to have a very specific model for each one?" Talk about his response and your feelings about his response.

Lasse: I agree with his response that it's very important to have a very robust model that works across a number of different securities. It's often tempting to tailor your strategy so it looks like it's the best for every asset. You might want one particular managed futures [industry term for time-series momentum or trend following] strategy for gold, another strategy for wheat, yet another strategy in commodities and so on. If you try to do something like that, you might get extremely good performance in your back test, in your simulation of what would have happened in the past, because you're able to tailor this. But you might be exploiting a lot of noise, a lot of randomness, and you might end up with a model that works less well going forward in the future, when it really matters, when you're trading with live ammunition and when it's really important that your model works.

When you're truly in the dark, the best-laid plans will be the simplest. When our expectations are uncertain and the data are noisy, the best bet is to paint with a broad brush, to think in broad strokes.
Brian Christian[8]

To avoid that kind of data mining or overfitting of your model, it's often better to have a simpler strategy. How do you get confidence that your strategy has a chance to work going forward? Well, if the same strategy has worked for gold, not just last year or the last 10 years, but perhaps the last 50 or 100 years, and it's the same strategy that has worked across all the commodities, not just all the commodities, it's worked for a bunch of currencies . . . If it's worked for equities, if it's worked also in fixed-income markets . . . Then you start to get a conviction that this strategy is not randomness, it's not just a coincidence of the past that will not repeat itself in the future. Then you start to get some conviction that this type of trend following strategy or managed futures strategy has a chance to work in the future.

Michael: You are part of the AQR study, "A Century of Evidence on Trend-Following Investing"?

Lasse: Yes.

Michael: Were there any elements or insights going through that process, doing that research, doing that study, that surprised you?

Lasse: It was quite an exciting project because we had been doing a lot of research on what are the best trend following strategies, and showing that some relatively simple trend following strategies actually performed extremely well over the last 20 to 30 years. And they've worked on average, not every year or every day, but on average, for every instrument we looked at, which is sort of unusual.

You think that it's going to work perhaps at the portfolio level, but not necessarily for every instrument in the portfolio. But we found this very consistent performance even at the instrument level. We were thinking, "Wow, this looks really robust, but how can we get even more conviction? How can we get another out-of-sample study?"

Of course, one out-of-sample study is just waiting and looking at the live performance going forward. We didn't have the patience for that, so we said, "Let's actually go ahead and collect data. Historical data on prices that are earlier than what we looked at before. Rather than looking just over the last 20, 30 years, let's look at a full century of data." We were a little bit worried, of course, that what had seemed like such a robust result maybe didn't work in the 60 to 70 years prior. But to our surprise it worked extremely well, and also historically about as well as in the more recent sample.

Michael: You talk about the arms race in high-frequency trading. There's an arms race amongst trend following managers to see how many centuries they can go back! [Laughter] You guys inspired with your first paper. Several others have come right after.

Lasse: That's right, yes.

Michael: One of the things in your conversation with George Soros . . . He says that you should not risk a significant part of your capital, but if you have a good run and you're making a lot of profit, you can risk your profits more than you can risk your [original] capital. That's a very classic time-series momentum trend following type thinking, a very quant thinking. Did you talk to Soros about the implementation of his strategies?

I'm focusing on what can I do for our players so we can have a chance to win the SEC championship tomorrow. That's really all I'm focusing on. I've talked about, 'Be where your feet are.' I'm right here, right now. This is what's important and this is what we have to focus on.

Nick Saban
Alabama Football Coach

Lasse: Yes, he has a different way of implementing, not so quantitative, but he's also very concerned about the downside risk versus upside risk. What he's really hoping to find is a strategy or a bet that has a big upside potential and a limited downside potential and then put a lot of money into that bet, like he did on the British pound [see Soros 1992 pound trade].

He talks about [how] he had the courage to really put such an enormous position on the British pound, because if the pound broke he would make a lot of money. But given that it was trading in a band there was almost no risk that it would make a large move going against him. And that type of thinking, he told me, inspired John Paulson in the way he sized his subprime bet. I asked John Paulson whether it was true that he got the idea to size the bet he did, the way he did, from Soros, and he confirmed that in that interview.

Much as we bemoan the daily rat race, the fact that it's a race rather than a fight is a key part of what sets us apart from the monkeys, the chickens—and, for that matter, the rats.

Brian Christian[9]

Michael: Everyone has to look with deep admiration, because many of the traders that you talk about would not have the latitude to take those kinds of bets. There's obviously a certain discretionary element. I can use interesting sports metaphors and randy language to describe it, but let's just say it takes a certain amount of gusto to do what some of those guys [like Soros] do in terms of their big bets, doesn't it?

Lasse: It definitely does, yes. And to keep riding at them when they've made a lot of money. To not just fold and be satisfied, but keep the bet on until it's delivered its full potential.

Section III

Trend Following Research

Academicians settled on volatility as the proxy for risk as a matter of convenience. They needed a number for their calculations that was objective and could be ascertained historically and extrapolated into the future. Volatility fits the bill, and most of the other types of risk do not. The problem with all of this, however, is that I just don't think volatility is the risk most investors care about. Rather than volatility, I think that people decline to make investments primarily because they're worried about a loss of capital or an unacceptably low return. To me, "I need more upside potential because I'm afraid I could lose money" makes an awful lot more sense than "I need more upside potential because I'm afraid the price may fluctuate." No, *I'm sure "risk" is—first and foremost—the likelihood of losing money.*

—Howard Marks[1]

I never know where connective tissue to make a case for trend following will be found. It's always serendipity. For example, Bob Seawright was a guest on my podcast (episode #328) and he has this great blog passage that I admire:

> American virologist David Baltimore, who won the Nobel Prize for Medicine in 1975 for his work on the genetic mechanisms of

If you talk to these extraordinary people, you find that they all understand this at one level or another. They may be unfamiliar with the concept of cognitive adaptability, but they seldom buy into the idea that they have reached the peak of their fields because they were the lucky winners of some genetic lottery. They know what is required to develop the extraordinary skills that they possess because they have experienced it firsthand.
Anders Ericsson[2]

viruses, once told me that over the years (and especially while he was president of CalTech) he received many manuscripts claiming to have solved some great scientific problem or to have overthrown the existing scientific paradigm to provide some grand theory of everything. Most prominent scientists have drawers full of similar submissions, almost always from people who work alone and outside of the scientific community. Unfortunately, none of these offerings has done anything remotely close to what was claimed, and Dr. Baltimore offered some fascinating insight into why he thinks that's so. **At its best, he noted, good science is a collaborative, community effort. On the other hand, crackpots work alone.**[3]

Since I like to think of myself as no crackpot, this new section of *Trend Following* lays bare in detail a collaborative and community effort. Each of the following research papers adds new value and clarification to my main text and interviews.

19 A Multicentennial View of Trend Following

Alex Greyserman and Kathryn Kaminsky

Cut short your losses, and let your profits run on.
—David Ricardo, legendary
political economist
Source: The Great Metropolis, 1838

Trend following is one of the classic investment styles. This chapter tells the *tale of trend following* throughout the centuries. Before delving into the highly detailed analysis in subsequent chapters, it is interesting to discuss the paradigm of trend following from a qualitative historical perspective. Although data-intensive, this approach is by no means a bulletproof rigorous academic exercise. As with any long-term historical study, this analysis is fraught with assumptions, questions of data reliability, and other biases. Despite all of these concerns, history shapes our perspectives; history is arguably highly subjective, yet it provides contextual relevance.

This chapter examines a simple characterization of trend following using roughly 800 years of financial data. Despite this rather naïve characterization and albeit crude set of financial data throughout the centuries, the performance of "cutting your losses, and letting your profits run on" is robust enough to garner our attention. The goal of this chapter is not to quote *t*-statistics and make resolute assumptions based on historical data. The goal is to ask the question of whether the legendary David Ricardo, the famous TurtleTraders, and many successful trend followers throughout history are simply a matter of overembellished folklore or whether they may have had a point.

In recent times, trend following has garnered substantial attention for deftly performing during a period of extreme market distress. Trend following managers boasted returns of 15 to 80 percent during the abysmal period following the credit crisis and infamous Lehman debacle. Many have wondered if this performance is simply a fluke or if the strategy would have performed so well in other difficult periods in markets. For example, how would a trend follower have performed during past crises like those experienced in the Great Depression, the 1600s, or even the 1200s?

Given that this chapter engages in a historical discussion of trend following, it seems only fitting to begin with a rather controversial and relatively spectacular historical event, the Dutch Tulip Bubble of the early 1600s. Historical prices for tulips are plotted in Figure 19.1. One common type of trend following strategy is a channel breakout strategy. A channel breakout signal takes a long (short) position when a signal breaks out of a certain upper (lower) boundary for a range of values. Using a simple channel breakout signal, a trend following investor might have entered a long position before November 25th, 1636 and would have exited the trade (by selling tulip bulbs and eventually short selling if that was even possible) around February 9th, 1637. A trend following investor simply "follows the trend" and cuts losses when the trend seems to disappear. In the case of tulips, a trend following investor might have ridden the bubble upward and sold when prices started to fall. This approach would have led to a sizeable return rather than a handful of flower bulbs and economic ruin. Although it is one rather esoteric example, the tulip bulb example demonstrates that there may be something robust or fundamental about the performance of a dynamic strategy like trend following over the long run. It is important to note that in this example, as in most financial markets, the exit decision seems to be more important than the entry. The importance of *cutting your losses and taking profits* seems to drive performance. This is a concept that is revisited often throughout the course of this book.

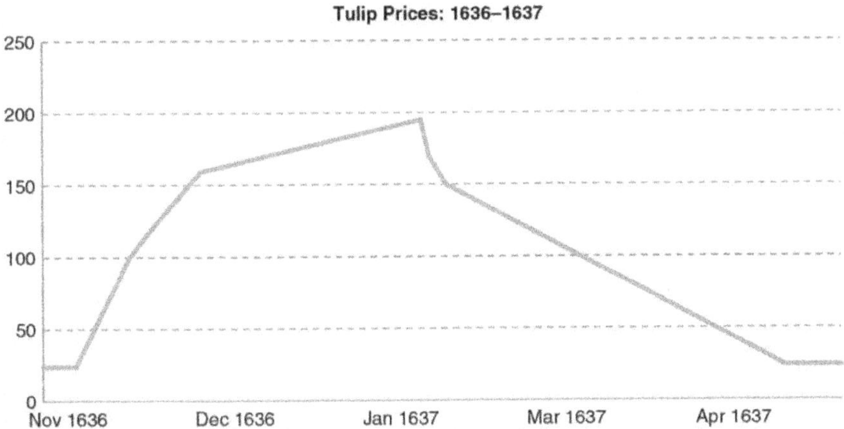

FIGURE 19.1: A standard price index for tulip bulb prices Source: Thompson (2007).

Trend following strategies adapt with financial markets. They find opportunities when market prices create trends due to many fundamental, technical, and behavioral reasons. As a group, trend followers profit from market divergence, riding trends in market prices, and cutting their losses across markets. Examples of drivers that may create trends in markets include risk transfer (or economic rents being transferred from hedgers to speculators), the process of information dissemination, and behavioral biases (euphoria, panic, etc.). Despite the wide range of explanations, the underlying reasons behind market divergence are *of little consequence* to a trend follower. They seek simply to be there when opportunity arises. Throughout history, opportunities do arise. The robust performance of trend following over the past 800 years helps to historically motivate this point.

The Tale of Trend Following: A Historical Study

Although almost two centuries have passed since the advice of legendary political economist David Ricardo, the same core principles of trend following have garnered significant attention in modern times. Using a unique dataset dating back roughly 800 years, the performance of trend following can be examined across a wide array of economic environments documenting low correlation with traditional asset classes, positive skewness, and robust performance during crisis periods.

The performance of trend following has been discussed extensively in the applied and academic literature (see Moskowitz, Ooi, and Pedersen 2012). Despite this, most of the data series that are examined are typically limited to actual track records over several decades or futures/cash data from the past century. In this chapter, an 800-year dataset is examined to extend and confirm previous studies. To examine trend following over the long haul, monthly returns of 84 markets in equity, fixed income, foreign exchange, and commodity markets are used as they became available from the 1200s through to 2013. There are several assumptions and approximations that are made to allow for a long-term analysis of trend following. For simplicity, an outline of assumptions and approximations as well as a list of included markets is included in the appendix.

Market behavior has varied substantially throughout the ages. To correctly construct a representative dataset through history, it is important to be particularly mindful of dramatic economic developments. This means that the dataset should, as closely as possible, represent investment returns that could have actually been investable. For a specific example, from the early seventeenth century to the 1930s, the United Kingdom (U.K.), the United States (U.S.), and other major countries were committed to the gold standard. During this period, the price of gold was essentially fixed. As a result, gold must be removed from the sample of investable markets during this particular time period. As a second example, during most of the nineteenth century, capital gains represented an insignificant portion of equity returns. On average, U.S. investors in the nineteenth century received only a 0.7 percent annualized capital gain, but a 5.8 percent dividend per annum (see Figure 19.2). In fact, up to the 1950s, stocks consistently paid a higher dividend yield than corporate bonds. As a consequence, total return indices must be used to represent equity market returns over time.

Using return data collected from as far back as 1223, a representative trend following system can be built for a period spanning roughly 800 years. A representative trend following system represents the performance of "following the trend" throughout the centuries in whatever markets might be available. Although certain commodity markets, such as rice, date all the way back to around 1000 A.D., the analysis begins in 1223 when there are at least a handful of available markets. At any point in time, to calculate whether a trend exists, the portfolio consists only of the markets that have at least a 12-month history. The trend following portfolio is assumed to be allowed to go both long and short. Monthly data is used for the analysis. Based on a set of simple liquidity constraints, the portfolio is constructed of available markets. Figure 19.3 depicts the number of markets in the portfolio over time. The growth of futures markets has facilitated trend followers by making more markets available for trading.

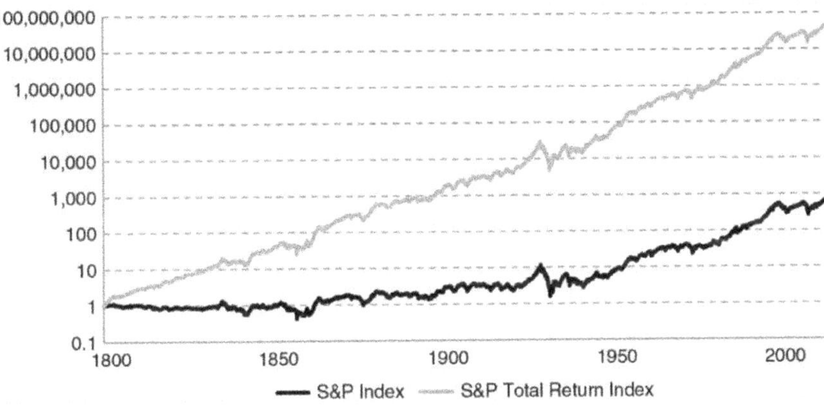

FIGURE 19.2: A historical plot of the S&P 500 Index and S&P 500 Total Return Index from 1800 to 2013 in log scale

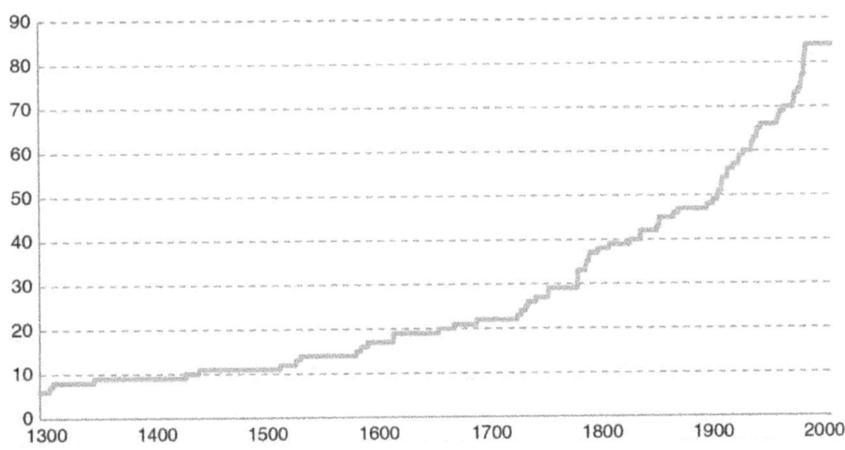

FIGURE 19.3: The number of included markets in the representative trend following program from 1300 to 2013

Return Characteristics over the Centuries

Trend following requires dynamic allocation of capital to both long and short trends across many different assets over time. Figure 19.4 plots the log scale performance of a trend following strategy for roughly 800 years. Over the entire historical period from the 1300s to 2013, the representative trend following system generates an annual return of 13 percent, with an annualized volatility of 11 percent. This results in a Sharpe ratio of 1.16.

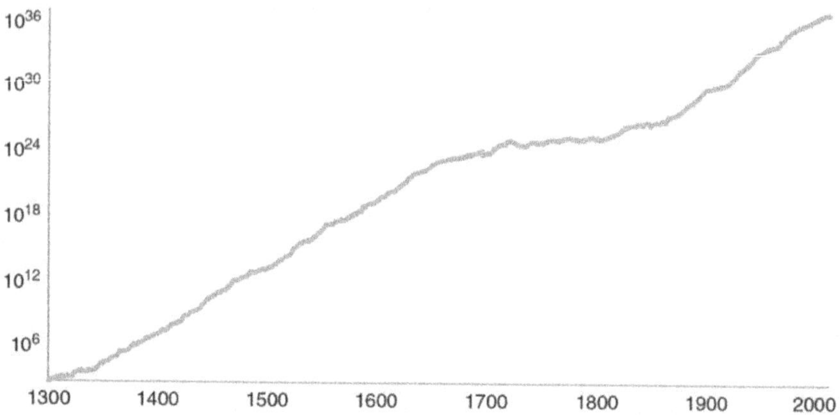

FIGURE 19.4: Cumulative (log) performance of the representative trend following portfolio from 1300 to 2013

Many finance experts have argued for the reduction of risks in the long run or that one should just simply buy and hold. Trend following strategies dynamically adjust positions according to trends, making them the counter to a buy-and-hold long-only strategy. The difference between these two can give insight into the value added of active management across asset classes. Position sizes for both trend following and a buy-and-hold strategy are rebalanced on a monthly basis to achieve equal risk. In contrast with the buy and hold, the trend following system is free to go short. For comparison, the buy-and-hold portfolio represents a diversified long-only portfolio consisting of equities, bonds, and commodities. Table 19.1 displays performance statistics for the long-only buy-and-hold portfolio and the representative trend following portfolio. In terms of Sharpe ratio, the total performance of trend following over the past 800 years is far superior. This suggests that there may be a premium to active management and directional flexibility in allowing short positions. Given the spectacular outperformance of trend following over a long-only buy-and-hold portfolio, it is only natural to take a closer look at various factors that may impact this performance. The role of interest rates, inflation, market divergence, and financial bubbles and crisis are examined in closer detail in the following sections.

TABLE 19.1: Performance Statistics for Buy-and-Hold and Trend Following Portfolios from 1223 to 2013

	Buy-and-Hold Portfolio	Trend Following Portfolio
Average Return (annual)	4.8%	13.0%
Standard Deviation (annual)	10.3%	11.2%
Sharpe Ratio	0.47	1.16

Interest Rate Regime Dependence

Because interest rates affect market participants' ability to borrow and lend as well as the time value of money, they are an important factor to examine for dynamic strategies. As interest rate regimes change, they can impact dynamic strategies in a plethora of ways. Interest rates are currently historically low, but interest rate regimes have varied substantially across history. Figure 19.5 plots government bond yields over the past 700 years. In this section, interest rate regimes are discussed from a 700-year perspective.

Since around 1300 A.D., the median long-term bond yield has averaged around 5.8 percent. Despite the intuitive/fundamental importance of interest rate regimes, the correlation between the level of interest rates and trend following returns is only 0.14. To see if different regimes have an impact on trend following performance, interest rate levels can be divided into high and low. A high interest rate regime can be defined by a year where the average yield is above the median, and a low-interest rate regime can be defined by a year where the average yield is below the median. Across both high- and low-interest rate regimes, on average, trend following performs better during high-interest rate regimes. This can be seen in Table 19.2.

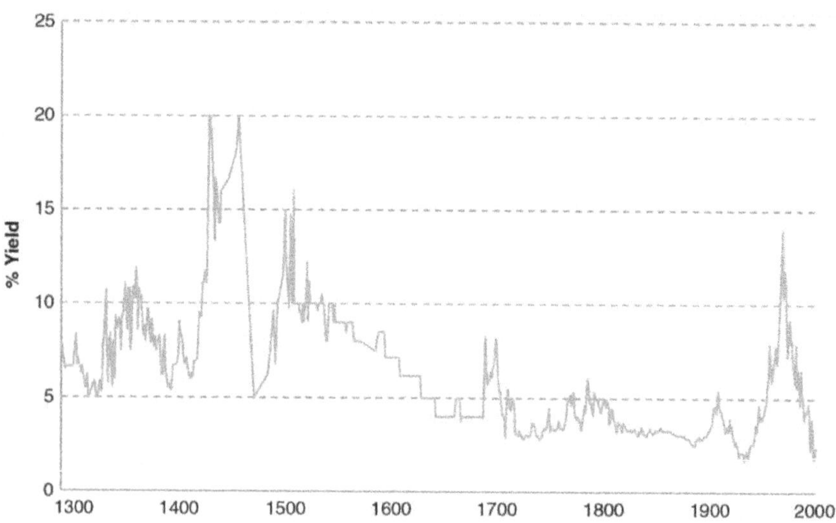

FIGURE 19.5: The GFD Long-Term Government Bond Yield Index from 1300 to 2013
Source: Global Financial Data.

TABLE 19.2: Performance of Trend Following over Different Interest Rate Regimes from 1300 to 2013

	High IR	Low IR	Rising IR	Falling IR
Average Return (annual)	15.5%	10.6%	11.9%	14.4%
Standard Deviation (annual)	9.9%	12.2%	11.2%	11.1%
Sharpe Ratio	1.56	0.86	1.06	1.30

In practice, it is not only the level of interest rates but also the relative movements in interest rates that impacts markets. To evaluate the impact of changes in interest rate, the yield differential from year-end to year-end can be computed. If the change over a time period is positive (negative), the year is defined as a rising (falling) interest rate year. The correlation between the change in yield and trend following returns is close to zero, suggesting that the difference in trend following performance, during periods of either rising or falling interest rates, does not seem to be significant.

Inflationary Environments

Having examined the impact of interest rate environments, it is also interesting to discuss inflation. Since both the buy-and-hold and trend following strategies allocate capital across asset classes, including commodities and currencies (buy and hold has only commodities), the inflationary environment may play an important role over time. Even outside this long-term historical study, in current times, threats of new, high-inflationary environments are rather pertinent. In light of the current *stimulative monetary policies* undertaken across the globe since the financial crisis of 2008, it may be reasonable to anticipate that these policies may eventually lead to higher inflation globally.

To examine the impact of different inflationary environments, using consumer price index and producer price index for the United States and the United Kingdom starting in 1720, a composite inflation rate index can be constructed. This composite inflation index is plotted in Figure 19.6.

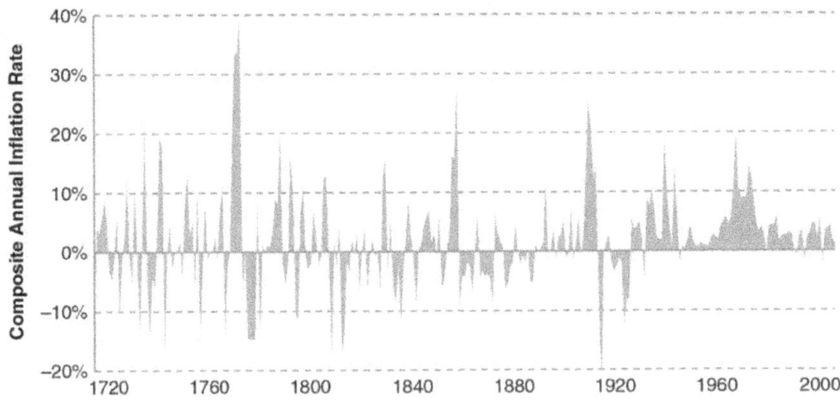

FIGURE 19.6: A composite annual inflation rate for the United States and the United Kingdom from 1720 to 2013 *Source:* Global Financial Data.

From 1720 to 2013, the composite inflation rate is above 5 percent more than 25 percent of the time and above 10 percent more than 13 percent of the time. Inflation can be divided into *low* (less than 5 percent), *medium* (between 5 percent and 10 percent), and *high* (above 10 percent). Performance can then be examined across different inflationary environments. Despite the large differences in inflationary environments, trend following performs roughly the same across all three types of inflationary environments: low, medium, and high. Table 19.3 summarizes the performance of trend following across different inflationary regimes. The robust performance for trend following across these inflationary regimes suggests that the strategy seems to be able to adapt to different inflationary regimes.

TABLE 19.3: Performance for Trend Following in Different Inflationary Environments during the Period from 1720 to 2013

	Inflation <5%	5% < Inflation < 10%	Inflation >10%
Average Return (annual)	10.4%	10.1%	14.9%
Standard Deviation (annual)	12.0%	9.90%	14.6%
Sharpe Ratio	0.87	1.02	1.02

Financial Bubbles and Crisis

As an illustrative example, the Dutch Tulip Bubble of the 1600s was briefly discussed in the chapter introduction. Over the centuries, numerous financial crises (or market bubbles) have plagued financial markets. Based on its global impact and severity, the 1929 Wall Street Crash (the notorious Black Monday of October 28, 1929) is another good example. Figure 19.7 plots the two-year period surrounding this date. Black Monday is the spectacular day when the Dow Jones Industrial index lost 13 percent.

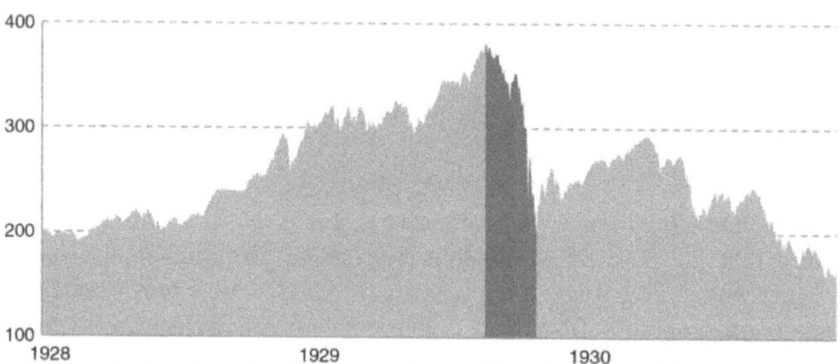

FIGURE 19.7: The Dow Jones Industrial index during the 1929 Wall Street Crash (Black Monday) *Source:* Global Financial Data.

Figure 19.8 plots the cumulative performance of the representative trend following system over the same period from Figure 19.7. During the month of October 1929, a month where the Dow Jones lost approximately half of its value, the representative trend following system had a slightly positive return. Even more astonishing during the two years pre- and post-crash, trend following earned a roughly 90 percent return with much of this return coming post-crash during the start of the Great Depression.

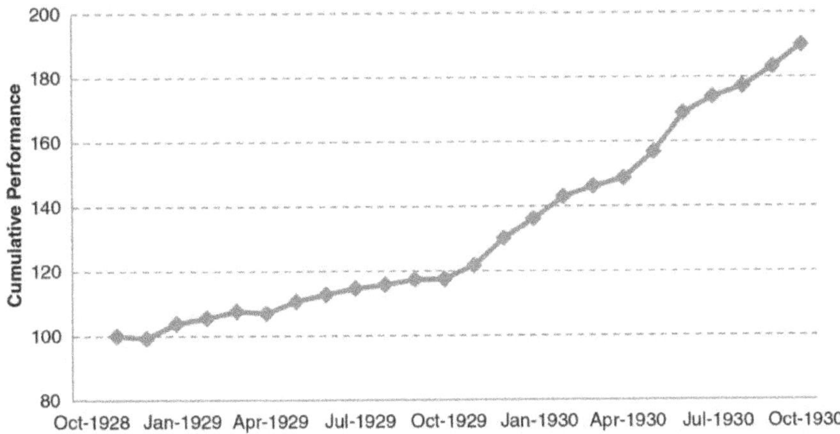

FIGURE 19.8: Cumulative performance for the representative trend following system pre and post the 1929 Wall Street Crash (Black Monday). The data period is October 1928 to October 1930.

The positive performance of trend following during crisis periods is not specific to the 1929 Wall Street Crash or the performance during the Dutch Tulip mania. In fact, the strategy seems to perform well during most of the difficult periods throughout history. Taking a closer look at negative performance periods for both fixed income and equity markets, the average performance for trend following is plotted in Figure 19.9. In this, the conditional average returns for trend following are positive for months when the equity index experienced negative performance. For example, in the top panel of Figure 19.9, the average trend following return is 0.2 percent for the 98 months when the equity portfolio return is between –4 and –6 percent. The bottom panel in Figure 19.9 shows a less consistent pattern with reference to the bond index. The mean return for trend following is positive for months when bond returns are negative. The performance of trend following seems to be good even when equity and bonds perform at their worst.

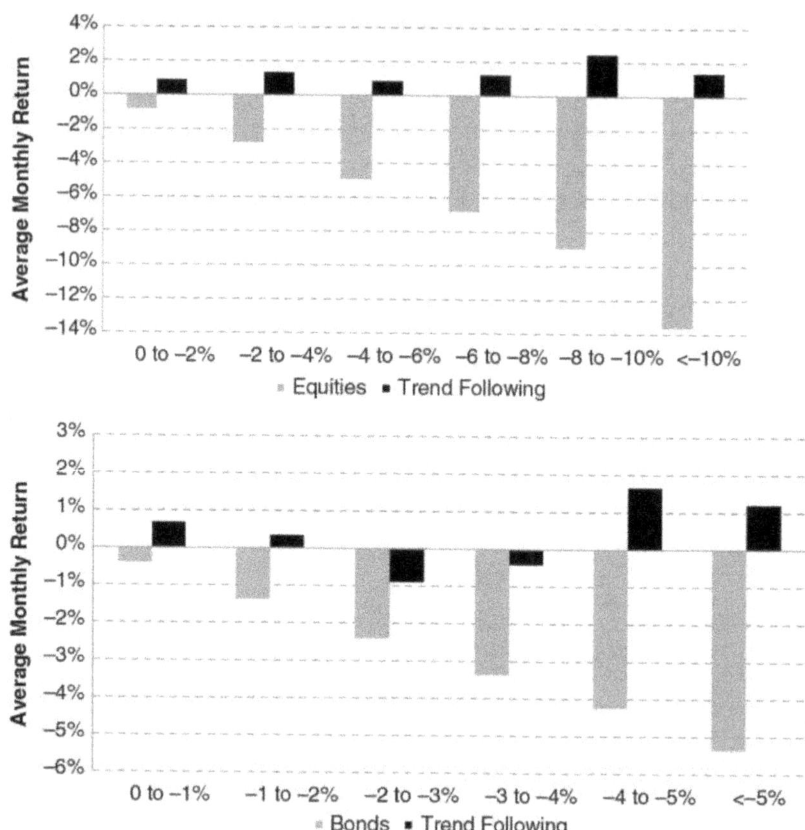

FIGURE 19.9: Average monthly returns for the representative trend following system during down periods in equity and bond portfolios

In addition to capturing trends outside equity markets, a portion of trend following performance during down periods can also come from the ability to short sell. For example, if short sales are restricted in equities, trend following will have a long bias in equities, and the performance (with and without the long bias) during down months in equities can be discussed for the past 300 years of the dataset. Figure 19.10 plots a comparison of with-and-without long bias to equities for down periods in equities. This demonstrates that a long equity bias reduces the performance of trend following during down equity months. For a concrete example, for months when the equity index was down more than 10 percent, the standard (balanced) trend following system returned 1.2 percent on average historically, while the system restricted to long equities returned a slightly negative average return. Slightly negative may seem disappointing, but putting this into the perspective of a pure long portfolio, slightly negative pales in magnitude when compared with the unfortunate long-only equity investor who lost roughly 14 percent.

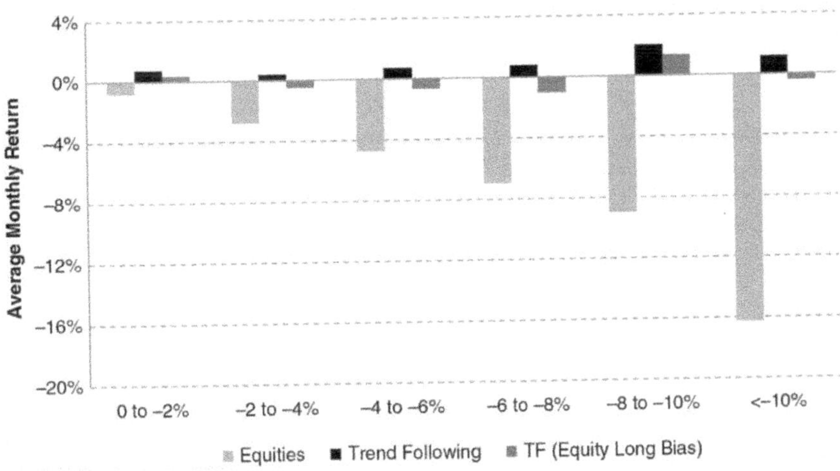

FIGURE 19.10: Average monthly returns for trend following when the equity index is down. Conditional performance is plotted for both with and without a long bias to the equity sector.

Market Divergence

Markets move and adapt over time. Periods when markets move the most dramatically (or periods of elevated market divergence) are those that provide "trends" suitable for trend following strategies. At the monthly level, the simplest way to demonstrate this is to divide performance into quintiles (five equal buckets). These buckets represent the worst equity return performance (1) to the best equity performance (5). Figures 19.11 and 19.12 plot the conditional performance of trend following for each of the five quintiles. Figure 19.11 plots the past 100 years of the dataset divided into two subperiods: 1913 to 1962 and 1963 to 2013. Figure 19.12 divides these two periods into two further 25-year subperiods: 1913–1937, 1938–1962, 1963–1987, and 1988–2013. These figures demonstrate a phenomenon practitioners often call the "CTA smile." Trend following returns tend to perform well during moments when market divergence is the largest. For example in the four 25-year time periods, the first period, which includes the Great Depression and the 1929 Wall Street Crash, exhibits the well-known "CTA smile": the best performance is during the best and worst moments for equities. The period after the Great Depression is a period when the best periods for equities were the best for a trend following strategy. The third time period also exhibits the smile. Finally, the past 25 years, a time period including the credit crisis and the tech bubble and other crises, is a time period when the most opportunities have come during the worst periods for equity markets. The convex performance (performance on both extremes) of trend following demonstrates the role of divergence or dislocation in markets (for good or for bad). [. . .]

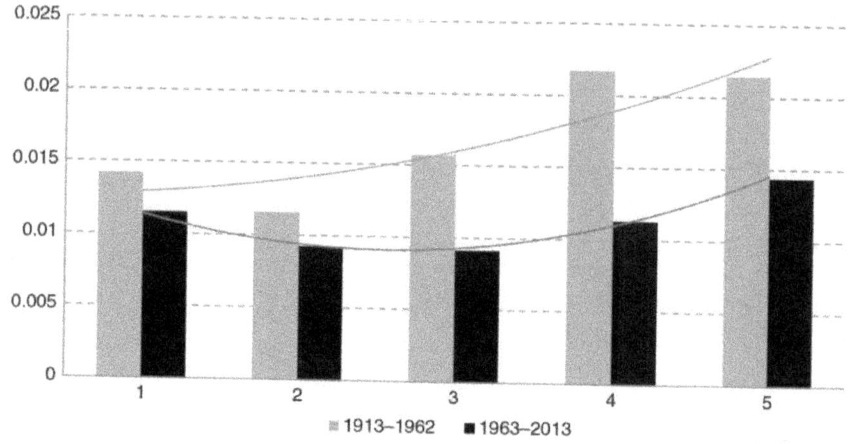

FIGURE 19.11: The "CTA Smile": Quintile analysis of trend following for 1913–1962 and 1963–2013. Returns are sorted by quintiles of equity performance from 1 (worst) to 5 (best).

Because the "CTA smile" demonstrates a convex relationship between trend following and equity markets, it is not surprising that many investors label trend following as "long volatility." Although trend followers perform well at the extremes, not all volatility is created equal. If volatility increased and there were trends across markets, trend followers are long volatility. If volatility increases and there are no trends, trend followers may be flat or even look like short volatility. Put more simply, trend following is long market divergence. Market divergence and volatility are related but they are by no means the same. [. . .]

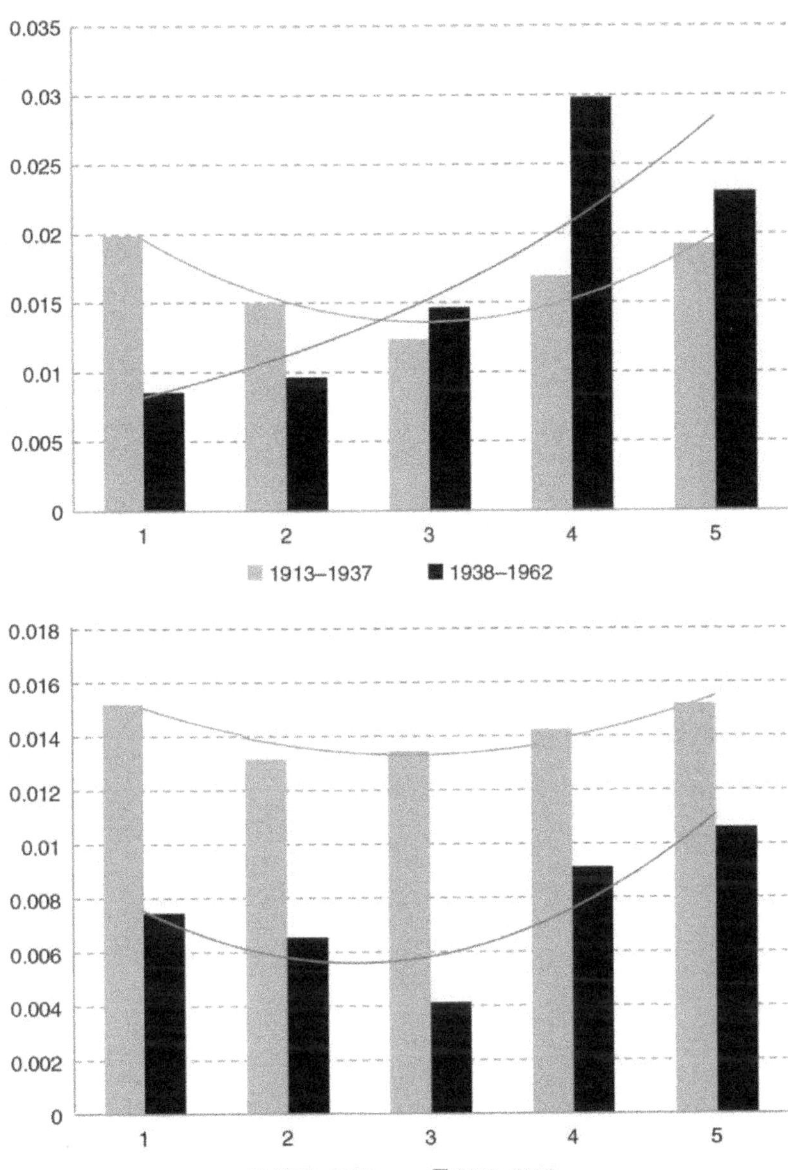

FIGURE 19.12: The "CTA Smile": Quintile analysis of trend following for 1913–1937, 1938–1962, 1963–1987, and 1988–2013. Returns are sorted by quintiles of equity performance from 1 (worst) to 5 (best).

Risk Characteristics over the Centuries

The principle of "let profits run and cut short your losses" enables trend following to achieve a desirable risk profile with more small losses as opposed to large drawdowns. In statistical terms, trend following returns exhibit positive skewness. Over the roughly 800-year period, the skewness for monthly returns is 0.30. Positive skewness indicates that the chance for left tail risk or large drawdowns in trend following is relatively small. This characteristic is somewhat unique to trend following. Most asset classes and strategies exhibit negative skewness.

In addition to positive skewness for the same roughly 800-year period, trend following has low correlation with traditional asset classes. To quantify the relationship between trend following and the traditional asset classes, a simple equity index and a simple bond index can be constructed by averaging the monthly returns of several global equity indices and bond markets. The overall correlation between the monthly returns of the representative trend following system and the equity index is 0.05, and 0.09 with the bond index. Given that these correlations are a proxy for the relationship between trend following with bond and equity markets, it is not surprising that the betas for trend following with both equity and fixed income are generally extremely low.

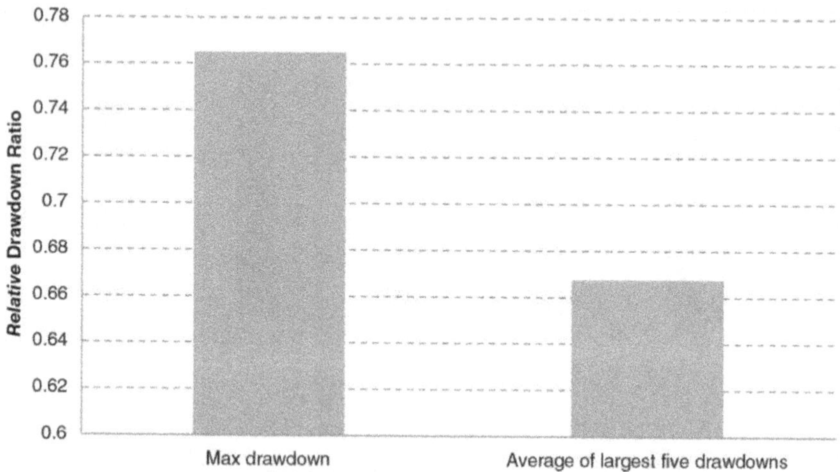

FIGURE 19.13: The maximum and average of the largest five relative drawdowns as a percentage for trend following relative to the buy-and-hold portfolio. The maximum drawdown of trend following is 75 percent of the magnitude of the maximum drawdown for the buy-and-hold portfolio.

Outside of skewness and correlation, drawdown is another important concern for most trend following investors. Figure 19.13 plots the maximum drawdown and the average of the five largest drawdowns for the representative trend following system relative to the corresponding largest drawdowns of the buy-and-hold portfolio. Drawdowns for trend following are significantly lower relative to the buy-and-hold portfolio. The maximum drawdown for trend following is approximately 25 percent lower than the maximum drawdown of the buy-and-hold portfolio. The average of the top five drawdowns for trend following is roughly a third lower than the average of the top five drawdowns for buy and hold.

As shown in Figure 19.14, the drawdown durations for trend following are also substantially shorter than those experienced by the buy-and-hold portfolio. During the past 700 years, when compared to the buy-and-hold portfolio, the duration of the longest drawdown and the average duration of the longest five drawdowns are 90 percent and 80 percent shorter, respectively. The superior drawdown profile of trend following is related to the positive skewness of returns and the negative serial correlation. [. . .]

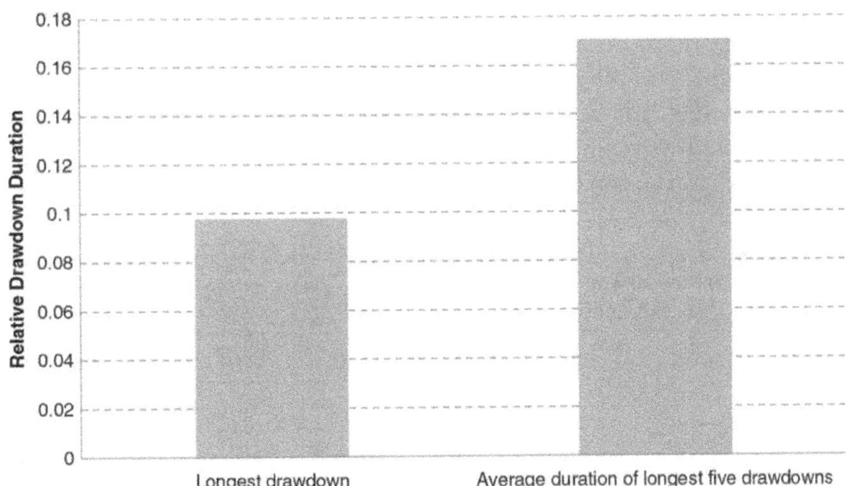

FIGURE 19.14: The relative size of the longest duration and average duration of the longest five drawdowns for trend following relative to the buy-and-hold portfolio. The longest drawdown duration is less than 10 percent of the length of the longest drawdown length for the buy-and-hold drawdown.

Portfolio Benefits over the Centuries

The previous sections discussed the return and risk characteristics of trend following over the centuries. Over an extensive 800-year period, trend following portfolios exhibit robust performance with a Sharpe ratio of 1.16. The strategy has low correlation with traditional asset classes, interest rate regimes, and inflation. In addition, performance during crisis periods is positive across the entire sample. A rough look across quintiles in equity markets demonstrates that divergence in market prices is a driver of trend following performance. The strategy also exhibits positive skewness and smaller drawdowns than buy-and-hold strategies. All of these characteristics make trend following a good candidate to diversify traditional portfolios.

During the period beginning in the 1690s up until 2013, the equity index achieves a reasonably high Sharpe ratio of 0.7. For an even longer period beginning in the 1300s up until 2013, the bond index also has a positive Sharpe ratio. Despite the fact that both indices are positive, the Sharpe ratio for trend following is still much higher than a combined buy-and-hold strategy. This suggests that adding some trend following may improve upon a buy-and-hold strategy. Table 19.4 displays the portfolio benefits created by combining the buy-and-hold portfolio (incorporating either the equity or bond indices) with an equal allocation to the representative trend following portfolio. The start dates for this analysis correspond to the first availability of data for equity and bond markets. In an equal risk allocated portfolio, the performance improvement (over both the traditional equity and bond portfolios) is relatively substantial.

TABLE 19.4: Performance for the equity index, bond index, trend following, and combined portfolios. The sample period is 1695–2013 for the equity index and 1300–2013 for the bond index.

	Equity and Trend Following: 1695–2013			Bond and Trend Following: 1300–2013		
	Equity	**TF**	**Equity+TF**	**Bond**	**TF**	**Bond+TF**
Average Return (annual)	7.85%	10.74%	9.68%	6.57%	12.97%	7.74%
Standard Deviation (annual)	11.28%	12.91%	8.81%	7.31%	11.21%	5.44%
Sharpe Ratio	0.7	0.83	1.1	0.9	1.16	1.42

Adding trend following to a traditional equity or bond portfolio improves the Sharpe ratio of both indices. To examine this from the perspective of a traditional investment portfolio, trend following can be added to a typical 60/40 equity bond portfolio. For example, a combined portfolio can be constructed such that it consists of 80 percent of a traditional 60/40 portfolio and 20 percent trend following. In this case, this translates to 48 percent of equities, 32 percent of bonds, and 20 percent of trend following. Figure 19.15 plots the performance in terms of Sharpe ratio for the individual portfolios, the trend following portfolio, the 60/40 portfolio, and the combined 60/40 and trend following portfolio. During the period of 1695 to 2013, a 20 percent allocation to trend following is able to boost the Sharpe ratio of a 60/40 portfolio from 1.0 to 1.2.

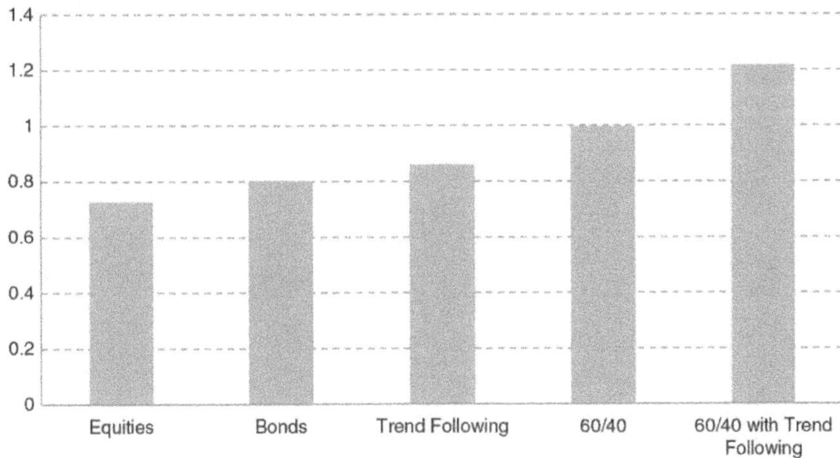

FIGURE 19.15: Sharpe ratios for individual asset classes including equity and combinations of the three asset classes from 1695 to 2013

Summary

The use of trend following as an alternative investment strategy has certainly grown over the past 30 years. Using roughly 800 years of market data, trend following can be viewed from a long-term perspective. Over the centuries, empirically, trend following has provided distinctly positive returns, a high Sharpe ratio, as well as low correlation with traditional asset classes, inflation, and interest rate regimes. The strategy provides consistently positive performance during crisis periods and the performance seems to be linked to divergence across markets. From a portfolio perspective, the combination of trend following with traditional portfolios such as a 60/40 portfolio significantly improves risk adjusted performance.

Appendix: Included Markets and Relevant Assumptions

Sector	Market	Sector	Market
Commodities	Aluminum	Commodities	Hops
	Brent Crude Oil		Iron Ore
	Butter		Lean Hogs
	Cheese		Live Cattle
	Coal		Malt
	Cocoa, NY		Manufactured Iron
	Cocoa, London		Natural Gas
	Coffee		Nickel
	Copper		Oat
	Corn		Orange Juice
	Cotton		Platinum
	Crude Oil		Rice
	Feeder Cattle		Rye
	French Gold Coin Mintage in Livres Tournois		Silver
	French Silver Coin Mintage in Livres Tournois		Soybeans
	Gas Oil-Petroleum		Soyameal
	Gold		Soyaoil
	Heating Oil		Sugar #11
			Sugar, White
			Tobacco
Commodities	Wheat	Currencies	Canadian Dollars per British Pound
	Wheat, Hard Red Winter		CHF/USD
	Wood		Dutch Guilders per British Pound
	Wool		EUR/USD (DEM/USD)
	Zinc		GBP/USD
Bonds	Bankers Acceptance Canada		Hamburg Mark for Paris Francs
	Canadian 10-Year Bond		Hamburg Mark for Vienna Crowns
	Euro-BUND		JPY/USD
	Eurodollar		Portugal Escudo per U.S. Dollar
	France 10-Year Bond		Swedish Krona per British Pound

Sector	Market	Sector	Market
	Gilts	Equities	Australian SPI200 Index
	Japanese Bond		CAC 40
	Long-Term Government Bond		DAX Index
			E-Mini Nasdaq 100 Index
	Netherlands 10-Year Bond		E-Mini Russell 2000 Index
	Short Sterling		E-Mini S&P 500 Index
	U.K. Consolidated		FTSE 100 Index
	U.S. 10-year T-Note		Hang Seng
	U.S. 2-year T-Note		Italy All Index
	U.S. 30-year T-Note		Nikkei
	U.S. 5-year T-Note		Singapore MSCI Index
	Venice Prestiti		
Currencies	AUD/USD		Taiwan MSCI Index
	CAD/USD		Tokyo Stock Exchange Index

Assumptions and Approximations

There are several assumptions and approximations, which are made to allow for a long-term analysis of trend following. For simplicity, these are listed below.

1. Futures Prices First: When available, futures market returns are used.
2. Equity and Fixed Income: Prior to the availability of futures data, index returns are used for both equity and fixed income markets. Total returns are constructed using the appropriate short-term interest rates.
3. FX: For currency markets, spot price returns are adjusted by the interest rates differential of the two relevant currencies. When interest rates are not available, spot returns for currencies are used without adjustment.
4. Commodities: For commodities in the absence of futures price data, cash market returns are used.
5. Excess Cash Return: The interest earned on collateral and cash returns is excluded from this analysis.

Two Centuries of Trend Following

20

Yves Lempérière, Cyril Deremble, Philip Seager, Marc Potters, and Jean-Philippe Bouchaud

Capital Fund Management

We establish the existence of anomalous excess returns based on trend-following strategies across four asset classes (commodities, currencies, stock indexes, and bonds) and over very long time scales. We use for our studies both futures time series that have existed since 1960 and spot time series that allow us to go back to 1800 on commodities and indexes. The overall t-statistic of the excess returns is approximately equal to five since 1960 and approximately equal to 10 since 1800, after accounting for the overall upward drift of these markets. The effect is very stable, across both time and asset classes. It makes the existence of trends one of the most statistically significant anomalies in financial markets. When analyzing the trend-following signal further, we find a clear saturation effect for large signals, suggesting that fundamentalist traders do not attempt to resist "weak trends," but step

This work is the result of many years of research at Capital Fund Management (CFM). Many colleagues must be thanked for their insights, in particular P. Aliferis, N. Bercot, A. Berd, D. Challet, L. Dao, B. Durin, P. Horvai, L. Laloux, A. Landier, A. Matacz, D. Thesmar, T. Tu, and M. Wyart.

in when their own signal becomes strong enough. Finally, we study the performance of trend following in the recent period. We find no sign of a statistical degradation of long trends, whereas shorter trends have significantly withered.

Introduction

Are markets efficient, in the sense that all public information is included in current prices? If this were so, price changes would be totally unpredictable in the sense that no systematic excess return based on public information could be achievable. After decades of euphoria in economics departments,[1] serious doubts were raised by behavioral economists, who established a long series of pricing "anomalies" (Schwert 2003). The most famous of these anomalies (and arguably the most difficult to sweep under the rug) is the so-called excess volatility puzzle, unveiled by Shiller and others (Leroy and Porter 1981; Shiller 1981). Strangely (or wisely?) the 2013 Nobel committee decided not to take sides, and declared that markets are indeed efficient (as claimed by laureate Eugene Fama), but that the theory actually makes "little sense" (as argued by Robert Shiller, who shared the same prize!).[2] [See also de Bondt and Thaler (1985), Black (1986), and Summers (1986) for insightful papers on this debate.] In the list of long-known anomalies, the existence of trends plays a special role.

First, because trending is the exact opposite of the mechanisms that should ensure that markets are efficient, i.e., reversion forces that drive prices back to the purported fundamental value. Second, because persistent returns validate a dramatically simple strategy, "trend following," which amounts to buying when the price goes up, and selling when it goes down. Simple as it may be (Covel 2009), this strategy is at the heart of the activity of commodity trading advisors (CTAs; Bartas and Kosowski 2012), an industry that now manages (as of 2013 Q4) no less than US$325 billion, representing around 16% of the total assets of the hedge fund industry, and accounting for several percent of the daily activity of futures markets (Mundt 2014).[3] These numbers are by no means small, and make it hard for efficient market enthusiasts to dismiss this anomaly as economically irrelevant.[4] The strategy is furthermore deployed over a wide range of instruments (indexes, bonds, commodities, currencies, etc.) with positive reported performance over long periods, suggesting that the anomaly is to a large extent universal, across both epochs and asset classes.[5] This reveals an extremely persistent, universal bias in the behavior of investors who appear to hold "extrapolative expectations," as argued in many papers coming from different strands of the academic literature (see, for example, Bouchaud and Cont 1998; DeLong et al. 1990; Greenwood and Shleifer 2014; Hirshleifer and Yu 2012; Hommes et al. 2008; Hong and Stein 1999; Kent et al. 1998; Kirman 1991, 1993; Smith et al. 1988 and the references therein).

Many academic studies have already investigated this trend anomaly on a wide range of assets, and have convincingly established its statistical significance in the last few decades (Clare et al. 2012; Szakmary et al. 2010). Recently, this time horizon has been extended to 100 years by Hurst et al. (2012), and the effect still exists unabated. The aim of the present paper is to extend the time horizon even further, to 200 years, as far in the past as we have been able to go in terms of data. We find that the amplitude of the effect has been remarkably steady over two centuries. This also allows us to assess the recent weakening of the effect (as testified by the relatively poor performance of CTAs over the last five years). We show that the very recent past is fully compatible with a statistical fluctuation. Although we cannot exclude that this recent period is a precursor of the "end of trends," we argue theoretically that this is an unlikely scenario. We give several mechanisms that could explain the existence and persistence of these trends throughout history.

Note that trends exist not only for market factors such as indexes, bonds, and currencies, but also cross-sectionally in stock markets. The so-called momentum anomaly consists in buying the past winners and selling the past losers in a market-neutral way, again with a high statistical significance across many decades and different geographical zones (see Barroso and Santa-Clara 2013; Kent and Moskowitz 2013; Narasimhan and Titman 1993; see also Narasimhan and Titman 2011 and Geczy and Samonov 2016 for recent reviews). Although interesting in its own right (and vindicating the hypothesis that trend following is universal (Asness et al. 2013), we will not study this particular aspect of trend following in the present paper.

The outline of the paper is as follows. First we define the trend-following indicator used for this study and test its statistical significance on available futures data. We start with futures since they are the preferred instruments of trend followers in finance. Also, their prices are unambiguously defined by transparent market trades, and not the result of a proprietary computation. Next we carefully examine, for each asset class, how the available time series can be extended as far in the past as possible. We then present our results over two centuries, and show how exceptionally stable long trends have been. We examine more deeply the linearity of the signal, and find that the trend predictability saturates for large values of the signal, which is needed for the long-term stability of markets. Last, we discuss the significance of the recent performance of the trend in light of this long-term simulation.

Trend Following on Futures since 1960

Measuring Trends

We choose to define our trend indicator in a way similar to simulating a constant risk trading strategy (without costs). More precisely, we first define the reference price level at time t, $\langle p \rangle_{n,t}$, as an exponential moving average of past prices (excluding $p(t)$ itself) with a decay rate equal to n months. Long simulations can often only be performed on monthly data, so we use monthly closes. The signal $s_n(t)$ at the beginning of month t is constructed as

$$s_n(t) = \frac{p(t-1) - \langle p \rangle_{n,t-1}}{\sigma_n(t-1)}, \tag{2.1}$$

where the volatility σ_n is equal to the exponential moving average of the absolute monthly price changes, with a decay rate equal to n months. The average strength of the trend is then measured as the statistical significance of fictitious profits and losses (P&Ls) of a risk managed strategy that buys or sells (depending on the sign of s_n) a quantity $\pm\sigma_n^{-1}$ of the underlying contract α[6]:

$$Q_n^\alpha(t) = \sum_{t'<t} \mathrm{sgn}[s_n(t')] \frac{p(t'+1) - p(t')}{\sigma_n(t'-1)}. \tag{2.2}$$

In the rest of the paper, we will focus on the choice $n = 5$ months, although the dependence on n will be discussed. Of course, different implementations can be proposed. However, the general conclusions are extremely robust against changes to the statistical test or to the implemented strategy (see, for example, Bartas and Kosowski 2012; Clare et al. 2012; Szakmary et al. 2010).

In the following, we will define the Sharpe ratio of the P&L as its average return divided by its volatility, both annualized. Since the P&L

does not include interest earned on the capital, and futures are self-financed instruments, we do not need to subtract the risk-free rate to compute the Sharpe ratio. The t-statistic of the P&L (i.e., the fact that the average return is significantly different from zero) is therefore given by the Sharpe ratio times $\sqrt{N}$, where N is the number of years over which the strategy is active. We will also define the drift μ of a time series as the average daily return of the corresponding instrument, which would be the P&L of the long-only strategy if financing costs were to be neglected.

The Pool of Assets

Since we wish to prove that trend following is a universal effect not restricted to any one asset, we would like to test this signal on as large a pool as possible. This is also important in practice, since diversification plays an important role in the performance of CTAs. However, since the purpose of this paper is to back-test the trend on a very large history, we voluntarily limit ourselves to the contracts for which a long data set is available. This naturally makes the inclusion of emerging markets more difficult. Therefore, for indexes, bonds, and currencies, we only consider the following seven countries: Australia, Canada, Germany, Japan, Switzerland, the United Kingdom, and the United States. We believe the results of this section would only be improved by the choice of a wider pool.

We also need to select a pool of commodities. In order to have a well-balanced pool, we chose the following seven representative contracts: crude oil, Henry Hub natural gas, corn, wheat, sugar, live cattle, and copper.

In summary, we have a pool made up of seven commodity contracts, seven 10-year bond contracts, seven stock index contracts and six currency contracts. All the data used in the current paper comes from Global Financial Data (GFD).[7]

The Results

Our history of futures starts in 1960, mostly with commodities. As we can see from Figure 20.1 on the next page, the aggregated performance $\sum_\alpha Q_n^\alpha(t)$ looks well-distributed in time, with an overall t-statistic of 5.9, which is highly significant. The Sharpe ratio and t-statistic are only weakly dependent on n (see Table 20.2).

However, we might argue that this comes from the trivial fact that there is an overall drift μ in most of these time series (for example, the stock market tends to go up over time). It is therefore desirable to remove this "long" bias, by focusing on the residual of the trend-following P&L when the β with the long-only strategy has been factored in. In fact, the correction is found to be rather small, since the trend-following P&L and the long-only strategy are only +15% correlated. Still, this correction slightly decreases the overall t-statistic of the trend-following performance, to 5.0.

In order to assess the significance of the above result, we break it down into different sectors and decades. As shown in Tables 20.2 and 20.3, the t-statistic of the trend-following strategy is above 2.1 for all sectors and all decades, and above 1.6 when debiased from the drift μ. Therefore, the performance shown in Figure 20.1 is well-distributed across all sectors and periods, which strongly supports the claim that the existence of trends in financial markets is indeed universal. One issue, though, is that our history of futures only goes back 50 years or so, and the first 10 years of those 50 is only made up of commodities. In order to test the stability and universality of the effect, it is desirable to extend the time series to go back further in the past, in order to span many economic cycles and different macroenvironments. This is the goal of the next section, which provides a convincing confirmation of the results based on futures.

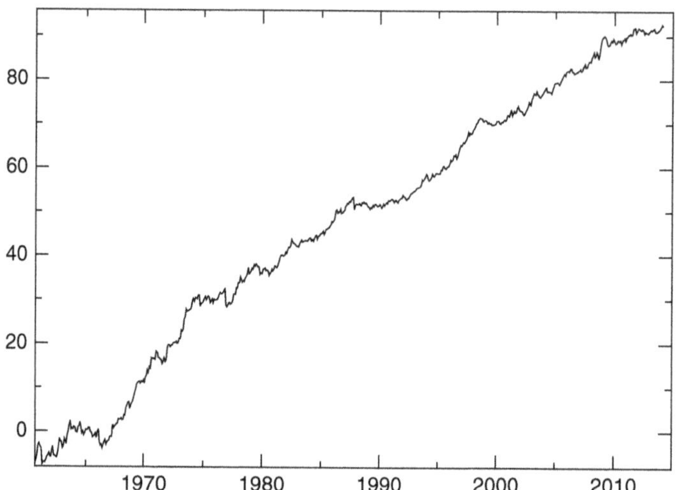

FIGURE 20.1: Fictitious P&L, as Described in Equation 2.2, of a Five-Month Trend-Following Strategy on a Diversified Pool of Futures

t-statistic = 5.9 (corresponding to a Sharpe ratio = 0.8). Debiased t-statistic = 5.0.

TABLE 20.1: Sharpe Ratio and *t*-Statistic of the Trend (*T*) and *t*-Statistic of the Debiased Trend (*T**) for Different Time Horizons *n* (in Months), since 1960

Time-Scale *n* (Months)	SR (*T*)	*t*-Statistic (*T*)	*t*-Statistic (*T**)
2	0.8	5.9	5.5
3	0.83	6.1	5.5
5	0.78	5.7	5.0
7	0.8	5.9	5.0
10	0.76	5.6	5.1
15	0.65	4.8	4.5
20	0.57	4.2	3.3

TABLE 20.2: Sharpe Ratio and *t*-Statistic of the Trend (*T*) for $n = 5$, of the Debiased Trend (*T**) and of the Drift Component μ of the Different Sectors, and the Starting Date for Each Sector

Sector	SR (*T*)	*t*-Statistic (*T*)	*t*-Statistic (*T**)	SR (μ)	*t*-Statistic (μ)	Start Date
Currencies	0.57	3.6	3.4	0.05	0.32	May 1973
Commodities	0.8	5.9	5.0	0.33	2.45	Jan 1960
Bonds	0.49	2.8	1.6	0.58	3.3	May 1982
Indexes	0.41	2.3	2.1	0.4	2.3	Jan 1982

TABLE 20.3: Sharpe Ratio and *t*-Statistic of the Trend (*T*) for $n = 5$, of the Debiased Trend (*T**) and of the Drift Component μ for Each Decade

Period	SR (*T*)	*t*-Statistic (*T*)	*t*-Statistic (*T**)	SR (μ)	*t*-Statistic (μ)
1960–1970	0.66	2.1	1.8	0.17	0.5
1970–1980	1.15	3.64	2.5	0.78	2.5
1980–1990	1.05	3.3	2.85	–0.03	–0.1
1990–2000	1.12	3.5	3.03	0.79	2.5
>2000	0.75	2.8	1.9	0.68	2.15

Extending the Time Series: A Case-by-Case Approach

We now try to find proxies for the futures time series that are reasonably correlated with the actual futures prices on the recent period but allow us to go back in the past a lot further. Natural candidates are spot prices on currencies, stock indexes and commodities, and government rates for bonds. We shall examine each sector independently. Before doing so, however, we should mention other important restrictions on the use of the historical data. First, we expect trends to develop only on freely traded instruments, where price evolution is not distorted by state interventions. Also, we require a certain amount of liquidity, in order to have meaningful prices. These two conditions, free-floating and liquid assets, will actually limit us when we look back in the distant past.

Currencies

The futures time series goes back to 1973. In the previous period (1944–71), the monetary system operated under the rules set out in the Bretton Woods agreements. According to these international treaties, the exchange rates were pegged to the U.S. dollar (within a 1% margin), which remained the only currency that was convertible into gold at a fixed rate. Therefore, no trend can be expected on these time series, where prices are limited to a small band around a reference value.

Prior to this, the dominant system was the Gold Standard. In this regime, the international value of a currency was determined by a fixed relationship with gold. Gold in turn was used to settle international accounts. In this regime we also cannot expect trends to develop, since the value of the currency is essentially fixed by its conversion rate with gold. In the 1930s, many countries dropped out of this system, massively devaluing in a desperate attempt to manage the consequences of the Great Depression (the "beggar thy neighbor" policy). This also led to massively managed currencies, with little hope of finding any genuine trending behavior.

All in all, therefore, it seems unlikely that we can find a free-floating substitute for our futures time series on foreign exchange prior to 1973.

Government Rates

Government debt (and default!) has been around for centuries (Reinhart and Rogoff 2009), but in order to observe a trend on interest rates we need a liquid secondary market, on which the debt can be exchanged at all times. This is a highly nontrivial feature for this market. Indeed, throughout most of the available history, government debt has been used mostly as a way to finance extraordinary liabilities, such as wars. In other periods of history, debt levels gradually reduced, as the principals were repaid, or washed away by growth (as debt levels are quoted relative to GDP).

As a typical example, we can see in Figure 20.2 that the U.S. debt, inherited from the War of Independence, fell to practically zero in 1835–6, during the Jackson presidency. There is another spike in 1860–65, during the American Civil War, which then gets gradually washed away by growth. We have to wait until World War I to see a significant increase in debt, which then persists until today. Apart from Australia, whose debt has grown at a roughly constant rate, and Japan, whose turning point is around 1905, during the Russo-Japanese War, the situation in all other countries is similar to that of the United States. From this point onward, the debt has never been repaid in its totality in any of the countries we consider in this study, and has mostly been rolled over from one bond issuance to the next.

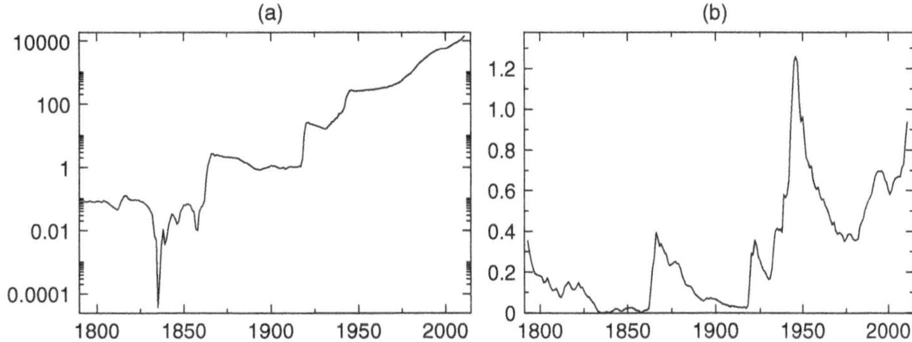

FIGURE 20.2: Global Debt of the U.S. Government (a) in Billions of U.S. Dollars and (b) as a Fraction of GDP

Another more subtle point can explain the emergence of a stable debt market: at the beginning of the twentieth century, the monetary policy (in its most straightforward sense: the power to print money) was separated from the executive instances and attributed to central banks, supposedly independent of the political power (see Figure 20.4). This move increased the confidence in the national debt of these countries, and helped boost subsequent debt levels.

All of this leads us to the conclusion that the bond market before 1918 was not developed enough to be considered as "freely traded and liquid." Therefore, we start our interest rate time series in 1918. We should note as well that we exclude from the time series World War II and the immediate post-war period in Japan and Germany, where the economy was heavily managed, therefore leading to price distortions.

TABLE 20.4: Starting Date of the Central Bank's Monopoly on the Issuance of Notes

Country	Start
United States	1913
Australia	1911
Canada	1935
Germany	1914
Switzerland	1907
Japan	1904
United Kingdom	1844

The Bank of England does not have this monopoly in Scotland and Ireland, but regulates the commercial banks that share this privilege.

Indexes and Commodities

For these sectors, the situation is more straightforward. Stocks and commodities were actively priced throughout the nineteenth century, so it is relatively easy to get clean, well-defined prices. As we can see from Tables 20.5 and 20.6, we can characterize trend following strategies for over two centuries on some of these time series. Apart from some episodes that we excluded, such as World War II in Germany and Japan, where the stock market was closed, or the period through which the price of crude oil was fixed (in the second half of the twentieth century), the time series are of reasonably good quality, i.e., prices are actually moving (no gaps) and there are no major outliers.

TABLE 20.5: Starting Date of the Spot Index Monthly Time Series for Each Country

Country	Start
United States	1791
Australia	1875
Canada	1914
Germany	1870
Switzerland	1914
Japan	1914
United Kingdom	1693

TABLE 20.6: Starting Date of the Spot Price for Each Commodity

Commodity	Start
Crude oil	1859
Natural gas	1986
Corn	1858
Wheat	1841
Sugar	1784
Live cattle	1858
Copper	1800

Validating the Proxies

We now want to check that the time series selected above, essentially based on spot data on 10-year government bonds, indexes, and commodities, yield results that are very similar to those we obtained with futures. This will validate our proxies and allow us to extend, in the following section, our simulations to the pre-1960 period. In Figure 20.3 we show a comparison of the trend applied to futures prices and to spot prices in the period of overlapping coverage between the two data sets. From 1982 onward we have futures in all four sectors and the correlation is measured to be 91%, which we consider to be acceptably high. We show the correlations per sector calculated since 1960 in Table 20.7

and observe that the correlation remains high for indexes and bonds but is lower for commodities, with a correlation of 65%. We know that the difference between the spot and futures prices is the so called "cost of carry," which is absent for the spot data, this additional term being especially significant and volatile for commodities. We find, however, that the level of correlation is sufficiently high to render the results meaningful. In any case the addition of the cost of carry can only improve the performance of the trend on futures and any conclusion regarding trends on spot data will be further confirmed by the use of futures data.

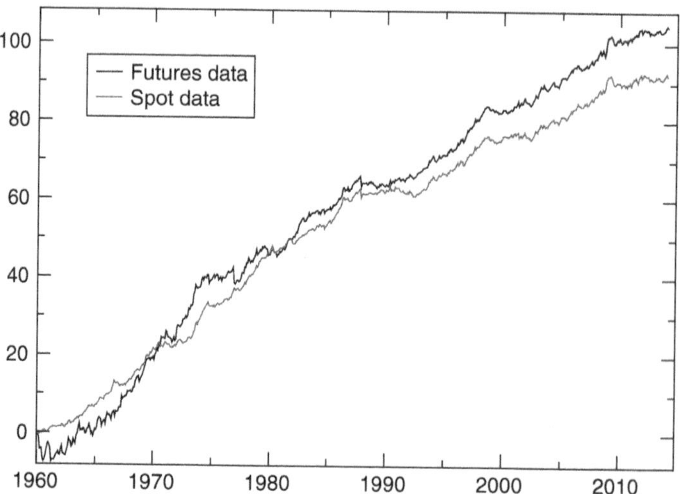

FIGURE 20.3: Trend on Spot and on Futures Prices

The overall agreement since the late 1960s (when the number of traded futures contracts becomes significant) is very good, although the average slope on spots is slightly smaller, as expected.

TABLE 20.7: Correlation between Spot and Futures Trend Following Strategies

Sector	Spot–Future Correlation
Commodities	0.65
Bonds	0.91
Indexes	0.92

Even though the "cost of carry" plays an important role for commodities, the trends are still highly correlated.

We therefore feel justified in using the spot data to build statistics over a long history. We believe that the performance will be close to (and in any case, no worse than) that on real futures, in particular because average financing costs are small, as illustrated by Figure 20.3.

Trend over Two Centuries

Results of the Full Simulation

The performance of the trend-following strategy defined by Equation 2.2 over the entire time period (two centuries) is shown in Figure 20.4. It is visually clear that the performance is highly significant. This is confirmed by the value of the t-statistic, which is found to be above 10, and 9.8 when debiased from the long-only contribution, i.e., the t-statistic of "excess" returns. For comparison, the t-statistic of the drift μ of the same time series is 4.6. As documented in Table 20.8, the performance is furthermore significant on each individual sector, with a t-statistic of 2.9 or higher, and 2.7 or higher when the long bias is removed. Note that the debiased t-statistic of the trend is in fact higher than the t-statistic of the long-only strategy, with the exception of commodities, where it is slightly worse (3.1 versus 4.5).

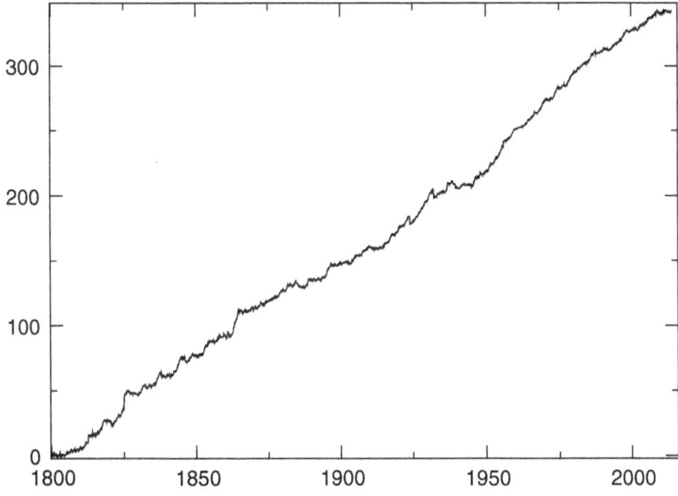

FIGURE 20.4: Aggregate Performance of the Trend on All Sectors
t-statistic = 10.5. Debiased t-statistic = 9.8. Sharpe ratio = 0.72.

TABLE 20.8: Sharpe Ratio and t-Statistic of the Trend (T), of the Debiased Trend (T^*) and of the Drift Component μ of the Different Sectors, with the Starting Date for Each Sector

Sector	SR (T)	t-Statistic (T)	t-Statistic (T^*)	SR (μ)	t-Statistic (μ)	Start Date
Currencies	0.47	2.9	2.9	0.1	0.63	1973
Commodities	0.28	4.1	3.1	0.3	4.5	1800
Bonds	0.4	3.9	2.7	–0.1	–1	1918
Indexes	0.7	10.2	6.3	0.4	5.7	1800

The performance is also remarkably constant over two centuries: this is obvious from Figure 20.4, and we report the t-statistic for different periods in Table 20.9. The overall performance is in fact positive over every decade in the sample (see Figure 20.7). The increase in performance in the second half of the simulation probably comes from the fact that we have more and more products as time goes on (indeed, government yields and currencies both start well into the twentieth century).

TABLE 20.9: Sharpe Ratio and t-Statistic of the Trend and of the Drift μ over Periods of Fifty Years

Period	SR (T)	t-Statistic (T)	SR (μ)	t-Statistic (μ)
1800–1850	0.6	4.2	0.06	0.4
1850–1900	0.57	3.7	0.43	3.0
1900–1950	0.81	5.7	0.34	2.4
After 1950	0.99	7.9	0.41	2.9

A Closer Look at the Signal

It is interesting to delve deeper into the predictability of the trend-following signal $s_n(t)$, defined in Equation 2.1. Instead of computing the P&L given by Equation 2.2, we can instead look at the scatter plot of $\Delta(t) = p(t + 1) - p(t)$ as a function of $s_n(t)$. This gives a noisy blob of points with, to the naked eye, very little structure. However, a regression line through the points leads to a statistically significant slope, i.e., $\Delta(t) = a + bs_n(t) + \xi(t)$, where $a = 0{:}018 \pm 0.003$, $b = 0{:}038 \pm 0.002$, and ξ is a noise term. The fact that $a > 0$ is equivalent to saying that the long-only strategy is, on average, profitable, whereas $b > 0$ indicates the presence of trends. However, it is not *a priori* obvious that we should expect a linear relation between Δ and s_n. Trying a cubic regression gives a very small coefficient for the s_n^2 term and a clearly negative coefficient for the s_n^3 term, indicating that strong signals tend to flatten, as suggested by a running average of the signal shown in Figure 20.5. However, the strong mean reversion that such a negative cubic contribution would predict for large values of *sn* is suspicious. We have therefore instead tried to model a nonlinear saturation through a hyperbolic tangent (Figure 20.5):

$$\Delta(t) = a + bs^* \tanh\left(\frac{s_n(t)}{s^*}\right) + \xi(t), \tag{4.1}$$

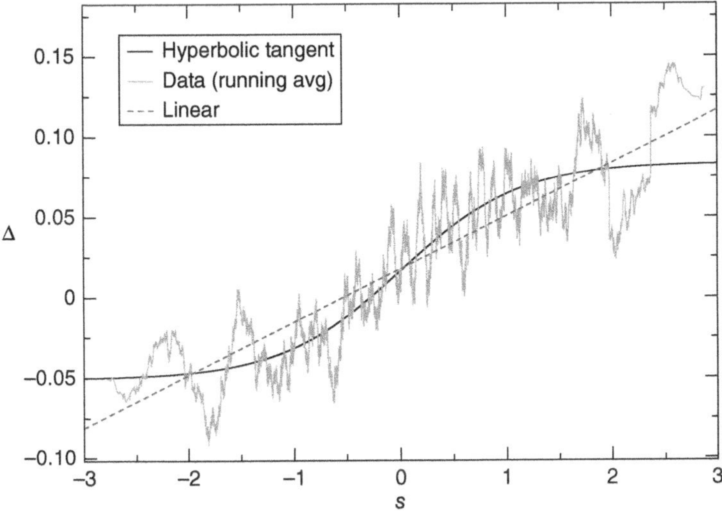

FIGURE 20.5: Fit of the Scatter Plot of $\Delta(t) = p(t+1) - p(t)$ as a Function of $s_n(t)$, for $n = 5$ Months, and for Futures Data Only

We do not show the 240,000 points on which the fits are performed, but rather show a running average over 5,000 consecutive points along the *x*-axis. We also show the results of a linear and hyperbolic tangent fit. Note the positive intercept $a \approx 0.02$, which indicates the overall positive long-only bias. The best fit to the data is provided by the hyperbolic tangent, which suggests a saturation of the signal for large values.

which recovers the linear regime when $|s_n| \ll s^*$ but saturates for $|s_n| > s^*$. This nonlinear fit is found to be better than the cubic fit as well as the linear fit, as it prefers a finite value $s^* \approx 0.89$ and now $b \approx 0.075$ (a linear fit is recovered in the limit $s^* \to \infty$). Interestingly, the values of a, b, and s^* hardly change when n increases from 2.5 months to 10 months.

A Closer Look at the Recent Performance

The plateau in the performance of the trend over the last few years (see Figure 20.6) has received a lot of attention from CTA managers and investors. Among other explanations, the overcrowdedness of the strategy has frequently been evoked to explain this relatively poor performance. We now want to reconsider these conclusions in the context of the long-term simulation.

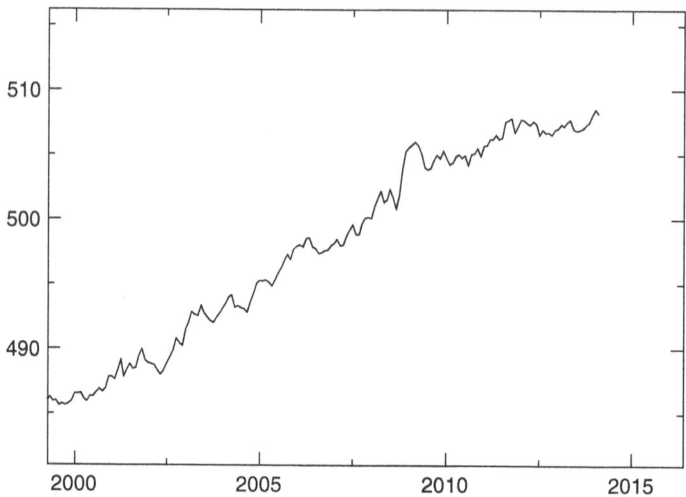

FIGURE 20.6: Recent Performance of the Trend
Since 2011, the strategy is virtually flat.

First, it should not come as a surprise that a strategy with a historical Sharpe ratio below 0.8 shows relatively long drawdowns. In fact, the typical duration of a drawdown is given by $1 = S^2$ (in years) for a strategy of Sharpe ratio S. This means that, for a Sharpe of 0.7, typical drawdowns last two years, while drawdowns of four years are not exceptional (see Bouchaud and Potters 2003 and Seager et al. 2014 for more on this topic).

To see how significant the recent performance is, we have plotted in Figure 20.7 the average P&L between time t – 10Y and time t. We find that, though we are currently slightly below the historical average, this is by no means an exceptional situation. A much worse performance was in fact observed in the 1940s. Figure 20.7 also reveals that the 10-year performance of trend following has, as noted above, never been negative in two centuries, which is again a strong indication that trend following is ingrained in the evolution of prices.

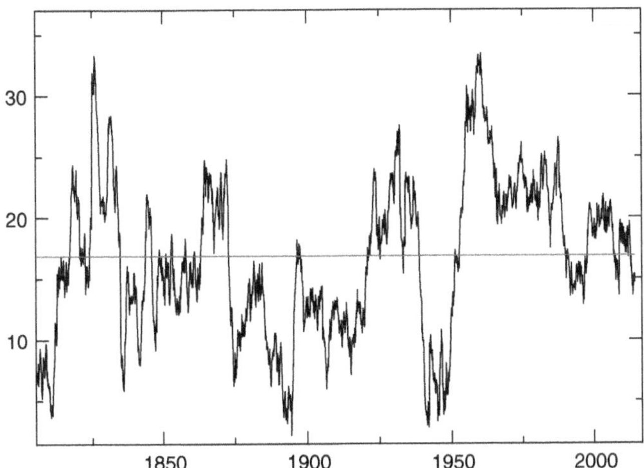

FIGURE 20.7: Ten-Year Cumulated Performance of the Trend (Arbitrary Units)
The horizontal line is the historical average.

The above conclusion is however only valid for long-term trends, with a horizon of several months. Much shorter trends (say, over three days) have significantly decayed since 1990 (see Figure 20.8). This is perfectly in line with a recent study by the Winton group (Duke et al. 2013). We will now propose a tentative interpretation of these observations.

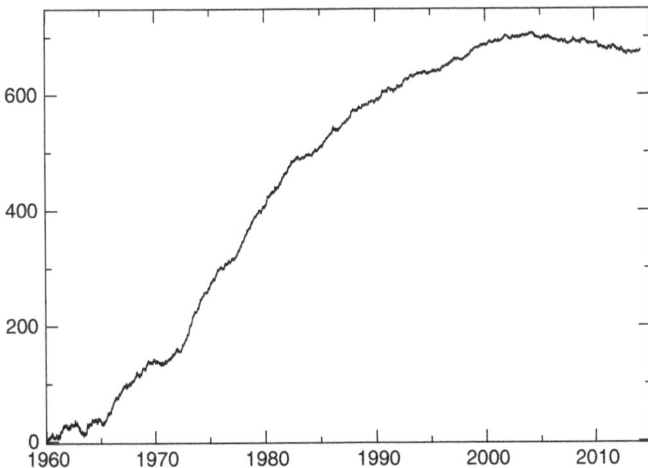

FIGURE 20.8: Performance of a Three-Day Trend on Futures Contracts since 1970
The effect seems to have completely disappeared since 2003 (or has maybe even inverted).

Interpretation

The above results show that long-term trends exist across all asset classes and are stable in time. As mentioned in the Introduction, trending behavior is also observed in the idiosyncratic component of individual stocks (Barroso and Santa-Clara 2013; Kent and Moskowitz 2013; Narasimhan and Titman 1993, 2011; Geczy and Samonov, 2016). What can explain such universal, persistent behavior of prices? We can find two (possibly complementary) broad families of interpretation in the literature. One explanation assumes that agents underreact to news and only progressively include the available information in prices (Hong and Stein 1999; Kent et al. 1998). An example of this could be an announced sequence of rate increases by a central bank over several months, which is not immediately reflected in bond prices because market participants tend to only believe in what they see and are slow to change their previous expectations ("conservatism bias"). In general, changes of policy (for governments, central banks, or indeed companies) are slow and progressive. If correctly anticipated, prices should immediately reflect the end point of the policy change. Otherwise, prices will progressively follow the announced changes and this inertia leads to trends.

Another distinct mechanism is that market participants' expectations are directly influenced by past trends: positive returns make them optimistic about future prices and vice versa. These "extrapolative expectations" are supported by "learning to predict" experiments in artificial markets (Hommes et al. 2008; Smith et al. 1988), which show that linear extrapolation is a strongly anchoring strategy. In a complex world where information is difficult to decipher, trend following—together with herding—is one of the "fast and frugal" heuristics (Gigerenzer and Goldstein 1996) that most people are tempted to use (Bouchaud 2013). Survey data also points strongly in this direction (Greenwood and Shleifer 2014; Menkhoff 2011; Shiller 2000).[8] Studies of agent-based models in fact show that the imbalance between trend following and fundamental pricing is crucial in accounting for some of the stylized facts of financial markets, such as fat tails and volatility clustering (see, for example, Barberis et al. 2013; Giardina and Bouchaud 2003; Hommes 2006; Lux and Marchesi 2000).[9] Clearly, the perception of trends can lead to positive-feedback trading, which reinforces the existence of trends rather than making them disappear (Bouchaud and Cont 1998; DeLong et al. 1990; Wyart and Bouchaud 2007).

On this last point, we note that the existence of trends far predates the explosion of assets managed by CTAs. The data shown above suggests that CTAs have neither substantially increased nor substantially reduced the strength of long-term trends in major financial markets. While the degradation in recent performance, although not statistically significant, might be attributed to overcrowding of trending strategies, it is not entirely clear how this would happen in the "extrapolative expectations" scenario, which tends to be self-reinforcing (see, for example, Wyart and Bouchaud 2007 for an explicit model). If, on the other hand, underreaction is the main driver of trends in financial markets, we may indeed see trends disappear as market participants better anticipate long-term policy changes (or indeed policy makers become more easily predictable). Still, the empirical evidence supporting a behavioral trend following propensity seems to us strong enough to advocate extrapolative expectations over underreactions. It would be interesting to build a detailed behavioral model that explains why the trending signal saturates at high values, as evidenced in Figure 20.5. One plausible interpretation is that, when prices become more obviously out of line, fundamentalist traders start stepping in, and this mitigates the impact of trend followers, who are still lured in by the strong trend (see Bouchaud and Cont 1998, Lux and Marchesi 2000, and Greenwood and Shleifer 2014 for similar stories).

Conclusions

In this study, we established the existence of anomalous excess returns based on trend following strategies across all asset classes and over very long time scales. We first studied futures, as is customary, then spot data that allows us to go far back in history. We carefully justified our procedure, in particular by comparing the results on spot data in the recent period, which shows a strong correlation with futures, with very similar drifts. The only sector where we found no way to extend the history is for foreign exchange, since the idea of a free-floating currency is a rather recent one. We found that the trend has been a very persistent feature of all the financial markets we looked at. The overall t-statistic of the excess returns has been around 10 since 1800, after accounting for the long-only bias. Furthermore, the excess returns associated to trends cannot be associated to any sort of risk premium (Lempérière et al. 2014; Narasimhan and Titman 2011). The effect is very stable, across both time and asset classes. It makes the existence of trends one of the most statistically significant anomalies in financial markets. When analyzing the trend-following signal further, we found a clear saturation effect for large signals, suggesting that fundamentalist traders do not attempt to resist "weak trends," but might step in when their own signal becomes strong enough.

We investigated the statistical significance of the recent mediocre performance of the trend, and found that this was actually in line with a long historical back-test. Therefore, the suggestion that long-term trend following has become overcrowded is not borne out by our analysis and is compatible with our estimate that CTAs only contribute a few percent of market volumes. Still, the understanding of the behavioral causes of trends, and in particular the relative role of "extrapolative expectations" versus "underreaction" or "conservative biases," would allow us to form an educated opinion on the long-term viability of trend following strategies. It is actually not obvious how crowdedness would deteriorate trend following strategies, since more trend following should speed up trends as managers attempt to "front-run" the competition. Figure 20.8, however, adds to the conundrum by showing that faster trends have actually progressively disappeared in recent years, without ever showing an intermediate period where they strengthened. Coming up with a plausible mechanism that explains how these fast trends have disappeared would be highly valuable in understanding the fate of trends in financial markets.

21

Trend Following
Quality, Not Quantity

Anthony Todd and Martin Lueck
Aspect Capital

Overview

Investors typically seek to exploit the power of diversification: It is possible to improve risk-adjusted returns simply by combining different diversifying strategies of similar risk and return. In this paper, we ask if this approach should be applied to trend following models. There are many different methods of creating trend following models, and we consider a wide range of common approaches to investigate whether the combination of several of these models can lead to improved performance, or whether there is a better way to construct a trend following system.

We show how different trend following models, when applied to the same portfolio of markets and operated at similar speeds, generally have high correlations with each other and thus offer limited diversification benefits. We also demonstrate that a better approach to trend following is to apply a holistic methodology which aims to capture the most effective features of many different techniques and to integrate them in a single high-calibre model. We demonstrate that Aspect's own trend following model, which has evolved over many years through innovative research that essentially combines the benefits of multiple different approaches, is such an example.

Introduction to Different Trend Following Models

In this paper we consider a group of 13 different trend following models. All the models have been applied to the same portfolio of 146 markets and have been parameterized such that they all capture medium-term trends of approximately two to three months in duration and generate the same levels of annualised return volatility. For the purposes of this analysis we do not include the impact of trading costs, as we are purely focused on the difference between various trend following approaches, and they will be broadly equivalent across the set of consistent time-scale models.

The origins of these 13 models are varied, but all are in the public domain. They include models popularized by the "TurtleTraders" of the 1980s,[1] models that have been regularly cited in recent years in academic literature, and a number of other well-known trend-capture techniques including look-back and look-forward windows, moving average approaches, technical indicators, and other statistical methods.

Figure 21.1 compares the performance of all these models over the period January 1999 to June 2016, and Figure 21.2 compares the models' information ratios, a measure of return for a given level of risk. The performance of the different models is generally fairly consistent and the average information ratio achieved in simulation by the 13 trend following models is 0.95, with the maximum being 1.10. (Explanations of all abbreviations used in the figures can be found in the Appendix of this chapter.)

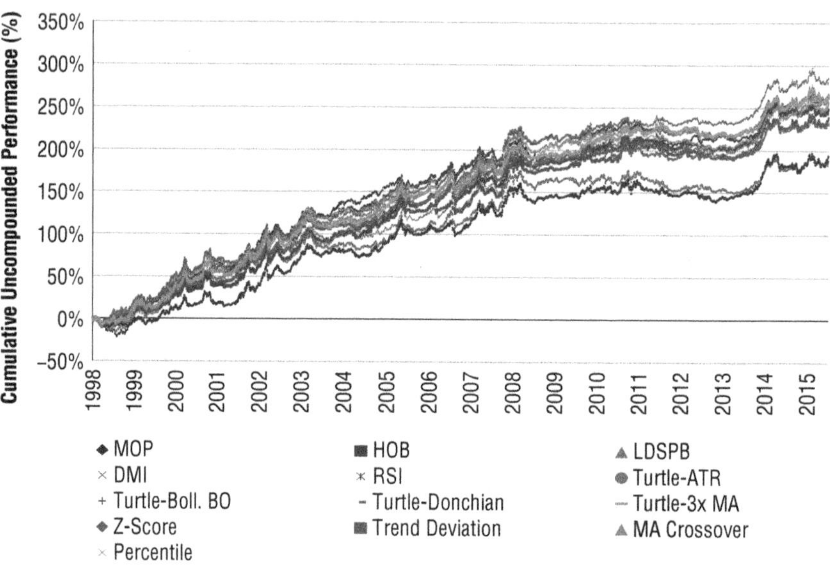

FIGURE 21.1: Simulated Performance of Trend Following Models: January 1999 to June 2016

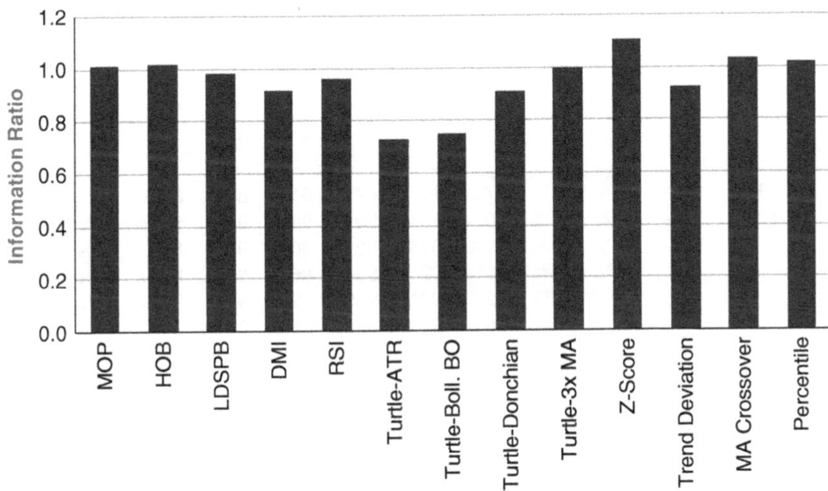

FIGURE 21.2: Simulated Risk-Adjusted Performance of Trend Following Models: January 1999

Diversification between Different Trend Following Models

When different diversifying strategies of similar risk and return are combined, better risk-adjusted returns might be expected through the lower volatility achieved as a result of the diversification. In this section we consider whether the combination of different trend following models can lead to improved performance.

While the 13 models we have introduced represent a broad range of different approaches to systematic medium-term trend capture, we find that they are highly correlated to each other. Figure 21.3 shows the correlations between the 13 models, again over the January 1999 to June 2016 period. The lowest correlation we see is 67% (between the MOP and Turtle-ATR models), while the average correlation between models is 89%.

As a first step in investigating whether a combination of these models is preferable, Figure 21.4 shows the performance of a strategy which is a simple average of all the 13 models, obtained by blending the output returns from each on a daily basis (and adjusting for the slight reduction in volatility that results).

	MOP	HOB	LDSPB	DMI	RSI	Turtle-ATR	Turtle-Boll. BO	Turtle-Donchian	Turtle-3x MA	Z-Score	Trend Deviation	MA Crossover	Percentile
MOP	100%	86%	90%	67%	75%	67%	71%	67%	81%	86%	80%	83%	85%
HOB		100%	95%	88%	94%	90%	89%	90%	94%	95%	93%	97%	95%
LDSPB			100%	81%	88%	81%	83%	82%	90%	92%	87%	94%	91%
DMI				100%	94%	90%	92%	90%	86%	88%	87%	89%	88%
RSI					100%	92%	92%	93%	92%	92%	91%	94%	94%
Turtle-ATR						100%	91%	92%	89%	88%	89%	91%	89%
Turtle-Boll. BO							100%	88%	88%	89%	88%	90%	88%
Turtle-Donchian								100%	85%	91%	83%	92%	90%
Turtle-3x MA									100%	90%	96%	94%	93%
Z-Score										100%	89%	97%	96%
Trend Deviation											100%	93%	92%
MA Crossover												100%	95%
Percentile													100%

FIGURE 21.3: Simulated Correlations between Trend Following Models: Jan 1999 to Jun 2016

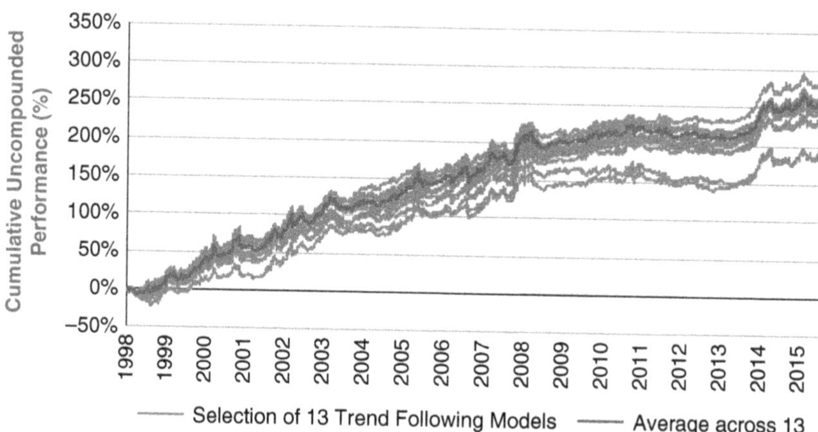

FIGURE 21.4: Simulated Performance of Trend Following Models and Average across all 13: Jan 1999 to Jun 2016

We see from Figure 21.4 that the performance of the averaged strategy is comparable to the performance of some of the individual models. In addition, its information ratio is 1.00, which is only slightly better than the average of the individual model information ratios of 0.95. As a consequence of the high levels of correlation between the individual models, the diversification benefit that arises from combining them is only slight.

To investigate this further, we consider all possible equally weighted combinations of the 13 models under consideration and determine the average risk-adjusted return as the number of models combined is varied. We start with just one model (of which there are 13 to choose from), and then in turn consider combinations of two, three, four, etc. up to the final combination of 13 models. Significantly, Figure 21.5 shows that there is very little diversification benefit to be had from combining models, as the impact on average risk-adjusted performance is insignificant.

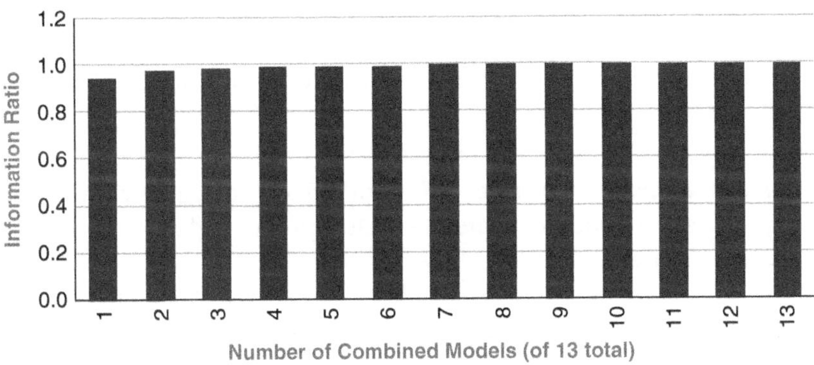

FIGURE 21.5: Simulated Average Information Ratios from Combining Different Trend Following Models: January 1999 to June 2016

Aspect's Approach to Trend Following

The results of the previous section suggest that, due to the high levels of correlation, diversification between different trend following models is illusory. Instead, Aspect takes the holistic view that if the goal is to maximize performance from trend following, it is better to build the best possible single trend following model that integrates distinguishing features of many different approaches.

Aspect's trend following model has been developed over many years of rigorous, scientific, and hypothesis-based research, incorporating features of multiple different approaches in a carefully considered, coherent framework. (Aspect's trend following model referenced in this paper is that which has an allocation of 80% within the Aspect Diversified

Programme.*) One of the major research innovations in Aspect's history was its move in 2005 from a multi-model approach to trend following to a single, holistic approach.

As an example of an Aspect innovation capitalizing on a feature of one family of models, some breakout models use methods to calculate a high and low range for their channels, but do so with a coarse binary signal construction. This observation led us to research more thoroughly the usefulness of considering channel data as part of our "data processing" stage, and has enabled us to refine the way our trend following model deals with specific market moves. This approach has enabled us to make the most of the diversifying features of breakout models, while at the same time avoiding its less desirable limiting features (i.e., its coarse binary signal construction).

Our research has led to a number of key trend following innovations over the years, which fall into three main stages within our single holistic model.

- *Data processing*: This stage deals with the way in which market data is processed in order to create the most appropriate data series for the trend measurement stage.
- *Trend measurement*: This stage filters the processed data, in order to measure the strength and direction of trends.
- *Position mapping*: Having determined appropriate trend measurements, these are then mapped to appropriately sized positions.

Figure 21.6 shows the performance of a base trend following model built by Aspect which still benefits from many of Aspect's portfolio construction, position-sizing, and risk management processes, but uses a simple trend following approach. Its performance is similar to some of the 13 strategies considered earlier. The chart also shows the simulated performance enhancements that arise from Aspect's research improvements over this base trend following model. Each of these enhancements adds value to Aspect's trend following model incrementally and consistently; the simulated information ratios also rise steadily from 0.76 for the base trend following model, to 1.41 for Aspect's full trend following model.

*The remaining 20% allocation comprises other complementary systematic models, carefully designed to modulate the trend following positions.

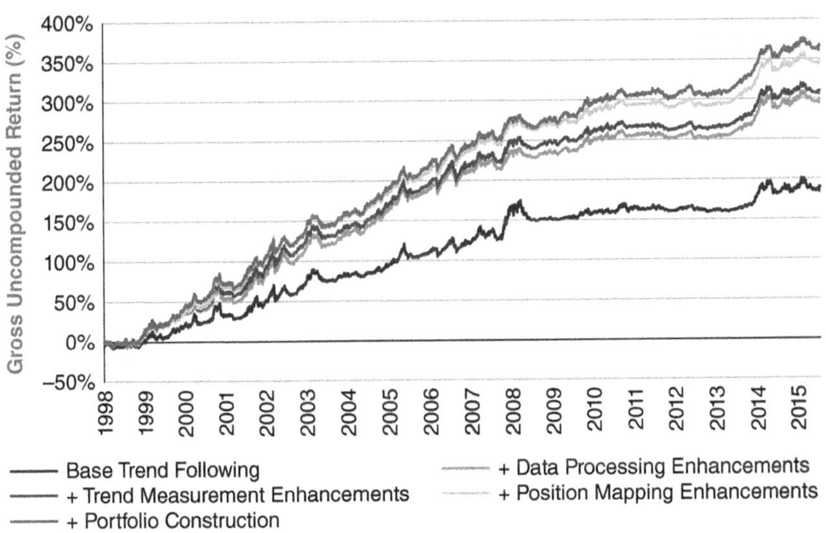

FIGURE 21.6: Aspect's Trend Following Model Simulated Performance Improvements: January 1999 to June 2016

Aspect's Model Compared to Other Trend Following Models

Our principled approach, in which we observe different features of trend following, learn from them, and integrate innovations to our model based on this research, is a key part of Aspect's systematic investment process. In our view, this approach is superior to combining multiple different trend following models.

In Figure 21.7 we compare the 13 models with Aspect's trend following model, developed over almost 20 years of evolutionary research. We see that Aspect's holistic trend following model outperforms all of the 13 models over the period under consideration. Aspect's information ratio of 1.41 is also superior to those of the other models.

The results support the argument that if the goal is to maximize performance from trend following, it is better to build the best possible single trend following model that integrates features of various approaches rather than relying on diversification from different models.

Additionally, if we subdivide the period into five-year windows, we see that Aspect's integrated approach outperforms in each individual window, as shown in Figure 21.8. By contrast, among the 13 other trend following models, there is almost no consistency in performance between the different five-year windows.

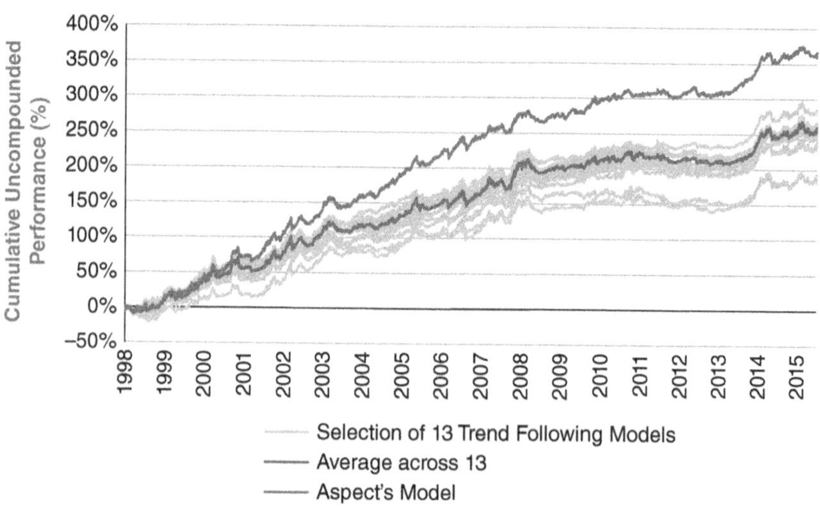

FIGURE 21.7: Simulated Performance of Trend Following Models versus Aspect's Trend Following Model: January 1999 to June 2016

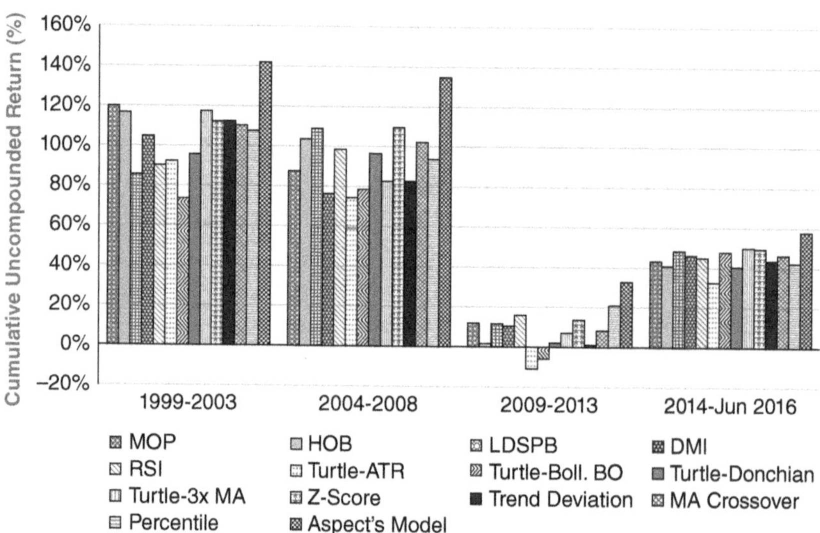

FIGURE 21.8: Simulated Performance of Trend Following Models versus Aspect's Trend Following Model: January 1999 to June 2016

Finally we demonstrate that Aspect's model cannot be improved by adding any of the 13 models considered earlier. Figure 21.9 shows the effect on the risk-adjusted return when Aspect's trend following model is blended with any of the other 13 models.

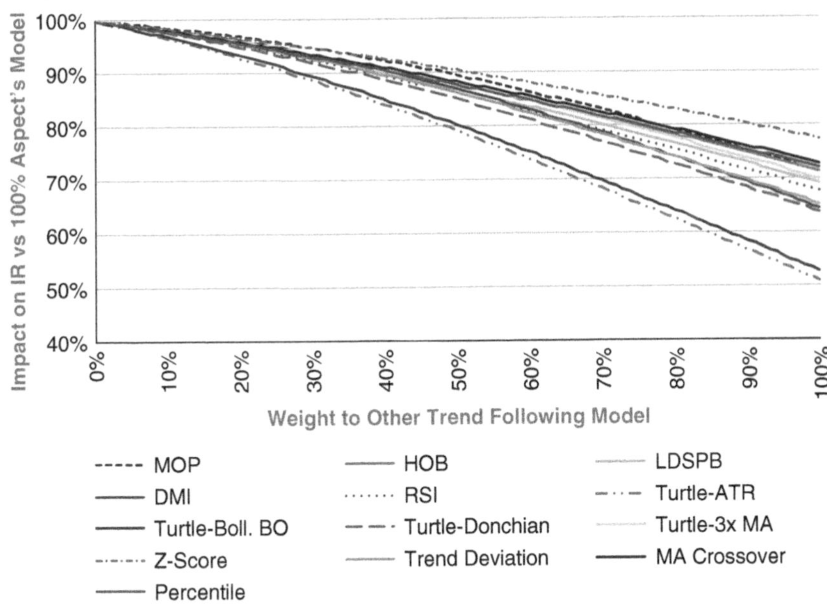

FIGURE 21.9: Simulated Impact on Aspect's Model Information Ratio from Adding Other Trend Following Models: Jan 1999 to Jun 2016

Again we see that the best option is to choose only Aspect's holistic trend following model, as any combination with other models will degrade its performance.

Conclusion

This paper considers the question of how to build the best trend following system: either to focus on building a single, high-quality model that combines the best features of other trend following approaches, or to adopt a multi-model approach to trend following, relying on diversification between models to improve the overall risk-return profile.

We have considered a wide range of different systematic models that all capture medium-term trend following, and have investigated whether any combinations of these models provide the best outcome. Given the high levels of correlation between the strategies, we actually find that there is very little diversification to be had.

In summary, the number of individual trend following models that comprise a trend following portfolio is not in itself a measure of its superiority. The best approach is to focus on building a single, well-researched trend following model that integrates key features of many different trend following approaches in a superior, coherent framework. Aspect applies an ongoing research effort in order to continue to enhance its trend following model in this way.

Chart Disclaimer

The 13 trend following models and aspect diversified's results are based on simulated or hypothetical performance results that have certain limitations. Unlike the results shown in an actual performance record, these results do not represent actual trading. Past performance is not necessarily indicative of future results.

22 Evaluating Trading Strategies

Campbell R. Harvey and Yan Liu

Consider the following trading strategy detailed in Figure 22.1.[1] While there is a minor drawdown in the first year, the strategy is consistently profitable through 2014. Indeed, the drawdowns throughout the history are minimal. Importantly, the strategy even does well during the financial crisis. Overall, this strategy appears very attractive and many investment managers would pursue this strategy.

Our research (see Harvey and Liu, 2014 and Harvey, Liu, and Zhu, 2014) offers some tools to evaluate strategies such as the one presented in Figure 22.1. It turns out that simply looking at average profitability, consistency, and size of drawdowns is not sufficient to give a strategy a passing grade.

Testing in Other Fields of Science

Before presenting our method, it is important to take a step back and determine whether there is anything we can learn in finance from other scientific fields. While the advent of machine learning is relatively new to

---

Campbell R. Harvey, Duke University, Durham, NC USA 27708; National Bureau of Economic Research, Cambridge, MA USA 02138; and Man Group, PLC, London, UK EC4R 3AD. Yan Liu, Duke University, Durham, NC USA 27708 and Texas A&M University, College Station, TX USA 77843. Version: August 25, 2014. First posted to SSRN: July 31, 2014. The paper has benefitted from comments from seminar participants at AHL as well as comments from Marco Buchmann.

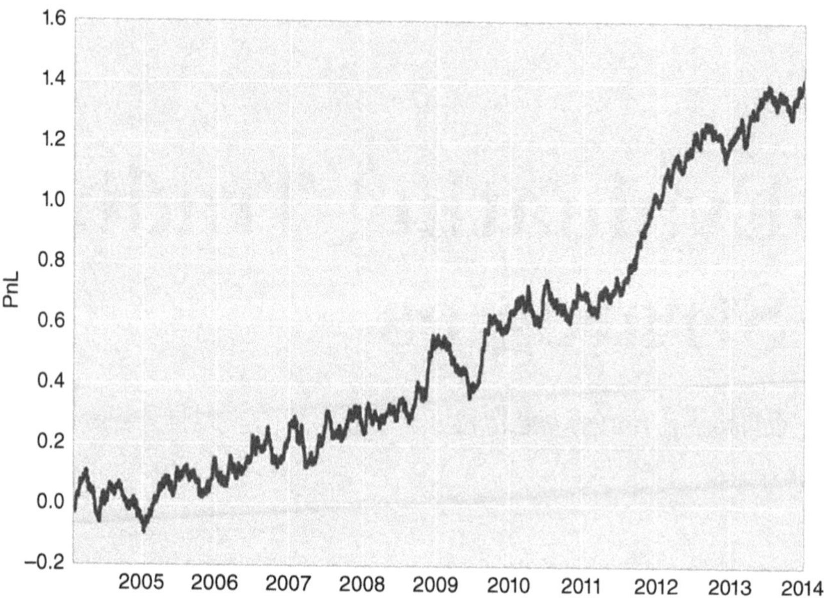

FIGURE 22.1: A Candidate Trading Strategy

investment management, similar situations involving a large number of tests have been around for many years in other sciences. It makes sense that there may be some insights outside of finance that are relevant for finance.

Our first example is the widely heralded discovery of the Higgs Boson in 2012. The particle was first theorized in 1964—the same year as William Sharpe's paper on the capital asset pricing model (CAPM) was published.[2] The first tests of the CAPM were published eight years later[3] and Sharpe was awarded a Nobel Prize in 1990. For Peter Higgs, it was a much longer road. It took years to complete the Large Hadron Collider (LHC) at a cost of about $5 billion.[4] The Higgs Boson was declared "discovered" on July 4, 2012 and Nobel Prizes were awarded in 2013.[5]

So why is this relevant for finance? It has to do with the testing method. Scientists knew that the particle was rare and that it decays very quickly. The idea of the LHC is to have beams of particles collide. Theoretically, you would expect to see the Higgs Boson in one in 10 billion collisions within the LHC.[6] The Boson quickly decays and key is measuring the decay signature. Over a quadrillion collisions were conducted and a massive amount of data was collected. The problem is that each of the so-called decay signatures can also be produced by normal events from known processes.

To declare a discovery, scientists agreed to what appeared to be [a] very tough standard. The observed occurrences of the candidate particle (Higgs Boson) had to be five standard deviations different from a world where there was no new particle. Five standard deviations is generally considered a tough standard. Yet in finance, we routinely accept discoveries where the *t*-statistic exceeds two—not five. Indeed, there is a hedge fund called Two Sigma.

Particle physics is not alone in having a tougher hurdle to exceed. Consider the research done in bio-genetics. In genetic association studies, researchers try to link a certain disease to human genes and they do this by testing the causal effect between the disease and a gene. Given that there are more than 20,000 human genes that are expressive, multiple testing is a real issue. To make it even more challenging, a disease is often not caused by a single gene but the interactions among several genes. Counting all the possibilities, the total number of tests can easily exceed a million. Given this large number of tests, a tougher standard must be applied. With the conventional thresholds, a large percentage of studies that document significant associations are not replicable.[7]

To give an example, a recent study in *Nature* claims to find two genetic linkages for Parkinson's disease.[8] About a half a million genetic sequences are tested for the potential association with the disease. Given this large number of tests, tens of thousands of genetic sequences will appear to affect the disease under conventional standards. We need a tougher standard to lower the possibility of false discoveries. Indeed, the identified gene loci from the tests have *t*-statistics that exceed 5.3.

There are many more examples such as the search for exoplanets. However, there is a common theme in these examples. A higher threshold is required because the number of tests is large. For the Higgs Boson, there were potentially trillions of tests. For research in bio-genetics, there are millions of combinations. With multiple tests, there is a chance of a fluke finding.

Revaluating the Candidate Strategy

Let's return to the candidate trading strategy detailed in Figure 22.1. This strategy has a Sharpe ratio of 0.92. There is a simple formula to translate the Sharpe ratio into a *t*-statistic[9]:

$$t\text{-statistic} = \text{Sharpe Ratio} \times \sqrt{\text{Number of years}}$$

In this case, the t-statistic is 2.91. This means that the observed profitability is about three standard deviations from the null hypothesis of zero profitability. A three-sigma event (assuming a normal distribution) happens only 1% of the time. This means that the chance that our trading strategy is a false discovery is less than 1%.

However, we are making a fundamental mistake with the statistical analysis. The statement about the false discovery percentage [is] conditional on an independent test. This means there is a single test. That is unlikely to be the case in our trading strategy and it was certainly not the case with the research conducted at the LHC where there were trillions of tests. With multiple tests, we need to adjust our hurdles for establishing statistical significance. This is the reason why the researchers at LRC used a five-sigma rule. This is the reason why bio-medical researchers routinely look for four-sigma events.

Multiple testing is also salient in finance—yet little has been done to adjust the way that we conduct our tests. Figure 22.2 completes the trading strategy example.[10]

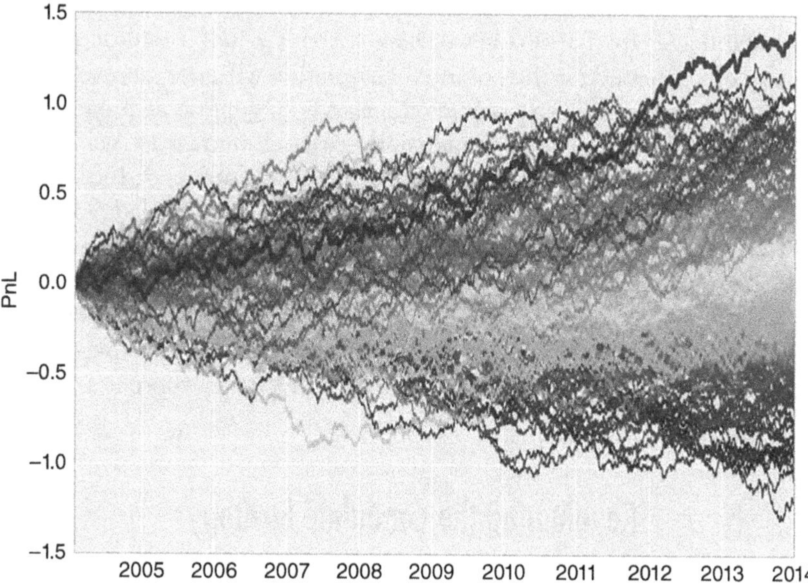

FIGURE 22.2: Two Hundred Randomly Generated Trading Strategies

Each of the trading strategies in Figure 22.2 was randomly generated at the daily frequency. We assumed an annual volatility of 15% (about the same as the S&P 500) and a mean return of zero. The candidate trading strategy highlighted in Figure 22.1 is the best strategy in Figure 22.2 (thick gray curve ending near top right corner of chart).

To be clear, all of the strategies in Figure 22.2 are based on random numbers—not actual returns. While the candidate trading strategy in Figure 22.1 seemed very attractive, it was simply a fluke. Yet the usual tools of statistical analysis would have declared this strategy "significant." The techniques we will offer in this paper will declare the candidate strategy, with the Sharpe ratio of 0.92, insignificant.

It is crucial to correct for multiple testing. Consider a simple example which has some similarities to the above. Suppose we are interested in predicting Y. We propose a candidate variable X. We run a regression and get a *t*-statistic of 2.0. Assuming that no one else had tried to predict Y before, this qualifies as an independent test and X would be declared significant at the 5% level. Now let's change the problem. Suppose we still want to predict Y. However, now we have 20 different X variables, X_1, X_2, . . . ,X_{20}. Suppose one of these variables achieves a *t*-statistic of 2.0. Is it really a true predictor? Probably not. By random chance, when you try so many variables, one might work.

Here is another classic example of multiple tests. Suppose you receive a promotional e-mail from an investment manager promoting a stock. The e-mail asks you to judge the record of recommendations in real time. Only a single stock is recommended and the recommendation is either long or short. You get an e-mail every week for 10 weeks. Each week the manager is correct. The track record is amazing because the probability of such an occurrence is very small ($0.5^{10} = 0.000976$). Conventional statistics would say there is a very small chance (0.00976% this is a false discovery, i.e., the manager is no good). You hire the manager.

Later you find out the strategy. The manager randomly picks a stock and initially sends out 100,000 e-mails with 50% saying long and 50% saying short. If the stock goes up in value, the next week's mailing list is trimmed to 50,000 (only sending to the long recommendations). Every week the list is reduced by 50%. By the end of the 10th week, 97 people would have received this "amazing" track record of 10 correct picks in a row.

If these 97 people had realized how the promotion was organized, then getting 10 in a row would be expected. Indeed, you get the 97 people by multiplying $100{,}000 \times 0.5.^{10}$ There is no skill here. It is random.

There are many obvious applications. One that is immediate is in the evaluation of fund managers. With over 10,000 managers, you expect some to randomly outperform year after year.[11] Indeed, if managers were randomly choosing strategies, you would expect at least 300 of them to have five consecutive years of outperformance.

Our research offers some guidance on handling these multiple testing problems.

Two Views of Multiple Testing

There are two main approaches to the multiple testing problem in statistics. They are known as the Family-wise Error Rate (FWER) and the False Discovery Rate. The distinction between the two is very intuitive.

In the Family-wise Error Rate, it is unacceptable to make a single false discovery. This is a very severe rule but completely appropriate for certain situations. With the FWER, one false discovery is unacceptable in 100 tests and equally as unacceptable in 1,000,000 tests. In contrast, the False Discovery Rate views "unacceptable" in terms of a proportion. For example, if one false discovery was unacceptable for 100 tests, then 10 are unacceptable for 1,000 tests. The FDR is much less severe than the FWER.

Which is the more appropriate method? It depends on the application. For instance, the Mars One foundation is planning a one-way manned trip to Mars in 2024 and has plans for many additional landings.[12] It is unacceptable to have any critical part fail during the mission. A critical failure is an example is a false discovery (we thought the part was good but it was not—just as we thought the investment manager was good but she was not).

The best known FWER test is called the Bonferroni test. It is also the simplest test to implement. Suppose we start with a two-sigma rule for a single (independent) test. This would imply a *t*-ratio of 2.0. The interpretation is that the chance of the single false discovery is only 5% (remember a single false discovery is unacceptable). Equivalently, we can say that we have 95% confidence that we are not making a false discovery.

Now consider increasing the number of tests to 10. The Bonferroni method adjusts for the multiple tests. Given the chance that one test could randomly show up as significant, the Bonferroni requires the confidence level increase. Instead of 5%, you take the 5% and divide by the number of tests, i.e., 5% / 10 = 0.5%. Again equivalently, you need to be 99.5% confident with 10 tests that you are not making a single false discovery. In terms of the *t*-statistic, the Bonferroni requires a statistic of at least 2.8 for 10 tests. For 1,000 tests, the statistic must exceed 4.1.

However, there are three issues with the Bonferroni test. First, there is the general issue about FWER error rate vs. FDR. Evaluating a trading strategy is not a mission to Mars. Being wrong could cost you your job and money will be lost—but it is unlikely a matter of life and death. However, reasonable people may disagree with this view.

The second issue is related to correlation among the tests. There is a big difference between trying 10 variables that are all highly correlated and 10 variables that are completely unrelated. Indeed, at the extreme, if the 10 tests were perfectly correlated, this is equivalent to a single, independent test.

The third issue is that the Bonferroni test omits important information. Since the work of Holm (1979), it has been known that there is information in the individual collection of test statistics and can be used to sharpen the test.[13] The Bonferroni test ignores all this information and derives a hurdle rate from the original level of significance divided by the total number of tests.

Let's first tackle the last issue. Holm (1979) provides a way to deal with the information in the test statistics. Again, suppose we have 10 tests. We know that the hurdle for the Bonferroni method would be 0.005 or 0.5%.

The Holm method begins by sorting the tests from the lowest p-value (most significant) to the highest (least significant). Let's call the first $k = 1$ and the last $k = 10$. Starting from the first test, the Holm function is evaluated.

$$pk = \frac{a}{M+1-k}$$

Where α is the level of significance (0.05) in our case and M is the total number of tests.

Suppose the most significant test in our example has a p-value of 0.001. Calculating the Holm function we get .05 / (10 + 1 – 1) = .005. The Holm function gives the hurdle (observed p-value must be lower than the hurdle). Given the first test has a p-value of 0.001, it passes the test. Notice the hurdle for the first test is identical to the Bonferroni. However, in contrast to the Bonferroni which has a single threshold for all tests, the other tests will have a different hurdle under Holm, for example, the second test would be 0.05 / (10 + 1 – 2) = 0.0055.

Starting from the first test, we sequentially compare the p-values with their hurdles. When we first come across the test such that its p-value fails to meet the hurdle, we reject this test and all others with higher p-values.

The Holm test captures the information in the distribution of the test statistics. The Holm test is less stringent than the Bonferroni because the hurdles are relaxed after the first test. However, the Holm still fits into the category of the FWER. Next, we explore the other approach.

As mentioned earlier, the False Discovery Rate approach allows an expected proportional error rate (see Benjamini and Hochberg, 1995 and Benjamini and Yekutieli, 2001). As such it is less stringent than both the Bonferroni and the Holm test. It is also easy to implement. Again, we sort the tests. The BHY formula is:

$$Pk = \frac{(k * a)}{M * c(M)}$$

where $c(M)$ is a simple function that is increasing in M and equals 2.93 when $M = 10$.[14] In contrast to the Holm test, we start from the last test (least significant) and evaluate the BHY formula.

For the last test, $k = M = 10$, the BHY hurdle is $0.05 / c(10) = 0.05 / 2.93 = 0.0171$. For the second last test, $k = M - 1 = 9$, the BHY hurdle is $9 \times 0.05 / 10 \times 2.93 = 0.0154$. Notice that these hurdles are larger and thus more lenient that the Bonferroni implied hurdle (i.e., 0.0050).

Starting from the last test, we sequentially compare the p-values with their threshold. When we first come across the test such that its p-value falls below its threshold, we declare this test significant and all tests that have a lower p-value.

Similar to the Holm test, BHY also relies on the distribution of test statistics. However, in contrast to the Holm test that begins with the most significant test, the BHY approach starts with the least significant test.[15] There are usually more discoveries with BHY. The reason is that BHY allows for an expected proportion of false discoveries, which is less demanding than the absolute occurrence of false discoveries under the FWER approaches. We believe the BHY approach is the most appropriate for evaluating trading strategies.

False Discoveries and Missed Discoveries

So far we have discussed false discoveries which are trading strategies that appear to be profitable—but they are not. Multiple testing adjusts the hurdle for significance because some tests will appear significant by chance. The downside of doing this is that some truly significant strategies might be overlooked because they did not pass the more stringent hurdle.

This is the classic tension between Type I errors and Type II errors. The Type I error is the false discovery (investing in an unprofitable trading strategy). The Type II error is missing a truly profitable trading strategy. Inevitably there is a tradeoff between these two errors. In addition, in a multiple testing setting it is not obvious how to jointly optimize these two types of errors.

Our view is the following. Making the mistake of using the single test criteria for multiple tests induces a very large number of false discoveries (large amount of Type I error). When we increase the hurdle, we greatly reduce the Type I error at minimal cost to the Type II (missing discoveries). Figure 22.3 illustrates this point.

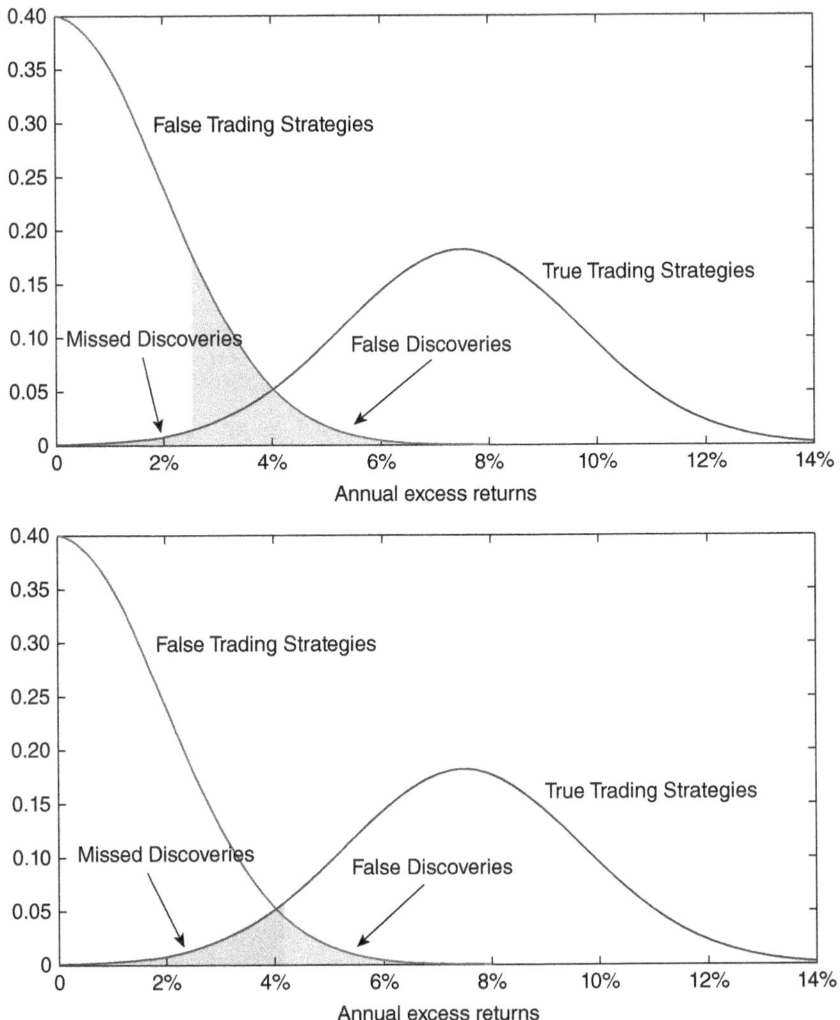

FIGURE 22.3: Panel A: False Trading Strategies, True Trading Strategies.
Panel B: False Trading Strategies, True Trading Strategies.

Panel A denotes the mistake of using single test methods. There are two distributions. The first is the distribution of strategies that don't work. It has an average return of zero. The second is the distribution of truly profitable strategies which has a mean return greater than zero. Notice that there is a large amount of Type I error (false discoveries).

Panel B shows what happens when we increase the threshold. Notice the number of false discoveries is dramatically reduced. However, the increase in missed discoveries is minimal.

Haircutting Sharpe Ratios

Harvey and Liu (2014) provide a method for adjusting Sharpe Ratios to take into account multiple testing. Sharpe Ratios based on historical backtests are often inflated because of multiple testing. Researchers explore many strategies and often choose to present the one with the largest Sharpe Ratio. But the Sharpe Ratio for this strategy no longer represents its true expected profitability. With a large number of tests, it is very likely that the selected strategy will appear to be highly profitable just by chance. To take this into account, we need to haircut the reported Sharpe Ratio. In addition, the haircut needs to be larger if there are more tests tried.

Take the candidate strategy in Figure 22.1 as an example. It has a Sharpe Ratio of 0.92 and a corresponding t-statistic of 2.91. The p-value is 0.4% and hence, if there were only one test, the strategy would look very attractive because there is only a 0.4% chance it is a fluke. However, with 200 tests tried, the story is completely different. Using the Bonferroni multiple testing method, we need to adjust the p-value cutoff to 0.05 / 200 = 0.00025. Hence, we would need to observe a t-statistic of at least 3.66 to declare the strategy a true discovery with 95% confidence. The observed t-statistic, 2.92, is well below 3.66—hence, we would pass on this strategy.

There is an equivalent way of looking at the Bonferroni test. To declare a strategy true, its p-value must be less than some predetermined threshold such as 5% (or 95% confidence that the identified strategy is not false):

$$p\text{-value of test} < \text{threshold}$$

Bonferroni divides the threshold (0.05) by the number of tests, our case 200:

$$p\text{-value of test} < .05/200$$

Equivalently, we could multiply the p-value of the individual test by 200 and check each test to identify which ones are less than .05, i.e.,

$$(p\text{-value of test}) \times 200 < 0.05$$

In our case, the original p-value is 0.004 and when [we] multiply by 200 the adjusted p-value is 0.80 and the corresponding t-statistic is 0.25. This high p-value is significantly greater than the threshold, 0.05. Our method asks how large the Sharpe Ratio should be in order to generate a t-statistic of 0.25. The answer is 0.08. Therefore, knowing that 200 tests have been tried and under Bonferroni's test, we successfully declare the candidate strategy with the original Sharpe Ratio of 0.92 as insignificant—the Sharpe Ratio that adjusts for multiple tests is only 0.08. The corresponding haircut is large, 91% (= (0.92 – 0.08) / 0.92).

Turning to the other two approaches, the Holm test makes the same adjustment as Bonferroni since the t-statistic for the candidate strategy is the smallest among the 200 strategies. Not surprisingly, BHY also strongly rejects the candidate strategy.

The fact that each of the multiple testing methods rejects the candidate strategy is a good outcome because we know all of these 200 strategies are just random numbers. A proper test also depends on the correlation among test statistics, as we discussed previously. This is not an issue in the 200 strategies because we did not impose any correlation structure on the random variables. Harvey and Liu (2014) explicitly take the correlation among tests into account and provide multiple testing adjusted Sharpe Ratios using a variety of methods.

An Example with Standard and Poor's Capital IQ

To see how our method works on a real dataset of strategy returns, we use the S&P Capital IQ database. It includes detailed information on the time-series of 484 strategies for the U.S. equity market. Additionally, these strategies are catalogued into eight groups based on the types of risks to which they are exposed. We choose the most profitable strategy from each of the three categories: "Price Momentum," "Analyst Expectations," and "Capital Efficiency." These trading strategies are before costs and, as such, the Sharpe Ratios will be overstated.

The top performers in the three categories generate Sharpe Ratios of 0.83, 0.37, and 0.67, respectively. The corresponding t-statistics are 3.93, 1.14, and 3.17 and their p-values (under independent testing) are

0.00008, 0.2543, and 0.0015.[16] We use the BHY method—our recommended method—to adjust the three p-values based on the p-values for the 484 strategies (we assume the total number of tried strategies is 484, i.e., there are no missing tests). The three BHY adjusted p-values are 0.0134, 0.9995, and 0.1093 and their associated t-statistics are 2.47, 0.00, and 1.60. The adjusted Sharpe Ratios are 0.52, 0.00, and 0.34, respectively. Therefore, by applying the BHY method, we haircut the Sharpe Ratios of the three top performers by 37% (= (0.83 – 0.52) / 0.83), 100% (= (0.42 – 0) / 0.42) and 49% (= (0.67 – 0.34) / 0.67).[17]

In Sample and Out of Sample

Until now, we evaluate trading strategies from an in-sample (IS) testing perspective, that is, we use all the information in the history of returns to make a judgment. Alternatively, one can divide the history into two sub-samples—one in-sample period and the other out-of-sample (OOS) period—and use OOS observations to evaluate decisions made based on the IS period.

There are a number of immediate issues. First, often the OOS period is not really out-of-sample because the researcher knows what has happened in that period. Second, in dicing up the data, we run into the possibility that, with fewer observations in the in-sample period, we might not have enough power to identify true strategies. That is, some profitable trading strategies do not make it to the OOS stage. Finally, with few observations in the OOS period, some true strategies from the IS period may not pass the test in the OOS period and be mistakenly discarded.

Indeed, for the three strategies in the Capital IQ data, if we use the recent five years as the OOS period for the OOS approach, the OOS Sharpe Ratios are 0.64, –0.30, and 0.18, respectively. We see that the third strategy has a small Sharpe Ratio and is insignificant (p-value = 0.53) for this five-year OOS period, although it is borderline significant for the full sample (p-value = 0.11), even after multiple testing adjustment. The problem is that with only 60 monthly observations in the OOS period, a true strategy will have a good chance to fail the OOS test.

Recent research by López de Prado and his coauthors pursues the out-of-sample route and develops a concept called the Probability of Backtest Overfitting (PBO) to gauge the extent of backtest overfitting (see Bailey et al., 2013a,b and López de Prado, 2013). In particular, the PBO measures how likely it is for a superior strategy that is fit IS to underperform in the OOS period. It succinctly captures the degree of backtest overfitting from a probabilistic perspective and should be useful in a variety of situations.

To see the differences between the IS and OOS approach, we again take the 200 strategy returns in Figure 2 as an example. One way to do OOS testing is to divide the entire sample in halves and evaluate the performances of these 200 strategies based on the first half of the sample (IS), i.e., the first five years. The evaluation is then put into further scrutiny based on the second half of the sample (OOS). The idea is that strategies that appear to be significant for the in-sample period but are actually not true will likely to perform poorly for the out-of-sample period. Our IS sample approach, on the other hand, uses all 10 years' information and makes the decision at the end of the sample. Using the method developed by López de Prado and his coauthors, we can calculate PBO to be 0.45.[18] Therefore, there is high chance (i.e., a probability of 0.45) for the IS best performer to have a below median performance in the OOS. This is consistent with our result that based on the entire sample, the best performer is insignificant if we take multiple testing into account. However, unlike the PBO approach that evaluates a particular strategy selection procedure, our method determines a haircut Sharpe Ratio for each of the strategies.

In principle, we believe there are merits in both the PBO as well as the multiple testing approaches. A successful merger of these approaches could potentially yield more powerful tools to help asset managers successfully evaluate trading strategies.

Trading Strategies and Financial Products

The multiple testing problem greatly confounds the identification of truly profitable trading strategies and the same problems apply to a variety of sciences. Indeed, there is an influential paper in medicine by Ioannidis (2005) called "Why Most Published Research Findings Are False." Harvey, Liu, and Zhu (2014) look at 315 different financial factors and conclude that most are likely false after you apply the insights from multiple testing.

In medicine, the first researcher to publish a new finding is subject to what they call the "winner's curse." Given the multiple tests, subsequent papers are likely to find a lesser effect or no effect (which would mean the research paper would have to be retracted). Similar effects are evident in finance where Schwert (2003) and McLean and Pontiff (2014) find that the impact of famous finance anomalies is greatly diminished out of sample—or never existed in the first place.

So where does this leave us? First, there is no reason to think that there is any difference between physical sciences and finance. Most of the empirical research in finance, whether published in academic journals or put into production as an active trading strategy by an investment manager, is likely false. Second, this implies that half the financial products (promising outperformance) that companies are selling to clients are false.

To be clear, we are not accusing asset managers of knowingly selling false products. We are pointing out that the statistical tools being employed to evaluate these trading strategies are inappropriate. This critique also applies to much of the academic empirical literature in finance—including many papers by one of the authors of this paper (Harvey).

It is also clear that investment managers want to promote products that are most likely to outperform in the future. That is, there is a strong incentive to get the testing right. No one wants to disappoint a client and no one wants to lose their bonus—or their job. Employing the statistical tools of multiple testing in the evaluation of trading strategies reduces the number of false discoveries.

Limitations and Conclusions

Our work has two important limitations. First, for a number of applications the Sharpe Ratio is not appropriate because the distribution of the strategy returns is not normal. For example, two trading strategies might have identical Sharpe Ratios but one of them might be preferred because it has less severe downside risk.

Second, our work focuses on individual strategies. In actual practice, the investment manager needs to examine how the proposed strategy interacts with the current collection of strategies. For example, a strategy with a lower Sharpe might be preferred because the strategy is relatively uncorrelated with current strategies. The denominator in the Sharpe Ratio is simply the strategy volatility and does not measure the contribution of the strategy to the portfolio volatility. The strategy portfolio problem, i.e., adding a new strategy to a portfolio of existing strategies, is the topic of Harvey and Liu (2014).

In summary, the message of our research is simple. Researchers in finance, whether practitioners or academics, need to realize that they will find seemingly successful trading strategies by chance. We can no longer use the traditional tools of statistical analysis that assume that no one has looked at the data before and there is only a single strategy tried. A multiple testing framework offers help in reducing the number of false strategies adapted by firms. Two sigma is no longer an appropriate benchmark for evaluating trading strategies.

Black Box Trend Following—Lifting the Veil

23

Nigol Koulajian and Paul Czkwianianc
Quest Partners LLC

The goal of this research series is to demystify specific black box CTA trend following strategies and to analyze their characteristics both as a stand-alone product as well as within a portfolio of typical financial instruments.

Synopsis

The goal of this paper is to help CTA investors familiarize themselves with black box trend following strategies. The paper highlights the sensitivity of returns to some of the optimizations that are available.

Specifically, we will

1. Provide transparent CTA black box trend following trading strategies, including specific parameters, markets to be traded, and risk management strategies.

The authors of this paper are principals of Quest Partners LLC. This paper does not constitute advice or recommendation to enter into any transaction. This work is intended for educational and informational purposes only.

2. Analyze the source of returns of such trading strategies and compare their returns to the Barclays BTOP 50 Managed Futures Index (BTOP50) and the S&P 500 Index (SP500).
3. Break down performance per sector and per trade direction (long vs. short).
4. Investigate the stability of the parameters used.
5. Explore the capacity of such strategies to hedge stock market risk.

Some of our findings are:

1. Simple, liquid, and fully transparent CTA strategies such as moving average crossovers and channel breakouts explain most of the returns of the BTOP50. These strategies are stable across parameters.
2. These simple strategies compare favorably to the BTOP50 and the SP500 both in terms of returns and risk-adjusted returns.
3. These strategies have positive skew. They tend to benefit from increases in volatility and SP500 down moves.
4. In the past 20 years, most of the returns of these strategies have come from long trades, the fixed income sector, and longer-term trading frequencies. Optimizing around these data points should be done with care.
5. The SP500 lost about 130% in its worst four drawdowns of the past 20 years. In these same four periods, the two strategies we proposed generated over +140% each.

The Strategies

Strategy Mechanics

The two technical indicators that are most commonly used as trend following filters are Channel Breakout and Simple Moving Average Crossovers. These two indicators have been used since the early '70s or before. Both these indicators have high correlation to CTA indexes and traditional CTAs. As such, they are a great proxy for the strategies that CTAs use in their portfolios. We can use their performance to study the performance of CTAs in general. Both strategies, in the form that we are going to discuss, are pure reversal strategies; they are always in the market long or short. Both strategies use daily data for their computations. Both strategies are stable across parameters as will be shown. For our purposes, we will specifically use the 50 Day Channel Breakout (CB50) and the 10x100 Simple Moving Average Crossover (MA10x100) strategies. These are the trading rules for the models:

50 Day Channel Breakout (CB50):

C = close of today

HC(50) = highest close in the last 50 days (including today)

LC(50) = lowest close in the last 50 days (including today)

Long Signal: If C = HC50 then go Long tomorrow market on open

Short Signal: If C = LC50 then go Short tomorrow market on open

10x100 Simple Moving Average Crossover (MA10x100):

MA10 = average of the last 10 closes (including today)

MA100 = average of the last 100 closes (including today)

Long Signal: If MA10 > MA100 then go Long tomorrow market on open

Short Signal: If MA10 < MA100 then go Short tomorrow market on open

Markets Traded

We apply each of the two trend following models to a diversified portfolio of 24 foreign exchange and futures markets. These markets comprise four distinct sectors: foreign exchange, fixed income, equity indexes, and commodities. Risk is allocated equally to all sectors. There are six markets in each sector:

Foreign Exchange	Fixed Income	Equity Index	Commodity
EUR/USD	U.S. Bond (30Y)	S&P 500	Light Crude Oil
GBP/USD	U.S. Note (10Y)	Nasdaq 100	Heating Oil
EUR/GBP	German Bund (10Y)	Euro Stoxx 50	Natural Gas
EUR/JPY	Japanese Govt Bond	Dax	Gold
USD/JPY	Eurodollar (3M)	Nikkei 225	Silver
GBP/JPY	Euribor (3M)	Hang Seng	Corn

Data Notes

Daily sampled data was used. Continuous price series for futures contracts were created using a standard back-adjusting mechanism relying on contract open interest as roll trigger. Bloomberg was used as a source for historical cash foreign exchange data. For the sake of simplicity, interest rate differences between currencies were ignored as they have negligible impact on our results.

Trade Sizing

All markets are allocated equal risk at trade entry. Position sizing is proportional to account size and inversely proportional to market volatility. The measure of volatility that was used is the standard deviation of daily price changes (not the standard deviation of daily percentage price changes). Volatility was measured over a 100-day period preceding each trade. All 24 markets were treated identically. Position size was determined at trade inception and was kept constant until trade was closed.

$$TS = 0.001 \times AS/(VOL \times PV)$$

TS = Trade Size in # contracts at trade initiation

AS = Account Size in USD at beginning of the month

VOL = Volatility as measured by standard deviation of daily price changes over the preceding 100 days

PV = Point Value in USD for 1.0 point move in price for 1 contract

This methodology of trade sizing is simple and robust. Unlike some other trade sizing methods such as fixed number of contracts per trade or fixed USD face value allocation per trade, it is independent of nominal price level and it can be applied in identical fashion across several market sectors.

Sector Weights

The selected markets are highly liquid. They comprise the majority of the liquidity available within each respective sector and are representative of the exposure of a typical CTA today. It is important to note that from the late '80s to the early '90s, CTAs shifted a considerable amount of risk exposure from the commodity and FX sectors to the financial and stock indexes sectors. We assume a fixed sector allocation over time in our simulations.

Time Span

The time period of our study spans over 20 years starting January 1990 and ending June 2010. Some markets that we used in our tests did not exist in 1990. In these cases, we used data from market inception onwards. Of the markets we chose to use, 22 were active as of December 1990, and all were active by December 1998. Special consideration was given to the Euro currency which was introduced January 1, 1999. Prior to January 1, 1999, the German Mark was used instead of the Euro in the relevant foreign exchange crosses.

Commission and Slippage

Throughout the study, we used conservative commission and slippage assumptions. Commissions were assumed to be $24 per round turn for futures contracts. Slippage assumptions were contract specific and averaged $87 per round turn. For the CB50 and MA10x100 strategies, this translates into slippage and commission costs of 2% and 2.58% per annum respectively. We note that in the '80s and '90s, prior to introduction of electronic exchanges, markets weren't as liquid as they have been over the past decade. The execution cost assumptions used in this study are significantly higher than those experienced during the past 10 years of live trading at Quest Partners but are appropriate for the overall study period.

Interest

Assuming a fully funded trading account, full interest was included in the simulated performance results. The 1-month USD Libor was used to calculate the interest return on the cash held in the trading account.

Fees

Where indicated, fees of 1% management and 20% incentive were charged on the strategies' accounts.

Performance Results and Graphs

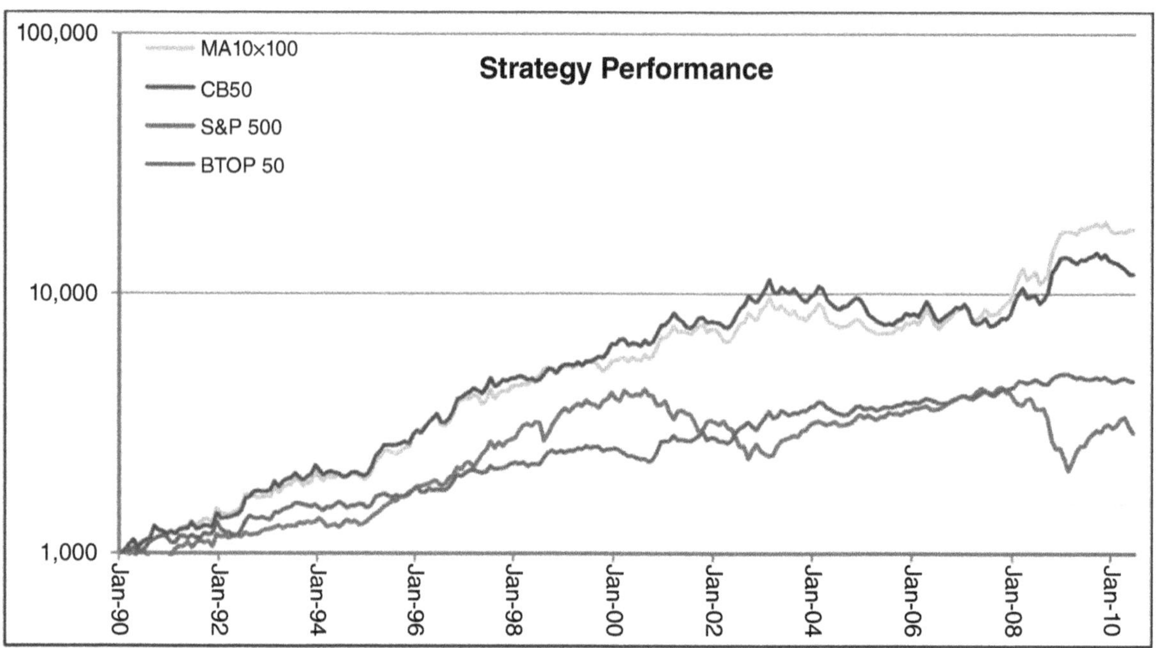

The above logarithmic scale chart shows cumulative NAV curves for the two trend following strategies, the SP500 and the BTOP50.

	MA10x100	MA10x100 (with fees)	CB50	CB50 (with fees)	SP500	BTOP50
Annual Compounded Return	15.1%	11.2%	12.8%	9.5%	5.4%	7.7%
Worst Peak-to-Trough Drawdown	–28.2%	–24.3%	–33.7%	–29.9%	–52.6%	–13.3%
Annual Standard Deviation	15.8%	12.6%	15.3%	12.2%	15.0%	9.5%
Annual Return/Max P/T Drawdown	0.53	0.46	0.38	0.32	0.10	0.58
Sharpe Ratio (Avg RFR = 4.26%)	0.68	0.55	0.56	0.43	0.07	0.37

	MA10x100	MA10x100 (with fees)	CB50	CB50 (with fees)	SP500	BTOP50
Skew	0.25	0.25	0.29	0.29	–0.65	0.43
Correlation to SP500	–14.3%	–14.3%	–12.4%	–12.4%	NA	–11.9%
Alpha to SP500	11.0%	7.1%	8.7%	5.3%	NA	3.6%
Correlation to BTOP50	70.2%	70.2%	68.2%	68.2%	–11.9%	NA
Alpha to BTOP50	6.7%	3.7%	4.8%	2.2%	1.8%	NA
Beta to BTOP50	1.16	0.93	1.09	0.88	–0.19	NA
Avg # of Trades Per Year Per Market	4.0	4.0	3.0	3.0	NA	NA
Avg # of Days Per Trade	60	60	81	81	NA	NA

The *returns* of the two simple trend following strategies are attractive. Gross as well as net of fees, these simple models outperform the SP500 and BTOP50 indexes. The MA10x100 and the CB50 respectively annualized 15.1% and 12.8% over the 20 year period of study.

On a *return to maximum peak-to-trough drawdown* basis, the strategies outperform the SP500 by a factor of 3 or more. The strategies' return to maximum peak-to-trough drawdown is slightly less than that of the BTOP50. The index's outperformance can be explained by the fact that a substantial portion of its returns is due to interest earned on the funding capital rather than actual trading. We estimate that the interest earned on cash is about 4.26% out of the 7.7% return of the index.

The strategies' *Sharpe ratios* over the period are superior to SP500 and BTOP50 indexes. This holds even after management and incentive fees are deducted from the returns.

The *skew* of the strategies' returns is between 0.25 and 0.29, slightly under the skew of the BTOP50 but substantially higher than the negative skew of the SP500 returns. This implies that the strategies are a good hedge for surprises or increases in volatility. This is a valuable characteristic from a portfolio construction perspective. We will address skew and its importance in risk measurement and portfolio construction in a separate research note. Note that the negative skew on the SP500 implies that surprises tend to be negative for the stock market.

The *correlation of the strategies to the SP500* is slightly negative indicating that they are a good diversifier to the SP500. The *Alpha of the strategies to the SP500* is substantial at 5% to 11% per year. The ability of these strategies to hedge the SP500 is discussed in the Summary of this paper and will be further analyzed in a separate research note.

The *correlation of the strategies to the BTOP50* is high at around 70%. The *Beta of the strategies to the BTOP50* is around 1. These strategies are therefore very good proxies for CTAs and the CTA index in general. The models have 2.2% to 6.7% *Alpha to the CTA index*. A good portion of this Alpha is due to high fee structures and high commission rates that were prevalent in CTAs in the first 10 years of the study.

The returns of these strategies can be improved by diversifying the portfolio across more markets than the current 24. Another way to easily improve the results is by trading a diversified portfolio of these models using a range of parameters rather than the current fixed chosen values.

Sector Performance

We now point our attention to the performance of the strategies within specific sectors.

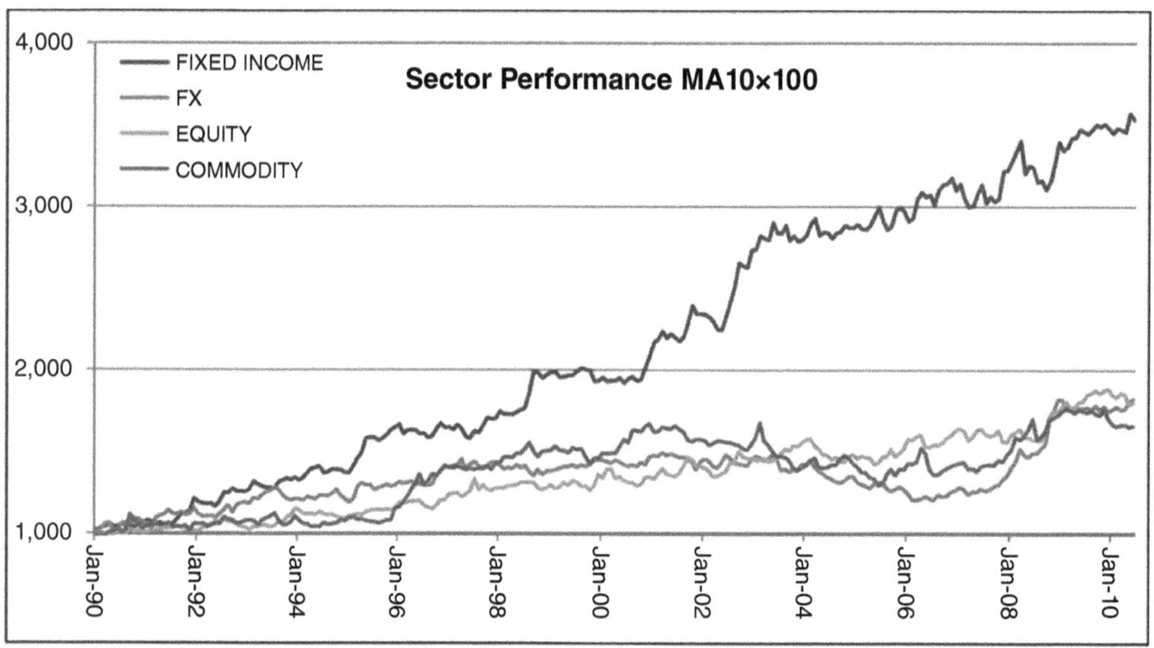

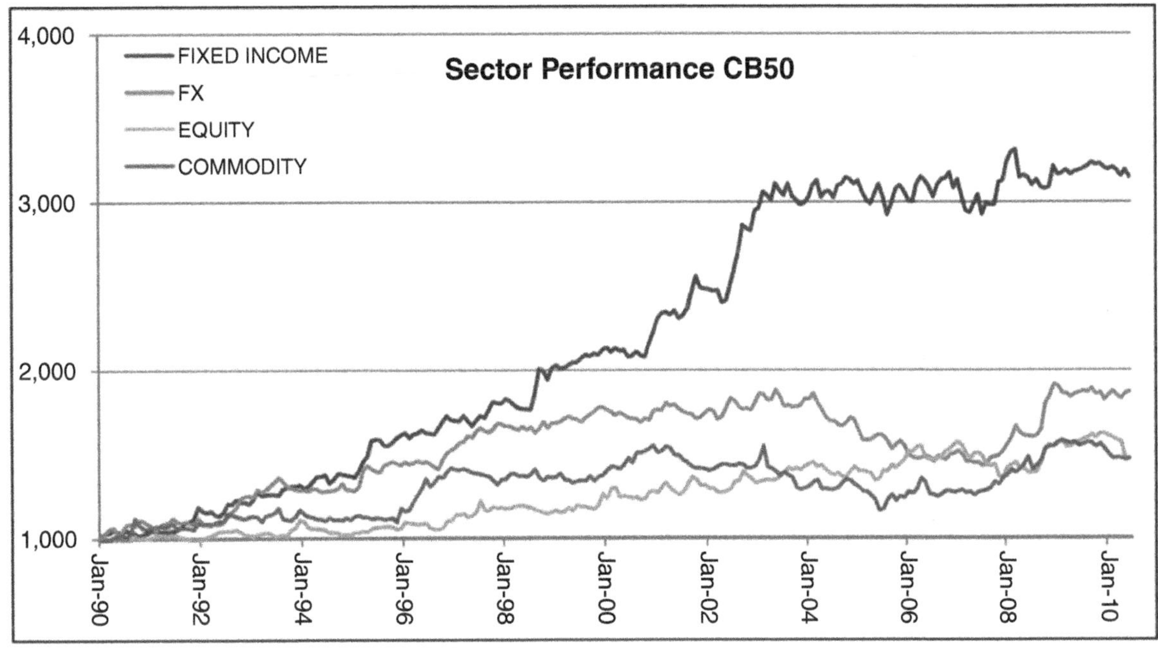

	MA10x100 FX	CB50 FX	MA10x100 Fixed Income	CB50 Fixed Income	MA10x100 Equity	CB50 Equity	MA10x100 Commodity	CB50 Commodity
Annual Compounded Return	3.0%	3.1%	6.3%	5.7%	2.9%	1.9%	2.5%	1.9%
Worst Peak-to-Trough Drawdown	−19.2%	−24.0%	−8.8%	−7.9%	−9.9%	−13.2%	−22.7%	−24.8%
Annual Standard Deviation	6.5%	6.2%	6.6%	6.6%	6.0%	6.1%	7.4%	7.0%
Annual Return/Max P/T Drawdown	0.15	0.13	0.72	0.73	0.29	0.15	0.11	0.08
Sharpe Ratio (Avg RFR = 4.26%)	0.29	0.33	0.80	0.71	0.31	0.14	0.20	0.12

(Continued)

	MA10x100 FX	CB50 FX	MA10x100 Fixed Income	CB50 Fixed Income	MA10x100 Equity	CB50 Equity	MA10x100 Commodity	CB50 Commodity
Skew	0.65	0.73	0.41	0.51	0.18	0.14	0.15	0.18
Correlation to SP500	−11.2%	−8.1%	−11.2%	−6.5%	−2.0%	−1.9%	−9.1%	−12.0%
Alpha to SP500	2.0%	2.1%	5.3%	4.7%	1.9%	0.9%	1.5%	0.9%
Correlation to BTOP50	53.3%	50.1%	53.2%	51.4%	33.9%	32.2%	27.9%	27.3%
Alpha to BTOP50	0.6%	0.9%	4.0%	3.4%	1.1%	0.1%	0.7%	0.1%
Beta to BTOP50	0.36	0.33	0.37	0.36	0.21	0.21	0.22	0.20
Avg # of Trades Per Year Per Market	4.7	3.2	3.7	3.0	4.0	3.0	4.2	3.2
Avg # of Days Per Trade	55	79	65	81	61	78	59	77

Individual Sector portfolios are assumed to be funded at 25%. If they were each fully funded, their annual compounded returns would each be higher by 3.19%.

It is clear that the best-performing sector over the last 20 years is fixed income followed by FX, equities, and commodities. For both models, over 45% of the overall return is derived from trading in this single market sector. This is an important factor to consider when comparing CTAs with a large portfolio weighting in fixed income as their outperformance might be confused with superior trading methodologies. Large CTAs tend to have outsized allocations to the fixed income sector due to its liquidity. The last 20 years have been a stellar environment for fixed income trading. The yields on the 30-year U.S. Treasury bonds have gone down from 8% in January 1990 to 4% in July 2010. It is highly unlikely that yields continue to drop as they have in the last 20 years. An up-trending fixed income market (yields going down) is highly favorable to a down-trending fixed income market due to the positive carry that is earned while being long (in a typically positively sloped yield curve).

Performance of Long versus Short Trades

Since the two strategies are entirely symmetric between the long and short side from a trading perspective, it is surprising to see how profitable the long trades are compared to the shorts.

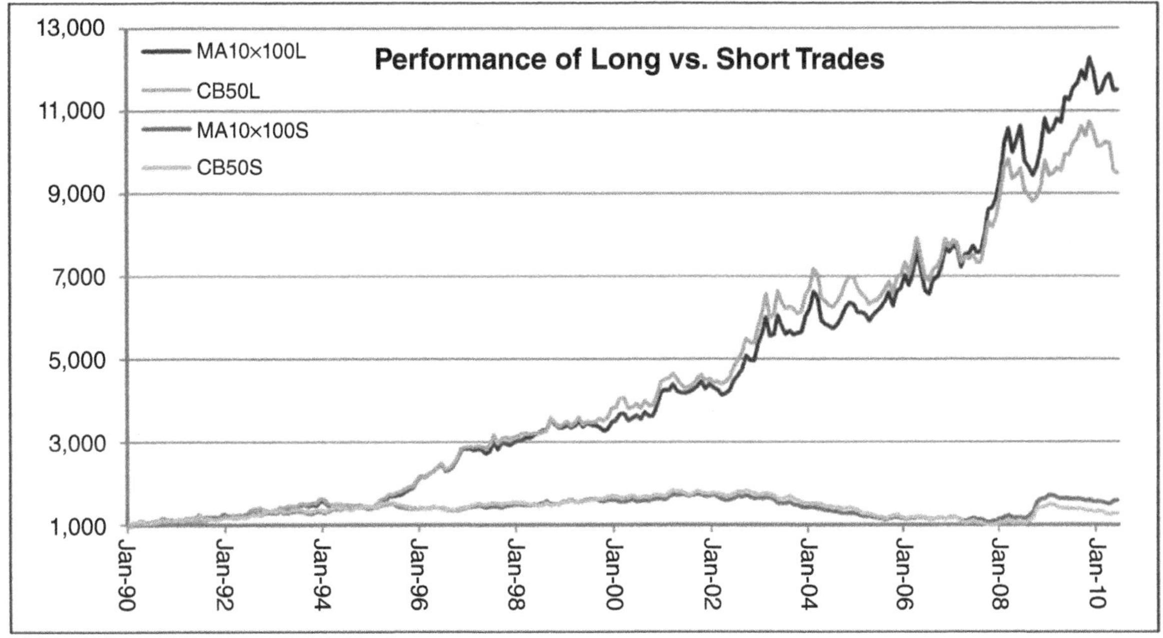

	MA10x100	MA10x100 Long	MA10x100 Short	CB50	CB50 Long	CB50 Short
Annual Compounded Return	15.1%	12.7%	2.3%	12.8%	11.6%	1.2%
Worst Peak-to-Trough Drawdown	–28.2%	–13.7%	–39.9%	–33.7%	–13.6%	–46.1%
Annual Standard Deviation	15.8%	12.2%	8.9%	15.3%	12.0%	8.7%
Annual Return/Max P/T Drawdown	0.53	0.92	0.06	0.38	0.85	0.03
Sharpe Ratio (Avg RFR = 4.26%)	0.68	0.87	0.02	0.56	0.79	–0.11

(Continued)

	MA10x100	MA10x100 Long	MA10x100 Short	CB50	CB50 Long	CB50 Short
Skew	0.25	0.00	1.66	0.29	0.09	1.56
Correlation to SP500	–14.3%	12.7%	–42.9%	–12.4%	14.1%	–41.3%
Alpha to SP500	11.0%	10.4%	0.4%	8.7%	9.4%	–0.7%
Correlation to BTOP50	70.2%	65.7%	34.7%	68.2%	64.0%	31.5%
Alpha to BTOP50	6.7%	7.6%	–1.0%	4.8%	6.7%	–1.9%
Beta to BTOP50	1.16	0.84	0.32	1.09	0.81	0.29
Avg # of Trades Per Year Per Market	4.0	2.0	2.0	3.0	1.5	1.5
Avg # of Days Per Trade	60	67	54	81	74	88

Individual Long and Short portfolios are assumed to be funded at 50%; if they were fully funded their annual compounded returns would each be higher by 2.13%.

The *returns* and *risk-adjusted returns* of the long side of the two strategies are superior to the short side of the strategies. Both strategies produce over 85% of profits from trading on the long side of the market. The strategies spend about 45% of time on the short side of the market.

The long side of the trading strategies has a much higher *correlation to the SP500* than the short side and is therefore not as valuable as an addition to a portfolio of financial assets.

The long side of the trading strategies also has a much lower *skew* than the short (0 vs. 1.66 for the MA10x100 and 0.09 vs. 1.56 for the CB50). It is therefore not as stable in a volatile environment. The long side of the strategies has a neutral convexity while the short side is positively convex. Positive convexity should be a very high priority for CTA strategies as they are typically used as a hedge or diversifier in volatile and falling stock market environments. Skew is a very important factor in predicting the hedging potential of an investment.

It is critical for investors into CTA strategies to be aware of the optimization risks that they are taking should they invest in a CTA who has improved his returns and risk-adjusted returns through the trading of the long side of the markets only. We will discuss this anomaly in more detail in a future research note. We will also provide methods of return analysis that could shed light on whether a CTA is taking advantage of this characteristic to improve returns.

Stability of Parameters

We shifted the parameters of the MA10x100 and CB50 models to get a sense of how dependent our analysis is on the particular parameter choice we made.

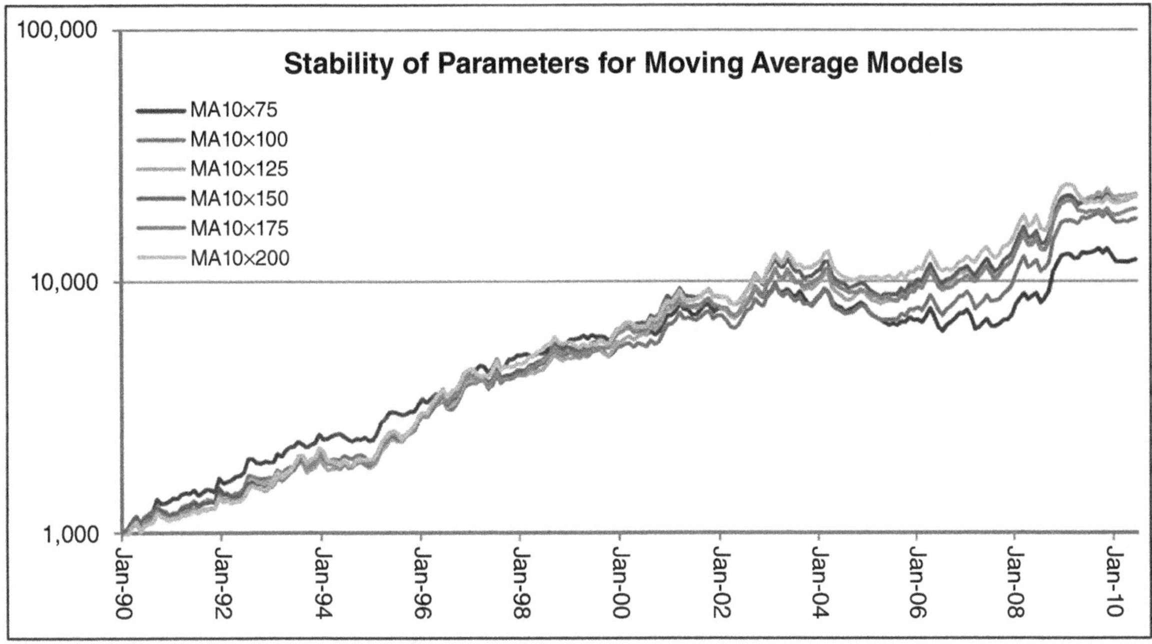

	MA10x75	MA10x100	MA10x125	MA10x150	MA10x175	MA10x200
Annual Compounded Return	13.0%	15.1%	16.3%	16.2%	15.6%	16.2%
Worst Peak-to-Trough Drawdown	–35.4%	–28.2%	–27.8%	–30.1%	–26.8%	–23.4%
Annual Standard Deviation	15.1%	15.8%	16.1%	15.9%	15.7%	16.1%
Annual Return/Max P/T Drawdown	0.37	0.53	0.59	0.54	0.58	0.69
Sharpe Ratio (Avg RFR = 4.26%)	0.58	0.68	0.75	0.75	0.72	0.74

(Continued)

	MA10x75	MA10x100	MA10x125	MA10x150	MA10x175	MA10x200
Skew	0.27	0.25	0.25	0.10	0.19	0.07
Correlation to SP500	–14.8%	–14.3%	–14.6%	–13.3%	–13.4%	–12.9%
Alpha to SP500	8.9%	11.0%	12.2%	12.1%	11.5%	12.1%
Correlation to BTOP50	68.8%	70.2%	68.8%	68.3%	65.2%	63.2%
Alpha to BTOP50	4.9%	6.7%	8.0%	8.0%	7.6%	8.2%
Beta to BTOP50	1.09	1.16	1.17	1.14	1.08	1.07
Avg # of Trades Per Year Per Market	4.7	4.0	3.5	3.1	2.8	2.5
Avg # of Days Per Trade	51	60	68	78	86	95

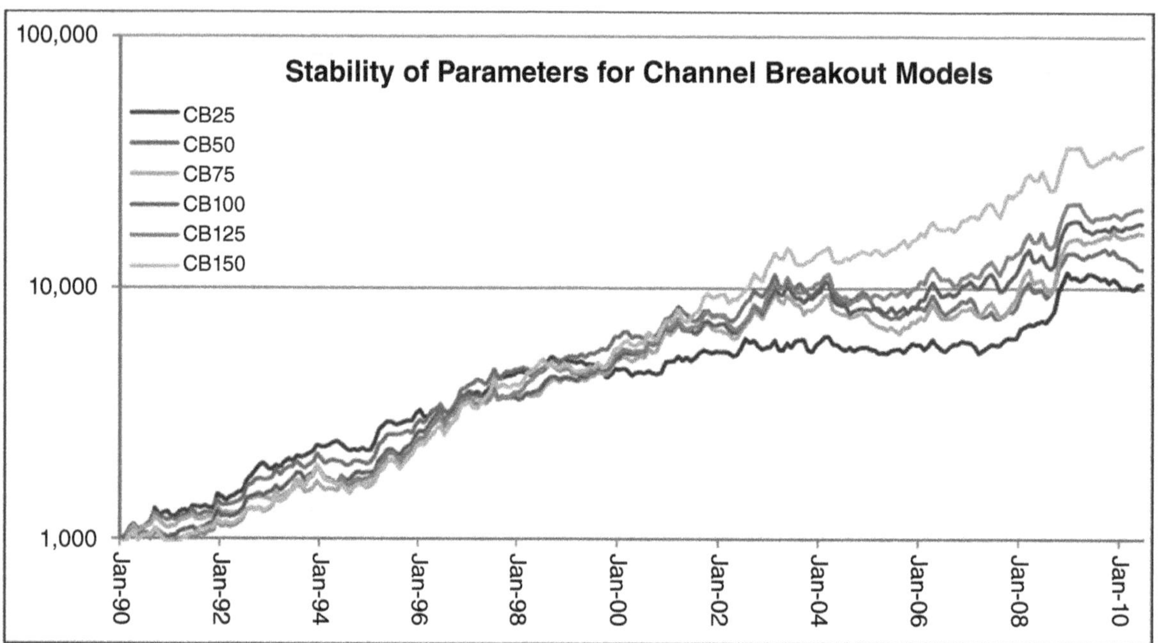

	CB25	CB50	CB75	CB100	CB125	CB150
Annual Compounded Return	12.1%	12.8%	14.7%	15.2%	15.9%	19.2%
Worst Peak-to-Trough Drawdown	–17.4%	–33.7%	–31.3%	–25.1%	–24.1%	–22.6%
Annual Standard Deviation	13.8%	15.3%	15.9%	15.8%	16.1%	16.8%

	CB25	CB50	CB75	CB100	CB125	CB150
Annual Return/Max P/T Drawdown	0.70	0.38	0.47	0.60	0.66	0.85
Sharpe Ratio (Avg RFR = 4.26%)	0.57	0.56	0.65	0.69	0.72	0.89
Skew	0.71	0.29	0.46	0.11	0.02	0.05
Correlation to SP500	−14.7%	−12.4%	−15.7%	−13.5%	−9.6%	−4.0%
Alpha to SP500	8.0%	8.7%	10.6%	11.1%	11.8%	15.0%
Correlation to BTOP50	63.2%	68.2%	66.9%	62.2%	58.1%	53.0%
Alpha to BTOP50	4.7%	4.8%	6.5%	7.3%	8.2%	11.7%
Beta to BTOP50	0.91	1.09	1.12	1.04	0.99	0.94
Avg # of Trades Per Year Per Market	6.0	3.0	1.9	1.4	1.1	0.8
Avg # of Days Per Trade	40	81	126	171	222	292

Both the moving average crossover and the channel breakout models are stable across parameters. For both the MA and CB models, the longer-term time frames had higher returns and risk-adjusted returns. As an example, the 150-day Channel Breakout model compounded at over 19% per year vs. just under 13% for the 50-day Channel Breakout. The Sharpe ratio of the CB150 was 0.89 vs. 0.56 for the CB50.

It would be obvious that one should be trading the longer-term strategies if it was not for the less positive skew that these strategies exhibit. Indeed these very long-term strategies are much more vulnerable to dramatic reversals than their shorter-term counterparts. As an example, in the large trend reversals of August 2007, the CB50 was up +0.5% while CB150 was down −5.79%. Similarly, the MA10x100 was up +0.95% while the MA10x200 was down −3.45%.

A point to consider is that large CTAs, due to their more significant slippage costs, tend to focus on the longer-term frequencies of trading. This does not give them access to the positive skew which translates into strong hedging characteristics that are valuable in portfolios.

CTAs are typically expected to shine during such dramatic market reversals as those that occurred in August 2007. The longer-term models do not have the reactivity that is necessary to meet such an expectation.

Are CTAs a Diversifier or a Hedge to the SP500?

It is common knowledge that CTAs have only a slight negative correlation to the SP500 and are therefore not a hedge for the stock market and stock-market-related investments. CTAs are typically considered a diversifier for stock market risk and are therefore allocated a minor portion of typical financial portfolios.

On further analysis of this correlation number, one notices that in months when the SP500 is down –3% or more, the correlation of the CB50, MA10x100, and BTOP50 to the SP500 is actually a significant –45% to –56%. In other words, CTAs have a tendency to hedge stock market corrections without necessarily giving back returns during the SP500 up months. This makes CTAs a good hedge to stock-market-related investments. This strength is further compounded by the fact that our models and BTOP50 generate +4% to +7% annual Alpha to the SP500 and have substantial returns on their own. In effect, CTA strategies have long-term positive returns and strong insurance characteristics. This is an exceptionally powerful combination that should be utilized in most portfolios.

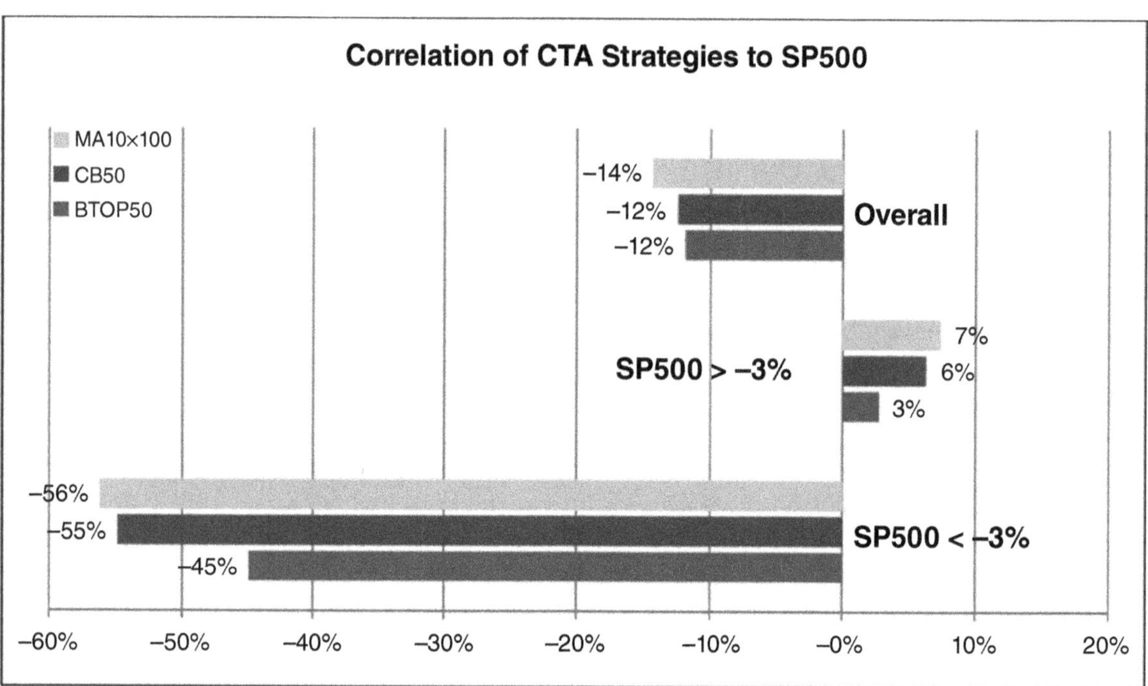

Next we consider the absolute returns of the CTA strategies during the worst four drawdowns of the SP500. In four periods when the SP500 lost a total of over –130%, the CTA strategies made +142% and +166%

respectively. Few hedge funds' strategies succeeded in generating positive returns during significant SP500 drawdowns in the past 20 years. As will be further analyzed in future research notes, these returns are a by-product of the positive skew that CTA strategies display. In effect, CTA strategies tend to benefit not only from trends, but also from the increases in volatility that inevitably occur during SP500 drawdowns. What is even more surprising is that this characteristic is not the by-product of option Gamma exposure but due to direct, liquid, and transparent futures trading.

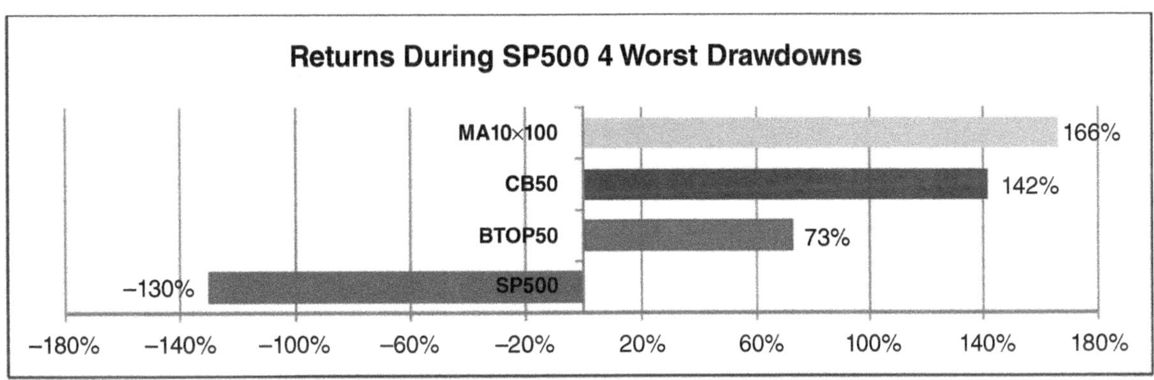

Returns During SP500 4 Worst Drawdowns

100%
80%
60%
40%
20%
0%
−20%
−40%
−60%

MA10×100
CB50
BTOP50
SP500

96.33%
70.28%
14.47%
−52.56%

6/90→10/90
SP500 : −15.84%

7/98→8/98
SP500 : −15.57%

9/00→9/02
SP500 : −46.28%

11/07→2/09
SP500 : −52.56%

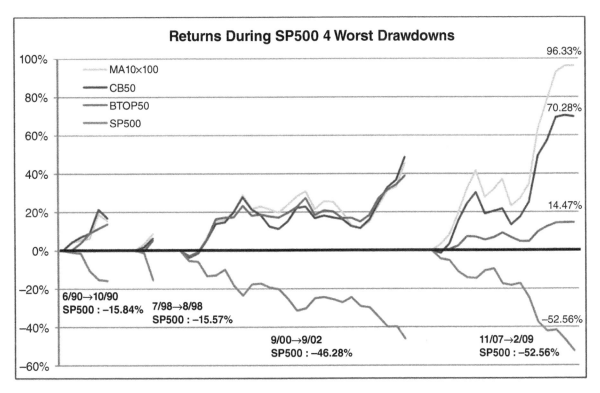

For illustration, we also include the returns of the two discussed CTA strategies and the BTOP50 during the 10 worst quarters and 20 worst months for the SP500. Both graphs confirm the hedge quality of CTAs during strong down quarters and down months for the SP500.

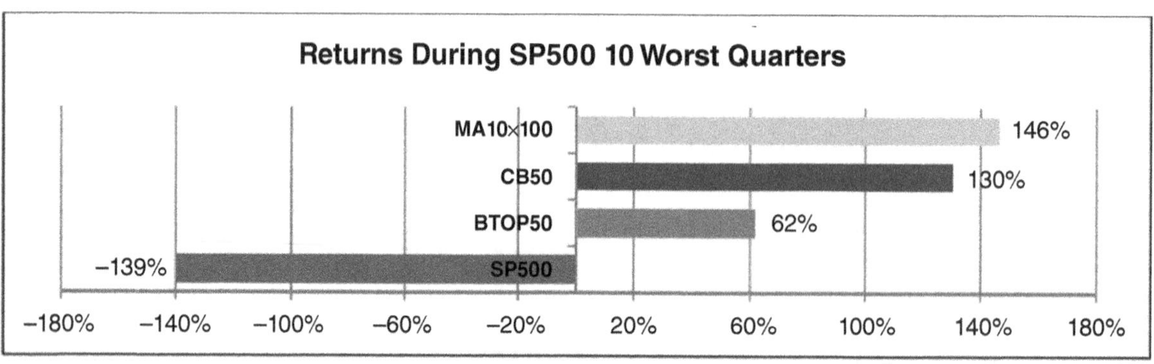

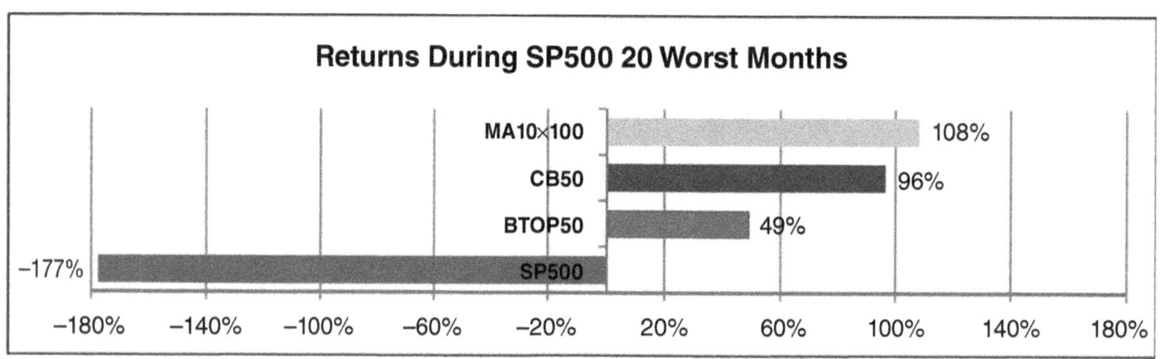

Summary

1. The typical CTA and the CTA indexes can easily be duplicated using simple, well-known trend following filters such as moving averages and channel breakouts.
2. Models based on these trend filters have performed well as stand-alone investments.

3. These models have approximately –50% correlation to the SP500 when it is down more than –3% in a month. The hedging characteristic of these models comes without a commensurate downside during strong stock market periods.

4. During the last 20 years, three shifts in these models would have considerably improved performance relative to benchmarks. These shifts are: 1) increasing the weight of the fixed income sector (accounts for over 50% of the performance of the typical CTA portfolio), 2) trading the long side only (accounts for over 85% of the performance of the typical CTA portfolio) and 3) trading longer-term frequencies than the typical portfolio. All three of these shifts negatively affect the ability to hedge stock market downturns. However, they improve risk-adjusted returns during typical low volatility periods such as the ones that were experienced in the last 20 years. As we will discuss in future papers, these style drifts are apparent in the CTA index. Investors should evaluate CTA outperformance with special attention to these three variables.

Risk Management 24

Ed Seykota

Risk

RISK is the possibility of loss. That is, if we own some stock, and there is a possibility of a price decline, we are at risk. The stock is not the risk, nor is the loss the risk. The possibility of loss is the risk. As long as we own the stock, we are at risk. The only way to control the risk is to buy or sell stock. In the matter of owning stocks, and aiming for profit, risk is fundamentally unavoidable and the best we can do is to manage the risk.

Risk Management

To manage is to direct and control. Risk management is to direct and control the possibility of loss. The activities of a risk manager are to measure risk and to increase and decrease risk by buying and selling stock.

The Coin Toss Example

Let's say we have a coin that we can toss and that it comes up heads or tails with equal probability. The Coin Toss Example helps to present the concepts of risk management.

The *PROBABILITY* of an event is the likelihood of that event, expressing as the ratio of the number of actual occurrences to the number of possible occurrences. So if the coin comes up heads, 50 times out of 100, then the probability of heads is 50%. Notice that a probability has to be between zero (0.0 = 0% = impossible) and one (1.0 = 100% = certain).

Let's say the rules for the game are: (1) we start with $1,000, (2) we always bet that heads come up, (3) we can bet any amount that we have left, (4) if tails comes up, we lose our bet, (5) if heads comes up, we do not lose our bet; instead, we win twice as much as we bet, and (6) the coin is fair and so the probability of heads is 50%. This game is similar to some trading methods.

In this case, our *LUCK* equals the probability of winning, or 50%; we will be lucky 50% of the time. Our *PAYOFF* equals 2:1 since we win 2 for every 1 we bet. Our *RISK* is the amount of money we wager, and therefore place at risk, on the next toss. In this example, our luck and our payoff stay constant, and only our bet may change.

In more complicated games, such as actual stock trading, luck and payoff may change with changing market conditions. Traders seem to spend considerable time and effort trying to change their luck and their payoff, generally to no avail, since it is not theirs to change. The risk is the only parameter the risk manager may effectively change to control risk.

We might also model more complicated games with a matrix of lucks and payoffs, to see a range of possible outcomes. This matrix might model a put-and-take game with a six-sided spinning top, or even trading. See Figure 24.1.

Luck	Payoff
10%	lose 2
20%	lose 1
30%	break even
20%	win 1
10%	win 2
10%	win 3

FIGURE 24.1: A Luck-Payoff matrix, showing six outcomes For now, however, we return to our basic coin example, since it has enough dimensions to illustrate many concepts of risk management. We consider more complicated examples later.

Optimal Betting

In our coin toss example, we have constant luck at 50%, constant payoff at 2:1, and we always bet on heads. To find a risk management strategy, we have to find a way to manage the bet. This is similar to the problem confronting a risk manager in the business of trading stocks. Good managers realize that there is not much they can do about luck and payoff and that the essential problem is to determine how much to wager on the stock. We begin our game with $1,000.

Hunches and Systems

One way to determine a bet size is by *HUNCH*. We might have a hunch and and bet $100.

Although hunch-centric betting is certainly popular and likely accounts for an enormous proportion of actual real-world betting, it has several problems: The bets require the constant attention of an operator to generate hunches, and interpret them into bets, and the bets are likely to rely as much on moods and feelings as on science.

To improve on hunch-centric betting, we might come up with a betting *SYSTEM*. A system is a logical method that defines a series of bets. The advantages of a betting system over a hunch method are (1) we don't need an operator, (2) the betting becomes regular, predictable, and consistent and, very importantly, (3) we can perform a historical simulation, on a computer, to *OPTIMIZE* the betting system.

Despite almost universal agreement that a system offers clear advantages over hunches, very few risk managers actually have a definition of their own risk management systems that is clear enough to allow a computer to back-test it.

Our coin-flip game, however, is fairly simple and we can come up with some betting systems for it. Furthermore, we can test these systems and optimize the system parameters to find good risk management.

Fixed Bet and Fixed-Fraction Bet

Our betting system must define the bet. One way to define the bet is to make it a constant fixed amount, say $10 each time, no matter how much we win or lose. This is a *FIXED BET* system. In this case, as in fixed-betting systems in general, our $1,000 *EQUITY* might increase or decrease to the point where the $10 fixed bet becomes proportionately too large or small to be a good bet.

To remedy this problem of the equity drifting out of proportion to the fixed bet, we might define the bet as as *FIXED-FRACTION* of our equity. A 1% fixed-fraction bet would, on our original $1,000, also lead to a $10 bet. This time, however, as our equity rises and falls, our fixed-fraction bet stays in proportion to our equity.

One interesting artifact of fixed-fraction betting, is that, since the bet stays proportional to the equity, it is theoretically impossible to go entirely broke so the official risk of total ruin is zero. In actual practice, however the disintegration of an enterprise has more to do with the psychological *UNCLE POINT*; see below.

Simulations

In order to test our betting system, we can *SIMULATE* over a historical record of outcomes. Let's say we toss the coin 10 times and we come up with five heads and five tails. We can arrange the simulation in a table such as Figure 24.2

Pyramiding and Martingale

In the case of a random process, such as coin tosses, streaks of heads or tails do occur, since it would be quite improbable to have a regular alternation of heads and tails. There is, however, no way to exploit this phenomenon, which is, itself random. In nonrandom processes, such as secular trends in stock prices, pyramiding and other trend-trading techniques may be effective.

Pyramiding is a method for increasing a position, as it becomes profitable. While this technique might be useful as a way for a trader to pyramid up to his optimal position, pyramiding on top of an already-optimal position is to invite the disasters of over-trading. In general, such micro-tinkering with executions is far less important than sticking to the system. To the extent that tinkering allows a window for further interpreting trading signals, it can invite hunch trading and weaken the fabric that supports sticking to the system.

The Martingale system is a method for doubling-up on losing bets. In case the doubled bet loses, the method redoubles and so on. This method

	Fixed Bet $10	Fixed-Fraction Bet 1%
Start	1000	1000
Heads	1020	1020
Tails	1010	1009.80
Heads	1030	1030
Tails	1020	1019.70
Heads	1040	1040.09
Tails	1030	1029.69
Heads	1050	1050.28
Tails	1040	1039.78
Heads	1060	1060.58
Tails	1050	1049.97

FIGURE 24.2: Simulation of fixed-bet and fixed-fraction betting systems

Notice that both systems make $20.00 (twice the bet) on the first toss, which comes up heads. On the second toss, the fixed bet system loses $10.00 while the fixed-fraction system loses 1% of $1,020.00 or $10.20, leaving $1,009.80. Note that the results from both these systems are approximately identical. Over time, however, the fixed-fraction system grows exponentially and surpasses the fixed-bet system, which grows linearly. Also note that the results depend on the numbers of heads and tails and do not at all depend on the order of heads and tails. The reader may prove this result by spreadsheet simulation.

is like trying to take nickels from in front of a steam roller. Eventually, one losing streak flattens the account.

Optimizing—Using Simulation

Once we select a betting system, say the fixed-fraction betting system, we can then optimize the system by finding the *PARAMETERS* that yield the best *EXPECTED VALUE*. In the coin toss case, our only parameter is the fixed-fraction. Again, we can get our answers by simulation. See Figures 24.3 and 24.4.

% Bet	Start	Heads	Tails	Heads	Tails	Heads	Tails	Heads	Tails	Heads	Tails
0	1000.00	1000.00	1000.00	1000.00	1000.00	1000.00	1000.00	1000.00	1000.00	1000.00	1000.00
5	1000.00	1100.00	1045.00	1149.50	1092.03	1201.23	1141.17	1255.28	1192.52	1311.77	1246.18
10	1000.00	1200.00	1080.00	1296.00	1166.40	1399.68	1259.71	1511.65	1360.49	1632.59	1469.33
15	1000.00	1300.00	1105.00	1436.50	1221.03	1587.33	1349.23	1754.00	1490.90	1938.17	1647.45
20	1000.00	1400.00	1120.00	1568.00	1254.40	1756.16	1404.93	1966.90	1573.52	2202.93	1762.34
25	1000.00	1500.00	1125.00	1687.50	1265.63	1898.44	1423.83	2135.74	1601.81	2402.71	1802.03
30	1000.00	1600.00	1120.00	1792.00	1254.40	2007.04	1404.93	2247.88	1573.52	2517.63	1762.34
35	1000.00	1700.00	1105.00	1878.50	1221.03	2075.74	1349.23	2293.70	1490.90	2534.53	1647.45
40	1000.00	1800.00	1080.00	1944.00	1166.40	2099.52	1259.71	2267.48	1360.49	2448.88	1469.33
45	1000.00	1900.00	1045.00	1985.50	1092.03	2074.85	1141.17	2168.22	1192.52	2265.79	1246.18
50	1000.00	2000.00	1000.00	2000.00	1000.00	2000.00	1000.00	2000.00	1000.00	2000.00	1000.00
55	1000.00	2100.00	945.00	1984.50	893.03	1875.35	843.91	1772.21	797.49	1674.74	753.63
60	1000.00	2200.00	880.00	1936.00	774.40	1703.68	681.47	1499.24	599.70	1319.33	527.73
65	1000.00	2300.00	805.00	1851.50	648.03	1490.46	521.66	1199.82	419.94	965.85	338.05
70	1000.00	2400.00	720.00	1728.00	518.40	1244.16	373.25	895.80	268.74	644.97	193.49
75	1000.00	2500.00	625.00	1562.50	390.63	976.56	244.14	610.35	152.59	381.47	95.37

FIGURE 24.3: Simulation of equity from a fixed-fraction betting system

At a 0% bet there is no change in the equity. At 5% bet size, we bet 5% of $1,000.00 or $50.00 and make twice that on the first toss (heads) so we have an expected value of $1,100. Then our second bet is 5% of $1,100.00 or $55.00, which we lose, so we then have $1,045.00. Note that we do the best at a 25% bet size. Note also that the winning parameter (25%) becomes evident after just one head–tail cycle. This allows us to simplify the problem of searching for the optimal parameter to the examination of just one head–tail cycle.

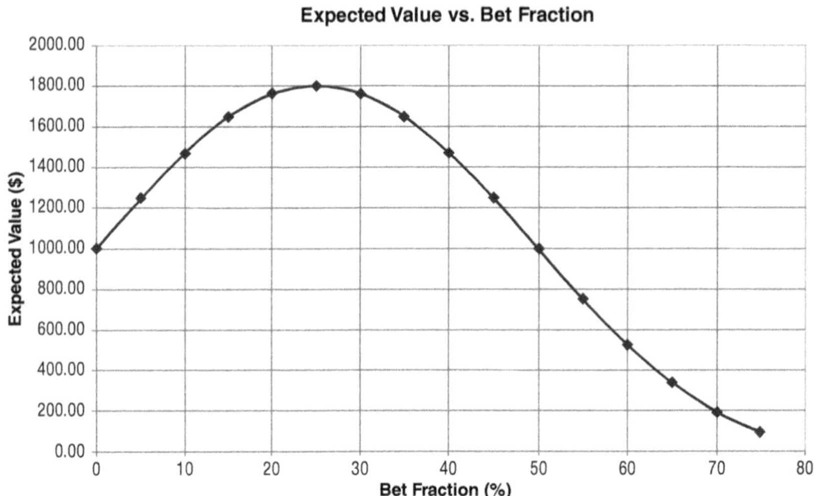

FIGURE 24.4: Expected value (ending equity) from 10 tosses, versus bet fraction, for a constant-bet fraction system, for a 2:1 payoff game, from the first and last columns of Figure 24.3

Notice that the expected value of the system rises from $1,000.00 with increasing bet fraction to a maximum value of about $1,800 at a 25% bet fraction. Thereafter, with increasing bet fraction, the profitability declines. This curve expresses two fundamental principles of risk management: (1) The Timid Trader Rule: If you don't bet very much, you don't make very much; and (2) The Bold Trader Rule: If you bet too much, you go broke. In portfolios that maintain multiple positions and multiple bets, we refer to the total risk as the portfolio heat.

Note: The chart illustrates the Expected Value / Bet Fraction relationship for a 2:1 payoff game. For a graph of this relationship at varying payoffs, see Figure 24.8.

Note: The coin-toss example intends to illuminate some of the elements of risk, and their interrelationships. It specifically applies to a coin that pays 2:1 with a 50% chance of either heads or tails, in which an equal number of heads and tails appears. It does not consider the case in which the numbers of heads and tails are unequal or in which the heads and tails bunch up to create winning and losing streaks. It does not suggest any particular risk parameters for trading the markets.

Optimizing—Using Calculus

Since our coin flip game is relatively simple, we can also find the optimal bet fraction using calculus. Since we know that the best system becomes apparent after only one head–tail cycle, we can simplify the problem to solving for just one of the head–tail pairs.

The stake after one pair of flips:

$$S = (1 + b \times P) \times (1 - b) \times S_0$$

S—the stake after one pair of flips

b—the bet fraction

P—the payoff from winning, 2:1

S_0—the stake before the pair of flips

$(1 + b \times P)$—the effect of the winning flip

$(1 - b)$—the effect of the losing flip

So the effective return, R, of one pair of flips is:

$$R = S / S0$$

$$R = (1 + bP) \times (1 - b)$$

$$R = 1 - b + bP - b2P$$

$$R = 1 + b(P - 1) - b2P$$

Note how for small values of b, R increases with b(P – 1) and how for large values of b, R decreases with b^2P. These are the mathematical formulations of the Timid and Bold Trader Rules.

We can plot R versus b to get a graph that looks similar to the one we get by simulation, above, and just pick out the maximum point by inspection. We can also notice that at the maximum, the slope is zero, so we can also solve for the maximum by taking the slope and setting it equal to zero.

Slope = dR / db = (P – 1) – 2bP = 0, therefore:

$$b = (P - 1) / 2P, \text{ and, for } P = 2{:}1,$$

$$b = (2 - 1)/(2 \times 2) = .25$$

So the optimal bet, as before, is 25% of equity.

Optimizing—Using the Kelly Formula

L. Kelly's seminal paper, *A New Interpretation of Information Rate*, 1956, examines ways to send data over telephone lines. One part of his work, the Kelly Formula, also applies to trading, to optimize bet size.

The Kelly Formula
K = W – (1 – W) / R
K = Fraction of Capital for Next Trade W = Historical Win Ratio (Wins/Total Trials) R = Winning Payoff Rate For example, say a coin pays 2:1 with 50-50 chance of heads or tails. Then K = .5 – (1 – .5) / 2 = .5 – .25 = .25. Kelly indicates the optimal fixed-fraction bet is 25%.

FIGURE 24.5: The Kelly Formula
Note that the values of W and R are long-term average values, so as time goes by, K might change a little.

Some Graphic Relationships Between Luck, Payoff, and Optimal Bet Fraction

Optimal Bet vs Y = Luck and X = Payoff

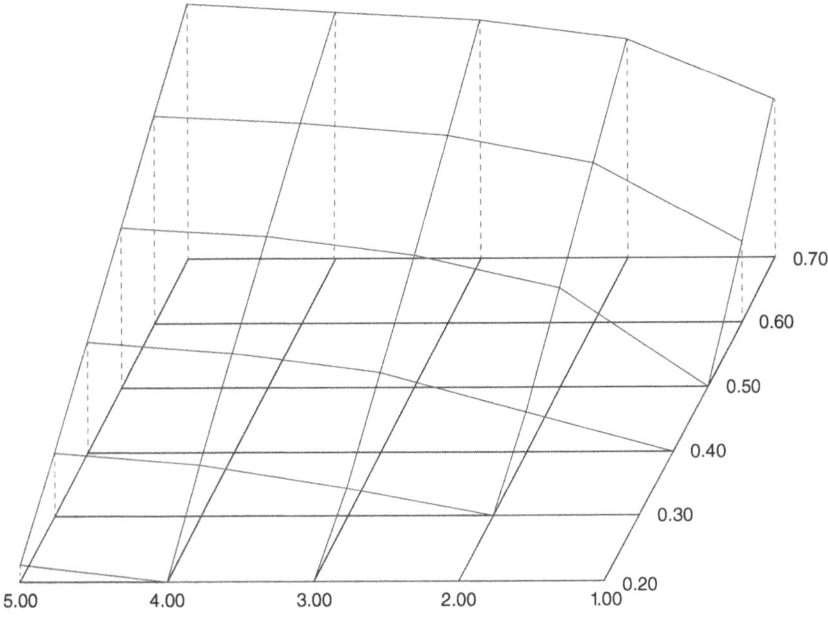

FIGURE 24.6: Optimal bet fraction increases linearly with luck, asymptotically to payoff.

The Optimal Bet Fraction Increases with Luck and Payoff

This graph shows the optimal bet fraction for various values of luck (Y) and payoff (X). Optimal bet fraction increases with increasing payoff. For very high payoffs, optimal bet size equals luck. For example, for a 5:1 payoff on a 50–50 coin, the optimal bet approaches about 50% of your stake.

Nonbalanced Distributions and High Payoffs

So far, we view risk management from the assumption that, over the long run, heads and tails for a 50–50 coin will even out. Occasionally, however, a winning streak does occur. If the payoff is higher than 2:1 for a balanced coin, the expected value, allowing for winning streaks, reaches a maximum for a bet-it-all strategy.

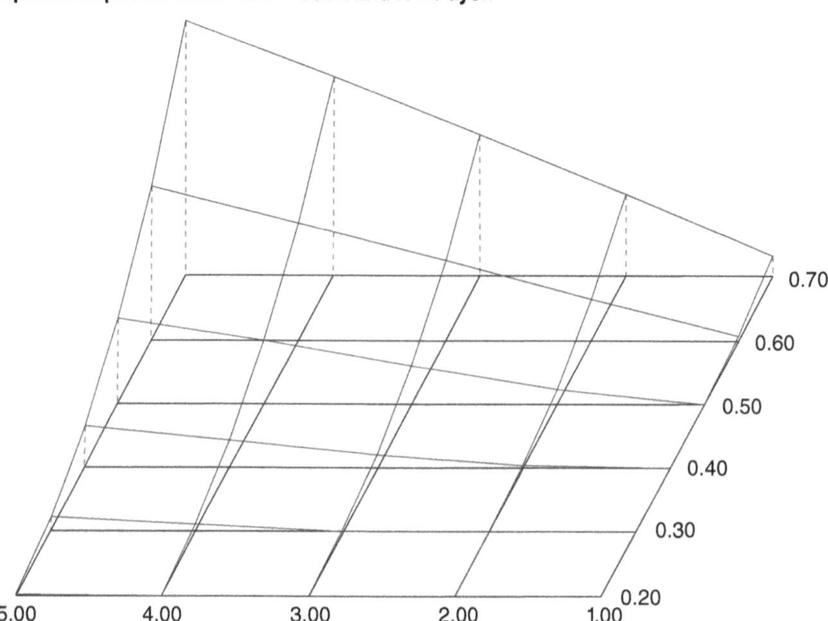

FIGURE 24.7: The optimal expected value increases with payoff and luck.

The Expected Value of the Process, at the Optimal Bet Fraction
This graph shows optimal expected value for various values of luck and payoff, given betting at the optimal bet fraction. The higher the payoff (X: 1:1 to 5:1) and the higher the luck (Y: .20 to .70), the higher the expected value. For example, the highest expected value is for a 70% winning coin that pays 5:1. The lowest expected value is for a coin that pays 1:1 (even bet).

For example, for a 3:1 payoff, each toss yields an expected value of payoff-times-probability of 1.0. Therefore, the expected value for 10 tosses is \$1,000 × $(1 + 1)^{10}$ or about \$1,024,000. This surpasses, by far, the expected value of about \$4,200 from optimizing a 3:1 coin to about a 35% bet fraction, with the assumption of an equal distribution of heads and tails.

Almost-Certain-Death Strategies

Bet-it-all strategies are, by nature, almost-certain-death strategies. Since the chance of survival for a 50–50 coin equals $(.5)^N$ where N is the number of tosses, after 10 tosses, the chance of survival is $(.5)^{10}$, or about one chance in one thousand. Since most traders do not wish to go broke, they are unwilling to adopt such a strategy. Still, the expected

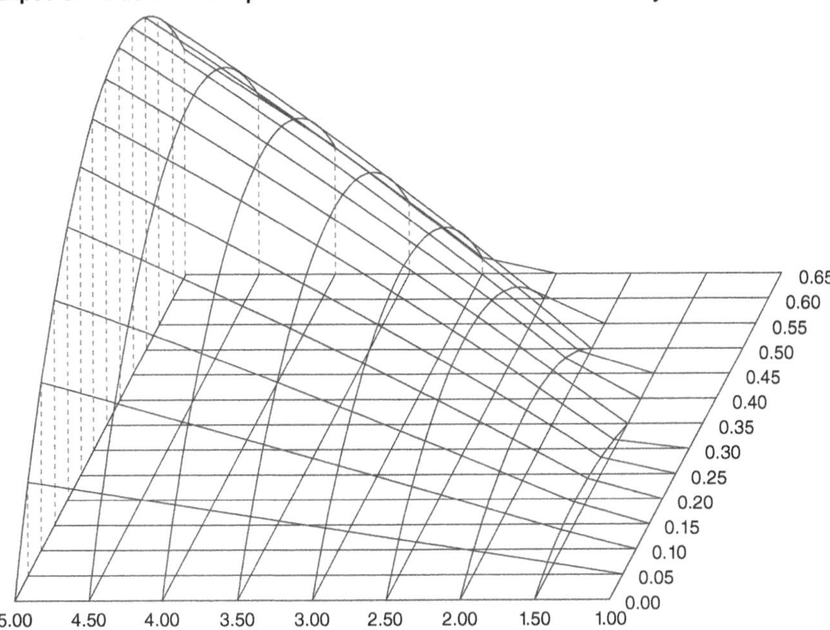

FIGURE 24.8: For high payoff, optimal bet fraction approaches luck.

Finding the Optimal Bet Fraction from the Bet Size and Payoff
This graph shows the expected value of a 50% lucky (balanced) coin for various levels of bet fraction and payoff. The expected value has an optimal bet fraction point for each level of payoff. In this case, the optimal bet fraction for a 1.5:1 payoff is about 15%; at a 2:1 payoff the optimal bet fraction is about 25%; at a 5:1 payoff, the optimal bet fraction is about 45%.
Note: Figure 24.4 is the cross section of Figure 24.8, at the 2:1 payoff level.

value of the process is very attractive, so we would expect to find the system in use in cases where death carries no particular penalty other than loss of assets.

For example, a general, managing dispensable soldiers, might seek to optimize his overall strategy by sending them all over the hill with instructions to charge forward fully, disregarding personal safety. While the general might expect to lose many of his soldiers by this tactic, the probabilities indicate that one or two of them might be able to reach the target and so maximize the overall expected value of the mission.

Likewise, a portfolio manager might divide his equity into various sub-accounts. He might then risk 100% of each sub-account, thinking that while he might lose many of them, a few would win enough so the overall expected value would maximize. This, the principle of *DIVERSIFICATION*, works in cases where the individual payoffs are high.

Diversification

Diversification is a strategy to distribute investments among different securities in order to limit losses in the event of a fall in a particular security. The strategy relies on the average security having a profitable expected value, or luck-payoff product. Diversification also offers some psychological benefits to single-instrument trading since some of the short-term variation in one instrument may cancel out that from another instrument and result in an overall smoothing of short-term portfolio volatility.

The Uncle Point

From the standpoint of a diversified portfolio, the individual component instruments subsume into the overall performance. The performance of the fund then becomes the focus of attention, for the risk manager and for the customers of the fund. The fund performance then becomes subject to the same kinds of feelings, attitudes, and management approaches that investors apply to individual stocks.

In particular, one of the most important and perhaps under-acknowledged dimensions of fund management is the *UNCLE POINT*, or the amount of drawdown that provokes a loss of confidence in either the investors or the fund management. If either the investors or the managers become demoralized and withdraw from the enterprise, then the fund dies. Since the circumstances surrounding the Uncle Point are generally disheartening, it seems to receive, unfortunately, little attention in the literature.

In particular, at the initial point of sale of the fund, the Uncle Point typically receives little mention, aside from the requisite and rather obscure notice in associated regulatory documentation. This is unfortunate, since a mismatch in the understanding of the Uncle Point between the investors and the management can lead to one or the other giving up, just when the other most needs reassurance and reinforcement of commitment.

In times of stress, investors and managers do not access obscure legal agreements, they access their primal gut feelings. This is particularly important in high-performance, high-volatility trading where drawdowns are a frequent aspect of the enterprise.

Without conscious agreement on an Uncle Point, risk managers typically must assume, by default to safety, that the Uncle Point is rather close and so they seek ways to keep the volatility low. As we have seen above, safe, low-volatility systems rarely provide the highest returns. Still, the pressures and tensions from the default expectations of low-volatility performance create a demand for measurements to detect and penalize volatility.

Measuring Portfolio Volatility: Sharpe, VaR, Lake Ratio, and Stress Testing

From the standpoint of the diversified portfolio, the individual components merge and become part of the overall performance. Portfolio managers rely on measurement systems to determine the performance of the aggregate fund, such as the Sharpe Ratio, VaR, Lake Ratio, and Stress Testing.

William Sharpe, in 1966, creates his "reward-to-variability ratio." Over time it comes to be known as the "Sharpe Ratio." The Sharpe Ratio, S, provides a way to compare instruments with different performances and different volatilities, by adjusting the performances for volatilities.

S = mean(d) / standard_deviation(d) . . . the Sharpe Ratio, where

d = Rf – Rb . . . the differential return, and where

Rf—return from the fund

Rb—return from a benchmark

Various variations of the Sharpe Ratio appear over time. One variation leaves out the benchmark term, or sets it to zero. Another, basically the square of the Sharpe Ratio, includes the variance of the returns, rather than the standard deviation. One of the considerations about using the Sharpe Ratio is that it does not distinguish between up-side and down-side volatility, so high-leverage/high-performance systems that seek high upside volatility do not appear favorably.

VaR, or Value-at-Risk is another currently popular way to determine portfolio risk. Typically, it measures the highest percentage drawdown that is expected to occur over a given time period, with 95% chance. The drawbacks to relying on VaR are that (1) historical computations can produce only rough approximations of forward volatility and (2) there is still a 5%

chance that the percentage drawdown will still exceed the expectation. Since the most severe drawdown problems (loss of confidence by investors and managers) occur during these "outlier" events, VaR does not really address or even predict the very scenarios it purports to remedy.

A rule-of-thumb way to view high-volatility accounts, by this author, is the Lake Ratio. If we display performance as a graph over time, with peaks and valleys, we can visualize rain falling on a mountain range, filling in all the valleys. This produces a series of lakes between peaks. In case the portfolio is not at an all-time high, we also erect a dam back up to the all-time high, at the far right, to collect all the water from the previous high point in a final, artificial lake. The total volume of water represents the integral product of drawdown magnitude and drawdown duration.

If we divide the total volume of water by the volume of the earth below it, we have the Lake Ratio. The rate of return divided by the Lake Ratio gives another measure of volatility-normal return. Savings accounts and other instruments that do not present drawdowns do not collect lakes so their Lake-adjusted returns can be infinite.

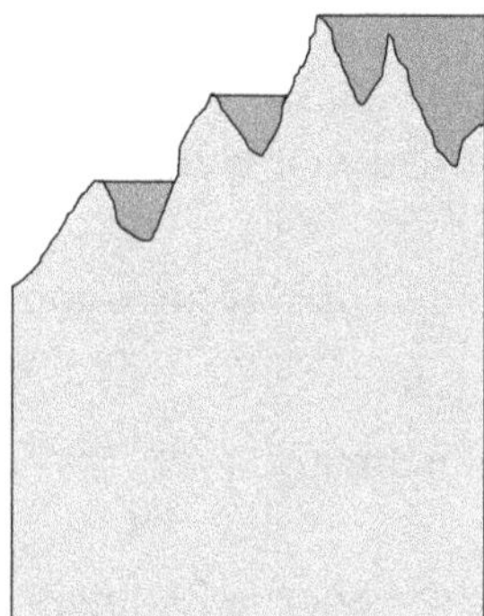

FIGURE 24.9: The Lake Ratio = Blue / Yellow

Getting a feel for volatility by inspection.
Reference for Sharpe Ratio: http://www.stanford.edu/~wfsharpe/art/sr/sr.htm

Stress Testing

Stress Testing is a process of subjecting a model of the trading and risk management system to historical data, and noticing the historical performance, with special attention to the drawdowns. The difficulty with this approach is that few risk managers have a conscious model of their systems, so few can translate their actual trading systems to computer code. Where this is possible, however, it provides three substantial benefits: (1) a framework within which to determine optimal bet-sizing strategies, (2) a high level of confidence that the systems are logical, stable, and efficacious, and (3) an exhibit to support discussions to bring the risk/reward expectations of the fund managers and the investors into alignment.

The length of historical data sample for the test is likely adequate if shortening the length by a third or more has no appreciable effect on the results.

Portfolio Selection

During market cycles, individual stocks exhibit wide variations in behavior. Some rise 100 times while others fall to 1% of their peak values. Indicators such as the DJIA, the S&P Index, the NASDAQ, and the Russell have wide variations from each other, further indicating the importance of portfolio selection. A portfolio of the best performing stocks easily outperforms a portfolio of the worst performing stocks. In this regard, the methods for selecting the trading portfolio contribute critically to overall performance and the methodology to select instruments properly belongs in the back-testing methods.

The number of instruments in a portfolio also affects performance. A small number of instruments produces volatile, occasionally very profitable performance while a large number of instruments produces less volatile and more stable, although lower, returns.

Position Sizing

Some position sizing strategies consider value, others risk. Say a million-dollar account intends to trade 20 instruments, and that the investor is willing to risk 10% of the account.

Value-Basis position sizing divides the account into 20 equal subaccounts of $50,000 each, one for each stock. Since stocks have different prices, the number of shares for various stocks varies.

Stock	Price/Share	Shares	Value
A	$50	1000	$50,000
B	$100	500	$50,000
C	$200	250	$50,000

Value-Basis Position Sizing
Dividing $50,000 by $50/share gives 1000 shares

Risk-Basis position sizing considers the risk for each stock, where risk is the entry price minus the stop-out point. It divides the total risk allowance, say 10% or $100,000 into 20 sub-accounts, each risking $5,000. Dividing the risk allowance, $5,000 by the risk per share, gives the number of shares.

Stock	Price/Share	Risk/Share	Shares	Risk	Value
A	$50	$5	1000	$5,000	$50,000
B	$100	$10	500	$5,000	$50,000
C	$200	$5	1000	$5,000	$200,000

Risk-Basis Position Sizing
Dividing $5,000 by $5 risk/share gives 1000 shares

Note that since risk per share may not be proportional to price per share (compare stocks B & C), the two methods may not indicate the same number of shares. For very close stops, and for a high risk allowance, the number of shares indicating under Risk-Basis sizing may even exceed the purchasing power of the account.

Psychological Considerations

In actual practice, the most important psychological consideration is ability to stick to the system. To achieve this, it is important (1) to fully understand the system rules, (2) to know how the system behaves, and (3) to have clear and supportive agreements between all parties that support sticking to the system.

For example, as we noticed earlier, profits and losses do not likely alternate with smooth regularity; they appear, typically, as winning and losing streaks. When the entire investor-manager team realizes this as natural, it is more likely to stay the course during drawdowns, and also to stay appropriately modest during winning streaks.

In addition, seminars, support groups, and other forms of attitude maintenance can help keep essential agreements on track, throughout the organization.

Risk Management—Summary

In general, good risk management combines several elements:

1. Clarifying trading and risk management systems until they can translate to computer code.
2. Inclusion of diversification and instrument selection into the back-testing process.
3. Back-testing and stress-testing to determine trading parameter sensitivity and optimal values.
4. Clear agreement of all parties on expectation of volatility and return.
5. Maintenance of supportive relationships between investors and managers.
6. Above all, stick to the system.
7. See #6, above.

How to GRAB a Bargain Trading Futures . . . Maybe 25

Mark Sleeman

Introduction

My name is Mark Sleeman. I live in Auckland, New Zealand and am the sole principal of CTA firm M.S. Capital Management Limited.

The next few pages detail a research project I originally undertook in conjunction with Ed Seykota in 2009 to contribute to the research on his "Trading Tribe" website (www.seykota.com). This is an updated version (September 2016). It has similar findings as the original version, but utilizes more up-to-date examples of market action to illustrate its points.

The project creates and tests a computerized trading system that buys retracements and sells rallies—the opposite of how common

Disclaimer: The GRAB a Bargain Research Project text shown here is a white paper written by Mark Sleeman detailing the process he followed during the project as well as his findings upon completion. It is provided for informational purposes only and should not be construed as an offer to sell or purchase any investment product or trading strategy.

trend following systems work. While I know that the buy-low, sell-high approach feels good to many traders, I wish to find out if it is actually profitable when subject to rigorous testing.

How to GRAB a Bargain Trading Futures

I love to grab a bargain. The problem is my trend following system—like all trend following systems—doesn't. It waits around until it sees a new uptrend and only then does it buy. Invariably, the buy signal comes long after the bottom. I find this extremely frustrating, and often wonder if it is possible to build a system that buys the bottoms and sells the tops.

Following Trends Is Hard Work

It is early January 2016 and I am watching the E-mini S&P 500 futures fall sharply against a background of plummeting oil prices and fears of a slowdown in China. Down and down the price goes. By January 20 it is at the August/September 2015 support level and I am thinking to myself, "This is cheap; I can jump in here and grab myself a bargain." I really want to buy, but my boring old trend following system says "Stay out." Prices jiggle sideways for a few weeks, then suddenly turn around and head up. Each day the market rallies, and each day I feel a growing knot in the pit of my stomach as I replay the situation over and over, only with me happily holding a long position, rather than watching hopelessly from the sidelines. As the price swiftly rises my feelings of anger and frustration rise with it. But, I listen to my system and do nothing. The price continues to rally. By early April the price is no longer a bargain, it is back up to resistance levels and looks expensive. I no longer want to buy, I want to sell short. But, what does my system do? It signals a buy. Reluctantly, I take the trade.

Initially the market rallies for a few days, but then it starts to fall. Down and down it goes—it as if "they" know I am finally long. I watch my losses mount; the knot in my stomach a few days ago is nothing compared to what I am feeling now. I curse myself, and my system, for buying at the top. Eventually prices are looking cheap again. But is my system buying? No, it is selling. The trade is hitting its stop-loss point, and it is time to get out.

Of course, prices then immediately rally again to new highs and my system goes long again. On June 24 the shock result of the Brexit vote

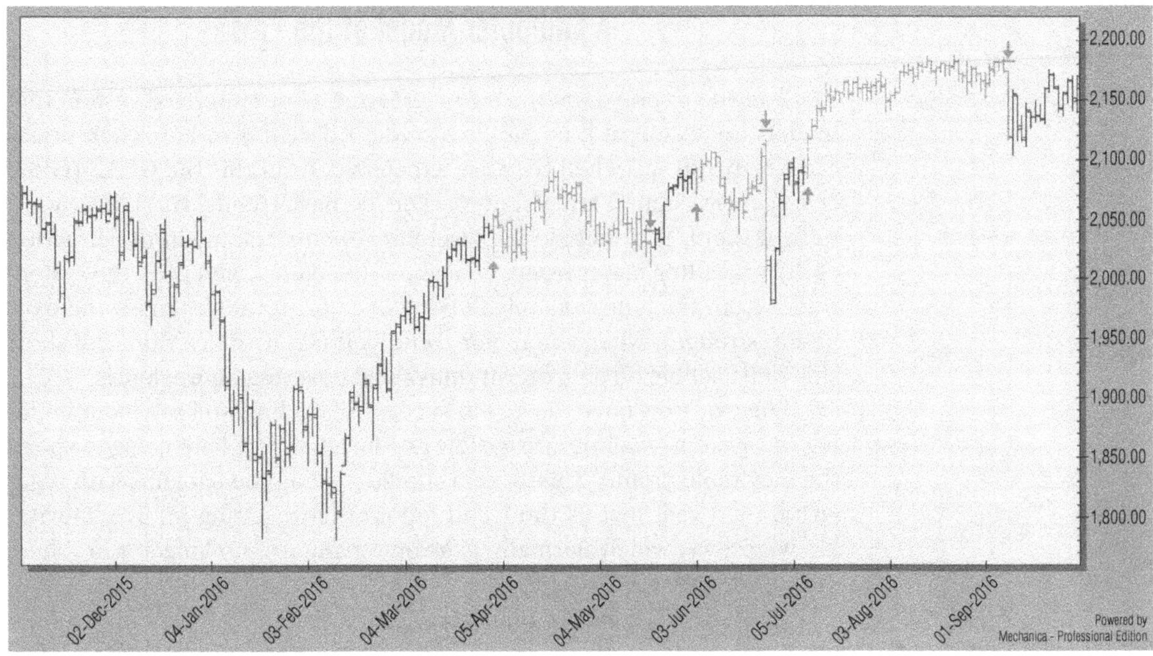

FIGURE 25.1: Trend Following System, E-Mini S&P 500 (Back-Adjusted)

sends prices into freefall: a heaven-sent opportunity to buy. What does my system do? It sells out. This happens one more time, with the system exiting on the big down day of September 9. I feel like an idiot; I seem to always be buying high and selling low. It is a zero-sum game, right? Someone must be making all the money that I am losing, but who? Who takes the money out of these markets? On reflection I figure it must be the "Pros." I am sick of throwing my money away; it is time for me to figure out how the Pros trade—then I can start trading like they do!

Figuring Out How the Pros Do It

Just how do the Pros do it? I think about how smart operators succeed in other businesses. Then I remember the old adage that to sell right, you must first buy right. That's it! That must be how the Pros trade. Not for them this silly game of buying at highs. I figure they wait patiently for bargains, and then pounce. All they have to do then is wait for the subsequent rally and sell. They can do this time and time again. And who are they selling to at the tops, and buying from at the bottoms? The sucker trend followers of course just like me.

A Computer Model of the Pros

I decide to prove my theory by creating a computerized system that models my vision of how the Pros trade. I design it to buy when prices are cheap and sell when they are expensive. I call this the GRAB (GRab A Bargain) system. I know that markets do have trends, and I don't want to fight them. So I include the discipline of only trading in the direction of the prevailing major trend, i.e., when the major trend is up the system trades from the long side only, buying on short-term weakness and exiting on strength; when the major trend is down it trades from the short side only, selling on short-term rallies and covering on weakness.

I figure I now have the key to successful trading, so I set about building the system—feeling a rosy glow as I imagine how I am going to spend the inevitable profits. This system should pick up the bargains with regularity, then sell, just as the trend followers are getting in. The inevitable whipsaws, which normally cause me pain, are no longer a problem; rather they are a source of profit.

The GRAB system is complete; to run, it requires two values (parameters), which are simply the number of days the system looks back to determine support and resistance levels (see "GRAB Trading System Details").

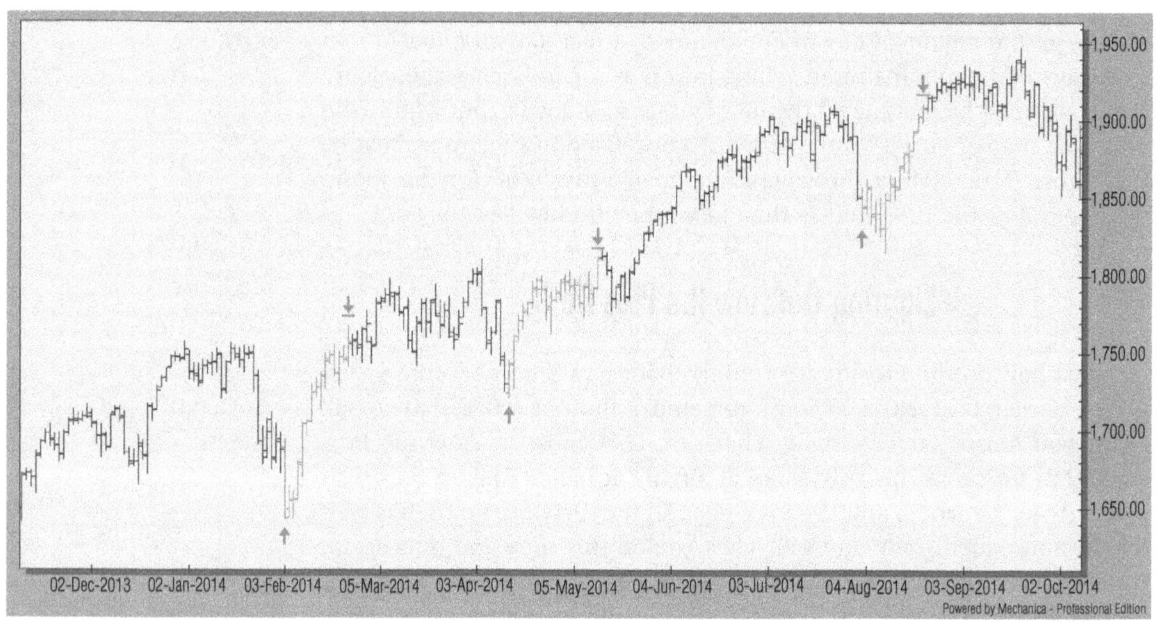

FIGURE 25.2: E-Mini S&P 500 (Back-Adjusted)

I set about optimizing these parameters. With experimentation I find values that allow the system to pick off the highs and lows just as I wish.

This looks great. Now the GRAB system is ready for back-testing. I am eager to see just how well this system performs. I select a diversified portfolio of 40 futures markets and 30 years of price history. I run the computer test and wait impatiently for the results.

A Terrible Discovery

When I run the system, in addition to finding it buys dips and sells rallies as I expect, I notice something else that makes my blood freeze. Despite the "Pro" trading strategy, this system does not make money, it loses money.

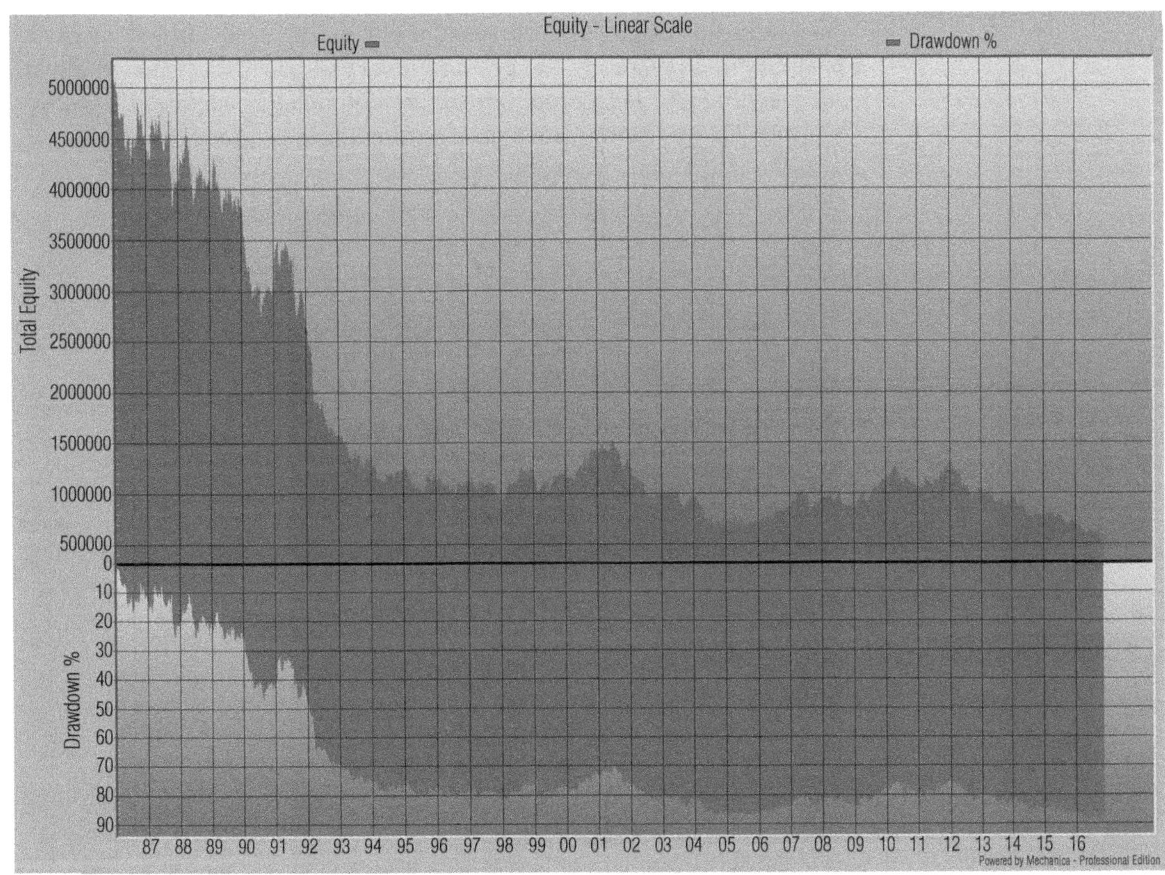

FIGURE 25.3: GRAB System; Parameter Values 40, 80

I am flabbergasted! Far from being the money machine I imagine, this system looks like a path to the poor house. To confirm the initial findings I run many more tests.

The results are conclusive: The GRAB system is a loser. I do not understand this mystery: How can something that looks so good lose money?

Solving the Mystery—Why Does the GRAB System Lose?

Clearly the GRAB system is not always picking off the highs and lows as I hope. As I investigate further, I see that the system behavior is highly dependent on the fit between the parameter values and the price action.

Often It Is Out of Sync with the Market

If the parameters are even slightly out of sync with the price action, the system no longer works as I want. It either enters too early or not at all. When it enters too early the position loses as it rides the reaction down, often exiting just before the bottom and completely missing the subsequent move up. Often this happens several times in succession, in a similar fashion to a trend following system suffering a series of whipsaw losses.

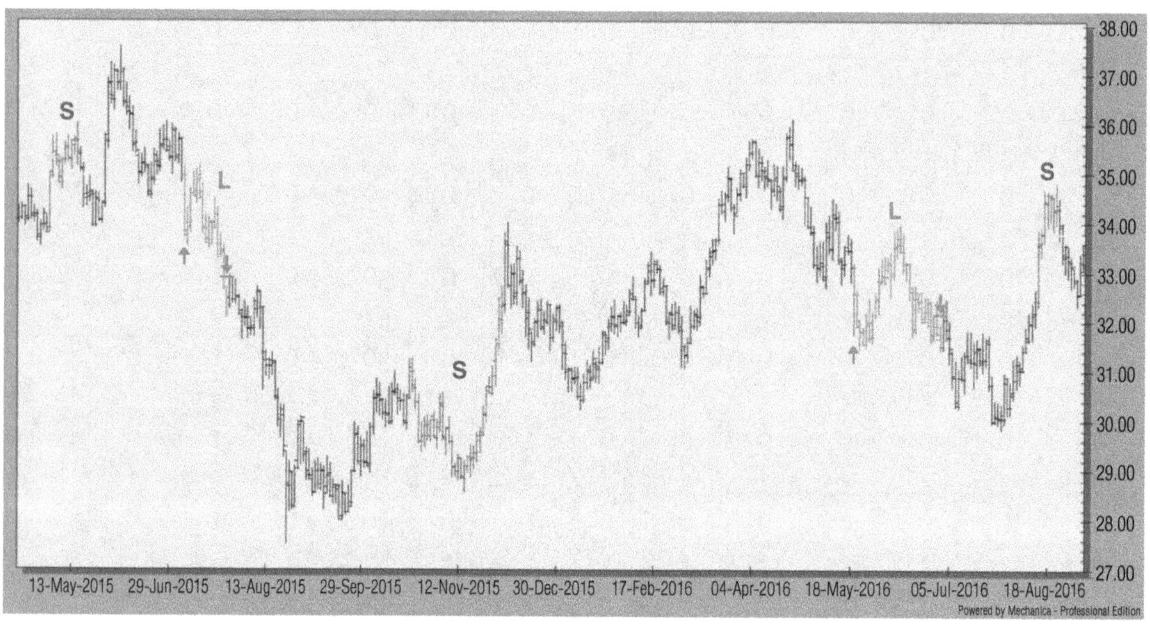

FIGURE 25.4: GRAB System; Parameter Values 40, 80 Soybean Oil (Back-Adjusted)
"L": Long Trades, "S": Short Trades

Worse Still, It Misses the Best Moves!

However, it is the case of the system not entering at all that really degrades the performance.

The GRAB system relies on reactions against the trend to enter a move. However, the strongest trends often have the smallest reactions; if these reactions are too small the GRAB system is not able to enter. Even if it does manage to enter the move once or twice, it quickly exits again on strength. Therefore, the GRAB system requires a series of substantial reactions to have any chance of catching a significant portion of a large move. The strongest moves often do not have deep enough reactions to allow this system to get on board, leaving it in the dust as the price rockets skywards. Note how, during the massive 2014 rally in bond prices, the GRAB system completely misses the move up in Euro German Bund prices. The enormous profits it misses out on in this case, and many others like it, wreck the system performance.

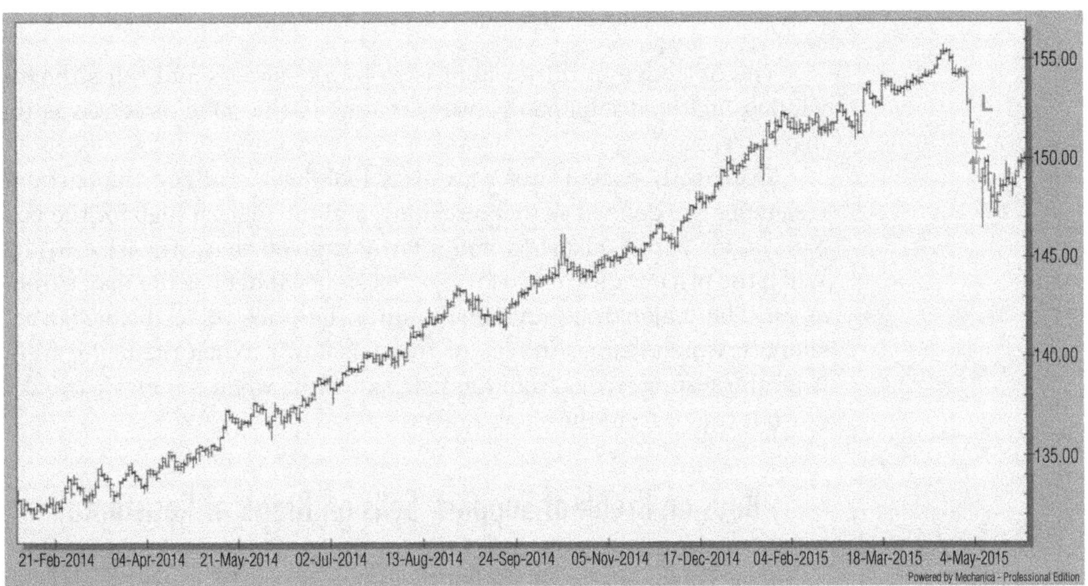

FIGURE 25.5: GRAB System; Parameter Values 40, 80 Euro German Bund (Back-Adjusted)

"L": Long Trades, "S": Short Trades

The GRAB system only works well during the rare times that its parameters are in sync with the market action. The rest of the time it either mistimes the reactions or fails to get aboard the large moves—missing out on huge profits as it sits on the sidelines.

Maybe Being Profitable Means Being Uncomfortable?

These results shatter my day-dreams of systematically picking up bargains in the futures markets. The strategy of buying cheap and selling when prices look expensive feels good to me and, I expect, to many other people. But when I test it on computer it is clearly a loser. In contrast, I often feel uncomfortable operating my trend following system, with its strategy of buying at highs and selling at lows. But, the big difference is that it is generally profitable. It appears that in futures trading (like other endeavors), profits do not come easily, because they require the trader to absolutely stick to a system that is sometimes very difficult to follow.

GRAB Trading System Details

The objective of this system is to buy weakness and sell strength, while using the discipline of always trading in the same direction as the major trend.

The GRAB system uses a two-box look-back strategy. Support and resistance are defined as the lowest low and the highest high for the past N days, for both a near-box and a far-box, given that N(near) < N(far). When the price trades above far-box resistance it defines the major trend as up. The major trend remains up until the price trades below far-box support, which defines the major trend as down. When the major trend is up the system trades from the long side only; when the major trend is down it trades from the short side only.

Buys on Break of Support, Sells on Break of Resistance

Thus far the system is similar to a support/resistance trend following system. The difference is that, within a major uptrend, GRAB *buys* weakness and *sells* strength (in a downtrend the procedure reverses). When the major trend is up, the system buys (during a reaction) on a break of near-box support, and sells (during a rally) on a break of near-box resistance, using limit orders. It keeps doing this until, rather than rallying to near-box resistance, prices break below far-box support, at which point the major trend definition changes to down and the position exits (on a stop). The system is then ready to trade short, by selling on a break of near-box resistance.

See "GRAB Trading System Code" for the code behind the GRAB system.

FIGURE 25.6: Near-Box Look-Back: 20 Days. Far-Box Look-Back: 100 Days, Corn (Back-Adjusted)

"L": Long Trades, "S": Short Trades, "NBR": Near Box Resistance, "NBS": Near Box Support, "FBS": Far Box Support

The GRAB system is inherently different to standard trend following systems, which buy strength and sell weakness. At first glance I think it should generate a number of small profits from trading within the trend, followed by a larger loss as the trend reverses. This likely has the effect of increasing the Win/Loss rate over that of a trend following system, while reducing the Average Win/Average Loss ratio. I also believe the slippage costs should be smaller, as a result of much of the trading executing via limit orders, rather than the stop orders trend following systems use.

Testing Reveals Some Behavior I Do Not Expect

In back-testing I find some things I do not expect (the following assumes the trend is up):

1. Sometimes the near-box and far-box support levels are the same. This happens more often when the two parameter values are close together. In these cases the system wants to buy (enter) and sell (exit) at the same price. I see that the back-test does not enter these trades. This is a reasonable approximation of actual trading—as the trader can cancel both orders, rather than send them to the broker.
2. A losing trade does not accompany every major trend reversal, as not all trend reversal trades enter [see (1) above].
3. Not all of the trades within the major trend are profitable. Sometimes the exit level (near-box resistance) moves below the entry level during the life of the trade. This is more likely to occur when the near- and far-box parameters are further apart.
4. It is possible, although unlikely, that a position exit that occurs on a major trend change (break of far-box support) is actually profitable. This occurs when the far-box support moves above the entry price during the life of the trade. This is more likely to occur when the parameters are close together.

Difference between Parameter Values Defines Character of GRAB System

The distance between the parameters defines the character of the GRAB system. When the parameters are far apart, only a small reaction against the major trend breaks near-box support, and triggers an entry. Similarly, only a small profitable move breaks near-box resistance, and triggers the exit. Conversely, the system requires a large losing move to break far-box support and signal a major trend change from up to down. This produces frequent trading, with many small wins and a few large losses. This may appeal to a trader's desire to be "right."

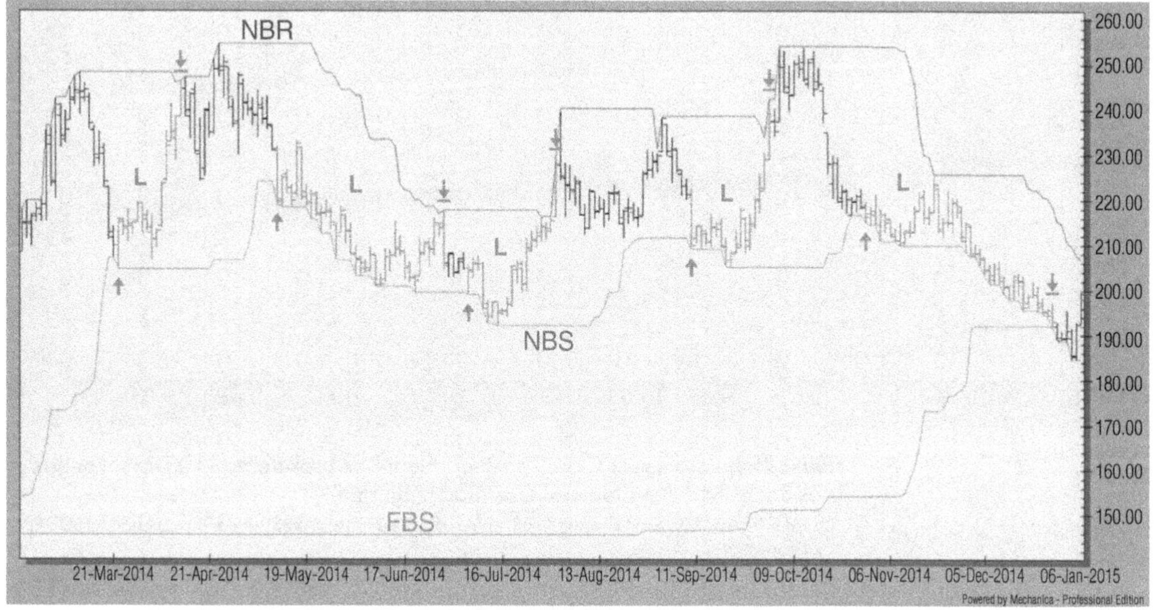

FIGURE 25.7: Parameters Far Apart: Near-Box Look-Back: 20 Days. Far-Box Look-Back: 200 Days, New York Coffee (Back-Adjusted)

"L": Long Trades, "S": Short Trades, "NBR": Near Box Resistance, "NBS": Near Box Support, "FBS": Far Box Support

When the parameters are close together, the GRAB system requires a large reaction against the major trend to enter a position, hence trading is less frequent. Once in a position the system requires a large profitable move to reach near-box resistance, and trigger an exit. Conversely, it requires only a small losing move to break far-box support and trigger a trend-change exit. This configuration skips many of the trend-change trades as in (1) above. This produces infrequent trading, with few winners. However the trades that do win enter very near the bottom of the reaction and exit near the top of the ensuing move. This may appeal to a trader's desire to be "smart."

FIGURE 25.8: Parameters Close Together: Near-Box Look-Back: 110 Days. Far-Box Look-Back: 140 Days Natural Gas (Back-Adjusted)

"L": Long Trades, "S": Short Trades, "NBR": Near Box Resistance, "NBS": Near Box Support, "FBS": Far Box Support

GRAB Trading System Code

The following is the code for the grab system in a semi-English format. An apostrophe at the beginning of a line denotes a comment.

Indicator Setup

```
'GRAB System.
'Two-box system. Far box defines major trend; system
trades only in same direction as major trend,
'meanwhile fading the signals of near box.
'Last trade in each trend exits at break of far box - at
the same time as the trend reverses.
'All trades, except the last in the trend, use a limit
order, as they are fading the near box.
'The last trade exits on a stop, as the trend changes.
'Assign entry and exit break out parameters using
integers "X" and "Y".
```

```
'Set X = Far box lookback
X = 80
'Set Y = Near box lookback
Y = 40
'Create the far and near box support/resist levels.
FAR_BOX_RESISTANCE = MAX[H,X,0]
FAR_BOX_SUPPORT = MIN[L,X,0]
NEAR_BOX_RESISTANCE = MAX[H,Y,0]
NEAR_BOX_SUPPORT = MIN[L,Y,0]
'Initialize long term trend value to 0 so that it does
not set until indicators up to speed.
'See if high TODAY breaks yesterday's look back high, or
if low breaks yesterday's look back low.
IF FAR_BOX_RESISTANCE = 0 THEN
  TREND = 0
ELSE IF HIGH >= FAR_BOX_RESISTANCE[1] THEN
  TREND = 1
ELSE IF LOW <= FAR_BOX_SUPPORT[1] THEN
  TREND = -1
ELSE
  TREND = TREND[1]
```

Position Entry

```
'If the trend is up buy on a break of near box support.
IF TREND[1] = 1 THEN BUYLIMIT = NEAR_BOX_SUPPORT[1]
'If the trend is down sell on a break of near box
resistance.
IF TREND[1] = -1 THEN SELLIMIT = NEAR_BOX_RESISTANCE[1]
```

Position Exit

```
IF LONG = 0 THEN JUMPTO[1]
'If long either, sell (at a limit) on a break up from
the near box or, sell (on a stop) on a break down 'from
the far box - a change in trend from up to down.
SELLLIMIT = NEAR_BOX_RESISTANCE[1]
SELLSTOP = FAR_BOX_SUPPORT[1]
JUMPTO[2]
[1]
' Vice-versa if short.
BUYLIMIT = NEAR_BOX_SUPPORT[1]
BUYSTOP = FAR_BOX_RESISTANCE[1]
[2]
```

Position Sizing

```
'Use Fixed Fractional Position sizing. Positions size
inversely to the risk they present at entry.
'Set the risk budget.
RISK_BUDGET = .01
STARTDATE = 19860101
ENDATE = 20161010
STARTUPCASH = 1000000
NEWCONTRACTS = TOTALEQUITY * RISK_BUDGET / NEWRISK
```

Why Tactical Macro Investing Still Makes Sense

26

Jason Gerlach, Rick Slaughter, Chris Stanton
Sunrise Capital Partners

Introduction

In November 2002, Cass Business School Professor Harry M. Kat, Ph.D. began to circulate a working paper entitled "Managed Futures and Hedge Funds: A Match Made in Heaven." The *Journal of Investment Management* subsequently published the paper in the First Quarter of 2004. We consider Dr. Kat's paper to be one of the seminal works in the tactical macro investing or "managed futures" space. In the paper, Kat noted that while adding hedge fund exposure to traditional portfolios of stocks and bonds increased returns and reduced volatility, it also produced an undesirable side effect—increased tail risk (lower skew and higher kurtosis). He went on to analyze the effect of adding managed futures to the traditional portfolios, and then of combining hedge funds and managed futures, and finally the effect of adding both hedge funds and managed futures to the traditional portfolios. He found that managed futures were better diversifiers than hedge funds, that managed futures

Note: Why Tactical Macro Investing Still Makes Sense—Further Revisiting Kat's "Managed Futures and Hedge Funds: A Match Made in Heaven." Additional contributions from M. Odo, M. Schauben, T. Rollinger.

reduced the portfolio's volatility to a greater degree and more quickly than did hedge funds, and that managed futures achieved this without the negative side effect of increased tail risk. He concluded that the most desirable results were obtained by combining both managed futures and hedge funds with the traditional portfolios.[1]

Kat's original period of study was June 1994–May 2001. In our paper, we revisit and update Kat's original work. Hence, our primary period of study is the "out-of-sample" period since then, which is January 2001–December 2015. In two appendices, we also include our findings for two other periods. Due to the availability of the data and our choice of it, in Appendix A, we share our results for the entire period from 1990–2015.

This encompasses the almost four and a half years prior to Kat's original study period, Kat's original study period, and the out-of-sample period since then. In Appendix B, we share our results for the exact same period that Kat studied in his paper (June 1994–May 2001). It is important to note that our paper in general and Appendix B specifically is not meant to be an exact replication of Kat's original work.

Managed Futures

Managed futures may be thought of as a collection of liquid, transparent, tactical macro hedge fund strategies which focus on exchange-traded futures, forwards, options, and foreign exchange markets. Trading programs take both long and short positions in as many as 400 globally diversified markets, spanning physical commodities, fixed income, equity indices, and currencies. Daily participants in these markets include hedgers, traders, and investors, many of whom make frequent adjustments to their positions, contributing to substantial trading volume and plentiful liquidity. These conditions allow most managed futures programs to accommodate large capacity and provide the opportunity to diversify across many different markets, sectors, and time horizons.[2]

Diversification across market sectors, active management, and the ability to take long and short positions are key features that differentiate managed futures strategies not only from passive, long-only commodity indices, but from traditional investing as well.[3] Although most managed futures programs trade equity index, fixed income, and foreign exchange futures, their returns have historically been uncorrelated to the returns of these asset classes.[3] The reason for this is that most managers are not simply taking on systematic beta exposure to an asset class, but are attempting to add alpha through active, tactical management and the freedom to enter short or spread positions, tactics which offer the potential for completely different return profiles than long-only, passive indices.[3]

Early stories of futures trading can be traced as far back as the late 1600s in Japan.[4] Although the first public futures fund started trading in 1948, the industry did not gain traction until the 1970s. According to Barclays (2012), "a decade or more ago, these managers and their products may have been considered different than hedge funds; they are now usually viewed as a distinct strategy or group of strategies within the broader hedge fund universe. In fact, managed futures represent an important part of the alternative investment landscape," commanding approximately 12% of all hedge fund assets, which equated to $333.4 billion at the end of Q3 of 2015.[5]

Managed futures can be thought of as a subset of global macro strategies that focuses on global futures and foreign exchange markets and is likely to utilize a highly tactical, systematic approach to trading and risk management. The instruments that are traded tend to be exchange-listed futures or extremely deep, liquid, cash-forward markets. Futures facilitate pricing and valuation and minimize credit risk through daily settlement, enabling hedge fund investors to mitigate or eliminate some of the more deleterious risks associated with investing in alternatives. Liquidity and ease of pricing also assist risk management by making risks easier to measure and model.[3] In research conducted before the Global Financial Crisis, Bhaduri and Art (2008) found that the value of liquidity is often underestimated, and, as a result, hedge funds that trade illiquid instruments have underperformed hedge funds that have better liquidity terms.[6]

The quantitative nature of many managed futures strategies makes it easy for casual observers to mistakenly categorize them as "black box" trading systems.[3] According to Ramsey and Kins (2004), "The irony is that most CTAs will provide uncommonly high levels of transparency relative to other alternative investment strategies."[7] They go on to suggest that CTAs are generally willing to describe their trading models and risk management in substantial detail during the course of due diligence, "short of revealing their actual algorithms." CTAs are also typically willing to share substantial position transparency with fund investors. Through managed accounts, investors achieve real-time, full transparency of positions and avoid certain custodial risks associated with fund investments. Ramsey and Kins conclude that, "It is difficult to call CTAs black box, considering they disclose their methodology and provide full position transparency so that investors can verify adherence to that methodology."

Separately managed accounts, common among managed futures investors, greatly enhance risk management by providing the investor with full transparency, and in extreme cases, the ability to intervene by liquidating or neutralizing positions.[3] In addition, institutional investors who access CTAs via separately managed accounts substantially reduce operational risks and the possibility of fraud by maintaining custody of assets. Unlike the products traded in other hedge fund strategies, those traded by CTAs allow investors to customize the allocation by targeting a specific level of risk through the use of notional funding. The cash efficiency made possible by the low margin requirements of futures and foreign exchange allows investors to work with the trading manager to lever or delever a managed account to target a specific level of annualized volatility or other risk metric. Some CTAs offer funds with share classes with different levels of risk. Unlike traditional forms of leverage, which require the investor to pay interest to gain the additional exposure, assets used for margin in futures accounts can earn interest for the investor.

Another advantage of trading futures is that there are no barriers to short selling. Two parties simply enter into a contract; there is no uptick rule, there is no need to borrow shares, pay dividends, or incur other costs associated with entering into equity short sales. Thus, it is easier to implement a long-short strategy via futures than it is using equities.[3]

Defining Managed Futures and CTAs

"Managed futures" is an extremely broad term that requires a more specific definition. Managed futures traders are commonly referred to as "Commodity Trading Advisors" or "CTAs," a designation which refers to a manager's registration status with the Commodity Futures Trading Commission and National Futures Association. CTAs may trade financial and foreign exchange futures, so the Commodity Trading Advisor registration is somewhat misleading since CTAs are not restricted to trading only commodity futures.[3]

Where Institutional Investors Position Managed Futures and CTAs

According to a survey in the Barclays February 2012 Hedge Fund Pulse report, institutional investors view the top three key benefits of investing in CTAs as:

1. Low correlation to traditional return sources
2. The risk-mitigation/portfolio-diversifying characteristics of the strategy
3. The absolute-return component of the strategy and its attributes as a source of alpha

Also, 50% of the investors surveyed have between 0% to 10% of their current hedge fund portfolio allocated to CTA strategies, and 50% of investors surveyed plan to increase their allocations to the strategy in the next six months.[5]

Skewness and Kurtosis

When building portfolios using the Modern Portfolio Theory (MPT) framework, investors focus almost solely on the first two moments of the distribution: mean and variance. The typical MPT method of building portfolios appears to work well, as long as historical correlations between asset classes remain stable.[8] But in times of crisis, asset classes often move in lock-step, and investors who thought they were diversified experience severe "tail-risk" events. By only focusing on mean return and variance, investors may not be factoring in important, measurable, and historically robust information.

Skewness and kurtosis, the third and fourth moments of the distribution, can offer vital information about the real-world return characteristics of asset classes and investment strategies. The concepts of skewness and kurtosis are paramount to this study.

- Skewness is a measure of symmetry and compares the length of the two "tails" of a distribution curve.
- Kurtosis is a measure of the peakedness of a distribution—i.e., do the outcomes produce a "tall and skinny" or "short and squat" curve? In other words, is the volatility risk located in the tails of the distribution or clustered in the middle?

To understand how vital these concepts are to the results of this study, we revisit Kat's original work. Kat states that when past returns are extrapolated, and risk is defined as standard deviation, hedge funds do indeed provide investors with the best of both worlds: an expected return similar to equities, but risk similar to that of bonds. However, Amin and Kat (2003) showed that including hedge funds in a traditional investment portfolio may significantly improve the portfolio's mean-variance characteristics, but during crisis periods, hedge funds can also be expected to produce a more negatively skewed distribution.[9] Kat (2004) adds, "The additional negative skewness that arises when hedge funds are introduced [to] a portfolio of stocks and bonds forms a major risk, as one large negative return can destroy years of careful compounding."[1]

Kat's finding appears to be substantiated in Koulajian and Czkwianianc (2011), which evaluates the risk of disproportionate losses relative to volatility in various hedge fund strategies[10]:

"Negatively skewed strategies are only attractive during stable market conditions. During market shocks (e.g., the three largest S&P 500 drawdowns in the past 17 years), low-skew strategies display:

- Outsized losses of –41% (vs. gains of +39% for high-skew strategies);
- Increases in correlation to the S&P 500; and
- Increases in correlation to each other"

Skewness and kurtosis may convey critical information about portfolio risk and return characteristics, something that should be kept in mind when reading this study. [A more thorough review of skewness and kurtosis can be found in Appendix C.]

Data

Like Kat, our analysis focuses upon four asset classes: stocks, bonds, hedge funds, and managed futures.

Stocks—represented by the S&P 500 Total Return Index. The S&P 500 has been widely regarded as the most representative gauge of the large cap U.S. equities market since the index was first published in 1957. The index has over US$7.8 trillion benchmarked against it, with index-replication strategies comprising approximately US$2.2 trillion of this total. The index includes 500 leading companies in leading industries of the U.S. economy, capturing 80% of the capitalization of equities. The S&P 500 Total Return Index reflects both changes in the prices of stocks as well as the reinvestment of the dividend income from the underlying constituents.

Bonds—represented by the Barclays U.S. Aggregate Bond Index (formerly the Lehman Aggregate Bond Index). It was created in 1986, with backdated history to 1976. The index is the dominant index for U.S. bond investors, and is a benchmark index for many U.S. index funds. The index is a composite of four major sub-indexes: the U.S. Government Index; the U.S. Credit Index; the U.S. Mortgage-Backed Securities Index (1986); and (beginning in 1992) the U.S. Asset-Backed Securities Index. The index tracks investment-quality bonds based on S&P, Moody, and Fitch bond ratings. The index does not include High-Yield Bonds, Municipal Bonds, Inflation-Indexed Treasury Bonds, or Foreign Currency Bonds. As of late 2015, the index is comprised of about 8,200 bond issues.

Hedge Funds—represented by the HFRI Fund Weighted Composite Index, which includes over 2,300 constituent hedge funds. It is an equal-weighted index that includes both domestic and offshore funds—but no funds of funds. All funds report in USD and report net of all fees on a monthly basis. The funds must have at least $50 million under management or have been actively trading for at least 12 months.

Managed Futures—represented by the Barclay Systematic Traders Index. This index is an equal-weighted composite of managed programs whose approach is at least 95% systematic.

Closing 2015, there are 454 systematic programs included in the index.

Basic Statistics

The basic performance statistics for our four asset classes are shown in Table 26.1. Similar to Kat's results, but to a much lesser extent, our results show that managed futures have a lower mean return than hedge funds. Managed futures also have a higher standard deviation. However, they exhibit positive instead of negative skewness and much lower kurtosis. This is a critical point: the lower kurtosis conveys that less of the standard deviation is coming from the tails (lower tail risk), and the positive skewness indicates a tendency for upside surprises, not downside. From the correlation matrix, we see that hedge funds are highly correlated to stocks (0.80), managed futures are somewhat negatively correlated to stocks (–0.17), and the correlation between managed futures and hedge funds is low (0.07).

TABLE 26.1: Monthly Statistics for Stocks, Bonds, Hedge Funds, and Managed Futures for the Period June 2011–December 2015

	Stocks	Bonds	Hedge Funds	Managed Futures
Mean (%)	0.50	0.42	0.45	0.33
Standard Deviation (%)	4.32	1.01	1.72	2.25
Skewness	–0.63	–0.33	–0.84	0.22
Excess Kurtosis	1.17	1.37	2.06	0.43
Correlations				
Stocks	1.00			
Bonds	–0.11	1.00		
Hedge Funds	0.80	–0.03	1.00	
Managed Futures	–0.17	0.24	0.07	1.00

Stocks, Bonds, Plus Hedge Funds or Managed Futures

In order to study the effect of allocating to hedge funds and managed futures, we form a baseline "traditional" portfolio that is 50% stocks and 50% bonds ("50/50"). We then begin adding hedge funds or managed futures in 5%-allocation increments. As in Kat's original paper, when adding in hedge funds or managed futures, the original 50/50 portfolio will reduce its stock and bond holdings proportionally. This produces portfolios such as 40% stocks, 40% bonds, and 20% hedge funds, or 35% stocks, 35% bonds, and 30% managed futures. (Note: All portfolios throughout the paper are rebalanced monthly.) Similar to Kat, we studied the differences in how hedge funds and managed futures combine with stocks and bonds. Kat found that during the period he studied, adding hedge funds to the 50/50 portfolio of stocks and bonds lowered the standard deviation, as hoped for. Unfortunately, hedge funds also increased the negative tilt of the distribution. In addition to the portfolios becoming more negatively skewed, the return distribution's kurtosis increased, indicating "fatter tails." However, Kat found that when he increased the managed futures allocation, the standard deviation dropped faster than with hedge funds, the kurtosis was lowered, and, most impressively, the skewness actually shifted in a positive direction (see Table 26.2). Kat (2004) summarized by saying, "Although [under the assumptions made] hedge funds offer a somewhat higher-than-expected return, from an overall risk perspective, managed futures appear to be better diversifiers than hedge funds."[1]

TABLE 26.2: Monthly Return Statistics for 50/50 Portfolios of Stocks, Bonds, and Hedge Funds or Managed Futures for the Period January 2001–December 2015

HEDGE FUNDS					MANAGED FUTURES				
HF (%)	Mean (%)	StDev (%)	Hedge Funds	Kurtosis	HF (%)	Mean (%)	StDev (%)	Hedge Funds	Kurtosis
0	0.46	2.17	Skew	2.27	0	0.46	2.17	Skew	2.27
5	0.46	2.13	–0.80	2.28	5	0.45	2.05	–0.74	2.05
10	0.46	2.09	–0.81	2.3	10	0.45	1.94	–0.69	1.79
15	0.46	2.05	–0.82	2.31	15	0.44	1.83	–0.63	1.49
20	0.46	2.02	–0.84	2.32	20	0.43	1.74	–0.55	1.16

(Continued)

HEDGE FUNDS					MANAGED FUTURES				
HF (%)	Mean (%)	StDev (%)	Hedge Funds	Kurtosis	HF (%)	Mean (%)	StDev (%)	Hedge Funds	Kurtosis
25	0.46	1.98	–0.85	2.33	25	0.43	1.66	–0.45	0.82
30	0.46	1.95	–0.86	2.34	30	0.42	1.59	–0.35	0.49
35	0.46	1.92	–0.87	2.35	35	0.41	1.53	–0.24	0.19
40	0.46	1.89	–0.88	2.35	40	0.41	1.49	–0.13	–0.03
45	0.46	1.87	–0.89	2.35	45	0.40	1.47	–0.04	–0.18
50	0.46	1.84	–0.90	2.35	50	0.39	1.47	0.04	–0.23

Note. HF% = hedge fund allocation percentage; StDev(%) = standard deviation.

Our results show that Kat's observations have held up during the period since his original study. When we increased the hedge fund allocation, the portfolio return went up and the standard deviation went down. However, the previously discussed "negative side effect" of adding hedge funds was present, as the skewness of the portfolio fell and the kurtosis went up. On the other hand, when we added managed futures into the traditional portfolio, we observed more impressive diversification characteristics. In fact, managed futures appear to have improved the performance profile even more in this period, compared to the one Kat studied. Adding managed futures exposure increased mean return and simultaneously increased the skewness of –0.78 of the traditional portfolio to –0.04 at the 45% allocation level. The standard deviation dropped more and faster than it did with hedge funds, and kurtosis also improved, dropping from 2.27 to –0.18 at the 45% allocation level.

Hedge Funds Plus Managed Futures

Table 26.3 summarizes the results of combining only hedge funds and managed futures. The mean monthly return for managed futures is lower than hedge funds, so we may expect adding them in will reduce the expected return of the portfolio. The standard deviation of managed futures is higher than hedge funds, so one might expect upward pressure on volatility from the addition of managed futures. However, this is not

TABLE 26.3: Monthly Return Statistics for Portfolios of Hedge Funds and Managed Futures for the Period January 2001–December 2015

MF(%)	Mean(%)	StDev(%)	Skew	Kurtosis
0	0.45	1.72	–0.84	2.06
5	0.45	1.64	–0.73	1.73
10	0.44	1.58	–0.61	1.37
15	0.43	1.52	–0.48	1.00
20	0.43	1.48	–0.34	0.65
25	0.42	1.44	–0.21	0.33
30	0.42	1.42	–0.09	0.09
35	0.41	1.41	0.02	–0.08
40	0.40	1.42	0.10	–0.18
45	0.40	1.44	0.16	–0.20
50	0.39	1.47	0.19	–0.17

Note. MF% = managed fund allocation percentage; StDev(%) = standard deviation.

what happens when they are combined. Due to their positive skewness and significantly lower kurtosis, adding managed futures to hedge funds appears to provide a substantial improvement to the overall risk profile. With 40% invested in managed futures, the standard deviation drops from 1.72% to 1.42%, but the expected return only declines by 5 basis points. At the same allocation to managed futures, skewness increases from –0.84 to 0.10, while kurtosis drops noticeably from 2.06 to –0.18. Hedge funds are impressive on their own, but managed futures demonstrate that they are the ultimate teammate by improving the return characteristics of the overall portfolio.

Stocks, Bonds, Hedge Funds, and Managed Futures

The last step in our analysis is to study the effects of combining all four asset classes in one portfolio. Like Kat, we accomplish this in two steps. First, we combine hedge funds and managed futures into what we call the "alternatives portfolio." Next, we combine this alternative portfolio with increasing amounts of a static 50/50 stocks and bonds "traditional portfolio." With this advanced analysis, we are trying to answer two questions simultaneously. First, "What is the best combination of traditional and alternative investments?" (see axis in Figure 26.1 labeled "% in Alternatives") and second, "What is the best mix of hedge funds and managed futures within the alternatives portfolio?" (see axis in Figure 26.2 labeled "% in Managed Futures").

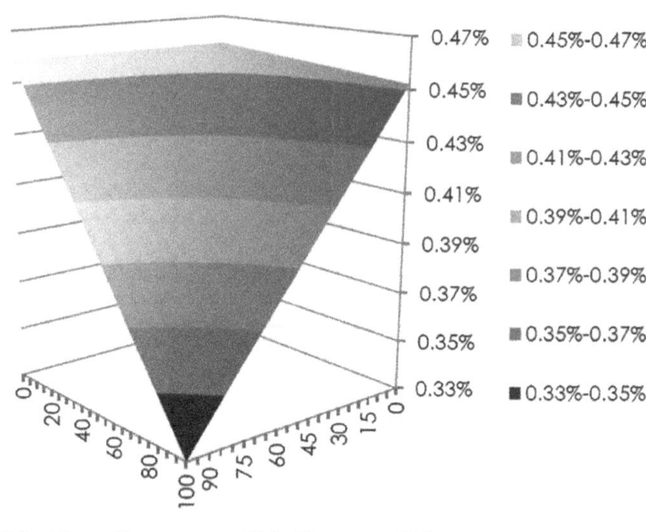

FIGURE 26.1: Mean return of varying allocation between traditional and alternative portfolios, while changing the alternative portfolio's Managed Futures/Hedge Fund composition, for the period January 2001–December 2015

Figure 26.1 shows that the highest mean return is obtained when the portfolio is not allocated to managed futures. Adding managed futures has a downward effect on mean return because its return is lower (0.33% vs. 0.45% for hedge funds and 0.46% for stocks and bonds). This is to be expected, as managed futures firms weigh the minimization of their standard deviation and drawdown just as heavily into their investment decisions as they do maximizing their return.

Figure 26.2 begins to tell a more intriguing story. Very similar to Kat's results, we find that adding alternatives to traditional portfolios of stocks and bonds significantly reduces the portfolio's standard deviation of returns. (Note: Regarding the axis labels on the figures, the author selected the viewing angle that best conveys the information in each

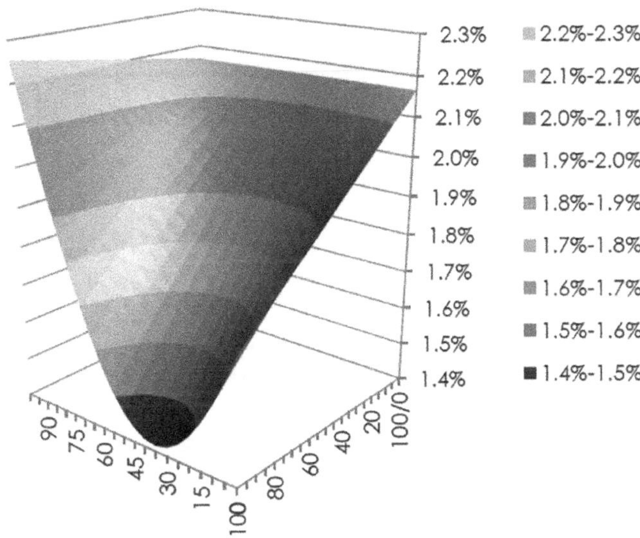

FIGURE 26.2: Standard deviation of varying allocation between traditional and alternative portfolios, while changing the alternative portfolio's Managed Futures/ Hedge Fund composition for the period January 2001–December 2015

figure. Hence, beginning with Figure 26.2, the axis labels are not necessarily consistent with those of other figures.) Moreover, this effect would have historically been optimal at a 100% allocation to alternatives with 35% of the alternatives portfolio allocated to managed futures.

Figure 26.3 shows the results of dividing returns by standard deviation, a common risk-adjusted return metric. It can be argued that the consistency of an investor's returns is just as important as the average amount returned, or in other words, the most upside per unit of risk. We can see a maximum risk-adjusted return when invested in 100% with about 30% of that in managed futures.

Figure 26.4 shows the skewness results for the combined portfolios. We find that adding exposure to alternatives exerts a desirable upward effect on skewness. In turn, as the managed futures allocation is increased, the positive effect on skewness is increased. At levels starting at approximately 80% allocation to alternatives, the skewness of the portfolios actually becomes positive. The highest levels of skewness were found at an 100% allocation to alternatives with more than half allocated to managed futures.

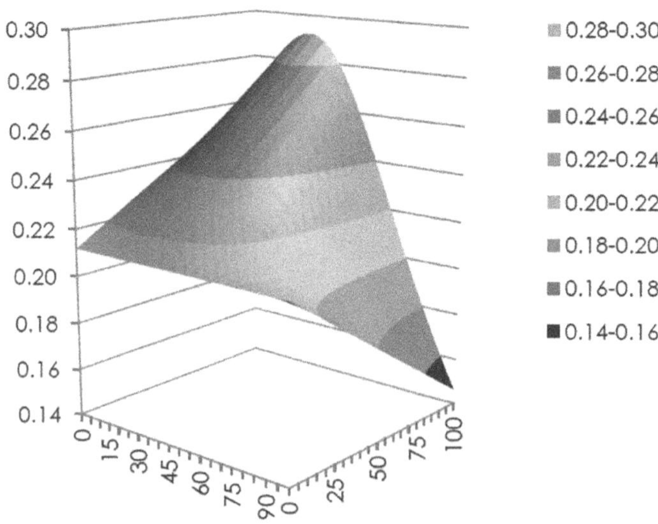

FIGURE 26.3: Risk-adjusted return of 50/50 portfolios of stocks, bonds, hedge funds, and managed futures for the period of January 2001–December 2015

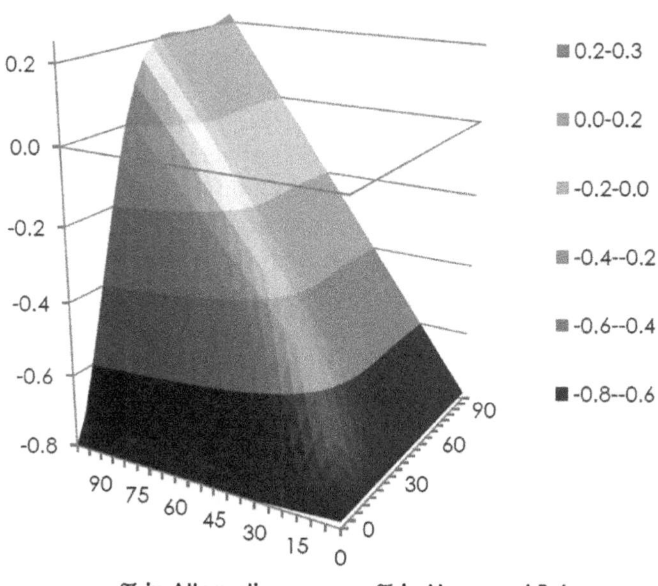

FIGURE 26.4: Skewness of 50/50 portfolios of stocks, bonds, hedge funds, and managed futures for the period June 2001–December 2015

Finally, Figure 26.5 shows the results as they pertain to kurtosis. Like Kat, we find that allocation of managed futures favorably decreases the portfolio's kurtosis, and with 95%–100% allocated to alternatives and 40%–55% of the alternatives portfolio allocated to managed futures it actually produces a negative kurtosis of –0.19.

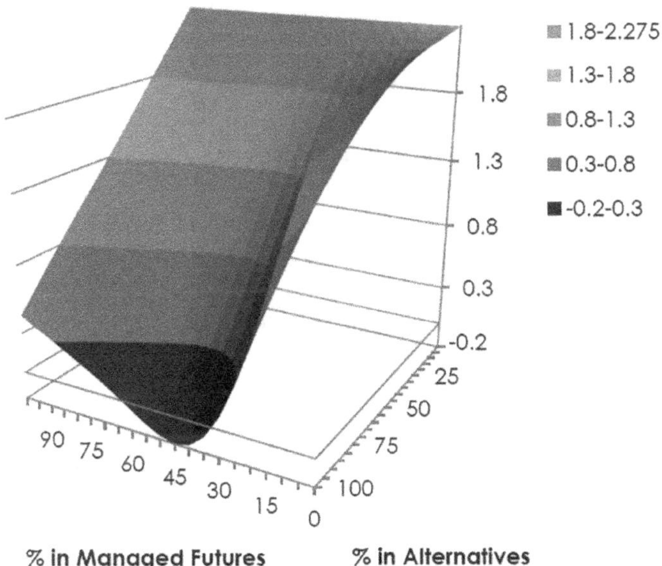

FIGURE 26.5: Kurtosis of 50/50 portfolios of stocks, bonds, hedge funds, and managed futures for the period June 2001–December 2015

We repeated the analysis above with several other CTA indices to make sure that our results were not specific to one index in particular. In all cases, the results were very similar to what we found above, suggesting that our results are robust irrespective of the choice of managed futures index.

Conclusion

In this study, we used the framework introduced by Dr. Harry M. Kat in his paper *Managed Futures and Hedge Funds: A Match Made in Heaven* to analyze the possible role of managed futures in portfolios of stocks, bonds, and hedge funds. Our aim with this paper was to discover whether or not Kat's findings have held up in the years since.

Managed futures have continued to be very valuable diversifiers. Throughout our analysis, and similar to Kat, we found that adding managed futures to portfolios of stocks and bonds reduced portfolio standard deviation to a greater degree and more quickly than did hedge funds alone, and without the undesirable side effects of skewness and kurtosis.

The most impressive results were observed when combining both hedge funds and managed futures with portfolios of stocks and bonds. Figures 26.1 to 26.5 showed that the most desirable levels of mean return, standard deviation, skewness, and kurtosis were produced by portfolios with allocations of 90%–100% to alternatives and 40%–55% of the alternatives portfolio allocated to managed futures.

As a finale, we thought it would be instructive to show performance statistics for portfolios that combine all four of the asset classes: stocks, bonds, managed futures, and hedge funds. Table 26.4 shows the results for portfolios ranging from a 100% Traditional portfolio (50% stocks/50% bonds) to a 100% Alternatives portfolio (50% hedge funds/50% managed futures) in 10% increments.

TABLE 26.4: Performance Statistics for Portfolios Ranging from 100% Traditional Portfolio to 100% Alternatives Portfolio in 10% increments for the Period January 2001–December 2015

Stocks(%)	Bonds(%)	HF(%)	MF(%)	Mean(%)	StDev(%)	Skew	Kurt	Return/Risk
50	50	0	0	0.46	2.66	–0.47	1.29	0.17
45	45	5	5	0.45	2.59	–0.46	1.28	0.17
40	40	10	10	0.45	2.53	–0.44	1.28	0.18
35	35	15	15	0.44	2.46	–0.42	1.28	0.18
30	30	20	20	0.43	2.39	–0.41	1.27	0.18
25	25	25	25	0.42	2.32	–0.39	1.27	0.18
20	20	30	30	0.42	2.26	–0.37	1.26	0.19
15	15	35	35	0.41	2.19	–0.36	1.26	0.19
10	10	40	40	0.40	2.12	–0.34	1.25	0.19
5	5	45	45	0.40	2.05	–0.32	1.25	0.19
0	0	50	50	0.39	1.99	–0.31	1.25	0.20

Note. Return/Risk calculated using annualized mean and standard deviation. HF(%) = hedge fund allocation percentage, MF(%) = managed futures allocation percentage, StDev(%) = standard deviation, Kurt = kurtosis.

In Table 26.4 and Figure 26.6 (an efficient frontier based on the data in Table 26.4), the benefits of allocating to alternatives with a sizable percentage allocated to managed futures are quite compelling. As the contribution to alternatives increases, all metrics benefit:

1. Risk-adjusted return increases
2. Standard deviation decreases
3. Skewness increases
4. Kurtosis decreases

Overall, our analysis is best summarized by the following quote from Dr. Kat (regarding his own findings almost 10 years ago): "Investing in managed futures can improve the overall risk profile of a portfolio far beyond what can be achieved with hedge funds alone. Making an allocation to managed futures not only neutralizes the unwanted side effects of hedge funds, but also leads to further risk reduction. Assuming managed futures offer an acceptable expected return, all of this comes at quite a low price in terms of expected return foregone."[1]

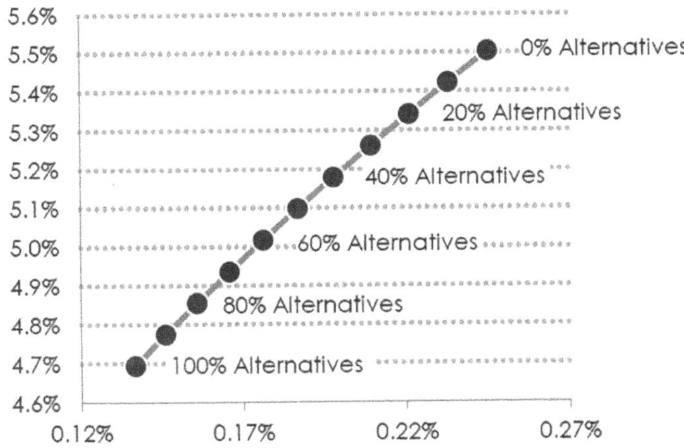

FIGURE 26.6: Efficient frontier for portfolios ranging from 100% Traditional portfolio to 100% Alternatives portfolio in 10% increments for the period June 2001–December 2015

Appendix A

In this appendix, we present the results of our analysis via data tables and graphics in the same format as the main body of the study, but for the period January 1990–December 2015. The data we used in our study, particularly the hedge fund and CTA indices, allowed us to go back to 1990, almost four and a half years prior to the start of Kat's study period. Besides analyzing the out-of-sample period since Kat's study period, we thought analyzing the entire period from 1990–2015 would be both instructive and interesting (Table A-1).

TABLE A-1: Monthly Statistics for Stocks, Bonds, Hedge Funds, and Managed Futures for the Period January 1990–December 2015

	Stocks	Bonds	Hedge Funds	Managed Futures
Mean (%)	0.83	0.52	0.83	0.54
Standard Deviation (%)	4.2	1.05	1.94	2.86
Skewness	–0.58	–0.22	–0.62	0.75
Excess Kurtosis	1.19	0.74	2.54	2.11
Correlations				
Stocks	1.00			
Bonds	0.11	1.00		
Hedge Funds	0.74	0.09	1.00	
Managed Futures	–0.11	0.21	0.02	1.00

TABLE A-2: Monthly Return Statistics for 50/50 Portfolios of Stocks, Bonds, and Hedge Funds or Managed Futures for the Period January 1990–December 2015

HF(%)	Mean(%)	StDev(%)	Skew	Kurt	MF(%)	Mean(%)	StDev(%)	Skew	Kurt
0	0.67	2.32	4	1.46	0	0.67	2.32	–0.54	1.46
5	0.68	2.18	–0.57	1.50	5	0.67	2.11	–0.46	1.33
10	0.69	2.15	–0.60	1.55	10	0.66	2.01	–0.37	1.24
15	0.70	2.11	–0.64	1.60	15	0.65	1.92	–0.25	1.22
20	0.70	2.08	–0.67	1.65	20	0.65	1.84	–0.10	1.30
25	0.71	2.04	–0.71	1.70	25	0.64	1.78	0.06	1.50
30	0.72	2.02	–0.74	1.75	30	0.63	1.74	0.23	1.83
35	0.73	1.99	–0.76	1.81	35	0.63	1.72	0.40	2.25

HF(%)	Mean(%)	StDev(%)	Skew	Kurt	MF(%)	Mean(%)	StDev(%)	Skew	Kurt
40	0.74	1.97	–0.79	1.87	40	0.62	1.71	0.56	2.71
45	0.74	1.95	–0.81	1.93	45	0.61	1.73	0.70	3.12
50	0.75	1.93	–0.82	1.99	50	0.61	1.77	0.79	3.42

Note: StDev(%) = standard deviation, Kurt = kurtosis.

In Table A-2, adding managed futures to a 50/50 portfolio of stocks and bonds increased the kurtosis for this period due to a single data point. In December 1991 managed futures produced a 14.49% return for the month, which substantially increased both the skew and kurtosis for the period. This is a prime example of our contention that skewness and kurtosis are connected and should not be analyzed in isolation. The significantly higher kurtosis, in this case, is due to the significantly higher skew caused by one positive outlier (i.e., upside volatility), in December 1991.

To help gauge the effect of that one particular data point, we recalculated the statistics for the period, intentionally omitting the December 1991 data point. In doing so we found that at the 50% allocation level to managed futures, the skewness of the portfolio decreased slightly from 0.78 to 0.5 and kurtosis dropped from 1.54 to 1.16. Said another way, without the effect of the December 1991 data point, the statistics are more in line with our other two periods of study in this paper.

TABLE A-3: Monthly Return Statistics for Portfolios of Hedge Funds and Managed Futures for the Period January 1990–December 2015

MF(%)	Mean(%)	StDev(%)	Skew	Kurt
0	0.83	1.94	–0.62	2.54
5	0.81	1.85	–0.51	2.14
10	0.80	1.78	–0.38	1.72
15	0.78	1.71	–0.22	1.32
20	0.77	1.67	–0.05	0.99
25	0.76	1.63	0.14	0.79
30	0.74	1.62	0.32	0.73
35	0.73	1.63	0.48	0.82
40	0.71	1.65	0.61	1.02
45	0.70	1.69	0.71	1.28
50	0.68	1.74	0.78	1.54

Note: StDev(%) = standard deviation, Kurt = kurtosis.

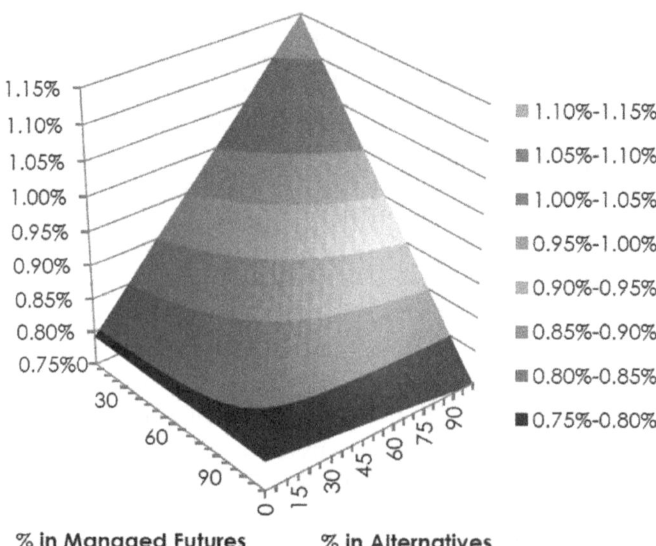

FIGURE A-1: Mean return of 50/50 portfolios of stocks, bonds, hedge funds, and managed futures for the period January 1990–December 2015

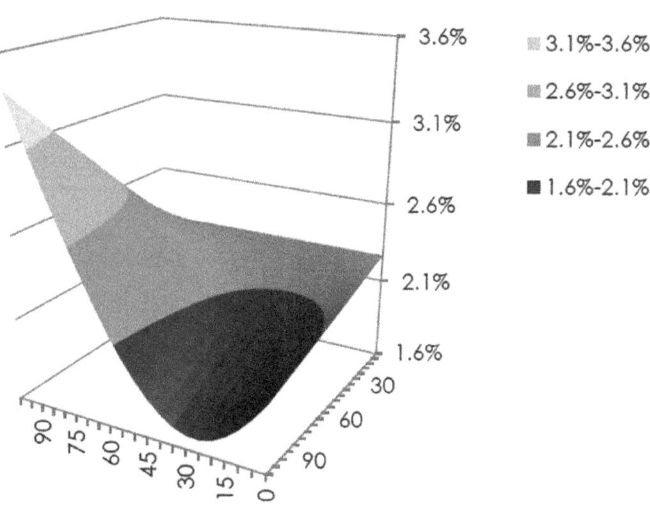

FIGURE A-2: Standard deviation of 50/50 portfolios of stocks, bonds, hedge funds, and managed futures for the period January 1990–December 2015

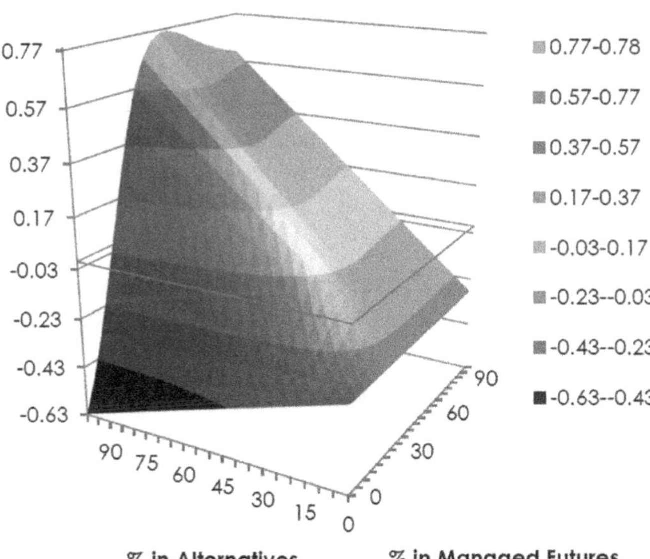

FIGURE A-3: Skewness of 50/50 portfolios of stocks, bonds, hedge funds, and managed futures for the period January 1990–December 2015

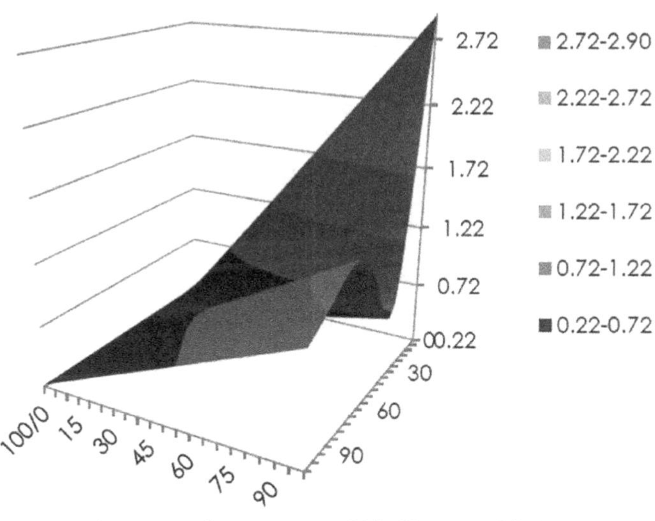

FIGURE A-4: Kurtosis of 50/50 portfolios of stocks, bonds, hedge funds, and managed futures for the period January 1990–December 2015

Appendix B

In this appendix, we present the results of our analysis via data tables and graphics in the same format as the main body of the study, but for the exact same period that Kat studied in his paper (June 1994–May 2001). It is important to keep in mind that we used different data than Kat:

1. To represent "bonds," Kat used a 10-year Government Bond Index, while we used the Barclays U.S. Aggregate Bond Index (formerly the Lehman Aggregate Bond Index).
2. For "hedge funds," Kat used his own methodology to build hedge fund portfolios with data from Tremont TASS, while we used the HFRI Fund Weighted Composite Index.
3. While we and Kat both used the S&P 500 Total Return Index to represent "stocks," Kat capped its mean return at 1% per month, while we used its exact return stream.
4. For "managed futures," Kat used the Stark 300 Index and we used the Barclay Systematic Traders Index.

After factoring in all of these differences, we were pleasantly surprised at how closely our results resembled Kat's work from over 10 years ago.

TABLE B-1: Monthly Statistics for Stocks, Bonds, Hedge Funds, and Managed Futures for Kat's Study Period of June 1994–May 2001

	Stocks	Bonds	Hedge Funds	Managed Futures
Mean (%)	1.46	0.63	1.16	0.65
Standard Deviation (%)	4.39	1.03	2.36	2.89
Skewness	–0.81	0.12	–0.67	0.34
Excess Kurtosis	1.05	0.38	2.95	0.31
Correlations				
Stocks	1.00			
Bonds	0.22	1.00		
Hedge Funds	0.70	0.01	1.00	
Managed Futures	–0.05	0.32	–0.02	1.00

TABLE B-2: Monthly Return Statistics for 50/50 Portfolios of Stocks, Bonds, and Hedge Funds or Managed Futures for Kat's Study Period of June 1994–May 2001

HF(%)	Mean(%)	StDev(%)	Skew	Kurt	MF(%)	Mean(%)	StDev(%)	Skew	Kurt
0	1.04	2.36	–0.59	0.04	0	1.04	2.36	–0.59	0.04
5	1.05	2.32	–0.64	0.17	5	1.02	2.25	–0.53	–0.14
10	1.06	2.30	–0.70	0.32	10	1.01	2.20	–0.46	–0.29
15	1.06	2.25	–0.75	0.48	15	0.99	2.06	–0.38	–0.40
20	1.07	2.23	–0.81	0.52	20	0.97	1.99	–0.30	–0.45
25	1.07	2.20	–0.85	0.85	25	0.95	1.93	–0.22	–0.43
30	1.08	2.18	–0.90	1.05	30	0.93	1.88	–0.13	–0.34
35	1.09	2.17	–0.94	1.26	35	0.91	1.86	–0.06	–0.21
40	1.09	2.15	–0.97	1.47	40	0.89	1.85	0.02	–0.05
45	1.10	2.15	–0.99	1.68	45	0.87	1.86	0.07	0.10
50	1.10	2.14	–1.01	1.88	50	0.85	1.89	0.12	0.21

Note: HF(%) = hedge fund allocation percentage, MF(%) = managed futures allocation percentage, StDev(%) = standard deviation, Kurt = kurtosis.

TABLE B-3: Monthly Return Statistics for Portfolios of Hedge Funds and Managed Futures for Kat's Study Period of June 1994–May 2001

MF(%)	Mean(%)	StDev(%)	Skew	Kurt
0	1.16	2.36	–0.67	2.95
5	1.14	2.24	–0.56	2.41
10	1.11	2.13	–0.44	1.82
15	1.09	2.04	–0.31	1.20
20	1.06	1.96	–0.18	0.60
25	1.04	1.89	–0.05	0.07
30	1.01	1.85	0.07	–0.34
35	0.99	1.82	0.18	–0.60
40	0.96	1.81	0.25	–0.70
45	0.93	1.82	0.29	–0.67
50	0.91	1.84	0.31	–0.55

Note: MF(%) = managed futures allocation percentage, StDev(%) = standard deviation, Kurt = kurtosis.

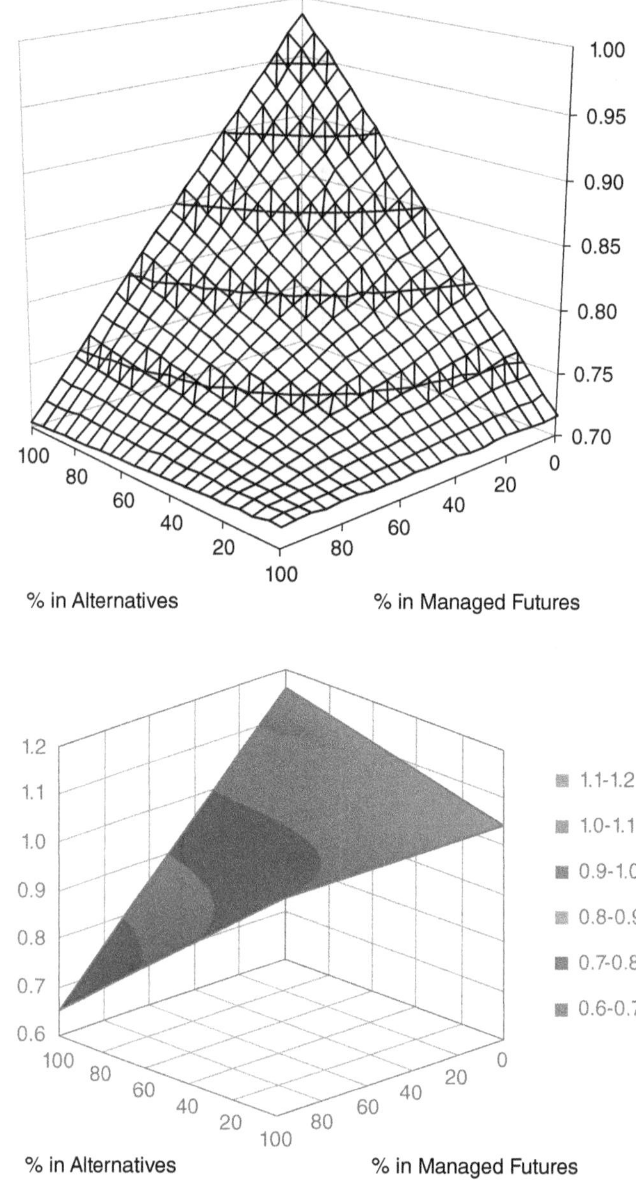

FIGURE B-1: Mean return of 50/50 portfolios of stocks, bonds, hedge funds, and managed futures for Kat's study period of June 1994–May 2001 (top, Kat's original graphic;[11] ours is on bottom). Note: Our image looks different than Kat's, primarily because he constrained the equity returns for the period and we did not.

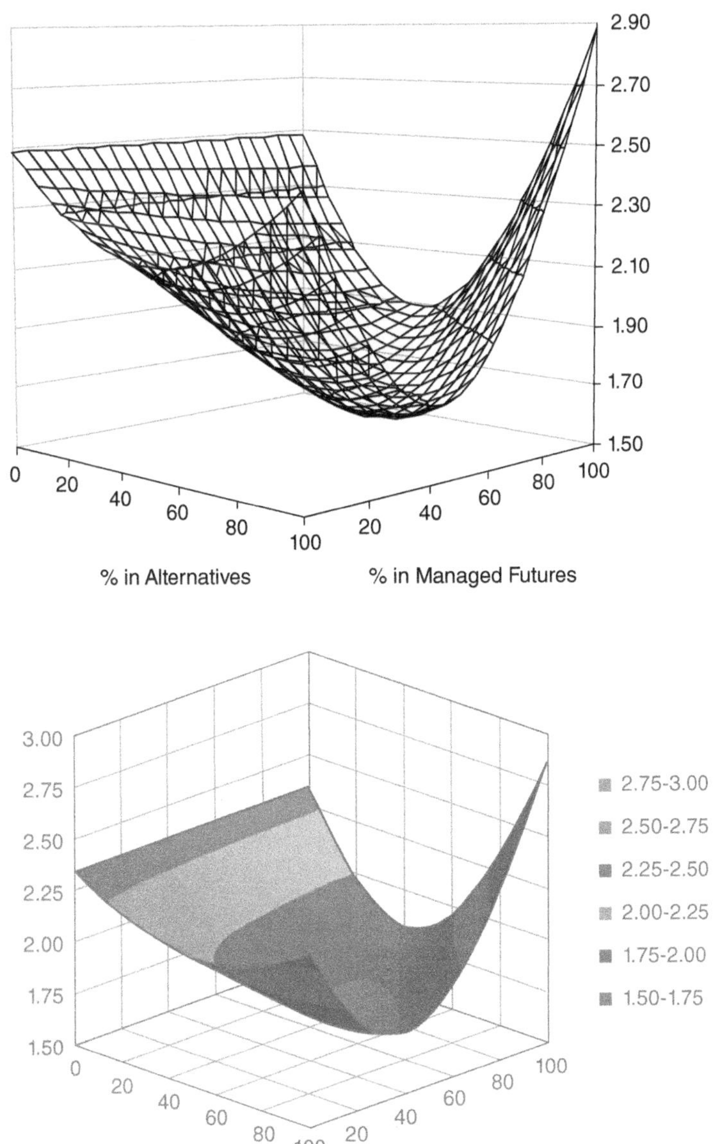

FIGURE B-2: Standard deviation of 50/50 portfolios of stocks, bonds, hedge funds, and managed futures for Kat's study period of June 1994–May 2001 (top, Kat's original graphic;[11] ours is on bottom)

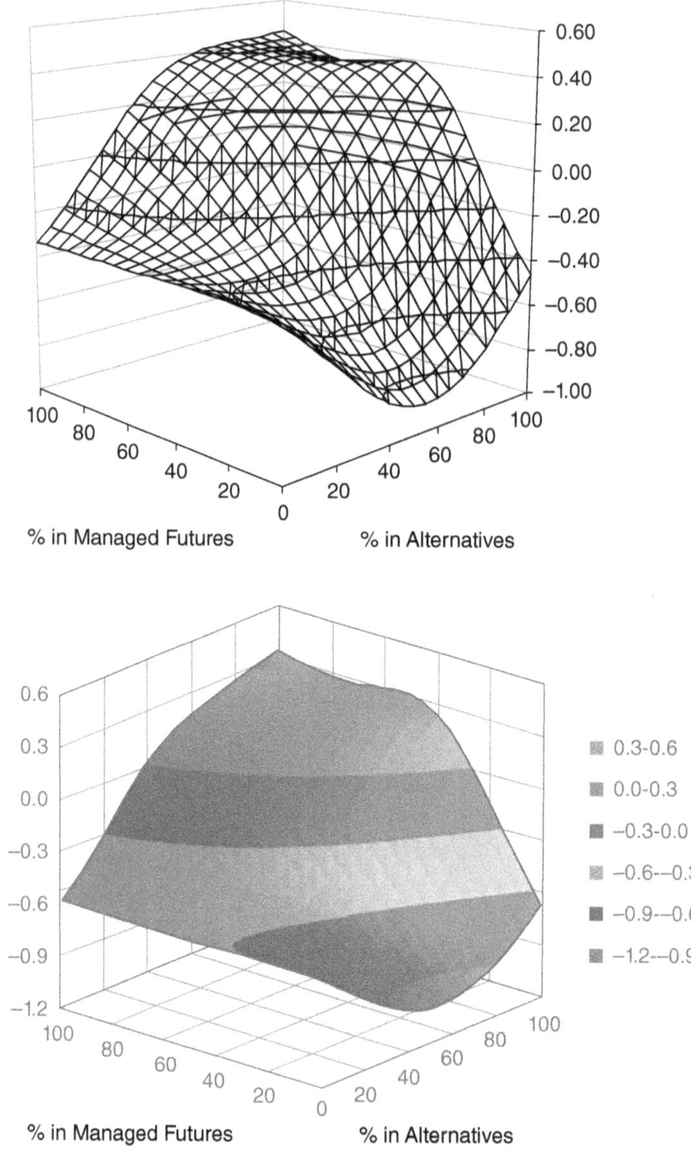

FIGURE B-3: Skewness of 50/50 portfolios of stocks, bonds, hedge funds, and managed futures for Kat's study period of June 1994–May 2001 (top, Kat's original graphic;[11] ours is on bottom)

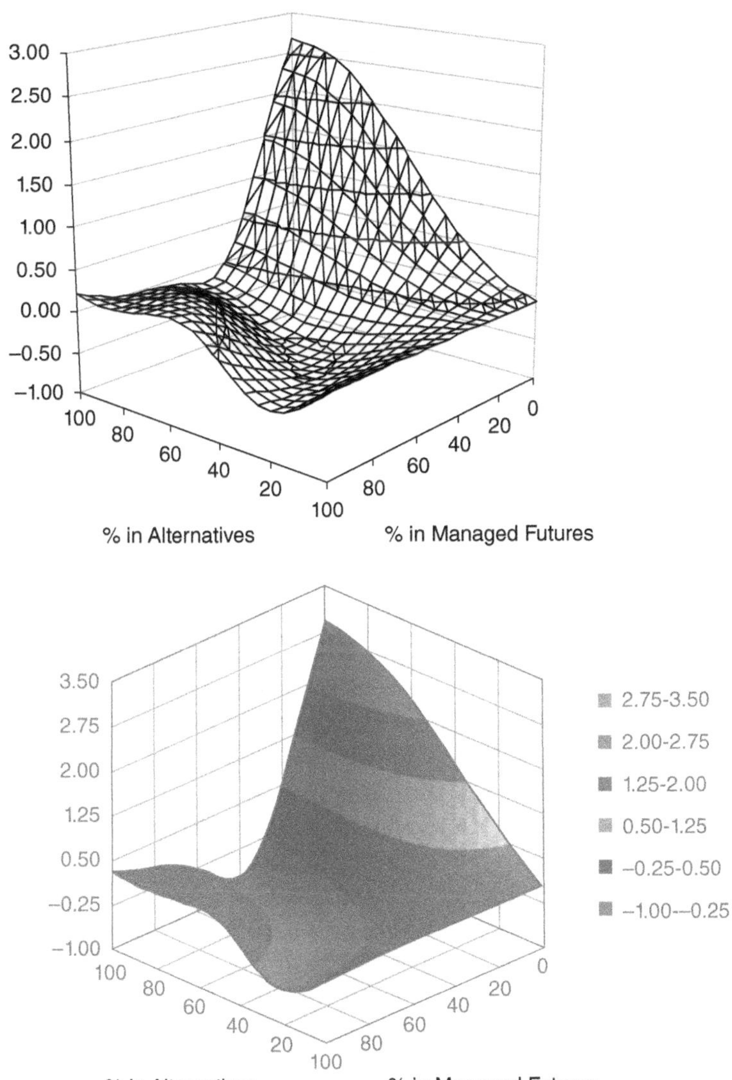

FIGURE B-4: Kurtosis of 50/50 portfolios of stocks, bonds, hedge funds, and managed futures for Kat's study period of June 1994–May 2001 (top, Kat's original graphic below;[11] ours is on bottom)

APPENDIX C

Review of Skewness and Kurtosis*

The first four "moments" that describe data distributions are:

1. Mean
2. Variance
3. Skewness
4. Kurtosis

Most investment professionals focus only on the first two moments, and in a theoretical world where investment returns are assumed to be normally distributed, focusing only on the relationship of returns to volatility may suffice.[8] However, we know that market returns, and more importantly in this case, alternative investment returns, are rarely normally distributed. The Dot-com crash and the Global Financial Crisis have left investors wondering just how often "100-Year Storms" actually occur. Standard measures of risk did not seem to prepare investors for the extreme nature of the two bear markets in the first decade of the 2000s. The rapid growth in hedge funds and other forms of alternative investments resulted in a proliferation of products with return profiles that did not fit standard definitions of return and risk described by normal distributions.[8]

Although well-established in statistical theory, skewness and kurtosis are often ignored or misunderstood in performance analysis. This is not surprising, given that skewness and kurtosis take a bit more effort to understand. It is our contention that skewness and kurtosis are connected and should not be analyzed in isolation from one another or other performance statistics.

Skewness

Skewness is a measure of symmetry, or more precisely, lack of symmetry, of a random variable's probability distribution of returns around

*A special note of appreciation to Marc Odo, CFA, CAIA, CHP of Zephyr Associates for assistance with Appendix C.

the mean. Stated a different way, skewness compares the length of the two "tails" of the distribution curve. If the distribution is impacted more by negative outliers than positive outliers (or vice versa), the distribution will no longer be symmetrical. Therefore, skewness tells us how outlier events impact the shape of the distribution.

- A positive skew value indicates a tendency for values to fall below the mean with the "tail" of the distribution to the right ("a tendency for upside surprises")
- A negative skew value indicates a greater chance that values will fall above the mean ("a propensity for downside volatility")

Kurtosis

Kurtosis is a measure of whether a random variable's probability distribution is "tall and skinny" or "short and squat" as compared to the normal distribution of the same variance. It conveys the extent to which the distribution is dominated by outlier events—those extreme events distant from the mean.

There are differing conventions on how kurtosis should be scaled. Pearson's original calculation for kurtosis produces a value of 3.0 for a normal distribution. Therefore, it is common practice to use an adjusted version called "excess" kurtosis that subtracts 3.0 from Pearson's calculation to produce a value of 0.0 for a normal distribution (Microsoft Excel's kurtosis function, "KURT( )", returns excess kurtosis).

- Positive excess kurtosis describes a leptokurtic distribution with a high peak, thin midrange, and fat tails indicating an increased chance of extreme observations
- Negative excess kurtosis describes a platykurtic distribution with a low peak and fat midrange on both sides
- Zero excess kurtosis is called mesokurtic—a normally distributed, bell-shaped curve

Sometimes referred to as "the volatility of volatility," kurtosis conveys where in the distribution the standard deviation resides, not the overall level of standard deviation.[8]

Carry and Trend in Lots of Places

27

Vineer Bhansali, Josh Davis, Matt Dorsten, and Graham Rennison

There is a long history of using yields as the baseline for prospective asset returns for a wide variety of asset classes. For instance, Cochrane points out that yields predicting future returns is a "pervasive phenomenon" across markets (Cochrane [2011]) and Leibowitz [2014] applies this systematically to various types of bond portfolios. "Carry" is used by practitioners in an analogous way to yield, especially for derivatives markets like futures, and indeed is more general than yield in that it incorporates the cost of funding the investment. For fixed income investments, this distinction between yield and carry can be important, for instance, when yield curves are inverted.

Investors intuitively know two fundamental principles of investing: (1) Don't fight the trend, and (2) don't pay too much to hold an investment. But do these simple principles actually lead to superior returns? In this paper we report the results of an empirical study covering 20 major markets across four asset classes, and an extended sample period from 1960 to 2014. The results confirm overwhelmingly that having the trend and carry in your favor leads to significantly better returns, on both an absolute and a risk-adjusted basis. Furthermore, this finding appears remarkably robust across samples, including the period of rising interest rates from 1960 to 1982. In particular, we find that while carry predicts returns almost unconditionally, trend following works far better when carry is in agreement. We believe that this simple two-style approach will continue to be an important insight for building superior investment portfolios.

If we decompose the total return of any investment as the sum of returns from change in the underlying pricing factors and from the passage of time, then carry can be best thought of as the return attributable to the second component, i.e., the expected return from the passage of time. Carry is defined by Koijen [2007] as the "expected return on an asset assuming that market conditions, including its price, stay the same." Thus, carry may be thought of as a naïve, yet robust, model-free measure of the risk premium in a given asset class. In this regard, it is plausible that being on the side of positive carry should earn a higher return, on average, but accepting potentially greater risk as well since the assumption of static prices is rarely true in practice.

Historically, the literature has focused on the concept of carry mainly in the currency markets. Following the collapse of Bretton Woods, market practitioners started broadly pursuing currency carry trade strategies in the 1980s and 1990s. Academia has followed this closely, and a host of plausible explanations have been put forth for the effectiveness and persistence of currency carry as a predictor of future returns. In a no-arbitrage finance setting, for currency carry to predict returns, it must be compensation for "market" risk that cannot be diversified away. Academic finance posits that the currency risk premium is a direct consequence of the co-variation of returns with the stochastic discount factor. Lustig [2007] observes that currency carry tends to work empirically due to the co-variation of the payoff on carry trades with consumption growth. Viewing currency carry through the lens of locally hedged option prices, Bhansali [2007] and Menkhoff [2012] offer an intuitive connection between this carry risk premium as compensation for exposure to volatility risk.

In his seminal work "Treatise on Money" [1930], Keynes proposed that backwardation in commodities, or the tendency of futures contracts to trade below spot contracts, is normal and related to producers of commodities seeking to hedge by locking in future prices, thus constructing a premium that can be earned by speculators who provide the insurance. Gorton [2012] provides a comprehensive analysis of the drivers of these risk premia (including current and future levels of inventories) and shows that price measures, such as the futures basis (a measure of carry), contain relevant information for predicting future returns.

In fixed income markets, the nominal U.S. Treasury bond risk premium is often directly measured by the steepness of the yield curve, which is related to the term premium. Fama and Bliss [1987] show that expected returns on bonds vary through time and the variation of the term premium is closely related to the business cycle. Cochrane and Piazzesi [2005] and Campbell, Sunderam, and Viciera [2013] relate the bond risk premium directly to the concavity in the yield curve, defined loosely as the level of intermediate interest rates relative to the average of short- and longer-term bond yields. Using an empirical data set spanning 150 years, Giesecke, Longstaff, Schaefer, and Strebulaev [2011] show that, on average, at least half of the carry on corporate bonds, given by credit spread corresponding to the yield difference between corporate bonds and duration-matched Treasury bonds, is a risk premium. Furthermore, these authors show that actual defaults are closely related to equity returns and volatility.

While the computation of carry in equities is less analogous, in equity futures, the implied dividend yield less the local risk-free rate is one determinant of carry. Fama and French [1988] document that dividend yields help to forecast equity returns, with better predictive ability at longer horizons. Because carry as a concept is less popular in equity markets, our approximation used below should be taken as one attempt at making it similar to the one used for other assets, with further room for improvement.

In contrast to carry, where there is a naturally intuitive explanation in terms of a compensation for risk transfer, trend following (or its cross-sectional cousin, momentum) has long been a conundrum of financial markets, potentially delivering returns over multiple decades (and even centuries, according to some recent studies, e.g., Geczy [2013], Lemperiere [2014], Moskowitz [2012]). While there are numerous behavioral explanations for returns from trend following, it is hard to find explanations that are consistent with classical finance, and thus, trend following has been largely thought of as a persistent anomaly in the classical context.

Despite this lack of a convincing model to explain trend following, there is much evidence that in the portfolio construction context, carry and trend are mutually diversifying, especially in extreme states. Thus, it is intuitively appealing to combine them. Conceptually, we can think of carry as a position that harvests risk premiums, and thus, performs best when prices don't move much, whereas trend following is a long-tail option-replicating strategy (Fung [2002]), which benefits when prices move as a consequence of fat-tail events such as those experienced during the financial crisis. Thus, combining these two strategies should intuitively result in better portfolio outcomes in a broad set of states.

We view this work as highly complementary to that of Asness, Moskowitz, and Pedersen [2013]. In that work, the authors investigate the ability of value and momentum signals to predict returns across markets and asset classes. These authors focus on value from the perspective of "book value," or a measure of long-run value relative to its current market value. Thus, their work implicitly depends on invoking some model for valuation. We believe that in most asset classes, focusing on model-independent carry and time-series properties of asset prices that are basically arithmetic operations provides essentially the same gains to portfolio construction. Further, due to the practical ease of implementation of both carry and trend portfolio using plain-vanilla futures contracts, our work is likely to be of appeal to a wider variety of investors.

Carry and Trend: Definitions, Data, and Empirical Study

To assess the empirical relevance of carry and trend to futures returns, we assembled an extensive dataset covering the four major asset classes: equities, bonds, currencies, and commodities. We selected five markets in each asset class that represent the major, most liquid markets available now and historically. For equity indices we use the S&P 500, Euro Stoxx 50, Nikkei 225, FTSE 100, and S&P ASX 200.[1] For bond markets, we use U.S. 10-year, German 10-year, Japan 10-year, U.K. 10-year, and Australian 10-year government bonds. In currencies we use the euro (switching to the Deutsche mark prior to 1999), Japanese yen, British pound, Australian dollar, and Swiss franc. And lastly, in commodities we use corn, WTI crude, gold, copper, and natural gas.

To make this study relevant for actual implementation, and since we are interested only in excess returns above risk-free rates, we used primarily futures data, where available, though more efficient implementation with swaps is frequently possible and should be undertaken. To avoid biases associated with the long recent period of falling interest rates, we wanted to cover, to the extent possible, also the period of rising interest rates in the 1970s and early 1980s. In order to do so, we had to extend some data sets back before futures data was available using simple proxies from cash security markets. Table 27.1 provides data sources and summary statistics. For each market we have used actual futures data, where available (the majority of each sample), and proxy futures returns prior to that (for the S&P 500, bonds and

TABLE 27.1: Data Sources and Summary Statistics

Market	Begins	Data Sources	Avg Excess Return/yr	Volatility/yr	Avg Ex-Ante
Commodities					
Corn	Jun-60	Bloomberg	–2.2%	22.0%	–4.7%
Oil	Apr-87	Bloomberg	9.7%	34.8%	4.1%
Gold	Jan-76	Bloomberg	2.2%	19.6%	–5.1%
Copper	Dec-89	Bloomberg	8.7%	26.5%	3.6%
Nat Gas	Mar-91	Bloomberg	–7.1%	49.7%	–6.9%
Equities					
Nikkei	May-93	Bloomberg	2.4%	24.4%	0.5%
S&P 500	Jan-60	Bloomberg, Haver	5.5%	16.9%	–2.0%
EuroStoxx	Jun-99	Bloomberg	3.1%	25.0%	1.0%
S&P ASX	Apr-01	Bloomberg	5.6%	16.4%	–0.7%
FTSE 100	May-93	Bloomberg	5.9%	18.6%	–1.0%
Currencies					
AUD	Dec-77	Bloomberg, R.B.A.	2.5%	11.2%	2.7%
GBP	Dec-72	Bloomberg, IMF, DMS*	1.6%	9.7%	2.1%
EUR	Dec-72	Bloomberg, IMF, DMS*	1.2%	10.3%	–0.9%
JPY	Dec-72	Bloomberg, IMF, DMS*	0.1%	10.6%	–2.6%
CHF	Dec-72	Bloomberg, IMF, DMS*	1.3%	11.8%	–2.6%
Bond Futures					
UK Gilt	Nov-83	Bloomberg	2.8%	7.4%	1.1%
JGB	Aug-75	Bloomberg, B.O.J.	2.9%	4.6%	1.3%
Bund	Jul-92	Bloomberg	4.6%	5.5%	1.6%
US 10Y Note	Aug-72	Bloomberg, GSW**	2.9%	7.1%	1.4%
Australia 10Y	Jun-02	Bloomberg	2.4%	7.6%	0.5%

*Dimson, Marsh, and Staunton database. **Gurkaynak, Sack, and Wright database.

currencies only). Proxy futures returns are calculated from corresponding cash market data as follows:

> S&P 500: We take total returns, including reinvested dividends, minus the 3-month T-bill return.
>
> Bond futures: Using yield data, we calculate the returns of a 10-year bond financed at the short-term interest rate, and including roll-down.
>
> Currencies: We use return from spot exchange rates plus the difference between domestic and foreign deposit rates as carry.

Consistent with the definitions above, we define (ex-ante) carry in each market as the annualized excess return assuming that spot prices remain unchanged. This quantity is calculated daily for each market.[2] Market specific definitions of carry are as follows:

> *Commodities*: Roll yield measured between 1) the first future with an expiry greater than one year, and 2) the nearby future, to eliminate seasonality effects.
>
> *Currencies*: Roll yield between first and second future (since no seasonality concern) or, prior to futures data being available, the short-term deposit rate differential.
>
> *Equities*: Trailing 12-month total dividend divided by current spot index level, minus local short-term interest rate (we do not use futures roll yield since futures beyond one year to expiry are not available and therefore there is no way to adjust for seasonality in dividend payments).
>
> *Bond futures*: Calculated directly from the yield curve (not from futures prices), defined as the yield, plus roll-down the curve, minus the short-term interest rate.

We define trend in the simplest way possible, by setting trend as positive if the futures price today is above the one-year trailing moving average futures price, adjusted for rolls, and negative if the price is below. More sophisticated methods of identifying trends can certainly improve the performance of trend following strategies, but the benefit of our approach is to capture the beta of such strategies without any sign of data mining.

For each market, we can categorize each day then into one of four groups: 1) positive carry and positive trend, 2) positive carry and negative trend, 3) negative carry and positive trend, or 4) negative carry and negative trend. Finally, we can calculate average subsequent excess returns for each market, in each group, and annualize these. As described above, this computation is not only intuitively clean, but is similar to how these measures have been used in a model-independent way by investors for long periods.

Carry and Trend in Interest Rate Futures

To set the stage, we will first consider U.S. 10-year Treasury note futures. These futures started trading in June 1982, but we extend back to 1972 using proxy futures returns based on yield data. Figure 27.1 shows an index of excess returns of rolling futures positions beginning at 1 in August 1972. The chart also shows the estimated carry on the right-hand axis. The carry is positive 1.4% on average, but varies significantly and indeed goes negative in various episodes in the 1970s, late '80s and '90s, and in 2006. These episodes roughly correspond to periods of inverted yield curves.

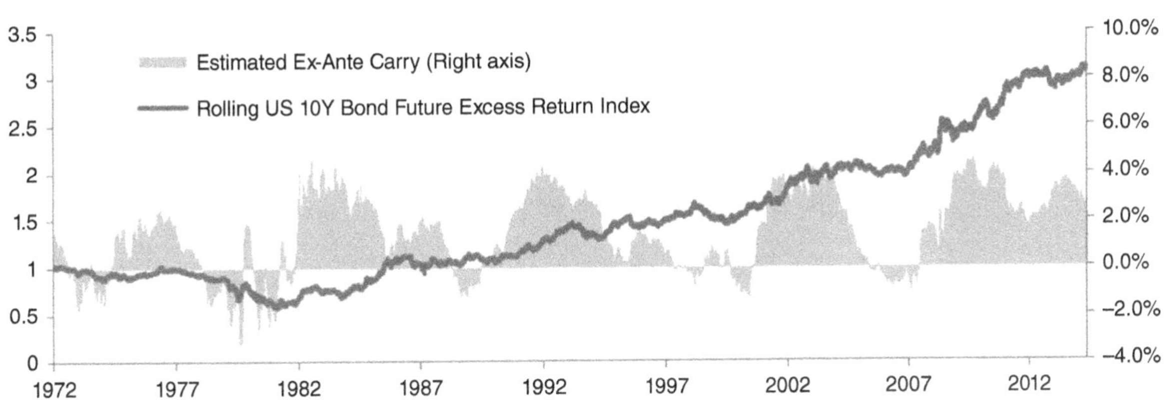

FIGURE 27.1: Excess Return Index and Estimated Carry for Rolling U.S. 10-Year Note Futures Source: Bloomberg, PIMCO.

Figure 27.2 shows a decomposition of the history of returns for the 10-year futures contract into our four groups listed above. We find that positive-carry, positive-trend periods were the most common over this window (53% of the sample), consistent with the bull market in bonds

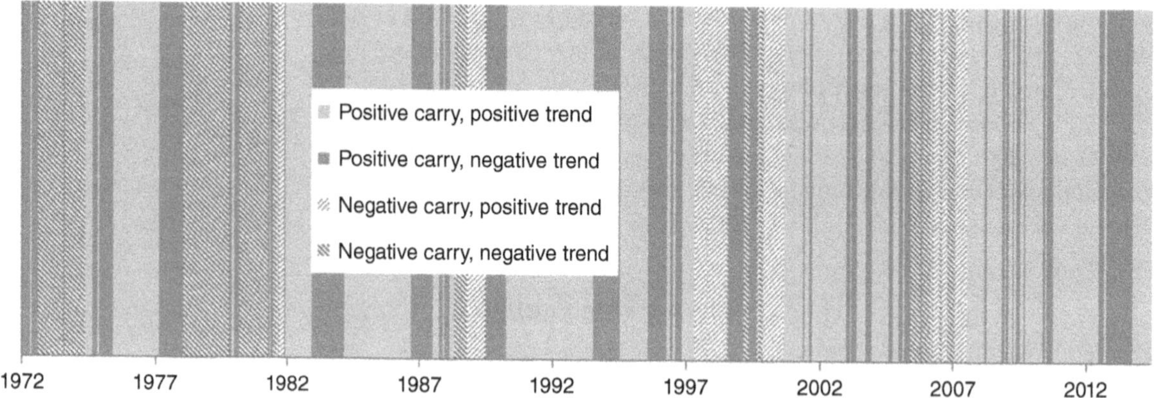

FIGURE 27.2: Decomposing History of U.S. 10-Year Note Futures by Carry and Trend Source: Bloomberg, PIMCO.

from 1982—present. However, 24% of the episode was positive carry but trending negative (i.e., interest rates rising and bonds selling off). Of the negative-carry episodes (the remaining 23% of the sample), this was split roughly equally between trending up and down.

Table 27.2 shows the average excess returns (annualized) for each group, as well as for the full sample. Over the full sample, the average excess return was 2.9% per year, but in periods when both trend and carry were in favor (i.e., positive), the average annualized excess return was almost double the average, at 5.2% per year. Conversely, when both trend and carry were against the position, the average return was –4.2%. The mixed categories, with one of trend and carry against, and one

TABLE 27.2: Average Returns and Risk-Adjusted Returns by Category, U.S. 10-Year Note Futures, 1972–2014

			Annualized Returns by Category				Annualized Return/Volatility by Category			
			Carry>0		Carry<0		Carry>0		Carry>0	
Market	Begins	Full Sample Avg Return	Trend>0	Trend<0	Trend>0	Trend<0	Trend>0	Trend<0	Trend>0	Trend<0
US 10Y Note	Aug-72	2.9%	5.2%	1.6%	3.0%	–4.2%	0.8	0.2	0.5	–0.5

in favor, the returns were in between, at 1.6% and 3.2%, respectively. We also report the returns normalized by volatility since we will compare the risk-adjusted returns in each of the different quadrants across assets. The same pattern is visible, and in fact enhanced, since not only were the positive-carry, positive-trend periods the highest returning, they also had lower volatility on average.

Trend and Carry across Asset Classes

The rest of this paper generalizes these results to other asset classes to see if the same pattern holds, i.e., the best returns are when trend and carry are mutually reinforcing, and the worst returns are when they are opposing. We also detail the results for different interest rate regimes and find that the results favor being in positive-trend, positive-carry investments even when rates are rising.

Table 27.3 shows the proportion that falls into each category split by sector into commodities, equities, currencies, and bonds. Table 27.4 details the performance of each asset class within the four combinations of trend and carry highlighted above.

TABLE 27.3: Proportion of History in Each Carry and Trend Category by Market

		Frequency by Category			
		Carry>0		Carry<0	
Market	**Begins**	***Trend>0***	***Trend<0***	***Trend>0***	***Trend<0***
Commodities					
Corn	Jun-60	17.5%	8.6%	19.5%	54.4%
Oil	Apr-87	47.7%	11.4%	11.1%	29.7%
Gold	Jan-76	0.0%	0.0%	48.4%	51.6%
Copper	Dec-89	37.6%	11.7%	17.3%	33.4%
Nat Gas	Mar-91	26.0%	10.2%	7.5%	56.4%
Sector Average		**25.8%**	**8.4%**	**20.8%**	**45.1%**
Equities					
Nikkei	May-93	41.4%	35.2%	10.8%	12.5%
S&P 500	Jan-60	17.9%	7.2%	48.1%	26.8%

(Continued)

		Frequency by Category			
		Carry>0		Carry<0	
Market	**Begins**	***Trend>0***	***Trend<0***	***Trend>0***	***Trend<0***
EuroStoxx	Jun-99	44.9%	18.8%	18.0%	18.3%
S&P ASX	Apr-01	21.5%	12.6%	44.2%	21.7%
FTSE 100	May-93	21.9%	7.7%	44.6%	25.9%
Sector Average		**29.5%**	**16.3%**	**33.1%**	**21.0%**
Currencies					
AUD	Dec-77	51.9%	31.7%	6.0%	10.5%
GBP	Dec-72	54.0%	35.8%	3.2%	7.1%
EUR	Dec-72	19.8%	10.7%	33.3%	36.1%
JPY	Dec-72	8.1%	3.4%	43.3%	45.2%
CHF	Dec-72	6.1%	4.1%	44.9%	44.9%
Sector Average		**28.0%**	**17.1%**	**26.1%**	**28.8%**
Bond Futures					
UK Gilt	Nov-83	38.1%	15.5%	25.8%	20.6%
JGB	Aug-75	68.0%	16.1%	6.7%	9.1%
Bund	Jul-92	65.5%	22.4%	9.5%	2.6%
US 10Y Note	Aug-72	52.9%	23.6%	10.0%	13.5%
Australia 10Y	Jun-02	34.9%	27.4%	17.5%	20.2%
Sector Average		**51.9%**	**21.0%**	**13.9%**	**13.2%**

TABLE 27.4: Full Table of Results by Market, Maximum Available Sample Periods 1960–2014

			Annualized Returns by Quadrant				Annualized Return/Volatility by Quadrant			
			Carry>0		Carry<0		Carry<0		Carry>0	
Market	**Begins**	**Full Sample *Avg Return***	***Trend>0***	***Trend<0***	***Trend>0***	***Trend<0***	***Trend>0***	***Trend<0***	***Trend>0***	***Trend<0***
Commodities										
Corn	Jun-60	–2.2%	21.2%	–8.9%	–5.7%	–7.4%	0.8	–0.4	–0.2	–0.4
Oil	Apr-87	9.7%	27.6%	29.6%	–15.4%	–17.1%	0.8	0.9	–0.5	–0.4

Market	Begins	Full Sample Avg Return	Annualized Returns by Quadrant				Annualized Return/Volatility by Quadrant			
			Carry>0		Carry<0		Carry<0		Carry>0	
			Trend>0	Trend<0	Trend>0	Trend<0	Trend>0	Trend<0	Trend>0	Trend<0
Gold	Jan-76	2.2%	—	—	7.1%	–2.4%	—	—	0.3	–0.1
Copper	Dec-89	8.7%	20.6%	8.1%	1.9%	–0.9%	0.8	0.3	0.1	0.0
Nat Gas	Mar-91	–7.1%	10.5%	–46.8%	32.4%	–13.3%	0.2	–1.1	0.9	–0.3
Sector Average		**2.3%**	**20.0%**	**–4.5%**	**4.1%**	**–8.2%**	**0.6**	**–0.1**	**0.1**	**–0.3**
Equities										
Nikkei	May-93	2.4%	9.1%	1.9%	–15.6%	–2.5%	0.5	0.1	–1.0	–0.1
S&P 500	Jan-60	5.5%	13.4%	21.4%	6.0%	–4.9%	1.1	0.8	0.5	–0.2
EuroStoxx	Jun-99	3.1%	6.7%	27.4%	7.3%	–35.2%	0.4	0.8	0.4	–1.1
S&P ASX	Apr-01	5.6%	14.9%	10.4%	5.7%	–6.7%	1.2	0.4	0.5	–0.3
FTSE 100	May-93	5.9%	8.4%	29.2%	5.8%	–3.2%	0.6	1.0	0.4	–0.1
Sector Average		**4.5%**	**10.5%**	**18.1%**	**1.9%**	**–10.5%**	**0.8**	**0.6**	**0.1**	**–0.4**
Currencies										
AUD	Dec-77	2.5%	5.2%	2.1%	–6.5%	–4.6%	0.5	0.2	–0.9	–0.4
GBP	Dec-72	1.6%	4.7%	–2.1%	–1.5%	–2.0%	0.5	–0.2	–0.2	–0.2
EUR	Dec-72	1.2%	5.8%	3.2%	6.2%	–6.6%	0.6	0.3	0.6	–0.6
JPY	Dec-72	0.1%	5.1%	11.7%	4.7%	–6.1%	0.6	2.3	0.4	–0.6
CHF	Dec-72	1.3%	0.8%	7.4%	4.9%	–2.9%	0.1	0.6	0.4	–0.3
Sector Average		**1.3%**	**4.3%**	**4.5%**	**1.6%**	**–4.4%**	**0.4**	**0.6**	**0.1**	**–0.4**
Bond Futures										
UK Gilt	Nov-83	2.8%	2.8%	4.9%	2.2%	2.0%	0.4	0.6	0.3	0.3
JGB	Aug-75	2.9%	3.7%	5.3%	–2.1%	–3.4%	0.9	0.9	–0.4	–0.6
Bund	Jul-92	4.6%	4.7%	2.6%	6.6%	11.8%	0.9	0.5	1.2	2.1
US 10Y Note	Aug-72	2.9%	5.2%	1.6%	3.0%	–4.2%	0.8	0.2	0.5	–0.5
Australia 10Y	Jun-02	2.4%	7.3%	1.6%	–6.8%	3.1%	0.9	0.2	–0.8	0.5
Sector Average		**3.1%**	**4.7%**	**3.2%**	**0.6%**	**1.8%**	**0.8**	**0.5**	**0.2**	**0.4**

The results are striking and intuitive. In all but one case (Bund futures), the positive-carry, positive-trend buckets significantly outperform the negative-trend, negative-carry positions. The Bund futures example is from a shorter sample period (July 1992–December 2014), and the negative-carry, negative-trend category has less than six months of observations, far fewer than the other markets. While we do not claim to have an exhaustive set of assets, and indeed it is possible that one can find assets where the strategy of having positive trend and positive carry is not the best performer, we expect that such occurrences are relatively rare.

In addition, looking at just the "with-the-trend" trades, we find that positive-trend trades are much more profitable when also positive carry versus negative carry. Going sector by sector, commodities show remarkably strong decomposition results, with the same pattern observed as in U.S. 10-year bond futures. Some of these are worth highlighting due to specific idiosyncratic characteristics. It is worth noting that corn futures have data stretching back to June 1960 in which these results hold. Natural gas shows an extreme negative return in the positive-carry, negative-trend category (however, coming from a relatively small number of observations). Gold has always been in contango so has no positive-carry observations. Importantly, risk-adjusted returns maintain the same pattern across all five commodity markets.

In equity markets the same patterns are evident, including for the S&P 500, for which we have data back to January 1960. In some markets the positive-carry, negative-trend returns are higher than the positive-carry, positive-trend category, but the negative-carry, negative-trend returns are uniformly negative, which confirms that for portfolio construction being against the market and paying too much for this privilege is not a good strategy. Interestingly, for equity markets, the volatilities are higher in negative-trend periods (which include stock market crashes), so that on average risk-adjusted returns of the positive-carry, positive-trend strategy are the highest, and are lowest in the negative-carry, negative-trend strategy.

Results for currencies are straightforward and cover a uniformly good sample period from the early-to-mid-1970s to the present. The same pattern persists, i.e., Japanese yen has seen outlier returns in the positive-carry, negative-trend category, but again, this was from a small set of observations and indeed can be traced to an extremely active and interventionist central bank.

Lastly, bond futures show more mixed results, although again, in every case except Bunds the positive-trend, positive-carry group outperforms the negative-carry, negative-trend group. Because the majority of the sample period occurs within the 30-year declining-rates regime, the average returns are naturally higher, even in the left-hand category. The three longest histories are for the U.S., Japan, and U.K. The first two markets show fairly consistent patterns. The U.K. results are weaker—possibly due to technical demand factors in the long end of the gilts curve.

Carry and Trend across Rate Regimes

One important and natural question that leaps out from this analysis, however, is the extent to which these results are simply driven by the period of falling rates. We have addressed the general performance of trend following strategies in rising rates in another paper (Rennison et. al. [2014]). Admittedly, the statistical analysis is challenging due to the limited availability of data in the early part of the sample. Nonetheless, we do have sufficient data for roughly half the markets to restrict the analysis only to the period of broadly rising interest rates from 1960–December 1982. Table 27.5 shows these results in the same format as Table 27.4.

TABLE 27.5: Full Table of Results by Market, Maximum Available Sample Period from 1960–1982

			Annualized Returns by Category				**Sharpe Ratios by Category**			
			Carry>0		**Carry>0**		**Carry>0**		**Carry<0**	
Market	**Begins**	**Full Sample Avg Return**	***Trend>0***	***Trend<0***	***Trend>0***	***Trend<0***	***Trend>0***	***Trend<0***	***Trend>0***	***Trend<0***
Commodities										
Corn	Jun-60	–0.9%	42.6%	–0.9%	–7.6%	–11.4%	1.6	0.0	–0.4	–0.8
Gold	Jan-76	6.0%			30.8%	–20.6%			1.0	–0.8
Sector Average		**2.6%**	**42.6%**	**–0.9%**	**11.6%**	**–16.0%**	**1.6**	**0.0**	**0.3**	**–0.8**
Equities										
S&P 500	Jan-60	1.8%	16.0%	12.9%	5.2%	–11.6%	1.9	0.7	0.5	–0.8
Sector Average		**1.8%**	**16.0%**	**12.9%**	**5.2%**	**–11.6%**	**1.9**	**0.7**	**0.5**	**–0.8**
Currencies										
AUD	Dec-77	–0.3%	1.2%	–5.2%	–0.5%	1.9%	0.3	–1.3	–0.1	0.6
GBP	Dec-72	–0.5%	7.9%	–6.9%	–15.5%	–39.1%	1.1	–0.7	–1.8	–3.3

(Continued)

			Annualized Returns by Category				Sharpe Ratios by Category			
			Carry>0		Carry>0		Carry>0		Carry<0	
Market	**Begins**	**Full Sample Avg Return**	**Trend>0**	**Trend<0**	**Trend>0**	**Trend<0**	**Trend>0**	**Trend<0**	**Trend>0**	**Trend<0**
EUR	Dec-72	1.4%	13.9%	3.0%	5.4%	–6.4%	3.3	0.6	0.5	–0.6
JPY	Dec-72	0.4%	1.9%	4.8%	9.8%	–10.6%	0.5	1.4	0.9	–1.0
CHF	Dec-72	2.0%			5.8%	–1.8%			0.4	–0.2
Sector Average		0.6%	6.2%	–1.1%	1.0%	–11.2%	1.3	0.0	0.0	–0.9
Bond Futures										
JGB	Aug-75	0.1%	6.0%	–1.9%	–2.9%	–2.2%	2.7	–0.6	–0.9	–0.5
US 10Y Note	Aug-72	–1.9%	4.7%	–3.8%	–5.6%	–6.6%	0.7	–0.6	–0.8	–0.7
Sector Average		–2.4%	5.4%	–2.9%	–4.2%	–4.4%	1.7	–0.6	–0.8	–0.6

We find the same patterns broadly hold, albeit with some slightly more dramatic results due to smaller sample sets and a generally volatile period. All markets except the Australian dollar (which only has data for five years in this test) show the same pattern of positive carry, positive trend outperforming negative carry, negative trend. In our view, this analysis provides ample evidence in other regimes that the baseline strategy of being on the positive side of the trend and positive carry is indeed the superior strategy.

Conclusions

In this paper we first identified that the returns to carry and trend are robust over periods and asset classes. In particular, the combination of positive-carry and positive-trend positions is without exception better than negative-carry and negative-trend positions over each historical period and for (almost) every asset class and across rate regimes. In addition, we find that while carry in itself is a positive expected return strategy, positive-trend strategies can match and even exceed positive-carry strategies over a wide combination of periods and assets, but the best combination ex-ante is to build portfolios that democratically harvest the best trends and best carry.

The investment implications are straightforward: Combining positive-carry and positive-trend positions has high positive risk-adjusted expected returns. As a corollary, if positive-carry positions cannot be found, then by extension of our results, positive-trend positions that minimize negative carry are high-expected-return strategies. This has significant impact for portfolio construction at a high level. In summary, it reminds us that the best strategy for long-term portfolio construction is: "Be on the right side of the trend, and don't pay too much while you are at it."

28

The Great Hypocrisy

Josh Hawes and Paul King
Hawking Alpha LLC

As it's told, Albert Einstein had three rules that guided his work: One, out of clutter find simplicity; two, from discord, find harmony; and three, in the middle of difficulty lies opportunity. For a while I have become more and more frustrated with the financial industry, and in this paper I hope to provide a few points of clarity amidst the mess. While the street has learned how to sell "simple," sadly simple in its profitable form is not always easy.

Many investors have been complaining loudly about the performance of their funds and the huge capital gains taxes that are tacked on by the IRS. Investors from the small retail client to the ultra-high-net-worth investor would like more transparency in their funds so they could find out what specific stocks that they are invested in. Most investors are feeling like they have lost control over the decision-making process regarding their investments at every level. I truly believe that there are better wealth-building opportunities that an investor can adopt to protect their assets and financial well-being.

In my opinion, the financial investment community, from mutual funds to hedge funds, has become bloated and lethargic. The majority of investors have been slowly losing their wealth for many years in mutual funds as well as hedge funds after 2008; fees and excessive costs are taking a toll in their pursuit to "beat the market." During the bull market of the 1990s we saw plenty of double-digit returns, and there seemed to be a happy marriage between the investor and mutual funds. We see now at the beginning of the twenty-first century, there are red flags flying high and bright giving a warning to investors.

Mutual funds have a record of underperformance, hidden fees, higher income tax consequences, and a lack of investor control, and hedge funds aren't far behind. Informed investors are now beginning to realize that they're wasting their time and wealth in many of these "structured" products.

Don't get me wrong, mutual funds did not start out as a bad investment. In fact, mutual funds have provided many Americans the opportunity to amass fortunes during their working life in their retirement accounts since the 1940s, when the Securities and Exchange Commission founded the Investment Company Act that created the concept of putting multiple stocks and/or bonds in separate funds. Since their invention, mutual funds have been good for Americans for many decades. Mutual funds were supposed to create an opportunity for the average middle-class American to invest like those with more substantial resources, and those with substantial resources were supposed to be able to use hedge funds to, well, hedge. These funds became the investor's new best friend, offering professional management, many choices, and, for a long time, stress-free investing. It was truly a powerful force in the marketplace.

These pools of equities offered investors diversification and more safety than most individual securities at a price that was affordable. It was a shift from brand-name investing for the generations, where Mom and Dad would invest in one company like General Motors and hold for life, to broad-based baskets from the academic community.

This shift can really be attributed to Morningstar when in the '90s it came out with its "style box." This was a feeble attempt at simplifying something academic like the Capital Asset Pricing Model. Instantly people could "see" how a fund was "managed" in relation to other "styles." Due to our inherent nature it was practically a dollar-printing shop for the industry, as it provided an easily understood graphic to articulate a vocabulary that was relatively nonexistent in describing client product demand. Yet as Eugene Fama and Kenneth French showed that bets on "style" frequently masquerade as skill and can attribute away many manager's returns![1]

Soon mutual funds increased even more in popularity due to the government-offered retirement plan. We know these plans as our 401(k)s, SEPs, and IRAs. The fact is, today, over 40% of mutual fund assets come from these retirement plans. This sum is a major reason that vast sums of money were pumped into mutual funds. American investors finally had an affordable investment for the middle class family, but as the title of one famous book said, "where are all the customer yachts?"[2]

Times have changed. The mask is off and the real face of the industry is being exposed. If you read this full paper you will see what I am talking about. In the early years, funds were all about making money for clients, but now it seems that they're focused only on gathering as many assets as they possibly can all while under the mandate of beating a "benchmark" rather than making money. Now they are sidestepping the spirit that was born in the 1940s, and it's no different in the hedge fund industry, where A. W. Jones was to hedge the downside of his long portfolio. The industry is also optimizing as much market share as they can get even if they have to break a few laws to do it.

Let's look at some statistical facts. In 1980, there were 500 mutual funds available to choose from with a total of $100 billion invested. As of June 2014, there are 8,300 mutual funds with a total of $26.8 trillion invested according to the Investment Company Institute. In 1990 the hedge fund industry only had $40 billion in assets under management, but now there are over 8,000 hedge funds managing more than $2.4 trillion.[3] This is not a misprint; this monster keeps growing and growing. An investment pattern with this concept originally developed slowly.

Americans put about 20% of their discretionary wealth into mutual funds during the 1970s and 1980s. By the time the 1990s rolled around, investors were investing at a rate of 25%. In 1996, that rate rose to 60%. At the end of the century, the rate of investment in the mutual funds by Americans climbed to a staggering 82%! It's not surprising that the firms that you see as "leaders" today were the early risers during the boom between 1980 and 2000.

Sadly this increase in the number of choices available has led to the inevitable expectation of better outcomes. As psychology has shown today, though, more (in the form of choice) equals less for us in the end. As Sheena Iyengar points out, satisfaction comes from the perception of control.[4] But the desire for choice is not a choice in and of itself, even though the ability to choose well is one of our most powerful tools. Thus for most people, they are SELF-defeated before they even begin as they are overwhelmed by all their options with no means of process or TRUE measurement.

Before 2003, the worst thing we could say about a mutual fund was that most of them lost money and hedge funds were levered, scary instruments because of the lasting effects from Long-Term Capital Management. From 2003 onwards, we can now say something even worse about the group as a whole: a large number of mutual funds are now losing money fraudulently! In 2003, New York State Attorney General Eliot Spitzer crusaded ineffectively to put the brakes on the likes of major financial companies for improper trading of mutual fund shares. Blue-chip companies such as Bank of America, Strong Capital Management, and Bank One were implicated along with small-trader hedge fund Canary Capital Partners in schemes to milk investors of billions each year, according to Spitzer. Spitzer exposed more than 60 years of backsliding. In 2008 we had the largest Ponzi scheme in history exposed with regards to Bernie Madoff's company. Of course just a few years later we have one of the strongest hedge fund performers with Steven Cohen and SAC Capital getting in trouble for insider trading! What this does as a result is leave people worrying about *choosing* the right options.

An industry entrusted with nearly $8.1 trillion of the American public's money, mutual funds used to be the investment vehicles that investors relied on to finance the American dream of a home in the suburbs, good education for the kids, and a comfortable retirement.[5] Hedge funds were supposed to be tools to help wealthy individuals protect themselves, not risk blowing up and losing their capital, and what is rule number one for a family office? Protect the principal.

Today we see that the nation's 93 million mutual fund investors are basically overwhelmed by the competing claims of some 8,000+ mutual funds. Just look at the two powerhouses in the industry: Vanguard and Fidelity. Each of them has a different core message. Vanguard believes in low cost and that beating the market is stupid, so being cost focused is key. At the same time Fidelity is focused on its ability to distribute its "stars." These two names became masters at selling their unique selling points.

Most of the time investors are clueless about how to enhance their wealth using mutual funds. The average equity fund lost 12% during the year 2000, 2001, and 2002. Since that time the results have not been much better. In fact if we look at the last 10 years of the general market, which most mutual funds and even hedge funds track, we can see an eerie indication about the weakness of their viability to grow your assets in a stable manner in relation to purchasing power.

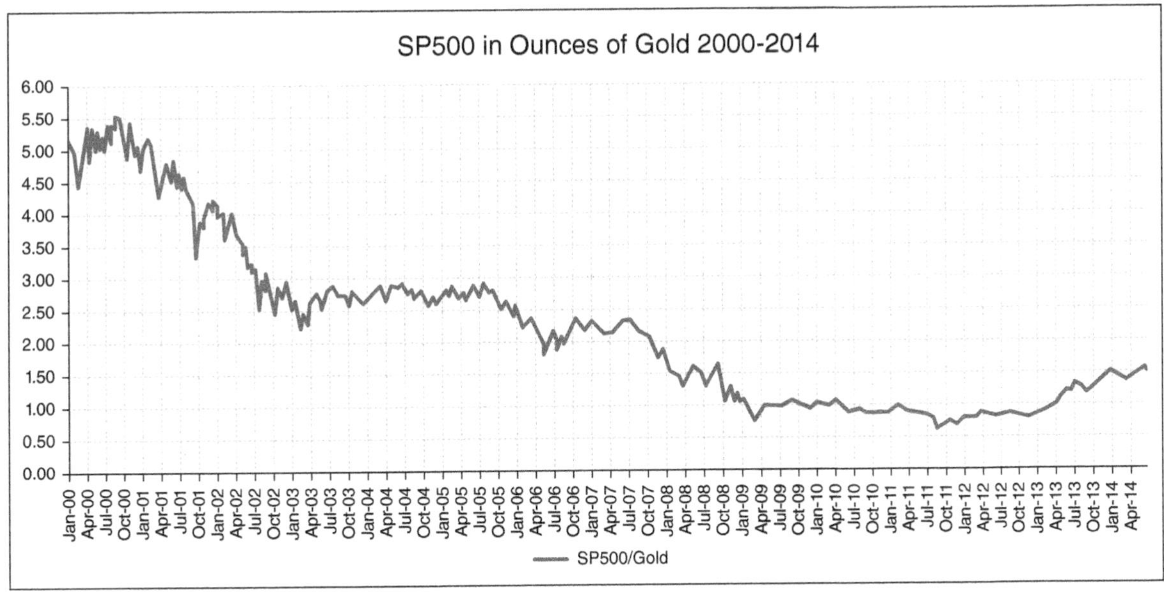

S&P 500 in Ounces of Gold 2000–2014

We can see in this chart that the compound annual growth rate has actually been negative! The fact that economists even mention the term "wealth effect" should tell you something! This measure of return in relation to the purchasing power is shockingly bad. It's not the stars nor is it the cost, it's the manager's process that one invests in, not some little box. As Warren Buffett has said, "If in a game of poker you don't know who the patsy is, you're the patsy." I give no ill face toward Fidelity or Vanguard, as they did their job: Make money for the company. The responsibility lies on the investor's shoulders. It's a sad day when people spend more time choosing their next refrigerator than their investments. For people across the gamut, from mutual fund to hedge fund investor, I recommend a paper by Andrew Weisman called, "Informationless Investing and Hedge Fund Performance Bias."[6] It does a great job of describing the fallacy of using the Sharpe ratio as a measure of goodness, especially for hedge funds. As Ronald Reagan used to say, "Trust but verify," and in our opinion you need to be verifying with at least the right tools.

But that's just about return and doesn't include the hidden killer, either. Let's get to the real problem in this industry: fees in relation to risk. It is the expenses that kill returns. Average investors are so confused by these expenses that they have no idea what they're paying, and high net worth investors are willing to accept unfair deals. The sales commissions for the most active managed funds are tacked on by the brokers and are usually around 6%. The fund deducts at least half a percentage point on average from your account for its service. Cash drag, a reserve set aside for opportunity cost or to pay off redemptions, will add another 0.6%. Rich people with hedge funds aren't out of the woods, either; don't forget about funds of funds. A third of hedge fund investors use these outsourced instruments and they have their own added costs wrappers as well. A question I constantly ask people is that it's not how much are you paying for your return, but how much are you paying for your drawdown?

The point is that investors pay billions in costs and fees per year. What do they get in return? They almost always receive mediocre performance and yet all the risk when you factor in taxes, and many actually suffer a financial loss. A stable bond fund, real estate, individual stock, or even a treasury bill may perform as well as the average mutual fund trading equities. Sadly, over the last few years, this is even true for most hedge funds as well. More and more when one digs under the hood, one just discovers "closet indexers"—those just trying to match an index and not wanting to stray too far from it "in case" they are wrong and their performance lags the benchmark index. What does Jones say? "Losers average losers."

The churn (turnover) of stocks that fund managers perform all year long causes these transaction costs. In fact, the average turnover of the stock is 80% or higher yearly for nearly every stock and mutual fund portfolio.[7] By conservative estimates, this wraps up an expense of 0.7%, not including capital gains tax, which also eats away at your profits. On top of this, add another 1.5% for management fees and expenses including the dreaded 12b-1 that those outside the industry strongly criticize. You better believe that those inside the industry continue to exploit it for all that they are worth! In a hedge fund, the transaction costs are socialized due to being commingled vehicles. This makes it very hard to measure costs in relation to net asset value.

Let's take an example. Assume your fund is generating a good return in today's market with an assumption of 12% compound annual growth rate of total assets (as a long-term buy-and-hold investor). The commissions, costs, cash drag, and fees reduce this to 8.7%. In short, the cost of your fund manager is close to 3.3%. Therefore, the fund is underperforming the market by at least 3.3%. After taxes, which I estimate conservatively to be around 0.7%, you will have no more than 8% of the original 12% return. This is only two-thirds of your fund's return that you get to take home and put in your pocket, but in reality it is probably much less than this. Now this type of performance isn't bad and should be paid up for IF the manager is able to manage risk and thus the drawdown is less than the market's risk in relation to the generated return. Sadly, as history has shown, the bottom line is that mutual funds cost way too much in relation to their return to the risk taken, and hedge funds aren't doing their mandate—hedging—either.

The typical investor is averaging 3.5% in cost. What always shocks me is that most people balk at the typical 2/20 structure with hedge funds, and yet if we assume an average return of 12% for the hedge fund, the total cost comes out to only 4.4%; that's less than one point greater than the cost of a supposed "fee friendly" fund. A lot of people will ask, "Well, where's the value?" To that I say, simple, let's take a look at the market's MAR ratio (remember the one from before?) to the fund's MAR ratio. As we have seen in our chart, the market's MAR ratio is around 0.1—well, at Hawking, for us, an acceptable MAR ratio is 0.5. That means that we provide a 400 times value for only a 1% increase in cost! At least with a hedge fund they don't get paid their 20% unless they MAKE the investor money. The reason that you see conflicting fee charges for mutual funds is that there are multiple fee revenue streams and many fees that are charged, but are hidden to you.

Sadly, we can look at mutual funds as a billing iceberg. Most of an iceberg is unseen, underwater. Mutual fund companies have become increasingly adept at applying extra hidden revenue streams to their funds, in addition to the standard fees, which are also going up over time. In fact, as returns have diminished during the post-2000 era, mutual fund companies have actually been raising fees. The average mutual fund investor isn't even aware of the fees he is paying, disclosed or undisclosed. In fact, shareholders are paying for mutual fund advertising and promotions through 12b-1 fees. At least hedgies have to pay for their marketing out of their own cash flow. Unfortunately, as mentioned earlier, most investors don't read their mutual fund prospectus, where a lot of essential fee information can be found. All 93 million mutual fund investors reward mutual fund companies annually with about $70 billion in operating cost—and most investors don't realize they're paying it.[8]

What is investing in funds really costing you? You can expect to pay approximately 3% to 4% of your fund assets yearly in total cost (upfront or backend cost) for a load fund. For no-load fund, you'll still be paying around 3% to 3.5% for your portfolio mutual funds. If you do some serious checking into these costs over the life of your portfolio, you'll see some serious money going into the coffers of the mutual fund companies over and over again.

Unlike paying your gas bill or your electricity bill regularly, you'll hardly ever receive a bill from your mutual fund company. Your costs are simply deducted from your portfolio returns right off the top when the broker executes a trade. You may scream if your daughter makes an unauthorized credit card purchase, but where are you when you pay a 5% load on a $25,000 mutual fund investment? With the boom of mutual fund returns in the 1990s, wouldn't you think the fund companies with these huge infusions of cash coming in and internal expenses going down would reduce fees for their shareholders? Don't count on it. The resulting discovery of this has seen the rise of low-cost funds or ETF's and the use of research to expound upon the virtues of "passive" investing. How "riding it out" is a sound strategy. Since when did passive anything work in your life? You got here by your sweat and hard work. In fact, just a little elbow grease can go a long way. The problem is that "passive" is not a USP, it's a solution to fees, and the truth is it's turned into preying on the fear of investors of "missing out." As a wise manager once told me, just because exposure is there, doesn't mean you need it.

In fact, due to the fixed cost of fund companies (staffing, accounting, research, and so forth) becoming smaller (thank you, technology), fees actually could have been reduced, much like trading costs were squeezed by low-cost brokers. Remember, fund companies increased revenues many times when AUM went in the year 2000 from 371 billion in 1984.[9] John Bogle says "the drive to make money for others—the fund's shareholders—may not be as powerful as the drive to make money for oneself through ownership participation in the management company. There are two sides pulling against each other in mutual fund companies: the shareholders (the investors in the mutual funds) and the stockholders (the investors in the mutual fund company)."[10] For the hedge fund industry and its structure, an important question to be asking your manager is what they are looking for in a strategic partner, as most funds are in the form of a partnership, aren't they? When dealing with someone's money, from $100 to $1 billion, a form of partnership is entrusted and should be viewed and PROTECTED as such. There shouldn't be a pulling of conflicting goals, there should be an alignment of them. When everyone is aligned together, everyone is most likely to come out ahead. This establishes the most critical element, which is trust. One way to confirm that is by making sure that managers invest in their own funds or at least that the performance structure in place aligns the manager with the investor not against them.

"Investors today are being fed lies and distortions, and are being exploited and neglected," says Arthur Levitt, former chairman of the SEC. "In the wake of the last decade's rush to invest by millions of households, and Wall Street's obsession with short-term performance, a culture of gamesmanship has grown amongst corporate management, financial analysts, brokers, and mutual fund managers, making it hard to tell financial fantasy from reality, and salesmanship from honest advice." A study by Dreman and Berry showed that there was a significant gap between Wall Street analyst's estimates and actual corporate profits.[11] What was more striking was that they found that this gap is increasing as time AND TECHNOLOGY go on and becomes more sophisticated. Sadly, we live in an era where a manager touts his AUM and not his risk-adjusted return.

Did you know that around 15 years ago there was not one TV channel that covered detail market news? Today there are, according to Robert B. Jorgensen[12]:

- Hundreds of radio stations that report financial news
- Specialized financial newspapers and magazines
- Three major cable channels that are devoted to financial news
- Most major and minor newspapers have business pages
- Thousands of newsletters that cover financial topics
- Hundreds of thousands of websites that pertains to financial investments
- Financial salespeople to make calls
- Advertisers, slick brochures, and mailing pieces abound with financial offers

Literally hundreds of websites are positioned to reveal the latest hot investment opportunity for investors at every level; those worth thousands to those worth millions to hundreds of millions. All these triggering devices want you to believe they're rubbing the lamp with one rub that will propel you to untold riches with, as most look for, no hassle and no requirement to understand the investment. But, as psychology experts have shown, the more we use "experts" the higher we set our expectations, without any quality metric and the larger the potential for disappointment.

It's time for you to come to the truth about the industry and not just accept it for the "norm" or you will suffer the consequences:

- The tax consequence—If fund managers sell stock at a profit, you take a capital gains hit even if your fund lost money.
- The quick change consequence—You invest in the fund to fulfill a certain investment strategy. Be careful; the manager can change the strategy.
- The no-diversification consequence—Unless you're diversified across fund sectors, you may wind up owning the same stock in different funds.
- The name's the game consequence—A stock fund's name doesn't always reflect its investing intentions.
- The moving manager consequence—Managers come and go. If you lose your manager, your account will probably suffer, if the team isn't being built to take over the roles of leadership at every level of management.
- The huge-fund consequence—The more assets a fund takes in, the higher the chances of lower performance.
- The fee consequence—You'll pay myriad fees and commissions.

The bottom line is that most fund management companies fall short in regard to performance and returns with investors' stock funds. At the same time they are a master at sneaking in fees and add-on charges. In short, most funds are a marketing success, not an investing success, and ride the coattails of those that do perform, and why would those that perform care? It's their edge for outperformance!

Former SEC chairman Arthur Levitt says, "Investors simply do not get what they pay for when they buy into a mutual fund; most investors don't even know what they're paying for. The industry has often misled investors into buying funds on the basis of past performance. Fees, along with the effect of annual expenses, sales loads, and trading costs, are hidden. Fund directors as a whole exercise scant oversight over management. The cumulative effect of this has manifested itself in the form of late trading, market timing, insider trading, and other instances of preferential treatment that cut at the very heart of investor trust. It would be hard not to conclude that the way funds are sold and managed reveals a culture that thrives on hype, promotes short-term trading, and withholds important information."

Results come from having a method to the madness, not a checklist or box. Investment satisfaction doesn't come from great performance, and truthfully would be okay with all the fees and costs IF expectations are fulfilled. That's why I have talked about trust, because trust is the foundation of confidence, and that should be the objective of the Street; to instill confidence once again by setting the right expectations.

What does this mean to you as an investor of your hard-earned money into mutual funds and hedge funds? You've entrusted your money and your wealth to these managers, but you're getting the short end of the stick when it comes to them doing their number one job of managing risk first. This is surprising because we've always been told that the stock market is the single best place to build wealth for your families and your retirement. This is true if you're getting the most value for your dollar from managers that concentrate on risk-adjusted returns. If you're not, your portfolio is on a hamster wheel going nowhere along with the assets of millions of other dejected mutual fund and hedge fund investors. My purpose here is to get you off of the wheel, and I hope by this point I at least got you starting to think outside of just return, and at least realizing that you can't do what everyone else is doing and get "outperformance."

So how can something go so wrong? In 2013, mutual fund assets totaled over $13 trillion.[13] This increase can only naturally call for companies' priorities to shift. It's evident that the mutual fund industry does not hold the individual investor in the highest regard and the hedge fund industry is not far behind. John Bogle, an outspoken critic of mutual funds and the founder of Vanguard Financial, says his biggest complaint of the mutual fund industry is that it's now run like a business where cash flow from asset fees rather than return is the priority. Bogle traces the industry's demise to a 1956 federal court ruling allowing mutual fund firms to become public enterprises. This changed the playing field, according to Bogle. "That opened the door to look at this business as an entrepreneurial business in which the focus was on making money for the stockholders," he said. "Once you change the investment profession into a marketing service business, you put management in the backseat and marketing in front."

People have been waking up to this, as the mass exodus in 2008 showed, and the lack of volume back in the markets in the subsequent years. This doesn't mean that mutual funds and the companies that produce and market them are going to become extinct. In fact the opposite is true. At the time of this writing, mutual fund companies are evolving. They're developing new alternatives and investment strategies like low-cost ETFs and replication structures in order to hold on to their client base and secure new clients. Eventually, though, mutual funds will take a backseat to new forms of investing for the emerging affluent investors. Brian Portnoy said it best, "'Convergence' is upon us.[14] The once-distinct traditional and alternative investment worlds are colliding rapidly. Traditional asset-management firms, fighting shrinking margins on their core business, are building new forms of investment risk that can be packaged and sold at premium margins. Meanwhile, hedge fund shops, generally tiny in comparison, see massive yet untouched markets that can be potentially accessed by delivering more investor friendly structures. Alternatives are going mainstream, and fast!"

Mutual funds are dying in their original state because of the unfairness of fees, unnecessary taxes, lack of investor control, and a host of other reasons. Don't think hedge funds are any different, though, as the industry has seen its fees shrink from the normally 2% down to an average of 1.5%. Investors have never grasped these points until now. Today, a lot of investors understand the drawbacks of mutual funds because the events of the last five years have brought the message home. They discovered that they're paying out millions of dollars in excessive cost in running needless risk, all in the hope of outperforming the market based on return without even properly considering risk.

We need government to rise to the occasion, but know it won't, even as the government examines more critically the operating policies of mutual funds; things will only slowly change. Increased federal and state scrutiny will trigger more reforms that will probably get the ball rolling in Congress, like the Mutual Funds Integrity and Fee Transparency Act that the mutual fund industry successfully lobbied against.

Meanwhile, underperformance is the norm for mutual funds and 95% of most hedge fund managers. In recent years, the mutual fund companies could perhaps be forgiven for the huge marketing expenses and increased salaries of their star managers if the product delivered as advertised. But this is no longer the case. Underperformance is the norm rather than the exception. It's a fact. In spite of our respectable pass during the 1980s and 1990s, the average mutual fund returned 2% less than the returns of the market each and every year while still participating fully in the downside moves.[15] Sharpe, Treynor, and Jensen showed that a sample of mutual funds from the '40s to the '60s could not outperform buy and hold, nor even a randomly generated portfolio![16] It's not just the mutual fund industry, though. One study found that only 21.2% of fund of funds managers find alpha after fees, and only 5.6% of them add value above the alpha from what they are investing in! At the very least one should be asking for a manager's aggregate profit and loss to see if his constituents have actually made any money.

"In the mutual fund industry, we used to be in the business of long-term investing; now we're in the business of short-term speculation" said Bogle. Not only do the fund managers tend to underperform the S&P 500 yearly, but the underperformance also has grown more pronounced over the years. The individual managers responsible for funds are now marketed as stars. The truth is that most market outperformance lies in the hedge fund industry and even in that niche only a few dozen like George Soros, John Paulson, David Harding, Jerry Parker, Bruce Kovner, David Tepper, and Louis Bacon have made their clients money. More staggering is that these few have also produced most of the return for the whole industry! Even more surprising is that only 7% of funds that are better than the sixteenth percentile manage to repeat that performance every year of their life. This means that attempting to pick THE best fund to ALWAYS outperform is futile, as there's no evidence to support that it is possible. However, finding managers for a particular objective can be done. As Brian Portnoy points out, it revolves around trust, risk, skill, and fit.[17]

Investors and potential investors are subject to the billions of dollars of advertising promoting the virtue of funds and mutual fund managers who are supposedly skilled in handling their money. With the new JOBS ACT, don't expect this to be any different in the future, as hedge funds get into the marketing game more and more. The chances of the fund manager beating the market are small, so small that the average mutual fund only outperforms the market two times out of every five, according to mutual fund researchers. If you're still not convinced, consider this[18]:

- Through the end of 2001, there were 1,226 actively managed stock funds with a five-year record. Their average annualized performance trailed the S&P index by 1.9% per year (8.8% for the funds and 10.7% for the index).
- Through the end of 2001, there were 623 active managed stock funds with a 10-year record. Their average annualized performance trailed the S&P 500 by 1.7% per year (11.2% for the funds and 12.9% for the index).

- The figures above include the sales loads charged by many funds. Loads are akin to brokerage commissions, which come straight out of your returns. They are charged when you buy or sell shares of your fund. Even with these load funds excluded, the five-year average trailed the S&P 500 by 1.4% per year, and the 10-year average return trailed by 1.4% as well.
- These figures didn't include discarded mutual funds, which would reflect poor performance and bring these averages down significantly. The exclusion of these mutual funds is called "survivorship bias." With returns corrected for survivorship bias, average actively managed funds trailed the market by about 3% per year. This self-selection bias isn't just inherent in the mutual industry but shows up in the hedge fund world as well, as Dichev in 2009 was able to show.[19] The reason being is that as a fund dies off the last few months of underperformance never get reported and thus logged. The estimates of this effect on true return for these indexes ranges from about 3% to 5%.

Cost will drag down your performance. Fund managers are supposed to be good, and some of them certainly are, except we don't know which ones are good until the returns come in. Most managers, unfortunately, will only equal the market as a whole before costs. As famous fund manager Paul Tudor Jones said, "Losers average losers." What drags performance down is the management fees, trading costs, sales loads, and other incidentals. And thus, direct and indirect costs defeat the performance of most funds before you get your feet wet.

Mutual funds must disclose that past performance is not indicative of future results. Unfortunately, most investors and financial media use past performance as their primary selection criteria. I once sat in a room with a major institutional allocator who got on the phone to say, "The only thing that's indicative of the future for me is past results." I was shocked as these guys were supposed to have some type of system for this kind of thing, but sadly this is what most people can only use as a means to measure "good" without proper education of what "good" is.

The truth is, most mutual funds rarely outperform the markets for a significant period of time. Only eight funds in the history of mutual funds have outperformed the S&P 500 for more than 10 years straight![20]

Next let's take a look at taxes associated with mutual funds. There are no tax advantages to mutual funds, only disadvantages. If you pay taxes in all mutual funds, you have created a natural adversarial relationship. You'll probably have to pay taxes when your stocks are sold in the portfolio. Not only that, you may also have to pay taxes when your stock fund loses money. Mutual fund companies during the tax year are required to distribute capital gains and the dividends to their shareholders. Unless you own a non-taxable mutual fund (i.e., municipal bond fund, retirement account, etc.), you probably are going to have capital gains.

Mutual fund companies are not looking out for you when it comes to taxes. Shareholders pay capital gains taxes; mutual fund companies don't. In 2013 your capital gains are taxed at the standard tax rate: 28% to 36%, depending on your reported income, for stocks held less than one year.[21] If you hold funds for more than a year, it's 15% across the board.

Statistics show that American households paid $345 billion in capital gains taxes on mutual funds in the year 2000.[22] These gains have accumulated throughout the 1990s. When the air came out of technology stocks, portfolio managers began dumping them. But even if the stocks have lost their original value, they still accumulated capital gains. Remember, even if your stock fund loses money, you're still liable for capital gains because during the fund's history it made money, making its capital gains embedded. I haven't even mentioned dividends. Even if you reinvest your dividends back into the fund, the IRS says you're still subject to tax on your dividends.[23]

There are ways to cut your tax bill with mutual funds if the companies were responsible. Critics charge that fund companies could lower their capital gains distributions if they wished. One way is through improved bookkeeping. If the fund companies were programmed to sell their highest-cost years first once they reduce the large block of stock, it could result in the tax savings for the investors. This is called HIFO (highest in, first out) accounting, according to Vanguard, the low-cost index fund company, because it could save investors as much as 1% of assets each year due to lower cost. Trading this often would hinder the capital gains explosion, but because the average mutual fund turns over its stocks once in the course of a year (on which the commission is on average five cents a share every time a share is traded), this seems unlikely.

The mutual fund structure prevents "tax harvesting," the timing of securities by its manager to utilize capital losses or defer capital gains. Regardless of when you buy into a mutual fund, you become the proud owner of the liabilities that were incurred before you even put your money down. So you buy into a fund for $10,000 on December 12 at $10 a share.

Shortly before the year ends, your mutual fund company calculates a yearly capital gain of two dollars a share. Guess what? Because you have 1,000 shares, you will shortly receive the distribution of $2,000, all taxable to you. Even though you've only been in the fund for a couple weeks, you will have to pay the same amount of taxes as the fellow that had been in it all year. Your original $10,000 investment may still be intact, but now you have a $2,000 tax bill. That's why you should never buy into a fund in December when mutual fund companies record the year's performance (my full opinion is that you should never buy a mutual fund, period). Yet a focus on taxes is really just a moot point that sidetracks one from thinking in risk-adjusted terms.

Always examine funds by their after-tax returns, rather than pre-tax. Even then you still have things like basis risk and gross exposure (don't just look at net) which tilts analysis into the realm of the complicated. You won't find these figures in the fund advertisement or the colorful brochures. You can find these figures in the fund's prospectus, in very small print. Thanks to the SEC's February 2003 ruling requiring mutual fund companies to include pre-tax and post-tax information in their prospectus, companies cannot conceal this information.[24] The only problem is that most investors don't read the prospectus. For example, a lot of investors who bought into a popular fund that year saw the capital gains were spread amongst a lot of people. A bear market emerged because many investors rushed to liquidate that particular fund and its manager had no choice but to sell as many stocks as possible to raise enough capital for those redemptions. A huge capital distribution was left for the remaining stockholders. There are examples of investors who put a few thousand dollars into a fund and later were hit by Uncle Sam for a five-figure tax bite.

Was there a chance that the mutual fund managers could have foreseen the taxpayer's dilemma and altered their selling strategy? Not a chance. Mutual fund managers are not paid to maximize tax efficiency, only to generate returns, and I wouldn't want it any other way considering how big our tax code is. Which means that they need to concentrate on incentive-aligned structures. Once you've identified those structures then it's all about looking at how the manager aligns himself in what Brian Portnoy distinguished as the five keys: concentration, leverage, directionality, illiquidity, and complexity.[25] The "perfection" of what you are trying to look for is whether the manager is diversified (by systems too?), market neutral, unlevered, highly liquid, and simply executed.

The mutual fund industry profits by keeping the spotlight off such issues mentioned above. As long as the fund companies keep you ignorant, the negative elements of mutual funds won't ever be brought to light. Most investors traditionally have to make do with minimum information. That's the bare minimum ruled by the SEC. Twice a year, you get to see what's going on in your account. Investors said they want their financial information 24 /7. Even though the Internet has sped up the tracking of investments considerably, major fund companies have been painfully slow to keep investors current. This means that when you check your holdings on the Web, your figures are out of date, and possibly flat-out wrong or altogether missing because fund managers are changing your portfolio so rapidly. This is why we utilize our own proprietary risk management software that runs and monitors every position in every portfolio by our stringent risk controls. Each of these is compiled in a risk report that allows us to make sure that our return drivers are not evincing false diversification by having the same underlying risk even if we are perfectly hedged long and short with excellent returns.

This is why communication between investor and manager is paramount. With our clients we are able to give them access to their own portfolio, and they see their own risk all the way from a trade-by-trade level to portfolio level within our own front end we call *positive alpha.* This allows us to engage in a conversation that each party must have with regards to answering the question, what do you do and are you the right fit for me? As an aside, this has little to do with return as the basis for the relationship, and that is because that is the manager's job (or at least should be), and since we have shown that performance chasing doesn't work, then each party, manager and investor alike, must be able to answer the question, what is MY personal objective in the context of the risk being taken?

We must never underestimate the rich man's appeal of mutual funds. Many older and wealthier Americans in this country own mutual funds and are comfortable with the investment process that has been around for some 60 years. That feeling is disappearing. Today's investors are more comfortable with change. Today, those with emerging affluence are asking themselves if they should stay with the ultimate retail investment—one that is associated with mass-market investing and that is now viewed by many as a commodity. Mutual fund managers don't differentiate between one investor and another. Their job is to boost the inflow from the account and to get the numbers regardless of who's investing in the fund. The bottom line is mutual funds do not treat their investors like the good old days.

Unless you are totally shut out from the world, you have, like most of us, regular contact with people. Family and friends are a given. You like human contact and feel goodwill towards people most of the time. This leads to the inevitable interaction of crowds. The downside of human contact is when you find yourself in the overstuffed elevator and get stuck between floors. It's uncomfortable, stressful, intimidating, and even scary. The same can be said of mutual funds. You'll have crowded elevator contact but you still have contact with people.

Dealing with other investors in your mutual fund can invoke feelings similar to the overcrowded elevator—stress and intimidation. The inflows and outflows caused by human nature may be some of the more subtle difficulties of mutual funds. Fellow investors panic when the markets fall and become greedy as the markets rise. Instead of following the traditional words of investor wisdom—buy low and sell high—just the opposite occurs with disastrous effects for everybody.

Every investor feels the impact of a bloated fund with too much cash. It becomes too unwieldy for good management control. This causes funds to grow too quickly, turning good-performing funds into bad performers from one year to the next. In one important study done on long-only managers, it was found that the trading in and out of funds by pension plans, the "pickers" would've been better off sticking with their original choice.[26] This is a classic example of gambler's fallacy, where we are constantly trying to find patterns and "reasons" where none exist. Two books I highly recommend all people read are *The Invisible Gorilla* and *Fooled by Randomness*.[27] Each of these books discusses the dangers of how our mind operates and "sees" things and the many errors that plague everyone from the genius to the working man.

The better question is why attempt to "game" a system that doesn't seem to work to begin with?

"One advantage of mutual funds that's really a disadvantage is it's easy to get out of them," remarked Peter F. Tedstrom, of Brown and Tedstrom, Inc. "This makes it simple for an investor to call in an order as soon as the market dips," said Tedstrom. "Consequently, in the end, the investor suffers poor performance returns by frequently trading in and out of his or her portfolio." This is on top of the fact that we've already shown managers have very high churn ratios in and of themselves! This effect is apparent in hedge funds too, as 2008 showed when funds of funds were pulling their capital out of hedge funds and the result of such large client redemptions was an effect on return as well. Even a legendary investor with one of the longest track records, Paul Tudor Jones, had to put a restriction on withdrawals from clients so as not to adversely affect results.[28] That was how much the madness had crept into all aspects of the financial industry. This very story above shows that even the world's elite, as investors in hedge funds, are momentum investors, trying to chase performance.

One thing I constantly harp on about to people is that hedge funds and mutual funds are NOT asset classes and people have to get that into their head. Stocks and investing are an ALTERNATIVE to excess cash that one has. This is a problem much of the world doesn't even have! The point is that investing in liquid assets is for an alternative to cash. People will always want access to their hard earned greenbacks as quickly as possible when things FEEL the slightest bit bad. As I tell people all the time, humans think linearly but react emotionally and don't think that there isn't emotion tied with money. This ease, portrayed as an advantage, is really a disadvantage due to its effect on our decision making and must be taken into account. As an old trader on the floor once told me, "It's always easy to get in, it's never really as easy to get out."

It's time to start asking the tough questions no matter the fund, style, or manager name.

What is the market risk, the liquidity risk, operational risk, is there any style drift? All of these things as well as the core we mentioned above need to be carefully considered. I personally am a fan of Portnoy, in his book *The Investor's Paradox*,[29] where he mentions the 5 P's: portfolio, people, process, performance, and price. As he says, it's all about method over storytelling (something this industry is fond of). What one needs to be focusing on is finding someone with a repeatable coherent process. There's more to proper choice than just fees and pedigree, as Vanguard and Fidelity have shown us, as well as checking off style boxes and number of allocations.

It's time for action and to ask the tough questions of why have results for clients been so poor. What kind of transparency should I get? What kind of fee structure aligns me with my manager's goals?

Is this the end of investment bank and brokerage domination? I don't think so. You must understand that mutual funds are an American icon. Since the first mutual fund was formed, it has been the building block of our country's investment strategy and home to some 93 million Americans today. Habits die hard, even in the face of the facts given above. My guess is that only half of the readers take any significant action.

Let's face it; millions of Americans will continue to put their hard-earned wealth into the mutual fund vehicle seeking magic returns, and wealthy people will continue to chase protection in hedge funds. They don't get the message. Did your parents ever ask you, "If everyone else jumps off a bridge, are you going to do it also?" Just because most people are too lazy to do their homework does not mean you have to be. We now have better options out there for one to accumulate future wealth. Ultimately an alignment of goals and skill at meeting expectations is what brings fruitful results. With hedged solutions beginning to be offered in 401(k)s, people are beginning to ask the right questions. But each person must come to their own conclusion regarding a manager's integrity, stability, and investment process.

As you go down the road of looking for the best risk-adjusted returns, remember the old saying, "You can't eat a Sharpe ratio." Look for those that have the ability to robustly adapt and not just data-mine within the context of their edge. Align yourself with the manager that is able to deliver consistent risk exposure for you, and since one can't have return without risk, you are going to want to see a process for effectively handling risk.

You can leave a legacy and you can break the chains of bondage that hold a lot of investors down. It must always be remembered that growth is not a given. We could very well be in a unique episode of human experience these past 200 years. The world and its returns from the past are no longer here today and the unique social and economic drivers are not here to support them anymore. To look at return without also looking at downside risk is a dangerous bet that I am not willing to make.

Smart people are looking to merely answer the questions of what can go wrong and what are the results if that occurs.

Epilogue

If a problem can be solved at all, to understand it and to know what to do about it are the same thing. On the other hand, doing something about a problem which you do not understand is like trying to clear away darkness by thrusting it aside with your hands. When light is brought, the darkness vanishes at once.
—Alan Watts[1]

Books are never finished. They are merely abandoned.
—Oscar Wilde

The truth is you can't rely on anyone but yourself to make your possible fortune or prepare for a comfortable retirement. The safest, most profitable way to prepare for your future is by following the trend, not following some talking head's opinion or your momentary emotional whim. Everything else beyond *trend* is white noise.

For example, think about the next Fed meeting, as there is always a next. And you know the drill. Expect sophisticated talk from [fill in the blank with name of odd looking *economist* that now leads the Fed] about this or that data, economic indicators by the bushel, assorted indecipherable mumblings and an army of TV talking heads lapping it all up as if an economic God has arrived. Let me blunt: No politician or economist will fix anything for you. However, you can fix your own situation, or at least put much better odds on your side. You can get ahead and ultimately leave nonsense behind, i.e., Fed watching.

To receive my free interactive trend following presentation send a picture of your receipt to receipt@trendfollowing.com.

Look, nothing is easy, but the sooner you get off the passive investing train, the government promises merry go round, the sooner you can find peace of mind, and possibly real money. Imagine decades into the future to visualize interest income. You can't. And like it or not, your Social Security benefits (or pension if you have one) will be cut big time. Or you'll be working well into your 80s. Or both. Don't make it to your 80s? Well, that's arguably the State's real plan for your golden years.

In theory, theory and practice are the same. In practice, they're not.
Yoggi Berra

But, what if I am dead wrong? What if I am overly pessimistic? I could be, sure. Anyone can be wrong about future market events, especially when trying to analyze a financially engineered landscape going back to Netscape's 1995 IPO. That leaves us with a conundrum: If we don't know what is coming next, how can we prepare for what's coming next?

That is why trend following can't be ignored.

Sometimes in trying to make the case I stumble into that perfect story that makes me smile. At the end of a 2016 presentation, I blurted out what must have sounded like an unexpected sign off to the audience: "Pray for trends!"

If you want to have an impact, be prepared to say the same thing for a decade.
David Heinemeier Hansson

One of my associates got a kick out of that. He needled me, and at first I felt silly for invoking a religious ritual as a possible path to profit. Let me be clear: that's not how trend following works.

And I did not mean to push prayer as strategy, but concluding with that sign off, being very clear that none of us have control over the markets, *letting go* was my point bubbling up from my subconscious. Letting go in the form of trend following philosophy can be summarized:

Most of the Ivy League guys I know are so used to being right *they get very uncomfortable dealing with uncertainty—when there is no right answer. Their egos often make them so afraid of being* wrong, *that they're unable to make good bets. They aren't comfortable with the idea of risk, because they don't know how to assess it or measure it. [They have been] taught to absorb knowledge, not what to do with it.*
Larry Hite

- No one can predict the future;
- If you can take the would-be, could-be, should-be out of life and look at what actually is, you have a big advantage over most;
- What matters can be measured, so keep refining your measurements;
- You don't need to know when something will happen to know it will;
- Prices can only move up, down, or sideways;
- Losses are a life; and
- There is only now.[2]

That's a more complete explanation than my call for prayer. But I know that some become upset at those seven points. They see them as trite:

> "Too simple."
>
> "They are not complex enough."

"There must be more!"

"Covel is el diablo!"

Look, even with the evidence supplied in *Trend Following*, there will be those who cry for the *secret*, or alternatively bemoan me, the messenger, not the message. After 13 years of living this work, confusion, critics, skeptics, and trolls abound—it's expected. A *shatter-the-earth-is-flat* point of view such as this book will leave many in cognitive dissonance, because if trend following makes you feel not so smart, not so wise, then it will be hard to accept if your self-image is PhD brilliant.

There are still others who will never cross the Rubicon even if they half-believe and half want to try. Yet indecision won't work—it's the reason why behaviorists like Daniel Kahneman are as important to a trend following understanding as the system math. It's all in or you definitely won't make it.

But even if you have the right approach, you better have patience too. Altegris, an investment firm based in La Jolla, California, has placed over $1 billion with trend following traders like David Harding, Ewan Kirk, and William Eckhardt. I spent time with the founder of Altegris, Jon Sundt. He put forth a conundrum:

Our response to this environment has to be disciplined. If disagreement of opinions leads to trends, we need to maintain our positions. Similarly, we must be willing to close or change positions without ambiguity if called for. Risk management is especially opportune at this time. Will Rogers summed it up succinctly: "Even if you are on the right track, you'll get run over if you just sit there."

Mark S. Rzepczynski

> Can a great trader have great skill and no opportunity to make money?
>
> Can a bad trader have no skill and tons of opportunity to make money?
>
> The answer is yes to both questions. Luck is at play in the short-term for most traders. There will always be "some guy" with a great one-year return, but the sustained edge appears only over time.

What happens when the bad trader with no skill finally finds no opportunity? Know that answer or go to Las Vegas. And trust me, Vegas can be super fun, so there is a consolation prize if trend following is not your cup of tea.

Oz Behind the Curtain

Believing in *price* alone will never be accepted by the masses, and the size of assets under management in passive index funds confirms that belief. Trend following is not a provocative enough narrative for investors raised on crystal balls and disingenuous media selling ads for brokers.

We will merely chart our course and steer our ship in the direction of the prevailing wind. When the economic weather changes, we will change our course with it and will not try to forecast the future time or place at which the wind will change.
William Dunnigan (1954)

On the other hand, if you want to avoid acute pain in your trading account when the next investment Black Plague rears its head, and avoid bleeding out, and if you are ready to disconnect from a state-sponsored feeding tube, then acceptance of price as the only fact is the starting and logical first step. Do that and it becomes easy.

You say, "No way, trend following is too complicated!"

Not true.

Listen to David Harding's incredulity as he explains his early lack of computing sophistication: "I had a very deep understanding of the ideas involved in running trend following trading systems [and] it was very easy for me to set up. As a matter of fact, we set it all up using spreadsheets. We didn't have any sophisticated computers, we had no computer languages."[3]

That revelation alone might cause the folks chasing secrets a myocardial infarction. But Harding was not done:

> In fact, we didn't employ any programmers at all. One of my old friends who has no training of any sort wrote all the systems and everything on a single spreadsheet, and we were able to run [our firm] just on a spreadsheet program in Excel with three people. That spreadsheet continued in operations the next nine or ten years. (Laughter.) I'm really letting the secrets out of the bag here. Maybe it was more than ten years, but yes, nine or ten years. But I was able to run that very easily and didn't indeed have to work..... We were creating a track record.[4]

All trends are historical; none are in the present. There is no way to determine the current trend, or even define what current trend might mean; we can only determine historical trends. The only way to measure a now-trend (one entirely in the moment of now) would be to take two points, both in the now and compute their difference. Motion, velocity, and trend do not exist in the now. They do not appear in snapshots. Trend does not exist in the now, and the phrase, "the trend" has no inherent meaning.
Ed Seykota

He then went theoretical-physicist on the deeper meaning at play within a trend following philosophy: "[Trend following is] much more profound than many hedge fund strategies because it's talking about the very exploitable effect in the price movements of whole asset classes. People talk about anomalies; it's not like some small anomaly. It's about the way the whole world works. It's a theory about the way the world works, which is different from the theory that everybody in the financial world has about how the world works."[5]

Daniel Dennett, a cognitive scientist with zero connection to trend following, compounds Harding's insights:

> Here is something we know with well-nigh perfect certainty: nothing physically inexplicable plays a role in any computer program, no here-

> tofore unimagined force fields, no mysterious quantum shenanigans, no élan vital. There is certainly no wonder tissue in any computer. We know exactly how the basic tasks are accomplished in computers, and how they can be composed into more and more complex tasks, and we can explain these constructed competences with no residual mystery. So although the virtuosity of today's computers continues to amaze us, the computers themselves, as machines, are as mundane as can-openers. Lots of prestidigitation, but no *real magic*.[6]

Now, there's one thing that you men will be able to say when you get back home, and you may thank God for it. Thirty years from now when you're sitting around your fireside with your grandson on your knee, and he asks you, "What did you do in the great World War Two?" You won't have to say, "Well, I shoveled shit in Louisiana." Alright now, you sons of bitches, you know how I feel. I will be proud to lead you wonderful guys into battle anytime, anywhere. That's all.

General George S. Patton, 3rd Army speech—May 31, 1944

No real magic . . . indeed.

I am under no illusions with trend following. There will always be critics and cheerleaders. And there will always be controversy with an alternative moneymaking strategy. Religious versus atheist. Hatfields versus McCoys. Democrat versus Republican. Shoot, plain jealousy and envy, those drivers will always have a seat at the table too.

Nevertheless, beyond histrionics and misinformation, I find solace in the decades, even hundreds of years of trend following performance numbers. That is the real story, the truth Wall Street can't accept, match, or wants buried because it casts considerable doubt on their real agenda—typical commission business regardless whether you make money or lose it all.

You see, no matter how many agree or disagree with this content, the philosophy and rules, backed by positive performance numbers, especially from historic winning times like October 2008 and Brexit 2016—it paints a picture of *Homo sapiens*' moneymaking reality you accept or reject.

Trends become more apparent as you step further away from the chart.

Ed Seykota

While this is the fifth edition of *Trend Following*, it will not be the last. Some massive, unexpected surprise will unfold, some calamitous and unforeseen implosion where trend following makes a fortune so massive that politicians demand it be outlawed. And then I will need to get that *trend* into these pages posthaste before they lock me up for causing too many to see the *light*.

Afterword

No good decision was ever made in a swivel chair.
—General George S. Patton Jr.

When I started trading in the commodity futures markets over 40 years ago, the industry didn't even have a name. Today the business has grown to the point where there are myriad ways to describe the funds that operate and their many styles of investing. The particular discipline of trading that I practiced, even before the nomenclature existed, is now plainly and aptly termed "trend following." In fact, while I have seen many strategies come and go, most of the other managers that I have known to survive and thrive over the past few decades in global futures markets are also trend followers. For having made my living as a trend follower, I've yet to come across a more compelling study, so clearly distilled, than has been offered by Michael Covel in *Trend Following*.

The Teacher Retirement System of Texas made 9% in 2013, but paid out over $600 million in fees. Fire people please.

Michael Covel

I first met Michael Covel when he was working on this book. I was a little hesitant at first about sharing some of the rather simple secrets of my trade. And I didn't make it easy on Covel. I started interviewing him on his investments and how he managed his risk. He quickly made me realize that he not only understood trend following, but that he embraced it much like me. We delved into the roots of trend following and my investment strategies to explore why they work rather than just accepting the results. In reading *Trend Following*, I now see how well he was able to translate his knowledge, and the perspectives of many of my colleagues, to paper.

Back in the 1970s, most of the guys I knew traded individual markets. The ones who traded wheat did not talk to the guys who traded sugar. And the guys who invested stocks did not care to talk to either one, because commodities were for "speculators" and not "investors." Further, the bond crowd thought the stock guys were cowboys. Each group had developed its own superiority complexes and fundamentally believed that only industry experts like them could understand the subtle dynamics of their markets. I guess that's part of the reason that no one cared much for trend followers like me—I viewed every market the same way and each represented nothing more than a trade to me. Today, for all the different facets, I believe everyone has come to speak the same language. It's the language of *risk*.

In my early days, there was only one guy I knew who seemed to have a winning track record year after year. This fellow's name was Jack Boyd. Jack was also the only guy I knew who traded lots of different markets. If you followed any *one* of Jack's trades, you never really knew how you were going to do. But if you were like me and actually counted *all* of his trades, you would have made about 20 percent a year. So, that got me more than a little curious about the idea of trading futures markets "across the board." Although each individual market seemed risky, when you put them together, they tended to balance each other out and you were left with a nice return with less volatility.

It is difficult to get a man to understand something when his salary depends upon his not understanding it.
Upton Sinclair

I could always see, after I got to Wall Street, how, for all the confusion, markets were driven by people and their emotions. That was what all of these markets had in common—people—and people just don't change. So, I set out to understand similarities in the way that markets moved. When I added up Jack's trades, only a few big trades made him all the money. For each of these big winners, I was there when "experts" told Jack that these markets couldn't go any higher, but they did. Then, when I looked at Jack's losses, they tended to be relatively small. Although it took me many years to put it all together—remember, there were no books like this back then—these seemingly small observations became the foundation for me of two important, intertwined investment themes: trend following and risk management. Jack was not so much a trend follower, but he did practice the first rule of trend following: Cut your losers and let your winners run.

Most of the guys that I knew who lost a lot of money actually tended to be more right than wrong. They just lost a lot on a few big losers. I believe that people put too much of a premium on being right. In some ways, it's one of the drawbacks for people who went to the best schools and always got straight A's—they are too used to always being right. It gets back to people and emotions. Everyone is happy to take lots of little winners—it makes them feel good. When their trades go against them, on the other hand, they hold on because they don't want to accept being wrong. Many times, these trades come back and they are able to capture their small profit. To me, that kind of trading is a little bit like picking up nickels in front of a steamroller.

Thankfully, the markets don't care about me or you or where we went to school. They don't care if you're short or tall. I was never very good in school and I wasn't a good athlete, either. With my background, the way I saw it, I never had any problem with the idea that I could be wrong. So, I have always built in an assumption of wrongness to anything that I do. We now kindly refer to this practice as risk management, but I just wanted to answer the question: "What's the worst thing that could happen to me?" I never wanted to do anything that could kill me. Knowing that I was not likely to be right that often, I had to trade in a way that would make me a lot of money when I was right and not lose me a lot of money when I was wrong. If that wasn't enough, it also had to be simple enough for me to understand.

Innocence is a kind of insanity.
Graham Greene, *The Quiet American*

After many years of searching and learning things the hard way, I evolved my own version of trend following. The idea made sense and I had some good examples to follow. Still, I wanted to prove to myself that it worked without betting real money. I had to test what would have happened had I traded that way in the past. These were the early days of computers and we even had to "borrow" time on university computers to test and prove our theories. It was a painstaking task, but it gave me the comfort that I needed. Now, in reading *Trend Following*, the do-it-yourselfers might argue that having a book that illustrates these same basic principles takes some of the fun out of it.

Actually, Covel, like any good trend follower, has not focused solely on the endpoint. He gives you a deep understanding of the most important part: the path. Unlike so many other books that have been written about investing, *Trend Following* goes beyond the results to explore the journey of this outstanding group of traders.

We're all puppets, Laurie. I'm just a puppet who can see the strings.
Alan Moore, *Watchmen*

For my staff, Covel's *Trend Following* is required reading. For my daughters at home, it has finally settled the question I seemed never to have been able to clearly answer myself, "Daddy, what do you do for a living?" This book captures and conveys what so many traders have taken careers and large losses to learn. And lucky for all of us, you don't have to be Phi Beta Kappa to understand it.

We no longer live in that world of wheat guys, sugar guys, and stock guys. Trend following trading is an important force in every market and should be a part of any diverse investment portfolio. For me, the discipline of trend following goes beyond trading and money management. Trend following is a way of thinking that can be employed in many parts of life as we all tend to continue to do the things that work for us and stop doing those activities that don't.

From a crash-only perspective, falling off the wagon (and getting back on) isn't the main thing. It's the only thing.
Ribbonfarm.com

The way I see it, you have two choices—you can do what I did and work for 30-plus years, cobbling together scraps of information, seeking to create a moneymaking strategy, or you can spend a few days reading Michael Covel's book and skip that three-decade learning curve.

—Larry Hite
Larry Hite founded Mint Investments in 1983 and by 1990 Mint Investments had become the largest commodity trading advisor (CTA) in the world in terms of assets under management. The classic, *Market Wizards*, dedicated an entire chapter to Hite's trading and risk management philosophy.

Note: I reached out to an associate of mine, Steve Burns, for extra Larry Hite feedback. Steve, who is one of the go-to voices for new traders, reminded me of these Hite gems left out of this edition of *Trend Following*:

- "Frankly, I don't see markets; I see risks, rewards, and money."
- "The truth is that, while you can't quantify reward, you can quantify risk."
- "If you argue with the market, you will lose."
- "If you diversify, control your risk, and go with the trend, it just has to work."

Trend Following Podcast Episodes

We weren't afraid to make changes. We weren't afraid to fail. We tried to do things very cheaply, very quickly. And if it wasn't working, we would kill it quickly. It meant making quick decisions, fixing things that were broken and scaling things that worked.
—Jared Kushner on running the Donald Trump campaign

My trend following podcast has generated over 5 million listens across 500+ episodes. Please enjoy a sampling on iTunes and at www.trendfollowing.com:

- Ep. 516 Wesley Gray
- Ep. 507 Lanny Bassham
- Ep. 505 Daniel Crosby
- Ep. 503 John Miller
- Ep. 499 Jenny Blake
- Ep. 498 Norton Reamer
- Ep. 495 Ted Parkhill
- Ep. 493 Adam Khoo
- Ep. 491 Brian Christian
- Ep. 489 Chris Voss
- Ep. 487 Robert Cialdini
- Ep. 485 Jared Dillian
- Ep. 483 Paul Tough
- Ep. 481 Chris Zook
- Ep. 479 Zen DeBrucke
- Ep. 477 Morgan Wright
- Ep. 475 Chase Jarvis
- Ep. 473 Chris Lochhead
- Ep. 471 Emma Seppala
- Ep. 467 David Burkus
- Ep. 465 Sunrise Capital
- Ep. 461 Robin Hanson
- Ep. 459 Tucker Max
- Ep. 457 Amy Herman
- Ep. 456 Josh Hawes
- Ep. 455 Ryan Holiday
- Ep. 453 Daniel Shapiro
- Ep. 451 Daehee Park
- Ep. 449 Neil Pasricha
- Ep. 448 Mike Lofgren

Your questions were excellent questions. I enjoyed this very much.
Vernon Smith
Nobel Prize in Economics

Michael Covel's podcast is great for those looking for alternative views on the market, those who are tired of hearing the same old stories told on CBNC and other traditional outlets. This is highly recommended if you are looking to expand your mind in investing. Covel has had some incredible guests, to include multiple Nobel Prize winners and world-famous investors.
Wall Street Journal

- Ep. 445 Parag Khanna
- Ep. 443 Simon Black
- Ep. 441 Jesse Lawler
- Ep. 437 Anders Ericsson
- Ep. 436 Tom Bilyeu
- Ep. 435 Steven Pinker
- Ep. 431 Bill Bonner
- Ep. 429 Jim Rogers
- Ep. 427 Michael Ellsberg
- Ep. 425 Philip Tetlock
- Ep. 423 Angus Deaton
- Ep. 405 Didier Sornette
- Ep. 403 Barbara Fredrickson
- Ep. 402 Charles Faulkner
- Ep. 401 Ben Carlson
- Ep. 400 Tom Basso
- Ep. 399 Brett Steenbarger
- Ep. 396 Kathleen Eisenhardt
- Ep. 395 Rob Walling
- Ep. 391 Charles Poliquin
- Ep. 385 Paul Slovic
- Ep. 383 Lawrence McMillan
- Ep. 377 Annie Duke
- Ep. 375 Mark Sleeman
- Ep. 373 Lasse Pedersen
- Ep. 371 Alexander Ineichen
- Ep. 368 Taylor Pearson
- Ep. 365 Chris Clarke
- Ep. 363 Blair Hull
- Ep. 361 Francisco Vaca
- Ep. 359 Campbell Harvey
- Ep. 357 Jonathan Fader
- Ep. 355 Ed Seykota
- Ep. 353 Steve Burns
- Ep. 352 Tim Larkin
- Ep. 350 Michael Melissinos
- Ep. 349 Donald MacKenzie
- Ep. 347 Kathryn Kaminski
- Ep. 345 Spyros Makridakis
- Ep. 344 Martin Lueck
- Ep. 343 Ryan Holiday
- Ep. 342 Victor Ricciardi
- Ep. 341 Michael Dever
- Ep. 340 Tim Ferriss
- Ep. 339 Tim Price
- Ep. 338 K. D. Angle
- Ep. 337 William Ury
- Ep. 336 Colin Camerer
- Ep. 333 Gary Dayton
- Ep. 332 Brian Proctor
- Ep. 331 Douglas Emlen
- Ep. 330 Nigol Koulajian
- Ep. 329 Terrance Odean
- Ep. 328 Robert Seawright
- Ep. 327 Susan Polgar
- Ep. 324 David Stockman
- Ep. 322 Sophia Roosth
- Ep. 320 Mike Shell
- Ep. 319 Salem Abraham
- Ep. 318 Christopher Chabris
- Ep. 316 Gary Antonacci
- Ep. 315 Michael Mauboussin
- Ep. 314 Peter Larson
- Ep. 310 Daniel Simons
- Ep. 309 Mark Mobius
- Ep. 307 Bryan Caplan
- Ep. 302 Z. Hermaszewski
- Ep. 301 Jim Rogers
- Ep. 300 Travis Jamison
- Ep. 298 Emanuel Derman
- Ep. 297 Gabriele Oettingen
- Ep. 296 Ewan Kirk
- Ep. 295 Gerd Gigerenzer
- Ep. 294 Nigol Koulajian
- Ep. 292 Chris Cruden
- Ep. 291 Steven Kotler
- Ep. 290 Mark Rzepczynski
- Ep. 287 Toby Crabel

- Ep. 286 Alex Greyserman
- Ep. 285 Anthony Todd
- Ep. 284 Jason Fried
- Ep. 282 Kathryn Kaminski
- Ep. 281 Vineer Bhansali
- Ep. 279 Mark Broadie
- Ep. 278 Larry Swedroe
- Ep. 275 Joel Mokyr
- Ep. 274 Guy Kawasaki
- Ep. 273 Rande Howell
- Ep. 270 Laurie Santos
- Ep. 269 Robert Aumann
- Ep. 268 Gregory Morris
- Ep. 267 Dennis Gartman
- Ep. 265 Leo Melamed
- Ep. 264 John H. Cochrane
- Ep. 263 Meir Statman
- Ep. 262 Terry Burnham
- Ep. 261 Andy Puddicombe
- Ep. 260 Sally Hogshead
- Ep. 259 Bucky Isaacson
- Ep. 258 Megan McArdle
- Ep. 257 Cullen Roche
- Ep. 256 Mike Harris
- Ep. 255 Tyler Cowen
- Ep. 254 William Poundstone
- Ep. 253 Perry Kaufman
- Ep. 252 Ben Hunt
- Ep. 250 Hersh Shefrin
- Ep. 248 Mark Miller
- Ep. 247 Van Tharp
- Ep. 246 David Ryan
- Ep. 245 Jerry Parker
- Ep. 244 Walter Williams
- Ep. 242 Jean-Philippe Bouchaud
- Ep. 240 Nir Eyal
- Ep. 239 Brett Steenbarger
- Ep. 238 Larry Hite
- Ep. 237 Sharon Moalem
- Ep. 236 Robin Hanson
- Ep. 235 Harry Markowitz
- Ep. 234 Ryan Holiday
- Ep. 230 Mark Minervini
- Ep. 227 Justin Fox
- Ep. 226 Larry Tentarelli
- Ep. 225 Thomas Gilovich
- Ep. 224 Tom Dorsey
- Ep. 223 Marc Faber
- Ep. 222 Martin Bergin
- Ep. 221 Howard Lindzon
- Ep. 220 Victor Sperandeo
- Ep. 219 Carl Richards
- Ep. 215 Al Abaroa
- Ep. 212 Daniel Kahneman
- Ep. 211 John Bollinger
- Ep. 205 Chris Ducker
- Ep. 203 Bobby Casey
- Ep. 202 Barry Schwartz
- Ep. 197 Jack Horner
- Ep. 194 Dan Ariely
- Ep. 193 Gerd Gigerenzer
- Ep. 185 Tom DeMark
- Ep. 184 Cal Newport
- Ep. 183 Yaron Brook
- Ep. 178 Vernon Smith
- Ep. 177 Brad Rotter
- Ep. 175 Dylan Evans
- Ep. 168 Larry Williams
- Ep. 166 Harry Binswanger
- Ep. 165 Tom O'Connell
- Ep. 164 Richard Noble
- Ep. 162 Tim Dyer
- Ep. 160 Peter Borish
- Ep. 152 Dan Andrews
- Ep. 144 Jon Boorman
- Ep. 140 Tom Asacker
- Ep. 139 Steve Burns
- Ep. 134 Brendan Moynihan

People don't want more information. They are up to their eyeballs in information. They want faith. Faith in you, your goals, your success and in the story you tell.

Unknown

Here's the essential conundrum: investing requires us to decide how to position for future developments, but the future isn't knowable.
Howard Marks

- Ep. 121 Jason Russell
- Ep. 112 Larry Tentarelli
- Ep. 111 Nick Radge
- Ep. 090 Richard Weissman
- Ep. 089 Tadas Viskanta
- Ep. 085 Barry Ritholtz
- Ep. 080 Robert Greene
- Ep. 076 Jack Schwager
- Ep. 073 Peter L. Brandt
- Ep. 068 Mark Shore
- Ep. 056 Steve Brechtel
- Ep. 049 David Cheval
- Ep. 048 Michael Gibbons
- Ep. 046 Ralph Vince
- Ep. 033 David Stendahl
- Ep. 029 Mike Dever
- Ep. 022 Mike Aponte
- Ep. 017 James Rohrbach
- Ep. 011 Tim Pickering
- Ep. 007 Michael Shannon
- Ep. 002 Bob Pardo

Have a great guest idea? Send an e-mail: www.trendfollowing.com/contact.

Endnotes

Preface

1. Ernest Shackleton, "Men Wanted (advertisement)," *Times*, London, 1913.
2. Timothy W. Martin, "What Does Nevada's $35 Billion Fund Manager Do All Day? Nothing," *Wall Street Journal,* October 19, 2016, www.wsj.com/articles/what-does-nevadas-35-billion-fund-manager-do-all-day-nothing-1476887420.
3. Jason Zweig, "Making Billions with One Belief: The Markets Can't Be Beat," *Wall Street Journal*, October 20, 2016, www.wsj.com/articles/making-billions-with-one-belief-the-markets-cant-be-beat-1476989975.
4. "Efficient Market Hypothesis," *Wikipedia*, last modified December 11, 2016, https://en.wikipedia.org/wiki/Efficient-market_hypothesis.
5. Jean-Philippe Bouchaud and Damien Challet, "Why Have Asset Price Properties Changed So Little in 200 Years," May 2, 2016.
6. Jean-Philippe Bouchaud, "Economics Needs a Scientific Revolution," Capital Fund Management, December 1, 2008.
7. David Harding, "Efficient Market Theory: When Will It Die," Winton Capital Management, February 2016.
8. "David Harding (financier)," *Wikipedia*, last modified December 11, 2016, https://en.wikipedia.org/wiki/David_Harding.
9. Harding, "Efficient Market Theory."
10. Katie Allen, "Nobel Prize-Winning Economists Take Disagreement to Whole New Level," *The Guardian,* December 12, 2013, www.theguardian.com/business/2013/dec/10/nobel-prize-economists-robert-shiller-eugene-fama.
11. David Harding, "Efficient Market Theory: When Will It Die," Winton Capital Management (February 2016).
12. Van K. Tharp, *Trade Your Way to Financial Freedom* (New York: McGraw-Hill, 1999).
13. Richard D. Donchian, "Trend-Following Methods in Commodity Price Analysis," *Commodity Year Book* (1957), 35.

14. Ari Levine and Lasse Heje Pedersen, "Which Trend Is Your Friend," *Financial Analysts Journal* 72, no. 3 (May/June 2016).
15. Miles Kimball, "Robert Shiller: Against the Efficient Markets Theory," *Confessions of a Supply-Side Liberal* (blog), April 14, 2014, http://blog.supplysideliberal.com/post/82659078132/robert-shiller-against-the-efficient-markets.
16. John Plender, "A New Paradox Found in Markets Theory," *Financial Times,* December 9, 2012, www.ft.com/content/8e2ae5b2-3e14-11e2-91cb-00144feabdc0.
17. Eugene F. Fama and Kenneth R. French, "Q&A: Market Timing with Moving Averages," *Fama/French Forum*, https://famafrench.dimensional.com/questions-answers/qa-market-timing-with-moving-averages.aspx.
18. Eric Johnson, "Benchmark's Bill Gurley Says He's Still Worried about a Bubble," *Recode*, September 12, 2016, www.recode.net/2016/9/12/12882780/bill-gurley-benchmark-bubble-venture-capital-startups-uber.

Chapter 1

1. Ludwig von Mises, *Human Action: A Treatise on Economics* (4th rev. ed.) (Irvington-on-Hudson, NY: The Foundation for Economic Education, 1996).
2. Robert Koppel, *The Intuitive Trader* (Hoboken, NJ: John Wiley & Sons, Inc., 1996), 88.
3. von Mises, *Human Action.*
4. George Francis Train, *Young America on Wall Street* (London: Sampson Low, 1857), 209.
5. Arthur Crump, *The Theory of Stock Exchange Theory* (New York: S. A. Nelson, 1903), 50.
6. Albert Williams, *How to Win and How to Lose* (Chicago: 1883).
7. Ibid.
8. *The Art of Investing* (New York: Appleton, 1888).
9. John Hill Jr., *Gold Bricks of Speculation* (Chicago: Lincoln Book Concern, 1904).
10. Louis Guenther, *Investments and Speculation* (Chicago: La Salle Extension University, 1910), 121.
11. G. C. Selden, *Psychology of the Stock Market* (New York: Ticker Publishing Company, 1912), 12.
12. *Wall Street: Money Never Sleeps,* directed by Oliver Stone (Los Angeles: 20th Century Fox, 2010).
13. Jack Schwager, *Market Wizards: Interviews with Top Traders* (New York: HarperCollins, 1993).
14. von Mises, *Human Action.*

15. Keith Campbell, "Barclay Managed Futures Report," *Barclay Managed Futures Report* 3, no. 3 (third quarter 1992), 3.
16. Allison Colter, "Dow Jones" (July 13, 2001).
17. "Trading System Review" (Futures Industry Association Conference, November 2, 1994).
18. Jack Schwager, *Getting Started in Technical Analysis* (Hoboken, NJ: John Wiley & Sons, Inc., 1999).
19. "The History of the Motley Fool," *Fool.com*, November 4, 2003.
20. "The State of the Industry," *Managed Account Reports, Inc.* (June 2000).
21. John Allen Paulos, *A Mathematician Plays the Stock Market* (New York: Basic Books, 2003), 47.
22. "Quantitative Strategy: Does Technical Analysis Work?" *Equity Research, Credit Suisse First Boston* (September 25, 2002).
23. Bob Bryan, "RED ALERT—Get Ready for a 'Severe Fall' in the Stock Market, HSBC says," *Business Insider*, October 12, 2016, www.businessinsider.com/hsbc-red-alert-get-ready-for-a-severe-fall-in-the-stock-market-2016-10.
24. Martin Estlander, "Presentation for the Association of Provident Fund of Thailand & Partners" (Association of Provident Fund of Thailand & Partners, Bangkok, February 26, 2015).
25. Mebane Faber, "A Quantitative Approach to Tactical Asset Allocation," *The Journal of Wealth Management* (Spring 2007).
26. Daniel P. Collins, "Kevin Bruce: Improving on a Passion," *Futures* (October 2003).
27. "Disclosure Document," John W. Henry & Company, Inc. (August 22, 2003).
28. Ibid.
29. Carla Cavaletti, "Top Traders Ride 1996 Trends," *Futures* (March 1997), 68.
30. Jack Schwager, *Getting Started in Technical Analysis* (Hoboken, NJ: John Wiley & Sons, Inc., 1999).
31. Ewan Kirk, "Ewan Kirk of Cantab on Trend Following," *Trend Following* (blog), August 15, 2016, www.trendfollowing.com/2016/08/15/ewan-kirk-cantab-trend-following/.
32. Mathew Bradbard, "Q&A with Todd Hurlbut and Ted Parkhill for Incline Investment Management," *RCM Futures—Manager's Corner*, www.rcmfutures.com/managed-futures/incline-investment.
33. Morningstar, "Interview: Cliff Asness Explains Why He Started a Managed Futures Fund," *Business Insider*, March 5, 2010, www.businessinsider.com/cliff-asness-new-fund-is-for-wimps-who-cant-handle-the-market-swings-2010-3.
34. Jack Schwager, *Hedge Fund Market Wizards* (Hoboken, NJ: John Wiley & Sons, Inc., 2012).
35. Ginger Szala, "Abraham Trading: Trend Following Earns Texas Sized Profits," *Futures* (March 1995), 61.

36. Desmond MacRae, "Valuing Trend-Followers' Returns," *Managed Account Reports,* No. 242 (April 1999), 12.
37. John W. Henry (presentation given to financial consultants, November 17, 2000).
38. John W. Henry (presentation, Geneva, Switzerland, September 15, 1998).
39. Charles Faulkner, *Futures* 22, no. 12 (November 1993), 98.
40. Patrick Welton, "Has Trend Following Changed," *AIMA Newsletter* (June 2001).
41. Morton S. Baratz, *The Investor's Guide to Futures Money Management* (Columbia, MD: Futures Publishing Group, 1984).
42. Guest Article, *Managed Account Reports* 249 (November 1999), 9.
43. John W. Henry (presentation given to financial consultants, November 17, 2000).
44. Brian Hurst, Yao Hua Ooi, and Lasse H. Pedersen, "A Century of Evidence on Trend-Following Investing," *AQR Capital Management* (Fall 2014).
45. Peter Borish, "Upstairs/Downstairs Seminar with Tom Baldwin," *Futures Industry Association* (1994).
46. "Performance Review," John W. Henry & Company (February 1999).
47. William Eckhardt, "Tass Twenty Traders Talk," (presentation, Montreal Ritz Carlton Hotel, Montreal, Canada, June 29, 1996).
48. Schwager, *Market Wizards*.
49. Riva Atlas, "Macro, Macro Man," *Institutional Investor Magazine* (1996).
50. Robert Murray, "Trend Following: Performance, Risk and Correlation Characteristics" (white paper), Graham Capital Management.
51. Ibid.
52. Christopher Cruden, "Trends in Currency Markets: Which Way the $?" *AIMA Newsletter* (June 2002).
53. "The Trading Tribe" (forum response), *The Trading Tribe*, www.seykota.com/tribe/.
54. Mary Greenebaum, "Funds: The New Way to Play Commodities," *Fortune* (November 19, 1979).
55. Carol Dweck, "What Is Mindset," *Mindset,* accessed December 17, 2016, http://mindsetonline.com/whatisit/about/.
56. Brett N. Steenbarger, *The Psychology of Trading* (Hoboken, NJ: John Wiley & Sons, Inc., 2002), 316–17.
57. Brenda Ueland, *How to Write,* 10th ed. (New York: Graywolf Press, 1997).
58. Bruce Cleland, "Campbell and Company," *Futures* (March 2004): 72.
59. David Whitford, "Why Owning the Boston Red Sox Is Like Running a Successful Hedge Fund," *Fortune Small Business* (October 25, 2003).
60. "The Whizkid of Futures Trading," *Businessweek*, December 6, 1982, 102.
61. Van Tharp, *Super Trader: Make Consistent Profits in Good and Bad Markets* (New York: McGraw-Hill Education, 2010).

Chapter 2

1. Jim Rogers, *Investment Biker* (New York: Random House, 1994).
2. Thomas Friedman, *The Lexus and the Olive Tree* (New York: Farrar, Straus and Giroux, 1999).
3. Leah McGrath Goodman, *Trader Monthly*, www.traderdaily.com/magazine/article/17115.html.
4. Ibid.
5. Ibid.
6. David Harding, *The Winton Papers*, Winton Capital Management, www.wintoncapital.com.
7. Daniel P. Collins, "Seeding Tomorrow's Top Traders; Managed Money; Dunn Capital Management Provides Help to Commodity Trading Advisor Start-ups," *Futures* 32, no. 6 (May 1, 2003): 67.
8. J. R. Newman (ed.), *The World of Mathematics* (New York: Simon & Schuster, 1956).
9. Jim Collins, *Good to Great* (New York: Harper Business, 2001).
10. Robert Koppel, *The Intuitive Trader* (Hoboken, NJ: John Wiley & Sons, Inc., 1996), 74.
11. The Reason Foundation, www.reason.org.
12. Collins, "Seeding Tomorrow's Top Traders."
13. Bill Dunn, "Tricycle Asset Management," (presentation, Market Wizards Tour, May 15, 2003, Saskatoon, Saskatchewan).
14. Ibid.
15. Ibid.
16. Amy Rosenbaum, "1990s Highs and Lows: Invasions, Persuasions and Volatility," *Futures* 19, no. 14 (December 1990): 54.
17. Andrew Osterland, "For Commodity Funds, It Was as Good as It Gets," *Businessweek*, September 14, 1998.
18. Jack Reerink, "Dunn: Slow Reversal Pays Off," *Futures* 25, no. 3 (March 1996).
19. Mike Mosser, "Learning from Legends," *Futures* 29, no. 2 (February 2000).
20. "How Managed Money Became a Major Area of the Industry; Futures Market," *Futures* 21, no. 9 (July 1992): 52.
21. *No Country for Old Men*, directed by Ethan Coen and Joel Coen (Santa Monica, CA: Miramax Films, 2007).
22. Denise G. Shekerjian, "Uncommon Genius" (New York: Penguin, 1990).
23. Mary Ann Burns, "Industry Icons Assess the Managed Futures Business," *Futures Industry Association* (May/June 2003).
24. Reerink, "Dunn: Slow Reversal Pays Off."

25. Carla Cavaletti, "Comeback Kids: Managing Drawdowns According to Commodity Trading Advisors," *Futures* 27, no. 1 (January 1998): 68.
26. "Dunn Capital Management Monthly Commentary," Dunn Capital Management (February 2003).
27. Keith Campbell, "Barclay Managed Futures Report," *Barclay Managed Futures Report* 3, no. 3 (third quarter 1992): 2.
28. "Job Wanted" (advertisement), Dunn Capital Management, www.monster.com.
29. Ginger Szala, "John W. Henry: Long-Term Perspective," *Futures* (1987).
30. John W. Henry (presentation, Geneva, Switzerland, September 15, 1998).
31. Lois Peltz, *The New Investment Superstars* (New York: John Wiley & Sons, Inc., 2001).
32. Mary Ann Burns, "Industry Icons Assess the Managed Futures Business," *Futures Industry Association* (May/June 2003).
33. Mark S. Rzepczynski, "John W. Henry & Co. Year in Review," (December 2000).
34. Oliver Conway, cover story about John W. Henry & Company, Inc., *Managed Derivatives* (May 1996).
35. W. H. Auden and L. Kronenberger, eds., *The Viking Book of Aphorisms* (New York: Viking, 1966).
36. Michael Peltz, "John W. Henry's Bid to Manage the Future," *Institutional Investor* (August 1996).
37. Szala, "John W. Henry."
38. Peltz, *The New Investment Superstars*.
39. John W. Henry (presentation, November 17, 2000).
40. Peltz, *The New Investment Superstars*.
41. "2002 Year in Review," John W. Henry & Company, Inc. (2002).
42. "Futures Industry Association Conference Seminar," *Trading System Review* (November 2, 1994).
43. John W. Henry (presentation, Morgan Stanley Dean Witter Achieve Conference, Naples, Florida, November 17, 2000).
44. Azeez Mustapha, "Leda Braga: A High Earning Hedge Fund Manager," *ADVFN Financial News*, May 8, 2014, http://uk.advfn.com/newspaper/azeez-mustapha/26204/leda-braga-a-high-earning-hedge-fund-manager.
45. John W. Henry (presentation, Geneva, Switzerland, September 15, 1998).
46. Ibid.
47. Ibid.
48. FIA Research Division dinner, New York, April 20, 1995.
49. "The Alternative Files, History of Managed Futures," Attain Capital Management (January 2014).
50. Jack Schwager, *Market Wizards: Interviews with Top Traders* (New York: Harper Business, 1989), 172.

51. "The Trading Tribe" (forum response), *The Trading Tribe*, www.seykota.com/tribe/.
52. E-mail, www.TurtleTrader.com.
53. Daniel P. Collins, "Long-Term Technical Trend-Following Method for Managed Futures Programs," *Futures* 30, n. 14 (November 2001): 22.
54. Ed Seykota, "The Trading Tribe," www.seyokota.com/tribe/.
55. Thom Hartle, ed., "Ed Seykota of Technical Tools," *Technical Analysis of Stocks & Commodities* 10, no. 8 (August 1992): 328–31. (Used with permission; www.traders.com.)
56. Ibid.
57. Ibid.
58. Ibid.
59. Shawn Tully, "Princeton's Rich Commodity Scholars," *Fortune*, February 9, 1981, 94.
60. "The Trading Tribe" (forum response), *The Trading Tribe*, www.seykota.com/tribe/.
61. "System Dynamics," last modified June 23, 1997, http://web.mit.edu/sysdyn/sd-intro/.
62. J. L. Kelly Jr., "A New Interpretation of Information Rate," *Bell System Technical Journal* (July 1956): 917–26.
63. "The Trading Tribe" (forum response), *The Trading Tribe*, www.seykota.com/tribe/.
64. Jack Reerink, "The Power of Leverage," *Futures* 24, no. 4 (April 1995): 59.
65. Gibbons Burke, "How to Tell a Market by Its Covers: Financial Market Predictions Based on Magazine Covers," *Futures* 22, no. 4 (April 1993): 30.
66. *Your Trading Edge*, www.yte.com.au.
67. Joe Niedzielski, "Wild Market Swings Take Toll on Commodity Trading Advisers," *Dow Jones Newswires*, April 25, 2000.
68. I. Gordon and S. Sorkin, eds., *The Armchair Science Reader* (New York: Simon & Schuster, 1959).
69. Darrell R. Jobman, "How Managed Money Became a Major Area of the Industry," *Futures* 21, no. 9 (July 1992): 52.
70. "Campbell & Company (presentation, excerpt)," *Futures Industry Association Conference*.
71. Mary Ann Burns, "Industry Icons Assess the Managed Futures Business," *Futures Industry Association* (May/June 2003).
72. "Value of Adding Managed Futures" (marketing documents), Campbell & Company.
73. "2003 Disclosure Document," Campbell & Company.
74. Desmond McRae, "31-Year Track Record of 18.1%," *Managed Futures* (March 2003).

75. "Barclay Managed Futures Report," *Barclay Trading Group, Ltd.* 2, no. 3 (third quarter 1991): 2.

76. The Futures and Industry Association's Future and Options Expo '98, Sheraton Chicago Towers & Hotel, Chicago, October 14–16, 1998.

77. Ibid.

78. Ibid.

79. Ibid.

80. Ibid.

81. Chuck Epstein, "The World According to J. Parker," *Managed Account Reports* (November 1998).

82. "Barclay Managed Futures Report," *Barclay Trading Group, Ltd.* 2, no. 3 (third quarter 1991): 7.

83. Ibid.

84. Simon Romero, "A Homespun Hedge Fund, Tucked Away in Texas," *New York Times*, December 28, 2003, 1.

85. *Futures* (March 1995).

86. Romero, "A Homespun Hedge Fund."

87. "Program Description: Trading Methods and Strategies," Abraham Trading Company, www.abrahamtrading.com.

88. Ayn Rand, *The Fountainhead* (New York: Bobbs-Merrill, 1943).

89. Romero, "A Homespun Hedge Fund."

90. Jack Schwager, *Market Wizards: Interviews with Top Traders* (New York: New York Institute of Finance, 1989).

91. Stanley W. Angrist, "Commodities: Winning Commodity Traders May Be Made, Not Born," *Wall Street Journal*, September 5, 1989.

92. Greg Burns, "Rich Dennis: A Gunslinger No More," *Businessweek*, April 7, 1997.

93. Susan Abbott, "Richard Dennis: Turning a Summer Job into a Legend," *Futures*, September 1983, 58.

94. Ibid., 59.

95. Ibid., 57.

96. Ibid., 58.

97. Paul Rabar, "Managed Money: Capitalizing on the Trends of 1990," *Futures* 20, no. 3 (March 1991).

98. Schwager, *Market Wizards*.

99. Barbara Dixon, "Richard Donchian: Managed Futures Innovator and Mentor," *Futures Industry Association*.

100. William Baldwin, "Rugs to Riches (Section: The Money Men)," *Forbes* (March 1, 1982).

101. Dixon, "Richard Donchian."

102. Ibid.

103. Ibid.
104. Baldwin, "Rugs to Riches."
105. Dixon, "Richard Donchian."
106. Baldwin, "Rugs to Riches."
107. "Futures Industry Association Review: Interview: Money Managers," *Futures Industry Association*, www.fiafii.org.
108. Barbara S. Dixon, "Discretionary Accounts," *Managed Account Reports*, Report No. 20, no. 14: 5.
109. Barbara S. Dixon, "Discretionary Accounts," *Managed Account Reports*, Report No. 20, no. 14: 5.
110. Edwin Lefèvre, "Reminiscences of a Stock Operator," (New York: George H. Doran Company, 1923).
111. Andrew Leckey, "Dabble, Don't Dive, in Futures," *Chicago Tribune* (October 2, 1986, C1).
112. Dickson G. Watts, *Speculation as a Fine Art* (reprint, Flint Hill, Virginia: Fraser Publishing Co., 1997).
113. Eric Johnson, "Benchmark's Bill Gurley says he's still worried about a bubble," *Recode* (September 12, 2016), www.recode.net/2016/9/12/12882780/bill-gurley-benchmark-bubble-venture-capital-startups-uber.

Chapter 3

1. Sir Arthur Conan Doyle, *The Adventures of Sherlock Holmes* (New York: A. L. Burt, 1892).
2. Alexander M. Ineichen, *Absolute Returns* (New York: John Wiley & Sons, Inc., 2003): 19.
3. "Disclosure Document," John W. Henry & Company, Inc. (August 22, 2003).
4. "BMFR," *Barclay Trading Group* (first quarter 2003).
5. "International Traders Research Star Ranking System Explanation," *International Traders Research*, http://managedfutures.com.
6. Ludwig von Mises, *Human Action: A Treatise on Economics*, 4th rev. ed. (Irvington-on-Hudson, NY: The Foundation for Economic Education, 1996).
7. Larry Harris, *Trading and Exchanges: Market Microstructure for Practitioners* (New York: Oxford University Press, 2003).
8. David Greising, "How Managed Funds Managed to Do So Poorly," *Businessweek*, November 23, 1992, 112.
9. Daniel P. Collins, "The Return of Long-Term Trend Following," *Futures* 32, no. 4 (March 2003): 68–73.
10. Desmond McRae, "Top Traders," *Managed Derivatives* (May 1996).
11. "Trend Following: Performance, Risk and Correlation Characteristics" (white paper), Graham Capital Management.

12. Larry Harris, *Trading and Exchanges: Market Microstructure for Practitioners* (New York: Oxford University Press, 2003).
13. "Schroder GAIA BlueTrend," *Schroders Expert*, Issue 1 (February 2016).
14. Ben Warwick, "The Holy Grail of Managed Futures," *Managed Account Reports*, no. 267 (May 2001): 1.
15. "The Trading Tribe" (forum response), *The Trading Tribe*, www.seykota.com/tribe/.
16. "Drawdowns," Institutional Advisory Services Group, www.iasg.com.
17. Laurie Kaplan, "Turning Turtles into Traders," *Managed Derivatives* (May 1996).
18. "Marketing Materials," Dunn Capital Management, Inc.
19. Carla Cavaletti, "Comeback Kids: Managing Drawdowns According to Commodity Trading Advisors," *Futures* 27, no. 1 (January 1998): 68.
20. Michael Peltz, "John W. Henry's Bid to Manage the Future," *Institutional Investor* (August 1996).
21. D. Harding, G. Nakou, and A. Nejjar, "The Pros and Cons of Drawdown as a Statistical Measure of Risk for Investments," *AIMA Journal* (April 2003): 16–17.
22. Cavaletti, "Comeback Kids."
23. Ibid.
24. Thomas F. Basso, "When to Allocate to a CTA?—Buy Them on Sale" (1997).
25. *InvestorWords*. See http://investorwords.com.
26. "New Fans for Managed Futures," Euromoney Institutional Investor PLC (February 1, 2003): 45.
27. Julius A. Staniewicz, "Learning to Love Non-Correlation. Investor Support," John W. Henry & Company.
28. Ginger Szala, "Tom Shanks: Former 'Turtle' Winning Race the Hard Way," *Futures* 20, no. 2 (January 15, 1991): 78.
29. Carla Cavaletti, "Turtles on the Move," *Futures* 27 (June 1998): 79.
30. Laurie Kaplan, "Turning Turtles into Traders," *Managed Derivatives* (May 1996).
31. Harris, *Trading and Exchanges.*
32. Larry Harris, "The Winners and Losers of the Zero-Sum Game: The Origins of Trading Profits, Price Efficiency and Market Liquidity (Draft 0.911)" (Los Angeles: University of Southern California, May 7, 1993).
33. Ibid.
34. Danny Hakim, "Huge Losses Move Soros to Revamp Empire," *New York Times*, May 1, 2000.
35. Enoch Cheng, "Of Markets and Morality . . ." *Café Bagola* (blog), August 27, 2002, https://web.archive.org/web/20041019121710/.

36. Ayn Rand, "Philosophical Detection," *Philosophy: Who Needs It?* (Indianapolis, IN: Bobbs-Merrill, 1998).
37. Lawrence Parks (presentation, Hearing on Hedge Funds before the Subcommittee on Capital Markets, Securities, and GSEs; House Committee on Banking and Financial Services, United States House of Representatives, March 3, 1999).
38. Hakim, "Huge Losses."
39. Ibid.
40. "Merrill Lynch & Co. Inc. Research Reports Securities Litigation, 02 MDL 1484" (Ruling by Federal Judge Milton Pollack dismissing class-action claims brought against Merrill Lynch & Co. and its former analyst Henry Blodgett).
41. Gregory J. Millman, "The Chief Executive," (January–February 2003).
42. Bill Dries, *Futures* (August 1995): 78.
43. Mark Rzepczynski, "The Weatherstone Approach to Hedge Fund Investing," *Disciplined Systematic Global Macro Views* (blog), October 13, 2016, http://mrzepczynski.blogspot.com/2016/10/the-weatherstone-approach-to-hedge-fund.html.

Chapter 4

1. Nassim Taleb, *Fooled by Randomness* (New York: Texere, 2001).
2. Herb Greeenberg, "Answering the Question—Who Wins from Derivatives Losers," *San Francisco Chronicle*, March 20, 1995, D1.
3. Ibid.
4. Alexander M. Ineichen, *Absolute Returns* (New York: John Wiley & Sons, Inc., 2003): 416.
5. Michael J. Mauboussin and Kristen Bartholdson, "Integrating the Outliers: Two Lessons from the St. Petersburg Paradox," *The Consilient Observer* 2, no. 2 (January 28, 2003).
6. Jason Russell, www.acorn.ca.
7. "Trend Following: Performance, Risk, and Correlation Characteristics" (white paper), Graham Capital Management (April 2013).
8. William Poundstone, *Fortune's Formula: The Untold Story of the Scientific Betting System That Beat the Casinos and Wall Street* (New York: Farrar, Straus & Giroux): 213.
9. Thomas S. Y. Ho and Sang Bin Lee, *The Oxford Guide to Financial Modeling* (Oxford, UK: Oxford University Press, 2004): 559.
10. Ginger Szala, "Barings Abyss," *Futures* 24, no. 5 (May 1995): 68.
11. Carolyn Cui and Ann Davis, "Some Trend-Following Funds Are Winners in Rough Market," *Wall Street Journal*, November 5, 2008.
12. Corporate brochure, John W. Henry & Company, Inc. (1998), www.jwh.com.

13. Mark S. Rzepczynski, "President, John W. Henry and Co." (presentation), www.jwh.com.
14. Erin E. Arvedlund, "Swinging for the Fences: John W. Henry's Managed Futures Funds Are Striking Out," *Barron's*, December 4, 2000.
15. Presentation, John W. Henry and Co., November 17, 2000, www.jwh.com.
16. Erin E. Arvedlund, "Whiplash! Commodity-Trading Advisers Post Sharp Gains," *Barron's*, January 15, 2001.
17. "Fast Finish Makes 2000 a Winner," *Managed Account Reports*, no. 263 (January 2001).
18. Presentation, John W. Henry and Co., November 17, 2000, www.jwh.com.
19. Pallavi Gogoi, "Placing Bets in a Volatile World," *Businessweek*, September 30, 2002.
20. "Enron Employee Feedback," *TurtleTrader*.
21. "Barclay Managed Futures Report," *Barclay Trading Group* (fourth quarter 2002).
22. Larry Swedroe, "Buckingham Asset Management," www.bamstl.com/.
23. "The Trading Tribe" (forum response), *The Trading Tribe*, www.seykota.com/tribe/.
24. Paul Barr, "Trending Markets Lead to Profit: September 11 Example Will Go in Case Studies," *Money Management World* (September 25, 2001).
25. *Trillion Dollar Bet*, transcript, *Nova*, no. 2075 (February 8, 2000).
26. Ibid.
27. Kevin Dowd, "Too Big to Fail? Long-Term Capital Management and the Federal Reserve," Cato Institute Briefing Paper, no. 52 (September 23, 1999).
28. Lowenstein, *When Genius Failed*, 34.
29. Ibid., 69.
30. Ibid.
31. Clay Harris and Wiliam Hall, "Top-Tier Departures Expected at UBS," *Financial Times: London Edition* (October 2, 1998): 26.
32. "The LTCM Crisis and Its Consequences for Banks and Banking Supervision," Organization for Economic Cooperation and Development (June 1999).
33. Jerry Parker (The Futures and Industry Association's Future and Options Expo '98, Sheraton Chicago Towers & Hotel, Chicago, Ill., October 14–16, 1998).
34. John W. Henry (presentation, Geneva, Switzerland, September 15, 1998).
35. *Trillion Dollar Bet*.
36. "Black-Scholes Model," *Wikipedia*, last modified December 14, 2016, https://en.wikipedia.org/wiki/Black--Scholes_model.
37. Lowenstein, *When Genius Failed*, 71.

38. Andrew Osterland, "For Commodity Funds, It Was as Good as It Gets," *Businessweek*, September 14, 1998.
39. John W. Meriwether, "Letter to Investors," (September 1998).
40. *Trillion Dollar Bet.*
41. Bruce Cleland, "Campbell and Company, The State of the Industry," *Managed Account Reports, Inc.* (June 2000).
42. Robert Lenzner, "Archimedes on Wall Street," *Forbes* (October 19, 1998).
43. Kevin Dowd, "Too Big to Fail? Long-Term Capital Management and the Federal Reserve," Cato Institute Briefing Paper, no. 52 (September 23, 1999).
44. Malcolm Gladwell, "Blowing Up," *The New Yorker*, April 22 and 29, 2002.
45. G. K. Chesterton, *The Scandal of Father Brown* (London: Cassell and Company, 1935).
46. W. B. Arthur, S. N. Durlaf, and D. A. Lane, eds., *The Economy as an Evolving Complex System II*, (Reading, MA: Addison-Wesley, 1997), 566.
47. James Rickards, *The Road to Ruin: The Global Elites' Secret Plan for the Next Financial Crisis* (London: Penguin, 2016).
48. Dan Colarusso, "Gray Monday's First Casualty: Famed Soros Confidant Victor Niederhoffer," *The Street* (October 29, 1997), www.thestreet.com.
49. Mark Etzkorn, "Bill Dunn and Pierre Tullier: The Long Run (Trader Profile)," *Futures* 26, no. 2 (February 1997).
50. David Henry, *USA Today*, October 30, 1997.
51. Victor Niederhoffer, Letter to shareholders.
52. "Niederhoffer 1997 Performance," *Barclay Managed Futures Report.*
53. Etzkorn, "Bill Dunn and Pierre Tullier."
54. *The Stark Report* (second quarter 1997).
55. Greg Burns, "Whatever Voodoo He Uses, It Works: Trader Victor Niederhoffer Is as Eccentric as He Is Contrarian," *Businessweek*, February 10, 1997.
56. Ibid.
57. George Soros, *Soros on Soros* (New York: John Wiley & Sons, Inc., 1995).
58. Victor Niederhoffer and Laurel Kenner, "Why the Trend Is Not Your Friend," *The Speculator: MSN Money*, May 2, 2002, www.moneycentral.msn.com.
59. Victor Niederhoffer and Laurel Kenner, *Practical Speculation* (Hoboken, NJ: John Wiley & Sons, Inc., 2003): 74.
60. Ibid.
61. Victor Niederhoffer, *The Education of a Speculator* (New York: John Wiley & Sons, Inc., 1997).
62. Greg Burns, "Whatever Voodoo He Uses, It Works: Trader Victor Niederhoffer Is as Eccentric as He Is Contrarian," *Businessweek*, February 10, 1997.
63. Gladwell, "Blowing Up."
64. IFCI International Financial Risk Institute.

65. Mark Hawley, "Dean Witter Managed Futures," (presentation, Futures Industry Association Dinner, New York City, April 20, 1995).
66. James Simons, *The Greenwich Roundtable* (June 17, 1999).
67. John W. Henry (presentation, Geneva, Switzerland, September 15, 1998).
68. Sharon Reier, "Easy to Beat Up, Hard to Kill," *The International Herald Tribune* (March 23, 2002), www.iht.com.
69. Ed Krapels, "Re-examining the Metallgesellschaft Affair and Its Implication for Oil Traders," *Oil & Gas Journal*, March 26, 2001.
70. Ibid.
71. John Digenan et al., "Metallgesellschaft AG: A Case Study," *The Journal of Research and Ideas on Financial Markets and Trading*.
72. Lewis Carroll, *Through the Looking Glass*, 1872.
73. "The Value of a JWH Investment as a Portfolio Diversifier" (marketing materials), John W. Henry and Company (September 1998).
74. Arthur Conan Doyle, *The Sign of Four* (London and New York: Pitman and Sons, 1890).
75. "Computers Challenge the Stockmarket Gurus," *The Economist*, March 1987.
76. Christopher L. Culp, *Media Nomics*, April 1995, 4.
77. "The Coming Storm," *The Economist*, February 17, 2004, www.economist .com/node/2440313.
78. Emanuel Derman, *The Journal of Derivatives* (Winter, 2000): 64.
79. Frederic Townsend, *Futures* (December 2000): 75.
80. Rickards, *The Road to Ruin*.
81. "Another Two Bites the Dust," *Derivative Strategies* (May 16, 1994): 7.
82. Luke Kawa and Andrea Wong, "Broken Indicators Mean It's Growing Harder to Spot Troubles in the Market," Bloomberg (October 19, 2016), www.bloomberg.com/news/articles/2016-10-19/wall-street-sees-graveyard-of-broken-indicators-in-reform-s-wake.

Chapter 5

1. Michael J. Mauboussin and Kristen Bartholdson, "The Babe Ruth Effect: Frequency versus Magnitude," *The Consilient Observer* 1, no. 2 (January 29, 2002).
2. Michael Lewis, *Moneyball: The Art of Winning an Unfair Game* (New York: W.W. Norton, 2003).
3. Sam Caldarone, "Emotions Can Lie, Numbers Don't," *The Varsity*, October 17, 2016, http://thevarsity.ca/2016/10/17/emotions-can-lie-numbers-dont/.
4. Leigh Steinberg, "Changing the Game: The Rise of Sports Analytics," *Forbes*, August 18, 2015, www.forbes.com/sites/leighsteinberg/2015/08/18/changing-the-game-the-rise-of-sports-analytics/#724ae5c231b2.

5. Lewis, *Moneyball*.
6. Ibid.
7. Earnshaw Cook, *Percentage Baseball* (Baltimore: Waverly Press, 1964).
8. Rob Neyer, "A New Kind of Baseball Owner," *ESPN.com*, August 15, 2002.
9. "The Trading Tribe" (forum response), *The Trading Tribe*, www.seykota.com/tribe/.
10. Richard Driehaus, "Unconventional Wisdom in the Investment Process" (presentation, 1994).
11. John Dorschner, "Boca Raton, Fla.-Based Firm Is a Standout in Futures," *Miami Herald*, January 27, 2001.
12. Greg Burns, "Former 'Turtle' Turns Caution into an Asset," *Chicago Sun-Times*, May 29, 1989, 33.
13. Rob Neyer, "Examining the Art of Evaluating: Q&A with Michael Lewis," *ESPN.com*, May 13, 2003.
14. Lewis, *Moneyball*.
15. Steinberg, "Changing the Game."
16. James Surowiecki, "The Buffett of Baseball," *The New Yorker*, September 23, 2002.
17. Rob Neyer, "Red Sox Hire James in Advisory Capacity," *ESPN.com*, November 7, 2002.
18. Bill James, "Red Sox Hire. Baseball Abstract," *USA Today*, November 15, 2002.
19. Surowiecki, "The Buffett of Baseball."
20. David Grabiner, "The Sabermetric Manifesto," *SeanLahman.com* (1994), http://seanlahman.com/baseball-archive/sabermetrics/sabermetric-manifesto/.
21. Caldarone, "Emotions Can Lie."
22. Bill James, *1981 Baseball Abstract* (Bill James, 1981).
23. Ibid.
24. Ibid.
25. Ben McGrath, "The Professor of Baseball," *The New Yorker*, July 14, 2003, 38.
26. *New York Times*, September 26, 2002.
27. Neyer, "Red Sox Hire James."
28. Jon Birger, "Baseball by the Numbers," *Money*, April 2003, 110.
29. Ibid.
30. Thomas Boswell, "Evaluation by Numbers Is Beginning to Add Up," *Washington Post*, May 29, 2003, D1.
31. Jon Birger, "Baseball by the Numbers," *Money*, April 2003, 110.
32. Neyer, "Red Sox Hire James."
33. Eric Perlmutter, "Little Not Big Enough for Sox," *The Brown Daily Herald*, October 29, 2003.

34. Michael Lewis, "Out of Their Tree," *Sports Illustrated*, March 1, 2004, 7.
35. Stephen Jay Gould, *Triumph and Tragedy in Mudville: A Lifelong Passion for Baseball* (New York: W.W. Norton, 2003): 176–7.
36. Ibid.
37. Jeff Merron, "The Worst Sports Moves of 2003," *ESPN.com*.
38. Sam Miller, "Are Statheads Responsible for the Most Exciting Postseason in Years?" *ESPN.com* (October 24, 2016), www.espn.com/mlb/story/_/id/17870355/are-statheads-responsible-most-exciting-postseason-years.
39. Steinberg, "Changing the Game."
40. Ben Cohen, "The Golden State Warriors Have Revolutionized Basketball," *Wall Street Journal* (April 6, 2016), www.wsj.com/articles/the-golden-state-warriors-have-revolutionized-basketball-1459956975.
41. Ibid.
42. Rob Arthur, "How Baseball's New Data Is Changing Sabermetrics," *FiveThirtyEight* (March 17, 2016), http://fivethirtyeight.com/features/how-baseballs-new-data-is-changing-sabermetrics/.
43. Ibid.
44. Bill Belichick, New England Patriots Press Conference, October 2016.
45. Caldarone, "Emotions Can Lie."
46. Howard W. Eves, *Mathematical Circles Squared* (Boston: Prindle, Weber and Schmidt, 1972).

Chapter 6

1. *Financial Trader* 1, no. 7 (September/October 1994): 26.2.
2. Jason Russell, www.acorn.ca.
3. Brian Hurst, Yao Hua Ooi, and Lasse H. Pedersen, "Understanding Managed Futures," *AQR Capital Management* (Winter 2010).
4. Gerard Jackson, *Brookesnews.com*, April 21, 2003.
5. Jason Zweig, "Do You Sabotage Yourself?" *Business 2.0*, May 2001.
6. David Dreman, *Contrarian Investment Strategies* (New York: Simon & Schuster, 1998).
7. Lao Tsu, "Verse XXXIII," *Tao Te Ching*.
8. Steven Pearlstein, "The New Thinking about Money Is That Your Irrationality Is Predictable," *Washington Post*, January 27, 2002, H1.
9. Daniel Goleman, "What Makes a Leader?" *Harvard Business Review* (1998).
10. Harris Collingwood, "The Sink or Swim Economy," *New York Times*, June 8, 2003.
11. Jack D. Schwager, *The New Market Wizards* (New York: Harper Business, 1992).

12. Ayn Rand, *Atlas Shrugged* (New York: Random House, 1957).
13. *Animal House*, directed by John Landis (Universal City, CA: Universal Pictures, 1978).
14. Daneen Skube, "Self Knowledge Keys," *The Seattle Times* (2002).
15. *Futures* 22, no. 12. (November 1993): 98.
16. Alexis de Tocqueville, *Democracy in America* (New York: Vintage, 1959).
17. Daniel Goleman, *Emotional Intelligence* (New York: Bantam, 1995).
18. Goleman, "What Makes a Leader?"
19. Ibid.
20. Rand, *Atlas Shrugged*.
21. Denise G. Shekerjian, *Uncommon Genius* (New York: Penguin Books, 1990).
22. Goleman, "What Makes a Leader?"
23. Tom Girard, "The Wizards Cast a Spell," *Financial Trader*, No. 4 (July 1995).
24. Gustave Le Bon, *The Crowd: A Study of the Popular Mind* (London: T. F. Unwin, 1925).
25. Rand, *Atlas Shrugged*.
26. Girard, "The Wizards Cast a Spell."
27. Ibid.
28. Schwager, *The New Market Wizards*, 416.
29. "The Trading Tribe" (forum response), *The Trading Tribe*, www.seykota.com/tribe/.
30. Ludwig von Mises, *Human Action* (New Haven, CT: Yale University Press, 1963).
31. Jack Schwager, *Getting Started in Technical Analysis* (New York: John Wiley & Sons, Inc., 1999).
32. Robert Koppel, *The Intuitive Trader* (New York: John Wiley & Sons, Inc., 1996), 74.
33. David Nusbaum, "Mind Games; Trading Behavior," *Futures* 23, no. 6 (June 1994): 60.
34. Michelle Conlin, *Businessweek*, June 30, 2003.
35. Michael J. Mauboussin and Kristen Bartholdson, "All Systems Go: Emotion and Intuition in Decision-Making," *The Consilient Observer* 3, no. 2 (January 27, 2004).
36. Schwager, *The New Market Wizards*.
37. Michael Crichton, *The Lost World* (New York: Knopf, 1995).
38. Lee Kuan Yew.
39. Alan Greenberg, *Memos from the Chairman* (New York: Workman, 1996).
40. Anna Muoio, "All The Right Moves—If You See a Good Idea, Look for a Better One," *Fast Company*, No. 24 (May 1999): 192.

41. Jason Russell, www.acorn.ca.
42. Robert B. Zajonc, "Feeling and Thinking: Preferences Need No Inferences," *American Psychologist* (1980): 151–75.
43. Antonio R. Damasio, *Descartes' Error: Emotion, Reason, and the Human Brain* (New York: Avon, 1994), xii.
44. David Warsh, "Paul Samuelson's Secret," *Economic Principals* (January 23, 2011), www.economicprincipals.com/issues/2011.01.23/1225.html.
45. Shawn Tully, "Princeton's Rich Commodity Scholars," *Fortune*, February 9, 1981.
46. Sam Carpenter, *Work the System: The Simple Mechanics of Making More and Working Less* (Austin, TX: Greenleaf, 2011).

Chapter 7

1. Lewis Carroll, *Alice's Adventures in Wonderland* (1865).
2. Gerd Gigerenzer and Peter M. Todd, *Simple Heuristics That Make Us Smart* (New York: Oxford University Press, 1999), 28.
3. Robert Rubin (Harvard Commencement Address before the graduating class of 2001), www.treasury.gov/press-center/press-releases/Pages/rr3152.aspx.
4. Carla Fried, "The Problem with Your Investment Approach," *Business 2.0* (November 2003): 146.
5. "The Trading Tribe" (forum response), *The Trading Tribe,* www.seykota.com/tribe/.
6. Thomas A. Stewart, "How to Think with Your Gut," *Business 2.0* (November 2002), www.marketfocusing.com/b20_5.html.
7. www.2think.org.
8. Gerd Gigerenzer and Peter M. Todd, *Simple Heuristics That Make Us Smart* (New York: Oxford University Press, 1999): 14.
9. Stephen Hawking, *A Brief History of Time* (New York: Bantam Books, 1988).
10. Gigerenzer and Todd, *Simple Heuristics,* 358.
11. Futures 22, no. 12 (November 1993): 98.
12. Gigerenzer and Todd, *Simple Heuristics,* 361.
13. Gerd Gigerenzer, "Smart Heuristics," *Edge Foundation, Inc.* (March 31, 2003), www.edge.org/conversation/gerd_gigerenzer-smart-heuristics.
14. Bruce Bower, "For Sweet Decisions, Mix a Dash of Knowledge with a Cup of Ignorance," *Science News* 155, no. 22 (May 29, 1999), www.sciencenews.org.
15. Mark Rzepczynski (presentation, New York Mercantile Exchange).
16. Anna Muoio, "All The Right Moves—If You See a Good Idea, Look for a Better One," *Fast Company,* No. 24 (May 1999): 192.

17. Ari Levine and Lasse Heje Pedersen, *Financial Analysts Journal* 72, no. 3 (May/June 2016).
18. "Market Commentary," John W. Henry and Company.
19. Daniel P. Collins, "Building a Stronger Fort," *Futures* 21, no. 6 (May 1, 2003): 82.
20. Gigerenzer, "Smart Heuristics."
21. Larry Swedroe, "Swedroe: A Persistent Kind Of Momentum," *ETF.com* (September 16, 2016), www.etf.com/sections/index-investor-corner/swedroe-persistent-kind-momentum.
22. Clayton M. Christensen, *The Innovator's Dilemma* (Boston: Harvard Business School Press, 1997).
23. Tom Girard, "The Wizards Cast a Spell," *Financial Trader,* No. 4 (July 1995).
24. Michael J. Mauboussin and Kristen Bartholdson, "Be the House: Process and Outcome in Investing," *The Consilient Observer* 2, no. 19 (October 7, 2003).
25. J. Edward Russo and Paul J. H. Schoemaker, *Winning Decisions* (New York: Doubleday, 2002).
26. Leigh Buchanan and Andrew O'Connell, "A Brief History of Decision Making," *Harvard Business Review* (January 2006), https://hbr.org/2006/01/a-brief-history-of-decision-making.

Chapter 8

1. Thomas Harris, *The Silence of the Lambs* (New York: St. Martin's Press, 1988).
2. *Webster's Revised Unabridged Dictionary* (Springfield, MA: G. C. Merriam, 1913).
3. "The Trading Tribe" (forum response), *The Trading Tribe*, www.seykota.com/tribe/.
4. Jessica James and Neil Johnson, "Physics and Finance. Visions: Briefing Papers for Policy Makers," *Institute of Physics and IOP Publishing Ltd.* (1999–2000).
5. Richard Feynman, "Feynman on Scientific Method," (presentation, Cornell University, 1964), www.youtube.com/watch?v=EYPapE-3FRw.
6. Pierre Simon, Marquis de Laplace, *Theorie Analytique des Probabilites* (Paris, Ve. Courcier, 1812).
7. www.criticalthinking.org.
8. Ibid.
9. Darrell Huff, *How to Take a Chance* (New York: W. W. Norton, 1959).
10. Manus J. Donahue III, "An Introduction to Chaos Theory and Fractal Geometry," (1997).
11. "Daniel Patrick Moynihan," *Wikipedia*, last modified December 12, 2016, https://en.wikipedia.org/wiki/Daniel_Patrick_Moynihan.

12. Gerd Gigerenzer, "Smart Heuristics," *Edge Foundation, Inc.* (March 31, 2003), www.edge.org/conversation/gerd_gigerenzer-smart-heuristics.
13. "Elementary Concepts in Statistics," http://statsoftinc.com/textbook/stathome.html.
14. National Institute of Standards and Technology, www.itl.nist.gov.
15. Michael J. Mauboussin and Kristen Bartholdson, "A Tail of Two Worlds, Fat Tails and Investing," *The Consilient Observer* 1, no. 7 (April 9, 2002).
16. Ha Lux, "The Secret World of Jim Simons," *Institutional Investor* 34, no. 11 (November 1, 2000): 38.
17. Ibid.
18. Jerry Parker, "The State of the Industry," *Managed Account Reports, Inc.* (June 2000).
19. Daniel P. Collins, "Chenier: Systematizing What Works (Trader Profile)," *Futures* 32, no. 9 (July 1, 2003): 86.
20. Roger Lowenstein, *Wall Street Journal*, June 13, 2003.
21. Benoit B. Mandelbrot, "A Multifractal Walk down Wall Street," *Scientific American* 280, no. 2 (February 1999): 70–73.
22. Larry Swedroe, Buckingham Asset Management, www.bamstl.com/.
23. Ibid.
24. Mark Rzepczynski, "Return Distribution Properties of JWH Investment Programs, Stock and Bond Indices, and Hedge Funds," John W. Henry and Co., No. V (June 2000).
25. *National Institute of Standards and Technology,* www.itl.nist.gov.
26. Ibid.
27. Jim Rogers, *Investment Biker* (New York: Random House, 1994).
28. Larry S. Liebovitch, "Two Lessons from Fractals and Chaos," *Complexity* 5, no. 4 (2000): 34–43.
29. Per Bak, "Narrative Physics," *The Paula Gordon Show* (February 1, 2000), www.paulagordon.com/shows/bak/.
30. Donald H. Rumsfeld, "DoD News Briefing—Secretary Rumsfeld and Gen. Myers," (U.S. Department of Defense, February 12, 2002), http://archive.defense.gov/Transcripts/Transcript.aspx?TranscriptID=2636.
31. Bill Bonner, "Understanding the Nature of the Fat Tail Phenomenon," *American Writers and Artists Inc.*

Chapter 9

1. "Of Pimps, Punters and Equities," *The Economist*, March 24, 2001.
2. "Crossfire," *CNN*, December 21, 1999.
3. Richard Rudy, "Buy and Hold: A Different Perspective," *Barclay Managed Futures Research* (fourth quarter 2001).

4. James Glassman, "Buy It Now! For a Fine Keepsake of the Internet Boom!" (Review of *Dow 36000*, Amazon.com, November 7, 2001).
5. Jerry Parker, "The State of the Industry," *Managed Account Reports, Inc.* (June 2000).
6. Rudy, "Buy and Hold."
7. William R. Gallacher, *Winner Take All* (New York: McGraw-Hill, 1994).
8. David Dukcevich, *Forbes* (May 6, 2002).
9. James Cramer, *CNBC: Kudlow and Cramer* (television interview, *Yahoo! Chat*, September 7, 2000).
10. "News Release," Berkshire Hathaway, Inc. (May 22, 2002).
11. *Washington Post* (March 6, 2003): E1.
12. Courtney Comstock, "Michael Steinhardt Bashes Warren Buffett: 'He's Just The Greatest PR Person Of All Time . . . How He Treated John Gutfreund Was Disgusting,'" *Business Insider* (April 5, 2011), www.businessinsider.com/michael-steinhardt-bashes-warren-buffett-greatest-pr-person-of-all-time-conned-everybody-2011-4.
13. James K. Glassman, *Washington Post*, December 9, 2001.
14. "Moneyline," *CNN*, December 23, 1999.
15. James K. Glassman, *Washington Post*, February, 17, 2002.
16. "Street Sweep," *CNN* (April 4, 2000).
17. Jennifer Karchmer, "Tiger Management Closes: Julian Robertson Plans to Return Money to Shareholders after Losses in Value Stocks," *CNNfn* (March 30, 2000: 6:59 p.m. EST).
18. Aaron L. Task, "Requiem for a Heavyweight," *TheStreet.com*.
19. "Larry King Live," *CNN*, March 2001.
20. Edward Clendaniel, "After the Sizzle Comes the Fizzle," *Forbes.com*, March 25, 2002.
21. Allan Sloan, "Even with No Bull Market, Baby Boomers Can Thrive," *Washington Post*, March 26, 2002, E1.
22. Alan Abelson, "Up and Down Wall Street," *Barron's*, December 15, 2003.
23. B. Luke, "WorldCom: The Accounting Scandal; JR Kuhn Jr.," *The Charlotte Observer* (2006).
24. David Rode and Satu Parikh, "An Evolutionary Approach to Technical Trading and Capital Market Efficiency," The Wharton School, University of Pennsylvania (May 1, 1995).
25. "The Trading Tribe" (forum response), *The Trading Tribe*, www.seykota.com/tribe/.
26. "Harding: Master of the Markets," (video clip, *CNBC*, April 8, 2011), http://video.cnbc.com/gallery/?video=3000015574.
27. Ibid.
28. Ibid.
29. Ibid.

30. Ibid.
31. Ibid.
32. Ibid.
33. Ibid.
34. Ibid.
35. Ibid.
36. "Defining Critical Thinking," *The Critical Thinking Community*, www.criticalthinking.org/aboutCT/define_critical_thinking.cfm.
37. "General Form for Registration of Securities: Pursuant to Section 12(b) or 12(g) of the Securities Exchange Act of 1934," United States Securities and Exchange Commission, www.sec.gov/Archives/edgar/data/1309136/000090514804005334/efc4-2070_form1012g.txt.
38. "What Happened? What's Next? Merrill Lynch Review and Forecast (marketing flyer)," Merrill Lynch.
39. Jerry Garcia and Robert Hunter, "Casey Jones" (The Grateful Dead, *Workingman's Dead*, 1970).
40. David Whitford, "Why Owning the Boston Red Sox Is Like Running a Successful Hedge Fund," *Fortune Small Business* (October 25, 2003).
41. Dave Barry (February 3, 2002).
42. Jean-Philippe Bouchaud and Damien Challet, "Why Have Asset Price Properties Changed So Little in 200 Years" (May 2, 2016).
43. Ibid.

Chapter 10

1. "The Trading Tribe" (forum response), *The Trading Tribe*, www.seykota.com/tribe/.
2. "Marketing Materials," Dunn Capital Management, Inc.
3. Leon G. Cooperman, "CNBC Interview with Ron Insana."
4. Charles Sanford, "Commencement address," (University of Georgia, June 17, 1989).
5. Gibbons Burke, "Managing Your Money," *Active Trader* (July 2000).
6. Mark Rzepczynski, "Portfolio Diversification: Investors Just Don't Seem to Have Enough," *JWH Journal*.
7. Jack Reerink, "The Power of Leverage," *Futures* 24, no. 4 (April 1995).
8. Edward O. Thorp, *The Mathematics of Gambling* (Hollywood, CA: Gambling Times, 1984).
9. Larry Harris, *Trading and Exchanges: Market Microstructure for Practitioners* (New York: Oxford University Press, 2003).
10. "Going Once, Going Twice," *Discover*, August 2002, 23.

11. Jim Little and Sol Waksman, "A Perspective on Risk," *Barclay Managed Futures Report*.

12. Craig Pauley, "How to Become a CTA," (June 1994).

13. Thomas L. Friedman, *The Lexus and The Olive Tree* (New York: Farrar, Straus & Giroux, 1999).

14. Gibbons Burke, "Managing Your Money," *Active Trader* (July 2000).

15. Craig Pauley, "How to Become a CTA" (June 1994).

16. Ed Seykota and Dave Druz, "Determining Optimal Risk," *Technical Analysis of Stocks and Commodities Magazine* 11, no. 3 (March 1993): 122–124, www.traders.com.

17. Gibbons Burke, "Gain Without Pain: Money Management in Action," *Futures* 21, no. 14 (December 1992): 36.

18. Tom Basso, "How to Become a CTA" (June 1994).

19. Carla Cavaletti, "Comeback Kids: Managing Drawdowns According to Commodity Trading Advisors," *Futures* 27, no. 1 (January 1998): 68.

20. Michael Peltz, "John W. Henry's Bid to Manage the Future," *Institutional Investor* (August 1996).

21. InterMarket, *The Worldwide Futures and Options Report* (Chicago: InterMarket Publishing Group, July 1984).

22. "The Trading Tribe" (forum response), *The Trading Tribe*, www.seykota.com/tribe/.

23. Oliver Conway, "Cover story about John W. Henry & Company, Inc.," *Managed Derivatives* (May 1996).

24. Ted Williams, *The Science of Hitting* (New York: Simon & Schuster, 1986), 7.

25. Desmond McRae, "31-Year Track Record of 18.1%: Managed Account Reports: Extracting Inherent Value," *Managed Futures* (March 2003).

26. Daniel Colton, "Trading the Pain Threshold (Trader Profile: Mark van Stolk)," *Futures* (November 2003): 98.

27. Ludwig von Mises, *Human Action: A Treatise on Economics,* 4th rev. ed. (Irvington-on-Hudson, NY: The Foundation for Economic Education, 1996).

28. Ellyn E. Spragins, "Gary Weiss, and Stuart Weiss, Contrarians," *Businessweek,* December 29, 1986, 74.

29. *Washington Post* (December 9, 2001).

30. Jack D. Schwager, *The New Market Wizards* (New York: Harper Business, 1992).

31. "Bruce Kovner," *Wikipedia*, last modified October 14, 2016, https://en.wikipedia.org/wiki/Bruce_Kovner.

32. "John W. Henry," *Wikipedia*, last modified December 15, 2016, https://en.wikipedia.org/wiki/John_W._Henry.

33. Hedgeable, "Lesson 4.3: Biggest Winners & Losers of 2008," www.hedgeable.com/education/highest-paid-investment-managers-4.3.

34. "Michael Marcus," *Wikipedia*, last modified May 9, 2016, https://en.wikipedia.org/wiki/Michael_Marcus_%28trader%29.
35. "David Harding," *Wikipedia*, last modified December 11, 2016, https://en.wikipedia.org/wiki/David_Harding_%28financier%29.
36. Erin E. Arvedlund, "On the Right Track," *Barron's* (November 30, 2009), www.barrons.com/articles/SB125935481888466969.
37. Jerry Parker, "The State of the Industry," *Managed Account Reports, Inc.* (June 2000).
38. Bruce Terry, *Managed Account Reports* (September 2001).
39. Morton Baratz, "Do Trend Followers Distort Futures Prices?" *Managed Account Reports*, No. 43: 9.
40. Sharon Schwartzman, "Computers Keep Funds in Mint Condition: A Major Money Manager Combines the Scientific Approach with Human Ingenuity," *Wall Street Computer Review* 8, no. 6 (March 1991): 13.
41. Ibid.
42. Friedman, *The Lexus and the Olive Tree*.
43. "Barclay Trading Group, Ltd.," *Barclay Managed Futures Report* 4, no. 1 (first quarter 1993): 3.
44. Ibid., 10.
45. John W. Henry (presentation, Geneva, Switzerland, September 15, 1998).
46. "Trading System Review," (Futures Industry Association Conference Seminar, November 2, 1994).
47. Tom Basso, "How to Become a CTA," (June 1994).
48. Leo Melamed, *Escape to the Futures* (New York: John Wiley & Sons, Inc., 1996).
49. Miles Johnson, "Hedge Fund Nightmare Turns into a Dream," *Financial Times* (November 5, 2014), www.ft.com/content/7953c1f8-64e7-11e4-bb43-00144feabdc0.
50. Tony Robbins, *Money: Master the Game. 7 Simple Steps to Financial Freedom* (Simon & Schuster, 2014).

Chapter 11

1. "The Trading Tribe" (forum response), *The Trading Tribe*, www.seykota.com/tribe/.
2. Alexander M. Ineichen, *Absolute Returns* (New York: John Wiley & Sons, Inc., 2003): 64.
3. Keith Campbell, "Campbell & Company," *Managed Account Reports*.
4. Carla Cavaletti, "Turtles on the Move," *Futures* 27, no. 6 (June 1998): 77.
5. Jerry Parker, "The State of the Industry," *Managed Account Reports, Inc.* (June 2000).

6. "Who's to Blame Next?" *Asterias Info-Invest*, Asterias, Ltd.
7. Parker, "The State of the Industry."
8. Richard Dennis, "The State of the Industry," *Managed Account Reports, Inc.* (June 2000).
9. Bill Dunn (presentation, MAR's Mid Year Conference on Alternative Investment Strategies, June 22–24, 1999).
10. Van K. Tharp, "Interview with Two Super Traders."
11. Max Gunther, *The Zurich Axioms* (New York: New American Library, 1985).
12. W. H. Auden and L. Kronenberger, eds., *The Viking Book of Aphorisms* (New York: Viking Press, 1966).
13. William Deresiewicz, "Don't Send Your Kid to the Ivy League," *New Republic* (July 21, 2014), https://newrepublic.com/article/118747/ivy-league-schools-are-overrated-send-your-kids-elsewhere.

Section II: Trend Following Interviews

1. Stephen Mitchell, *The Second Book of the Tao* (New York: Penguin Books, January 5, 2010).

Chapter 12

1. "Ed Seykota," *Wikipedia*, last modified August 5, 2016, https://en.wikipedia.org/wiki/Ed_Seykota.
2. Tobias J. Moskowitz, Yao Hua Ooi, and Lasse Heje Pedersen, "Time Series Momentum," *Journal of Financial Economics* 104 (July 11, 2011), 228–250.
3. Ross Lincoln, "Blumhouse and the Calculus of Low Budget Horror—Produced By," *Deadline* (May 30, 2015), http://deadline.com/2015/05/blumhouse-panel-produced-by-conference-1201435034/.
4. Spyros Makridakis, *Dance with Chance: Making Luck Work For You* (London: Oneworld Publications, 2010).
5. Charles Mackay, *Extraordinary Popular Delusions and the Madness of Crowds* (New York: Dover, 2003).

Chapter 13

1. "Martin Lueck," Aspect Capital, www.aspectcapital.com/about-aspect/team/martin-lueck.
2. Fred Schwed, *Where Are the Customers' Yachts?: or A Good Hard Look at Wall Street* (Hoboken, NJ: John Wiley & Sons, Inc., January 10, 2006).

Chapter 14

1. "Jean-Philippe Bouchaud," *Wikipedia*, last modified October 25, 2016, https://en.wikipedia.org/wiki/Jean-Philippe_Bouchaud.
2. Charles Mackay, *Extraordinary Popular Delusions and the Madness of Crowds* (New York: Dover, 2003).

Chapter 15

1. "Ewan Kirk," *Wikipedia*, last modified July 1, 2016, https://en.wikipedia.org/wiki/Ewan_Kirk.
2. Peter King, "Upsetting Developments," *Sports Illustrated*, December 28, 2015, http://mmqb.si.com/mmqb/2015/12/28/peyton-manning-hgh-allegations-nfl-week-16-upsets.

Chapter 16

1. "Alex Greyserman," ISAM, www.isam.com/management-team/alex-greyserman.
2. Nassim Taleb, *The Black Swan: The Impact of the Highly Improbable* (New York: Random House, May 11, 2010).

Chapter 17

1. "Campbell Harvey," *Wikipedia*, https://en.wikipedia.org/wiki/Campbell_Harvey.

Chapter 18

1. "Lasse Heje Pedersen," *Wikipedia*, last modified November 10, 2016, https://en.wikipedia.org/wiki/Lasse_Heje_Pedersen.
2. Paul Johnson, "When Excess Is A Virtue," *Forbes*, March 23, 2016, www.forbes.com/sites/currentevents/2016/03/23/when-excess-is-a-virtue/#502ecfdc34b5.
3. Nassim Taleb, *The Black Swan: The Impact of the Highly Improbable* (New York: Random House, 2010).

4. Andy Greenberg, "Want to Know Julian Assange's Endgame? He Told You a Decade Ago," *Wired*, October 14, 2016, www.wired.com/2016/10/want-know-julian-assanges-endgame-told-decade-ago/.
5. John Allen Paulos, "The Mathematics of Changing Your Mind," *New York Times* (August 5, 2011), www.nytimes.com/2011/08/07/books/review/the-theory-that-would-not-die-by-sharon-bertsch-mcgrayne-book-review.html.
6. David Harding, Winton Capital Management (May 2015).
7. Brian Christian and Tom Griffiths, *Algorithms to Live By: The Computer Science of Human Decisions* (New York: Brilliance Audio, 2016).
8. Ibid.
9. Ibid.

Section III: Trend Following Research

1. Howard Marks, *The Most Important Thing* (New York: Audible Studios on Brilliance Audio, March 8, 2016), 36.
2. Anders Ericsson, *Peak: Secrets from the New Science of Expertise* (New York: Eamon Dolan/Houghton Mifflin Harcourt, 2016).
3. Robert P. Seawright, "A Hierarchy of Advisor Value," *Above the Market*, February 12, 2016, https://rpseawright.wordpress.com/2016/02/12/a-hierarchy-of-advisor-value/.

Chapter 19

Bailey, D., and M. Prado, "Drawdown–Based Stop–Outs and the 'Triple Penance' Rule" (working paper), 2013.

Grant, J. *The Great Metropolis* (Philadelphia: E. L. Carey & A. Hart, 1838).

Greyserman, A., "The Multi-Centennial View of Trend Following," ISAM white paper (2012).

Jegadeesh, N., and S. Titman. "Returns to Buying Winners and Selling Losers: Implications for Stock Market Efficiency," *Journal of Finance* 48, no. 1 (1993): 65–91.

Kaminski, K., "Managed Futures and Volatility: Decoupling a 'Convex' Relationship with Volatility Cycles," CME Market Education Group (May 2012).

Moskowitz, T., T. Ooi, and L. Pedersen, "Time Series Momentum," *Journal of Financial Economics*, no. 104 (May 2012).

Taylor, B., "The GFD Guide to Total Returns on Stocks, Bonds, and Bills (working document)," *Global Financial Data*, www.globalfinancialdata.com/News/Articles/The_GFD_Guide_to_total_returns.doc.

Thompson, Earl. "The Tulipmania: Fact or Artifact?" *Public Choice* 130, nos. 1–2 (2007): 99–114.

Chapter 20

1. "There is no other proposition in economics which has more solid empirical evidence supporting it than the efficient market hypothesis," as M. Jensen famously wrote in 1978.
2. Together with a third scientist, Lars Hansen, who had not directly taken part in the debate.
3. Futures markets allow traders to go short as easily as going long. Therefore, both up-trends and down-trends can be exploited equally.
4. Jensen (1978) actually stressed the importance of trading profitability in assessing market efficiency. In particular, if anomalous return behavior is not definitive enough for an efficient trader to make money trading on it, then it is not economically significant.
5. Note that the excess return of trends cannot be classified as a risk premium either (see Lempérière et al. 2014; Narasimhan and Titman 2011). On the contrary, trend following is correlated with "long-vol" strategies.
6. We call this a fictitious P&L since no attempt is made to model any realistic implementation costs of the strategy.
7. See www.globalfinancialdata.com.
8. Anecdotally, based on a long history of Capital Fund Management (CFM) inflows and outflows, our experience suggests that professional investors have a strong tendency to "chase performance," i.e., to invest in CFM's funds after a positive rally and redeem after negative performance.
9. Within their model, Giardina and Bouchaud (2003) show that, without an element of trend following, markets quickly reach an "efficient" stationary state where nothing much happens.

References

Asness, C. S., T. J. Moskowitz, and L. H. Pedersen, "Value and Momentum Everywhere," *Journal of Finance* 58 (2013): 929–85.

Barberis, N., R. Greenwood, L. Jin, and A. Shleifer, "X-CAPM: An Extrapolative Capital Asset Pricing Model" (Working Paper), (2013).

Barroso, P. and P. Santa-Clara, "Momentum Has Its Moments" (working paper) (2013).

Bartas, N. and R. Kosowski, "Momentum Strategies in Futures Markets and Trend-Following Funds" (EUROFIDAI-AFFI Finance Meeting, Paris, December 2012), http://dx.doi.org/10.2139/ssrn.1968996.

Black, F., "Noise," *Journal of Finance,* 41 (1986): 529–43.

Bouchaud, J. P., "Crises and Collective Socio-economic Phenomena: Simple Models and Challenges," *Journal of Statistical Physics*, 151 (2013): 567.

Bouchaud, J. P. and R. Cont, "A Langevin Approach to Stock Market Fluctuations and Crashes," *European Physical Journal B* 6, no. 4 (1998): 543–50.

Bouchaud, J. P. and M. Potters, "Theory of Financial Risk and Derivative Pricing," *Cambridge University Press* (2003).

Clare, A., J. Seaton, P. N. Smith, and S. Thomas, "Trend Following, Risk Parity and Momentum in Commodity Futures" (working paper), http://dx.doi.org/10.2139/ssrn.2126813.

Covel, Michael, *The Complete TurtleTrader* (New York: HarperCollins, 2009).

de Bondt, W. and R. H. Thaler, "Does the Stock Market Overreact?" *Journal of Finance,* 42 (1985): 557–81.

DeLong, J., A. Bradford, A. Shleifer, L. H. Summers, and R. J. Waldmann, "Positive Feedback Investment Strategies and Destabilizing Rational Speculation," *Journal of Finance* 45 (1990): 379–95.

Duke, J., D. Harding, and K. Land, "Historical Performance of Trend Following" (working paper) (December 2013).

Giardina, I. and J. P. Bouchaud, "Bubbles, Crashes and Intermittency in Agent Based Market Models," *European Physics Journal B* 31 (2003): 421.

Gigerenzer, G. and D. Goldstein, "Reasoning the Fast and Frugal Way: Models of Bounded Rationality," *Psychological Review* 103 (1996): 650.

Greenwood, R. and A. Shleifer, "Expectations of Returns and Expected Returns," *Review of Financial Studies* 27, no. 3 (2014): 714–46.

Hirshleifer, D. and J. Yu, "Asset Pricing in Production Economies with Extrapolative Expectations" (working paper) (2012).

Hommes, H., "Heterogeneous Agent Models in Economics and Finance," *Handbook of Computational Economics,* Vol. 2.

Hommes, H., J. Sonnemans, J. Tuinstra, and H. van de Velden, "Expectations and Bubbles in Asset Pricing Experiments," *Journal of Economic Behavior and Organization* (2008): 116–33.

Hong, H., and J. Stein, "A Unified Theory of Underreaction, Momentum Trading, and Overreaction in Asset Markets," *Journal of Finance* (1999): 2143–84.

Hurst, B., Y. H. Ooi, and L. H. Pedersen, "A Century of Evidence on Trend-Following Investing" (working paper), *AQR* (2012).

Kent, D. and T. J. Moskowitz, "Momentum Crashes," *Swiss Finance Institute Research Paper Series* (2013): 13–61.

Kent, D., D. Hirshleifer, and A. Subrahmanyam, "Investor Psychology and Security Market Under and Overreactions," *Journal of Finance* 53 (1998): 1839–85.

Kirman, A., "Ants, Rationality and Recruitment," *Quarterly Journal of Economics* 108 (1991): 137–56.

Kirman, A., "Epidemics of Opinion and Speculative Bubbles in Financial Markets," *Money and Financial Markets* (1993).

Lempérière, Y., C. Deremble, P. Seager, M. Potters, and J. P. Bouchaud, "Two Centuries of Trend Following," *Journal of Investment Strategies* 3 (2014): 41.

Lempérière, Y., "What Is Risk Premium and How Does It Differ from Alpha Strategies?" (working paper) (2014).

Leroy, S. F., and R. D. Porter, "The Present Value Relation: Tests Based on Implied Variance Bounds," *Econometrica* 49 (1981): 555.

Lux, T., and M. Marchesi, "Volatility Clustering in Financial Markets: A Microsimulation of Interacting Agents," *International Journal of Theoretical and Applied Finance* 3 (2000): 675–702.

Menkhoff, L., "Are Momentum Traders Different? Implications for the Momentum Puzzle," *Applied Economics* 43 (2011): 4415–30.

Mundt, M., "Estimating the Capacity of the Managed Futures Industry," *CTA Intelligence* (March 30, 2014).

Narasimhan, J. and S. Titman, "Returns to Buying Winners and Selling Losers: Implications for Stock Market Efficiency," *Journal of Finance* 48 (1993): 65–91.

Narasimhan, J. and S. Titman, "Momentum" (working paper), http://ssrn.com/abstract=1919226.

Reinhart, M. and K. S. Rogoff, *This Time Is Different: Eight Centuries of Financial Folly*, (Princeton, NJ; Princeton University Press, 2009).

Schwert, G. W., "Anomalies and Market Efficiency," *Handbook of the Economics of Finance* B 1 (2003): 939–74.

Seager, P., "The Statistics of Drawdowns" (working paper) (2014).

Shiller, R. J., "Do Stock Prices Move Too Much to Be Justified by Subsequent Changes in Dividends?" *American Economic Review* 71 (1981): 421–36.

Shiller, R. J., "Measuring Bubble Expectations and Investor Confidence," *Journal of Psychology and Financial Markets* (2000): 49–60.

Smith, V. L., G. L. Suchanek, and A. W. Williams, "Bubbles, Crashes and Endogenous Expectations in Experimental Spot Asset Markets," *Econometrica* 56 (1988): 1119–51.

Summers, L., "Does the Stock Market Rationally Reflect Fundamental Values?" *Journal of Finance* 41 (1986): 591.

Szakmary, A. C., Q. Shen, and S. C. Sharma, "Trend-Following Strategies in Commodity Futures: A Re-examination," *Journal of Banking and Finance* 34, no. 2 (2010): 409–26.

Wyart, M. and J. P. Bouchaud, "Self-referential Behaviour, Overreaction and Conventions in Financial Markets," *Journal of Economic Behavior and Organization* 63 (2007): 1.

Chapter 21

C. M. Faith, *Way Of The Turtle* (New York: McGraw-Hill, 2007).

Moskowitz, Ooi, and Pedersen, "Time Series Momentum," *Journal of Financial Economics* Vol. 104, Issue 2 (May 2012).

Hutchinson and O'Brien, "Is This Time Different? Trend-Following and Financial Crises," *The Journal of Alternative Investments*, Vol. 17, no. 2 (Fall 2014).

Y. Lemperiere, C. Deremble, P. Seager, M. Potters, and J. P. Bouchaud, "Two Centuries of Trend Following," *Journal of Investment Strategies* Vol. 3, no. 3 (June 2014).

Appendix

The 13 trend following models used in the paper are as follows:

1. *MOP*: The strategy goes long/short each market for one month, based on the sign of its past 12 month return. Based on the "Time Series Momentum" paper by Moskowitz, Ooi, and Pedersen.[2]
2. *HOB*: Applies a similar methodology to MOP but considers an average of look-back periods ranging from 1 to 12 months. Based on the "Is This Time Different? Trend Following and Financial Crises" paper by Hutchinson and O'Brien.[3]
3. *LDSPB*: Captures the direction of price deviations from a long-term exponentially weighted moving average. Based on the "Two Centuries of Trend Following" paper by Lemperiere et al. of Capital Fund Management.[4]
4. *DMI*: Directional movement indicator, designed to differentiate between strong and weak trends.
5. *RSI*: Relative strength index, a technical momentum indicator designed to compare the magnitude of recent gains to recent losses.
6. *Turtle-ATR*: Channel breakout strategy which uses the Average True Range, an alternative to standard deviation to measure price volatility.
7. *Turtle-Boll. BO*: Breakout strategy that uses Bollinger Bands® to identify breakouts, a tool which involves a moving average approach and setting upper and lower bands based on standard deviations above and below the moving average.
8. *Turtle-Donchian*: Breakout strategy that includes an additional trade entry condition based on comparing short and long exponential moving averages.
9. *Turtle-3x MA*: Moving average using three time horizons: fast, medium and slow, to determine trade entry and exit.
10. *Z-Score*: Statistical model designed to estimate price drift, relative to the volatility of returns.
11. *Trend Deviation*: Double exponentially weighted moving average approach.
12. *MA Crossover*: Uses the difference between a moving average over a short window, and one over a longer window.
13. *Percentile*: Uses percentiles of recent prices averaged over a short window, from a longer-term distribution.

Chapter 22

1. See AHL Research (2014).
2. Sharpe (1964) for the CAPM. Higgs (1964) for the Higgs Boson.
3. See Black, Jensen, and Scholes (1972) and Fama and MacBeth (1973).
4. A 2009 brochure put the cost of the machine at about $4 billion and this does not include all other costs. See http://cds.cern.ch/record/1165534/files/CERN-Brochure-2009-003-Eng.pdf, retrieved July 10, 2014.

5. CMS (2012) and ATLAS (2012).
6. See Baglio and Djouadi (2011).
7. See Hardy (2002).
8. See Simon-Sanchez et al. (2009).
9. When returns are realized at higher frequencies, Sharpe Ratios and the corresponding *t*-statistics can be calculated in a straightforward way. Assuming that there are N return realizations in a year and the mean and standard deviation of returns at the higher frequency is μ and σ, the annualized Sharpe Ratio can be calculated as $(\mu \times N) / (\sigma \times \sqrt{N}) = (\mu / \sigma) \times \sqrt{N}$. The corresponding *t*-statistic is $(\mu / \sigma) \times \sqrt{(N \times \text{Number of years})}$. For example, for monthly returns, the annualized Sharpe Ratio and the corresponding *t*-statistic are $(\mu / \sigma) \times \sqrt{12}$ and $(\mu / \sigma) \times \sqrt{(12 \times \text{Number of years})}$, respectively, where μ and σ are the monthly mean and standard deviation for returns. Similarly, assuming μ and σ are the daily mean and standard deviation for returns and there are 252 trading days in a year, the annualized Sharpe Ratio and the corresponding *t*-statistics are $(\mu / \sigma) \times \sqrt{252}$ and $(\mu / \sigma) \times \sqrt{(252 \times \text{Number of years})}$.
10. See AHL Research (2014).
11. See Barras, Scaillet, and Wermers (2010).
12. See www.mars-one.com/mission/roadmap, retrieved July 10, 2014.
13. See Schweder and Spjotvoll (1982).
14. More specifically, $c(M) = 1 + 1/2 + 1/3 \ldots + 1/M = \Sigma MM1/ii$ and approximately equals log(M) when M is large.
15. For the *p*-value thresholds, whether or not BHY is more lenient than Holm depends on the specific distribution of *p*-values, especially when the number of tests M is small. When M is large, BHY implied hurdles are usually much larger than Holm.
16. We have 269 monthly observations for the strategies in the "Price Momentum" and "Capital Efficiency" groups and 113 monthly observations for the strategies in the "Analyst Expectations" group. Therefore, the *t*-statistics are calculated as $0.83 \times \sqrt{(269 / 12)} = 3.93$, $0.37 \times \sqrt{(113 / 12)} = 1.14$ and $0.67 \times \sqrt{(269 / 12)} = 3.17$.
17. Applying the Bonferroni test, the three *p*-values are adjusted to be 0.0387, 1.0, and 0.7260. The corresponding adjusted Sharpe Ratios are 0.44, 0, 0.07 and the haircuts are 47%, 100%, and 90%. These haircuts are larger than under the BHY approach.
18. See AHL Research (2014). The 0.45 is based on 16 partitions of the data.

References

ATLAS collaboration, "Observation of a New Particle in the Search for the Standard Model Higgs Boson with the ATLAS Detector at the LHC," *Physics Letters B* 716, no. 1 (2012): 1–29.

"Strategy Selection," AHL internal research paper (2014).

Bailey, D., J. Borwein, M. López de Prado, and Q. J. Zhu, "Pseudo-Mathematics and Financial Charlatanism: The Effects of Back Test Over Fitting on Out-of-Sample" (working paper), *Lawrence Berkeley National Laboratory* (2013a).

Bailey, D., J. Borwein, M. López de Prado, and Q. J. Zhu, "The Probability of Backtest Overfitting" (working paper), *Lawrence Berkeley National Laboratory* (2013b).

Barras, L., O. Scaillet, and R. Wermers, "False Discoveries in Mutual Fund Performance: Measuring Luck in Estimated Alphas," *Journal of Finance* 65 (2010): 179–216.

Baglio, J. and A. Djouadi, "Higgs Production at the IHC," *Journal of High Energy Physics* 1103, no. 3 (2011): 55.

Benjamini, Y., and Y. Hochberg, "Controlling the False Discovery Rate: A Practical and Powerful Approach to Multiple Testing," *Journal of the Royal Statistical Society* Series B 57 (1995): 289–300.

Benjamini, Y. and D. Yekutieli, "The Control of the False Discovery Rate in Multiple Testing under Dependency," *Annals of Statistics* 29 (2001): 1165–88.

Black, F., M. C. Jensen, and M. Scholes, *Theory of Capital Markets* (New York: Praeger, 1972): 79–121.

CMS collaboration, "Observation of a New Boson at a Mass of 125 GeV with the CMS Experiment at the LHC," *Physics Letters B* 716, no. 1 (2012): 30–61.

Fama, E. and J. D. MacBeth, "Risk, Return, and Equilibrium: Empirical Tests," *Journal of Political Economy* 81 (1973): 607–36.

López de Prado, M., "What to Look for in a Backtest" (working paper), *Lawrence Berkeley National Laboratory* (2013).

McLean, R. D. and J. Pontiff, "Does Academic Research Destroy Stock Return Predictability?" (working paper), University of Alberta (2014).

Ioannidis, J. P., "Why Most Published Research Findings Are False," *PLoS Medicine* 2, e124 (2005): 694–701.

Hardy, J., "The Real Problem in Association Studies," *American Journal of Medical Genetics* 114, no. 2 (2002): 253.

Harvey, C. R., and Y. Liu, "Backtesting" (working paper), Duke University (2014), https://papers.ssrn.com/sol3/papers.cfm?abstract_id=2345489.

"Multiple Testing in Economics" (working paper), Duke University (2014).

"Incremental Factors" (working paper), Duke University (2014).

Harvey, C. R., Y. Liu, and H. Zhu, ". . . and the Cross-section of Expected Returns" (working paper), Duke University (2014), https://papers.ssrn.com/sol3/papers.cfm?abstract_id=2249314.

Higgs, P., "Broken Symmetries and the Masses of Gauge Bosons," *Physical Review Letters* 13, no. 16 (1964): 508–9.

Schweder, T. and E. Spjotvoll, "Plots of P-values to Evaluate Many Tests Simultaneously," *Biometrika* 69 (1982): 439–502.

Schwert, G. W., "Anomalies and Market Efficiency," *Economics of Finance* (2003): 937–72.

Simon Sanchez, J., C. Schulte, and T. Gasser, "Genome-wide Association Study Reveals Genetic Risk Underlying Parkinson's Disease," *Nature Genetics* 41 (2009): 1308–12.

Chapter 24

Sharpe, William F., "The Sharpe Ratio," *The Journal of Portfolio Management* (Fall 1994).

Chapter 26

1. Harry M. Kat, "Managed Futures and Hedge Funds: A Match Made in Heaven," *Journal of Investment Management* 2, no. 1 (2004), 32–40.
2. Peter Park, Oguz Tanrikulu, and Guodong Wang, "Systematic Global Macro: Performance, Risk and Correlation Characteristics" (February 24, 2009), http://ssrn.com/abstract=1348629 or http://dx.doi.org/10.2139/ssrn.1348629.
3. Ryan Abrams, Ranjan Bhaduri, and Elizabeth Flores, "Lintner Revisited—A Quantitative Analysis of Managed Futures for Plan Sponsors, Endowments and Foundations," *CME Group* (May 2012).
4. Henry H. Bakken, "Futures Trading—Origin, Development, and Present Economic Status" (Madison, WI: Mimir Publishers, 1966), 3.
5. Barclays Capital, "Trending Forward: CTAs/Managed Futures," *Hedge Fund Pulse* (February 2012).
6. Ranjan Bhaduri and Christopher Art, "Liquidity Buckets, Liquidity Indices, Liquidity Duration, and their Applications to Hedge Funds," *Alternative Investment Quarterly* (second quarter, 2008).
7. Neil Ramsey and Aleks Kins, "Managed Futures: Capturing Liquid, Transparent, Uncorrelated Alpha," *The Capital Guide to Alternative Investment* (2004): 129–35.
8. Marc Odo, "Skewness and Kurtosis" (working paper), Zephyr Associates, Inc. (August 2011), www.styleadvisor.com.
9. Gaurav Amin and Harry M. Kat, "Stocks, Bonds and Hedge Funds: Not a Free Lunch!" *Journal of Portfolio Management* (Summer 2003): 113–20.
10. Nigol Koulajian and Paul Czkwianianc, "Know Your Skew—Using Hedge Fund Return Volatility as a Predictor of Maximum Loss," *AlphaQuest CTA Research Series #2* (June 2011).
11. Harry M. Kat, "Managed Futures and Hedge Funds: A Match Made in Heaven," *ISMA Centre Discussion Papers* (November 2002), http://ssrn.com/abstract=34758.

Chapter 27

1. Since our focus is generally on derivatives markets, we do not cover single stocks in this study.
2. To guard against occasional bad data in the early part of the sample, we in fact use a trailing average of the last 10 days, with the two biggest outliers removed (i.e., a central 8/10 mean).

References

Asness, Clifford S., Tobias J. Moskowitz, and Lasse Heje Pedersen, "Value and Momentum Everywhere," *Journal of Finance* 68, no. 3 (2013): 929–85.

Bhansali, Vineer, "Volatility and the Carry Trade," *Journal of Fixed Income*, 17, no. 3 (2007): 72–84.

Campbell, John, Adi Sunderam, and Luis M. Viceira, "Inflation Bets or Deflation Hedges: The Changing Risks of Nominal Bonds?" (working paper), *NBER* (February 2009).

Cochrane, John H., "Presidential Address: Discount Rates," *Journal of Finance* 66, no. 4 (2011): 1047–1108.

Cochrance, John H. and Monika Piazzesi, "Bond Risk Premia," *American Economic Review* 95 (2005): 138–60.

Fama, Eugene F. and Kenneth French, "Dividend Yields and Expected Stock Returns," *Journal of Financial Economics* 22, no. 1 (1988): 3–25.

Fama, Eugene, F. Fama and Robert R. Bliss, "The Information in Long-Maturity Forward Rates." *American Economic Review* 77, no. 4 (1987): 680–92.

Fung, D. and D. A. Hsieh, "The Risk in Hedge Fund Strategies: Theory and Evidence from Trend Followers," *The Review of Financial Studies* 14, no. 2 (2002): 313.

Geczy, C., and M. Samonov, "212 Years of Price Momentum" (working paper), *Financial Analysts Journal* 72, no. 5 (September/October 2016), http://ssrn.com/abstract=2292544.

Giesecke, Kay, Francis A. Longstaff, Stephen Schefer, and Ilya A. Strebulaev, "Macroeconomic Effects of Corporate Crisis: A Long-Term Perspective," *Journal of Financial Economics*, 111 (2014): 297–310.

Gorton, Gary B., Fumio Hayashi, and Geert K. Rouwenhorst, "The Fundamentals of Commodity Futures Returns (working paper)," *Yale ICF*, No. 07-08 (February 2012).

Gurkaynak, R., B. Sack, and J. Wright, "The U.S. Treasury Yield Curve: 1961 to the Present" (Finance and Economics Discussion Series, Divisions of Research & Statistics and Monetary Affairs, Federal Reserve Board, 2006).

Keynes, John M. *Treatise on Money* (Eastford, CT: Martino Fine Books, June 2, 2011).

Koijen, Ralph S. J., Tobias J. Moskowitz, Lasse Heje Pedersen, and Evert B. Vrugt, "Carry" (working paper), *Fama-Miller* (November 2007).

Leibowitz, M., A. Bova, and S. Kogelman, "Long-Term Bond Returns under Duration Targeting," *Financial Analysts Journal* 70, no. 1 (January/February 2014).

Lemperiere, Y., C. Deremble, P. Seager, M. Potters, and J. P. Bouchaud, "Two Centuries of Trend Following," *Journal of Investment Strategies* (2014): 41.

Lustig, Hanno and Adrien Verdelhan, "The Cross Section of Foreign Currency Risk Premia and Consumption Growth Risk," *American Economic Review* 97 (March 2007): 89–117.

Menkhoff, Lukas, Lucio Sarno, Maik Schmeling, and Andreas Schrimpf, "Carry Trades and Global Foreign Exchange Volatility," *Journal of Finance* 67, no. 2 (April 2012): 681–718.

Moskowitz, T. J., Y. H. Ooi, and L. H. Pedersen, "Time Series Momentum," *Journal of Financial Economics* (2012): 228.

Rennison, G., M. Dorsten, and V. Bhansali, "Trend Following and Rising Rates," *PIMCO* (September 2014).

Chapter 28

1. Eugene F. Fama and Kenneth R French, "Common Risk Factors in the Returns on Stocks and Bonds," *Journal of Financial Economics* (1993): 3–56.
2. Simon Lack, "The Hedge Fund Mirage," (Hoboken, NJ: John Wiley & Sons, Inc., 2012).
3. *Investment Company Fact Book*, www.icifactbook.org/fb_ch2.html.
4. Sheena Iyengar, *The Art of Choosing* (New York: Twelve Books, 2010): 7.
5. *Investment Company Fact Book*, www.icifactbook.org/fb_ch7.html.
6. Andre Weisman, "Informationless Investing and Hedge Fund Performance Measurement Bias," *The Journal of Portfolio Management* 28, no. 4 (Summer 2002): 80–91.
7. Zeke Ashton, "The Real Costs of Turnover," *Fool.com* (November 21, 2003), www.fool.com/investing/general/2003/11/21/the-real-costs-of-turnover.aspx.
8. *Investment Company Fact Book*, www.icifactbook.org/fb_ch6.html.
9. *Investment Company Fact Book*, www.icifactbook.org/fb_data.html#section1.
10. John C. Bogle, "The First Index Mutual Fund: A History of Vanguard Index Trust and the Vanguard Index Strategy," Bogle Financial Markets Research Center (1997), www.vanguard.com/bogle_site/lib/sp19970401.html.

11. David N. Dreman and Michael A. Berry, "Analyst Forecasting Errors and Their Implications for Security Analysis," *Financial Analysts Journal* (1995): 30–41.

12. Robert B. Jorgensen, *Individually Managed Accounts* (Hoboken, NJ: John Wiley & Sons, Inc., 2003).

13. *Investment Company Fact Book*, www.icifactbook.org/fb_ch2.html#us.

14. Brian Portnoy, *The Investors Paradox* (New York: Palgrave McMillan, 2013).

15. Bill Barker, "The Performance of Mutual Funds," *The Motley Fool*, www.fool.com/School/MutualFunds/Performance/Record.htm.

16. William F. Sharpe (1966), "Mutual Fund Performance," *Journal of Business*, supplement on Security Prices, 39 (January), 119–138; Jack L. Treynor (1966), "How to Rate Management Investment Funds," *Harvard Business Review*, 43 (January–February); Michael C. Jensen (1967), "Performance of Mutual Funds in the Period 1945–1964," *Journal of Finance*, 23(2), 389–416.

17. Brian Portnoy, *The Investor's Paradox* (New York: Palgrave McMillan, 2013).

18. Don Wilkinson, *Stop Wasting Your Wealth in Mutual Funds: Separately Managed Accounts—The Smart Alternative* (Chicago: Dearborn Trade Publishing, 2006).

19. Ilia D. Dicheve and Gwen Yu, "Higher Risk, Lower Returns: What Hedge Fund Investors Really Earn," *Journal of Financial Economics* (July 1, 2000).

20. "Only 8 Funds Have Beaten the S&P 500 for 10 Years," *MarketWatch*, November 17, 2011, http://blogs.marketwatch.com/thetell/2011/11/17/only-8-funds-have-beaten-the-sp-500-for-10-years/.

21. "Topic 409—Capital Gains and Losses," IRS (September 20, 2016), www.irs.gov/taxtopics/tc409.html.

22. Wilkinson, *Stop Wasting Your Wealth*.

23. "Topic 404—Dividends," *IRS* (September 20, 2016), www.irs.gov/taxtopics/tc404.html.

24. *Investment Company Fact Book*, www.icifactbook.org/fb_appa.html.

25. Portnoy, *The Investor's Paradox*.

26. Amit Goyal and Sunil Wahal, "The Selection and Termination of Investment Management Firms by Plan Sponsors," *Journal of Finance* (August, 2008): 63.

27. Christopher Chabris and Daniel Simons, *The Invisible Gorilla: How Our Intuitions Deceive Us* (New York: Crown, 2009).

28. "Hedge Funds Extend Redemption Ban," *Financial Times* (November 29, 2008).

29. Portnoy, *The Investor's Paradox*.

Epilogue

1. Alan Watts, *The Wisdom of Insecurity* (New York: Knopf, 2011).
2. Charles Faulkner, "Inside the Counterintuitive World of Trend Followers: It's Not What You Think. It's What You Know," *Stocks, Futures & Options Magazine,* April 2005.
3. Ken Durr, "Interview with David Harding," Securities and Exchange Commission Historical Society, June 18, 2013.
4. Ibid.
5. Ibid.
6. Daniel C. Dennett, *Intuition Pumps and Other Tools for Thinking* (New York: W. W. Norton, 2013).

About the Author

1. Denise G. Shekerjian, *Uncommon Genius* (New York: Penguin, 1990).

Bibliography

Abbott, Susan. "Turning a Summer Job into a Legend." *Futures* 12, no. 9 (September 1983): 57–59.

Abrams, Ryan, Ranjan Bhaduri, and Elizabeth Flores. "Lintner Revisited—A Quantitative Analysis of Managed Futures for Plan Sponsors, Endowments and Foundations." *CME Group*, May 2012.

Amin, Gaurav, and Harry M. Kat. "Stocks, Bonds and Hedge Funds: Not a Free Lunch!" *Journal of Portfolio Management* (Summer 2003): 113–20.

Amin, Gaurav S., and Harry M. Kat. "Who Should Buy Hedge Funds? The Effects of Including Hedge Funds in Portfolios of Stocks and Bonds." Working Paper Series, ISMA Centre for Education and Research in Securities Markets, 2002.

Angrist, Stanley W. *Sensible Speculation in Commodities or How to Profit in the Bellies, Bushels and Bales Markets*. New York: Simon & Schuster, 1972.

Aronson, Mark. "Learning from a Legend." *Trading Advisor Review* (June 1997).

Ashton, Zeke. "The Real Costs of Turnover." *Fool.com* (November 21, 2003). www.fool.com/investing/general/2003/11/21/the-real-costs-of-turnover.aspx.

Asness, C. S., T. J. Moskowitz, and L. H. Pedersen. "Value and Momentum Everywhere." *Journal of Finance* 58 (2013): 929–85.

ATLAS Collaboration. "Observation of a New Particle in the Search for the Standard Model Higgs Boson with the ATLAS Detector at the LHC." *Physics Letters B* 716, no. 1 (2012): 1–29.

Baglio, J., and A. Djouadi. "Higgs Production at the IHC." *Journal of High Energy Physics 1103*, no. 3 (2011): 55.

Bailey, D., J. Borwein, M. López de Prado, and Q. J. Zhu. "The Probability of Backtest Overfitting." Working paper, Lawrence Berkeley National Laboratory, 2013.

Bailey, D., J. Borwein, M. López de Prado, and Q. J. Zhu. "Pseudo-Mathematics and Financial Charlatanism: The Effects of Backtest Overfitting on Out-of-Sample." Working paper, Lawrence Berkeley National Laboratory, 2013.

Bakken, Henry H. "*Futures Trading—Origin, Development, and Present Economic Status*." Madison, WI: Mimir Publishers, 1966.

Baratz, Morton S. *The Investor's Guide to Futures Money Management*. Columbia, MD: Futures Publishing Group, 1984.

Barber, Brad, and Terrance Odean. "Trading Is Hazardous to Your Wealth: The Common Stock Investment Performance of Individual Investors." *Journal of Finance LV*, no. 2 (April 2000): 773–806.

Barberis, N., R. Greenwood, L. Jin, and A. Shleifer. "X-CAPM: An Extrapolative Capital Asset Pricing Model" Working paper, 2013.

Barclays Capital. "Trending Forward: CTAs/Managed Futures." *Hedge Fund Pulse* (February 2012).

Barker, Bill. "The Performance of Mutual Funds." *The Motley Fool*. Accessed December 18, 2016. www.fool.com/School/MutualFunds/Performance/Record.htm.

Barras, L., O. Scaillet, and R. Wermers. "False Discoveries in Mutual Fund Performance: Measuring Luck in Estimated Alphas." *Journal of Finance* 65 (2010): 179–216.

Barroso, P., and P. Santa-Clara. "Momentum Has Its Moments." Working paper, 2013.

Bartas, A. N., and R. Kosowski. "Momentum Strategies in Futures Markets and Trend-Following Funds." EUROFIDAI-AFFI Finance Meeting, Paris, December 2012. http://dx.doi.org/10.2139/ssrn.1968996.

Basso, Thomas F. "The Driving Force behind Profits in the Managed Futures Industry." Trendstat Capital Management, 1998.

Basso, Thomas F. "Some Leverage Is Good, Too Much Is Dangerous." Trendstat Capital Management, March 1999.

Basso, Thomas F. "Study of Time Spent in Trending and Sideways Markets." Trendstat Capital Management, 1999.

Basso, Thomas F. "When to Allocate to a CTA? Buy Them on Sale" (1997).

Benjamini, Y., and Y. Hochberg. "Controlling the False Discovery Rate: A Practical and Powerful Approach to Multiple Testing." *Journal of the Royal Statistical Society* Series B 57 (1995): 289–300.

Benjamini, Y., and D. Yekutieli. "The Control of the False Discovery Rate in Multiple Testing Under Dependency." *Annals of Statistics* 29 (2001): 1165–88.

Bernstein, Peter L. *Against the Gods: The Remarkable Story of Risk*. Etobicoke, Ontario: John Wiley & Sons, Inc., 1996.

Bhaduri, Ranjan, and Christopher Art. "Liquidity Buckets, Liquidity Indices, Liquidity Duration, and Their Applications to Hedge Funds." *Alternative Investment Quarterly* (second quarter, 2008).

Bhansali, Vineer. "Volatility and the Carry Trade." *Journal of Fixed Income* (2007): 72–84.

Black, F., M. C. Jensen, and M. Scholes. *Theory of Capital Markets*. New York: Praeger, 1972.

Black, F. "Noise." *Journal of Finance* (1986): 529–43.

Bogle, John C. *Common Sense on Mutual Funds.* New York: John Wiley & Sons, Inc., 1999.

Bogle, John C. "The First Index Mutual Fund: A History of Vanguard Index Trust and the Vanguard Index Strategy." Bogle Financial Markets Research Center, 1997. www.vanguard.com/bogle_site/lib/sp19970401.html.

Borish, Peter. "Managed Money." *Futures* 27, no. 3 (March 1998).

Bouchaud, J. P. "Crises and Collective Socio-economic Phenomena: Simple Models and Challenges." *Journal of Statistical Physics* (2013): 567.

Bouchaud, J. P., and R. Cont. "A Langevin Approach to Stock Market Fluctuations and Crashes." *European Physical Journal* B (1998): 543–50.

Bouchaud, J. P., and M. Potters. "Theory of Financial Risk and Derivative Pricing." *Cambridge* University Press (2003).

Brealey, Richard, and Stewart C. Myers. *Principles of Corporate Finance* 5th ed. New York: Irwin McGraw Hill, 1996.

Brooks, Chris, and Harry M. Kat. "The Statistical Properties of Hedge Fund Index Returns and Their Implications for Investors." *Journal of Alternative Investment* 5 (2002): 26–44.

Brorsen, B. W., and S. H. Irwin. "Futures Funds and Price Volatility." *Review of Futures Markets* 6 (1987): 119–35.

Burke, Gibbons. "Your Money." *Active Trader* (July 2002): 68–73.

Burns, Greg. "A Gunslinger No More." *Businessweek* (April 7, 1997): 64–72.

Calderini, Pablo. "Systematic Global Macro: Performance, Risk, and Correlation Characteristics." April 2013. https://papers.ssrn.com/sol3/papers.cfm?abstract_id=2271659.

Campbell, John, Adi Sunderam, and Luis M. Viceira. "Inflation Bets or Deflation Hedges: The Changing Risks of Nominal Bonds?" National Bureau of Economic Research working paper, February 2009.

Canoles, W. Bruce, Sarahelen R. Thompson, Scott H. Irwin, and Virginia G. France. "An Analysis of the Profiles and Motivations of Habitual Commodity Speculators." Working Paper 97–01, Office for Futures and Options Research, University of Illinois, Champaign-Urbana, 1997.

Cavaletti, Carla. "1997's Home Run Hitters." *Futures* 27, no. 3 (March 1998).

Chabris, Christopher, and Daniel Simons. *The Invisible Gorilla: How Our Intuitions Deceive Us*. New York: Crown, 2009.

Chandler, Beverly. *Managed Futures*. West Sussex, England: John Wiley & Sons, Inc., 1994.

Chang, E. C., and B. Schachter. "Interday Variations in Volume, Variance and Participation of Large Speculators." Working paper, Commodity Futures Trading Commission, 1993.

Christensen, Clayton M. *The Innovator's Dilemma: When New Technologies Cause Great Firms to Fail.* Boston: Harvard Business School Press, 1997.

Christensen, Clayton M. and Matt Verlinden. "Disruption, Disintegration, and the Dissipation of Differentiability." Harvard Business School working paper, 2000.

Clare, A., J. Seaton, P. N. Smith, and S. Thomas. "Trend Following, Risk Parity and Momentum in Commodity Futures." Working paper. http://dx.doi.org/10.2139/ssrn.2126813.

Clendaniel, Edward. "Bubble Troubles." *Forbes* (March 25, 2002).

CMS Collaboration. "Observation of a New Boson at a Mass of 125 GeV with the CMS Experiment at the LHC." *Physics Letters B* 716, no. 1 (2012): 30–61.

Cochrane, John H. "Presidential Address: Discount Rates." *Journal of Finance* (2011): 1047–1108.

Cochrane, John H., and Monika Piazzesi. "Bond Risk Premia." *American Economic Review* (2005): 138–60.

Collins, James C., and Jerry I. Porras. *Built to Last: Successful Habits of Visionary Companies*. New York: Harper Business, 1994.

Collins, Jim. *Good to Great*. New York: Harper Business, 2001.

Commodity Futures Trading Commission, Division of Economic Analysis. "*Survey of Pool Operators in Futures Markets with an Analysis of Interday Position Changes*." Washington, DC: Commodity Futures Trading Commission, 1991.

Covel, Michael. *The Complete TurtleTrader*. New York: HarperCollins, 2009.

de Bondt, W., and R. H. Thaler. "Does the Stock Market Overreact?" *Journal of Finance* (1985): 557–81.

DeLong, J., A. Bradford, A. Shleifer, L. H. Summers, and R. J. Waldmann. "Positive Feedback Investment Strategies and Destabilizing Rational Speculation." *Journal of Finance* 45 (1990): 379–95.

Dennett, Daniel C. *Intuition Pumps and Other Tools for Thinking*. New York: W. W. Norton, 2013.

de Prado, M. López. "What to Look for in a Backtest." Working paper. Lawrence Berkeley National Laboratory, 2013.

de Tocqueville, Alexis. *Democracy in America*. New York: Vintage, 1959.

Dicheve, Ilia D., and Gwen Yu. "Higher Risk, Lower Returns: What Hedge Fund Investors Really Earn." *Journal of Financial Economics* (July 1, 2000).

Diz, Fernando. "How Do CTAs' Return Distribution Characteristics Affect Their Likelihood of Survival?" *Journal of Alternative Investments* 2, no. 2 (Fall 1999): 37–41.

Douglas, Mark. *The Disciplined Trader: Developing Winning Attitudes*. New York: New York Institute of Finance, 1990.

Dreman, David N., and Michael A. Berry. "Anlayst Forecasting Errors and Their Implications for Security Analysis." *Financial Analysts Journal* (1995): 30–41.

Duke, J., D. Harding, and K. Land. "Historical Performance of Trend Following." Working paper, December 2013.

Durr, Ken. "Interview with David Harding" Securities and Exchange Commission Historical Society, June 18, 2013.

Eales, J. S., B. K. Engel, R. J. Hauser, and S. R. Thompson. "Grain Price Expectations of Illinois Farmers and Grain Merchandisers." *American Journal of Agricultural Economics*, 72 (1990): 701–8.

Ecke, Robert. "Allocation to Discretionary CTAs Grow as Market Stalls." *Barclay Trading Group Roundtable* 9, no. 3 (third quarter, 1998).

Eckhardt, William. "The C-Test." *Stocks and Commodities* 12, no. 5 (1994): 218–21.

Edwards, Franklin R., and Mustafa Onur Caglayan. "Hedge Fund and Commodity Fund Investment Styles in Bull and Bear Markets." *Journal of Portfolio Management*, 27 (2001): 97–108.

Ellis, Charles D. *Winning the Loser's Game.* 3rd ed. New York: McGraw-Hill, 1998.

"Energy Traders on the Verge of Extinction." *Barclay Trading Group Roundtable* 8, no. 3 (third quarter, 1997).

Epstein, Richard A. *The Theory of Gambling and Statistical Logic.* San Diego, CA: Academic Press, 1995.

Fabozzi, Frank J., Francis Gupta, and Harry M. Markowitz. "The Legacy of Modern Portfolio Theory." Institutional Investor, 2002.

Fama, Eugene, and J. D. MacBeth. "Risk, Return, and Equilibrium: Empirical Tests." *Journal of Political Economy* 81 (1973): 607–36.

Fama, Eugene F., and Kenneth R. French. "Common Risk Factors in the Returns on Stocks and Bonds." *Journal of Financial Economics* (1993): 3–56.

Fama, Eugene F., and Kenneth French. "Dividend Yields and Expected Stock Returns." *Journal of Financial Economics* 22, no. 1 (1988): 3–25.

Fama, Eugene F., and Robert R. Bliss. "The Information in Long-Maturity Forward Rates." *American Economic Review* (1987): 680–92.

Faulkner, Charles. "Inside the Counterintuitive World of Trend Followers: It's Not What You Think. It's What You Know." *Stocks, Futures & Options Magazine*, April 2005.

Feynman, Richard P., as told to Ralph Leighton. *"What Do You Care What Other People Think?" Further Adventures of a Curious Character.* New York: W. W. Norton, 1988.

Fleckenstein, Bill. "The Long and Short of Short-Selling." *MSN Money*, September 2002. http://moneycentral.msn.com.

Forrester, Jay W. *Principles of Systems.* Cambridge, MA: Wright-Allen Press, 1968.

Forrester, Jay W. "System Dynamics and the Lessons of 35 Years." In *The Systemic Basis of Policy Making in the 1990s*, edited by Kenyon B. de Greene, 1991.

Friedman, Thomas L. *The Lexus and the Olive Tree.* New York: Farrar, Straus & Giroux, 1999.

Fung, William, and David A. Hsieh. "Asset-Based Hedge-Fund Styles and Portfolio Diversification." *Financial Analyst Journal* (September 2001).

Fung, William, and David A. Hsieh. "Hedge-Fund Benchmarks: Information Content and Biases." *Financial Analyst Journal* (2002).

Fung, William, and David A. Hsieh. "Pricing Trend Following Trading Strategies: Theory and Empirical Evidence" (1998).

Fung, William, and David A. Hsieh. "The Risk in Hedge Fund Strategies: Theory and Evidence from Fixed Income Funds." *Journal of Fixed Income*, 14 (2002).

Gadsden, Stephen. "Managed the Future." *The MoneyLetter* 25, no. 20 (October 2001).

Gallacher, William R. *Winner Take All.* New York: McGraw-Hill, 1994.

Gann, W. D. *How to Make Profits Trading in Commodities*. Pomeroy, WA: Gann Publishing, 1951.

Garber, Peter M. *Famous First Bubbles: The Fundamentals of Early Manias.* Cambridge, MA: MIT Press, 2000.

Gardner, B. L. "Futures Prices in Supply Analysis." *American Journal of Agricultural Economics* 58 (1976): 81–84.

Gary, Loren. "The Right Kind of Failure." *Harvard Management Update*.

Geczy, C., and M. Samonov. "212 Years of Price Momentum." *Financial Analysts Journal* 72, no. 5 (September/October 2016). http://ssrn.com/abstract=2292544.

Giardina, I., and J. P. Bouchaud. "Bubbles, Crashes and Intermittency in Agent Based Market Models." *European Physics Journal B* 31 (2003): 421.

Giesecke, Kay, Francis A. Longstaff, Stephen Schefer, and Ilya A. Strebulaev. "Macroeconomic Effects of Corporate Crisis: A Long-Term Perspective." *Journal of Financial Economics* 111, (2014): 297–310.

Gigerenzer, G., and D. Goldstein. "Reasoning the Fast and Frugal Way: Models of Bounded Rationality." *Psychological Review* (1996): 650.

Gigerenzer, Gerd, and Peter M. Todd. *Simple Heuristics That Make Us Smart.* Oxford: Oxford University Press, 1999.

Gilovich, Thomas, Robert Valone, and Amos Tversky. "The Hot Hand in Basketball: On the Misperception of Random Sequences." *Cognitive Psychology*, 17 (1985): 295–314.

Ginyard, Johan. "*Position-Sizing Effects on Trader Performance: An Experimental Analysis*." Uppsala, Sweden: Department of Psychology, Uppsala University, 2001.

Goldbaum, David. "Technical Analysis, Price Trends, and Bubbles."

Gorton, Gary B., Fumio Hayashi, and Geert K. Rouwenhorst. "The Fundamentals of Commodity Futures Returns." *Yale ICF,* Working Paper No. 07–08, February 2012.

Gould, Stephen Jay. *Full House.* New York: Three Rivers Press, 1996.

Gould, Stephen Jay. "The Streak of Streaks." *The New York Review of Books*, August 18, 1988. See www.nybooks.com/articles/1988/08/18/the-streak-of-streaks/.

Goyal, Amit, and Sunil Wahal. "The Selection and Termination of Investment Management Firms by Plan Sponsors." *Journal of Finance* (August 2008): 63.

Greenwood, R., and A. Shleifer. "Expectations of Returns and Expected Returns." *Review of Financial Studies* (2014): 714–46.

Greyserman, Alex, and Kathryn Kaminski. *Trend Following with Managed Futures: The Search for Crisis Alpha*. Hoboken, NJ: John Wiley & Sons, Inc., 2014.

Grof, Stanisslav. *The Adventure of Self-Discovery: Dimensions of Consciousness and New Perspectives in Psychotherapy and Inner Exploration.* Albany: State University of New York Press, 1988.

Gurkaynak, R., B. Sack, and J. Wright. "The U.S. Treasury Yield Curve: 1961 to the Present." Finance and Economics Discussion Series, Divisions of Research & Statistics and Monetary Affairs, Federal Reserve Board, 2006.

Hakim, Danny. "Hedging Learned at the Family Farm." *New York Times*, July 26, 2002.

Hardy, J. "The Real Problem in Association Studies." *American Journal of Medical Genetics* 114, no. 2 (2002): 253.

Harlow, Charles V., and Michael D. Kinsman. "The Electronic Day Trader & Ruin." *The Graziadio Business Report* (Fall 1999).

Harris, Larry. *Trading and Exchanges.* New York: Oxford University Press, 2003.

Harris, Lawrence. *The Winners and Losers of the Zero-Sum Game: The Origins of Trading Profits, Price Efficiency and Market Liquidity (Draft 0.911).* Los Angeles: University of Southern California, May 7, 1993.

Harvey, C. R., and Y. Liu. "Backtesting." Working paper, Duke University, 2014. http://papers.ssrn.com/sol3/papers.cfm?abstract_id=2345489.

Harvey, C. R., Y. Liu, and H. Zhu. ". . . and the Cross-section of Expected Returns." Working paper, Duke University, 2014. See https://papers.ssrn.com/sol3/papers.cfm?abstract_id=2249314.

Haun, Bruce. "Rebalancing Portfolios Lowers Volatility and Stabilizes Returns." B. Edward Haun & Company, June 1994.

"Hedge Funds Extend Redemption Ban." *Financial Times* (November 29, 2008).

Higgs, P. "Broken Symmetries and the Masses of Gauge Bosons." *Physical Review Letters* 13, no. 16 (1964): 508–9.

Hirshleifer, D., and J. Yu. "Asset Pricing in Production Economies with Extrapolative Expectations." Working paper, 2012.

Hommes, C. H. "Heterogeneous Agent Models in Economics and Finance." *Handbook of Computational Economics*, Vol. 2.

Hommes, C. H., J. Sonnemans, J. Tuinstra, and H. van de Velden. "Expectations and Bubbles in Asset Pricing Experiments." *Journal of Economic Behavior and Organization* (2008): 116–33.

Hong, H., and J. Stein. "A Unified Theory of Underreaction, Momentum Trading, and Overreaction in Asset Markets." *Journal of Finance* (1999): 2143–84.

Hurst, B., Y. H. Ooi, and L. H. Pedersen. "A Century of Evidence on Trend-Following Investing." Working paper, *AQR*, 2012.

Hutchinson, Mark C., and John O'Brien. "Is This Time Different? Trend-Following and Financial Crises." *The Journal of Alternative Investments* 17, no. 2 (Fall 2014).

"Incremental Factors." Working paper, Duke University, 2014.

Internal Revenue Service. "Topic 404—Dividends." September 20, 2016. www.irs.gov/taxtopics/tc404.html.

Internal Revenue Service. "Topic 409—Capital Gains and Losses." September 20, 2016. www.irs.gov/taxtopics/tc409.html.

Ioannidis, J. P. "Why Most Published Research Findings Are False." *PLoS Medicine* 2, e124 (2005): 694–701.

Irwin, Scott H., and Satoko Yoshimaru. "Managed Futures Trading and Futures Price Volatility" (1996).

Iyengar, Sheena. *The Art of Choosing*. New York: Twelve Books, 2010.

Jaeger, Lars. *Managing Risk in Alternative Investment Strategies*. Upper Saddle River, NJ: Financial Times Prentice Hall, 2002.

Jakiubzak, Ken. "KmJ: Ready for Anything." *Futures* 29, no. 3 (March 2000).

Jensen, Michael C. "Performance of Mutual Funds in the Period 1945–1964." *Journal of Finance* (1967): 389–416.

Jorgensen, Robert B. *Individually Managed Accounts.* Hoboken, NJ: John Wiley & Sons, Inc., 2003.

Kahneman, Daniel, and Amos Tverksy. "Prospect Theory: An Analysis of Decision Under Risk." *Econometrica* 47 (1979): 263–91.

Kaplan, Laurie. "Turning Turtles into Traders." *Managed Derivatives* (May 1996).

Karas, Robert. "Looking behind the Non-Correlation Argument," www.aima.org/.

Kat, Harry M. "Managed Futures and Hedge Funds: A Match Made in Heaven." Working paper, November 2002.

Kaufman, Perry. *Trading Systems and Methods.* 3rd ed. New York: John Wiley & Sons, Inc., 1998.

Kent, D., D. Hirshleifer, and A. Subrahmanyam. "Investor Psychology and Security Market Under and Overreactions." *Journal of Finance* 53 (1998): 1839–85.

Kent, D., and T. J. Moskowitz. "Momentum Crashes." *Swiss Finance Institute Research Paper Series* (2013): 13–61.

Keynes, John M. *Treatise on Money*. Eastford, CT: Martino Fine Books, 2011.

Kirman, A. "Ants, Rationality and Recruitment." *Quarterly Journal of Economics* (1991): 137–56.

Kirman, A. "Epidemics of Opinion and Speculative Bubbles in Financial Markets." *Money and Financial Markets* (1993).

Klein, Gary. *Sources of Power: How People Make Decisions.* Cambridge, MA: MIT Press, 1998.

Koijen, Ralph S. J., Tobias J. Moskowitz, Lasse Heje Pedersen, and Evert B. Vrugt. "Carry." Working paper. *Fama-Miller* (November 2007).

Koulajian, Nigol, and Paul Czkwianianc. "Know Your Skew—Using Hedge Fund Return Volatility as a Predictor of Maximum Loss." *AlphaQuest CTA Research Series #2* (June 2011).

Lack, Simon. *The Hedge Fund Mirage.* Hoboken, NJ: John Wiley & Sons, Inc., 2012.

Le Bon, Gustave. *The Crowd: A Study of the Popular Mind.* Atlanta: Cherokee Publishing Company, 1982.

Lefèvre, Edwin. *Reminiscences of a Stock Operator.* Etobicoke, Ontario: John Wiley & Sons, Inc., 1994.

Leibowitz, M., A. Bova, and S. Kogelman. "Long-Term Bond Returns under Duration Targeting." *Financial Analysts Journal* 70, no. 1 (January/February 2014).

Lempérière, Y. "What Is Risk Premium and How Does It Differ from Alpha Strategies?" Working paper, 2014.

Lempérière, Y., C. Deremble, P. Seager, M. Potters, and J. P. Bouchaud. "Two Centuries of Trend Following." *Journal of Investment Strategies* 3, no. 3 (June 2014).

Lerner, Robert L. "The Mechanics of the Commodity Futures Markets, What They Are and How They Function." Mount Lucas Management Corp., 2000.

Leroy, S. F., and R. D. Porter. "The Present Value Relation: Tests Based on Implied Variance Bounds." *Econometrica* (1981): 555.

Liebovitch, L. S. *Fractals and Chaos Simplified for the Life Sciences.* New York: Oxford University Press, 1998.

Liebovitch, L. S., A. T. Todorov, M. Zochowski, D. Scheurle, L. Colgin, M. A. Wood, K. A. Ellenbogen, J. M. Herre, and R. C. Bernstein. "Nonlinear Properties of Cardiac Rhythm Abnormalities." *Physical Review*, 59 (1999): 3312–19.

Livermore, Jesse L. *How to Trade in Stocks: The Livermore Formula for Combining Time Element and Price.* New York: Duel, Sloan & Pearce, 1940.

Lukac, L. P., B. W. Brorsen, and S. H. Irwin. "The Similarity of Computer Guided Technical Trading Systems." *Journal of Futures Markets*, 8 (1988): 1–13.

Lungarella, Gildo. "Managed Futures: A Real Alternative." White paper.

Lustig, Hanno, and Adrien Verdelhan. "The Cross Section of Foreign Currency Risk Premia and Consumption Growth Risk." *American Economic Review* 97 (March 2007): 89–117.

Lux, T., and M. Marchesi. "Volatility Clustering in Financial Markets: A Microsimulation of Interacting Agents." *International Journal of Theoretical and Applied Finance* 3 (2000): 675–702.

Mackay, Charles. *Extraordinary Popular Delusions and the Madness of Crowds*. New York: Dover, 2003.

MacRae, Desmond. "Dealing with Complexities." *Trading Focus* (July 1998).

Martin, George. "Making Sense of Hedge Fund Returns: What Matters and What Doesn't." *Derivatives Strategies* (2002).

Maubossin, Michael, and Kristen Bartholdson. "Whither Enron? Or Why Enron Withered." *The Consilient Observer* 1, no. 1 (January 2002).

Mauboussin, Michael J., Alexander Schay, and Stephen Kawaja. "Counting What Counts." Credit Suisse First Boston Equity Research (February 4, 2000).

Mauboussin, Michael J., and Kristen Bartholdson. "Stress and Short-Termism." *The Consilient Observer* 1, no. 9 (May 2002).

McLean, R. D., and J. Pontiff. "Does Academic Research Destroy Stock Return Predictability?" Working paper, University of Alberta, 2014.

Menkhoff, L. "Are Momentum Traders Different? Implications for the Momentum Puzzle." *Applied Economics* 43 (2011): 4415–30.

Menkhoff, Lukas, Lucio Sarno, Maik Schmeling, and Andreas Schrimpf. "Carry Trades and Global Foreign Exchange Volatility." *Journal of Finance* 67, no. 2 (April 2012): 681–718.

Moskowitz, T., T. Ooi, and L. Pedersen. "Time Series Momentum." *Journal of Financial Economics* 104, no. 2 (May 2012).

Mosser, Mike. "Learning from Legends." *Futures* 29, no. 2 (February 2000).

"Multiple Testing in Economics." Working paper, Duke University, 2014.

Mundt, M. "Estimating the Capacity of the Managed Futures Industry." *CTA Intelligence* (March 30, 2014).

Nacubo Endowment Study. Washington, DC: National Association of College and University Business Officers, 1999.

Narasimhan, J., and S. Titman. "Momentum." Working paper, August 29, 2011. https://papers.ssrn.com/sol3/papers.cfm?abstract_id=1919226.

Narasimhan, J., and S. Titman. "Returns to Buying Winners and Selling Losers: Implications for Stock Market Efficiency." *Journal of Finance* 48 (1993): 65–91.

Niederhoffer, Victor, and Laurel Kenner. *Practical Speculation.* Hoboken, NJ: John Wiley & Sons, Inc., 2003.

Odean, Terrance. "Are Investors Reluctant to Realize Their Losses?" *Journal of Finance* 53 (October 1998): 1775–98.

Odo, Marc. "Skewness and Kurtosis." Working paper, Zephyr Associates, August 2011. www.styleadvisor.com.

O'Donoghue, Ted, and Matthew Rabin. "Choice and Procrastination." Working Paper E00–281. Berkeley: University of California Department of Economics, June 3, 2001.

"Oldest CTAs in the Industry Have Survived and Thrived." *Barclay Trading Group Roundtable* 6, no. 3 (third quarter, 1995).

"Only 8 funds Have Beaten the S&P 500 for 10 years." *MarketWatch.* November 17, 2011. http://blogs.marketwatch.com/thetell/2011/11/17/only-8-funds-have-beaten-the-sp-500-for-10-years/.

Peltz, Lois. "The Big Global Macro Debate." *Market Barometer* (April 1998): 9–13.

Peltz, Lois. *The New Investment Superstars.* Etobicoke, Ontario: John Wiley & Sons, Inc., 2001.

Peters, E. E. *Fractal Market Analysis.* New York: John Wiley & Sons, Inc., 1994.

Portnoy, Brian. *The Investor's Paradox.* New York: Palgrave Macmillan, 2013.

Ramsey, Neil, and Aleks Kins. "Managed Futures: Capturing Liquid, Transparent, Uncorrelated Alpha." *The Capital Guide to Alternative Investment* (2004): 129–35.

Rand, Ayn. *Atlas Shrugged.* New York: Random House, 1957.

Rand, Ayn. *The Fountainhead.* New York: Bobbs-Merrill, 1943.

Rappaport, Alfred. *Creating Shareholder Value: A Guide for Managers and Investors.* New York: Free Press, 1998.

Rappaport, Alfred, and Michael J. Mauboussin. *Expectations Investing.* Boston: Harvard Business School Publishing, 2001.

Reerink, Jack. "Seidler's Returns Fuel Comeback." *Futures* 24, no. 3 (March 1995).

Reinhart, C. M., and K. S. Rogoff. *This Time Is Different: Eight Centuries of Financial Folly.* Princeton, NJ: Princeton University Press, 2009.

Rennison, G., M. Dorsten, and V. Bhansali. "Trend Following and Rising Rates." *PIMCO* (September 2014).

Rogers, Jim. *Investment Biker.* New York: Random House, 1994.

Russo, J. Edward, and Paul J. H. Schoemaker. "Managing Overconfidence." *Sloan Management Review* (Winter 1992).

Rzepczynski, Mark. "The End of the Benign Economy and the New Era for Managed Funds." *MFA Reporter* (John W. Henry & Company, Inc., 2001).

Rzepczynski, Mark S. "Market Vision and Investment Styles: Convergent versus Divergent Trading." *Journal of Alternative Investments* 2, no. 1 (Winter 1999): 77–82.

Schneeweis, Thomas, and Georgi Georgiev. "The Benefits of Managed Futures." CISDM and School of Management at University of Massachusetts (2002).

Schneeweis, Thomas, and Spurgin, Richard. "Quantitative Analysis of Hedge Fund and Managed Futures Return and Risk Characteristics." In *Evaluating and Implementing Hedge Fund Strategies*, edited by R. A. Lake. 2nd ed. London: Nestor House, 2002.

Schwager, Jack D. *Getting Started in Technical Analysis.* New York: John Wiley & Sons, Inc., 1999.

Schwager, Jack D. *Market Wizards: Interviews with Top Traders.* New York: Harper Business, 1989.

Schwager, Jack D. *The New Market Wizards: Conversations with America's Top Traders*. New York: Harper Business, 1992.

Schwed, Fred Jr. *Where Are the Customers' Yachts?* Etobicoke, Canada: John Wiley & Sons, Inc., 1995.

Schweder, T., and E. Spjotvoll. "Plots of P-values to Evaluate Many Tests Simultaneously." *Biometrika* 69 (1982): 439–502.

Schwert, G. W. "Anomalies and Market Efficiency." *Handbook of the Economics of Finance* 1, Part B. (2003): 939–74.

Seager, P. "The Statistics of Drawdowns." Working paper, 2014.

Sender, Henny. "Why Hedge Funds Are Clinging to Investors' Cash," *Financial Times* (December 13, 2008). www.ft.com/cms/s/0/66ef9630-c8b8-11dd-b86f-000077b07658.html?ft_site=falcon&desktop=true#axzz4TEKivVUk.

Seykota, Ed, and Dave Druz. "Determining Optimal Risk." *Stocks and Commodities Magazine* 11, no. 3 (March 1993): 122–4.

Shapiro, Carl, and Hal R. Varian. *Information Rules: A Strategic Guide to the Network Economy.* Boston: Harvard Business School Press, 1999.

Sharpe, William F. "Mutual Fund Performance." *Journal of Business* (January 1966): 119–38.

Sharpe, William F. "The Sharpe Ratio," *The Journal of Portfolio Management* (Fall 1994).

Shefrin, Hersh, and Meir Statman. "The Disposition to Sell Winners Too Early and Ride Losers Too Long: Theory and Evidence." *Journal of Finance* 40 (1985): 777–90.

Shekerjian, Denise. *Uncommon Genius.* New York: Penguin, 1990.

Shiller, Robert J. *Irrational Exuberance.* Princeton, NJ: Princeton University Press, 2000.

Shiller, Robert J. "Do Stock Prices Move Too Much to Be Justified by Subsequent Changes in Dividends?" *American Economic Review*, 71 (1981).

Shiller, Robert J. "Measuring Bubble Expectations and Investor Confidence." *Journal of Psychology and Financial Markets* (2000): 49–60.

Simon-Sanchez, J., C. Schulte, and T. Gasser. "Genome-wide Association Study Reveals Genetic Risk Underlying Parkinson's Disease." *Nature Genetics* 41 (2009): 1308–12.

Sloan, Allan. "Even with No Bull Market, Baby Boomers Can Thrive." *Washington Post,* March 26, 2002, E1.

Slywotzky, Adrian J. *Value Migration: How to Think Several Moves Ahead of the Competition.* Boston: Harvard Business School Press, 1996.

Smith, V. L., G. L. Suchanek, and A. W. Williams. "Bubbles, Crashes and Endogenous Expectations in Experimental Spot Asset Markets." *Econometrica* 56 (1988): 1119–51.

Soros, George. *The Alchemy of Finance: Reading the Mind of the Market.* New York: John Wiley & Sons, Inc., 1994.

Spurgin, Richard. "Some Thoughts on the Source of Return to Managed Futures." CISDM and School of Management at University of Massachusetts, 2005.

Steinhardt, Michael. *No Bull: My Life In and Out of Markets.* Etobicoke, Ontario: John Wiley & Sons, Inc., 2001.

Stendahl, David, "Staying Afloat." *Omega Research* (1999).

"Strategy Selection." AHL internal research paper, 2014.

Summers, L. "Does the Stock Market Rationally Reflect Fundamental Values?" *Journal of Finance* 41 (1986): 591.

Szakmary, A. C., Q. Shen, and S. C. Sharma. "Trend-Following Strategies in Commodity Futures: A Re-examination." *Journal of Banking and Finance* 34, no. 2 (2010): 409–26.

Szala, Ginger. "William Eckhardt: Doing by Learning." *Futures* 21, no. 1 (January 1992).

Taleb, Nassim Nicholas. *Fooled by Randomness.* New York: Texere, 2001.

Teweles, Richard J., and Frank J. Jones. *The Futures Game. Who Wins? Who Loses? Why?* New York: McGraw-Hill, 1987.

Thaler, Richard H. "Mental Accounting Matters." *Journal of Behavioral Decision Making*, 12 (1999): 183–206.

Thaler, Richard H. "Saving, Fungibility, and Mental Accounts." *Journal of Economic Perspectives* 4, no. 1 (Winter 1990): 193–205.

Tharp, Van K. *Trade Your Way to Financial Freedom.* New York: McGraw-Hill, 1999.

Thorp, Edward O. *Beat the Dealer.* New York: Vintage, 1966.

Toffler, Alvin. *Future Shock.* New York: Bantam, 1971.

Treynor, Jack L. "How to Rate Management Investment Funds." *Harvard Business Review* (January–February 1966).

Tully, Shawn. "Princeton's Rich Commodity Scholars." *Fortune*, 9 (February 1981): 94.

Tversky, Amos, and Daniel Kahneman. "Belief in the Law of Small Numbers." *Psychological Bulletin*, 76 (1971): 105–10.

Tzu, Sun. *The Art of War.* Boston and London: Shambhala, 1988.

Ueland, Brenda. *If You Want to Write: A Book About Art, Independence and Spirit.* Saint Paul, MN: Graywolf Press, 1937.

Vince, Ralph. *The New Money Management.* New York: John Wiley & Sons, Inc., 1995.

Vince, Ralph. *Portfolio Management Formulas.* Etobicoke, Ontario: John Wiley & Sons, Inc., 1990.

von Mises, Ludwig. *Human Action: A Treatise on Economics.* New York: The Foundation for Economic Education, 1996. First published 1949.

Watts, Alan. *The Wisdom of Insecurity.* New York: Knopf, 2011.

Watts, Dickson G. *Speculation as a Fine Art and Thoughts on Life.* New York: Traders Press, 1965.

Weisman, Andre. "Informationless Investing and Hedge Fund Performance Measurement Bias." *Journal of Portfolio Management* 28, no. 4 (Summer 2002): 80–91.

"Where, Oh Where Are the .400 Hitters of Yesteryear." *Financial Analysts Journal* (November/December 1998): 6–14.

Wilkinson, Don. *Stop Wasting Your Wealth in Mutual Funds: Seperately Managed Accounts—The Smart Alternative*. Chicago: Dearborn Trade Publishing, 2006.

Williamson, Christine. "Liquidity Hunt Hits Managers." *Pensions and Investments*, November 10, 2008. See www.pionline.com/article/20081110/PRINT/311109937/liquidity-hunt-hits-managers.

Williamson, Porter B. *General Patton's Principles for Life and Leadership*. Tuscon, AZ: MSC, 1988.

Wolfram, Stephen. *A New Kind of Science*. Champaign, IL: Wolfram Media, Inc., 2002.

Wolman, William, and Anne Colamosca. *The Great 401(k) Hoax*. Cambridge, MA: Perseus Publishing, 2002.

Wyart, M., and J. P. Bouchaud. "Self-Referential Behaviour, Overreaction and Conventions in Financial Markets." *Journal of Economic Behavior and Organization* 63 (2007): 1.

Yeung, Albert, Mika Toikka, Pankaj N. Patel, and Steve S. Kim. "Quantitative Strategy. Does Technical Analysis Work?" Credit Suisse First Boston. September 25, 2002.

Acknowledgments

I asked them, "How many of you have ever taken the lid off a toilet tank to see how it works?" None of them had. How do you get to M.I.T. without having ever looked inside a toilet tank?

—Jay W. Forrester

I want to thank the 100,000-plus readers since 2004 that have read an edition of this book. You are the only reason I am here 13 years later onto my 5th edition.

For this 5th edition a big thank you goes out to Barry Ritholtz for his new foreword contribution. And, thank you to Larry Hite and Charles Faulkner for their earlier edition forewords.

It is a pleasure to recognize the traders, colleagues, mentors, writers, and friends who contributed directly or indirectly to *Trend Following*:

Fundamentals that you read about are typically useless as the market has already discounted the price, and I call them funny-mentals. However, if you catch on early, before others believe, you might have valuable surprise-a-mentals.

Ed Seykota

Mark Abraham, Kate Abraham, Salem Abraham, James Altucher, Dan Andrews, Will Andrews, Ngo Thi Anh, Gerald Appel, Jeanette Arango, Christian Baja, Hunter Baldwin, Tom Basso, David Beach, Martin Bergin, Laurent Bernut, Vineer Bhansali, John Boik, Peter Borish, Jean-Philippe Bouchaud, Wade Brorsen, Gibbons Burke, Holly Burns, Steve Burns, Jim Byers, Melissa Cantrell-Sprafkin, Jake Carriker, Patrick Cheo, Michelle Cheung, Michael Clarke, Art Collins, Cory Colvin, Allan Como, Larry Connors, Justin Cooke, Jerome Covel, Johanna Covel, Mary Covel, Toby Crabel, Jonathan Craven, Richard Cripps, Frank Curzio, James R. Dailey, Jurgen Dhaese, Edward Dobson, Woody Dorsey, Bernard Drury, David Druz, Bill Dunn, Daniel Dunn, Tim Dyer, William Eckhardt, Jonas Elmerraji, Alistair Evans, Marc Faber, Steve Flato, Nelson Freeburg, William Fung, Charles Gaudet, Jason Gerlach,

Nate Ginsburg, Dave Goodboy, Wesley Gray, Alex Greyserman, David Harding, Mike Harris, Campbell Harvey, Josh Hawes, Mark Hawley, John W. Henry, Scott Hicks, John Hoade, Jonathan Hoenig, Ryan Holiday, James Holter, Gary Hopkinson, Scott A. Houdek, Grace Hung, Ta Hoang Diem Huong, Virginia Hurley, Brian Hurley, John Hurley, Patrick Hurley, Withers Hurley, Robert (Bucky) Isaacson, Travis Jamison, JonPaul Jonkheer, Perry Jonkheer, Shaun Jordan, Kathryn Kaminski, Easan Katir, Carol Kaufman, Jenny Kellams, Adam Khoo, Paul King, Alejandro Knoepffler, Jeff Kopiwoda, Nigol Koulajian, Anton Kraly, Brandon Langley, Fabian Lim, Martin Lueck, Dinh Van Luu, Bill Mann, Jane Martin, Lucy Mattinen, Michael Mauboussin, John Mauldin, Leo Melamed, John Melvin, Todd Miller, Bill Miller, Larry Mollner, James Montier, Mr. Sun, Paul Mulvaney, Michelle Murphy, Georgia Nakou, Peter Navarro, Hung Nguyen, Oanh Nguyen, Vincent Nguyen, Nguyen Thi Kim Nhung, William W. Noel, III, John O'Donnell, Matt Osborne, Michael Panzner, Bob Pardo, Jerry Parker, Ted Parkhill, Taylor Pearson, Lasse Heje Pedersen, Dick Pfister, Mai Pham, Baron Robertson, Jon Robinson, Jim Rogers, Leon Rose, Mark Rosenberg, Brad Rotter, Murray Ruggiero, Jason Russell, Mark Rzepczynski, Marlene Salinas, Ian Schoen, Greg Schuett, Michael Seneadza, Ed Seykota, Tom Shanks, Doug Short, Howard Simons, Barry Sims, Rick Slaughter, Mark Sleeman, Aaron Smith, Grant Smith, Bob Spear, Chris Stanton, Brett Steenbarger, Clint Stevens, Richard Straus, Jon Sundt, Nassim Nicholas Taleb, Stephen Taub, Larry Tentarelli, La Thi Thao, Anthony Todd, Ken Tower, Irve Towers, Adam Tremper, Ken Tropin, Justin Vandergrift, Thomas Vician, Jr., Danny Walsh, Michelle Zichao Wang, Antoni Watts, Robert Webb, Addison Wiggin, Raphael Wilhelm, Gabriel Wisdom, Terence Yao, Patrick L. Young, and Steven Zhang.

My great concern is not whether you have failed, but whether you are content with your failure.
Abraham Lincoln

I want to thank everyone who has appeared on my podcast since January 2012. You can find all of their names in the "Trend Following Podcast Episodes" section. I also want to thank the firms and individuals who contributed to my new "Research" chapters 19–28.

And thank you to the following publications and writers: Sol Waksman and Barclay Managed Futures Report, *Futures* magazine, Managed Account Reports, Graham Capital Management, and *Technical Analysis of Stocks and Commodities Magazine.*

I am indebted to the following authors, whose works continue to be treasure troves of information and insight: Morton Baratz, Peter Bernstein, Clayton Christensen, Jim Collins, Jay Forrester, Tom Friedman, Gerd Gigerenzer, Daniel Goleman, Stephen Jay Gould, Alan Greenberg, Larry Harris, Robert Koppel, Edwin Lefèvre, Michael Lewis, Jesse Livermore, Roger Lowenstein, Ludwig von Mises, Lois Peltz, Ayn Rand, Jack Schwager, Denise Shekerjian, Robert Shiller, Van Tharp, Edward Thorp, Peter Todd, Brenda Ueland, and Dickson Watts.

A thank you goes to Wiley for bringing my 2017 mega edition to the market. Laura Gachko, Tula Weis, Michael Henton, Susan Cerra, Stacey Fischkelta, Kathryn Hancox, and Judy Howarth all contributed their expertise over many hours.

Money does not buy you happiness, but lack of money certainly buys you misery.

Daniel Kahneman

The original edition of this book could have only come to fruition with the editorial guidance of Celia Straus and Jim Boyd. I also owe a special debt of gratitude to Paul Donnelly at Oxford University Press, for seeing potential in my 2003 proposal, and introducing me to my first editor. And to Michelle Murphy? An eye for detail!

Finally, to Amy Neidlinger, thank you for my *rights*.

—Michael W. Covel
April 2017

About the Author

Fear touches everyone—even the successful people, the golden boys, the people who give the appearance of passing through life with their hands deep in their pockets, a whistle on their lips. To take on risk, you need to conquer fear, at least temporarily, at least occasionally. It can be done, especially if you look outside yourself for a strong ledge to stand on.
—Denise Shekerjian[1]

Michael Covel searches. He digs. He goes behind the curtain to reveal a state of mind the *system* doesn't want you in.

Characterized as *essential* and *required reading*, Michael teaches beginners to seasoned pros how to generate profits with straightforward and repeatable rules. He is best known for popularizing the counterintuitive and controversial trading strategy, trend following.

There are many who find a good alibi far more attractive than an achievement. For an achievement does not settle anything permanently. We still have to prove our worth anew each day: we have to prove that we are as good today as we were yesterday. But when we have a valid alibi for not achieving anything, we are fixed, so to speak, for life.
Eric Hoffer

An avowed entrepreneur, Michael is the author of five books including the international bestseller, *Trend Following*, and his investigative narrative, *TurtleTrader.* Fascinated by secretive traders that have quietly generated spectacular returns for seven decades, those going against the investment orthodoxy of *buy and hope*, he has uncovered astonishing insights about the right way to think, develop, and execute trend following systems.

Michael's perspectives have garnered international acclaim and have earned him invitations with a host of organizations: China Asset Management, GIC Private Limited (a Singapore sovereign wealth fund), BM&F Bovespa, the Managed Funds Association, Bank of China Investment Management, the Market Technicians Association, and multiple hedge funds and mutual funds. He also has the distinction of having interviewed five Nobel Prize winners in economics, including Daniel Kahneman and Harry Markowitz, and he has been featured in major media outlets, including the *Wall Street Journal*, Bloomberg, CCTV, *The Straits Times*, and Fox Business.

Take risks: if you win, you will be happy; if you lose, you will be wise.
Anonymous

Michael posts on Twitter, publishes a blog, and records his podcast weekly. His consulting clients are across hedge funds, sovereign wealth funds, institutional investors, and individual traders in more than 70 countries. He splits his time between the United States and Asia:

www.trendfollowing.com

Note: How is Covel pronounced? Co-vell. "Co" rhymes with toe. "Vell" rhymes with bell. Equally accented each syllable. It was shortened from Covalesky, which was shortened originally from Kavaliauskas. Michael's direct contact: www.trendfollowing.com/contact.

Index